Georgia Women

Georgia Women

THEIR LIVES AND TIMES

Volume 2

EDITED BY

Ann Short Chirhart and Kathleen Ann Clark

The University of Georgia Press   *Athens and London*

Published with the generous support of Dr. M. Louise McBee

© 2014 by the University of Georgia Press
Athens, Georgia 30602
www.ugapress.org
Set in Minion Pro by Graphic Composition, Inc.
Printed and bound by Thomson-Shore, Inc.
The paper in this book meets the guidelines for
permanence and durability of the Committee on
Production Guidelines for Book Longevity of the
Council on Library Resources.

Most University of Georgia Press titles are
available from popular e-book vendors.

Printed in the United States of America
14 15 16 17 18 P 5 4 3 2 1

The Library of Congress has cataloged the first volume of this book as follows:
Georgia women : their lives and times / edited by Ann Short Chirhart and Betty Wood.
v. cm.
Includes bibliographical references and index.
Contents: Introduction / Ann Short Chirhart with Betty Wood—Mary Musgrove (ca. 1700–1765) : maligned
mediator or mischievous malefactor / Julie Anne Sweet—Nancy Hart (ca. 1735–ca. 1830) : "Too good not to tell
again" / John Thomas Scott—Elizabeth Lichtenstein Johnston (1764–1848) : "Shot round the world but not heard" /
Ben Marsh—Ellen Craft (ca. 1826–1891) : the fugitive who fled as a planter / Barbara McCaskill—Fanny Kemble
(1809–1893) and Frances Butler Leigh (1838–1910) : becoming Georgian / Daniel Kilbride—Susie King Taylor
(1848–1912) : "I gave my services willingly" / Catherine Clinton—Eliza Frances Andrews (1840–1931) : "I will have
to say Damn! yet, before I am done with them" / Christopher J. Olsen—Amanda America Dickson (1849–1893) :
a wealthy lady of color in nineteenth-century Georgia / Kent Anderson Leslie—Mary Gay (1829–1918) : sin, self,
and survival in the post–Civil War South / Michele Gillespie—Rebecca Latimer Felton (1835–1930) : the problem
of protection in the new South / LeeAnn Whites—Mary Latimer McLendon (1840–1921) : "Mother of suffrage
work in Georgia" / Stacey Horstmann Gatti—Mildred Lewis Rutherford (1851–1928) : the redefinition of new
South White womanhood / Sarah Case—Nellie Peters Black (1851–1919) : Georgia's Pioneer Club woman / Carey
Olmstead Shellman—Lucy Craft Laney (1855–1933) and Martha Berry (1866–1942) : lighting fires of knowledge /
Jennifer Lund Smith—Corra Harris (1869–1935) : the storyteller as folk preacher / Donald Mathews—Juliette
Gordon Low (1860–1927) : late-blooming daisy / Anastatia Hodgens Sims.
ISBN-13: 978-0-8203-3336-6 (hardcover : alk. paper) ISBN-10: 0-8203-3336-0 (hardcover : alk. paper) ISBN-13:
978-0-8203-3337-3 (pbk. : alk. paper) ISBN-10: 0-8203-3337-9 (pbk. : alk. paper)
1. Women—Georgia—Biography. 2. Women—Georgia—History. 3. Georgia—Biography. I. Chirhart, Ann
Short. II. Wood, Betty.
CT3262.G4 G46 2009
975.8092'2—dc22
[B] 2009008552

Volume 2
ISBN: 978-0-8203-3784-5 (hardcover : alk. paper)
ISBN: 978-0-8203-3785-2 (paperback : alk. paper)
ISBN: 978-0-8203-4700-4 (e-book)

British Library Cataloging-in-Publication Data available

Contents

Acknowledgments

This volume relied on the research of all contributors, and we would like to thank them for their patience and contributions to Georgia women's history. Indiana State University provided funding to Ann Short Chirhart with a grant from the Indiana State University Research Grant that allowed her to read collections at the Robert W. Woodruff Library at the Atlanta University Center; and a Gregory Research Award from the University of Georgia helped to fund Kathleen Clark's research at the New York Public Library in Manhattan and at the Harry Ransom Center at the University of Texas in Austin. Without the support of Nancy Grayson at the University of Georgia Press, this entire series on southern women would not exist. We thank her for her commitment to bringing southern women's stories to the public and for the opportunity to work with her on *Georgia Women*.

Special thanks to Cornell University Press for permission to reprint portions of work published by Kathryn Nasstrom in *Everybody's Grandmother and Nobody's Fool: Frances Freeborn Pauley and the Struggle for Social Justice*.

Finally, Ann Short Chirhart would like to thank Ken Chirhart for living with both volumes on Georgia women and reminding her about the joys of marriage. Kathleen Clark would like to thank David, Sam, and Eleanor Dean for their patience, love, and support.

Georgia Women

Introduction

ANN SHORT CHIRHART AND KATHLEEN ANN CLARK

This is the second of two volumes that together explore the diverse and changing patterns of Georgia women's lives. Volume 2 focuses on eighteen Georgia women from the turn of the century to the 1980s. In volume 1, black and white women responded to dramatic changes in their lives during and after the Civil War by grasping new opportunities as professionals, writers, and leaders of organizations. Volume 2 follows this trajectory and illuminates how women during the twentieth century expanded these opportunities, pushed for equality, promoted various organizations and political interests, pioneered women's roles in some professions, and became leading writers and artists in the nation. They grappled with the ongoing oppressions of Jim Crow, the legacy of two world wars, the Great Depression, the Cold War era, the civil rights movement, the growth of conservatism, and the memory of the Civil War. How do these women's stories help us understand these dramatic changes in the South and the United States? How did modernity change their lives as communities fragmented, secularization spread, urbanization grew, industrialization expanded, and equality and rights were demanded? Did Georgia women of different classes, races, and religions who lived during these tumultuous years share a common identity? Did they see themselves as distinct from other southern women or women across the nation? Or in the age of modernity, did they come to see themselves as part of national movements, professions, and ideas? These questions, among others, are at the heart of these volumes, and the essays explore the lives of women often marginalized, frequently misunderstood, and always at the forefront of change or the preservation of tradition at the local, state, and even national level.

As these essays show, Georgia women participated in the dramatic changes in the twentieth century in multiple ways. Their work for reforms, literature and the arts, and professional choices were shaped by broader movements for suffrage, equal rights for African Americans, and new opportunities for professional work, artistic expression, and political activism, among others, but they engaged these changes in complex ways. For some, the past represented restrictions on what they could do or say, virulent racism in Jim Crow, and domination by men in the home and public life. For others, Georgia's past retained a conflicted hold on them as they sought to preserve what they believed were the best of traditions in the home, Christianity, and society at the same time that they, too, challenged dominant perceptions of women's roles. Withal, Georgia women, black and white, were vital actors in the myriad changes that transformed families, communities, and society in the South and the nation at large over the course of the twentieth century.

For many Americans, World War I marked the nation's shift to modernity in the twentieth century. Yet most Georgians were already confronting transformations in their social order. Georgians who were alive September 22–24, 1906, never forgot the Atlanta Race Riot, when white mobs tore through Atlanta's streets attacking blacks and black businesses. At least twenty-five blacks were murdered and possibly more. For black women like Lugenia Burns Hope, it marked the destruction of already fragile interracial ties; hope for shared efforts to improve African Americans' status dimmed considerably when "their white friends had planned to destroy them."[1] For some white women, like Margaret Mitchell, it was a time for lawful white Atlantans to defend themselves against the threats of violence, disorder, and mob rule. For other white women, like Vara Majette, the riot captured distorted power relations between blacks and whites and demonstrated how white patriarchal authority lessened the potential for all women to challenge dependent relations. While distinct in their particular perspectives and prescriptions for change, all three women shared the fear of mob violence and what could instantaneously erupt when the Southern order of class and race was threatened.

In the wake of the riot's days of terror and murder, the event marked shifts in turn-of-the-century Georgia. Atlanta in particular was a site of increased industrialization and urban growth. From a small city formed by the intersection of railroads in 1846, Atlanta hosted a population of more than ninety thousand people by 1900. Twenty years later, more than two hundred thousand people lived there—the largest city in Georgia and the third largest in the Southeast.[2] Called the Gate City, Atlanta embodied New South boosterism with New South business advocates like Henry Grady calling for industrial growth. Unlike other southern cities like Birmingham, Atlanta spawned a diverse economy of railroads, industry, construction, higher education, sports, and the promotion of the arts. Because of its extraordinary development after the Civil War, Atlantans often imagined themselves to be different from other Georgians, and the city's business elite from the 1920s through the 1960s sought to create a city that would gain national prominence. Eventually it did, and its business culture often framed distinctions between Georgia and its neighboring states like Alabama and South Carolina.

Yet Atlanta's growth also meant that thousands of residents, notably blacks, lived in segregated neighborhoods that lacked paved streets or sewer systems and had to send their children to overcrowded schools. Although black reformers and educators in Atlanta, Savannah, and Macon sought assistance from white business elites and politicians, little was forthcoming. Instead, social and economic opportunities for blacks shrank. The localism and extended kinship ties of rural areas began to break down in Atlanta, Macon, Savannah, and Augusta, and business elites emerged as new power brokers in the state. Urban and town whites paid higher taxes for better schools, which meant that more white women attended schools and often graduated from high schools. Black women, often selected by their families over sons to remain in school, took advantage of the limited educational opportunities offered to them. Even in cities and towns, black women attended public schools with fewer resources than white schools. It also meant that for postsecondary education, many attended private schools funded by northern philanthropists, local black communities, or evangelical Protestant missionary organizations. In a state still dominated by evangelical Protestants, some Georgia women drew on Christian beliefs to underscore their commitment to reform; some even looked for ways to reconstruct tentative alliances across hardened racial lines. And as many black and white women gained more education, they looked beyond traditional feminine roles of marriage or teaching to propel them into public spaces of reform and new professions. Yet black and white working-class women frequently contested these notions of reform and propriety. Working-class women—the domestics, factory workers, and prostitutes—found new forms of leisure in cities and frequently perceived family and independence differently from politicians and reformers who wanted to change them.

Women like Vara Majette and Viola Ross Napier embody one version of the "New Woman" in the early twentieth century—the educated woman who became a professional and voted. To be sure, their original choice was marriage and a version of domestic life, but because of a variety of circumstances, Majette and Napier went beyond teaching to obtain an income. Both became lawyers, and, like Lugenia Burns Hope, focused on social reforms improving schools, abolishing child labor, and temperance. Majette later turned to writing "to liberate her and bring back the magic of living" (see Leslie Dunlap's article in this volume). Often articulating their own expression of the Social Gospel movement, reformers like Hope insisted their faith in redemption demanded nothing less of them

(see Ann Short Chirhart's article). For Majette, these decisions included criticism of the white patriarchal order that insisted white women must be protected
at home, notably from black male rapists. On occasion, black and white women
worked together in organizations like the Commission on Interracial Cooperation, founded in 1921, and shared commitments to end lynchings of black men
and women. Still, interracial work had its limits, as Hope learned. Few white
women supported black women's goals for universal suffrage even after women
obtained the right to vote. Fewer still supported equality or justice for blacks.

Indeed, reforms in Progressive Era Georgia resembled those across the
South. Black men lost voting rights, and lynching rates increased. The convict
lease system, used predominantly with black prisoners, was replaced with labor
from chain gangs across the state. Believing alcohol to be part of the cause of
the Atlanta Race Riot, and certainly other moral failings, the Georgia legislature banned the manufacture and sale of alcohol in 1907. As more Georgians in
urban and rural areas drove cars, the Georgia Highway Department began to
pave roads in the state, thereby streamlining state authority over local county
highway projects. White urban and town Georgians benefited more from state
education reforms. By 1920 the state made high schools part of public schools,
began to mandate some requirements for teacher training, and allowed local
school districts to raise taxes for schools. In some instances, black Rosenwald
schools, funded by philanthropist Julius Rosenwald and black communities,
shamed whites into building better schools. Nonetheless, black students in cities
and black and white students in rural areas continued to attend poorly funded
schools that seldom had more than eight grades, often had ill-trained teachers,
and lacked basic resources like desks and textbooks.

Changes in education and culture in modern Georgia affected women like
artist Lucy Stanton and performer Gertrude "Ma" Rainey, women from different class and race backgrounds who made their mark in painting and singing
the blues, respectively. Like other middle-class white women, Stanton's father
ensured his daughter received an education, and she eventually developed her
talents in painting portraits using innovative techniques like painting ordinary
people of Georgia, including African Americans, rather than elites (see Betty
Alice Fowler's article in this volume). "Ma" Rainey captured the ears of recording producers and sang about women's relationships with men, their lives as
working women, and domestic violence. "I woke up this mornin', my head was
as sore as a boil / My main beat me last night with five feet of copper coil," she
wailed in "Sweet Rough Man" (see Steve Goodson's article). Notwithstanding
both women's ability to gain from modern culture and new technologies like
the radio and records, the differences between them highlight the problems

black women still faced. Stanton travelled to Europe and eventually painted in her own studio; Rainey's popularity declined with the Great Depression, and she returned home to try to survive on her prior earnings.

Not all Georgians welcomed modern challenges to families, communities, the authority of churches, and local control. In Georgia, the virulent mix of white paternalism, nativism, and hostility against other religions sealed the fate of Jewish factory owner Leo Frank, who was lynched by a nascent offshoot of the Ku Klux Klan for the murder of the young worker Mary Phagan in 1915. At the time, the majority of white Georgians believed that justice had been done. At rallies to support Frank's execution, they sang Fiddlin' John Carson's ballad: "Down upon her knees / To Leo Frank she plead; / He taken a stick from the trash-pile / And struck her across the head."[3]

The 1920s saw the reemergence of the Ku Klux Klan in Georgia. Valorized in the appallingly racist film *The Birth of a Nation*, the Klan not only battled to preserve white supremacy but also to uphold what they believed to be sacrosanct traditions in the South—conservative evangelical Protestantism, paternal authority in the home, and local control of schools and communities. So widespread was the Klan's influence that during the 1920s most major political leaders, including Georgia's governor, were associated with the organization. The Klan sought to underscore their understanding of traditional values and enforce temperance, which they believed were under assault from modern forces, including business elites.

Efforts to preserve traditions were rarely simply upheld by violence from terrorist groups like the Klan, nor were they uncomplicated efforts to resist all change. At the same time that cities like Atlanta, Columbus, Augusta, and Macon witnessed the growth of the textile industry, some women sought to preserve the art of home crafts. Building on shifting ideas and new opportunities for women's work, some women like Mary Hambidge and Catherine Evans Whitener promoted home production of such goods as bed spreads by women. But Whitener's craft, which itself reflected new techniques, soon became more than the production of bedspreads in the home. With modern methods of advertising and increasing mechanization, bedspread production moved right out of the home into expanding factories in northwest Georgia. With this change, most women like Whitener lost control of a craft as it became mass-produced, even as the popularity of bedspreads rested in part with their identification with a "traditional" female craft (see Randall L. Patton's article in this volume). In contrast, Hambidge, a textile weaver and social reformer, sought to preserve rural life by establishing the Hambidge Center as a retreat for creative thinkers from around the world (see Rosemary M. Magee's article).

For all of the remarkable growth of cities like Atlanta, most Georgians still lived in rural areas, attended rural evangelical Protestant churches, tried to give their children at least seven to eight years of school, and lived and died by the cotton crop. Sharecropping and tenancy had limited black and white small farmers after Reconstruction, but the 1920s signaled doom for many of these farmers. Often in debt in 1919, they now battled the boll weevil that threatened to destroy cotton production in the early 1920s. Production expanded again in 1926, but now farmers confronted competition from foreign markets and from California. Even before the stock market crash in 1929, many Georgia farmers knew that cotton held the flimsiest thread on which to base their future. Thousands left farms for small towns and cities; others, like thousands of African Americans in the South, headed north in order to find better jobs, vote, allow their children to attend schools, and maybe find a better life.

By 1930 most Georgians no longer worked on farms. For the first time in the state's history, a majority of the workforce now worked in nonagricultural jobs.[4] This counted for extraordinary changes in the way Georgians thought about themselves, their families, their communities, and their futures. No longer did sons and daughters expect to live their lives in the same community as their parents. Nor did they look to cotton for their livelihood. Blacks and whites, men and women, Georgians sought new jobs that paid more than a fickle crop and possibly provided new opportunities for schools and other conveniences of urban areas. Along the way, they met new neighbors from different parts of the state and indeed from different states. They worshiped in new fundamentalist and holiness churches like the Pentecostal Church; they tried to purchase cars that would take them around towns and cities as well as back to rural areas to visit families. Still, this split between rural and urban Georgians often resulted in tensions as rural Georgians sought to ensure that their urban cousins and former neighbors failed to control state politics. In 1917 Georgia voters approved the Neill Primary Act that codified informal agreements in the state. Known as the county unit system, the Neill Primary Act allocated votes to rural, urban, and town counties in a manner that ensured that expanding cities like Atlanta could never dominate state politics. Ruled by a political system that gave rural counties a disproportionate amount of clout, rural voters, courted and wooed by demagogue politicians from Tom Watson to Eugene Talmadge, ensured that many modern reforms were held at bay, most notably any effort to expand rights to African Americans.

But the Great Depression and New Deal programs challenged many Georgians' hold on traditions. For Georgians who tried to find better jobs in towns and cities and for those who still grabbed the hoe to chop cotton, the collapse of the nation's economy affected almost every Georgian. Even when the federal government offered assistance for towns and cities and price supports for rural areas, Governor Eugene Talmadge attacked relief efforts, believing that they destroyed an individual's desire to work and surely provided too much assistance for African Americans. "The way to handle a relief program," Talmadge insisted, "was like Mussolini was handling it in Italy, namely to line these people up and take the troops and make them work."[5] President Franklin Delano Roosevelt, long familiar with Georgia after numerous trips to Warm Springs for rehabilitation after he was stricken with polio, finally federalized the state, which allowed the appointment of Gay Shepperson as head of New Deal programs in Georgia. Now a woman, a "foreigner" to Talmadge, controlled federal assistance in Georgia and did her best to improve public schools, begin construction projects, and provide jobs for thousands of hungry and desperate people.

Like all Americans, Georgia women experienced the Great Depression differently. For Margaret Mitchell, the Great Depression marked the publication of her only published novel, *Gone With the Wind*, which remains one of the most popular novels written about the South, as well as the enormously successful release of the subsequent film produced by David Selznick (see Kathleen Ann Clark's article in this volume). For Frances Pauley, the Great Depression began her journey into public activism. "The first thing I ever remember organizing," she recalled, "was during the Depression" (see Kathryn L. Nasstrom's article). Because of her efforts, the DeKalb Clinic and a school lunch program were started in DeKalb County. For Hazel Raines, however, the Great Depression had little impact. Then a college graduate, she began taking flying lessons in Macon and became "a two bit Flight instructor and a gal trying to make her way in Aviation." Then, a few years later, "Bang," she recalled, "I was teaching flying when the telegram from Miss Jacqueline Cochran arrived asking me if I would be interested in flying planes in England" (see Paul Stephen Hudson's article). Raines launched into the job of her dreams as a pilot for the ferry service. For Mabel Murphy Smythe, as she attended Spellman College and watched her mother's friend, Lugenia Burn Hope, fight to obtain assistance for black Atlantans, the Great Depression and the New Deal were reminders that African Americans had yet to be recognized as full citizens with equal rights let alone voting rights (see Mary Rolinson's article).

In some respects, the New Deal changed Georgia. Now the state rather than local school boards controlled teacher certification. Agricultural programs increased the mechanization of cotton picking and displaced thousands of black and white tenants. Although Franklin Delano Roosevelt's commissioned report *The Report on the Economic Conditions of the South* noted the many ways in which the South ranked below the rest of the nation, it resulted in few structural reforms that could improve schools, health, and poverty. The cotton plantation system remained, albeit with wage laborers, and industries still paid minimal wages to workers. Most women, black and white, found few opportunities for employment outside of teaching or nursing even with the strides made by Majette and Napier. And blacks, even when the white primary was declared unconstitutional in *Smith v. Allright* in 1946, still had to pass literacy tests and pay poll taxes if they wanted to vote.

Georgia writers captured these tensions and conflicts throughout the twentieth century—only Mississippi claimed more writers. Georgians tackled a vast array of modern themes like sexuality, race, patriarchy, family, region, and religion. Characters' identities often roiled in turmoil even in Mitchell's *Gone With the Wind*, whose famous heroine embodied so many of the conflicts facing women as they struggled to reshape their identities to fit a more modern—and yet conservative—southern society. At times, life in Georgia became so difficult and grueling that some writers like Carson McCullers had to leave, although she occasionally returned "to renew my sense of horror" (see Carlos Dews's article in this volume). Through her characters, infused with southern attributes, McCullers used literature as a means of arguing with the South and its stultifying ideas about race, class, homosexuality, and women's roles. Lillian Smith embraced blacks' fight for equality and emphasized the sickness of both black and white southerners living under the regime of segregation in the South in her works (see John C. Inscoe's article). Others like Flannery O'Connor rejected any political commentary and focused on using novels and short stories to awaken her readers to religious faith and salvation (see Sarah Gordon's article), while Mitchell gently prodded readers to release some cherished ideals of a glorified southern past, even as she produced a seductive and powerful story that valorized white elite authority and black subservience. Born a decade later, Alice Walker absorbed erupting civil rights protests and "knew I would never be able to live in this country without resisting everything that sought to disinherit me" (see Deborah Plant's article). Her poems, essays, and novels depict the struggles of southern blacks, notably women, to define themselves as a people and as women.

World War II enhanced changes in Georgia's traditional social, cultural, political, and economic order. The expansion of military bases and defense industries brought better-paying jobs to Georgians and even created towns. Wellston, a train stop for local farmers, became Warner Robins, the site of one of the largest United States Air Force bases. Bell Bomber in Marietta later became Lockheed-Martin and helped fuel Georgia's expansion into modern industry by supplying managers with training in addition to training workers for new skills that they used to gain employment in other areas. Governor Ellis Arnall, elected in 1942, promoted educational reforms, accepted the decision to abolish the white primary in *Smith v. Allright*, and encouraged economic development during World War II. Black men grabbed new opportunities to serve in combat, insisted on black officers and better conditions at military camps and at the same time vowed to come home to a state that gave them equal rights and certainly voting rights. While black women often maintained and expanded NAACP chapters, black men joined them after the war and worked in massive voter registration campaigns. Fifty new branches of the NAACP joined larger branches in Atlanta, Savannah, and Macon, while one-fifth of the eligible black population registered to vote.[6] Chapters in Atlanta and Savannah drew from their chapters' origins in activism when John and Lugenia Burns Hope, among others, called for the right to vote back in 1917. Former students from black colleges, primarily located in Atlanta, returned to communities and focused on gaining positions of authority. Leaders of black colleges like Benjamin Mays of Morehouse University refused to use segregated facilities and encouraged his students to do the same. At Fort Valley State College, Horace Mann Bond reminded students that they were fighting a war for freedoms that they lacked.

Black and white women often took jobs in defense industries to earn better pay than many of them could earn in teaching or other jobs. Although women's opportunities were still restricted, their experiences during World War II changed them. Without husbands or steady beaus for four years and frequently living in towns or urban areas, some women began to see opportunities and possibilities they had never known. No longer monitored by neighbors or church members, women went to movies, looked in department store windows for consumer goods, and jitterbugged in aisles at swing music concerts. To be sure, most women still focused on getting married and having children, but they occasionally thought about what else they might do while married. Perhaps they could volunteer for the League of Women Voters (LWV) like Frances Pauley or the Southern Conference for Human Welfare (SCHW) like Lillian Smith. Or maybe life in the South was no longer an option. Certainly Coretta Scott King sought an independent life when she left the South for voice lessons at the New England Conservatory of Music in Boston. Mabel Murphy Smythe left Fort Valley Normal and Industrial School and, with her family, began her career as an international teacher and diplomat. Organizations like the LWV, SCHW, and the Southern Regional Council (SRC) focused on voter registration and gave women opportunities to organize campaigns. Still, other women, like Hazel Raines and Katherine Dunaway, had little to do with these organizations that called for social justice. Their lives were circumscribed by a profession or, in Dunaway's case, raising a family and volunteering in her community for the Parent Teacher Association, working in her Methodist Church, and eventually founding the North Fulton chapter of the Georgia Federation of Republican Women (see Robin Morris's article in this volume).

For all the efforts to push for increased rights and social justice during World War II, many whites fought back. The Georgia they knew valued traditions of community interaction, a hierarchical social order with African Americans at the bottom, evangelical Protestantism, and family structure. Modernity may have brought a growing economy, but to some Georgians it also brought the possibility that their social order might turn upside down. Voters returned Eugene Talmadge to the governor's office, but when he died before he could take office, a scandal known as the "Three Governors Controversy" in 1946 made Georgia the laughingstock of the nation as Georgians fought over who the governor should be. That same year, Maceo Snipes, a black World War II veteran, proudly voted in the primary and was killed by ten white men three days later. The following week, a mob murdered two black couples in Walton County. Even President Truman's best efforts failed to break the silences among those in Walton County who might have known what happened.

As in any period, responses to the swift return of white supremacy and violence varied across Georgia. On the whole, activism declined as NAACP chapters shrunk, the SCHW collapsed, and the SRC offered tepid support for equal rights. Little wonder that Mabel Murphy Smythe decided that she had to leave Georgia in order to live and accomplish what she believed she could do. Still, many African Americans like Coretta Scott King decided to remain in the South and try to change it (see Glenn T. Eskew's article in this volume). She agreed with new husband Martin Luther King Jr.'s decision to accept the pastorate at a church in Montgomery, Alabama, yet she had long decided to mark her own path to reform. Her Christian belief in duty to social justice and equality expanded to include human rights for the poor in the United States. So, too, Frances Pauley increased her work for equal rights as she met more blacks and agreed that segregated schools for blacks could never be equal to white schools. In Plains, Rosalynn Carter not only assisted her husband, Jimmy, run the family peanut farm after bearing four children, she also helped run his campaigns for political offices in Georgia (see Scott Kaufman's article).

During the civil rights movement in the 1950s and 1960s, black women fought to integrate public schools, ensure voting rights, and desegregate public spaces in Atlanta, Albany, and other towns and cities. Organizations like the NAACP, Southern Christian Leadership Conference (SCLC), and the Student Nonviolent Coordinating Committee (SNCC) provided opportunities for black women's activism, even though they were denied positions of leadership. At times some white women, like Frances Pauley and Rosalynn Carter, joined these efforts for open schools and human rights. Firmly rooted in the legacy of the Social Gospel, they could see no other way for their state to enter the modern world and realize its promise for all its residents, many of whom were unable to vote or have access to equal employment opportunities. This path later led some women to call for equal rights. Most vocal of the three, Carter championed the Equal Rights Amendment as First Lady of Georgia and First Lady of the United States. Still, to southern conservatives, the ERA seemed to eradicate the very core of womanhood, the differences that made women distinct and valued. Katherine Dunaway led the anti-ERA forces in Georgia and must have smiled when the amendment was defeated. After all, she battled a First Lady from her own state and won. Alice Walker, an activist in the NAACP Legal Defense and Education Fund, used her passion for writing to reach a public audience and redefine a position for black women in public spaces.

Conservative evangelical roots of Georgia women manifested themselves in multiple ways. Rejected by some, filtered and sifted by others, accepted by still others, Georgia women represented the national constellation of women's voices by the 1980s. Searching for the best and most appropriate ways to articulate and define what it meant to be a woman, they joined organizations, worked with or against one another, worshiped in congregations, and explored the meaning of family and community. Other women never joined an organization, and still others continued to share efforts to survive on minimal wages or low incomes from farms. None of their voices appear in either volume on Georgia women because they lacked the time or skills to write about their lives. Still, organizations from the Neighborhood Union to evangelical Protestant women's groups to the SCLC endeavored to represent them and include them in their work. From the colonial era that witnessed Mary Musgrove and Elizabeth Lichtenstein Johnson push for their beliefs in the future of specific future Georgians to Lucy Craft Laney and Mary Gay, who carved paths for women professionals and writers after the Civil War; to reformers like Lugenia Burns Hope and Vara Majette, who became public activists for social justice; to writers like Margaret Mitchell and Alice Walker, whose novels expressed the tensions within modern Georgia; to Rosalynn Carter and Katherine Dunaway, who perceived the ERA from different perspectives, Georgia women grabbed opportunities to articulate their beliefs in actions and writings. Their efforts mark the diverse roots of Georgia's history and the legacy of slavery, the Civil War, and patriarchal evangelical culture. Indeed, it is quite possible that Mildred Lewis Rutherford and Susie King Taylor, women who clearly had opposing views of slavery, would approve of what women accomplished after World War I. After all, Alice Walker and Katherine Dunaway echoed the multiple threads of gender, class, race, and religious beliefs that were spawned in Georgia from its colonial origins.[7]

NOTES

1. As quoted in Jacqueline Anne Rouse, *Lugenia Burns Hope: Black Southern Reformer* (Athens: University of Georgia Press, 1989), 43.

2. Andy Ambrose, "Atlanta," *New Georgia Encyclopedia*, February 16, 2012, http://www.georgia encyclopedia.org/nge/Article.jsp?id=h-2207 (accessed May 25, 2013).

3. Franklyn Bliss Snyder, "The Ballad of Mary Phagan," *Leo Frank Trial*, http://law2.umkc.edu/faculty/projects/ftrials/frank/frankballad.html (accessed June 30, 2012), reprinted from *Journal of American Folk-Lore* 31 (1918): 264–66.

4. Numan V. Bartley, *The Creation of Modern Georgia*, 2nd edition (Athens: University of Georgia Press, 1990), 170.

5. As quoted in William Anderson, *The Wild Man from Sugar Creek: The Political Career of Eugene Talmadge* (Baton Rouge: Louisiana State University Press, 1975), 120.

6. Stephen Tuck, *Beyond Atlanta: The Struggle for Racial Equality in Georgia, 1940–1980* (Athens: University of Georgia Press, 2003), 43–73.

7. For further reading on the central themes and topics in the history of Georgia between 1733 and the early twentieth century, see Kenneth Coleman, *History of Georgia* (Athens: University of Georgia Press, 1977); Bartley, *The Creation of Modern Georgia*; and *The New Georgia Encyclopaedia* at http://www.georgiaencyclopedia.org/nge/Home.jsp (accessed April 4, 2012). See also special issues on Georgia women in *The Georgia Historical Quarterly* 76 (Summer 1992), and 82 (Winter 1998). More specialized studies are to be found in the bibliography to this volume.

Lugenia Burns Hope

(1871–1947)

Fulfilling a Sacred Purpose

ANN SHORT CHIRHART

Within two years of moving to Atlanta in 1898, Lugenia Burns Hope emerged as a leader for race work in the African American community. Primarily remembered for founding the Neighborhood Union (NU) in 1908, Hope's work as a reformer originated during one of the most dire periods for African Americans in the South: race riots exploded, lynchings increased exponentially, citizenship rights were retracted, appalling labor conditions for sharecroppers expanded, and the promise of education for blacks collapsed as most white southerners found ways to remind black southerners of their inferior place in society. For four decades, Hope battled this trajectory at the local, state, and national levels. In addition to organizing the NU, she became a leader in the National Association for Colored Women (NACW), organized voter registration campaigns for the National Association for the Advancement of Colored People (NAACP), helped start the National Council of Negro Women (NCNW), and unabashedly promoted equal rights for blacks to the Commission on Interracial Cooperation (CIC). Like many other African American women reformers, she did this while raising a family. In addition to caring for two sons, she also promoted her husband John Hope's work at Morehouse College and later Atlanta University.[1]

While often overshadowed by black women like Mary Church Terrell or Mary McLeod Bethune, Hope has most frequently been recognized by scholars for her organization of the NU. These scholars contend that her motives for founding this group stemmed directly from the Atlanta Race Riot of 1906. To be sure, Hope's papers, the bulk of which contain NU records and a few personal reflections, contribute to this interpretation. Yet a more careful consideration of Hope's life and papers suggests a broader framework for interpreting her

LUGENIA BURNS HOPE

at the approximate time she founded the Neighborhood Union, circa 1908.

Neighborhood Union Collection, Woodruff Library, Emory University.

actions, and conveys greater significance to what she did—and did not—accomplish through her decades-long activism on behalf of African American communities. The NU represented only one way that Hope implemented her mission, and while the Atlanta Riot solidified Hope's commitment to local activism, the origins of the NU and her later work lay in her prior experiences in Chicago and her ongoing efforts to combine principles and practices of maternalism, Christian theology, and interracial organizing to contest the barriers facing African Americans in the Jim Crow South.

Throughout her life, Hope's perception of equality and citizenship drew on her interpretation of her mission and duty—a blend of social gospel theory, black and white women's reform agendas, commitment to black women's leadership, persistent efforts to achieve equality for African Americans, and the steadfast conviction that African Americans were the ones who practiced true Christianity. She believed that the right to vote and the empowerment of educated, professional African Americans would lead to social justice for all blacks. It did not. Hope's efforts, like that of many of her peers, failed to engage a broader base of working-class blacks.

Still, Hope's understanding of what a reformer should do and be evolved as she devised her vision for how a true Christian should act in the world.[2] Like Charlotte Hawkins Brown and Bethune, Hope countered white supremacists' language of Christianity with the black women's insistence that they were the real Christians—the most radical political response they could muster against white supremacy.[3] A community activist, she demanded equality, social justice, education, and citizenship for all African Americans—an understanding for the salvation of her race that she shared with leading black women reformers of her generation—and most often targeted white women reformers to work with them for interracial change. Above all, black women reformers like Hope understood that white women, those who continued to demand subservience and humility from black women in households and public spaces, held the key to undermining the white supremacist hierarchy.

Before Hope moved to Atlanta, she became acquainted with women's reform work and social gospel advocates in Progressive Era Chicago. Born on February 19, 1871, to Ferdinand and Louisa M. Bertha Burns in St. Louis, Missouri, Lugenia Burns was the youngest of the Burns' seven children. After Ferdinand's sudden death, the Burns moved to Chicago where Louisa hoped to provide Lugenia with a better education. But Louisa Burns was unquestionably concerned about other factors. During the 1880s, southern states began to enact a pernicious combination of de facto and de jure segregation. Chicago's economic prospects beckoned to many educated and skilled African Americans in the

1880s and 1890s. Here Lugenia attended high school, and afterward the Chicago Art Institute between 1890 and 1893, an education that set her apart from most African Americans.[4] To help support her mother, she quit school and worked as a secretary for the board of directors of the International Order of the King's Daughters and Sons (IOKDS), a white charity organization that provided instruction for young working girls and worked with the sick in Chicago. She then accepted a second position as secretary for the Silver Cross Club, a business that offered food for young working people. Through her connections with this organization, Hope became familiar with Jane Addams's work at Hull House.[5]

Lugenia Burns Hope's employment did more than serve as financial support for her mother and family.[6] Both jobs provided her with insight into the ways white reform organizations assisted young working-class women as well as the poor in Chicago's neighborhoods. She learned how educated, single women framed their public work within the context of Progressive Era themes of maternalism and the social gospel at the same time their careers offered them an independent life.[7] At the core of maternalism lay beliefs in women's unique values as nurturers, in addition to their responsibilities to the nation because of their shared capacity for motherhood.[8] Social gospel, often inadequately described as a movement, was an effort by some American Protestants to perform Christian mission work and create a cohesive community in order to bind society together at a time of divisions and violence.[9] How to accomplish this was described very differently by practitioners, on the one hand, and evangelical Protestant theorists—who ranged from Josiah Strong, Walter Rauschenbusch, and Jane Addams to Ida Wells-Barnett and Mary Church Terrell—on the other.

The IOKDS illustrated one way women social gospel practitioners tried to implement their understanding of a maternalist Christian mission. Founded in 1886 by a group of white women in New York City, the women formed a "sisterhood of service" in cities to develop spiritual life and create Christian activities.[10] Using a quotation from Mark 10:45 as their theme, "Not to be ministered unto, but to minister," the IOKDS built hospitals and offered education for the poor. The organization and its members drew from a variety of Protestant denominations and insisted that its Christian members practice Christian teachings.[11] Hope saw how these principles resulted in practical accomplishments in Chicago like cleaning up communities, providing day care for children, and offering health care.[12] Three nights a week, she directed course work for young working women.

Hope also knew about African American activism, notably black women's activism, because of her family's connections to Ida Wells. Wells, one of the most prominent black activists of the era, witnessed Burns's older sister's marriage in St. Louis in 1881, and became a leader in the National Association of Colored Women (NACW), which was founded in 1896.[13] An internationally renowned reformer by 1895, Wells led a passionate campaign against lynching and rape in the South. Two publications, *Southern Horrors* (1892) and *A Red Record* (1895), documented brutality against blacks and violence against black women in the South, and called out white southern Christians, including white women, for accepting the lie that all black men who were lynched had raped white women, while black women's rapists remained unpunished.[14]

So although Hope valued her work with white women reformers, she knew the limits of interracial work and understood the boundaries of white Christians.[15] She no doubt appreciated the work her white employers gave her, but she must have understood that interracial efforts focused on social improvements rather than equality between races. Still, by the late nineteenth century, interaction with white reformers and social gospel advocates provided some of the only opportunities for African Americans to interact with whites in order to open fissures in racial boundaries wherever blacks could crack them.[16]

Hope's early work for the IOKDS and the Silver Cross Club, in addition to her knowledge of black activism, reveals part of her personality that remained constant. A devout Christian, she chose employment opportunities deliberately and took pains to learn each organization's mission. Both women-centered organizations relied on educated women implementing reforms for women in homes and communities. Her work provided her with personal fulfillment and a sense of independence similar to other African American women reformers like Wells, Terrell, Brown, and Bethune, whom she met later.[17] As Hope later recalled, her work in Chicago provided her with a "rich and thrilling experience"—one that she described as one of the privileges of her life.[18] So essential were these experiences that they framed the core of her future goals.

These characteristics became more evident when Lugenia began dating her future husband, John Hope, whom she met during the World's Columbia Exposition in Chicago in 1893. John Hope, born in 1868, worked at the Lexington Hotel during the exposition while on summer break from his studies at Brown University in Rhode Island. Like Lugenia, John came from a mixed-race background, with free African American family members in Augusta, Georgia. He attended a preparatory school in Massachusetts followed by his acceptance at Brown University.

If John was quickly smitten with Lugenia, she had her doubts about the relationship. Here was Lugenia Burns, a young, independent woman who was already working and defining her goals. There was John Hope, a university senior who seemed uncertain about his future. John Hope's correspondence to

Lugenia indicates her reluctance to commit to their relationship, and he often complained about her silences that were "inexplicable and disturbing."[19]

In 1894, Hope accepted a position at Roger Williams University in Nashville, Tennessee, but his heart remained in Chicago with Lugenia. He wrote frequent letters to her each week, sometimes letters up to twenty pages, imploring her to write if "you still love me, if we are once more to embrace . . . if Genie is to make me a more nearly perfect man."[20] Because few of her letters remain, most of what we know about their courtship comes from John's lengthy letters, which often quote from her letters and address her questions. While John's letters are effusive with expressions of love, she often responded with concerns about their future, or with humor. He requested that she write to him twice a week. She did not.[21] Instead, she continued to date other men as she worked two jobs.

That Lugenia loved John is unquestionable, but her reservations ranged from fears of leaving her mother without financial support to her concern about living in the South. Equally important, she intended to preserve her independence in a marriage that would be based on mutual respect, allow her to run the household, and pursue what she understood as God's calling to serve the African American community. Through most of their four-year courtship, Lugenia Burns remained deliberate, patient, and cautious, and revealed little of John's torrent of emotions.

When John continued to write long, passionate letters that requested frequent responses from her, she sent him two blank postcards.[22] John, sober and shy, failed to understand her humor. "Did you make a mistake?" he asks.[23] During their courtship, Lugenia contemplated becoming a missionary to Africa, to which he replied that he would "become a nobler man by loving the memory of so saintly a woman."[24] Through the years, they shared their devout Christian faith, readings in literature and history, a commitment to serve their race, and their love for each other, beliefs that forged the groundwork for their extraordinary partnership.

At the end of summer in 1896, Lugenia finally accepted John's proposal on condition that they would keep it secret until the following year. Even then, she again briefly considered becoming a missionary to Africa.[25] If, as historians observe, Lugenia's primary concerns were supporting her mother and moving to the South, then her desire to become a missionary, something she considered twice during their courtship, challenges this interpretation, for surely here money was scarcely a concern. Numerous black and white women, including Brown, Bethune, and Wells, considered becoming missionaries to Africa and China during this period—an opportunity that would allow them to combine their commitment to Christian duty with independence and adventure.[26]

What Hope sought from John was assurance that he would accept her autonomy and be true to their relationship. Six days before John and Lugenia married, she poured her passions for him and her ideas about marriage in a letter.
"In just a few days we will be together and another we shall be as one to love
each other always," she writes. And she insists, "We must always work for the
other's good . . . contributing to the others welfare."[27] To her, a successful marriage meant that a husband should respect his wife's interests, and that included
some kind of missionary work.[28] They married in Chicago on December 29,
1897, and moved to Nashville.[29]

After a brief stay in Nashville, John Hope accepted a position at Atlanta Baptist College. The position fulfilled both his desire to return to Georgia, where
some of his family still lived, as well as his desire to become a faculty member
at a college (whose reputation was rapidly improving). Atlanta Baptist College
and Atlanta offered other possibilities for Lugenia's commitment to community
reform and teaching as well, and her agreement to this move was vital for their
marriage. A growing city after the Civil War, African Americans composed almost 40 percent of Atlanta's approximately ninety thousand residents in 1900,
and she must have known that she could draw from her experiences in Chicago
to assist young women and the poor.[30] In September 1898, the young couple
moved to Atlanta. Here their local and organizational work made them one of
the most formidable partnerships in American history.

Atlanta Baptist College, later renamed Morehouse College in 1913, joined
Spelman College, Atlanta University, Morris Brown College, and Clark University on the West End of Atlanta. These schools provided some of the best
education for African Americans in the South. Here in the West End, faculty
lived with some black business owners, like Alonzo Herndon of Atlanta Life
Insurance Company, and David T. Howard, owner of a prominent under-
taker service. The Hopes' economic status and social networks in fraternal
orders and churches placed them in the aspiring group within the African
American community in Atlanta. In most cases, their lighter skin, successful
business ventures, and education distinguished them from the majority of
Atlanta blacks who moved there to find jobs other than sharecropping. Some,
like John and Lugenia Burns Hope, came from families with no former slave
members.

The Hopes' social networks consisted of W. E. B. and Nina Du Bois, George
Towns of Atlanta University, Reverend H. H. Proctor of the First Congrega-
tional Church, and other black professionals, all of whom were committed to
race work and equality for African Americans.[31] The Hopes joined Friendship Baptist Church, which was affiliated with Atlanta Baptist College and was

organized quickly in Atlanta after the Civil War—Atlanta's first autonomous black Baptist church. Atlanta's black women initiated social reform work in the late nineteenth century when they established a chapter of the NACW by 1899, which Lugenia joined at some date unrevealed by the historical record.

As the Hopes and other members of Atlanta's aspiring African American community discovered, the degrees, property, income, and lighter skin meant little in the face of escalating racism and segregation in the 1890s. If Lugenia Burns Hope rode a streetcar, she, like African American working-class women, moved to segregated seating in the back of the car. If John Hope wanted to vote, he had to pay a poll tax, and by 1908, pass a literacy test just like darker-skinned African American men.[32] The black elite knew about the brutal use of black convicts at the Chattahoochee Brick Company in northwest Atlanta. Indeed, a columnist for the *Atlanta Independent* wrote in 1907 that black convicts' labor was easily observed from Atlanta University.[33]

Worse still were the rapid increases in lynching between 1890 and 1900—an appalling average of one African American a month.[34] The outrageous spectacle of Sam Hose's lynching in Coweta County in 1899, thirty miles southwest of Atlanta, shook African Americans in the region. So harrowing was this incident that Ida Wells hired a special investigator to learn what caused this grisly murder. Even though John and Lugenia Hope never mentioned it, their friends, W. E. B. and Nina Du Bois did, because W. E. B. later wrote that he saw Hose's knuckles displayed in an Atlanta store window.[35] The Du Bois also carried the painful knowledge of the lack of medical care for blacks in Atlanta when Burghardt, their two-year-old son, died of diphtheria in 1899. Even living on campus at Atlanta Baptist failed to shelter the Hopes from the stench and dirt on the West End. Here was a segregated neighborhood that lacked sewers and a paved street, served as the city's dumping grounds, and was home to various gambling and prostitution sites.

Hope drew upon her friendships in her West End early years to begin her own work. She participated in Atlanta University conferences in 1899 and 1900, sponsored by Atlanta University faculty, including Du Bois, on "The Welfare of the Negro Child."[36] Following the conferences, she immediately began to raise funds for a kindergarten for black children, Gate City Free Kindergarten, funded by black elites like Herndon and Howard. The birth of the Hopes' first son in 1901, Edward Swain Hope, added to Lugenia's recognition of the need for day care for black working-class families; and Hope, ever mindful of her mission work to God and her race, sought to organize additional day care centers. Hope also taught courses at Spelman College on sewing and millinery. In 1909 the Hopes' second son, John II, was born.

If Atlanta's race men and women ever believed that working with some white southerners would alleviate the worst aspects of Jim Crow, the 1906 Atlanta Race Riot surely changed their minds. Lugenia Hope's later recollections of the riot underscored the sense of betrayal and fear that Atlanta's blacks experienced on September 22, 1906. That night of terror, murder, and violence brought the reality of white supremacy to her front porch. Stoked by Atlanta newspaper reports of black men assaulting white women during a virulent Georgia gubernatorial election between Hoke Smith and Clark Howell, tensions erupted at Five Points in Atlanta that September night. African Americans walked to streetcar stops as they made their way home from shopping, dancing, work, or a break at a local saloon. On the way, they met an enraged mob of whites who attacked blacks on streetcars, destroyed black businesses, and killed an estimated twenty-five African Americans before the rampage slowed at three in the morning on September 23—the worst race riot of the era. The police and governor did little to stop the mob.

One-and-a-half miles away in the West End, John and Lugenia Burns Hope feared for their own lives and those of their son and neighbors.[37] Black families brought their children to Atlanta's black colleges for protection, but the white mob then headed for the West End. John Hope, one of many blacks armed with guns to protect themselves, patrolled the Morehouse campus in the face of the escalating pogrom. "Gangsters [camped] at our gates," seethed Lugenia Hope.[38] African Americans from other areas, even out of state, smuggled arms to Atlanta blacks in coffins and soiled laundry.

As the "gangsters" headed for Atlanta Baptist, they stopped short at the sight of armed black men. Hope recalled that white people nailed up their homes in fear of retribution because they knew "how they had treated the Negro all the while."[39] Blacks prepared to die. Then, Hope sardonically recalled, and only then did "the good Christian white people care what happened to the Negro."[40] The white churches' doors opened to admit blacks for protection. To Hope, their belated response came from fear—fear of blacks' response to the inexcusable racist actions from whites. Fear, not a commitment to Christian compassion and duty, pushed these "good Christians" to finally act.

The Atlanta Race Riot, Hope recalled, proclaimed to African Americans that "their white friends had planned to destroy them. The Negro[es] will never forget or forgive the shock of realizing that their white friends had betrayed them." This was one of the few times she ever publicly stated the consequences of racism in such stark terms.[41] Disease, lynchings, rape, and the convict lease system already threatened survival of the race. The hysterical mobs who mobilized against African Americans were bent on destroying it. African Americans became even more attentive to saving themselves.

Hope knew how to organize coalitions through her work in Chicago and with the Gate City Kindergarten. Now she focused on expanding that mission of neighborhood reform by galvanizing more women in the neighborhood. Nine neighbors gathered at her home in July 1908 to discuss how they could best serve Atlanta's West End. Naming their group the Neighborhood Union (NU), their motto was "Thy Neighbor as Thyself," words from Leviticus 19:18. Their primary purpose was to "elevate the moral, social, intellectual and spiritual standards in each neighborhood" in addition to helping mothers care for children, improving sanitation in homes, campaigning against "vice and disease," and teaching classes on cooking and housekeeping.[42] By noting the spiritual and physical needs of the neighborhood, the NU created their version of a settlement house.

Drawing from their motto, the use of which indicated how the IOKDS and the central role of black women in church mission work had influenced Hope, the founders of the NU referred to a story that compelled them to act. In a family residence in the West End, a young woman sat on the front porch while her husband and father worked and later became chronically ill. She died, leaving her three children without a mother. The women neighbors realized that they had neglected to pay attention to a shy neighbor, who might have lived had she received some medical assistance, but who was unaware of how to obtain it. Thus, the NU's motto recalled the women to their maternal and Christian duties to care for children and families around them.[43] Indeed, most historians rely on this story to account for the NU's origins.

Yet the motto meant more than that. Coming on the heels of the 1906 race riot, African American women, organized by Lugenia Burns Hope, used the verse not only to recall other African American women to their duties to each other but also to call out white Atlantans, white women in particular, of their responsibilities to blacks. If white southerners claimed to be Christians, and indeed most of them did, then who were their neighbors, and what exactly did it mean to love their neighbors as themselves? Surely this excluded mob violence and riots attacking black neighborhoods and businesses, as well as tolerating filthy slums and lynchings. From the outset, NU women politicized their public work by using a biblical verse with which southern Christians would be familiar, and insisted that neighbors included Atlanta's African Americans. African American women asserted that they, not white women, knew the true meaning of Christianity. That the NU used a Bible verse rather than a more overt political claim to equality marks the extent to which they also understood the limits of their political reach.

In Hope's recollections about the riot, she scolded "good Christian white people"—a comment that drew from black Christians' understanding of what

Christianity actually meant. Since slavery, African Americans interpreted Christianity differently than their white Christian owners—the owners who would face judgment for their sins against slaves.[44] "Slaves," thundered Frederick Douglas, "knew enough of the orthodox theology of the time to consign all bad slaveholders to hell."[45] Moreover, black women always claimed authority to interpret and preach Christianity in communities north and south.[46] Hope and NU members, then, sustained this tradition by using common biblical texts to force white evangelicals to confront alternative meanings.

As Hope wrote, any group created a community through face-to-face associations in neighborhoods. But to practice true Christianity, individuals needed to prepare their hearts, heads, and hands out of their love for Christ.[47] The story of the woman on the porch who later died became the NU's public promotional message. Certainly to Hope, however, the NU embodied her Christian duty to enact Christ's teachings about loving your neighbor as yourself. "Christ," she noted, "came not to call the religious but the sinners."[48] Like other social gospel practitioners, Hope believed the failure to transform a community was as venal a sin as a lack of faith. "We have to work to get people together," she wrote, "who have nothing in common and then get them sufficiently acquainted with each other to be able to work together."[49] Moreover, to Hope, women knew best about how to accomplish the work of preserving civilization because of their roles in the family and the community. "Who," she asked, "can better train and reform than a woman?"[50] Dating from the nineteenth century, black women rooted their fight against oppression and understanding of community and family needs in their Christian beliefs.[51]

Hope's perspective on social reform, then, drew from several sources: her Christian faith, her readings (which ranged from social gospel theorists to biblical commentaries), her ties with black women reformers, and her experiences with white maternalist reformers in Chicago. Thus, to Hope, the NU was more than a response to a neighbor woman's death or the Atlanta Race Riot. The NU was the public embodiment of her mission, and that mission was intended not only to aid the black community but also to convert white Christians to an equitable understanding of community. Hope and other black women reformers never simply attempted to replicate or emulate white standards; rather, they constructed their own values and beliefs from their experiences and interpretations of the Bible and hoped that whites might learn from them.

To that end, women in the NU initially investigated homes in the West Side and conducted surveys in order to determine what the community needs were and how the NU could best serve them.[52] Hope divided the West Side into ten districts, with two district leaders responsible for reporting to the NU on their district's conditions. In 1912 the NU had grown from nine to eighteen members. By 1914, the NU expanded its work into other black neighborhoods in Atlanta. Initially, members of the NU included members of Atlanta's professional, educated, and working-class women, although apparently working-class women did not stay in the organization. To Hope, the NU's goal was to create a "community[,] not simply a group of houses or families[,] but [with] those families knowing one another, assisting and ever loving another."[53] The intent of the NU's interactions with community women was to bridge intraracial class divisions and attempt to establish a grassroots, local organization that would implement an egalitarian agenda.[54] Soon the NU's funds sponsored various programs that ranged from day care to disease prevention to cleanliness and education classes.[55] NU members went door to door in their districts noting what food each family ate, the amount of milk they drank, how many people lived in each home, and who looked after the children during the day. They inquired about illnesses and whether family members knew how to prevent hookworms or whether they understood what typhoid fever and tuberculosis were.[56]

One of the most controversial aspects of the NU's work were the home visits that resulted in either evictions or reports to white police about suspected criminal activities in homes.[57] Minutes of the NU repeat concerns and fears about "houses of ill repute," specific dance halls that played blues or jazz music, "blind tigers" (places where alcohol was sold illegally), and children who lived in filthy homes or homes frequented by men where foul language was heard.[58] On September 9, 1909, the NU formed an investigative committee on the West Side to report menaces to the neighborhood. Using connections with white law enforcement and petitions to Atlanta's city council, this NU committee closed many brothels, poolrooms, and blind tigers. They evicted residents suspected of "bad" morals or living patterns that endangered community morals and health.[59]

As problematic as these actions may seem on the surface, Hope and NU members' approach to reform constituted more than simply mandating that all African Americans should replicate white middle-class standards of respectability.[60] The NU's face-to-face encounters with working-class blacks attempted to bridge the gap between them. Like Progressive reformers across the nation, the NU understood how diseases and poor diet led to high infant and adult mortality rates. Eugenicists' belief in Anglo-Saxon superiority, white supremacists' stereotypes of African Americans, and appalling conditions in black urban neighborhoods spawned real concerns about declining birthrates and the increase in diseases.

To the NU, investigating the home meant changing overcrowded, fetid conditions that created an environment ripe for bacteria and diseases like typhoid fever and tuberculosis that were killing blacks in urban communities.[61] They read about diseases and taught classes on cleanliness and ventilation not merely to shape morals but to promote health and prevent escalating deaths from diseases. They repeatedly helped sick families by bringing them food, sending doctors, holding health clinics, and caring for infants of sick mothers.[62]

One of the NU's successful interracial efforts was their campaign to reduce the spread of tuberculosis with the support of the white Atlanta Anti-Tuberculosis Association. Many white women relied on black domestic workers to clean their homes and care for their children, so reducing the spread of disease was obviously in everyone's best interest.[63] And white women who relied on black women for domestic labor insisted on strict standards of cleanliness and domestic education. Paradoxically, however, they associated black women with filth and immorality. One generation removed from the plantation household, white women nonetheless persistently sought ways to humiliate the black women who kept their homes clean, cooked their food, and cared for their children—even requiring education for making a bed (being told, for example, to avoid breathing on a pillowcase).[64]

Moreover, the home, as Hope stated and NU members agreed, was the key site of human development. To NU members, their sacred purpose included improving the moral community and promoting black interests by protecting the home. Family and community constituted the core of a civilization, and by creating a thriving community, civilization—black and white—could prosper. The black home must become an environment that not only preserved the race by preventing disease but also encouraged self-determination and self-help, key components for a fit race.[65] Here in their homes, black families must demonstrate self-respect and morality.[66] This included practicing Christian values in order to avoid sin.

Thus, the NU's mission included efforts to monitor working-class women's sexuality. They perceived that black working-class women needed to be protected and saved from venereal disease and rape. Often the result of white mob violence, raping black women became another means for white men to assert their dominance and humiliate blacks.[67] Worse still, sexual transgressions underscored racist beliefs in black women's immorality, as whites insisted that black women asked for white men's sexual assaults; it became the ultimate means of denying black women their right to their bodies. Still, NU members' attitudes about sexual behavior, similar to those promoted by the NACW, seemed to imply that their working-class sisters needed reminders about proper behavior with men, and at times, NU women's actions reinforced many whites' attacks on black working-class women's sexuality.[68] Certainly, the NU's ties to white police made the NU suspicious to some working-class blacks. Why would women of their own race cooperate with white police bent on assaulting them? How could they criticize working women who simply wanted to have some fun at a dance hall after working all day in a white woman's home?[69]

Yet rather than focusing on black women reformers' attempts to inculcate middle-class values in other black women, which is what some scholars have done, it seems just as likely that the reformers, bound by race and targets of white supremacists, sought to find the best way to instruct black women and preserve their safety at home and at work.[70] Familiar with the plethora of publications on morality and respectable behavior written by African Americans and women like Margaret Slattery, Hope and her NU cohorts targeted sexual behaviors of working-class black women in order to build Christian and healthy environments as well as preserve boundaries against the potential for violence from white men. Mothers knew more about the beginning of crime, noted Hope, and they certainly knew Christian behavior.[71] If children were the future of the race, then what they saw and heard in the home must be monitored. This meant that women needed to avoid having men other than their husbands in their homes or being paid for sexual favors. Yet by directing attention to younger, working-class women, the NU implied that women alone bore the burden of the race's future. Both the "agents and targets of reform," black women became the focus of black and white organizations, and their sexuality caused endless angst, for most reformers assiduously avoided public criticism of black and white male sexuality. The NU may have failed to address economic circumstances that often forced working-class women into low-paying jobs or even prostitution, but the NU lacked the means for direct political action though which to address such concerns.[72]

Notwithstanding the NU's shortcomings, the women successfully reduced diseases and improved the neighborhood by providing day care, classes for women, and recreation. They continued to redefine their mission. In Hope's most direct writings, she specified how she understood the connection between Christianity, women, and reform. At some time in the 1920s, the peak years of her interracial reform efforts, she organized and revised her readings and beliefs in four lessons. Here she became the evangelical teacher as she grounded the NU's purpose in black women's construction of true Christian theology and, more important, sought to challenge white women's Christian beliefs that tolerated white supremacy.

First, Hope selected New Testament readings from the Gospels and Epistles: Mark 1–3, Matthew 5, Luke 4 and 5, John 6–11 and 13, First Corinthians, and the Epistle of James.[73] Her comments on these readings referred to sinners' dilemmas, service Christ did, and what real Christians should do to follow his example. For example, after the reading on Mark 2, Hope wrote that "no one can forgive sin but God," a comment that underscores her understanding that all Christians were accountable to God for their actions.[74] She noted that when Christ was criticized for eating with sinners, he responded that he came for the sinners and not the righteous. Matthew 5 includes the beatitudes and other comments from Jesus about how to live, which were "'Jesus' standards for righteousness," and therefore standards for all Christians.[75]

Hope structured four lessons that centered on the ways in which a community organization fulfilled the mission of Jesus—redemption came from service to sinners. In Lesson I, Hope writes that community organizations dealing with groups "must have Christ's spirit."[76] By this she meant love thy neighbor as thyself. Reiterating this in Lesson II, Hope states that individuals had to prepare their heart, head, and hands; and to prepare the heart meant "faith in Christ and humanity."[77] Through Christian faith, reformers needed to believe that all things were possible, including neighborly love and organizational work. Lesson III again addresses women's community organizations whose spiritual motives for reform came from members' love of Christ. Here Hope includes readings from John 6–11 and 13 and First Corinthians, writing that "love was the only acceptable motive in service."[78]

This lesson also included a reference to Margaret Slattery's *The Girl and Her Religion*, written in 1913. Slattery wrote numerous Sunday school publications, and *The Girl and Her Religion* was directed to women who may attend college and then serve their community as their moral duty. Her examples of "handicapped," "privileged," "misunderstood," or "easily led" girls whose demise into poverty, despair, prostitution, and pride offered good reason for not only including Christian faith in one's life but also serving Christ through deeds.[79] That meant educating people about tuberculosis, making the home a good environment, teaching young girls about proper morals, and providing them with better education and work opportunities.

In Lesson IV Hope defines her own motives for community organization that combine her faith with writings from social gospel advocates, because an organization needed a "sacred purpose." "The home," Hope writes, "is the basis of a peoples' development. Here the fundamental lessons of system, thrift, law, and sacrifice are learned; and each community should try to bring its people together that they may discuss and apply these principles."[80] In another entry, Hope mentions several texts, such as George Holley Gilbert's *Revelation of Jesus*, Walter Rauschenbusch's *A Theology for the Social Gospel* (1918) and *Christianizing the Social Order* (1927), W. M. Arnold Stevens and Ernest Dewitt Burton's *A*

Harmony of the Gospels, A. T. Robertson's *Epochs in the Life of Jesus*, and Henry
Burton Sharman's *Jesus in the Records*. Sharman, Burton, Stevens, Robertson,
and Gilbert were theologians who attempted to organize Jesus's life and mission
by studying the Gospels, albeit in different ways.

Carefully cited chapters from white theologians and social gospel advocates
clarify how Hope's understanding of her mission evolved. For example, chapter 1
from both of Rauschenbusch's works challenged Christians to apply Christianity
in their communities, while later chapters describe how and why. Chapter 2 in
Robertson's work and chapters 4 and 14 in Sharman include references to Jesus's
demands on those who would follow his teachings and the criticism Jesus faced.
Hope's notes mention that the problem Sharman describes in Mark 2 and 3 was
"to find what acts of Jesus occasioned opposition and criticism from his contemporaries to learn also why these things were objected to by leaders of his day. . . .
He would not conform to Jewish laws."[81]

Hope never stated that what she intended to accomplish in her mission
would not conform to white southern laws, but she must have seen the parallels. Following Jesus's example of opposition to some Jewish laws, Hope sought
to solve social problems, and that meant she would not conform to Jim Crow
boundaries. Nor would she risk committing a sin by failing to act, because she
knew what Christians should do. The various dates of these texts, ranging from
1899 (Gilbert) to 1927 (Rauschenbusch's *Christianizing the Social Order*), demonstrate that Hope persistently revised her approach to uplift and reform.

To be sure, part of what Hope sought to accomplish in these lessons was
intended for fellow reformers in the NU. Yet to see these lessons as applicable
to only black women misses Hope's definition of Christianity and community.
She frequently referred to "community" in the broadest sense to encompass
whites as well; and certainly pointing out sin in the home was meant to call
out white women for their shortcomings as Christian mothers. Her citations
from the New Testament countered white evangelicals' use of Old Testament
passages that ostensibly supported white supremacy. Hope's readings, her previous work in Chicago, and her friendships in the NACW led to her unique
insight into what the NU could accomplish.[82] The NACW's motto, "Lifting as
We Climb," undoubtedly included racial uplift and community improvement,
as most historians note.

But NACW members believed they were true Christians who needed to demonstrate how real Christians should act.[83] Hope's friend Charlotte Hawkins
Brown distinguished between "Christian propaganda" about race relations (as
characterized in newspapers) and the realities of housing, education, and economic opportunities denied to northern and southern blacks by calling out

"so-called Christians"—those who clearly misunderstood the "very kernel of the teaching of Jesus."[84] Intraracial and interracial reform constituted nothing less than enacting social justice for all people because of Christian beliefs. Still, Hope's beliefs encountered repeated challenges in the 1920s and 1930s, and more often than not, her vision of reform, the best possibility for change in the rigid Jim Crow South, met with limited success.

Because NU members sought to expand their mission, in 1913 they formed a Social Improvement Committee to promote attendance in public schools. In Atlanta, schools for blacks had double or triple sessions. Even then, over-crowded classrooms and lack of materials were standard fare in black schools, as they were in rural black and white schools. NU members worked with their husbands and black churches to petition the white school board regarding poor conditions. These efforts led to few changes. The school board's broader agenda in 1917 was to decrease public education for blacks and eliminate the seventh grade.[85] Fighting this action became the priority of the NU and Atlanta's newly formed NAACP chapter. Using the NU's studies of education for black students in Atlanta, the local NAACP, including John Hope and most of Atlanta's race men, successfully stopped the school board from dropping seventh grade. But the school board adamantly opposed granting additional funds to black schools.[86]

Determined to help the NAACP's campaign to increase public education for blacks, Lugenia Burns Hope headed a women's registration committee to in-crease the NAACP's chapter membership in 1918. Urging blacks to pay their poll taxes, Hope's committee managed to register enough black male voters, still eligible to vote in city bond elections, to defeat a bond measure twice in 1919. The city was pushed to a compromise measure that led to the construction of Atlanta's first black high school in 1924, Booker T. Washington High School, and increased funds for black and white schools in the next bond measure in 1921.[87] Still, one high school existed in 1924 for Atlanta's 18,000 black students. Teacher salaries remained low, double sessions at schools persisted, and Wash-ington High School accommodated at least 500 more students on opening day than the estimated 1,500 for which it was built.[88] Few whites expected the rest of eligible black children to attend high school. For them, six to seven grades of education sufficed for work as day laborers or domestics.

Interracial attempts to gain financial support for the NU met with similar mixed results. Hope turned to the Community Chest in 1924, which meant that the NU's programs would now be overseen by a white-controlled agency. But the alliance of the NU with the Community Chest led to disappointing results. In retrospect, some NU members perceived this as the moment that eventually led to the decline of the NU. The Community Chest benefitted from the NU's fund-raising abilities in the black community at the same time that it restricted its programs to preschool health clinics.[89] No longer did the NU have the autonomy to decide what programs to offer or fund, nor did it have the potential to organize black neighborhoods.

Yet as limited as the results were from interracial work, it was the only means of dealing with white moderates and powerbrokers in the early twentieth century. It must have tested the meaning of Thy Neighbor as Thyself and Hope's firm belief in her mission. As many of her friends and her husband understood all too well, white organizations and philanthropists had the means to accomplish results, yet ultimately they determined the ends. Surely Hope must have reminded herself repeatedly that through faith in Christ all things were possible, because so much was out of her control.

She nonetheless persevered in her advocacy for blacks' rights, determined to discover some way to crack Jim Crow's barriers. In 1920 Hope arranged a meeting of the NACW with two white women from the Methodist Women's Missionary Council for the purpose of creating a women's committee in the Commission on Interracial Cooperation (CIC). To black women like Hope and Brown, white women had to learn about the plight of blacks because white women held the key to unraveling white supremacy. As Christians, they could attack theological racism and join some efforts to improve conditions for blacks, whether that included preventing lynching or treating black domestic help better. In white homes across the South, white women continued to insist on standards and guidelines for cooking and cleaning designed to degrade black women.[90] They responded to black women's quest for independence by reasserting control of their labor. This meeting, to black women, yet again provided a time for Hope, Brown, and others to encourage white women to adhere to Christian ideals in their treatment of blacks and their domestic help.

Traveling to a subsequent meeting of the women's committee in Memphis, Tennessee, between black and white women, "twelve husky young white men" removed Brown from her seat in a Pullman car, and she, "in humiliation and some resentment," was forced to walk through three railroad cars to the Jim Crow car—past "southern white women passing for Christians" who were on their way to the very same meeting.[91] "You," Brown seethed at the white women in Memphis, "are going to reach out for the same hand that I am reaching out for, but I know that the dear Lord will not receive it if you are crushing me beneath your feet."[92] But the CIC's head of the Committee on Women's Work, Carrie Johnson, refused to recognize black women's demands for voting, and mitigated their call for an end to lynching. Hope, along with other black women, fumed. Black women deserved the rights and privileges of citizenship, for "what is good for one race is good for the other."[93] Praying together was a gesture from white women who misunderstood the gospel's message of social justice, and Hope wanted tangible results.

Given the negligible results from interracial reform, it often seemed more likely that black women might cease their efforts to teach and explain to whites how they could offer a modicum of support. Yet six years later, Hope again tried an interracial approach after the Mississippi Flood in 1927. Within days of catastrophic levee breaches on April 15, 1927, reports of African American forced labor and low food rations at Greenville, Mississippi, filtered north to black newspapers and the national NAACP office.[94] Herbert Hoover, Secretary of Commerce and probable Republican candidate for president in 1928, headed the federal government's flood relief effort and organized state flood commissions. Still, the NAACP continued to receive reports of abuse that ranged from peonage to rape.[95] In May, Hoover called for a Colored Advisory Commission (CAC) to investigate the conditions of African Americans in the camps and asked Robert Russa Moton, principal of the Tuskegee Institute, to head the commission, which included his friend, Lugenia Burns Hope.[96] Even at this early stage, however, Hoover's stunning indifference about African Americans revealed itself in his wires to Moton and Hope. Moton's name was spelled "Moulton"; Hope was spelled "Holt."[97]

As Hope traveled through Mississippi from May 29 to June 9, she saw the disastrous effects of the flood and immediately fought for changes. In Greenville, the location of more than thirteen thousand African American refugees, African Americans had to work in order to receive food rations, while white refugees did not.[98] When the local Red Cross decided black women and children would receive no food rations unless a man was present in the family, Hope made sure the order was rescinded.[99] In many camps, blacks slept on the ground or beds of hay; whites used cots donated by the Red Cross.[100]

Even so, Hope's report for the CAC indicated the limited possibilities for reform in the 1920s, a period when membership in the Ku Klux Klan carried more clout than interracial reform. Hope barely mentioned the vast economic gap between sharecroppers and landowners. She never cited blacks' inability to vote. What she questioned was "the flood of ignorance" in the Mississippi Valley because of poor education.[101] Her emphasis on the appalling lack of schools was included in the CAC final report in addition to criticism of the Red Cross relief effort. But the CAC's public report omitted criticism of the Red Cross in exchange for a promise from Hoover that he would allocate funds for educational and agricultural aid to blacks if they supported him in the 1928 election.[102] As the aftermath of the 1928 election proved, Moton's agreement with Hoover was a Faustian bargain indeed. Hoover did nothing, and once again interracial efforts accomplished little. With no support from white politicians in the 1920s, the potential for Hope's vision of Christian uplift seemed bleak.

Once she returned to Atlanta, Hope reenergized voter registration during the Great Depression in another effort to politicize her message. Again she chaired the organization committee for the 1930 membership drive, and her activism in the branch mobilized a women's auxiliary for the branch that had been dominated by men. By 1932 Hope gained members for the branch from her connections in the NU, the Atlanta university and college networks, black friends in the professions, and black educators at Booker T. Washington High School. The women's auxiliary of the Atlanta branch, headed by Hope's friend Josephine Dibble Murphy, targeted voter registration and education as their primary responsibilities.[103] As chair of the citizenship committee, Hope helped to develop a plan and write the primer for citizenship schools for black Atlantans. The primer and evening lectures described the responsibilities of voters, the branches of state and federal government, and the qualifications for voting.[104] The national office of the NAACP was so impressed with the primer that it requested copies of the brochure to distribute to other branches.

At Booker T. Washington High School, Hope and others taught thousands of black Atlantans and sponsored mock elections for students.[105] Yet the impact of her efforts was limited. Voter registration drives failed to register enough black voters to really change school reform, in part because the NAACP branch lacked the ability to connect with the majority of blacks. The primer Hope helped write, for example, was written in language often inaccessible to many working-class blacks. Nor did the NAACP explain how voting would actually help the majority of Atlanta's blacks even if they could pay the poll tax. Not until the late 1930s did the local branch set an agenda that appealed to blacks across economic lines.[106]

Hope's efforts during the Great Depression indicated the limitations of Thy Neighbor as Thyself because the NU did little to advocate for economic equality. Nor could it. With no help from the Community Chest or Atlanta's Family Welfare Society and limited assistance from New Deal agencies, the NU desperately tried to feed and clothe unemployed blacks by sponsoring its own fundraising drives. Out of these efforts came the West Side Unemployment Relief Committee in 1931, which combined black churches, organizations, and parent-teacher associations to raise funds for blacks. Funds from sponsored events provided some aid for West End blacks. Hope, her NU cohorts, and students and faculty from the Atlanta School of Social Work attempted to establish an independent organization in Atlanta that did not have to work with white-dominated organizations that had repeatedly failed them in the past.[107] But they could do little to force local white New Deal administrators to give blacks equitable benefits.

Nor did many working-class and unemployed blacks rally to Hope's efforts. Like Brown, Terrell, and Moton, Hope relied on a version of activism that failed to galvanize some blacks. As much as she longed for voting rights and citizenship for blacks, she and her peers defined how it would be accomplished. Voting would lead to full citizenship and then improved economic conditions. All too often, this excluded the voices of the poor and unemployed. Too many African Americans lacked the means to even pay a poll tax, let alone pass the literacy test in order to vote. Even the curriculum Hope developed for the citizenship schools resembled civics instruction, rather than more accessible readings on how to pass the literacy test in order to vote.[108] The NAACP and the citizenship schools failed to clarify how voting would actually benefit working-class blacks because they rarely spelled out how exactly voting could eliminate vagrancy laws, improve job opportunities, stop physical assaults of black women, or lead to hiring black men in Atlanta's police force—all of which were key issues for most blacks.

In 1935 Lugenia Burns Hope again offered her resignation from the NU, and this time her friends accepted it. In 1933 John Hope experienced a major heart attack following periods of bad health since 1929, and his appeal to NU members to accept her resignation along with her repeated efforts to change leadership finally convinced NU members. The Hopes believed that the NU needed a change in administration, and Lugenia, now sixty-four, reminded her colleagues of her other organizational and family duties. John Hope died on February 20, 1936, following a bout of the flu that developed into pneumonia. Lugenia Burns Hope, sick with a cold, failed to see him before he died.

As if to intentionally add to Hope's grief, Florence Read, the white president of Spelman College and close friend of John, insisted that Hope immediately vacate the family's residence at Atlanta University. She had to leave the residence so quickly that she later petitioned the Board of Trustees of Atlanta University and even First Lady Eleanor Roosevelt to obtain some of her personal belongings.[109] Hope left Atlanta in 1937 and only returned to visit her son John and his family. For the rest of her life, she divided her time between stays with family members in New York, Chicago, and Nashville. Within the turmoil of grief and dislocation from the home she had known for decades, Hope's gaze remained fixed on her mission for race work, and she insisted on preserving her husband's legacy through a biography written by Ridgely Torrence.

In 1935 Hope joined the National Council of Negro Women (NCNW), an organization founded by her friend Mary McLeod Bethune. Here she returned to her origins of social reform by working with black women for social justice. Bethune, Hope, Brown, and other black women sought to combine all black women's organizations—both religious and secular—into a nondenominational umbrella organization in order to articulate a clear, unified, political agenda for African Americans. Like Bethune, the women believed that if they could gain access to seats of power at the national level, then they could use those positions to improve black communities.

On April 4, 1938, Bethune convened a meeting of NCNW women at the East Room of the White House for an interracial conference, titled "On the Participation of Negro Women and Children in Federal Programs." First Lady Eleanor Roosevelt and Bethune gathered the heads of various New Deal agencies for NCNW women, including Hope and Brown. As leading black women reformers addressed cabinet officials and insisted that New Deal programs must include more blacks, Hope demanded voting rights for blacks so that they could force changes in their states and local communities.[110] Most New Deal officials supported increased opportunities for blacks, but total equality was far from the minds of President Franklin Delano Roosevelt and conservative politicians from the South. And certainly appointing more black women to government positions was scarcely a high priority. Even if black women other than Bethune had been given government positions, what they could have accomplished was circumscribed by most white Americans' reluctance to address the stark realities of blacks' lives.

While Hope lived in New York, she worked as an administrative assistant to Bethune in the National Youth Administration's Division of Negro Affairs in 1937. By 1940 Hope's health began to deteriorate. Throughout her life she suffered from asthma, and was later affected by heart disease. After a stroke in 1944 and increasing heart ailments, Lugenia Burns Hope died in Chicago on August 14, 1947. She specified memorial services before she died—one in Nashville, Tennessee, where she and John began their married life, and one at Morehouse College in Atlanta, where they had launched their careers and activism. But unlike John, Lugenia wanted to make sure that her ashes would never rest on Atlanta University property, even though her grave lies next to John's. Her friends from the NU who survived her scattered her ashes from the top of Grave Hall on the campus, a tribute to the woman who fought for Atlanta's black neighborhoods, women, and children.

NOTES

1. Jacqueline Anne Rouse, *Lugenia Burns Hope: Black Southern Reformer* (Athens: University of Georgia Press, 1989); Leroy Davis, *A Clashing of the Soul: John Hope and the Dilemma of African American Leadership and Black Higher Education in the Early Twentieth Century* (Athens: Univer-

sity of Georgia Press, 1998); Allison Dorsey, *To Build Our Lives Together: Community Formation in Black Atlanta, 1875–1906* (Athens: University of Georgia Press, 2004); David Fort Godshalk, *Veiled Visions: The 1906 Atlanta Race Riot and the Reshaping of American Race Relations* (Chapel Hill: University of North Carolina Press, 2005); Georgiana Hickey, *Hope and Danger in the New South City: Working-Class Women and Urban Development in Atlanta, 1890–1940* (Athens: University of Georgia Press, 2003); Elizabeth Lasch-Quinn, *Black Neighbors: Race and the Limits of Reform in the American Settlement House Movement, 1890–1945* (Chapel Hill: University of North Carolina Press, 1993), chap. 4; Michele Mitchell, *Righteous Propagation: African Americans and the Politics of Racial Destiny after Reconstruction* (Chapel Hill: University of North Carolina Press, 2004.

2. Numerous African Americans viewed their Christian beliefs as true Christianity, in contrast to the Christian beliefs of white supremacists. See, for example, Albert J. Raboteau, *Slave Religion: The "Invisible Institution" in the Antebellum South* (New York: Oxford University Press, 1978); and Ann Short Chirhart, "Charlotte Hawkins Brown (1883–1961): Living the Correct Way," in *North Carolina Women: Their Lives and Times*, vol. 2, ed. Sally McMillen and Michele Gillespie (Athens: University of Georgia Press, forthcoming).

3. Paul Harvey, *Freedom's Coming: Religious Culture and the Shaping of the South from the Civil War to the Civil Rights Era* (Chapel Hill: University of North Carolina Press, 2005), 47–49.

4. Rouse, *Lugenia Burns Hope*, chap. 1. On southern African American education, see Ann Short Chirhart, *Torches of Light: Georgia Teachers and the Coming of the Modern South* (Athens: University of Georgia Press, 2005); Adam Fairclough, *A Class of Their Own: Black Teachers in the Segregated South* (Cambridge, Mass.: Harvard University Press, 2007).

5. Rouse, *Lugenia Burns Hope*, chap. 1.

6. Lugenia Burns married John Hope in 1897; however, throughout this essay, I refer to her as Lugenia Burns Hope.

7. Robyn Muncy, *Creating a Female Dominion in American Reform* (New York: Oxford University Press, 1991); Molly Ladd-Taylor, *Mother-Work: Women, Child Welfare, and the State, 1890–1930* (Urbana: University of Illinois Press, 1994); Ralph E. Luker, *The Social Gospel in Black and White: American Racial Reform, 1885–1912* (Chapel Hill: University of North Carolina Press, 1991).

8. Ladd-Taylor, *Mother-Work*, 3–7. See also Muncy, *Creating a Female Dominion*.

9. Luker, *Social Gospel Black and White*, 4.

10. Sue Buck, "A Brief History of the International Order of the King's Daughters And Sons," International Order of the King's Daughters And Sons Website, http://www.iokds.org/history.html (accessed February 15, 2011).

11. "Who Are the King's Daughters and Sons?," International Order of the King's Daughters And Sons Website, http://www.iokds.org/index2.html (accessed February 15, 2011).

12. Muncy, *Creating a Female Dominion* chap. 1.

13. Rouse, *Lugenia Burns Hope*, 15.

14. Mia Bay, *To Tell the Truth Freely: The Life of Ida B. Wells* (New York: Hill and Wang, 2009), 122–29, 211–13. See also Paula J. Giddings, *Ida: A Sword among Lions* (New York, Amistad, 2008).

15. Lasch-Quinn, *Black Neighbors*, chap. 1.

16. Glenda E. Gilmore, *Gender and Jim Crow: Women and the Politics of White Supremacy in North Carolina, 1896–1920* (Chapel Hill: University of North Carolina Press, 1997), chaps. 2 and 7; Luker, *Social Gospel in Black and White*.

17. Gilmore, *Gender and Jim Crow*, chaps. 2 and 7; Deborah Gray White, *Too Heavy a Load: Black Women in Defense of Themselves, 1894–1994* (New York: W. W. Norton, 1999), chap. 2.

18. As quoted in Rouse, *Lugenia Burns Hope*, 17.

19. John Hope to Lugenia Burns, August 19, 1896, Providence, R.I., Papers of John and Lugenia Burns Hope, reel 13 (hereafter, Hope Papers).

20. Ibid.

21. John Hope to Lugenia Burns, November 22, 1896, Hope Papers, reel 13.

22. John Hope to Lugenia Burns, April 22, 1897, Hope Papers, reel 13.

23. Ibid.

24. John Hope to Lugenia Burns, December 6, 1896, Hope Papers, reel 13.

25. Rouse, *Lugenia Burns Hope*, 24; Davis, *A Clashing of the Soul*, 99.

26. Mitchell, *Righteous Propagation*, chap. 1; Barbara Reeves-Ellington, Kathryn Kish Sklar, and Connie A. Shemo, *Competing Kingdoms: Women, Mission, and the American Protestant Empire, 1812–1960* (Durham: Duke University Press, 2010), introduction. See also Charles W. Wadelington and Richard F. Knapp, *Charlotte Hawkins Brown and Palmer Memorial Institute: What One African-American Woman Could Do* (Chapel Hill: University of North Carolina Press, 1999); Rackham Holt, *Mary McLeod Bethune, a Biography* (New York: Doubleday and Company, 1964); Patricia A. Schechter, *Ida B. Wells-Barnett and American Reform, 1880–1930* (Chapel Hill: University of North Carolina Press, 2001).

27. Lugenia Burns to John Hope, December 23, 1897, Hope Papers, reel 13.

28. Ibid.

29. Rouse, *Lugenia Burns Hope*, 24; Davis, *Clashing of the Soul,* 100.

30. Ronald H. Bayor, *Race and the Shaping of Twentieth Century Atlanta* (Chapel Hill: University of North Carolina Press, 1996), 7.

31. Rouse, *Lugenia Burns Hope*, chap. 2; Davis, *Clashing of the Soul*, chap. 3.

32. Bayor, *Race and the Shaping of Twentieth Century Atlanta*, chaps. 1 and 2; Dorsey, *To Build Our Lives Together*, chap. 6; Godshalk, *Veiled Visions*, chap. 2.

33. Dorsey, *To Build Our Lives Together*, 147–50.

34. E. M. Beck and Stewart E. Tolnay, "Lynching," *The New Georgia Encyclopedia*, April 30, 2009, http://www.georgiaencyclopedia.org/nge/Article.jsp?id=h-2717 (accessed January 28, 2013).

35. Derrick P. Alridge, "W. E. B. Du Bois in Georgia," *The New Georgia Encyclopedia*, January 8, 2010, http://www.georgiaencyclopedia.org/nge/Article.jsp?id=h-905 (accessed January 28, 2013).

36. Rouse, *Lugenia Burns Hope*, 28–29.

37. Godshalk, *Veiled Visions*, chap. 4; Dorsey, *To Build Our Lives Together,* chap. 7; Mark Bauerlein, *Negrophobia: A Race Riot in Atlanta, 1906* (San Francisco: Encounter Books, 2001); Gregory Lamont Mixon, *The Atlanta Riot: Race, Class, and Violence in a New South City* (Gainesville: University of Florida Press, 2005).

38. As quoted in Rouse, *Lugenia Burns Hope*, 43.

39. As quoted in ibid., 44.

40. Ibid.

41. As quoted in ibid., 42–43.

42. "Treating Negro Women as Basis," *Atlanta Constitution* clipping, 1911, box 2, folder 4, "Clippings and Press Releases 1911," Neighborhood Union Collection 1908–1961 (hereafter referred to as NU).

43. "Stepping Stones to Today of the Neighborhood Union," no date, folder 17, Timeline 1933, box 2, NU. See also Godshalk, *Veiled Visions*, chap. 10; Hickey, *Hope and Danger*, chap. 4; Rouse, *Lugenia Burns Hope*, chap. 4.

44. Albert J. Raboteau, *Slave Religion: The "Invisible Institution" in the Antebellum South* (New York: Oxford University Press, 1974), 212–88; 290–318. See also Eugene D. Genovese, *Roll, Jordan, Roll: The World the Slaves Made* (Vintage: New York, 1976), book 2.

45. As quoted in Raboteau, *Slave Religion*, 291.

46. Schechter, *Ida B. Wells Barnett and American Reform*, 63–70.

47. Notes, no date, folder 18, box 1, NU.

48. Ibid.

49. Ibid.

50. Research notes, no date, folder 22, box 1, NU.

51. Bettye Collier-Thomas, *Jesus, Jobs, and Justice: African American Women and Religion* (New York: Alfred A. Knopf, 2010); Paula J. Giddings, *When and Where I Enter: The Impact of Black Women on Race and Sex in America* (New York: Bantam, 1985).

52. Godshalk, *Veiled Visions*, chap. 10; Rouse, *Lugenia Burns Hope*, chap. 4.

53. Notes, folder 18, box 1, NU

54. Notes, folder 18, box 1, NU; Lugenia Burns Hope's—Notes, folder 44, box 13 NU; Louie Delphia Shivery, "The History of Organized Social Work among Atlanta Negroes, 1890–1935," MA thesis, Atlanta University, 1936, 438; Godshalk, *Veiled Visions*, chap. 10; Rouse, *Lugenia Burns Hope*, chap. 4.

55. Neighborhood Union Minute Book 1908–1918, July 23, 1908, March 11, 1909, January 1911, February 1911, folder 1, box 4, NU; Meeting Notes—Neighborhood Union, folder 18, box 1, NU; Godshalk, *Veiled Visions*, chap. 10; Hickey, *Hope and Danger*, chap. 4; Lasch-Quinn, *Black Neighbors*, chap. 4; Shivery, "The History of Organized Social Work," 45–60; Rouse, *Lugenia Burns Hope*, chap. 4.

56. Meeting Notes—Neighborhood Union, no date, folder 18, box 1, NU.

57. Neighborhood Union Minute Book 1908–1918, October 14, 1909, folder 1, box 4, NU.

58. Neighborhood Union Minute Book 1908–1918, October 14, 1909, November 1909, August 1910, January 1911, February 1911, June 9, 1911, November 1911, August 8, 1912, March 7, 1912, folder 1, box 4, NU. See also Godshalk, *Veiled Visions*, chap. 10; Hickey, *Hope and Danger*, chap. 4; Rouse, *Lugenia Burns Hope*, chap. 4.

59. Hattie Rutherford Watson, "Work of the Neighborhood Union," *Spelman Messenger*, November 1916.

60. On divisions, see Hickey, *Hope and Danger*, chap. 4; White, *Too Heavy a Load*, chap. 2.

61. Mitchell, *Righteous Propagation*, 8–10 and chaps. 3 and 5; Peter A. Coclanis, "The World of Tuskegee in Economic Context," in *Booker T. Washington and Black Progress: Up from Slavery 100 Years Later*, ed. W. Fitzhugh Brundage, 81–106 (Gainesville: University of Florida Press, 2003).

62. Neighborhood Union Minute Book 1908–1918, July 23, 1908, January 1911, February 1911, October 12, 1911, November 9, 1911, March 7, 1912, April 10, 1913, January 9, 1914, folder 1, box 4, NU.

63. Annual Report of the Atlanta Anti-Tuberculosis Association, 1919, folder 6, box 10, NU; Neighborhood Union Minute Book, 1908–1918, September 9, October 11, November 1909, August 1910, February, June 9, November 1911, August 8, March 1912, folder 1, box 4, NU; Godshalk, *Veiled Visions*, 239–40; Hickey, *Hope and Danger in the New South City*, chap. 5; Hunter, *To 'Joy My Freedom*, chap. 9.

64. Chirhart, *Torches of Light*, chapter 3; Glymph, *Out of the House of Bondage*, Epilogue; Rebecca Sharpless, *Cooking in Other People's Kitchens*, chapter 3.

65. Mitchell, *Righteous Propagation*, chap. 5.

66. Notes, no date, folder 7, box 2, NU.

67. Godshalk, *Veiled Visions*, chap. 10; Mitchell, *Righteous Propagation*, chap. 4; Hannah Rosen, "Not That Sort of Woman," *Sex, Love, Race: Crossing Boundaries in North American Histories*, ed. Martha Hodes (New York: New York University, 1999), 267–93; Danielle L. McGuire, *At the Dark End of the Street: Black Women, Rape, and Resistance—a New History of the Civil Rights Movement from Rosa Parks to the Rise of Black Power* (Vintage: New York, 2011), prologue.

68. Hickey, *Hope and Danger*, chap. 4; Godshalk, *Veiled Visions*, chap. 10; White, *Too Heavy a Load*, chaps. 1 and 2; Lasch-Quinn, *Black Neighbors*, chap. 4.

69. Hunter, *To 'Joy My Freedom*, chapters 6 and 8. See also Mitchell, *Righteous Propagation,* chap. 5.

70. Karen Ferguson, *Black Politics in New Deal Atlanta* (Chapel Hill: University of North Carolina Press, 2002); Kevin Gaines, *Uplifting the Race: Black Leadership, Politics, and Culture in the Twentieth Century* (Chapel Hill: University of North Carolina Press, 1996).

71. Research notes, no date, folder 22, box 1, NU.

72. Research notes, no date, folder 22, box 1, NU; Godshalk, *Veiled Visions*, chap. 10; Mitchell, *Righteous Propagation,* 172; White, *Too Heavy a Load*, 71–86.

73. Notes, no date, folder 18, box 1, NU.

74. Ibid.

75. Ibid.

76. Ibid

77. Ibid.

78. Ibid.

79. Margaret Slattery, *The Girl and Her Religion* (Boston: Pilgrim Press, 1913). See, for example, chaps. 1–6.

80. Notes, no date, folder 18, box 1, NU.

81. Ibid.

82. White, *Too Heavy a Load*, chaps. 1 and 2. The NU invited Margaret Murray Washington to speak at one of their meetings. Neighborhood Union Minute Book 1908–1918, October 12, 1912, folder 1, box 4, NU.

83. White, *Too Heavy a Load,* chap. 1; Paula Giddings, *Where and When I Enter*, chap. 6.

84. Brown, "Where We Are in Race Relations," 1926, 1–2, Charlotte Hawkins Brown Papers, Arthur and Elizabeth Schlesinger Library on the History of Women in America, Radcliffe College, Cambridge, Massachusetts, Microfilm (hereafter Brown Papers), reel 1; Charlotte Hawkins Brown, *The Correct Thing to Do—to Say—to Wear* (New York: G. K. Hall, 1995), 65. See also Charlotte Hawkins Brown, "Some Incidents in the Life and Career of Charlotte Hawkins Brown Growing Out of Racial Situations, at the Request of Dr. Ralph Bunche," 3, Brown Papers, reel 1.

85. Minutes of the Women's Social Improvement Committee, August 19, September 2, October 28, 1913, folder 1, box 4, NU; Godshalk, *Veiled Visions*, 242–44; Rouse, *Lugenia Burns Hope*, 73–79.

86. Walter White to James Johnson, October 17, 1917, folder 8 box G43, NAACP; Walter White to Roy Nash, March 3, 1917, folder 8, G43, NAACP; T. K. Gibson to James Johnson, March 7, 1919, folder 11 G43, NAACP; Mary Gambrell Rolinson, "Community and Leadership in the First Twenty Years of the Atlanta NAACP, 1917–1937," *Atlanta History* 42 (Fall 1998): 5–21; Godshalk, *Veiled Visions,* 246–48.

87. Godshalk, *Veiled Visions*, 248–51.

88. "Schools Report September 29, 1923," no author, folder 9, box 6, NU; Bayor, *Race and the Shaping of Twentieth-Century Atlanta*, 205.

89. Shivery, "History of Organized Social Work," 518; Godshalk, *Veiled Visions*, 252–53; Karen Ferguson, *Black Politics in New Deal Atlanta* (Chapel Hill: University of North Carolina Press, 2002), 49–52.

90. Glymph, *Out of the House of Bondage*, 230. See Chirhart, *Torches of Light*, chap. 3.

91. Brown, "Some Incidents," 6, reel 1. Gilmore, 200–201.

92. As quoted in Gilmore, *Gender and Jim Crow*, 201.

93. Lugenia Burns Hope to Mrs. Archibald Davis, March 1, 1921, folder 37, box 10, NU. See also Jacquelyn Dowd Hall, *Revolt against Chivalry: Jesse Daniel Ames and the Women's Campaign Against Lynching* (New York: Columbia University Press, 1979), chap. 3; Rouse, *Lugenia Burns Hope*, chap. 5.

94. "Conscript Labor Gangs Keep Flood Refugees in Legal Bondage, Claimed," no author, Pittsburgh Courier, May 14, 1927, folder 15 box C380, National Association for the Advancement of Colored People Papers, Library of Congress (hereafter referred to as NAACP); "Charge Flood Zone Abuses," no author, New York Times, May 28, 1927, folder 15, box C380, NAACP. For more on the 1927 Mississippi Flood, see Pete Daniel, *Deep'n as It Come: The 1927 Mississippi River Flood* (New York: Oxford University Press, 1977); John M. Barry, *Rising Tide: The Great Mississippi Flood of 1927 and How It Changed America* (New York: Simon and Schuster, 1997), chaps. 13–17.

95. John T. Clark to Walter White, May 20, 1927, folder 17, box C380, NAACP.

96. The other women members of the Colored Advisory Commission were Eva Bowles, executive secretary of the National YWCA, and Mary E. Williams, public health nurse in the Tuskegee Chapter of the Red Cross. "The Final Report of the Colored Advisory Commission, Mississippi Valley Flood Disaster, 1927," 9–10, folder 19, box I C 380, NAACP.

97. Barry, *Rising Tide*, 322; Herbert Hoover to Mrs. John Holt, May 28, 1927, folder 3, box 1, NU.

98. "Rations in Greenville," no author, clipping from *Daily Democrat-Times*, May 23, 1927, folder 2, box 1, NU.

99. Ibid.

100. Untitled report, appendix, no author, folder 2, box 135, Robert Russa Moton Collection, Tuskegee University (hereafter referred to as RRM).

101. Appendix, 1927, by Mrs. John Hope, J. B. Martin, Miss M. E. Williams, and Mr. T. M. Campbell, folder 6, box 1, NU.

102. Herbert Hoover to Dr. R. R. Moton, June 17, 1927, folder 3, box 1, NU; "Memorandum for Committee," Robert Russa Moton, no date, folder 3, box 135, RRM; Barry, *Rising Tide*, chap. 32; Daniel, *Deep'n as It Comes*, 183–95.

103. Josephine Murphy to Walter White, February 14, 1934, folder 7, box G44, NAACP; Ferguson, *Black Politics*, chap. 1; Rouse, *Lugenia Burns Hope*, chap. 5.

104. "A Primer on Citizenship Prepared and Used by Citizenship Training School," Atlanta Branch NAACP, 1933, folder 5, Atlanta, April–December 1933, Box G 44, NAACP.

105. Ferguson, *Black Politics in New Deal Atlanta*, 152–56.

106. Ibid., 140–41. See, for example, T. Riggins to Walter White, September 14, 1933, folder 5 box G44, NAACP; "Work Done by Southern Branches of the NAACP in 1932," no author, folder 5, box G44, NAACP.

107. Ferguson, *Black Politics in New Deal Atlanta*, 49–53.

108. Ibid., chap. 6.

109. The relationship between Lugenia Burns Hope and Florence Read was contentious and fraught with tension although the reasons are unclear. See Davis, *Clashing of the Soul*, 327–29.

110. Series 4, box 1, folder 5, Conference on the Participation of Negro Women in Federal Welfare Programs, 69, Records of the National Council for Negro Women; National Archives for Black Women's History.

Vara A. Majette
(1875–1974)

"The Small Voice of a Dissenter" *in the Segregated South*

LESLIE DUNLAP

In September 1924, the Strand Theatre in Jesup, Georgia, screened the film *The Birth of a Nation* due to the efforts of the local chapter of the United Daughters of the Confederacy (UDC), whose members not only sponsored the showing but commended the movie to "every man, woman and child in [Wayne] county."[1] That very month, the vice president of Jesup's local UDC published a novel titled *White-Blood*.[2] Vara A. Majette's novel featured many of the same themes as D. W. Griffith's blockbuster, including rape, lynching, and segregation, but in a much different fashion.[3] The novel confronted certain of the film's—and the white South's—most cherished myths, especially the idea that chivalrous white men needed to protect virtuous white women from violent black men. Not surprisingly, *White-Blood* met a different reception than did the film. Whereas *The Birth of a Nation* was wildly popular among white filmgoers but boycotted by black organizations, *White-Blood* was dismissed or ignored by white readers but praised by African American reviewers.[4] The next year, Alain Locke included *White-Blood* in his survey of the literature of the "New Negro," and the NAACP sold the novel at its New York bookshop.[5] Four years later, Majette and *White-Blood* were applauded in a University of North Carolina extension bulletin as representative of "a new attitude toward the southern Negro" demonstrated by white "southern women who have attempted a fair portrayal of conditions and a sympathetic study of Negro character."[6]

Although reviewers at the time did not take note, Majette's novel also dramatized a new attitude toward sex exhibited by a transitional generation of white southern women. This generation came of age schooled in Victorian ideals of female sexual and racial purity but reached middle age in the new century, when a modern emphasis on female sexual expression came up against southern whites' determined insistence on racial purity.[7] Majette intended *White-Blood* as a "bitter indictment" of racial injustice in the South, but it was also an account of a white woman's political and sexual transformation. Publicized as an "ardent" romance of a modern white heroine, it was plotted as much for an audience of readers eager to read about modern love and sex as for serious, sociologically minded students of "the race problem."[8] Daughters of the Confederacy were better known for their efforts to prop up myths about the Old South than for the challenge they posed to those of the New.[9] How, then, to explain a reformer and novelist such as Majette, who believed in white supremacy but exposed racial injustice, with one foot in the tradition of the UDC and the other in emerging interracial reform networks?

Majette participated in the massive transformations of her time: the industrialization of the rural South, the solidification of racial segregation, the professionalization of social work, and the revolution of sexual manners and mores that accompanied the birth of the modern South. Yet many of Majette's experiences—in the isolated turpentine camps of piney woods Georgia, on the fringes of the middle class, as a rural social worker in urban reform networks, and as a female among male laborers, doctors, and lawyers—put her in uneasy relation to dominant ideas about southern social order. Her daily and close physical interactions with black turpentine workers, for example, were at odds with the social and physical distance prescribed by segregation, while her knowledge of the violence in southern households and communities contradicted claims about southern chivalry and "civilization." The dissonance between her experiences and racialized gender ideology generated profound anxiety in Majette, but it also animated her activism and analysis of southern politics. In her life as in her novel, Majette struggled to reconcile her commitment to democratic ideals and personal expression with her commitment to segregation and sexual propriety. These competing commitments located her between black and white reformers, rural and urban social workers, poor families and the state, clubwomen and male politicians.

Vara Swinney's childhood and early adulthood in the piney woods and railroad towns of southeastern Georgia in the last quarter of the nineteenth century were shaped by social contradictions that marked her entire life. As a daughter

VARA A. MAJETTE

Courtesy of Susan Majette Murphy.

and then a wife in logging and turpentine camps she was often the only woman among men, and one of a few whites among African Americans, which gave her unusual opportunities to see how white men and white supremacy worked. She developed an especially painful awareness of the compounded violence and intimacy that characterized relationships in southern households, workplaces, and communities.

Unlike many nineteenth-century white women, Vara Swinney did not grow up cradled in a "female world of love and ritual."[10] Her mother, Deborah Morgan Swinney, died in childbirth in 1882 when Vara was seven, leaving four young daughters in the care of their father in McRae, Georgia, a railroad junction connecting Atlanta to coastal Brunswick.[11] Growing up without a mother put Swinney out of line with middle-class Victorian family ideology that sentimentalized the purifying and "civilizing" influence of mothers, especially on daughters. The motherless girls must have felt loss and longing reading such prescriptive literature as *Mother, Home, and Heaven*, which lionized the mother as "the fountain-head of the home."[12] Her mother's death cast her "too much in the company of men," Majette later mused, leaving her vulnerable and untutored "in the qualities that go into the making of wife and mother."[13]

In her mother's absence, the influence of Swinney's father was profound. She identified so closely with him that she later entitled her own life story "A Country Doctor's Daughter."[14] William E. Swinney, a Civil War surgeon (and son of a surgeon before him) was a "horse and buggy" country doctor who traveled long rounds treating patients in the log-rafting, sawmill, and turpentine camps throughout the Ocmulgee River basin in southeast Georgia. Dr. Swinney came from a prominent family of Augusta slave owners, yet the family's postwar status was precarious.[15] Competition from younger physicians with professional medical training threatened to undercut Dr. Swinney's modest rural practice, while the death of Deborah Morgan Swinney undermined the family's emotional stability. The Swinneys were middle class, but only tenuously so. Her mother's piano stood out in Majette's memory as an emblem of the family's attempts to preserve the trappings of feminine influence and middle-class status in declining circumstances, and as a reminder of Majette's own distance from antebellum "ladyhood."[16]

William Swinney's own physical and emotional state contributed to the family's insecurity. Vara Swinney's first memory was of her father screaming as his right leg was amputated due to an injury sustained when he fell from a two-story building rescuing a woman from a fire. William Swinney's injuries led to a dependency on alcohol and opiates to relieve the pain, and on his daughter for personal care and assistance on his rounds.[17] For a Civil War veteran invested in heroic medicine, in a culture concerned that manhood had been lost with the Lost Cause, such debility and dependence must have been troubling. It certainly unnerved his daughter. Perhaps in response to his own vulnerability, the doctor asserted his authority over his daughters with force. "Weakness angered Father," Majette put it. "He could be very stern and sometimes almost brutal."[18] William Swinney insisted that Vara Swinney display stoicism in the face of pain and danger, engendering her lifelong insistence on female courage and physical fitness. He did so through hazing: in one memorable incident, he put her "to the test" by rigging a skeleton to fall on her when she opened a closet.[19] Living with her father's volatility and the threat of violence led Swinney to identify with others who were subject to her father's rage, such as a black child her father beat harshly with a leather bridle.[20]

A daughter's torn response to her father's pain and rage are dominant themes in Majette's unpublished novel, "Please, God," an autobiographical coming-of-age novel completed in 1956, when she was contemplating the course of her life over eight decades. The daughter responds to frequent thrashings by her father with a confusing combination of hatred and "the need to protect him," in the understanding that his drunken binges and violent outbursts are the result of his physical pain and loss of his wife. At one point she considers turning to the Klan to restrain her father; at another point neighbors summon agents from the Macon orphan home to remove the daughters.[21] In fiction, Majette reckoned with the psychic damage of domestic violence: "Something inside of her cringed even more than her flesh when the doctor mauled her body," she later wrote.[22] She also articulated her awareness of the connections between white men's domestic and racial power, and the violence that sustained both. The doctor lashes out at members of the household (pets, daughters, servants alike), leading them to try to protect one another from him.[23] Although corporal punishment was a typical aspect of childrearing in southern families and schools at this time, Majette presented her father's violence as out of bounds. In her understanding, this was a feature of southern patriarchy concealed by the dominant discourse of protection: white women and all African Americans might need protection *against* white fathers and husbands, not protection *by* them.

The discourse of protection was predicated on the ideal of white female sexual purity, an ideal strictly enforced by William Swinney even as he encouraged his daughter to buck expectations of white female delicacy. The subject of sex was surrounded by silence and shame. "My father had never mentioned the word sex to me," Majette later recalled. He barred his daughter from delivery rooms and made "no effort to instruct me as to what marriage entailed."[24] In "Please, God," secrecy around sex causes the protagonist confusion and trauma, from her mother's death in childbirth to unwanted sexual advances. Neither her father nor his volume on "female diseases," which she read clandestinely, offers her protection from the neighbor boy who exposes himself to her, the young doctor who strokes her arm, the old neighbor who gropes her thighs, or her teacher's husband who makes sexual suggestions to her.[25] At the same time, Majette noticed that black girls were denied even the "protection" that the discourse of purity was said to offer white women, and were especially vulnerable to powerful white men.[26]

In other ways, William Swinney raised his favored daughter as he might have a son. As his medical apprentice, she learned how to lance a boil, stitch a wound, pull teeth, apply leeches, improvise poultices, mix medicine, and lay out the dead, as well as how to ride a horse, ford a raging river, and fire a gun. Dr. Swinney treated patients with measles, pneumonia, "cramp colic," typhoid fever, and especially malaria. Just as often, he and his daughter tended wounds from workplace accidents and from knife and gunfights in the sawmill and in turpentine camps. Majette later described in detail her tasks: palpating swellings, cutting scorched skin, stitching flesh, clipping hair, pulling teeth, applying poultices, and removing stitches and bullets using homemade remedies and household tools, not medical instruments.[27] Such intimate physical relations with African American men and women must have stood out for a young middle-class white woman at a time when New South politicians were promoting strict racial separation as a modern solution to racial conflict.

Vara Swinney grew up, then, impressed with the imperatives of respectability, but also encouraged and determined to escape certain conventions of white southern femininity. She entertained ambitions to become a writer and travel "to see all there is of everything . . . to know why the world was like it was."[28] While her German music teacher seems to have moved her toward artistic and personal expression, her education at South Georgia College in McRae pushed her toward respectability.[29] Swinney studied art, drama, and elocution at the Methodist college, whose mission in the "illiterate wiregrass section of Georgia" was to shape and "refine" each student, "no matter how rough the diamond."[30] A prize-winning oration she gave probably sounded like the advice she soon gave a younger relative: "You can make yourself what you will. With courage and a brave determination to succeed there is no limit to your power of mind no height you cannot attain. Remembering always that 'tis not to the rich man's daughter only to whom the noble aspirations of life are given and that no diamond dust of the mine can compare with the sparkling gems of intellect."[31] In this spirit, she made plans to attend the American Academy of Dramatic Art in New York City.[32]

She did not get to New York. She got married. Edwin Smith Majette was the son of Virginia planters looking for his chance in Georgia in the burgeoning naval stores industry.[33] Vara Swinney seems to have resigned herself to marriage, expressing doubt to her future mother-in-law about her ability to manage household affairs and resolving to learn the "patience and self-denial" necessary "to meet the trials and cares I know must come in the new life that I am to enter." "I know that life is very seldom what we picture it when young," she reasoned even at the time.[34] She later remembered her October 1895 wedding as "a catastrophe": the cat delivered a litter of kittens on her dress and she had to wear a green one ("married in green, better never been seen"). That night she suffered an alarming nosebleed, preventing what she called "the events that would have usually followed," suggesting her association of sex with anxiety if not trauma. In hindsight she considered these premonitions of a marriage that turned out to be disappointing, at best.[35] Majette soon found herself isolated in a company house on a turpentine ranch in the remote piney woods, thirty miles from Jesup, the nearest town: "I know what the word 'lonely' means in its fullest sense," she wrote just two weeks after her wedding.[36]

Conditions in the turpentine industry resembled slavery.[37] Living in a turpentine shack in a camp overseen by her husband, Majette had a decade to consider this comparison, which she would later dramatize in *White-Blood*. As a "woodsrider" who patrolled workers on horseback with a gun, and then manager of a turpentine operation, Edwin Majette was responsible for disciplining workers in an "exceptionally ruthless" industry that depended on debt peonage and raw violence to compel black laborers to perform miserable work. As one labor historian describes the dynamics in what were essentially armed encampments, "the bull whip set the tone of daily life in the camps" where "alone in the wilderness [managers] could rule their camps with unquestioned authority" and with the connivance of southern sheriffs, judges, and officials. Such exploitative conditions precipitated violence among workers themselves in the quarters where employees lived and in company-owned juke joints where employers permitted and even promoted drinking, gambling, sexual competition, and violent forms of conflict resolution. "Everyone within the camp learned to live with the pervasive threat of violent death," one historian has concluded.[38] At the time, Savannah's black newspaper put it more bluntly, describing life in the turpentine camps as "Hell on Earth."[39] The piney woods were notorious for virulent white racism, heightened fears about miscegenation, and frequent outbursts of white mob violence. Between 1880 and 1924, there were close to one hundred recorded lynchings in the wiregrass and piney woods region, twenty-four of these in and immediately surrounding the counties where Majette lived.[40]

Living in a turpentine camp meant, in other words, that Majette was not "protected" or sheltered from knowledge of violence. Unlike another white wife of a turpentine operator who slept with a pistol when her husband was away, though, Majette expressed no worries over her own safety as the lone white woman among black laborers and their families.[41] Instead, she followed in her father's footsteps and assumed responsibility for the medical care of the camp's residents. Treatment included stitching wounds from accidents and razor fights, removing bullets, treating burns, delivering a baby, and possibly treating workers disciplined by her husband.[42]

Contrary to white southern propaganda about white women who couldn't leave their homes for fear of black men, Majette's fears lay closer to home. Pregnancy and childbirth exacerbated her sense of isolation and alienation. She attributed this to secrecy and shame around sex, attitudes that led to the confinement of pregnant women before and for a month after childbirth. Her fears were not unfounded, considering that both her mother and older sister had died in childbirth, that she endured a stillbirth and infant death, that her last breech delivery was a "do-it-yourself job," and that, if available, she found doctors unreliable to the point of "negligence."[43]

Although Majette seems to have found satisfaction in mothering a son and two daughters, she apparently found marriage demoralizing. While she passed over her husband in startling silence in her reminiscences, she devoted many pages of "Please, God" to the sexual dynamics of a relationship marked by "dull numbness" on the wife's part, who "disliked husbandly advances on his part and only permitted them as a matter of endurance," and "fits of fierce anger," infidelity, and drunkenness on the husband's.[44] Whether Majette wrote from personal experience or not, in retrospect she clearly identified sex as a source of tension if not danger in southern marriages, and husbands, not strangers, as threats to the women they supposedly protected. Judging by her 1956 novel, however, it was the psychological consequences as much as the physical toll of an incompatible marriage that troubled Majette, whose character is seized by a "spiritual fear" that she had "imprisoned herself" in an "inescapable net." Her father had taught her "contemptuousness for physical fear," her character observes, "but he had not taught her that life itself might become [something] to fear."[45]

Majette's disappointments were also economic. Edwin Majette did not realize his ambitions in the naval stores industry. His prospects were initially promising, as he moved from guard to manager to part owner of a turpentine business, moving his family in 1904 to Jesup, a railroad town and county seat in the piney woods.[46] In 1911 the *Savannah Morning News* cited Edwin Majette as an authority on the turpentine industry who boasted about its sure returns.[47] Just two years later Majette lost his still and his share in the business; he was soon employed as a general baggage master at the Jesup railroad station.[48] This was not what Vara Swinney had anticipated when she married a "Virginia gentleman," and the move pushed the family onto the margins of the middle class. Majette blamed the system of debt peonage but also pointed to personal failures on her husband's part, including drinking.[49] Majette's relationship with both her father and husband, then, shaped her analysis of white men and white supremacy.

As her husband's career wavered, Majette channeled her frustrations and fantasies into writing editorials, occasional newspaper stories, poetry, and novels. Writing promised "to liberate her and bring back the magic of living," she explained, offering an escape from the demands of domesticity and the restrictions of respectability.[50] Reform, on the other hand, reflected her aspirations to "climb upward," which she balanced uneasily against her inclination to dissent. In part, Majette sought respectability and social acceptance through membership in women's organizations, such as the United Daughters of the Confederacy and the Jesup Woman's Club—she called it "becoming a lady."[51] As a clubwoman, Majette presided over punch bowls, hosted lunches and socialized with the wives of the county seat's proprietors, professionals and politicians.[52] Yet her husband's dwindling economic circumstances would have undermined such social standing. So must have Majette's propensity to speak her mind, in person and in increasingly pointed editorials taking issue with everything from fine details of local politics to the foundational myths of twentieth-century white supremacy.[53]

In 1906 Majette marked her distance from Daughters of the Confederacy and most white southerners when she questioned the sources of racial and sexual violence in the region. That summer a wave of sensational rape stories fueled campaigns by white Georgians to lynch and disfranchise African Americans, inciting three days of white mob violence directed against black citizens in Atlanta.[54] Just before the riot Majette had published an editorial entitled "The White Man to Blame," based on her own experiences, in what appears to be her first published article. "I suppose in all the hue and cry of 'Lynch 'em!' 'Ku Klux 'em,' the small voice of a dissenter will not be heard, or if heard will be shouted down as an alienist in the cause of Southern womanhood," she opened.[55] In her editorial, Majette did not directly challenge the twin myth of the black rapist and the hypersexual black woman. The dissent she posed was to the idea that chivalrous white men needed to protect passive white women in order to preserve embattled white supremacy. First, she identified white women's "hysterical" fear and passivity as a pathological weakness, not a point of pride. "Are we a superior race when our womanhood [is] afraid in the presence of a negro?"

she doubted. White women's fear might actually "induce" some black men to rape, she reasoned, while in other cases "the cry of rape is started by some hysterical woman when there has never been a shadow of such, only in a frenzied imagination." She called on white women to exhibit "nerve" and "courage"— and never to show fear—in the face of a potential rapist.

Even more, she cast certain white men not just as unfit "guardians of the South's honor," but as threats to it, pointing to "hordes of mulatto children" as evidence of white men's "crimes"—not against black women but against racial purity. In her editorial, back men's rape of white women was the flip side of white men's "intercourse" with black women, which, she suggested incited black men's sexual revenge in the first place. Majette identified white men, not black men, as the primary threat to white supremacy and "Southern honor and justice." She identified white women as the solution. This strategy connected her to a generation of white reformers, such as Rebecca Latimer Felton, who identified white men's failure to preserve white supremacy as reasons for white women's political mobilization.[56]

But Majette's editorial also connected her to African American reformers, including Ida B. Wells, who had long pointed to white men and their sexual treatment of black women as evidence of the hypocrisies of white "chivalry" and the failures of white supremacy.[57] "The White Man to Blame" was reprinted in African American periodicals such as *Voice of the People*, where it prompted responses from reformers, who wrote to commend Majette for it, but also to correct her comments about "willing" black women. Baptist leader and temperance reformer Virginia W. Broughton wrote from Alabama to applaud Majette for her editorial, and then emphasized black girls' vulnerability to white men, especially as servants in white homes.[58] Washington, D.C., clubwoman Ethel Legre likewise complicated Majette's ideas about black women's consent, and the "*crime* of the white man toward Negro womanhood." "Modesty" offered no protection to black women from the "constant overtures" of the same white men who "refuse to sit by them in street cars," she commented. Legre turned white southern discourse around, calling for protection of black women by white women, who might teach white men "to respect all womanhood regardless of color."[59] Other African American readers also translated Majette's "blame" of white men into a defense of black women: her editorial was reprinted in northern African American papers even six years later under the headline "A Georgia White Woman Defends Her Colored Sisters."[60]

Such convictions about white men's sexual conduct and growing concerns about the sexual vulnerability of women and girls, including the vulnerability of black women to white men, drew Majette into the emerging profession of social work. Between 1920 and 1924 she worked as a probation and child welfare officer as the "eye and ear" of the county juvenile court, where she investigated hundreds of cases each year in black and white families.[61] Majette's investigations into the lives of her neighbors confirmed her ideas about white men's abuse of power, and likely resonated with her own experience of violence, addiction, and precarious respectability.[62] Majette was tied into a professional network of social workers forming across the state and nation. Indeed, representatives from the U.S. Children's Bureau came to Jesup to compile statistics and study her methods. At the same time, she appears to have been viewed by more genteel, urban colleagues as something of a rogue for her outspokenness and inclination "to play a lone hand in whatever she attempts."[63]

Majette confronted shocking cases of sexual abuse—"conditions that made her cheeks grow red"—but it seems to have been the garden-variety cases that troubled her most, alerting her to the systematic more than the sensational dynamics of white southern patriarchy.[64] In poems as well as editorials, Majette had criticized the conduct of inebriated and "lecherous leeches," as well as the "unctuous piety" and "false modesty" that permitted white men's sexual wrongdoing but penalized that of women.[65] Now she perceived the racial dynamics of this double standard. She discerned, for example, the secrets behind the screen of segregation: segregation enabled white men to father children with black women with impunity, excusing them from economic as well as moral responsibility for their children. African American women had no legal recourse against white men, she learned; women could not claim child support, nor even identify the father, since "to publish his name would endanger their lives."[66] Scores of white men hid behind her case reports marked "father unknown," she suspected.[67] In short, social work proved to Majette the accuracy of the analysis offered by Broughton and other African American reformers, and led her to question segregation, in practice though not in principle.

This dawning awareness led her into formal organization with reformers who shared her concerns with racial violence and sexual protection. In 1921 African American women in Jesup organized a Woman's Christian Temperance Union (WCTU) chapter, joining forty-seven other chapters organized by black women in the state, whose motto was "Give Us Protection."[68] Majette acted as an intermediary between the black and white unions in Jesup, and then throughout the state, as superintendent of "Work among Negroes" for the Georgia WCTU.[69] Temperance alliances translated into working relationships, such as when Annie E. Stafford, the president of Jesup's "colored" union, became a probation officer, responsible for supervising cases involving black families.[70] The month before *The Birth of a Nation* played in Jesup, Majette witnessed a production with a contrasting message. She attended the black women's WCTU convention in Atlanta, where members staged a performance of *Ethiopia at the Bar of Justice*, a pageant that combined a protest against peonage, lynching, and disfranchisement with an appeal for sexual protection for black women.[71] This appeal must have resonated with Majette, who two months later moved that the white state WCTU include black women in its provisions calling for the protection of girls. Majette included among these a call for a reform school for African American girls—a longstanding goal of African American reformers in the state.[72]

The WCTU seems also to have focused Majette's opposition to lynching. Since 1917 the state organization of white women had condemned lynching, and it questioned the use of rape charges as a poor "excuse for lynch law."[73] In 1920 the organization implored its white members to "each ask of her own conscience the question, 'what can I do to put a stop to this horror'?"[74] In the fall of 1921, Majette faced that very question when the young white wife of a turpentine operator charged two black men, one of whom was a war veteran, with rape. Majette and a handful of "good women" in the county attempted to intercede in the men's defense, based on evidence Majette had gathered.[75] Despite their efforts or the efforts of the Savannah NAACP, the men were lynched with the obvious collusion of local police.[76] Majette's attempt to "put a stop" to this lynching put her in line with women's branches of the Committee on Interracial Cooperation that were forming throughout the state, resulting in the formation of the Association of Southern Women for the Prevention of Lynching (ASWPL) a decade later.[77] Although Majette does not appear to have been active in the ASWPL, her actions anticipated a shift in white women's attitudes toward rape and lynching, marking her as a transitional figure in the history of southern women's activism. Certainly, the lynching cemented her conviction that violence subverted stability in the South, prompting her finally to finish the novel she had been working on since 1906, and which marked her departure from the pieties of the UDC.

Published in 1924 by a Boston publisher specializing in books on "Racial Contributions," *White-Blood* turned stock white southern scripts about vulnerable white ladies, upstanding white men, promiscuous black women, and rapacious black men on their head.[78] The novel features Ria Wharton, a "fresh-faced, frank, fun-loving" girl whose experiences in a turpentine camp in the piney woods of Georgia and in Atlanta during a race riot transform her into an outspoken critic of southern sexual and racial order. Ria is a thoroughly modern heroine who defies "the general and useless conventions that she thought hedged men and women in their social relationships," including the idea that white women need white men's protection.[79] The novel contrasts the athletic, independent, and sexually desirous "Girl of the Rebellious Heart" to "Princess of the Timid Heart," an "absurdly white and soft" blonde waif, who depends on white men to be her

"personal guardians."[80] "Lily-white" Louise ends up instigating the lynching of
an innocent man because of her "nervous imaginings" about black men, despite
Ria's valiant efforts to intervene.[81] Through this contrast Majette dramatized the
analysis of southern white womanhood she had introduced in her 1906 editorial, showing how the ideal of passivity and the discourse of protection fueled
violence and immobilized white women.

White southern gender ideals also debilitated white men and undermined
white control, in Majette's interpretation. *White-Blood* offered an extended
comment on white men's misconduct in business, politics, and intimate relationships. The novel pits lawyer Galan Kearns, Ria's love interest, against turpentine manufacturer Steve Wharton, her brother. At once virtuous and virile,
Kearns is the opposite of the "domineering" and "degenerate" Wharton, whose
"obsession of ownership and power" extends from his cruel labor practices to
his political campaigns, to his "perception that every negro woman . . . was a
prostitute and any white man's booty."[82] Kearns champions racial justice and
embodies the qualities Majette elsewhere extolled in "the man worthwhile," including "strength that dares defend / The priceless luster of a woman's name /
Yet just as strong with a strength within / That keeps his own from shame."[83]
Wharton, in contrast, foments sexual jealousy and racial violence, like the white
men "to blame" in her 1906 editorial.

Arrogant and powerful white men such as Wharton were a threat not just
to white women, Majette's novel suggested, but to black women as well. *White-
Blood* revealed Majette's half-awareness of black women's abuse by white men,
through the character Lissa and her relationships with Steve Wharton. On the
one hand, Majette drew the character nicknamed "Tiger Lily" according to
dominant white stereotypes about black female sexuality, the threatening effects of race mixing, and the traits associated with "white blood." On the other
hand, Majette presented Lissa as ambitious, frank, and noble, a characterization praised for its complexity in the NAACP review of the novel.[84] Indeed, Lissa
delivers some of the most powerful lines in the book about the personal and
social damage wrought by generations of white men who treat black women like
"plaything[s] . . . until they tire and cast us aside."[85] Black men in the novel also
expose the failures and hypocrisies of white men. Wharton realizes his own lack
"of manhood" and honor in a standoff with Lissa's husband, who leads a revolt
of the turpentine workers and is ultimately killed by a mob of armed white men,
while the old turpentine hand Megs offers subtly pointed commentary about his
"Boss" and the faults of white men.[86]

These failures were not isolated to individuals or confined to the piney woods
but encoded in southern politics, law, and customs. Ria Wharton discovers

this when she witnesses the campaign to disfranchise black citizens and the resulting Atlanta race riot. In a climactic chapter entitled "Rebirth," the "newly awakened" heroine finally reckons with the fundamental contradiction between democracy and the insistence that "this is a white man's country."[87] Animated by a new vision of social justice, she devotes herself to a career in social work and law, and in an ending befitting a modern romance novel, to her sensitive yet strong companion in marriage.

Despite its bodice-ripping qualities, Majette considered the novel an "unvarnished" sociological record of conditions in the South, based as it was on her own experiences as well as on actual historical events, and she recommended it to reformers such as Rebecca Latimer Felton and sociologist Howard Odum on that basis.[88] She also entertained hopes that it would become a bestseller, or at least repay the time and money she had poured into it. A few reviewers predicted a "howl of denunciation," "harsh epithets," and accusations that Majette had purposely "set out to make a stir and rip the fabric" of the South.[89] Contrary to these predictions, however, the novel seems to have been passed over in relative silence, including in Jesup, where one imagines the book must have caused a stir but where there was only passing reference to it in the newspaper (in contrast to the publicity surrounding *The Birth of a Nation*).[90] This may have been in part because, in the words of one reviewer, "the book is commonplace, ungrammatical, melodramatic, didactic," and in the words of another, "crudely written."[91] But this reception was also partly due to the very ideas about white female purity and propriety that the novel challenged. The *Macon Telegraph*, for example, criticized Majette's lack of tact in broadcasting matters that most female authors "have had the delicacy to forbid mentioning."[92] Majette, who prided herself on her "fearlessness of expression," explained the novel's disappointing reception as part of a concerted effort by white southern newspapers to cloak the secrets she courageously exposed.[93]

At the hopeful moment of its publication, though, and like her heroine at novel's end, Majette poised herself to transform the legal system and the racial and gender inequalities embedded in it. For three years she had studied law by correspondence courses through the University of California. When she failed the state bar examination, she identified male opposition as the reason, and announced her determination to take the exam until she passed, which she did in 1924.[94] Her recollections of her first case illustrate her understanding of white southern sexual myths and the kind of challenge she might pose to them. In an attempt to haze the new female lawyer, local attorneys and judges arranged for her to defend a black man accused of public indecency for exposing himself to white women on a train. Majette vowed to defend her client and her right to practice law at once. Her case rested on the argument that the train had no bathroom facilities in its Jim Crow car and on the assertion that since the women "could not see the accused then they could not be offended." And, as she had in her novel, Majette turned white men's accusations of black men's sexual impropriety back onto white men themselves, accusing the prosecution of using "obscenity" and "the crudest vulgarity" in the courtroom.[95] In this case, Majette's legal strategy resembled her literary strategy: upending stereotypes about threatening black men, vulnerable white women, and honorable white men.

Majette's highest-level case reached the Georgia Court of Appeals when she represented a poor white woman who charged Jesup's most prominent doctors with malpractice for mutilating her reproductive organs in a routine procedure and then lying to her about her condition. Majette paid for six trials out of her own pocket.[96] The case clearly touched a nerve with the country doctor's daughter. It probably also resonated with her own experiences with childbirth and reproductive health. Although Majette and her client eventually lost the case, it represented Majette's willingness to take on some of her town's most powerful white men.

Majette's practice of law was not as transformative as she had imagined. She lost the majority of her cases, beginning with her first. Many of her clients were charged with petty offenses, ranging from making liquor to stealing rides on trains.[97] Charges such as these were commonly used to indebt black workers by fixing them in the service of employers who paid their legal fines, and Majette worked against this practice on behalf of some of her black clients. But in an ironic twist for a former temperance woman and social worker, Majette also defended men charged with making and selling liquor, fornication and adultery, and at least one case of abandonment of minor children.[98] The irony was surely not lost on Majette, who soon announced her intention to be judge of the county juvenile court, a bid she lost.[99] Since the passage of woman suffrage and her involvement in the League of Women Voters, Majette ran for a range of city, county, and state offices (including for the Georgia House of Representatives in 1934), usually as the lone woman in the running and ultimately unsuccessfully.[100]

Political defeat merged with personal dissatisfaction. When she published *White-Blood*, Majette was on the verge of fifty, not a "fresh-faced" girl in search of love and adventure, and her novel may have reflected the aspirations and illusions of her daughters' generation more than her own. Her marriage had been quite unlike her modern heroine's, and she had enjoyed neither companionship nor sexual fulfillment. Just after the publication of *White-Blood*, her husband suffered a stroke and was paralyzed for the remainder of his life, a bitter punctuation to what she saw as his economic and emotional failings.[101] Read in the context of her biography, *White-Blood* is not entirely about exciting new opportunities opening up for modern women, but a sad reflection on the sexual constraints—what Majette called the "dull numbness"—imposed on the generation before.

Yet the sexual revolution of the 1920s was not lost on Majette, as she poured her longings into scores of poems about love, loss, desire and lust, and an affair with a man who signed his letters "Roma" (Gypsy).[102] After the death of her husband in 1932, Majette retired from law and moved to St. Simons, where she continued to write and to consider the themes of race and sex that had long gripped her. Her epic biography of the nineteenth-century critic of sexual exploitation in slavery Fanny Kemble revealed as much about Majette as about Kemble. The unpublished biography revolves around the conflict between Kemble's "love for personal freedom and her passion for justice," and her slaveholder husband's domination. "Mistress of a Thousand Slaves" was written in the romantic mold of *White-Blood*, imagining Kemble in the same prose and even some of the same scenes as that novel's modern heroine. Majette must have identified with Kemble's "experience of heart-breaking loneliness, outraged sense of justice, despair and estrangement," as well as her refusal to "hold her tongue" or conform to southern social conventions ("to think was to speak," Majette put it).[103]

The idea that southern history pivoted around questions of sexual desire, power, and competition infused "Daughters of Men," Majette's unpublished historical novel about European explorers' early conquest of the sea islands, told through the eyes of three generations of indigenous women. The women in the novel navigate between Indian, Spanish, and French worlds, brokering political and economic alliances through sexual relationships with chiefs and explorers, including Juan Ponce de Leon and Hernando de Soto. Majette presented the novel's "daughters" as strategists and diplomats who enjoy sexual power as well as desire, but she also offered comment on white men's "arrogant" treatment of native women.[104]

Although Majette continued to editorialize on politics—including her support of the Fair Employment Practices Commission as an expression of "the very essence of democracy,"—in her seventies she channeled her energies into writing and then painting.[105] In 1956 she began an autobiographical novel entitled "Please, God," in which she took critical stock of her life and especially the men in it. In this reckoning, she concluded glumly that "no one had ever read" her only published novel.[106] Majette held on to her ambitions for herself and her novel though, and in 1966 she proposed to publishers that conditions might now be ripe for the reissue of *White-Blood*.[107] By that time, however, Majette's antipathy toward miscegenation put her out of step with civil rights, the year before the Supreme Court determined that laws prohibiting interracial marriage were unconstitutional. Whereas in the 1920s she had been considered liberal for her advocacy of "segregated justice," from the 1960s forward her politics seemed reactionary. Indeed, in 1970 a Wayne County Daughter of the Confederacy discovered the novel and promoted it precisely for its antimiscegenation message.[108] And the novel's overwrought prose and romantic formulas were by then far outdated.

Still, Majette's faith in romance and politics reached into the 1970s, and changed even her mind. When her great-granddaughter (who had grown up in Jesup) returned from the University of North Carolina at Chapel Hill in 1969 with news that she was dating an African American intellectual and activist, with whom she had been organizing university service workers, Majette, then age ninety-four, was moved, not just by the romance, but by the couple's politics. Majette applauded her great-granddaughter's decision to protest her sorority's policy, which had barred her boyfriend from coming to dinner.[109] This was a romance Majette could not have imagined in the 1920s, but one she lived to appreciate.

NOTES

1. *Jesup Sentinel*, September 25, 1924; *Jesup Sentinel*, April 21, 1921, 1; *Jesup Sentinel*, June 2, 1921, 1.

2. Vara A. Majette, *White-Blood* (Boston: Stratford Publishing Co., 1924).

3. Michael Rogin, "'And the Sword Became a Flashing Vision': D. W. Griffith's *The Birth of a Nation*," *Representations* 9 (Winter 1985): 150–95; Melvyn Stokes, *D. W. Griffith's* The Birth of a Nation: *A History of the Most Controversial Motion Picture of All Time* (New York: Oxford University Press, 2007).

4. *Ashville (N.C.) Citizen*, March 8, 1925; *Columbia (S.C.) State*, March 8, 1925; *Birmingham (Ala.) Age Herald*, March 15, 1925; *The Crisis*, March 1925, all in box 1, folder 8, Vara A. Majette Papers, 1924–65, MS 3073, Hargrett Rare Book and Manuscript Library, University of Georgia Libraries (hereafter VAMP). See also Monroe N. Work, *Negro Year Book: An Annual Encyclopedia of the Negro, 1925–1926* (Tuskegee, Ala.: Negro Year Book Publishing Co., 1925), 114; and Guy B. Johnson, "Recent Literature on the Negro," *Journal of Social Forces* 3, no. 2 (1925), 315.

5. Alain Locke, *The New Negro: Voices of the Harlem Renaissance* (1925; New York: Touchstone, 1997), 427; *The Crisis*, May 1925.

6. Elizabeth Lay Green, *The Negro in Contemporary American Literature: An Outline for Individual and Group Study* (Chapel Hill: University of North Carolina Press, 1928), 43. Robert W. Bagnall wrote that *White-Blood* reflected "the new conception of race relations held by a growing minority of whites in the South" in *The Crisis*, May 1925.

7. Jacquelyn Dowd Hall, "The Mind That Burns in Each Body: Women, Rape, and Racial Violence," in *Powers of Desire: The Politics of Sexuality*, ed. Ann Snitow, Christine Stansell,

and Sharon Thompson (New York: Monthly Review Press, 1983), 328–49; Susan Cahn, *Sexual Reckonings: Southern Girls in a Troubling Age* (Cambridge, Mass.: Harvard University Press, 2007).

8. Stratford Company press release and book order form, box 1, folder 8, VAMP.

9. Karen L. Cox, *Dixie's Daughters: The United Daughters of the Confederacy and the Preservation of Confederate Culture* (Gainesville: University of Florida Press, 2003).

10. Carroll Smith-Rosenberg, "The Female World of Love and Ritual: Relation between Women in the Nineteenth Century," *Signs* 1 (Autumn 1975): 1–29.

11. Deborah Morgan Swinney (1855–82); the daughters were Immaroe Deborah (1873–93), Vara Anna (1875–1974), Emma Louvenia (1878–1959), and Riva (1881–1947).

12. *Golden Thoughts on Mother, Home, and Heaven: From Poetic and Prose Literature from All Ages and All Lands*, intro. by Rev. Theodore L. Cuyler (New York: E. B. Treat, 1878), mentioned in Majette, "Please, God," 87, unpublished novel, box 4, VAMP.

13. Majette, "The Test," unpublished poem, box 4, folder 5, VAMP.

14. Majette, "A Country Doctor's Daughter," unpublished reminiscences, Coastal Georgia Historical Society, St. Simon's Island (hereafter CGHS); Majette, "A Country Doctor's Daughter Ninety Years Ago," *St. Simons (Ga.) Islander*, August 22, 1983.

15. His parents Mark E. and Emeline Swinney owned two dozen slaves according to the 1850 and 1860 Federal Census Slave Schedules.

16. Majette, "Please, God," 23–25, 121, 128, 158–59.

17. Majette, "Country Doctor's Daughter," 1, 9; Margaret Quante, "Courage Is No Stranger to Vara Majette," *Savannah Morning News*, June 17, 1962; Majette, "Please, God."

18. Majette, "Country Doctor's Daughter," 4.

19. Majette, "Country Doctor's Daughter," 4; Majette, "Please, God," 205.

20. Robert West Jr., "Glimpses of the Past," *St. Simons (Ga.) Islander*, July 10, 1995; Majette, "Please, God," 200. Majette cited this incident as the source of her later interest in reforming race relations. The sight of a father beating servants was a staple in the autobiographical accounts of those who later became white racial liberals, such as Katharine DuPre Lumpkin and Lillian Smith. See Fred Hobson, *But Now I See: The White Southern Racial Conversion Narrative* (Baton Rouge: Louisiana State University Press, 1999).

21. Majette, "Please, God," 88, 2–3, 29, 16, 18, 27, 29, 33, 37–38, 45, 49, 85, 87, 88, 129, 136.

22. Ibid., 106.

23. Ibid., 29–30, 37–38, 45–48, 92–93, 106, 108, 128, 139–43.

24. Majette, "Country Doctor's Daughter," 14.

25. Majette, "Please, God," 16–17, 38–39, 41–42, 51, 86, 107, 111, 153, 181.

26. In "Please, God" Majette makes this point with the character of Doshia, a young black girl who dies in childbirth bearing a child fathered by the white son of an "up and coming" family (43, 45, 48, 55, 64, 87).

27. Majette, Country Doctor's Daughter," 1–13, 15–16.

28. Majette, "Please, God," 100, 105, 110.

29. Majette, "Please, God," 171–75, 181, 185–88; Majette, "The Shadow of the Turning," unpublished poem, box 4, folder 4, VAMP.

30. *Annual Catalogue of South Georgia College* (McRae, Ga.: Enterprise Job Print, 1893), 3, 5, 7, 12, 14, found in Arthur J. Moore Methodist Museum and Archives, St. Simons, Ga. (hereafter MMM); Necia Powell Cotter, "A Brief History of South Georgia College, 1892–1928" (1980), 1, 6, MMM; Alicia

Ryals and Ruth Mizell, eds., *The History of Telfair County, Georgia, 1807–1987* (Dallas: Curtis Media Corporation, 1988), 184–85.

31. Vara to Bettie (Mary Elizabeth Majette), October 25, 1895, Reel 17, Majette Family Papers (Mss 1M2886a), Southern Women and their Families in the 19th Century, Papers and Diaries, series D, Holdings of the Virginia Historical Society (hereafter MFP).

32. Linda Orr King, "Vara Swinney Majette," Georgia Women of Achievement Nomination, 1996, CGHS.

33. Ed to Mama, December 30, 1894–October, 13, 1895, Reel 15, MFP.

34. Vara to "Mama" (Mary Effa Smith Majette), July 30, September 9, October 13, 1895, Reel 15, MFP. See also Mary Effa Smith Majette to Vara, August 19, 1895, MFP.

35. Majette, "Country Doctor's Daughter," 14–15; Majette, "Please, God," 191; Emma to Vara, October 6, 1944, VAM Scrapbook, in Susan Majette Murphy's possession (hereafter VAM Scrapbook).

36. Vara to Bettie (Mary Elizabeth Majette), October 25, 1895, reel 17, MFP; Majette, "Country Doctor's Daughter," 17.

37. Michael David Tegeder, "Prisoners of the Pines: Debt Peonage in the Southern Turpentine Industry, 1900–1930," (PhD diss., University of Florida, 1996); Pete Daniel, *The Shadow of Slavery: Peonage in the South, 1901–1969* (Urbana: University of Illinois Press, 1972).

38. Tegeder, "Prisoners of the Pines," vii, 155, 159–80, 180–95. Tegeder characterizes woodsriders as "marginal men" bent on profit and intent on asserting their "superiority as white men" (156).

39. *Savannah Tribune*, quoted in W. Fitzhugh Brundage, *Lynching in the New South: Georgia and Virginia, 1880–1930* (Urbana: University of Illinois Press, 1993), 120.

40. Mark V. Wetherington, *The New South Comes to Wiregrass Georgia, 1860–1910* (Knoxville: University of Tennessee Press, 1994); Brundage, *Lynching in the New South*, 113–20, appendix.

41. Interview with Mrs. R. Allen (Ida Bethea) Willis, appendix C in Kenneth H. Thomas Jr., *McCranie's Turpentine Still* (Athens: University of Georgia Institute of Community and Arts Development, 1976), 1; Majette, "Please, God," 200.

42. Majette, "Country Doctor's Daughter," 15–18; Majette, "Please, God," 192–94.

43. Majette, "Country Doctor's Daughter," 18–21; Majette, "Please, God," 195–98, 236–37.

44. Majette, "Please, God," 190, 192, 199–201, 207, 212, 220–30, 240–47.

45. Ibid., 200, 205.

46. The still was in Gardi, seven miles outside of Jesup (*Jesup Sentinel*, September 11, 1913).

47. Bobby M. Martin, ed., *Wayne County, Georgia: Its History and Its People* (Dallas: Curtis Media, 1990) 45.

48. *Jesup Sentinel*, November 20, 1913, 1; *Jesup Sentinel*, January 8, 1925, 1; *Jesup Sentinel*, December 29, 1932, 1.

49. Majette, "Country Doctor's Daughter," 21; Majette, "Please, God," 243–45.

50. Majette, "Please, God," 214, 202–4.

51. Ibid., 278, 239–40.

52. *Jesup Sentinel*, February 2, 1911; *Atlanta Constitution*, April 7, 1912.

53. For example, see *Jesup Sentinel*, May 25, 1911; *Jesup Sentinel* June 8, 1911; *Jesup Sentinel*, July 25, 1911.

54. Charles Crowe, "Racial Massacre in Atlanta, September 22, 1906," *Journal of Negro History* 54 (April 1969): 150–73; Gregory Mixon, *The Atlanta Riot: Race, Class, and Violence in a New South City* (Gainesville: University Press of Florida, 2005); David F. Godshalk, *Veiled Visions: The 1906 Atlanta Race Riot and the Reshaping of American Race Relations* (Chapel Hill: University of North Carolina Press, 2005).

55. Majette, "The White Man to Blame," *Atlanta Georgian*, September 1, 1906, 9.

56. Crystal Feimster, *Southern Horrors: Women and the Politics of Rape and Lynching* (Cambridge, Mass.: Harvard University Press, 2009); LeeAnn Whites, "Rebecca Latimer Felton and the 'Problem' of Protection in the New South," in *Visible Women: New Essays in American Activism*, ed. Nancy Hewitt and Suzanne Lebsock (Urbana: University of Illinois Press, 1993), 41–61; LeeAnn Whites, "Love, Hate, Rape, Lynching: Rebecca Latimer Felton and the Gender Politics of Racial Violence," in *Democracy Betrayed: The Wilmington Race Riot of 1898 and Its Legacy*, ed. David Cecelski and Timothy B. Tyson (Chapel Hill: University of North Carolina Press, 1998), 143–62.

57. Ida B. Wells, *Southern Horrors and Other Writings*, ed. Jacqueline Jones Royster (New York: Bedford, 1997); Feimster, *Southern Horrors*.

58. Mrs. V. W. Broughton to VAM, October 25, 1906, VAM Scrapbook.

59. Legre to Majette [1906], VAM Scrapbook.

60. W. A. Williams to Majette, March 2, 1912, VAM Scrapbook.

61. For detailed summaries of her cases, see Majette, "Report of the Probation Officer of the Juvenile Court, Wayne County," Grand Jury Presentments, *Jesup Sentinel*, May 25, 1922, 1,4; Majette, "Report On the Juvenile Court," *Jesup Sentinel*, December 11, 1924, 8. Specific cases and their dispensation are recorded in Jesup City Court, Minute Book 2:throughout, and Jesup City Court, Minute Book 3:152–85, Wayne County Courthouse, Jesup, Georgia (hereafter WCC).

62. While many historians interpret social workers' zeal to intervene in poor families as evidence of middle-class social control and distance, Majette's experience suggests the possibility that some female reformers shared experiences of abuse and vulnerability with their clients.

63. Program, First Georgia Conference on Social Work, Georgia, March 18–29, 1924, box 1, folder 3, Rhoda Kaufman Papers, Georgia Division of Archives and History (hereafter GDAH); "State Conferences for Social Work," *Journal of Social Forces* 2, no. 3 (March 1924): 397; Rhoda Kaufman to Kate Burr Johnson, Secretary, Department of Public Welfare (enclosed to Howard W. Odum), January 20, 1925, box 22, Howard Washington Odum Papers, MS 3167, Southern Historical Collection, Manuscripts Department, Wilson Library, University of North Carolina at Chapel Hill.

64. Majette, "The Test."

65. Majette, "Does China Shame Us Here?" *Atlanta Georgian*, March 18, 1907, 4. Her poems on drinking and sexual double standards include "Do You Know," and "Wine First, then Woman," box 4, folder 7, VAMP.

66. Majette, *White-Blood*, 298.

67. Jesup City Court, Minute Book 2:135–36, 160–61, 391; Jesup City Court, Minute Book 3:171, WCC.

68. *Jesup Sentinel*, February 22, 1923, 1; *Minutes of the 38th Annual Convention of the WCTU of Georgia* (1921), 66, 149; *Minutes of 39th Annual Convention of the WCTU of Georgia* (1922), 28; *Minutes of the 40th Annual Convention of the WCTU of Georgia* (1923), 176; *Minutes of the 41st Annual Convention of the WCTU of Georgia* (1924), 165–71.

69. *Jesup Sentinel*, February 25, 1921; *Minutes of the 40th Annual Convention of the WCTU of Georgia* (1923), 6, 61, 169; *Minutes of the 41st Annual Convention of the WCTU of Georgia* (1924), 8, 52–53, 123, 132, 136.

70. Jesup City Court, Minute Book 2:160; Jesup City Court, Minute Book 3:160, 171, 181, 182, WCC.

71. *Minutes of the 41st Annual Convention of the WCTU of Georgia* (1924), 52–53, 164; Edward J. McCoo, "Ethiopia at the Bar of Justice" (1924), in Willis Richardson, ed., *Plays and Pageants from the Life of the Negro* (1930; Jackson: University of Mississippi Press, 1993), 345–73.

72. *Minutes of the 41st Annual Convention of the WCTU of Georgia* (1924), 136, 141.

73. *Georgia Bulletin*, January 1920, 3; *Minutes of the 36th Annual Convention of the WCTU of Georgia* (1919), 101; *Minutes of the 38th Annual Convention of the WCTU of Georgia* (1921), 136;

Minutes of the 39th Annual Convention of the WCTU of Georgia (1922), 156; *Minutes of the 40th Convention of the WCTU of Georgia* (1923), 148; *Minutes of the 41st Annual Convention of the WCTU of Georgia* (1924), 139; all in wctu Collection, Woodruff Library, Emory University.

74. *Georgia Bulletin*, January 1920, 3.

75. "Petition of Joe Jordan and James Harvey," n.d., group 1, series C, box c-355, Wayne County File, naacp Papers, lc; Wayne County Superior Court Minutes, record book 9, pp. 170–73, 248, wcc; Cynthia Parks, "Lawyer Majette Battled Prejudice, Ridicule," *Jacksonville (Fla.) Times-Union and Journal*, October 19, 1969, vam Scrapbook.

76. Brundage, *Lynching in the New South*, 232–33, 361.

77. There was a notice of such women's efforts in the cic in the *Jesup Sentinel*, September 15, 1921, 3; Jacquelyn Dowd Hall, *Revolt against Chivalry: Jesse Daniel Ames and the Women's Campaign against Lynching*, rev. ed. (New York: Columbia University Press, 1993).

78. The Stratford "Racial Contributions" series that year included W. E. B. Du Bois, *The Gift of Black Folk: The Negroes in the Making of America* (Boston: Stratford, 1924).

79. Majette, *White-Blood*, 110–11.

80. Ibid., 106–16.

81. Ibid., 133–35, 153–78.

82. Ibid., 51–51, 28.

83. Majette, "The Man Worthwhile," unpublished poem, box 4, folder 7, vamp.

84. *The Crisis*, May 1925.

85. Majette, *White-Blood*, 48–51, 144–51, 275–78.

86. The review in *The Crisis* made this point.

87. Majette, *White-Blood*, 233, 262–70.

88. Majette to Howard W. Odum, February 16, 1925, Howard Washington Odum Papers, Collection 3167, box 47, Southern Historical Collection, Manuscripts Department, Wilson Library, University of North Carolina, Chapel Hill; J. S. Lambert, Department of Education Rural School Agent (Montgomery, Ala.) to Stratford Company, January 24, 1925, box 1, folder 3, vamp.

89. *Wayne County Progress*, September 17, 1924; *Columbia (S.C.) State*, March 8, 1925, box 1, folder 8, vamp.

90. The *Jesup Sentinel* reported that *White-Blood* would be published in England, but this does not appear to have happened (*Jesup Sentinel*, April 16, 1925, 5).

91. *Ashville (N.C.) Citizen*, March 8, 1925; *The Crisis*, May 1925, box 1, folder 8, vamp.

92. Majette to Odum, February 16, 1925, Odum Papers.

93. Majette to Rebecca Latimer Felton, February 5, 1925, and Felton to Majette, February 6, 1925, box 8, folder 3 (microfilm reel 6), Rebecca Latimer Felton Papers, Hargrett Rare Book and Manuscripts Library, University of Georgia Libraries.

94. Application of Mrs. E. S. Majette for Admission to Bar, June 12, 1925, vam Scrapbook.

95. "Country Doctor's Daughter," 22–23; Majette, "Please, God," 283–84; "Lawyer Majette Battled Prejudice, Ridicule"; "Courage Is No Stranger."

96. *Colvin v. Warren*, Georgia Court of Appeals, Case 21393 (1931), and *Warren v. Colvin*, Georgia Court of Appeals, Case 23576 9 (1933), gdah, 56-2-2.

97. For examples, see *State v. Aspinwall* and *State v. Brice*, Wayne County Superior Court, Minute Book 10:138–39, 151; *State v. Lawrence Basket*, Jesup City Court, Minute Book 3, 305, 314, 335, 336, wcc.

98. *State v. V. L. Lane*, October 1929, Jesup City Court, Minute Book 4:402.

99. *Jesup Sentinel*, January 19, 1928, 1; *Jesup Sentinel*, March 1, 1928.

100. *Jesup Sentinel*, February 17, 1921, 1; *Jesup Sentinel*, October 2, 1924; *Jesup Sentinel*, May 10, 1934, 1.

101. *Jesup Sentinel*, January 8, 1925, 1; *Jesup Sentinel*, December 29, 1932, 1.

102. "The Fragrant Night," *Atlanta Constitution*, August 5, 1906, 4; "Transformation," "Do You Know" "Losing and Living," "The Years," "Her," "Love's Blindness," "I Would Love You," "To You, So Strong," "You Kissed Me In A Dream," "The Stranger," unpublished poems, box 4, folder 7, VAMP; "The Test," unpublished poem, box 4, folder 5, VAMP. "Roma" to "L.O.T.P." and to Vara (undated), VAM Scrapbook; V to Newton (c. 1929), VAM Scrapbook.

103. Majette, *Mistress of a Thousand Slaves*, preface, 395, 359, 350, 361, 363, box 3, VAMP.

104. Majette, "Daughters of Men," unpublished novel, box 2, folders 3–6, VAMP.

105. "Criticizes FEPC Filibuster," *Savannah Morning News*, January 31, 1946; "Explains Filibuster Stand," *Savannah Morning News*, February 2, 1946; Helen Jenkins, "Grandma Moses of the South," *Savannah Morning News*, January 1, 1961. Majette's paintings are held by CGHS.

106. Majette, "Please, God," 280, 298.

107. VAM to McMillan, June 10, 1966, VAM Scrapbook.

108. Martha M. Puckett, "Book Review: *White-Blood*," *Wayne County Press* [1970], box 1, folder 8, VAMP.

109. Susan M. Murphy comments, Vara A. Majette retrospective, Coastal Georgia Historical Society, St. Simon's Island, November 18, 2008. Thanks to Betty Majette Murphy and Susan Majette Murphy for sharing Majette's scrapbook with me. See also Betty Majette Murphy, "A Woman Ahead of her Time," *Coastal Senior* (February 2002).

Lucy May Stanton

(1876–1931)

New Forms and Ideas

BETTY ALICE FOWLER

Lucy May Stanton emerged as an American artist of significance at the beginning of the twentieth century. By 1902 she was regarded as one of the best artists in her hometown of Atlanta, known not only for her portraits of prominent men and women and their children but also as an artist who exhibited her work nationally in prestigious venues. For the next thirty years her paintings were seen in exhibitions in the United States and abroad, bringing high praise from critics and respect from her peers. Her sudden death in 1931 prompted renewed tributes to the originality of her subjects and her innovative artistic technique. Lucy Stanton worked in many media, but she is best remembered as a painter of miniature portraits in watercolor on ivory during a late nineteenth-century revival of the art form.

With her art she aimed, simply, "to dignify the immediate." Stanton chose as her subjects her family, friends, neighbors, and people she encountered in her life, including mountaineers, backwoodsmen, and, most notably, African Americans. Stanton has been called the first miniaturist with a social consciousness, and she may have been the last, since miniature painting was a dying art form when she was at the height of her career. Stanton revolutionized her medium, not only in what she chose to paint but also in her application of watercolor onto ivory, which utilized the fluid, painterly skills of the Impressionists, and transformed the miniature from a precious, often stilted piece of workmanship, into one that shared the conceptual qualities of full-scale works.[1]

Lucy Stanton's upbringing, experiences, and connections form a setting in which her art may be considered; and her art, in turn, reflects her life. What did it mean for her to be a Georgia woman? As an artist, it meant that she found her subject and inspiration around her, relating her time and place to the rest of the world. Though she had to leave Georgia for her training, she was able to develop her early career in Atlanta, a growing city in pursuit of culture, where women artists enjoyed equality with their male counterparts and the press was supportive of the visual arts. Being of the nonplanter merchant class, Stanton was not bound by traditional mores that would discourage a woman who wished to "engage in trade" by selling her paintings, though many times those paintings were bought by people outside of the state.

Stanton was a woman of contradictions. The very model of a southern lady, she was adventuresome and fiercely self-reliant. She observed the rituals of the Lost Cause yet preferred to live in the North. She was both open minded and conventional. Indeed, her nephew Stanton Forbes described her personality as impulsive yet controlled, and art historian Andrew Ladis called her a conservative revolutionary. Comments on her work by a New Orleans critic might also apply to her character: "She knows what she is doing and is following very definite ideas . . . she is doing something quite different and quite individual. She very likely stands alone in American art."[2]

Lucy Stanton's parents, William Lewis (W. L.) Stanton and Frances Louisa Cleveland Megee, were both from families who settled in the mountains of North Georgia. The Stantons were master farmers who did not own slaves; they produced all they needed and more on their abundant farm in Gordon County, with the help of overseers and hired hands; and their children learned the intricacies of farm and housework. Eight of the nine Stanton children attended college. W. L., the eldest, was the exception, as he joined the Confederate army at the age of seventeen. He would later follow the example set by his father and siblings, however, and devote his energies and resources to the advancement of education.[3]

W. L. Stanton fought gallantly as a sergeant in General Joseph Wheeler's Fourth Georgia Cavalry. After Lee's surrender at Appomattox in April 1865, he and Frances Megee were married. They subsequently joined a group of Georgians who immigrated to British Honduras to escape Reconstruction and the occupation of Georgia by federal troops.[4]

Proximity and the hope of prosperity drew thousands of refugees from the war-torn states to the English-speaking colony. The Stanton farm was not destroyed in the war, but with eight younger siblings, most of whom were probably still at home, W. L. Stanton may have relished the prospect of striking out on his own. New Orleans was the hub of the emigration activity, with 1866–70 the peak years of exodus. Most of the émigrés were sugar planters from Mississippi and Louisiana, many of considerable wealth, who sought to recreate their antebellum society under the British Crown. Former Confederate leaders,

LUCY MAY STANTON, 1929
Courtesy of the Hargrett Rare Book and Manuscript
Library, University of Georgia Libraries.

NEGRO BOY

A 1928 painting by Lucy May Stanton, watercolor
on ivory, $2^{15}/_{16} \times 2^{3}/_{16}$ inches, Manuscript, Archives,
and Rare Book Library, Emory University.

including Robert E. Lee and Jefferson Davis, called for submission to the U.S. government, and the *New Orleans Daily Picayune* echoed the popular sentiment that those contemplating leaving should instead stay home and help the South recover. The group migration to British Honduras failed within a few years because of the inhospitable climate and terrain, as well as cultural conflict. The long-term impact on the colony remained, however, in the dominance of the sugar industry in Belize. The *New Orleans Crescent* reported the return of Mr. and Mrs. W. L. Stanton and "Master Stanton" to the city aboard the *Trade Wind* in April 1868. Accounts differ regarding the male children of the Stantons, but this son apparently did not live to the time of the sisters' births.[5]

The Stantons settled in Atlanta around 1870, and by 1877, W. L. Stanton had opened a store at 89 South Broad Street selling lumber, hams, and other products of their parents' farms, as well as crockery, machinery, and tools. Atlanta, despite having been nearly obliterated in the Civil War, was experiencing tremendous growth in the postbellum years, led by energetic businessmen, mainly merchants and industrialists. The young city, with its upcountry location and commercial economy served by a railroad terminus rather than a navigable river, had a social profile different from that of the plantation South. Few of the economic elite were of the planter class. W. L. Stanton achieved success as a merchant, like many others, through real estate development. He built a Gothic Revival house on Gordon Street in the suburb of the West End, and Lucy May Stanton was born there on May 22, 1876.[6]

Lucy and her sister, Willie Marion Stanton ("TeWillie"), born in 1877, enjoyed a rich and active childhood. Frances Stanton encouraged Lucy to pursue her creative interests and gave her a set of watercolor paints when she was four years old. Within a few years Lucy had begun painting lessons, working in oils and instructed by Sally Seago, who taught her to paint from life and in full color. The children and their mother summered in the mountains at the grandparents' farms, and the Stantons spent many winters in New Orleans, where W. L. Stanton had a business brokering sugar and molasses from the Caribbean, possibly a remaining connection to British Honduras. Frances Stanton's health was declining, however, and at home she relied increasingly on the domestic help of Chloe Henderson to rear the girls.[7]

The Stantons were good friends with their neighbors, Joel Chandler Harris and his family, who lived across the street in the house that became known as The Wren's Nest. Harris, an editor for the *Atlanta Constitution*, published *Uncle Remus: His Songs and His Sayings* in 1880. With these and other stories, which were based on African American folklore, Harris soon gained a national audience. Meanwhile, he urged his fellow southern writers to create a new literature, using to their advantage, as he did, the unique, untouched materials surrounding them. Lucy and TeWillie heard the tales from the author himself. Lucy painted several portraits of Harris, as well as many others of his family. She maintained her strong friendship with the family for many years, and Julian Harris and his wife, Julia, hosted at least one exhibition of Stanton's work in their Atlanta home.[8]

Frances Megee Stanton died in June 1888 when Lucy was only twelve years old. An aunt came to live with the family, but the arrangement was not satisfactory. Within a few months, Mr. Stanton sold the house on Gordon Street, Chloe went to work for the Harrises, and the girls were sent to Southern Female College in LaGrange, Georgia. Thus, Lucy Stanton endured what must have been devastating losses as she entered her adolescence. Little is known of Lucy Stanton's mother except what her eulogist described as one who was "true to her country" and "a strong advocate of secession," nor are there any extant portraits of her by her daughter. Stanton did paint Chloe in 1922 or 1923, and it is among her most powerful portraits, created from a photograph and memory almost forty years after Chloe left the Stanton home. Although she is dressed as a servant, Chloe's direct gaze and elegant carriage belie her position. Her starched stole and mobcap might be the attire of a seventeenth-century Dutch merchant's wife, while Stanton establishes a psychological context through her painterly techniques that recall some of Rembrandt's most powerful portraits.[9]

W. L. Stanton was soon married again, in 1889, to Sallie Cox. Miss Cox was an accomplished violinist and a music instructor at Lucy and TeWillie's school, which was owned by her family and known as Cox College. She had taken the Stanton girls under her wing when they enrolled, and she quickly gained a place in their affections. She encouraged Lucy in her art, and figured largely in her growth by "teaching the conventionalities." The sisters accompanied the Stantons on their honeymoon in Europe and Britain, where Lucy had her first exposure to European art, as well as that of the ancient Greeks and Romans, whose cultures she would later study and revere. They visited schools and universities in Germany, Scotland, and England, as W. L. Stanton made plans to establish a Baptist college for women in Atlanta.[10]

A "college" for women in the nineteenth century might provide instruction either to university or high school students or both, as in the case of Cox College. Instruction in domestic pursuits was a focus of some schools, but collegiate education for women in the South had, since the antebellum period, also included the classical curriculum of men's colleges. Education was, indeed, a status symbol; but for women like Lucy Stanton, it also reinforced aspirations and imparted the self-assurance to expand their intellectual and social horizons.

Stanton chose the classics as her major area of study, and graduated with a master's degree and highest honors in Greek and Latin in 1893. She taught art and art history the following year at New Ebenezer College in Cochran, one hundred miles south of Atlanta, which was one of many small schools in Georgia that was associated with the Baptist Church. She returned to Cox College in 1894 as an assistant to James P. Field, her former instructor, who had trained in Paris and was one of Atlanta's top artists.[11]

Meanwhile, in 1892 W. L. Stanton had begun building the Southern Baptist College for Women. Atlanta was becoming the most populous city in the region, but before the war the city had, for the most part, lacked a gentry class and its associated cultural and educational institutions. W. L. Stanton was at the forefront of Atlanta's growth, and of the expansion in higher education that took place in the South between 1890 and 1920.[12]

Located in Manchester, a newly incorporated suburb eight miles from the city, Southern Baptist College for Women offered a full liberal arts curriculum. It was housed in a large brick and stone building crowned with a mansard roof and clock tower, which held a library, a museum of natural history and industrial sciences, a laboratory, an art studio, Steinway pianos, a chapel with pipe organ, and a mounted telescope. The college opened in the fall of 1894, but crucial promised support did not materialize, and the school operated only for that academic year. Stanton had to sell his assets to meet expenses, and he negotiated with his brother-in-law, Professor Charles Cox, to move the charter of Southern Female College from LaGrange to Manchester (later renamed College Park) and assume operation of the facility. According to his family he lost $125,000 in the venture. In nearby Decatur, Agnes Scott College had been founded by Presbyterians five years earlier for a similar amount, though its start-up costs were paid with donated, not pledged, funds. W. L. Stanton never recovered financially from his "heroic plunge into an effort to build a great Southern college for women in the name of the truth he loved." His remarkable commitment to women's education, while the cause of his reversal of fortune, shaped his daughter's confidence and independence. This legacy served her well, as a single woman and artist, to meet the challenge of supporting herself.[13]

Lucy Stanton continued teaching, and began to receive portrait commissions from Atlanta patrons, including her first order for a miniature from the world-famous soprano Adelina Patti. Patti was the aunt of Alfredo Barili, a pianist, music teacher, and leader in Atlanta's cultural community. The Barilis lived in College Park and were close friends of the Stantons. Madame Patti was pleased with the portrait, and Stanton produced two additional copies at her request. With this auspicious beginning, Stanton took her place as a professional artist.[14]

In the early years of her career she created the types of works through which she would distinguish herself: miniatures, self-portraits, and, by 1898, her first portrait of an African American. Teaching and commissions were practical necessities, but she also continued her education and traveled as often as possible. Two contemporary artistic trends influenced her entire artistic endeavor: Impressionism and the Arts and Crafts movement.

Impressionism was the dominant style of painting in America at the end of the nineteenth century. Its characteristic fluid technique was one that Lucy Stanton had adopted naturally from her earliest attempts at painting, and from her instructors, who were either French or French-trained Americans. Impressionism steered a course between the genteel and the new, combining traditional draftsmanship and modern aesthetic concepts. Its prevalence of domestic subject matter made Impressionism both appealing and accessible to women.[15]

Miniature portraits evolved from medieval manuscript illuminations. The art form achieved popularity in England in the late sixteenth century, and later in America. Demand for the miniature had faded by the 1840s, as the objective and affordable photograph replaced the miniature's functions of commemoration and the recording of private relationships. Portrait miniature painting was revived in England during the Arts and Crafts movement, however, and the trend spread to the United States in the late 1800s. Revival miniatures were appreciated as unique, handmade objects, in contrast to the mechanics of photography; and miniatures no longer served merely as a form of remembrance or personal adornment, but were treated as fine art, often hung on the walls of homes or galleries.[16]

The Arts and Crafts movement stressed the beautification of everyday life and the moral value of handwork, and within it women found unprecedented opportunity to fulfill their creativity. Art was an elevating activity suitable for engaging women in the home. Some women made their living as artists, while others used art to promote social reform. Women's production in ceramics, metalwork, stained glass, bookbinding, and textiles equaled and often surpassed men's, and the majority of the revival miniaturists were women. Artistic currents and early success thus favored Lucy Stanton as she began to build an independent career for herself. The portability of the miniature also must have made it an attractive medium for an artist who would lead a fairly itinerant life.[17]

Cultural growth in the late nineteenth-century South was hampered by the Civil War and its aftereffects, and by a lack of widespread patronage and large-scale philanthropy. The importance of art in the home was unquestioned, however, and women were responsible for their family's cultural well-being. In Atlanta, women were active as artists and arts supporters from the earliest years of the city. Though no detailed information exists on the first women artists of Atlanta, it is known that women were the city's first art teachers and award recipients at the agricultural fairs. Oscar Wilde made a significant impact in 1882 when he came to Atlanta and lectured on decorative art. His visit caused a stir in local cultural circles, resulting in increased momentum for art-related activities. The city became home for many professional artists, male and female, during the 1880s and 1890s, and "culture" was promoted in order to counterbalance Atlanta's reputation as a commercial center. Men and women artists were treated with equal regard by patrons and the press; both were judged on merit rather than gender, and won prizes at state fairs and expositions, and both studied in Europe and the northeast.[18]

Aspiring women artists in the late nineteenth-century South were no different from those in other parts of the country in following the trajectory for a professional career: study in New York or Boston, study more and travel in Europe, then return home to make a living. Since the South had no important collections of art and no acknowledged art centers for training in studio art, those who wished to improve their chances of success usually found a way to study at one of the northern schools. Around 1880, a generation of artists surfaced not only in the cities of the South but also in New York and elsewhere far from home. Some, such as Anne Goldthwaite of Alabama, gained national reputations, and their careers became touchstones for the younger artists who would be active participants in the Southern scene movement that followed in the 1930s and 1940s. Several, like Lucy Stanton, were miniaturists of note, such as Helen M. Turner of Kentucky, Elsie Motz Lowdon of Texas, and Sarah E. Cowan of Tennessee.[19]

Lucy Stanton was one of many Atlanta artists, men and women, who went to Europe to study during the late nineteenth century. Paris was the capital of the Western art world, and the destination of painters seeking serious instruction and prestige. Stanton arrived in 1896 for the first of two documented sojourns. A copy of *Hamlet* in a family collection, inscribed "Lucie M. Stanton, London, September 10, 1897, on the occasion of seeing Forbes Robertson in Hamlet," indicates a visit to England, and a temporary, French spelling of her name. James Field, her instructor, who had studied at the Académie Julien, may have advised her and provided introductions or information on suitable programs in Paris.[20]

Stanton studied under American artists Augustus Koopman and Virginia Richmond Reynolds. Reynolds introduced her students to a new way of painting miniatures using parallel brush strokes. In contrast to stippling, hatching, and evenly applied washes of color (tight, labored techniques practiced by most miniaturists since the sixteenth century), using parallel brush strokes enabled

Stanton to become more expressive within the confines of the miniature, pointing the way to her very loose, mature style. She also took classes at the École de la Grande Chaumière and the Académie Colarossi (two independent art schools open to women), studied anatomy at the Sorbonne, and is said to have had "some sessions with [James McNeill] Whistler," though the nature of her studies with him is not clear. Whistler was an important source of inspiration for many adventuresome American artists, and he was the painter she would come to admire above all others.[21]

Lucy Stanton created her first miniature portrait of an African American soon after her return to Atlanta from Paris. *Aunt Nicey Tuller* (1898) reveals Stanton's new technique of parallel brush strokes, as well as the influence of the Old Masters. In this image the sitter is depicted in a neoclassical-like profile and executed very much in a French manner, using a low-keyed palette. The emphasis is on the experience etched into her elderly countenance as opposed to a focus on her gender, race, or class. The subject was a significant choice, given the extreme racial intolerance and violence of the time. Indeed, four days of looting, lynching, and murder in Atlanta had followed the Georgia elections that year, which brought a complete reentrenchment of white supremacy. Seldom the subject of fine art, blacks were usually depicted committing atrocities or ridiculed in demeaning cartoons and photographs, all of which helped to popularize radical views. In contrast, Stanton portrays a human psychology that is independent and dignified. *Aunt Nicey Tuller* was shown the following year at the Philadelphia Academy of Fine Arts, the first work by Lucy Stanton to appear in a national exhibition.[22]

Surely Stanton was shocked and dismayed at the grim realities of black life, and perhaps wished to present another view through her art. Her anti-academic training stressed an interest in the commonplace and everyday life, and in her art she "[strived] to express as much of life as possible." Throughout her career she created portraits of African Americans. While her point of view was affectionate, the works are, above all, admiring character studies free of caricature or condescension. Though her exhibits were widely seen and commented on, whether her art changed race relations is not known. Perhaps her white audience, when exposed to such a new conception of the black image, came to view their neighbor more compassionately. Perhaps her black sitters were gratified by her beautiful and sensitive portraits of them, and her black audiences, however small, felt validated and strengthened by such positive depictions of humanity and individuality.[23]

In Atlanta, Stanton focused on teaching and portrait commissions. She worked again at Cox College (now located in Manchester), taught a drawing class at the

YMCA, and offered private lessons from her studio at the Grand Opera House. Among the successful women painters in Atlanta at this time were Mary Bland Rogers Gregory, Adelaide Everhart, Kate Edwards, and Lucy M. Thompson, another miniaturist. Some, like Stanton, had gone away to study, and all produced commissioned portraits of Atlanta's citizens and historical figures. Atlanta newspapers kept their readers informed of the travels and accomplishments of these and other "artistes." Stanton exhibited her paintings at the Atlanta Women's Club in March and at the 1899 Georgia State Fair in October. The *Atlanta Constitution* published her photograph, acknowledging her pictures as some of best at the fair.[24]

Soon Stanton began to travel to the North and establish important, lasting friendships and connections. She and her sister spent a year in New York City in 1901–2, and lived at the Bryant Park Studios on West Fortieth Street, near the New York Public Library. A photograph of their living space shows a "studio-salon" containing exotic textiles and furniture, with walls covered by dozens of miniatures and paintings, a current fashion. They, along with Polly Smith (an art student whom Lucy had met in Paris, and who lived in New York) took a course in practical charity nursing at the Episcopal Deaconess Hospital. The sisters took day trips up the Hudson River or to Coney Island, went to plays, and entertained at home with prepared food, cutlery, linens, and china from the restaurant downstairs, assisted by one of the waiters. Lucy painted, taught, and wrote in her diary of the city's wonderful essences and "marvelous advantages in the way of good pictures."[25]

Stanton also thrived in the wilderness. She became friends with the naturalist John Burroughs, an icon of the simple life espoused by adherents of the Arts and Crafts movement, and made the first of several visits to his home, *Slabsides*, during this time in New York. She also made excursions to remote settings such as rivers, lakes, caves, lodges, and rough cabins in the woods with her friends Polly Smith, Samuel Pillsbury of Boston, and others. An exuberant, fourteen-page letter describing a camping trip in Maine and many photographs attest to adventures and camaraderie, and suggest that she enjoyed unusual freedom for a young woman of her time.[26]

In November 1902, her work was shown in Boston at the annual exhibition of the Copley Society. The *Atlanta Constitution* reported on Stanton's achievement, noting that the jurors had rejected more than eight hundred paintings. The very same issue of the newspaper carried a disparaging syndicated article, "How the Bachelor Girls Overrun New York," on the futility of the yearly exodus to New York of young women in search of career opportunities. The author describes living arrangements and other specific details that closely resemble those of Lucy and TeWillie. Illustrated with a photograph of a young woman painting a portrait of two children, the writer describes the unfortunate girl, who, tired of life in a boarding house, "flees to the studio building." The writer then mentions that "a restaurant in the building does away with the necessity for cooking meals," and that "these makeshift homes are always attractive in their unconventional furnishings." According to the writer, the woman's life is "an odd Bohemian existence." The placement of the article may have been a coincidence or intended as a veiled criticism of a well-known, progressive young lady. Attacks in the press on single women and their professions represented commonly held views and were not unusual, but Stanton would not be deterred by such criticism. Her parents had supported her efforts to get an education, travel, and move into a profession, and she was not bound by the "family claim" that often kept unmarried women of the middle classes at home to look after parents and siblings. She was determined to forge a career and be independent.[27]

Willie Marion Stanton and Walter Tillou Forbes II were married in Atlanta in 1902. They made their home in Athens, Georgia, where Forbes was the general secretary of the YMCA. Lucy visited them and subsequently made Athens her home base. She was involved in the cultural development of the town and the University of Georgia, which was transforming from a small college into a modern state institution. She helped to organize traveling exhibitions and lectures, and appears to have written several newspaper articles aimed at encouraging support of the visual arts and the establishment of an art museum. When the Athens Art Association was founded in 1919, she was among the group's first invited speakers and was elected as a life member.[28]

In the late 1890s, Stanton's father, stepmother, and their three children moved to Los Angeles, where her brother Chapel Quillian Stanton and his wife, Ida, lived. In the spring of 1904, Stanton visited her family and stayed in California for nearly a year, painting and teaching. The press reported on her arrival and continued residence there, and featured a large illustration of *Aunt Nicey Tuller* in one article, which stated that a local patron had commissioned Stanton for a copy of the miniature. Featuring one of her portraits of African Americans is notable, as is the fact that she had a request for a copy. Both suggest that her non-stereotypical interpretations were of significant interest and beginning to reach a national audience.

She returned to Athens soon after the Forbeses' first child, a son, was born in January 1905, then departed in the spring, boarding a boat in Savannah that took her to Boston. She and Polly Smith met in New York and sailed for Europe. They toured England and Holland, and arrived in Paris in August. The young women lived for the next year at the Holy Trinity Lodge, 70 *bis*, rue Notre Dame des Champs, near the Luxembourg Gardens, and Stanton resumed her studies under the instruction of French painters Lucien Simon and J. Emile Blanche. Stanton and Smith ran the lodge, which was owned by a church and functioned as part-home and part-club for English-speaking women in Paris. They were able to put into practice their nursing training, since the lodge also provided rooms for women who were sick and required care and companionship, and they probably exchanged their services for housing at a reduced rate.[29]

The lodge sponsored an art league, which mounted its first annual exhibition of art by American and English women in Paris in February 1906, featuring works by sixty-five members and invitees. The *New York Herald* devoted a half page to the exhibition and a description of the lodge. Stanton was praised as a young Georgia woman of exceptional talent. A few months later she won a blue ribbon at the New Salon of the Société Nationale des Beaux Arts for *Mother and Child*, a miniature of her sister and nephew. Stanton had been exhibiting at the New Salon since 1896. Now, for the first time, her work was hung "on the line" at eye level—both the highest honor and especially advantageous in Salon galleries, which were hung floor to ceiling with pictures.[30]

By late 1906, Lucy Stanton was again back in Atlanta, which struggled for public order in the wake of the September race riots. Again, Stanton's thoughts on the brutality and killing that garnered international attention and nearly wiped out Atlanta's growing middle-class black community are unknown, but her paintings of African Americans, many of which were receiving national and international attention, contrasted startlingly with the racial violence that was occurring in the South and beyond. While there, she stayed with the Julian Harrisses and painted two portraits of Joel Chandler Harris, who sat for a large oil sketch and then a miniature. Not long after, she moved to Athens to live with her sister and her family.[31]

In Athens, Stanton painted many portraits of the Forbes family and an elderly African American couple who lived in a house on the alley behind the Forbeses' home. "Aunt Liza" and "Uncle George" are the subjects of at least seven miniatures, watercolors, and oil paintings, some of which have been seen by the author only in clippings of early newspaper articles on Stanton and her work. The portraits and paintings that are available for study in public and private collections demonstrate Stanton's sensitivity to the moods of her sitters, who are observed as wary, pensive, fatigued, or relaxed, and each work is a superb example of her technique in its respective medium. Her new wet-in-wet technique of "puddling" is used to great effect in her miniature of Aunt Liza, painted in 1908, in which she has translated the freedom and largeness of Impressionism into a tiny format. Dark and light puddles of pigments within a limited range create a broken surface rich in detail unlike any previous style of miniature painting. In an interview that same year, Stanton told an Atlanta newspaper reporter, "I believe the miniature ought to and can be a medium in abstract expression: that is, that it can be highly suggestive of ideas which it does not convey to the eye, and that it can teach a universal truth or principle as surely as can an oil painting." In her journals, Stanton cites Rembrandt, Frans Hals, and Goya for their depictions of common people. Like her European exemplars, she reveals the humanity of her subjects as she achieves one of her goals as a Southern artist, comprehending and capturing, in formats large and small, "the pathos of a departing negro life."[32]

Stanton exhibited her miniatures at least two times in Atlanta during this period, and was praised by reviewers, including one who noted both her technical originality as well as her subject matter. "'Aunt Liza Churning' is especially good in color. Several 'Negro Cabins' are as typical and picturesque as any Nomandie huts, and the young artist's very artistic treatment of them shows that the South offers abundant material. . . . A picture which attracted a great deal of attention was that of an old Southern mammy and two children designed for the cover of Uncle Remus's Home Magazine." The latter, *Afternoon on Cobb Street*, evokes the cherished image of the black servant who loved and cared for the white family—in this case, Stanton's niece and nephew. This mammy portrait, grouping in an idealized exterior setting painted from a studio photograph, is a departure for Stanton, who did not usually resort to stereotypes. The same is true of her ride in a Georgia Confederate veterans parade in 1909, though she certainly would have wished to honor her father, who was a veteran, and she probably enjoyed riding in a parade. There is no evidence that Stanton ever was a white supremacist, nor anything to suggest any such interest except a couple of flyers advertising a lecture by Mildred Lewis Rutherford to boys at the YMCA, "True Greatness," circa 1915.[33]

W. L. Stanton died in Los Angeles in March 1909, and Lucy received an inheritance that enabled her to build a small studio dwelling at the back of her property in Athens. After completing a portrait of Howell Cobb for the Fine Arts Committee of the U.S. House of Representatives, Stanton may have returned to Paris in 1911. She did continue to send her paintings to exhibitions at the Société Nationale des Beaux Arts through at least 1924; and in her notes, under the heading "Exhibitions for 1910–11," she lists *Uncle Jesse* as being shown at (or perhaps intended for) the New Salon. The only extant work by that title measures 50 x 30 inches, one of her few full-length portraits and the largest of her known easel paintings. A bearded, grizzled old black man, said to be a gravedigger, is somewhat stooped and dressed in heavy clothing, standing with

his knees slightly bent, holding a cap. He stares out over wire-rim glasses that
rest low on his nose, his attitude at once dignified and mysterious. Whether or
not she or *Uncle Jesse* went to Paris that year, Stanton surely would have savored
the reaction of international audiences to this remarkable work.[34]

During the summer of 1912, Stanton saw an exhibition of Whistler's works
at the National Gallery of Art in Washington, D.C., then went to Michigan to
study the history of Greek art and architecture at the University of Michigan.
In Detroit she visited Charles Lang Freer at his home, where she saw his extensive collection of Whistler's paintings and, presumably, Whistler's Peacock
Room, which Freer bought in 1904 from the Liverpool shipowner and collector,
Frederick R. Leyland, who had commissioned it. Her ability to arrange this encounter could mean, as has been suggested, that she had had a real connection
to Whistler in Paris.[35]

For several years, beginning in 1913 or 1914, Stanton, in need of separation
from family, friends, patrons, and critics, lived alone in the mountains of North
Carolina, first in Andrews, then at Valleytown. She painted in her one-room
cabin every morning, creating miniature portraits of neighbors and herself that
reveal her emerging technique of broad washes, in which each form is finished
in one brush stroke. Two self- portraits and *Mrs. Paris, a North Carolina Mountain Woman* are outstanding examples from this period, as is the half-length
portrait, *Joel Chandler Harris, Esq.* (now in the collection of the National Portrait Gallery), for which she was awarded the 1917 Medal of Honor of the Pennsylvania Society of Miniature Painters. Boston critic William Howe Downes
called *Mrs. Paris* "nothing less than a masterpiece of character."[36]

Stanton kept in touch with her wide circle of friends during her time in the
mountains, and a number of the letters she received during this period and after
suggest Stanton's interests and views. She seems to have had many activists and
social reformers among her correspondents and friends. A woman from the
University of Chicago, in preparing lectures on the mountain women of North
Carolina and Georgia, had learned of Stanton's retreat and wrote to her, asking
for human-interest stories that she could incorporate into her talks, which she
hoped would result in assistance for the mountaineers whom they both loved.
Another wrote of her fears about the war and the fate of art and artists in bomb-
ridden Europe.[37] Two letters from Scott Nearing in 1914 contain his side of what
appears to have been a lively discussion of Whistler's art. Nearing, an economist
at the University of Pennsylvania, was an outspoken, embattled social reformer
and antiwar activist who became a major figure in the socialist movement of the
1910s, and later, with his wife, in the countercultural, back-to-the-land movement of the 1970s and 1980s.[38] Her friendship with a community organizer,

ended when she refused to recommend him (whose "views" she did not agree with) as a sponsor for a young woman friend's employment at a settlement house in New York, while she was praised by a Baptist minister from South Georgia, as a "mystic in the land of beauty."[39]

TeWillie wrote scores of letters to her sister, sometimes daily or even more often, reporting on family, friends, business affairs, and life in Athens. Stanton sent her works to shows in New York and elsewhere, once prompting a column in the local weekly newspaper by a writer who was astounded to learn that a nationally famous artist was in residence, shipping her pictures to places far and wide from the town post office.[40]

After Stanton left the mountains in the fall of 1915, she decided to leave Georgia. She moved to New York and worked on commissions until June 1916, then went to Ogunquit, Maine, for the first of ten consecutive seasons. In September she moved to Boston, which, along with New York and Philadelphia, was a center for artists of the American miniature revival. Her prospects as a portraitist in a city full of wealthy patrons and collectors were far better than if she had stayed in the South. She lived in Boston for the next ten years.[41]

Women in Boston had a long history of achievement in many areas, including the visual arts, and Stanton's work had been featured in exhibitions there in 1902, 1912, 1914, and 1916. She was a member of the Copley Society and the Guild of Boston Artists, both important professional associations with galleries located on Newbury Street. During her years there she taught art and art history at several college preparatory schools. Her influence on her students was positive and memorable; as one wrote to her, "You created an atmosphere about yourself which every one of us girls admired and loved."[42]

Active in the cultural community, Stanton was part of a group that organized a series of lectures by Professor Jay Hambidge of Yale on the golden section and on his theory that certain ratios governed plant and shell growth. Her close friends were the artists Laura Coombs Hills and Mildred Dean Howells; the brothers Max and Harry Sand, and their sister, Alice (also an artist); Samuel Pillsbury and his family; George and Mable Sarton, and their daughter, May; and Dr. William L. Moss, a Cobb Street neighbor who taught at Harvard Medical School. Most of them, like Stanton, lived on Beacon Hill. Stanton was well suited to life in Boston, and she described to a friend the sense of belonging she felt "up North where living is highest."[43]

An exhibition by the American Society of Miniature Painters at New York's Montross Gallery in November 1916 elicited reviews that reveal how distinctive Stanton's paintings were. In contrast to the lack of originality, cloying sweetness, painstaking conscientiousness, and "somewhat fatiguing marvels of mi-

nuteness" that prevailed in most of the works, Stanton's, in one opinion, offered the possibility of a broader and freer manner of painting. The *New York
Sun* praised her "fine free touch" and her "happy gift of characterization." Her
first major Boston exhibition was in March 1919. William Howe Downes, the
prominent critic of the *Boston Transcript*, wrote: "Her portraits are on the scale
of miniatures, but they have none of the usual characteristics of miniatures,
being literally small portraits in watercolors on ivory, executed with a breadth
and looseness of handling that is combined with a distinctly marked personal
style and a fine sense of character. . . . In her Southern types, white and black,
Miss Stanton makes a contribution of real distinction to our art." Critics seldom
failed to discuss her portraits of blacks and regional types. Over the years the
tone of their remarks on Stanton's treatment of these subjects, whether written
for southern or northern readers, had evolved from general and patronizing to
astute and appreciative.[44]

Professor Linton Stephens Ingraham was a native of Sparta, Georgia, whom
Lucy Stanton painted in Boston in 1925. Ingraham, born a slave, became the
founder and director of the Sparta Agricultural and Industrial Institute, a
school for African Americans that was funded mainly by northern philanthropists. Ingraham's need for support of the school frequently led him to Boston
and other cities, and there are records of visits in 1923 and 1924 by him and his
wife, Anna, to the Concord Art Association, where they probably saw Stanton's
work, and it is likely that he saw her paintings in her studio. Ingraham is depicted as a well-dressed, middle-aged man who appears friendly and relaxed.
Were Stanton to have painted Mrs. Ingraham, her pair of miniatures would have
made an interesting comparison to the pendant portraits of William and Nancy
Lawson, free African Americans, painted by William Matthew Prior in Boston
in 1843. The Lawsons were successful merchants, who, like the Ingrahams, defined themselves by their intellectual abilities. Stanton also made sketches of a
black singer in concert. The subject is thought to be another Georgia native, the
tenor Roland Hayes, who had his first Boston recital at Symphony Hall in 1917
and went on to win international acclaim. Stanton delineated the character of
both of her compatriots, cultivated and confident, with the same understanding
and appreciation evident in her portraits of the more humble black subjects she
painted in Georgia.[45]

On many occasions, Stanton exhibited a group of works she called the *Southern Historical Series*, consisting of, along with self-portraits, various other miniature portraits of distinguished citizens (such as Joel Chandler Harris) and
African Americans. Among these were the *Little Murals*, five genre scenes of
African Americans at work on the street and in the cotton warehouse, and at

leisure, painted in Athens in 1921. Though finished works in their own right, the *Little Murals* were preliminary studies for full-size murals that Stanton hoped to execute on large, public walls. At least one, *Negroes Resting*, was copied from a photograph of slaves at the Turnwold Plantation in Eatonton, Georgia, where Joel Chandler Harris lived during the Civil War. The mural project was never realized, but it foreshadowed those commissioned by the Works Progress Administration during the 1930s and 40s, celebrating American laborers in farming and industry, installed in government buildings across the country. The series evolved as she created new works, such as *Negro Boy* in 1928. A pensive youth whose eyes are fixed on a distant point, he is said to have sat but once for the portrait. Stanton nevertheless captured, with a few colors on a slab of ivory that could fit within her hand, the aspiration of a young man with the prospect of a better life, in a bold series of strokes verging on modernism.[46]

In her lifetime, Stanton's pictures were shown in over forty different galleries, expositions, museums, and societies, many of which, in turn, presented her works on multiple occasions. The *Southern Historical Series* was seen and reviewed in Columbus, Georgia; Boston; Ogunquit, Maine; and Atlanta. The 1908 miniature *Aunt Liza* had been shown in twenty-five exhibitions by the time it was bought by the Concord Art Association in 1925, including venues in Paris, London, Liverpool, Boston, New York, Atlanta, Washington, and San Francisco, a pedigree perhaps the lengthiest of her works, but by no means the only long one.[47]

In 1925 Stanton left Boston and returned to Athens. She built the first floor of a permanent brick house on the front of her lot, but her financial situation was precarious, and after a year it was necessary for her to rent out the new house and move back into the old studio, where she lived for the rest of her life. She returned to New England and Nantucket Island each summer, and kept in touch with her friends and colleagues. She suffered from rheumatism in her hands, but neither the quality nor the quantity of her artistic production declined. The High Museum of Art in Atlanta presented an exhibition of her work in February 1927, the year after the museum opened, and she delivered a series of lectures on art history at the Atlanta Woman's Club during the same period. Her work was shown at the Guild of Boston Artists and in numerous group exhibitions in Georgia and elsewhere, and Stanton continued to receive commissions for portrait miniatures, though the popularity of the art form was waning.[48]

Stanton was a mentor to her niece Frances Forbes, who became a distinguished preschool teacher, and her nephew Stanton Forbes, an artist and writer. She shared her vast knowledge of art and literature with them and with other young people, whom she taught at no charge. Friends of all ages and occupations gathered at her studio for play readings or, sometimes, discussions of topics such as rural sociology or economics. As a self-described liberal Baptist and liberal Democrat, she continued, as always, to advance her views through action and persuasion. For example, one woman, whose friend Stanton had painted as a young girl, recalled the artist promoting women's suffrage during a portrait sitting in 1918, and Stanton's niece said that she had been a member of a local suffragette club as early as 1906. Like many Americans, Stanton feared the possibility of another world war after the United States failed to join the League of Nations. In response, she helped to found the Georgia Peace Society, and hosted meetings at her studio, one of which, in 1928, was attended by Count Carlo Sforza, an antifascist Italian expatriate who later represented his country in the formation of NATO. Such activities may have been unusual or unpopular in Georgia and the South, but it does not seem that Lucy Stanton was ever criticized or harassed as a result. Stanton Forbes later characterized his aunt as possessing "the crackling fire of an open mind."[49]

In a series of letters in 1930, Stanton and the director of the Georgia Department of Archives and History discussed a project in which she and fellow miniaturists Laura Coombs Hills and Elsie Pattee would paint portraits of as many as one hundred distinguished Georgians. Stanton expressed her desire to paint the late Mildred Lewis Rutherford, a fellow Athenian whom Stanton said she knew very well. Given her liberal leanings, it is curious that Stanton would want to paint Rutherford; but she was, after all, a professional artist, negotiating what she hoped would be a huge group of commissions. It is possible, though, that she felt inspired, maybe even compelled, to immortalize her on ivory; and a portrait of "Miss Millie" would round out her *Southern Historical Series*. Funding for the project had not yet been secured, however, when Stanton fell ill and died from double pneumonia in Athens on March 19, 1931.[50]

Lucy May Stanton, while herself a southern lady, was never on a pedestal, nor did she wish to be. "No strong womanly woman can be sullied by any contact with life," she wrote once in her journal. In *Self Portrait, Reading*, Stanton presents herself large, uncompromised by the public gaze of social conventions for female behavior. The nearly life-sized canvas was painted sometime before 1916, and was vividly described by a journalist who saw it in her studio in Ogunquit: "Wait! She will look up to you in a moment; isn't she tapping her foot as she reads?" *Arrangement in White and Green* is the alternate title, in homage to Whistler. Perhaps she is studying her French, or reading a Greek poet or a treatise against the war, pausing from time to time to envision her next journey, her next painting.[51]

NOTES

1. Lucy M. Stanton, diary, n.d., Lucy M. Stanton Papers, Hargrett Rare Book and Manuscript Library/University of Georgia Libraries, Athens, Ga. (hereafter referred to as LMS Papers); W. Stanton Forbes, *Lucy M. Stanton, Artist* (Atlanta: Special Collections Department, Robert W. Woodruff Library, Emory University, 1975), 1–2; Andrew Ladis, "A World in Little," *The Art of Lucy May Stanton* (Athens: Georgia Museum of Art, 2002), 30. Much of the information in this essay on Stanton's life, especially the early years, is from Forbes, *Lucy M. Stanton, Artist. The Art of Lucy May Stanton* contains additional biographical information, catalog entries, and illustrations of many of the Stanton paintings discussed in the essay.

2. Quoted in Forbes, *Lucy M. Stanton, Artist*, 1.

3. Mary I. Stanton, "Two Master Farmers of the Seventies," *Georgia Review* (Spring 1962): 23. W. L. Stanton was the son of John Wesley and Lucinda Hale Stanton. His parents were strong proponents of education, and in his will, J. W. Stanton provided for the support of a school at Fairmont, near the family home. Following his death in 1895, two buildings were erected for a high school, Fairmont Academy. One housed a museum, Stanton Hall, which exhibited relics from the Holy Land, collected by Peyton Lusby Stanton, a son who had gone to Palestine to establish a school for the blind. The school eventually closed and the properties were sold, with the proceeds used to benefit Young Harris College. Mary I. Stanton, the youngest child, graduated from Dahlonega College in 1884 and went to El Paso, Texas, where she taught in the Central School, established the public library, and later opened a business school.

4. "Cleveland Genealogy"; W. L. Stanton to W. H. Logan, College Park, Ga., June 28, 1895 (reprinted in *Atlanta Constitution*, April 12, 1897), LMS Papers.

5. Donald C. Simmons Jr., *Confederate Settlements in British Honduras* (Jefferson, N.C.: McFarland & Company, 2001), 15, 26–27, 121–22, 126; Forbes, *Lucy M. Stanton, Artist*, 5; Simmons, *Confederate Settlements in British Honduras*, 144; "Funeral of Mrs. Stanton," n.d., LMS Papers. In the eulogy a reference is made to two sons who died during the long, difficult stay in Honduras.

6. 1877 Atlanta City Directory; N. Lee Orr, *Alfredo Barili and the Rise of Classical Music in Atlanta* (Atlanta: Scholars Press, 1996), 51; Numan V. Bartley, *The Creation of Modern Georgia*, 2nd ed. (Athens: University of Georgia Press, 1990), 110; Lucy Stanton, information form for *The National Cyclopedia of American Biography*, Boston, October 15, 1925, Lucy Forbes Shevenell archives, Lexington, Mass.

7. Stanton, *National Cyclopedia* form; Research for this article has yielded new information on Sally Seago, who was born in Atlanta in 1859 and educated at Hollins College, Roanoke, Va. According to her obituary, Seago moved to New Orleans in 1890, apparently with her family, and was married there to James T. Callendar in 1891. One of their sons, Alvin Callender, was an aviation hero of World War I. See "Death Claims Mrs. Callender," *New Orleans Item*, October 31, 1940, and other related documents at the Williams Research Center, Historic New Orleans Collection, New Orleans, La.

8. Forbes, *Lucy M. Stanton, Artist*, 38–40; Edward L. Ayers, *The Promise of the New South: Life after Reconstruction* (New York: Oxford University Press, 1992), 342.

9. "Funeral of Mrs. Stanton," LMS Papers.

10. Forbes, *Lucy M. Stanton, Artist*, 9–11; Lucy Stanton, diary, 1910, LMS Papers.

11. Amy Thompson McCandless, *The Past in the Present: Women's Higher Education in the Twentieth-Century American South* (Tuscaloosa: University of Alabama Press, 1999), 6–18; Stanton, *National Cyclopedia* form, Shevenell archives; Willie Forbes, interview with Stanton Forbes, January 1958, transcript, LMS Papers; *Annual Report of Southern Female (Cox) College*, 1894–95 and

1895–96, Cox College Papers, Hargrett Rare Book and Manuscript Library/University of Georgia Libraries, Athens, Ga. (hereafter referred to as Cox College Papers), and LMS Papers; Carlyn Gaye Crannell, "In pursuit of Culture: A History of Art Activity in Atlanta, 1847–1926," (PhD diss., Emory University Institute of Liberal Arts, 1981), 229. Crannell cites Field as one of only two Atlanta artists listed in the official publication of the Cotton States and International Exposition of 1895. See also Betty Alice Fowler, "An Art in Living," *The Art of Lucy May Stanton*, 26n2, 26n7. The information on Stanton's college and early teaching career is inconclusive, as is the information regarding the year of her birth. New Ebenezer College later became Middle Georgia College.

12. Orr, *Alfredo Barili*, 143–44.

13. Willie Stanton Forbes, interview with Stanton Forbes, January 1958; Lynn D. Gordon, *Gender and Higher Education in the Progressive Era* (New Haven: Yale University Press, 1990), 170; "Obituary of W. L. Stanton," (March 1909), LMS Papers; *Annual Report of Southern Female (Cox) College*, 1895–96, Cox College Papers.

14. Crannell, "In Pursuit of Culture," 241; Lucy Stanton, Composition Book, vol. 2, Shevenell archives. Stanton later painted miniatures of Alfredo and Emily Barili, illustrated in Orr, *Alfredo Barili*, 98–99. Crannell cites the location of one of the miniatures of Adelina Patti.

15. Donald D. Keyes, *American Impressionism in Georgia Collections* (Athens: Georgia Museum of Art, 1993), 12; Erica E. Hirshler, *A Studio of Her Own: Women Artists in Boston 1870–1940* (Boston: MFA Publications, 2001), 83. Illustrations of works by Stanton are featured in both Keyes and Hirshler.

16. Robin Jaffee Frank, *Love and Loss: American Portrait and Mourning Miniatures* (New Haven: Yale University Press: 2000), 1–3; Lewis Hoyer Rabbage, "Absolutely Eulabee," *Eulabee Dix Portrait Miniatures: An American Renaissance* (Washington: National Museum of Women in the Arts, 1994), 29; Hirshler, *A Studio of Her Own*, 43, 64–65.

17. Heidi Nasstrom Evans, *Jane Byrd McCall Whitehead (1861–1955): Idealized Visions about Simple Living and Arts & Crafts* (Athens: Georgia Museum of Art, 2004), 17; Crannell, "In Pursuit of Culture," 210–11; Hirshler, *A Studio of Her Own*, 35–53.

18. Crannell, "In Pursuit of Culture," 45–54, 181, 347.

19. William U. Eiland, "Picturing the Unvictorious: The Southern Scene in Alabama, 1930–1946," 36–37; and Angela Culpepper and Alan Vannoy, "Biographies and Major Sources," 252–63, *The American Scene and the South: Paintings and Works on Paper, 1930–1946* (Athens: Georgia Museum of Art, 1996); Carrie Rebora Barratt and Lori Zabar, *American Portrait Miniatures in the Metropolitan Museum of Art* (New York: Metropolitan Museum of Art, 2010), 234–35, 255, 274–75.

20. Crannell, "In Pursuit of Culture," 212; Hirshler, *A Studio of Her Own*, 76; copy of *Hamlet* in collection of the artist's family; Forbes, *Lucy M. Stanton, Artist*, 11–12.

21. Stanton, *National Cyclopedia* form; Lucy M. Stanton, diaries, LMS Papers; Forbes, *Lucy M. Stanton, Artist*, 75; Willie Forbes, interviews with Stanton Forbes, Athens, Ga., 1960–61, transcript, LMS Papers; Forbes, "Peach Trees," LMS Papers; Barratt and Zabar, *American Portrait Miniatures*, 240. Stanton did not list Whistler as a teacher on any extant biographical information forms. She possibly lived near his studio, 86 rue Notre Dame des Champs, during her first stay in Paris, as that location is two blocks from Rue de la Grande Chaumiere, presumably the address of the art school of the same name that Stanton attended. She lived at 70 *bis* rue Notre Dame des Champs, when she went back to Paris in 1905, two years after his death.

22. Forbes, *Lucy M. Stanton, Artist*, 21–22; C. Vann Woodward, *Origins of the New South, 1877–1913* (Baton Rouge: Louisiana State University Press, 1971), 350–353. *Aunt Nicey Tuller* is in the collection of the Museum of Fine Arts, Boston.

23. Selene Armstrong, "Miss Stanton's Exhibit Is Admirable Display," *Atlanta Georgian and News*, February 20, 1908; Ladis, "A World in Little," 30; R. Bruce Bickley Jr., "Joel Chandler Harris (1845–1908)," *New Georgia Encyclopedia*, 30 March 2010, http://www.georgiaencyclopedia.org/nge/Article.jsp?id=h-525&sug=y (accessed October 1, 2011). See also Grace Elizabeth Hale, "'In Terms of Paint': Lucy Stanton's Representations of the South, 1890–1930," *Georgia Historical Quarterly* 77, no. 3 (1993): 577–92; and Hale, "'Some Women Have Never Been Reconstructed': Mildred Lewis Rutherford, Lucy M. Stanton, and the Racial Politics of White Southern Womanhood, 1900–1930," *Georgia in Black and White: Explorations in the Race Relations of a Southern State, 1865–1950*, ed. John C. Inscoe, 173–201 (Athens: University of Georgia Press, 1994). Hale has written extensively on Stanton within the context of race, class, and gender.

24. Crannell, "In Pursuit of Culture," 231–49, 210; Lucy Stanton, photo album and clipping, LMS Papers; *Annual Report of Southern Female College*, 1899, 1901, Cox College Papers.

25. Willie Forbes, interview with W. Stanton Forbes, 1960–61; photograph, May 1902, LMS Papers; Evans, *Jane Byrd McCall Whitehead*, 14; Lucy Stanton, notes, 1901, LMS Papers. See also *The Art of Lucy May Stanton*, 18, fig. 3.

26. Lucy Stanton, photograph album; Stanton to her family, Maine, September 5, 1902, LMS Papers.

27. "Atlanta Artist Is Honored: Miss Lucy May Stanton Has Work Hung Out at Copley Society Exhibit in Boston"; and Kate Masterson, "How the Bachelor Girls Overrun New York," *Atlanta Constitution*, November 30, 1902.

28. Stanton to Ida and Quillian Stanton, Paris, November 19, 1905, LMS Papers; Thomas G. Dyer, *The University of Georgia: A Bicentennial History, 1785–1985* (Athens: University of Georgia Press, 1985), 152–58; clippings, LMS Papers; Athens Art Association, "Selected Documents from Archives Portray a Historical Panorama of the Rise of Athens Art Association and Its Activities," 1984, 174. This folio can be found in the Louis T. Griffith Library, Georgia Museum of Art.

29. "Among the Studios," *Los Angeles Express*, May 21, 1904, and January 7, 1905; Stanton to Ida and Quillian Stanton, Rijsoord, Holland, undated (summer 1905); "Exhibition by the Art League of Holy Trinity Lodge . . . American and English Women Painters Hold First Annual Salon at American Art Association," *New York Herald*, February 4, 1906, Paris ed., LMS Papers.

30. "Exhibition by the Art League"; The Lodge Art League, exhibition catalogue, February 3, 1906, LMS Papers. *Mother and Child* (1896) is illustrated in Keyes, *American Impressionism in Georgia Collections*, 105.

31. David Fort Godshalk, *Veiled Visions* (Chapel Hill: University of North Carolina Press, 2005), 111–15.

32. Armstrong, "Miss Stanton's Exhibit."

33. Ibid.; for photograph of Stanton in the parade, see Emily Jean Doster and Gary L. Doster, *Athens* (Charleston, S.C.: Arcadia Publishing, 2011), 24; flyers in LMS Papers. Rutherford was an educator and historian of the Confederacy who, in her lectures around the country, advocated a remaking of the Old South, promoting white supremacy and an antisuffragist ideology for women. For her appearances, she often dressed in a hoop-skirted gown.

34. Willie Forbes, interviews with Stanton Forbes, 1960–61, transcript; Chester Harrison to Stanton, Washington, D.C., July 10, 1911; Lucy Stanton, notebook, Athens, Ga., February 1910, LMS Papers; Frances Forbes Heyn, interview with author, New Orleans, August 15, 2001.

35. Forbes, *Lucy M. Stanton, Artist*, 78–79; Lucy Stanton, small diary, February 19, 1915, LMS Papers.

36. William Howe Downes, "Miss Stanton's Portraits," *Boston Transcript*, March 7, 1919, Shevenell archives. *Mrs. Paris* is illustrated in Carrie Rebora Barratt and Lori Zabar, *American Portrait Miniatures*, 6, 256.

37. Emily Harrison to Lucy Stanton, Chicago, February 15, 1915; Helene Wood to Lucy Stanton, Albany, N.Y., January 13, 1915, LMS Papers.

38. Scott Nearing to Stanton, Elmira, New York, May 9, 1914; Scott Nearing to Stanton, September 28, 1914, LMS Papers; John A. Saltmarsh, "Scott Nearing," *American National Biography*, vol. 16, ed. Mark C. Carnes and John A. Garraty (New York: Oxford University Press, 1997), 263–64. In his earlier letter, Nearing refers to a visit to Athens, where Stanton may have met him.

39. Lucy Stanton to John Collier, Athens, Georgia, October 10, 1915; Lamar Sims to Lucy Stanton, Albany, Georgia, December 14, 1914, LMS Papers.

40. Nat H. Walker, "Miss Stanton," newspaper clipping, Andrews, N.C., December 10, 1914, LMS Papers. The LMS Papers contain many letters from Willie Forbes to Lucy Stanton, written during this period.

41. Willie Forbes to Stanton, Athens, February 16, 1916; Lucy Stanton, diary, February 18, 1916; Stanton to Sarah Moss, Ogunquit, Maine, July 28, 1916, LMS Papers; Lucy Stanton, Day Book, n.d., Shevenell archives.

42. Hirshler, *A Studio of Her Own*, 5–7, 65; Erica E. Hirshler, "'Sisters of the Brush': Artistic Education for Women in Nineteenth-Century Boston," *Laura Coombs Hills: A Retrospective* (Newburyport, Mass.: Historical Society of Old Newbury, 1996), 5–7; Lucy Stanton, exhibition records and newspaper clippings, 1902–16; Caroline Lyder to Stanton (n.d., c.1920), LMS Papers.

43. Forbes, *Lucy M. Stanton, Artist*, 31–34; Stanton to Sarah Moss, Ogunquit, Maine, June 20, 1921, LMS Papers.

44. Clipping (review of exhibition Montross Gallery, November 1916), Shevenell archives; "Miniature Painters' Exhibit at Montross's," *New York Sun*, n.d., LMS Papers; Downes, "Miss Stanton's Portraits."

45. Gwendolyn DuBois Shaw, *Portraits of a People: Picturing African Americans in the Nineteenth Century* (Andover, Mass.: Addison Gallery of American Art, 2006), 15; Susan J. Harrington, ed., *Cemeteries of Hancock County, Georgia* (Milledgeville, Ga.: Friends of Cemeteries of Middle Georgia, 2004), 232; Charles Scruggs and Lee VanDemarr, *Jean Toomer and the Terrors of American History* (Philadelphia: University of Pennsylvania Press, 1998), 9–15; Concord Art Association guest book, 1923, 1924; MacKinley Helm, *Angel Mo' and her Son, Roland Hayes* (Boston: Little Brown and Company, 1942), 46, 111–13. *Linton S. Ingraham, Ex-Slave* is illustrated in Forbes, *Lucy M. Stanton, Artist*, 59. During a trip north in 1921, Ingraham stopped in Washington, D.C. In need of a substitute to serve in his absence, he met a young man, Jean Toomer, who ran the school for him for three months during the fall. Two years later Toomer published the novel, *Cane*, based on his experiences in Sparta. Ingraham's school became the L. S. Ingraham High School in the 1950s.

46. Forbes, *Lucy M. Stanton, Artist*, 61–67; Bickley, "Joel Chandler Harris," October 1, 2011.

47. Forbes, *Lucy M. Stanton, Artist*, 82–83; Stanton to Elizabeth W. Roberts, Boston, November 23, 1925, LMS Papers. See also Forbes, *Lucy M. Stanton, Artist*, 54–56, for the exhibition history of *Mrs. Paris, a North Carolina Mountain Woman*, 1915.

48. Exhibition catalogs, LMS Papers; Lucy Stanton, composition book, Shevenell archives; "Miss Stanton Will Continue Art Lectures at Woman's Club," *Hearst's Sunday American*, February 13, 1927, LMS Papers.

49. Frances Forbes Heyn, interview with author, New Orleans, February 6, 1998; Mary Burnet Fradier, telephone interview with author, September 2001; Frances Forbes to Stanton, New York, December 30, 1929; Rollin Chambliss to Willie Forbes, Chattanooga, Tenn., March 21, 1931; J. L. Stephens to Stanton Forbes, Tifton, Ga., May 3, 1966, LMS Papers; Lucy May Stanton, *Biographical Information for the Department of Records of the State of Georgia*, August 1, 1926, Georgia Department

of Archives (RG 4–10–74), Morrow, Ga.; Susan Barrow Tate to Grace E. Hale, interview, October 9, 1990, in Hale, "In Terms of Paint," 577; Frances Forbes Heyn to Hale, interview, November 2, 1990, in Hale, "Some Women," 91; Forbes, *Lucy M. Stanton, Artist*, 80; Sforza to Stanton, Williamstown, Mass., August 16, 1928; W. Stanton Forbes, memoir, n.d., LMS Papers.

50. Stanton to Ruth Blair, Athens, January 10, 1930, Georgia State Archives; Blair to Stanton, Atlanta, February 1, 1930, LMS Papers; Stanton to Blair, Athens, February 3, 1930, LMS Papers; and Hale, "Some Women." In her earlier letter, Stanton also suggested to Blair a portrait of "Mrs. Felton," probably the journalist and suffragist Rebecca Lattimer Felton.

51. Lucy Stanton, diary, 1910; Ladis, "A World in Little," 33; "Miss Lucy Stanton, Artist," n.d. (newspaper article probably from Ogunquit, Maine), LMS Papers.

Catherine Evans Whitener

(1881–1964)

The Creation of North Georgia's Tufted Textile Industry

RANDALL L. PATTON

Catherine Evans was born in 1880 in the farming community of Reo in Whit-field County, Georgia. She grew up, as did most Georgia women in the late nineteenth century, on the farm. She was clearly a very talented girl, yet her horizons were limited by both the circumstances of her birth and her gender. Rural Georgians, male and female, faced few opportunities for education beyond the elementary grades, and Catherine Evans Whitener was no exception. Late in life, she mused about the restricted economic prospects for women of her generation. "When I was a girl I wished that I had been a boy," she wrote, "because a boy could find work to make money and there was nothing a girl could do to earn money."[1] Catherine Evans earned some money in her time and helped create an industry that earned fortunes for a few and provided employment for thousands. For anyone searching for a candidate to initiate a homegrown industrial revolution, Catherine Evans appeared a most unlikely candidate. Yet today she is widely credited as the mother of the region's carpet industry, the economic lifeblood of much of northwest Georgia. Dalton became, in turn, the tufted bedspread capital and the carpet capital of the world.

Announcements of the birth of a New South, a South boasting a more diversified economy complete with a thriving manufacturing sector, abounded in the late nineteenth and early twentieth centuries, but the economy of north Georgia remained predominantly agrarian. Whitfield County, home of Crown Cotton Mills, produced manufactured goods worth about three times the value of its farm products in 1900. Leaders in Dalton, county seat of Whitfield, had participated in the quintessential New South activity, the mill-building crusade of the 1880s, by founding the Crown Cotton Mill in 1884. Crown, like many of the mills in the late-nineteenth-century South, symbolized a commitment to industrialization through an act of will by local leadership. By the 1920s Crown had become one of the largest cotton mills in a Georgia landscape littered with the structures. But surrounding counties such as Catoosa, Murray, and Gordon remained overwhelmingly agricultural, producing three to ten times as much value in farm products as from manufactured goods, and even within Whitfield, most citizens were employed as farmers.[2]

Catherine Evans Whitener crafted a brief version of her own story in the late 1930s and edited it in the late 1950s. An early draft ("A History") and a later version ("Bedspread Beginning") have both been preserved at the Crown Archives in Dalton, Georgia. These two documents have been widely quoted and paraphrased (both with and without attribution) and form the bulk of the public record of her career. Indeed, these documents form the basis for virtually all written accounts of the origins of the tufted bedspread industry.

Examination of Catherine Evans Whitener's own version of her story has revealed much yet left many questions unanswered. "Mrs. William (Catherine Evans) Whitener" (as she styled herself in "A History") opened with a rationale for telling her story. "At the request of many friends," she wrote, "I am attempting to give a brief history of where, when, and how I began my tufted bed spread business." Catherine acknowledged she was "not a writer," but promised to "do my best to present the true facts in the interests of justice and truth."[3]

While visiting a cousin in 1893, twelve-year-old Catherine Evans saw an old candlewick bedspread that had been in the family for many years. The candlewick method created a pattern of raised tufts of thick yarn on the surface of the spread. She had never seen anything like it. Evans Whitener "admired it so much" that she decided that she would try to duplicate it when she got a little older. At age fifteen, in 1895, Evans Whitener kept her pledge. Rather than precisely duplicating the difficult candlewick method, she actually developed a new technique, a variation on candlewicking, called tufting (or turfing as most called it in the early twentieth century). Jean Manly, longtime interpreter of local lore for the local historical society in Dalton, alluded to Evans's variation on the traditional candlewick craft in a recent conversation, observing that her lack of any sort of formal training in the textile arts might have actually helped her create a somewhat simpler method for achieving a visual effect that closely mimicked candlewick.[4]

The work process for Evans Whitener's earliest spreads was tedious and time consuming. To form the initial piece of sheeting that would serve as a base for

CATHERINE EVANS WHITENER

as she displays some of her bedspreads, circa 1946.

Bandy Heritage Center.

the tufted design, Evans Whitener seamed together bits and pieces of material. She purchased white thread and used a spinning wheel, homemade by her father, to wind twelve strands together, forming a thick yarn; then, she notes: "I placed this thread in a bodkin needle and started working." At one point during this period, Evans Whitener's mother, Nancy, observed her daughter's intensive labor and offered a casual observation that proved prescient. "My mother told me I had started something I would never finish," Evans Whitener recalled. "But I did finish it." She referred matter-of-factly to the single spread that prompted her mother's observation, and her mother certainly meant her comment in the same way. Yet in a larger sense, Evans Whitener's labors initiated a process that came to define northwest Georgia and dominate the livelihoods of its people.[5]

Evans Whitener recalled that the process was so difficult that she nearly gave up after the first spread. The resilience of youth served her well, however, and a year later she noted, "I had forgotten the trouble and [had] enjoyed it so much that in 1896 I decided to make another one." After these two initial efforts, she put the craft aside until her eldest brother, Henry, planned to marry in 1900. Evans Whitener made a second spread for Henry and his bride as a wedding gift. Henry Evans's new sister-in-law, Mrs. John Lange, asked Evans Whitener if she could buy a similar spread. The request surprised Evans Whitener, who responded that she "had no idea what one would be worth because I had never heard of one being sold." Mrs. Lange told Evans Whitener "to make it and what ever I said it was worth would be all right." Evans Whitener recalled that the materials cost about $1.25. She doubled that figure to account for her labor, and offered Mrs. Lange a price of $2.50. Mrs. Lange "wanted to pay more but I did not want to charge too much." Mrs. Lange had thus made the first purchase of a tufted bedspread. Accounting for inflation, Evans Whitener's charge of $1.25 for her labor would have been worth about $35.80 in 2008, and the 2008 equivalent of the spread's total price would have been just over $70.50. She did not specify even an approximation of the hours she worked on these initial spreads.[6]

Mrs. Lange moved to Summerville, Georgia, soon after the wedding. Her friends and neighbors saw Evans Whitener's handiwork and asked if they, too, could buy such spreads. Soon Evans Whitener had a lucrative side business supplying her tufted spreads to households around north Georgia. Apparently, she also raised her prices somewhat, though the increase did not deter sales. Evans Whitener "kept making spreads and filling orders." During the early years of the twentieth century, she "worked in the cotton field" and "did house work of every kind between spread orders for several years after [she] quit going to school."[7]

Evans Whitener made use of the raw materials at hand, including patterns for her spreads. Meat skins made valuable tools for marking off spread patterns onto cotton sheeting. She drew from plates and saucers, quilts, washbowls, and curtains. Patterns borrowed from household china and other items became the basis for designs she called "The Washbowl," "Star Circles," "Wild Rose," "The Saveall," "Wedding Ring," and many more.[8] In her teen and young adult years, Catherine Evans demonstrated creativity and a desire to earn money. She created her own business from scratch.

Evans Whitener connected with Eugenia Jarvis in 1918 to market spreads more widely. Eugenia had married a local dentist at thirty-eight. Before her marriage, Eugenia Jarvis had worked as an agent for the Pruden Insurance Company. Eugenia stopped selling insurance when she married Harry Jarvis around 1917, but then she probably discovered that her new husband was a bit careless with money. Harry Jarvis brought two teenage daughters to the marriage, and the couple added a son to the family in 1919. "Dentists were often paid in produce," historian Thomas Deaton noted, "and what money Dr. Jarvis did make he spent on fancy cars." Eugenia Jarvis wanted to send her stepdaughters to the Georgia State College for Women, and she needed cash.[9] She benefited from her experience selling insurance, which had introduced her to a wider circle of acquaintances and boosted her self-confidence.

Eugenia Jarvis became Evans Whitener's primary selling agent. The partners made their first significant sale of spreads to Wanamaker's department store around 1918, and tufted bedspreads began the transition from home craft to industry. Catherine Evans Whitener's skill and industry had created a lucrative home-based business, but it took a partnership with someone who possessed perhaps greater confidence and wider experience to turn that home business into a cottage industry.[10]

Evans Whitener organized the production of spreads at her family's home. She began asking neighbors to come to the Evans farm in 1918 or 1919, shortly after initiating her partnership with Jarvis, to spread the work. Evans employed the women as helpers and taught them the new craft she had developed in the process. She planned meals for the group, scheduled household chores, and worked on bedspreads. Women would arrive in the morning and work all day. Organizing, teaching, directing, and feeding a group of women daily was a large undertaking for Evans Whitener, yet she enjoyed it, according to relatives. Many of the women she taught in those earliest years would go on to become her competitors, or perhaps more properly, members of a network of small-craft producers. Evans Whitener always insisted that there was more than enough work to go around as demand grew.[11]

Evans Whitener's legendary generosity helped a large number of north Georgians enter the bedspread business, among them Burl J. (B. J.) and Dicksie Bradley Bandy. B. J. Bandy and his wife owned and operated a series of dry goods stores in and around Calhoun, Georgia, about twenty miles south of Dalton. The serious recession that followed World War I nearly wiped them out. In search of a way to pay his creditors, Bandy sought out Catherine Evans Whitener, who "agreed to help them" and even "gave them three or four spread patterns with which to get started." B. J. put his wife on a train with one sample bedspread and sent her north in search of buyers. Her first stop was Washington, D.C. She walked into the first department store she could find, Woodward & Lothrop. She left with an order for four hundred spreads at four dollars each. After getting another order for two hundred spreads, she returned home to "hire the people to tuft those 600 spreads." Thus was B. J. and Dicksie Bandy's bedspread business launched. Bandy eventually became known as the first man to make a million dollars in the bedspread business. His son, Jack, would later be prominent among the local entrepreneurs who turned the bedspread and small rug industry toward carpet manufacture in the 1950s.[12]

Catherine Evans married Will Whitener in 1922 and moved out of her parents' home at the age of forty-two.[13] Little is known of Will Whitener's activities or contributions to the family income. Catherine and Will Whitener had no children, but remained close to many of their nieces and nephews. The absence of a second generation may have played a role in Evans Whitener's apparent exit from the business in the late 1930s.

By the mid-1920s Evans Whitener's spreads were "placed with nearly all the eastern shops." "Exclusive shops" often listed tufted bedspreads "among their choice offerings." By 1924, the *Atlanta Constitution* reported, "receipts for spreads shipped from Whitfield County exceeded the total value [of] the county's cotton crop." In perhaps the earliest journalistic recognition of the industry beyond the local newspaper, a *Constitution* writer profiled Dalton's industries, including such important firms as the Crown and American Thread cotton mills and the Manly Jail Works, but also noted the emergence of the bedspread industry. "If not first in importance financially," the author observed, the bedspread business was "at least first in romance and human interest." The spread industry was "fostered and built up largely by two practical but at the same time visionary women." As it grew, bedspread manufacture exerted a greater influence over other local industries. For example, Catherine Evans Whitener at first had to spin the heavy yarn for her spreads, but later she contracted with a local cotton mill for twenty-five pounds of specially twisted, thick yarn: "Now the mills of Dalton will not spin less than 2500 pounds of this yarn, which shows the progress of Mrs. Whitener's homegrown industry." Though some men were employed in the industry, it was "essentially a woman's occupation and has brought financial independence to hundreds of Whitfield county housewives."[14]

Catherine Evans Whitener, the rural craftworker, and Eugenia Jarvis, the better-educated town dweller with connections, partnered to take tufted bedspreads from a hobby to a thriving home-based business. Evans Whitener taught the craft to women first so that they could help her fill orders. Inevitably, with demand for "traditional crafts" expanding in the 1920s, many of those whom Evans Whitener had employed decided to strike out on their own. "Several of my friends began making spreads with all kinds of new designs," Evans Whitener wrote in 1938. "Many of them have become wealthy and for this I am proud."[15] Among these friends who became competitors was Eugenia Jarvis herself, who split with Evans Whitener and formed her own firm in the early 1930s. Jarvis and her family stamped spreads and farmed out the work to women in the countryside. Perhaps Catherine's most intriguing competitor, though, was her sister-in-law, Addie Evans.

Addie Lee Cavender was born in 1889; Catherine taught Addie Cavender the tufting technique, as she did with other women. Addie Cavender married Catherine Evans's brother, Eugene, in 1912. The newlyweds moved into a small farmhouse just across the road from Catherine Evans and her parents. Addie Evans related her early recollections of making spreads with her sister-in-law to her son, Washington Robert (generally known as W. R.), and daughter, Callie Ruth. "To begin with, my aunt and my mother stamped those bedspreads on the floor in our living room and I presume hers [Catherine's]," W. R. Evans remembered in a 1980 interview. Addie Evans eventually went into the bedspread business herself.

W. R. Evans insisted years later that his aunt, Catherine Evans Whitener, "just stayed at home . . . and made what few little spreads she could make. And she, as time went along, would train what lady or two that would come in. She never did go into any real training program. She never did really go to work on this thing and try to get production." W. R. Evans's recollections hinted at a split between the two women, perhaps generated by two distinctive styles. He probably exaggerated Evans Whitener's lack of interest in organizing a business. Evans Whitener's home-based operation seemed significantly larger than the shoestring operation characterized by W. R. Evans. She clearly organized a fairly large number of women in her own home and (with Eugenia Jarvis) put out some work to women in their own homes in the 1920s, and Evans Whitener accumulated some money through her bedspread making. But it seems certain that Addie Evans had some inner fire and confidence that drove her to create and build a larger-scale business operation.[16]

Addie Evans had a fifth-grade education and a "crippled foot" that limited her mobility. Yet, her granddaughter recalled, "to speak to Addie, you would never have known that her formal education was so limited." Addie Evans "was self-educated," and she worked hard at self-improvement, struggling to overcome her lack of education and limited rural background. And she worked hard to build a business out of tufting spreads. "I would put my young children in the buggy and go throughout the countryside and teach people how to tuft," Addie Evans recalled in a 1980 interview. She taught "the man, the woman, and the child if they showed that they wanted to learn." Addie Evans built her business by recruiting these home workers: "I took them the sheeting and the yarn and on a regular schedule I'd return and pick up the finished product."[17] The enduring image of the bedspread industry in northwest Georgia includes the figure of the hauler, the person who delivered raw materials to home workers in the countryside and returned later to collect semifinished goods. As far as we can tell, Addie Cavender Evans may have pioneered that "putting out" strategy for maximizing production within the bedspread industry.

This process of taking pre-stamped bedspreads and yarn into the countryside and recruiting home workers amounted to a vast putting-out system. First described as an integral phase of early industrialization in a European context in the Middle Ages, the system was characterized by a merchant taking raw materials into the countryside to be turned into cloth or other semifinished goods, then returning to gather up the goods and pay the home-based workers. "Proto-industrialization," as economic historians dubbed this system, was initially defined as a stage in the development of an industrial economy, but more recently scholars have developed a more nuanced view. Cottage industries often developed simultaneously with factory production in the same regions, rather than serving simply as a step on a ladder of industrial progress.[18] Similarly, Dalton was home to two large cotton mills in the early twentieth century, each of which employed hundreds. The proto-industry of bedspread manufacture emerged alongside these large factories.

In 1917 Addie Evans and her husband formed the Evans Manufacturing Company, still based in her home. This firm has often erroneously been characterized as a partnership between Catherine Evans Whitener and her brother Eugene. In fact, it represented a split between Addie Cavender Evans and her sister-in-law; by 1917 Catherine Evans Whitener's business was completely separate from that of Addie and Eugene Evans. Addie Evans began working from her home. Initially, the business was a small affair, marketing spreads to neighbors and a bit more widely by word of mouth. Among those who heard the word was Lizzie Maddox Parmalee, wife of Ohioan Frederic Parmalee, a Southern Railway agent. Born in 1885, Parmalee was the daughter of former Dalton mayor Sam Maddox. Parmalee later benefited from both her father's connections and from her husband's railroad experience in her efforts to find markets for Addie Evans's spreads.[19] Parmalee arrived at the Eugene Evans farmstead on July 3, 1918, just as the Evans family was "getting ready to go on a picnic." Addie Evans described Parmalee as "a fashionably dressed lady" who announced, "you don't know me, but I know about you and know about your bedspreads. I want to sell them for you." Carrying a sample spread, Parmalee quickly boarded a train for Atlanta. She soon convinced Rich's, Atlanta's signature department store, to try selling some of the spreads; Rich's ordered twenty-four spreads.[20] The initial order from Rich's was a huge success, and spurred Parmalee to market Addie Evans's spreads more widely.

Addie Evans began recruiting area women to help her "turf" (as the verb "tuft" was generally rendered in the local dialect). She typically worked late into the night preparing the spreads and yarn, and finished preparing breakfast before dawn. "Mother went out in the fields and helped Dad pick cotton until noon," her son recalled. After lunch, "we'd go on her bedspread trips. We'd get into that black buggy of Dad's" and make her rounds, teaching women and children to tuft and leaving sheeting and yarn, and visiting families who were finishing up spreads left on earlier trips for pickup. As the business grew, families began coming to Addie Evans's house to pick up materials and deliver tufted spreads. The Evans family erected a large tent to provide an outdoor space for marking off sheeting and boiling spreads to clean and fluff them. Callie Ruth Evans remembered her mother remarking, "We boiled them in huge pots and they came clean as a whistle and sold like hot cakes. Goodness we made money!"[21]

Addie Evans suspended the business briefly in the early days of the Great Depression. Both Catherine Evans Whitener and Addie Cavender Evans appear in the manuscript census of 1920 as "spreadmakers," but in 1930 each responded "none" when asked for an occupation. Addie Evans revived the business in 1933, and it was in this incarnation that Evans Manufacturing Company continued as a family enterprise for thirty years. Addie Evans's granddaughter recalled that her grandmother was "President, CEO, and everything else for that company." Addie Evans managed the business conservatively as it expanded and met new challenges. She used a chicken house that stood on her family's property for stamping spreads in early 1933, but built a spread house for stamping and laundering in the mid-1930s.

Addie Evans and her partner were among the first to use colored yarns in their spreads. Lizzie Parmalee identified a Delaware firm, Central Franklin Processing, which could dye thick yarn spun for tufting. But Addie Evans and

Parmalee, cautious businesswomen that they were, feared that their competitors would discover their connection with northern yarn mills and try to exploit it as well. Parmalee had the company's yarn shipped to her home in Kentucky, where she would unpack it from its marked wooden crates, then repack the yarn in unmarked crates and ship it to Addie Evans in Dalton, thus concealing from prying eyes the potential connection with outside yarn manufacturers. Evans Manufacturing was apparently "the sole spread business offering colored yarn for some three years" before competitors found their own sources.[22] The colored yarn anecdote illustrated as well as anything the differences between Evans Whitener and her sister-in-law. The personal characteristic most often used to describe Evans Whitener was generosity. Addie Evans has most often been remembered as a hard-driving, ambitious businesswoman who could be generous, but emphasized what was best for her business.

The emergence of home work in bedspread tufting in the early twentieth century mirrored developments in other crafts. As rural folk cultures faded in an increasingly urbanized America, consumers sought comfort in the consumption of handcrafted "traditional" products. Indeed, ads for tufted bedspreads often traded on this appeal. Sage-Allen & Co. of Hartford, Connecticut, marketed candlewick bedspreads in a typical ad in 1927 by observing that the spreads were "made by hand by the mountain people of Georgia."[23]

By the late 1920s, bedspread makers worked with department stores throughout the country to organize demonstration tours. These tours emphasized the rural roots and handicraft manufacture of tufted bedspreads. Spread makers and marketers tapped into the desire of American consumers for authentic folk products. Print advertisements for spreads throughout the 1920 and early 1930s often note that the spreads were made by hand in the mountains of Georgia or North Carolina. The Kingston, New York, *Daily Freeman* carried one of the earliest print advertisements for candlewick bedspreads in 1919. The Kingston Wanamaker's department store advertised "old-fashioned candlewick spreads made by hand in the old-fashioned way" for thirteen dollars each. Wanamaker's advertising emphasized the traditional nature of the handicraft as a selling point.[24] This ad quite likely referred specifically to some of Catherine Evans Whitener's early spreads made by groups of women in her home. Dalton's candlewick bedspreads quickly captured markets throughout the country. Taft and Pennoyer, self-described as Oakland, California's oldest dry goods establishment, hawked "candlewick colonial bedspreads" in 1922 advertisements.

Spread makers even arranged for local women to tour the country in the late 1920s and early 1930s, demonstrating the craft and emphasizing the homespun nature of the new product. Prominent women, including Dicksie Bandy, participated in some of these tours. Other young women also served as interpreters of rural southern and Appalachian culture. The *Hartford Courant* captured the essence of one such demonstration tour in 1930. The paper described Kitty Carter and Betty Lawson as "two attractive Georgia mountaineers" whose tufting demonstrations had taken them across the United States and into Mexico and Canada. According to the *Courant*, "the girls said their only criticism of northern cities is the sidewalks. Pavements hurt their feet," the reported explained, "as they are used to sand and dirt." The *Courant* summarized the reportage of Lawson and Carter's tour, noting that a Texas newspaper "reported them as being on a walking trip from Mexico to California." Another paper had reported that "one of the girls was working to get her pappy out of jail where the revenuers had put him." The girls were clearly (and probably with reporter's tongue firmly in cheek) portrayed as barefoot, naïve examples of the southern folk.[25]

Not all the tours emphasized the Ellie May Clampett stereotype of southern mountain girls. Jack Bandy recalled that his aunt and a friend had participated in some of these demonstration tours on behalf of B. J. Bandy's bedspread enterprise. He remembered being told that his aunt dressed in traditional colonial-era garb from head to toe, a far cry from the image conjured by the Lawson and Carter tour. A November 1929 *Los Angeles Times* advertisement neatly captured the spirit of this tour. The ad, headlined "A Native Handicraft," featured a sketch artist's rendition of a well-dressed colonial dame seated in a high-backed chair using a needle and thread to tuft a pattern onto a piece of sheeting. The ad invited customers to "a week's demonstration of American handicraft. . . . Native Georgia women have come to show you how Colonial American hand tufted spreads are made in the South." Bullock's department store touted the demonstration and offered a thousand handmade spreads at $3.45 each.[26]

It seems likely that this tour featured a member of the Bandy family. It appears quite different from the demonstration described above by the *Hartford Courant* a few months later. The Bandy tour presented the north Georgia craftswomen in colonial dress, while the tour described in Hartford presented a "hillbilly" image. Much of the detail surrounding these demonstrations has been lost, however, and the demonstrations may not have differed as much as the marketing. It does seem clear that, whatever the specific form, department stores used the craft nature and cottage industry image of hand tufting as a selling point.

The true nature of the emerging home-based industry differed somewhat from the image. Spread tufting in its twentieth-century incarnation emerged as a putting-out system rather than the product of skilled individual producers. Allen Eaton and others associated with the craft revival of the 1930s sought to use such home-based crafts to revitalize folk authentic cultures and as a way to fight the abject poverty that characterized much of rural America, particularly in southern Appalachia. In 1930 the Southern Highlands Handicraft Guild sought to promote mountain crafts to the public. Allen Eaton, an influential Friend member of the guild, published a survey of southern mountain crafts in 1937. He identified the hand-tufted bedspread craft of the Dalton, Georgia, area as a key source of potential for cultural revival and economic development. Eaton and those associated with the guild hoped that work could be both financially remunerative and socially regenerative, granting workers both an income and an enhanced sense of self-worth and dignity. In his review of the Southern Highlands handicraft revival of the 1930s, Eaton clearly saw bedspread manufacture as an opportunity for "building up of the handicrafts" of the people of the Southern Highlands. "The most concentrated home industry and the one employing the largest number of workers in the Southern Highlands," he observed, "is the candlewick bedspread industry." Eaton quoted J. Cooper Moorcock, county agent for Gordon County (just south of Whitfield County, home of Catherine Evans Whitener), who described the extent of the industry. "There are more than 2,000 farm families in this county," Moorcock observed. "In 90 percent you will find some members of the family doing bedspread work which they call tufting." The finished spreads were "disposed of through bedspread companies," which often hawked their wares "along the highway . . . at what you might call a curb market to the tourists who travel" U.S. Highway 41, often called the Dixie Highway. Eaton went on to note that the tufted bedspread industry was "one of the few handicrafts that have been commercially standardized."[27]

The home-based bedspread industry created by Catherine Evans Whitener and the women of northwest Georgia certainly provided cash incomes for farm families during the hard times of the 1920s and the Great Depression. Yet home tufters earned comparatively meager wages for their labors. Firms like those managed by Addie Cavender Evans and Eugenia Jarvis supplied raw materials and paid piece rates to home workers. Tufters could generally earn slightly more per spread if they came to pick up the sheeting and yarn themselves, perhaps $1.25 in the mid-1930s. Many had to wait for haulers to bring the materials out to the farms; these workers received about $1.10 per spread. These piece rates translated to hourly wages of about 10 to 15 cents. For comparative purposes, the first federally mandated minimum wage, established by the Fair Labor Standards Act of 1938, was set at 25 cents per hour.[28]

Eileen Boris found that women employed as home spread-tufters "complained about the difficulty of the work and the low pay" more often than other craftworkers. Yet some of these women also "experienced pleasure, if not in the making then in the aesthetics of their work." Spread tufters enjoyed the beauty of the designs and colors, but were critical of the work process and believed they deserved better pay. Jane Becker's close study of the Appalachian handicraft revival echoed Boris's conclusions. "Bedspread workers," Becker found, "invariably described their work as hard and tiring; they complained about pain in their backs, sides, shoulders, and hands." A woman who worked for Kenner and Rauschenberg, a prominent Dalton-based bedspread firm, observed in 1935, "We like the money we make, that's all." One of B. J. Bandy's tufters insisted, "It's the hardest work I ever did do." Boris concluded that "candlewick bedspread making was a sweated industry."[29]

Tufting bedspreads opened a new space that allowed many to turn traditional women's work into entrepreneurial opportunities or dearly prized cash incomes. As far as we can tell, it produced little in the way of cultural regeneration. It would perhaps be more accurate to characterize what emerged in the Dalton area as a new culture of enterprise rather than a revival of any sort of traditional culture. In the early days of the industry, women played a central role both as entrepreneurs organizing bedspread businesses and as home workers. In the 1930s first the National Recovery Administration and then the Fair Labor Standards Act threatened to force bedspread companies to boost compensation for home workers. Later that decade the industry mechanized and moved swiftly to factory production, with complementary increases in the speed of production and hourly wage rates.

Yet the story of the hand-tufted bedspread industry was complex. The stories of Catherine Evans Whitener, Addie Cavender Evans, and the women of the bedspread industry echoed the experiences of other southern rural women in the early twentieth century. Lu Ann Jones has chronicled the active participation involvement of southern farmwomen in the regional economy. The phrases used by women to describe their experiences displayed a complex set of motivations, from being able to purchase needed items to enhance the health and well-being of family members to a desire for greater financial security. "Mama learned us to work," according to one of Jones's interview subjects, highlighting the industriousness of southern farmwomen in this period. To purchase special shoes for a child and other items to contribute to her family's well-being, Lurline Stokes Murray recalled that her mother "decided that she'd get anything she could sell, and that's when she started to taking what she had and turning it into money." Southern farmwomen contributed to a family economy, but their earnings also could foster a sense of independence. A female correspondent to the *Progressive Farmer* noted in 1907 that no matter how generous and considerate the husband or father may be, there is always a feeling of dependence unless we have some way to make a little money of our own and spend it as we please."[30] Southern women developed poultry production as a profitable enterprise as part of this search for a measure of independence. And as the profitability of poultry products increased, men moved into the business in large numbers.[31]

North Georgia women developed the bedspread tufting home craft as yet another means of producing a cash income. Bertha Nienburg surveyed families associated with the Appalachian handicraft revival in the 1930s. Nienburg concluded that "*craft skill was looked upon by every worker visited as a possible means of earning money*" (emphasis in the original). When Nienburg asked "how they liked the work" (trying to ascertain what sort of aesthetic satisfaction might be gained from the labor), she observed that most home workers replied, "This is all we know how to do except work in the field." Nienburg cut to the heart of the dilemma of the handicraft revival movement when she observed that the creative work in the craft industries associated with homework was generally done by managers in production centers (such as Addie Evans's spread house), "while the mass of craftswomen and men were copyists working under instructions." Nienburg's study also emphasized that home work was not simply part-time labor, or something undertaken in a family's spare time. The labor allocated to spreads was not something done "when household tasks are done." Ten-hour days devoted to craftwork were common, according to Nienburg.[32]

The experiences recounted here perhaps contain hints of deeper transformations. Jan de Vries has argued that northwestern Europe and the United States have experienced at least two "industrious revolutions" since 1600. Briefly, de Vries describes changes in the allocation of household labor that resulted in greater involvement by the entire family in market production. Families shifted labor away from (unpaid but valuable) household production toward (paid) market-oriented labor in order to participate more fully in emerging new consumption patterns in the seventeenth century. The nineteenth-century Victorian "breadwinner-homemaker" household represented a strategic shift by families of female labor away from market labor and toward the production of new commodities that could not be easily purchased (health, cleanliness, education). A new industrious revolution—a shift of women's labor away from household production toward market labor—took hold in the 1960s, though there were signals of it as early as the Progressive era. De Vries's model does not deny gender-oriented exploitation or oppression, but it seeks to place the changing roles of women in capitalist labor markets within a new framework that emphasizes the agency of families and households. "Industrious revolutions" have exhibited "a vast expansion of households with multiple wage earners," "a pronounced redeployment of labor time from household to market production," and "reduced income pooling," among other characteristics.[33] The anecdotal evidence from the testimony of farmwomen might suggest a southern industrious revolution in the first half of the twentieth century. The emergence of "proto-industry," home-based work often organized into a putting-out system by merchants, typified the first industrious revolution.[34] The emergence of the bedspread home industry mirrored these earlier proto-industrial developments.

The industrious revolution represented by the dramatic expansion of the tufting industry in the 1920s and 1930s differed significantly from Dalton's earlier "industrial resolution." That act of will by local elites helped create a large cotton mill and promoted the idea of industrial growth. The industrious revolution of the early twentieth century emerged from households, led by women like Catherine Evans and Addie Cavender Evans, and employed thousands of women who sought home-based work to maintain their families in hard times and enhance family access to new consumption goods. If Dalton's "industrial resolution" of the 1880s was effectively a revolution from the top down, the emergence of tufting seemed a revolution from the ground up, encouraging entrepreneurial energy and providing a framework within which that energy could be expressed.

The emergence of new consumer desires should not be confused with simple materialism. The desire to consume goods associated with improving the health and well-being of the entire family or of particular family members should not be underestimated (as eloquently attested to in Lu Ann Jones's description of the story of Lurline Stokes Murray above). Bertha Nienburg observed that "small as the average earnings per home worker" may have been, those earnings made a crucial difference to families—"grocery money, money to send a child to school, money for shoes, money for a doctor's bill." Money earned from home craftwork was "so immediately translated into much needed articles" that the amount earned was generally "remembered by the purchases it made possible."[35]

The home work phase of the tufted textile industry's growth reached its peak in the mid-1930s. Despite apprehension that wage and hour laws would destroy the industry, business boomed. Tourists traveling a sixty-mile stretch of U.S. Highway 41 between Ringgold and Acworth were fascinated by "the sight of myriads of the candlewick bedspreads hung on lines and flapping in the breeze," as an *Atlanta Constitution* writer observed in 1935. The colorful peacock—perhaps the one design that came to characterize the tufted bedspread industry—appeared frequently in a host of variations. The reporter noted one reason cited by locals for the prevalence of the peacock. Tufters could use virtually any colors in any combination to create peacocks. This made the peacock a sort of "catch all" design that home tufters could use to consume small amounts of yarn left over from a variety of more disciplined designs.[36] This section of Highway 41 became known as "Bedspread Boulevard" and "Peacock Alley," as the spreads continued to flap in the breeze in large numbers through the 1960s. After 1970 the roadside business declined sharply. Yet even in the 1930s, while the Bedspread Boulevard/Peacock Alley idea conjured visions of a true home craft hawked by small makers on the roadside, more than 90 percent of tufted spreads were sold by manufacturers through department stores and distributors.

The *Atlanta Constitution* estimated that the Dalton area was home to about thirty bedspread firms, with nine of those "managed partly or entirely by women" such as Addie Cavender Evans and Eugenia Jarvis. (Catherine Evans Whitener's business was probably not included in this total. Evans Whitener always operated her business on a less formalized basis.) Manufacturers estimated that the industry's sales exceeded $2 million in 1935. Between 7,500 and 10,000 home workers labored in the industry, the vast majority of them women. The thirty manufacturers estimated a total payroll of about $600,000, or $60–80 per worker. The *Constitution's* Henry Nevins reported that the "wives and daughters" of tenant farmers were glad to have the needlework as a means of earning a livelihood." These earnings "in a great many cases" kept entire families "off relief rolls out of charity."[37]

Census records lend some credence to such claims. Just before the Great Depression, Whitfield County ranked seventh among Georgia counties in terms of the per capita value of manufactured products (about $502). A decade later, Whitfield had risen to third among Georgia counties. Per capita value in Whitfield grew as well (to about $528). Manufacturing suffered in the remainder of the state, with the value of shipments declining in most counties. While total manufacturing volume declined at both the state and national levels between 1929 and 1939, volume in Whitfield increased from $10.4 million to almost $14 million. Had Georgia matched Whitfield County's per capita manufacturing numbers, the state would have ranked eleventh among all U.S. states in 1939 (instead of thirty-second). Whitfield also ranked third in the state in value added per capita, and Georgia would have ranked ninth nationally (ahead of Pennsylvania, just behind Massachusetts) in this category had the state matched the tufted textile district's $263 average.

Income and consumption for workers in the Dalton area presented a cloudier picture. For all its growth, bedspread manufacture remained a labor-intensive, low-value-added industry. Workers in Whitfield County produced about $1,300 per year in value added compared to a national average of more than $3,100 (even Georgia averaged $1,600 at the state level). Bedspreads and other small tufted goods ranked as a low-value-added item even within the textile sector. Retail sales essentially split the difference between Whitfield's tremendous volume of goods and the low value added per capita. Consumers in Whitfield County spent a little more than the Georgia average; Whitfield Countians clearly had a bit more money in their pockets than the majority of Georgians ($228 for Dalton area residents as opposed to the $200 state average).[38]

The heyday of the handicraft industry passed in the mid- to late 1930s. The tufted bedspread industry began to mechanize in the 1930s. By 1939 companies like Cabin Crafts (consciously named by its founders to take advantage of the romance of handicraft production) had ceased the elaborate putting-out system in favor of concentrating workers in its factories. By the late 1930s the industry was characterized much less by home workers and more by rows of women seated at sewing machines specially adapted for inserting raised tufts of yarn in cotton sheeting. As Jane Becker has pointed out, spread-house owners increasingly experimented with and invested in machines to duplicate the hand tufting process. While earlier versions were in use by the late 1920s on a limited basis, Glenn Looper patented the first spread tufting machine rather late, in 1936. The Georgia Tech–trained textile engineer and other local mechanics in Dalton adapted surplus Singer sewing machines from the New York garment trades. The development of machinery was spurred in part by wage-and-hour laws, but spread-house owners also sought the efficiencies of factory production for other cost-related reasons. Eaton and other handicraft revivalists wanted to find a way to boost prices to increase wages for hand workers, but they also saw the dilemma inherent in that approach. Hand tufting would remain a low-value-added process as long as prices remained low. With the advent of machine production, the potential for faster production promised reduced costs and higher profits for manufacturers without a price increase. It was only the machines, moreover, that made possible the final, critical step in the development of this new industry: the transition to carpet manufacture.[39]

Catherine Evans Whitener had largely exited the industry by the time mechanization swept through it. By 1940 factories produced and sold $12 million worth of tufted spreads. More than three-quarters of tufted spreads were manufactured in the Dalton area. Yet Catherine Evans Whitener was "still unmechanized," according to a *Time* magazine profile in 1940. "Grey-haired and 60," the magazine reported, "she still produces for any friend who wants a handmade spread."[40] Evans Whitener may have still been producing for sale on a limited scale, but she did not follow the craft she helped create into the machine age.

Addie Cavender Evans and her family firm did move into the industry's machine age. Evans Manufacturing and other smaller firms faced difficult choices. Anxious about trying to compete with the volume production and cost structure of Cabin Crafts (and other new, larger firms such as Kenner-Rauschenberg), Evans could borrow and invest in expanding spread production to try and match Cabin Crafts at its own game. High-volume firms such as Cabin Crafts invested in bedspread yardage machines developed by firms like Chattanooga's Cobble Brothers. These machines could produce simple patterns on a continuous stream of sheeting. These sheets could be cut into shorter pieces as they rolled off the machine or from huge rolls at a later point. The development of this continuous production process threatened smaller manufacturers. In addition, Addie believed the wage provisions of the Fair Labor Standards Act in 1938 threatened to finish off the putting-out system she and other manufacturers still sometimes used by eliminating the advantage of cheaper home-based labor. Addie Evans invested in some small spread tufting machines, but began phasing out bedspread production to focus on small rugs.[41]

In 1943 Addie Evans bought a small rug-tufting factory and moved out of spreads and into the production of bath sets and small rugs. During the 1930s, as bedspread tufting machines were developed, Cabin Crafts and other local tufting firms worked to expand the tufting process to produce small floor coverings such as throw rugs (generally three-by-five feet or four-by-six feet), initially for bathroom use. The bath ensembles consisted of three-piece sets including a toilet tank cover, a contoured rug to fit around the bottom of the toilet, and a small decorative rug for the center of the bathroom floor. Cabin Crafts developed a unique needle-punch gun that enabled workers for that firm to produce intricate patterns on even larger rugs, but for most firms, these small rugs remained much simpler. For a time, Evans Manufacturing and other smaller firms helped create a competitive space for themselves. Larger firms had difficulty achieving cost advantages in the production of such small piece goods, at least until the volume of small-rug sales grew large enough to justify a capital investment in machinery. Addie Evans correctly interpreted the emerging patterns in her industry and made a wise, if only temporarily effective, strategic shift.

As Addie Evans and other firms mechanized and moved to factory production, the women (and some men) who came to work in the factories tried to organize. In the mid-1950s the Textile Workers Union of America made a major push to organize tufted textile workers centered on Dalton's large Belcraft Chenille plant.

That drive failed. Though it has gone largely unnoticed, the International Ladies Garment Workers Union apparently made some efforts to organize the mechanizing spread mills in the late 1930s. The ILGWU successfully negotiated a collective bargaining agreement with the Shenandoah Spread Manufacturing Company. Little else is known about the contract or the campaign, but this was clearly a rarity in Dalton's tufted textile industry. Southern manufacturers fought particularly hard to prevent union organization, and Dalton's managers were no exceptions.[42]

Evans Manufacturing apparently faced a union organizing campaign at some point, though the timing is uncertain. A family-approved account included a story about Addie Evans's response to unionization efforts. According to the story, upon receiving news that her employees were weighing the possibility of organization, Addie Evans "walked out to the plant . . . and pulled the electrical switch that powered all the machines. She then placed in the middle of the plant floor a wooden crate for use as a soapbox and stood on top of it." Addie Evans told the workers "there would not be an organized union coming into the Evans Manufacturing plant." The employees were free to organize if they chose, she said, but essentially threatened to close the plant if they did. "She continued to tell them that she didn't know if they had enough money to live on for the rest of their life, but that she did and planned to if she had to." Addie Evans's speech was followed by "complete silence." The union organizing effort fell apart in the face of this admonition.[43] Addie Evans had developed into a business leader as tough as any of the men who came to dominate management after mechanization, and she responded to labor unrest as her male counterparts in small manufacturing enterprises nearly universally did. The women who labored in the "sweated" home-tufting industry found it impossible to organize for better conditions in the new factories.

Evans Manufacturing, like all its competitors in bedspreads and small rugs, continued to employ an overwhelmingly female workforce even as they moved to mechanized factory production. Women constituted more than 80 percent of Addie Evans's roughly 120 workers in the late 1950s. "We employed some men to do the heavier work," Addie Evans's granddaughter remembered, but women operated the tufting machines. Anecdotal evidence suggested that this was common. Small-rug makers such as the Manor Rug Company, though owned and managed by men, used a predominantly female labor force in the 1950s.[44]

The small rugs that Evans began to make formed a bridge to broadloom carpet production. By the late 1940s, firms in the bedspread industry had adapted the machinery developed for speeding up the production of spreads to other purposes, including robes, small rugs (often called scatter rugs, generally four-by-six feet or smaller), bathroom tank sets, and the bare beginnings of larger rugs. In 1949 Cabin Crafts and the Cobble Brothers developed machines that could produce "broadloom" carpeting, essentially rugs that could cover most or all of an entire room. Carpet production would quickly revolutionize what was still a relatively new industry.

The chain of events that Catherine Evans Whitener began with her hand-tufted gift bedspread in 1896 led Dalton, Georgia, to become the "carpet capital of the world" by the 1960s. The link was the tufting process. Though the wall-to-wall carpeting produced by Dalton mills in the 1960s seemed far afield from the handmade spreads that Evans Whitener had produced, they shared a critical feature. In a sense, a modern piece of wall-to-wall carpeting is like a tufted bedspread—it is a sheet of pre-woven backing material completely covered in raised tufts of yarn. In between the handmade origins of the process and the carpet mills of the 1960s, the hand-tufting process was first adapted to small rugs (bathroom novelty items) and then mechanized.

Dalton became the carpet capital by the 1960s, but north Georgia firms did not invent large rugs or carpeting. From the mid-nineteenth through the mid-twentieth century, the production of carpeting had been among the highest-skilled, highest-value-added segments of the textile industry. Carpets were woven chiefly from wool on large power looms (hence the term "broadloom," which was applied, though a misnomer, to room-sized tufted rugs in the 1950s). Textile engineers had incrementally improved the weaving process over the years since the introduction of the power loom in the 1840s, but had produced no further breakthroughs in productivity. Catherine Evans Whitener's tufted bedspreads, a novelty item, led step by step toward the tufted production of wall-to-wall carpeting, a staple of middle-class American homes after World War II. Indeed, Cabin Crafts, the firm that led in the mechanization of the bedspread industry, also led in developing machine production of tufted rugs and pioneered in introducing tufted cotton room-sized rugs in late 1949.

Southern firms took over the U.S. textile industry segment by segment beginning early in the twentieth century. By the 1930s southern firms such as Burlington (the nation's largest textile concern) had taken the lead in most areas of textile production. Carpets remained, however, an exclusively New England/New York/Philadelphia product. Southern firms had exploited synthetic fibers such as rayon and nylon to surge forward in hosiery and other areas, and synthetic fibers were certainly important in the southern capture of carpet. But a new production process, based on Catherine Evans Whitener's handicraft revival, played the most critical role.

Mechanics at Cabin Crafts and a Chattanooga, Tennessee, company that manufactured bedspread machines developed tufting machines capable of making room-sized rugs and endless streams of wall-to-wall carpeting. These machines simply covered the entire surface of a piece of pre-woven backing material with raised tufts of thick yarn—first cotton, then synthetics like rayon, and finally nylon. Large northern carpet makers such as Bigelow-Sanford and Mohawk derided these tufted carpets as glorified bedspreads. The machine-tufting process made carpets much more quickly than the most efficient power looms. The early tufted carpets certainly could not match woven wool products for quality, appearance, or durability. But they easily trumped woven goods in terms of price. Cheap tufted carpets exploded onto the American market in the early 1950s just as the postwar housing boom took off. Woven carpets sold for $6.19 per square yard in 1955; tufted carpeting sold for just $3.36. American households bought an average of 1.97 square yards of carpeting per year in 1950, virtually all of it woven. That number had changed little from the level of the 1920s. In the late 1950s the DuPont company introduced a special type of nylon— bulked continuous filament, or BCF nylon—that made a much better substitute for wool than cotton. DuPont had been spurred to action by the increasing sales of tufted carpeting. In turn, DuPont's fiber innovation helped fuel even more explosive growth, helping the fledgling carpet makers of the Dalton area overcome at least some of the quality and durability problems associated with early tufted carpets. By 1970 U.S. families were purchasing 8.46 square yards of carpet annually, 90 percent of it tufted. The tufting process initiated by Catherine Evans Whitener and the women of northwest Georgia did not so much take over the U.S. carpet industry as create a new, much larger one.[45] Ironically, the hand-tufted bedspread had been replaced by a machine-made product designed to mimic a handcrafted product. The same machine technology enabled the creation of tufted carpeting, perhaps the ultimate mass-produced product of the 1960s and 1970s. Designed to appeal to the largest possible swath of homeowners, carpet factories churned out seemingly endless miles of continuously produced carpeting in simple patterns and mostly neutral colors for America's mass-produced suburban sprawl.

Tufted carpets were cheap compared to woven goods, but the same carpets dwarfed bedspreads in profitability and sales volume. In 1946 bedspreads had made up nearly 60 percent of all tufted textile products, while various sizes of tufted rugs accounted for only about a quarter (robes and miscellaneous items made up the remainder. By 1953 bedspreads as a share of tufted products had shrunk to 30 percent, while carpets and rugs—an amalgam of broadloom and small rugs—now amounted to 64 percent of sales. This transformation of product mix was due almost solely to growth in the carpet and rug segment; bedspread sales continued to rise into the 1950s. But the peacock spread had seen its brightest days by the mid-1950s. Bedspread sales crested and began to level off. Tufted spread makers sold $52 million in spreads in 1952, but just $48 million in 1964. The market for spreads had clearly reached its saturation point. Carpet continued to grow by leaps and bounds, with sales passing $1 billion in the early 1960s and topping $2 billion by 1970.[46]

Evans Manufacturing followed a middle path in the 1950s, specializing in small rugs but eschewing the capital investment that moving into full-scale broadloom carpeting would have required. The company got a boost in the late 1950s from a relatively rare phenomenon in a commodity industry—a patent on a new product. Brand identification and product identity were difficult to establish in the bedspread industry, but Evans managed to develop a method that at least slightly differentiated the company's bath sets from those of competitors. They modified the needles in some of their tufting machines so that additional yarn could be inserted into individual tufts, giving rugs a fuller, fluffier appearance reminiscent of poodle hair. Addie Evans dubbed the new process "poodle-tuft." Small firms such as Evans Manufacturing rarely were able to secure recognition for such innovations, however, and the department stores that bought and marketed tufted bedspreads, rugs, robes, and other products rarely attributed manufacturer names to these goods.

Advertisements for tufted textile goods began to appear in major newspapers around the country in the 1920s. It was rare, however, to attribute to particular manufacturers any of these products. Addie Evans's poodle-tuft rugs appeared in a number of newspaper ads beginning in 1957, probably the year she introduced the rugs. In November 1957, the Los Angeles–area May Company department stores ran ads for a "soft, fluffy poodle tuft" bath set, a three-piece ensemble that included a rectangular bath mat, a toilet seat cover, and a contour rug for placement around the toilet. In the early 1960s the Evans name appeared in several poodle-tuft rug ads.[47]

Even as Evans Manufacturing enjoyed the success of poodle-tuft rugs, the family was pondering its future in the tufted textile industry. Addie Evans's conservative business philosophy would not permit her to consider borrowing money on the scale necessary to move fully into the production of wall-to-wall carpeting by the mile. In the late 1950s and early 1960s, Callie Ruth and W. R., Addie's children, urged her to move into carpet production, but she feared it could not be done while clinging to her "no credit" rule. The company had purchased one broadloom machine around 1960, but it had been used exclusively to make large sheets of tufted carpet that were then cut into small rugs. Callie Ruth Roach, overseer of the company's finances, told Addie Evans it was time to invest heavily in such machinery or sell. Over seventy years of age by now,

Addie Evans chose to leave the tufted textile industry that she had helped create. She sold Evans Manufacturing in 1963. As her granddaughter (an adult working in the business at the time) remembered, Addie Evans and her children decided that "it was time to go."

As Addie Cavender Evans exited the industry and carpet took center stage, the labor force was transformed as well, though it has not yet been well documented. During the 1950s the bedspread and small-rug companies primarily employed women as production workers. Carpet manufacturers, except for a few job categories, preferred male employees. The testimony of workers from the era indicated that the two branches of tufted textile manufacture operated with very different workforces until the 1960s. As spread mills began to struggle in the early 1960s, women sought employment in the rapidly expanding carpet mills. Unlike the spread and small-rug mills, men occupied the top production jobs in the carpet mills: machine operators and inspectors. Carpet mills employed women largely as creelers, a difficult, repetitive, lower-paid job that involved keeping full spools of yarn attached to the creel rack that fed the tufting machines. Lower- and middle-management jobs were almost exclusively held by men. And the entrepreneurs who built the carpet mills were virtually all male. Though middle management and a greater variety of production jobs opened slowly for women, management jobs remained elusive through the 1990s.

Catherine Evans Whitener observed the growing dominance of men in the industry she made. B. J. Bandy, perhaps the most successful of them, had sought and received her aid. As the industry demonstrated its growth potential in the 1930s, men formed new firms that fully exploited machine technology. Evans Whitener observed of the early days of the industry, "The men began to notice that the ladies had something worth while and began talking about machines to make spreads." The men brought machines and technology into the industry, she recalled. "I never dreamed such a thing could happen."[48]

Yet the reality was more complex. Men already ran twenty-one of the thirty known spread companies as early as 1935, before mechanization had made much of an impact. B. J. and Dicksie Bandy began their business shortly after Evans Whitener's own. Jack Bandy, B. J. and Dicksie's son, used the capital his family had accumulated in the bedspread business in the 1920s, 1930s, and 1940s to invest heavily in carpet production in the 1950s. Jack Bandy helped form Coronet Carpets, a large firm that became a fixture in the carpet industry for decades. The potential for gain clearly attracted men to what had been considered women's work, and men clearly played a key role in mechanizing the industry and initiating carpet production. Addie Evans managed the transition to machine production and maintained a successful business in an industry that increasingly became a man's world, and she must have looked at Cabin Crafts and Barwick Mills and thought, "Why not me?" Beverly Whitfield, Addie Evans's granddaughter and a longtime loan officer for Dalton's First National Bank, insisted that Evans Manufacturing could have borrowed money "on Addie's name and reputation" as easily as a man might have in the 1950s. Yet for whatever reason, Addie Evans and other women who managed spread and small-rug mills did not make the transition to the truly big business of carpet production. Women continued to find work in the burgeoning industry to provide for their families, but they virtually disappeared as entrepreneurs.

Catherine Evans Whitener died in 1964 at the age of eighty-three. By that time, the Dalton-area tufted-carpet industry, which traced its origins to her handicraft revival, boasted more than $1 billion in annual sales. Evans Whitener's passing was noted by both *Time* magazine and the *New York Times*. The headline in the *Times* referred to Catherine as "Mrs. Will Whitener, founder of a Georgia textile trade."[49] Evans Whitener received recognition, but her identity was merged with that of her husband, who had played no role in the industry. Addie Cavender Evans died in 1990. No national media outlet reported her passing, or those of the innumerable women who had worked in the hand-tufted bedspread industry. Catherine Evans Whitener had come to stand for all those women who had worked so hard to provide for their families and, in the process, created a multibillion-dollar industry. In some ways, Evans Whitener was a safe symbol for the industry's origins. Evans Whitener's story seemed to conform to prevailing early and mid-twentieth-century gender norms. She engaged in traditional women's work—in her case, hand crafting textile products. She seemed appropriately overwhelmed by the emerging scale of the industry she helped make, and never attempted to make the transition to large-scale factory production.

As the bedspread industry faded, carpet mills sprang up in northwest Georgia. The tufted carpet industry that grew out of the roots of the spread business had generated hundreds of new businesses during the 1950s and 1960s. Some survived for decades, but many did not. Large firms such as Cabin Crafts, Barwick Industries, Coronet Carpets, and Shaw Industries grew alongside numerous small firms. In 2007 Georgia-based mills employed more than twenty-four thousand of the nation's thirty-seven thousand carpet mill workers; no other state accounted for as many as three thousand carpet mill workers. Georgia mills accounted for $9.5 billion of the industry's total of roughly $13 billion in wholesale shipments. Georgia's carpet mills accounted for 6 percent of the state's manufacturing workforce and 6.5 percent of the value of the state's manufacturing shipments. The work Catherine Evans Whitener began in the 1890s continued into the twenty-first century, helping to provide a livelihood for thousands.

The capital that built the industry was accumulated from the labors of women who worked long hours at home and received a small portion of the value of that labor. The wages earned by those women workers nevertheless made a critical difference for many rural families in the 1920s and 1930s. Those cash incomes helped north Georgia families weather low cotton prices in the 1920s, the Great Depression of the 1930s, and participate to a limited degree in an expanding consumer economy in the mid-twentieth century. The tufted bedspread industry offered a poignant example of the prospects and limitations faced by women in the first half of the twentieth century in Georgia, captured in Catherine Evans Whitener's words: "If I had been a boy." Implicit in that brief formulation was her recognition of possibilities lost. Yet the skill, industriousness, and labor of women built a foundation for one of Georgia's most important industries.

NOTES

1. Catherine Evans, "Bedspread Beginning," n.d., probably late 1950s, Catherine Evans Whitener File, Whitfield-Murray Historical Society, Dalton, Ga., hereafter referred to as Whitener File. In this essay, Catherine Evans Whitener is referred to as Evans Whitener, while her sister-in-law Addie Cavender Evans is referred to as "Addie Evans" throughout. Catherine Evans launched the tufted textile industry in Georgia before her marriage to Will Whitener, and her husband played no significant role in the business. Addie Cavender Evans, by contrast, had already married Catherine Evans's brother Eugene when she learned the craft, and she ran the business known as Evans Manufacturing for much of her adult life.

2. On the history of Crown and Dalton in the late nineteenth and twentieth centuries, see Douglas Flamming's exemplary community study, *Creating the Modern South: Millhands and Managers in Dalton, Georgia, 1884–1984* (Chapel Hill: University of North Carolina Press, 1992). For Flamming's characterization of Dalton's "industrial resolution," see chapter 2, "Dalton's Industrial Resolution," 36–55. For a complex evaluation of the New South ethos, much contested, see Numan Bartley, *The Creation of Modern Georgia*, 2nd ed. (Athens: University of Georgia Press, 1990), 83–87. The Crown Mill fit Henry Grady's prescription—a large cotton mill that employed local white labor yet did not seem to threaten the prevailing social structure, racial mores, etc.

3. Mrs. William (Catherine Evans) Whitener, "A History," n.d., probably late 1930s–early 1940s, Whitener File. The formulation suggests either a search for an elevated way of opening the story or a response to someone else's view, an effort to set straight a record doubted or distorted.

4. Catherine Amoroso Leslie, *Needlework through History: An Encyclopedia* (Westport, Conn.: Greenwood Press, 2007), 35–37; Jean Manly, interview by author, April 20, 2009.

5. Evans Whitener, "A History."

6. Evans, "Bedspread Beginning." For a valuable calculator for comparing the value of the dollar over time in a variety of ways, see Samuel H. Williamson, "Six Ways to Compute the Relative Value of a U.S. Dollar Amount, 1790 to Present," MeasuringWorth, 2009, http://www.measuringworth .com/uscompare/ (accessed May 20, 2009).

7. Evans Whitener, "A History."

8. Thomas M. Deaton, *Bedspreads to Broadloom: The Story of the Tufted Carpet Industry* (Acton, Mass.: Tapestry Press, 1993), 7.

9. Ibid., 7–8.

10. Ibid., 5–6.

11. Joe Evans, Catherine's great nephew, interview by author, June 15, 2009.

12. Deaton, *Bedspreads to Broadloom*, 8–9.

13. Evans Whitener, "Bedspread Beginning."

14. *Atlanta Constitution*, May 1, 1927, G10.

15. Evans Whitener, "A History."

16. Cheryl R. Wykoff, "Addie Lee Cavender Evans," article compiled for Prater's Mill Foundation, n.d. (probably early 1990s). This document is in the possession of Beverly Whitfield, Addie Evans's granddaughter. The bulk of the document consists of extended quotations from a 1989 speech by Callie Ruth Evans Roach (Addie's daughter) and a 1980 interview with W. R. Evans. Wykoff noted that Callie Ruth Roach approved a rough draft of the document, and Beverly Whitfield, Addie's granddaughter, confirmed this to the author.

17. Beverly Ann Whitfield, interview by author, June 10, 2009; Addie Evans quoted in Deaton, *Bedspreads to Broadloom*, 5.

18. An excellent overview of the putting-out system in medieval Europe is Marian Małowist, "Merchant Credit and the Putting-Out System: Rural Production during the Middle Ages," *Review (Fernand Braudel Center)* 4, no. 4 (1981): 667–81. The emergence of home-based craft production for the market, particularly in agricultural regions, is explored in Gay L. Gullickson, "Agriculture and Cottage Industry: Redefining the Causes of Proto-Industrialization," *Journal of Economic History* 43, no. 4 (1983): 831–50. On the continuing value of the concept of proto-industry, see Julie Marfany, "Is It Still Helpful to Talk about Proto-Industrialization? Some Suggestions from a Catalan Case Study," *Economic History Review* 63, no. 4 (2010): 942–73.

19. Bureau of the Census, 1920, 1930, accessed via Ancestry.com, June 15, 2009. Curiously, Lizzie listed no occupation in either the 1920 or 1930 census. By 1930 the Parmalee family had moved to Louisville, Ky. Addie's family believed that Parmalee lived in Louisville in 1918 and was simply in Dalton to visit family that July.

20. Wykoff, "Addie Lee Cavender Evans."

21. Quoted in ibid.

22. Beverly Whitfield interview; Wykoff, "Addie Lee Cavender Evans."

23. *Hartford Courant*, May 3, 1927, 5.

24. *Kingston Daily Freeman*, April 26, 1919, 5.

25. "Mountain Girls of Georgia Display Handicraft Skill," *Hartford Courant*, March 28, 1930, 3.

26. *Los Angeles Times*, November 17, 1929, 26.

27. Allen H. Eaton, *Handicrafts of the Southern Highlands* (New York: Dover Publications, 1937), 225–26.

28. Eileen Boris, "Crafts Shop or Sweatshop? The Uses and Abuses of Craftsmanship in Twentieth-Century America," *Journal of Design History* 2, nos. 2–3 (1989): 175, 187. Boris provides an insightful assessment of the craft revival of the 1930s.

29. Ibid., 186–87; Jane Becker, *Selling Tradition: Appalachia and the Construction of an American Folk* (Chapel Hill: University of North Carolina Press, 1998), 149–50 (workers quoted on 149).

30. Lu Ann Jones, *"Mama Learned Us to Work": Farm Women in the New South* (Chapel Hill: University of North Carolina Press, 2002), 49, 87–88.

31. North Georgians developed a thriving poultry industry in the 1920s and 1930s as well. See Carl Weinberg, "Big Dixie Chicken Goes Global," *Business and Economic History Online* 1 (2003), Business History Conference, http://www.thebhc.org/publications/BEHonline/2003/Weinberg.pdf; Monica Gisolfi, "From Crop Lien to Contract Farming: The Roots of Agribusiness in the American South, 1929–1939," *Agricultural History* 80 (Spring 2006): 167–89.

32. Bertha Nienburg, "Potential Earning Power of Southern Mountaineer Handicraft," *Bulletin of the Women's Bureau, Department of Labor*, no. 128 (Washington: U.S. Government Printing Office, 1935), 27–28.

33. See Jan de Vries, *The Industrious Revolution: Consumer Behavior and the Household Economy, 1650 to the Present* (New York: Cambridge University Press, 2008), esp. chap. 6, "A Second Industrious Revolution," 238–73 (quotes on 238–39).

34. Ibid., 97. Gavin Wright has adapted De Vries's concept specifically for the U.S. context. Wright emphasized the variations in size and region among American markets. Land abundance meant an increased and longer-lasting insistence on family farming within the U.S. context. Wright also observed that the United States might better be characterized as having experienced a number of industrious revolutions associated with such variation, including the "delayed commercialization in the South." See Wright, "The Industrious Revolution in America," Stanford Institute for Economic Policy Research Discussion Paper No. 10-007, September 2010, http://www.stanford.edu/group/siepr/cgi-bin/siepr/?q=system/files/shared/pubs/papers/pdf/10-007_Paper_Wright.pdf (accessed January 10, 2012). The emergence of the poultry industry followed a similar pattern, beginning as a home-based business and evolving along the lines of a sort of putting-out system, as described in the works by Weinberg and Gisolfi noted above. Contract poultry production represented in some ways a strategy used by small farmers to find an alternative to cotton, make their farms more productive, and thus enhance their ability to remain on the land, reflecting a strategy identified by Wright as particularly emerging in the land-abundant U.S. context.

35. Nienburg, "Potential Earning Power," 28.

36. Henry Nevins, "Bedspread Sales Reach High Mark in North Georgia," *Atlanta Constitution*, September 29, 1935, 13A.

37. Ibid.

38. Data gathered via the United States Historical Census Browser at http://fisher.lib.virginia.edu/census/ (accessed June 2, 2002).

39. Becker, *Selling Tradition*, 143; Randall L. Patton with David B. Parker, *Carpet Capital: The Rise of a New South Industry* (Athens: University of Georgia Press, 1999), 86–88.

40. "Catherine Evans' Bedspreads," *Time*, September 2, 1940, 8.

41. See Patton and Parker, *Carpet Capital*, 81–122, for an extended explication of this process. The emergence of the bedspread and later carpet industries exemplified the approach to industrialization advocated by Governor Ellis Arnall in the 1940s. Arnall argued that the South's insistence of wooing outside interests and northern capital was mistaken, and that Georgia and other southern states should focus on encouraging and promoting indigenous, internally generated industries. The dynamic growth of bedspreads and carpets exemplified that strategy while highlighting just how difficult it can be to catch such lightning in a bottle. Arnall's strategy is described in Bartley, *Creation of Modern Georgia*, 195–96.

42. *Kingsport Tennessee Times*, July 18, 1939, 15. Dalton had a history of successful union organization at the Crown Cotton Mill and the American Thread Company mill, ably chronicled in Douglas Flamming, *Creating the Modern South: Millhands and Mangers in Dalton, Georgia, 1884–1984* (Chapel Hill: University of North Carolina Press, 1992). The Dalton area's bedspread mills and carpet mills remained unorganized, however, with a couple of short-lived exceptions. See Patton, *Carpet Capital*, 123–48.

43. Wycoff, "Addie Evans." The source of the story is unclear but was probably Callie Ruth Roach.

44. Beverly Whitfield interview; James C. Patton, an employee of Manor Rug in the 1950s and early 1960s, interview by author, June 16, 1998.

45. Patton, *Carpet Capital*, 121, 257.

46. Ibid., 89; Patton, *Shaw Industries: A History* (Athens: University of Georgia Press, 2002), 41–42.

47. *Van Nuys News*, November 21, 1957, 22A. Similar ads appeared in other papers around the same time, including the *Los Angeles Times*, December 1, 1957, E7. The *Los Angeles Times* (January 2, 1963, E11) carried an ad featuring "Evans Poodle Tuft" in a list of products.

48. Whitener, "Bedspread Beginning."

49. *Time*, June 12, 1964, 5; *New York Times*, June 3, 1964, 43.

Viola Ross Napier
(1881–1962)

The Twentieth-Century Struggle
for Women's Equality

ELIZABETH GILLESPIE MCRAE

Viola Ross Napier, a mother of three children with another on the way, could not have known how fundamentally her life would change in 1919. For most Americans, the devastation of World War I had been something that they read about but did not experience directly. But the flu pandemic that swept across the nation brought war-like conditions—senseless death, fear, uncertainty, and sorrow—to rural hamlets, small towns, and bustling cities, including Macon, Georgia, Napier's hometown. The daily mail delivered distressing news throughout the winter of 1918–19. Her stepmother struggled against the flu, while her sister Hermie nursed her youngest son back to health only to watch her young daughter contract the flu and perish forty-eight hours later. In early April, Napier's father-in-law died, a victim of another recent menace: an automobile careening into a crowded downtown Macon street. The day after the funeral, her husband began suffering from flu-related cerebral meningitis. One week later Viola donned her black dress and buried her husband. Left with four children ranging in age from two months to eight years, very little savings, and a home, the thirty-eight-year-old Napier put her immediate affairs in order, and in the early summer of 1919 she headed to Virginia for a two-month visit with family. She could not support her family if she returned to her former career as a teacher in Georgia's poorly funded schools and feared that her children would be split up if she did not find a way to financial security.[1]

As she considered economic options, Congress passed the woman suffrage amendment and sent it to the states for ratification. This action would have an almost immediate effect on Napier's career possibilities as she first considered the legal profession and then in early 1922 a possible run for the state legislature. Her life, however, demonstrated the lengthy and ongoing struggle to make the promise of democracy into the reality of equal opportunity. Even with the vote, economic independence would remain an elusive goal for many black and white women. In the aftermath of suffrage, systemic and deeply rooted obstacles to women's equality, financial independence, and the promises of a greater democracy continued to shape the lives of Napier and others. These obstacles revealed the complicated relationship between political and economic opportunity, the very porous and perhaps indistinguishable lines between private and public spheres, and the issues that would shape second-wave feminism decades later.

When Napier returned to Macon in the late hot summer of 1919, she came home to a town that in many ways served as a microcosm of the possibilities and limitations of woman suffrage. As Lorraine Gates Schuyler has argued, in towns, cities, and counties across the South, women embraced suffrage to change their communities and wielded the vote with political sophistication. Countering older scholarship that lamented the failure of a woman's bloc in politics and often equated that failure with women moving away from political concerns, Schuyler's work shows the vibrancy women voters brought to the political sphere and the wide range of issues on which they acted, not in concert necessarily, but as active members of the body politic. This political shift, Schuyler has contended, would result in "the slow process of opening up the political system to newcomers."[2]

While politics did open up to women in Macon, "slow" was as important as "opening." Deep divisions between suffragists and antisuffragists, the South's reluctance to expand the electorate in the wake of decades of disenfranchisement campaigns, and the constant claims that woman suffrage would erode white supremacy remained visible and active on the political landscape. Two leaders of the Georgia Association Opposed to Woman Suffrage, Dolly Blount Lamar and Caroline Patterson, were both Maconites and moved immediately to defeat the suffrage amendment state by state. Successfully outdoing the efforts of suffragist Rebecca Latimer Felton, among others, they urged the Georgia General Assembly to consider the amendment in order to have the honor of being the first state to defeat it. Upon that victory, Lamar traveled to North Carolina to aid the Tarheel antisuffragists in their defeat of the Nineteenth Amendment. When Tennessee became the thirty-fourth and final state needed for ratification, Patterson and one of the most vociferous antisuffrage editors in the state, the *Macon Daily Telegraph*'s James Calloway, began a campaign against the femininity of the newly founded League of Women Voters.[3] Throughout 1919

VIOLA ROSS NAPIER

Courtesy of Middle Georgia Archives, Washington
Memorial Library, Macon, Ga.

and 1920, editorials in the Macon papers accused woman suffrage advocates of threatening white supremacy, of enfranchising black women, of wrecking the home, of neglecting their children, and of eroding the principle of states' rights.[4] While women urged the governor to make provisions for them to vote in 1920, the Georgia legislature would not act, and Georgia's women would not vote in the presidential election in 1920. It would be 1922 before they voted in a state-wide election.[5] Meanwhile, a reinvigorated Ku Klux Klan occupied the political mainstream in Macon, Athens, Atlanta, and even the statehouse. By 1922 the KKK could claim as members Governor Clifford Walker, chief justice of the State Supreme Court Richard Russell, and Atlanta mayor Walter B. Sims. By 1923 the KKK also claimed to control one-third of the votes of Georgia Democrats, members of the same party that had adopted many of the League of Women Voter's issues in their platform.[6] Bent on limiting the newfound freedoms of women as well as upholding racial segregation, the presence of the KKK had real effects on those anxious to make equality a reality.

Undaunted by such a political climate, some white women of Bibb County celebrated victory and moved to parlay suffrage into policy changes and political power. Helen Shaw Harrold, a mother and former suffragist, had formed Macon's Equal Suffrage Association in the wake of Congressional passage. In August of 1920 she transformed that club into the Bibb County League of Women Voters (LWV), with Napier by her side. Harrold had long refused to concede the political terrain to her antisuffrage sisters, and in September of 1920 Harrold, Napier, and thirty-eight other women tried to register to vote in the Democratic primary. With the support of U.S. senator Hoke Smith they marched to the registrar's office. A local newspaper described their effort as one conducted "in a manlike fashion," while a former antisuffragist accused the LWV members of advocating "sex antagonism." In a society that connected southern white womanhood to very specific characteristics, some went as far to question Harrold's femininity and racial identity in the racial- and class-coded language of the Jim Crow world, charging that she had big feet and wore cotton stockings. With a baby on her hip, Harrold noted that most LWV members were married, hardly advocates of sex antagonism, and, like Napier and herself, most were mothers. Responding to comments on her feet and legs, Harrold admitted to a crowd of a thousand that she had big feet and defended her use of cotton stockings as in line with her "belief in economy." Most effectively, however, she invoked the language of maternalism to justify women's political participation. In a thinly veiled attack on the spinsterhood of Patterson and the childless-ness of Lamar, Harrold noted, "Motherhood cannot foster sex antagonism and does foster interest in child welfare and in the ballot to protect the same." She also claimed the LWV members just believed that advice about political issues could be solicited from folks other than "their husbands and sweethearts." In a final tribute to the benefits of separate spheres and sexual difference to the political process, she celebrated gender-specific virtues that women would bring to politics.[7]

While Harrold posed for public photos with her children, Napier had marked her transition into widowhood with a public commitment to women's political equality and to a professional career in the law, both in the name of supporting her family. For Napier, the lines of demarcation between politics, economic opportunity, family life, and motherhood hardly seemed like borders at all. In addition to joining the League of Women Voters, seeking to register to vote in the primary, and speaking to groups of women about the necessity of casting their vote, Napier began practicing law in June of 1920. No longer bound by matrimony, its constraints as well as its security, Napier had joined the night law classes at her deceased husband's law firm in September of 1919. In class with eight or nine young men, she read during the day with her infant son on her lap. Later she remarked that she had always been interested in the law, but in the first decade of the twentieth century, she had taken the more conventional route for middle-class women and had become a teacher.[8] As a result, she had married a lawyer rather that becoming one. Even after marriage, she had expressed an interest in attending law school at her husband's office, but Hendley Varnier Napier had dismissed her wishes, claiming her place was at home. Perhaps, for similar reasons, he also said she could not learn to drive. Four children in eleven years maybe muted some of her wishes, but clearly, studying the law suited her.

As one writer had described Napier, "beneath the politeness was a will of steel, and directing the quiet voice as many who crossed swords with her learned was a first class brain."[9] While she was not the first female attorney in Georgia (Minnie Hale Daniel had been admitted to the bar in 1917), Napier was part of Georgia's first wave of female lawyers. Despite her first-class brain, Napier found that "there was no place for a woman lawyer in a man's office." So Napier hung a shingle with Miss Aline Hardin, a fellow graduate of E. W. Maynard's law school. Hardin would handle the office, and Napier would do the court cases.[10]

In 1920s Georgia, working as an attorney was more lucrative than teaching, but both male and female attorneys struggled to build new practices in a state that prevented lawyers from advertising. One Macon man remarked that Napier faced an uphill battle as he predicted that "nobody would go to a woman unless it was cheaper." As a result, he guessed that she probably made less than $1,000 per year. Extant correspondence upholds his estimation. He also noted that "most of Mrs. Napier's clients were blacks and women." In fact, one of her first inquiries was from a friend who asked her to represent Rosa, a black woman who cooked for her. Rosa's husband had died the very same day she paid the last premium on his life insurance policy, but the insurance agent had failed to honor the policy. Napier also represented black men who were wrongly imprisoned, who were held but not charged with a crime, and who were the recipients of unfair sentences. In letters from convict camps and jails, they implored her to find out their crime and to visit their white employers for character references. Unable to pay her while incarcerated, they promised to reimburse her in installments or work.[11]

As divorce rates rose across the nation and in Georgia, Napier also accepted divorce cases. When newspapers publicized one of her divorce cases, Napier's father noted that he had read about it and upon doing so smiled. Cognizant of the difficulties in building a practice, he predicted that she would be "called on often to make addresses to all sorts of women's meetings" and advised her that "practice makes perfect—don't turn any of them down when you can possibly accept."[12] He meant for this advice to be applied to court cases as well.

Napier's early cases indicated that she and her father were of like mind. While the Macon papers reported on court appearances, Napier and Hardin made headlines when they successfully defended a former student of Napier's who in his work as city detective was accused of murder. In another instance, an attorney from Wrightsville, Georgia, asked her to assist with the case of a poor white man who murdered his pregnant wife. The family of the murdered wife, the attorney informed her, were extremely poor people. "They are not able," he continued, "to pay an attorney to aid me." But, he assured her, this case "would bring her publicity." Publicity was critical since newspaper coverage and word of mouth were the only ways for attorneys to get their names before potential clients.[13]

The difficulties that Napier faced as a professional and politically active woman were only exemplified in the fate of one of her most notable clients, H. Augusta Howard. Howard had founded the Georgia Woman's Suffrage Association in the 1890s. In 1920 she lived alone in the family home in Columbus, Georgia, and had been convicted of the "unlawful shooting" of a small neighborhood boy who was hiding in her magnolia tree. Howard claimed that she was shooting high to scare trespassers and did not know that the boy was in the tree. Howard's brother, who was particularly anxious to acquire the family home, had helped to secure her conviction and apparently hoped that she would be committed to a mental institution. Upset with her representation, Howard solicited the services of Napier, hoping that a female attorney would be more inclined to provide quality legal services. Howard and some of her supporters

noted that her conviction was more about her progressive politics, spiritual independence, and family greed than criminal behavior. Howard wanted Napier
to conduct her appeal and to file "several enormous damage suits" on her behalf.
Despite Howard's prominence, this too would be a case that would not pay. In
her frequent contacts, Howard asked Napier to find "any man or woman . . .
who are not merely in favor of woman's rights, not that it is fashionable to appear so, but who have the manhood and womanhood to deeply resent woman's
WRONGS, they are the people to apply to for a silent loan which I can pay back
with interest when fully vindicated." She even asked Napier to finance her and
promised that "in the end it will finance you and several other lawyers hand-
somely." Acknowledging that enfranchisement was only one step in the struggle
for women's rights, Howard wrote Napier: "It is so little purpose that women
have the ballot in Georgia . . . if woman lawyers and women votes leave un-
redressed the outlawry of a woman for her service in every phase of woman's
cause." Appealing to Napier's commitment to women's rights, she also told Napier that her case was "[the case] of every woman in Georgia." Napier failed to
get an appeal, and it appeared that Howard would go to the state prison farm.
Napier, however, solicited letters for a pardon from friends, former suffragists,
attorneys, Governor Thomas Hardwick, and even the young boy's parents. In
the end, she had Howard pardoned before she served a single day of her sentence. While newspapers noted her accomplishment, Napier's success did not
result in immediate payment. In January 1922 Howard wrote to Napier that she
would "begin to handle your expense account (never forgotten) as soon as possible under my robbed and outlawed circumstances."[14]

While Napier's law practice resulted in some notable legal successes—she
was the first woman to argue a case before both the Georgia Court of Appeals
and the state Supreme Court—her law practice also educated her on the relationship between poverty, racial identity, and justice. Informed as well by social
science research on the causes of crime and the relationship between criminal
behavior and mental illness, Napier acknowledged that her practice taught her
to look differently at those accused and convicted of crimes. Time and time
again, she noted that her work had convinced her that those incarcerated were
most often mentally ill, poor, or black and could not afford appropriate legal
representation. In this assessment, she was in the company of many progressives and academics who were lobbying for a more scientific and research-based
understanding of factors contributing to crime, delinquency, violence, and poverty. In North Carolina, for example, Kate Burr Johnson and Nell Battle Lewis
published articles about the relationship between mental illness, poverty, and
crime in sociologist Howard Odum's new publication, *The Journal of Social*

Forces. In their articles, they echoed Napier's more impressionistic analysis. For Napier, the glaring discrimination in the justice system made her more and more interested in politics. Convinced that society could be improved by better social welfare institutions and that often environment, not genetic predisposition, contributed to criminal acts, poverty, and mental illness, Napier sought to change the way Georgia viewed and treated its most vulnerable populations, and she moved into state politics.[15]

Her initial venture into political activity was as president of Macon's LWV chapter, a position she inherited from Helen Shaw Harrold in 1920. In her hometown, this nonpartisan organization encouraged local women to register to vote and to educate themselves on political candidates. The LWV also maintained many Progressive era reforms in their platform, focusing on education, child labor, women's working conditions, and maternal protections. In interviews with political candidates, Napier asked them questions about their opinions on women holding public office, serving on juries, and working at night. She also questioned them on their attitudes toward child labor, international peacekeeping organizations, bonds for schools, prohibition, funding for the Children's Bureau, the Women's Bureau in the Department of Labor, federal aid to end illiteracy, and the Shepard-Towner Act, a piece of federal legislation dealing with infant and maternal health. Armed with their replies, Napier supplied the statewide LWV and local women voters with the various positions of the candidates. She called state legislator candidate Nat Winship's assertion that "women are better than men and the fact that they want a thing is sufficient for him . . . probably gas" and described another legislator candidate, J. F. Malone, as "a labor man . . . a plain but an honest one." She also discredited more paternalistic responses. In the spring of 1922, when a candidate for railroad commissioner offered that if elected he would "do all that lies within my power for the good and comfort of the Ladies on all the Street and Steam Railways and waiting rooms," she responded that "the influential women of the state [are] more interested in reform legislation than in their own personal comfort."[16]

As the female-led antisuffrage campaign had indicated, Napier not only had to convince men of women's political seriousness but also had to convince women to participate in the political process as a way to strengthen rather than undermine their role in society and their identities as women. Delivering a talk, "Why Women Should Vote" to a church group, Napier noted that the suffragists believed that enfranchised women could "reform the world." Their courage, she noted, earned them the ridicule and opposition of many women and men who depicted them as "mannish creatures, dressed in tight ungraceful clothes, entirely without feminine charm." Napier argued, however, that the vote was a duty akin to that of motherhood, implying that whether or not one desired such a duty, once handed it, one must exercise it. She encouraged them to register to vote and to cast an educated ballot because it was now their civic duty.[17] Conflating civic obligation and political participation with the duties of motherhood, Napier used maternal politics to work for a more progressive state.

As she encouraged and educated southern white women to get out to vote, Napier often found herself in Macon's newspaper offices submitting notices about the LWV. On one rainy day in the spring of 1922, the editor of the *Macon News*, R. L. McKenney, asked her to consider a run for the state legislature. In many ways, Napier was an ideal candidate. As an LWV member, she strengthened that organization's ties to the ruling Democratic Party. Her personal and family history offered impeccable credentials. A descendant of one of Georgia's first families and some of the earliest white settlers along the Ocmulgee River, Napier felt a sense of stewardship for her homeland. Born on February 14, 1881, Viola Felton Ross had attended Macon schools. Graduating from Gresham High, she then attended Wesleyan College and Elam Alexander Normal School, both in Macon. From 1901 until she was married in 1907, she taught in the public schools. While this experience gave her broad name recognition in Bibb County, it also cultivated a core belief in education as a panacea for many social ills, making her attractive to many progressive women's organizations.[18] As a widow she now evoked sympathy, and as an attorney her professional skills prepared her for the state legislature. Napier also recalled being excited by the possibility of political office and consulted with her family and friends about their willingness to share the responsibilities of raising her children, Marion Rose, John Blackmon, Viola Ross, and Hendley Varner, who ranged in age from eleven to three.[19] With no institutional childcare available, volunteers and her black domestic, Lena Fry, were her only options. Her sister in Atlanta offered lodging, easing that financial concern. With their encouragement, she decided to run and announced her candidacy in June 1922.[20]

While most of her correspondence congratulated her on her entrance into the race for legislature, others were less pleased. Going beyond accusations of big feet and cotton stockings, the *Butler Herald* identified Napier as the "negress, lawyer, and chairman of the Bibb County league of women voters," who was running for state legislature. Called on his mistake, the editor wrote and published an apology. He just could not explain how he could have suggested that Napier, "the highest type of Southern lady" was not white. Other opponents were not so apologetic. As her son John handed out handbills on election day, one man said his mother "oughta be home looking after her children," while a woman was more specific suggesting that her place was in the kitchen.[21]

Despite such opposition, Napier won her bid for the legislature. Her platform had closely resembled the legislative program of the League of Women Voters and included a plank to move the capital of Georgia from Atlanta to Macon, a proposal favored by most Bibb County residents. Of the seven candidates for office, she received the second highest number of votes and joined Nat Winship and J. F. Malone as the Bibb County delegation to the state legislature.[22] Numerous letters applauded the high moral standard that women and Napier would bring to politics. Several letters also pledged their support or asked her to consider specific pieces of legislation. Speaking to the organizational power of women's networks, the vice president of the WCTU, Mrs. Marvin Williams, proclaimed that she knew she could "expect the utmost consideration and cooperation for all bills looking toward the betterment of the women and children of the state." Williams noted that through the WCTU, "the state president can reach practically the entire body of Christian women of the state in twenty-four hours." Admitting that they were not a political organization, she added that "in order to carry out our purposes, [we] have always found it necessary to take a hand in the politics of the day."[23] Napier's presence in the statehouse gave women's organizations a potential advocate for issues they had long championed. For many middle-class reformers, white women in political offices were a necessary step in creating a more progressive state.

During her first term, her support for progressive legislation and her insistence that women voters be treated equally earned her respect and also made her prospects of reelection less certain. Napier and the other female legislator, Bessie Kempton of Fulton County, pushed the state legislature to repeal the general tax act that exempted women from the poll tax if they would not register to vote. While Napier argued that the law was confusing and disenfranchised many women, the chairman of the Ways and Means committee explained that the law was necessary for a white supremacist order that prevented "the voting of large numbers of negro women." Representative Ennis explained that the financial benefit of this exemption might keep black women away from the polls and preserve the Jim Crow order. He did not acknowledge that this might also be an incentive for working-class white women to avoid the polls. Napier's attempt failed, however, and in 1925 she was still urging the Business and Professional Woman's Club to include an amendment to the poll tax law on their legislative agenda.[24]

Napier had also campaigned on the promise to call for a statewide investigation of prison facilities. Perhaps hearing her pledge, one black man from Macon asked that she help start an investigation of the murder of his son in a Georgia convict camp. "Knowing your incessant stand for right and justice,"

William Miller appealed to Napier to find out the truth behind his son's death. In a state where the governor belonged to the Ku Klux Klan and where the KKK advertised on the inside cover of the legislative bulletin, Napier's previous and continued service to black men and women could not have helped endear her to those dedicated to racial inequality.[25]

More damaging, however, was her support for labor and her general progressive platform. She introduced the federal child labor amendment and was one of three legislators who supported it. She also supported a "Women in Industry" bill that would limit nighttime hours of women and give working women the protection to try to balance work and family responsibilities. Beginning in 1923 she worked for nearly three years on a committee of legislators to design a Child Welfare Code that would standardize the treatment of neglected, abandoned, and adjudicated youth, and revise the juvenile court system. When one constituent asked her to consider for Georgia a bill similar to Nebraska's antipicketing bill, Napier's response was unequivocal. "The prosperity of the nation is largely dependent on harmony between capital and labor," she reminded him. She expressed her doubt that a copycat bill for Georgia would create such harmony.[26]

Her support for education was more palatable to Georgia voters. During her first term, she successful introduced bills requiring fire escapes and the teaching of the state and federal constitutions in all public schools. Her fire escape bill earned her statewide praise after a Savannah school burned down but all the children and faculty escaped from an outside staircase built to comply with Napier's bill. She also advocated greater appropriations for Georgia State Women's College, training schools, and the state's School for the Blind. While these measures did not explicitly challenge white supremacy or the power of industry owners, they did meet the intransigence of a state known for its low appropriations for social services.[27]

As she made her stand in Atlanta for better treatment of Georgia youth, she did so at the cost of being with her own children. While the legislature was in session her children stayed with friends and family. In letters to her two youngest children, Napier described her daily visits to the legislature, told them about being one of the first women, promised little Viola a dress, and lamented that "there was no little boy there to hug me and tell me he loved me 4, 8, 9, eleven, seventy." The possibility of working in Macon and making more money led Napier to announce her candidacy for Bibb County tax collector in September of 1923, one session into her first legislative term. In a campaign advertisement, fourteen Macon Women urged the "Women of Bibb County" to come out and vote for "Viola Ross Napier, the only woman in the race." "She needs the office," the ad continued, "and is capable of running it." Napier lost her bid for tax collector, however. The *Macon Telegraph* expressed astonishment about the "failure of women voters to support the only woman . . . in the race," but surmised that Napier's late announcement meant that many women had already pledged their vote.[28]

She did, however, win her bid for reelection to the legislature in 1924. Despite spending a mere forty-five dollars on her campaign, she overcame the Ku Klux Klan's opposition to her candidacy and returned to Atlanta. Governor Clifford Walker called a special session to consider bond referendums for roads and education, adding even more time to the biennial meeting schedule. During her second term, she served on eight committees, including temperance, education, appropriations, and General Judiciary #1. Napier continued to try to secure greater funds for training schools and the creation of a training school for black girls. When the Colored Teachers' Association asked her to speak on school legislation at their annual meeting, she replied that she would speak on the need for a training school, hardly a topic that would address the serious inequities in Jim Crow education. Nevertheless, her consideration of black institutions and her quest for better educational facilities for black Georgians rooted her in the tradition of female educators who had long lobbied for better schools for all.[29]

As a middle-class progressive, she continued to push for the rights of labor, sponsoring a state child labor bill in 1925 and 1926. In 1925, at the culmination of three years of work, a group of legislators known as the Children's Code Commission—including Napier and another female legislator, Eugenia Zelda Richardson of Atlanta—introduced a collection of eight bills to the Georgia assembly. When Napier introduced the child labor bill on July 17, 1925, legislators complained that they had not had time to study the lengthy bill, and so Napier delayed the vote. On July 18 she introduced for a vote a bill that gave a favorable report on training schools and required the state to employ two factory inspectors instead of one, mandating that one inspector be a woman. Supported by the League of Women Voters, the Georgia Federation of Women's Clubs, the Woman's Christian Temperance Union, and the Parent-Teacher Association, the first bill of the Children's Code Commission nevertheless met defeat. Opposition led by a legislator from Culpepper County coalesced around the increase in state funding such legislation would require and that the second inspector's salary would tax the general treasury. The *Atlanta Georgian* lobbied for close consideration of Napier's bills, but the Child Commission was less than successful.[30] Continuing her efforts for labor reform, in the summer of 1926 she attended the South Regional meeting of the YWCA at the Methodist retreat of Lake Junaluska where she made a presentation on legislation for laborers. The industrial secretary, Louise Leonard, called Napier's presentation "the best one we have ever had." Upon her return, Napier urged her state to take "all steps to eliminate the causes of criminality, imbecility, and degeneracy."[31]

Of course, Georgia had a long way to go to improve such state services even for a southern state. Some statistics revealed that Georgia spent the smallest amount on education of ten southern states and only 28 cents per white inhabitant on institutions of higher learning. Between 1923 and 1926, North Carolina spent close to $10 million on improvements for institutions of higher learning, yet throughout the 1920s, Georgia spent only $10,000 in improvements at their flagship university in Athens. In fact Georgia's overall spending on common schools in the 1920s at times fell below 1900 spending. This meager spending, however, was not due to Georgia's relative poverty. In 1926, its per capita debt was less than seven southern sister states while coming in fifth in income, third in farm value of all crops, and fourth in the true value of property.[32]

Faced with a fiscal retrenchment in the legislature and a rising opposition to "maternal legislation," Napier lost her bid for the legislature in 1926, finishing fifth on the legislative slate of seven. While the newspapers did not speculate on the reasons for her defeat, she noted that the most votes she had ever received were before she served a single day. The KKK had campaigned against her in 1924, but Klan member and Governor Clifford Walker had pledged his public support for her, as had some leading judges, but just over nine hundred Bibb County citizens voted for her (the candidates who earned seats from Bibb County received around twelve hundred votes). Other legislators who had supported the Child Labor Amendment and legislation associated with the Children's Code Commission had also met defeat. Or perhaps it was her work for appropriations for black institutions, her steady advocacy for laborers, or her own fiscal conservatism in her campaign that led to her defeat. Her handwritten memoirs indicate that she was treated well by other legislators, some of whom had served during Reconstruction with black Georgians, but never with a woman. She had, however, criticized the legislature for its work ethic and the presence of too many members.[33]

After her defeat, Napier returned to her law practice, but then she closed her office in 1927, when Mayor Luther Williams appointed her to the post of city clerk—a position she would hold for the next twenty-seven years. As a professional woman—an attorney, businesswoman, and two-term legislator—she was overqualified for the position, but it had its benefits. She could remain in Macon, no longer scramble for childcare during legislative sessions, and make a steady income.

Even as a civil servant, Napier continued to engage in state politics, urging other women to broaden their political engagement as well. In 1927 she revived

Macon's LWV chapter, which had fallen apart after she left for Atlanta. She soon became the second vice president of the statewide LWV. She also served as their legislative chair, capitalizing on her contacts and experiences in the legislature to champion a reform of the tax code, a rise in the age of consent, a removal of the poll tax discrimination for women, an expansion of child and family services, and support for a state constitutional convention. She also became president of the Business and Professional Women's Club of Macon in the 1930s and worked with them on legislative issues and support networks for professional women.[34] Her fight for women's rights included financial as well as political equality and opportunity. In 1942 the Business and Professional Women's Club of Macon congratulated the *Macon Telegraph* editor on running an editorial that advocated "equal pay for equal work" and upheld the War Labor Board's ruling to that effect. The BPW's letter sounded very much like its former president Napier when they noted that "to pay women less than men are paid for doing the same work is discouraging, unjust and un-Christian. In fact, it is heathenish."[35]

As a former legislator, Napier still used her personal connections with members to protect and to advocate for certain legislation. When in 1927 Raymond Martin introduced legislation to dissolve the Department of Public Welfare, following an anonymous circular that derided its work and referred to the director as an "Atlanta Jewess," Napier wrote him a blistering letter. She noted that the director, Rhonda Kaufman, "knows more of the New Testament and lives up to its teaching more faithfully than the so-called Christian author or authors of that circular." She then attacked his apparent lack of manhood in circulating a petition with no authors that appealed to base prejudices. After attacking his religious devotion and masculinity, she then encouraged Martin to honor his professional ethics as a lawyer and not condemn someone before a trial. Instead, she encouraged him to go visit the department before launching such a harebrained proposal.[36]

Throughout the 1930s and 1940s Napier continued in her advocacy for women's rights, challenging widespread beliefs about masculine and feminine qualities. In a 1934 interview Rosemary Lyons Jones noted that Napier, "without having sacrificed her feminine charm and graciousness[,] . . . had taken on a certain masculinity that speaks of mental solidity, of standing squarely, and facing facts." Napier, however, denied that those characteristics were masculine. Instead, she argued that those characteristics were gained from experiences that were more accessible to men. "When women gain the same experience," she continued, "they develop the same qualities of thought." Moreover, she said that women "possess all of the mental qualities usually conceded to men."[37] Declared not to be a "women's libber" by her children, she nevertheless spoke to the cultural and economic structures that continued to limit women's experiences and their contributions to society.

Her primary duties, however, involved her position as city clerk. She wrote speeches for incumbent mayors, devised a city pension plan that lasted until Social Security, oversaw the city's dogcatcher, paid employees in Depression-era script, and even implemented a business licensure process that let entrepreneurs buy their licenses in installments. Meanwhile, she lost her savings when there was a run on the Luther Williams bank in 1932, and like other city employees she took several pay cuts during the lean years of the early 1930s.[38]

In 1946, in her nineteenth year as city clerk, Napier tried to make the city pay her an equitable salary. In a letter to John A. Jones, Chairman of the Finance Committee, Napier outlined the systemic salary discrimination she faced. She reminded him that when the pay of other city employees was restored in 1935, her office received a ten-dollar-a-month increase. They had, however, suffered twenty-five-dollar-per-month cuts between 1932 and 1935. Moreover, she reminded him that her pay had not been raised since 1935. Acting puzzled over this discrimination in light of her performance, Napier noted, "I have collected in insurance licenses and premium taxes which would not have otherwise been paid almost enough to pay my salary." In addition, since she had been clerk the revenue on auditorium rents had increased from $1,250 per year to $10,000 annually. She asked for a raise of $185 per year in addition to the proposed 10 percent raise already slated for 1946. To address the past inequity, she asked that the $185 be added to her base salary prior to the 10 percent increase. To further illuminate her point, she compared her salary to the office of city attorney from 1928 through 1946. Despite her efforts, she remained underpaid. When she retired in 1954, the next city clerk, her son recalled, received a significant raise, and his mother received her first pension check of $62.50.[39]

Throughout her life, Napier challenged barriers that inhibited white women's membership and activity in professional and political forums. It is important to remember that the context of her struggles was different in many ways than those of her white working-class and black southern sisters. In the Jim Crow era, she was white, a benefit hard to overestimate. She was educated. She had inherited a home. While her husband sought to narrow her opportunities, her father had offered encouragement, advice, and even delight as she entered public and political life. Her sisters and friends provided childcare, emotional advice, and an occasional shopping trip, and a black woman kept house for her. As an attorney, Napier had greater control over her work schedule than did her working-class counterparts in Georgia's factories. Her oldest daughter, Marion, recalled resenting her mother's work only on Sundays when Napier spoke at many different churches, and during the Augusta Howard case. When one in four Americans was out of work during the Great Depression, Napier's job as city clerk was secure.[40]

Despite these benefits, her accomplishments—political, legal, and maternal—were and remain impressive. While she challenged notions of a woman's sphere with her words, her legislation often upheld gender-specific ideas about women's issues and women's maternal instincts. Her politics, however, did not stop there, and she demonstrated that women as political figures had a wide range of interests and opinions. In her work as a Macon attorney and city clerk, she challenged the gender conventions of the day that celebrated women as appropriate advocates only for child and social policy.

Napier's life also speaks to the transformative power of political enfranchisement. The vote allowed her to be a political actor in the fullest sense and also expanded the possibilities of her professional life. In 1987, twenty-five years after her June 1962 death from several years of failing health, her portrait was hung in the Georgia State Capitol to commemorate her service to the state, and a Viola Ross Napier day was declared. Georgia politicians from Zell Miller to Max Cleland spoke and wrote about her contributions as the first woman legislator.[41]

But it is too comfortable to focus on the "firsts" of Napier and her notable career. Her life illuminates the deep roots of sexual inequality and the significant obstacles that working women faced and which they continue to face. Napier's consciousness about the women's second-class citizenship was clear. On Napier's retirement in 1954, Georgia's first female architect, Ellamae Ellis League, wrote: "I just want you to know that I feel it is women like you, who have created good public relations, who make it easier for women like me to get along in the world." Napier replied that League's letter "says that I have done that which I hoped and tried to do." "That is," she continued, "to make the world, my part of it at least, a better place for women, especially for business women." Napier knew that the journey was not finished and told League that "you are doing the same thing by proving that a woman architect can succeed even though she had to struggle to get that which any young man could have had as a matter of course, an architect's education and recognition."[42]

Napier could not parlay her professional education, her intelligence, her competence and her courage into a job that rewarded her with equitable pay or responsibilities commensurate with her experiences and talents. Her life reveals the futility of extracting the political, the economic, and the personal from one another. Her ability to support her family, the clientele she attracted as a lawyer, and her decision to trade electoral politics for a more secure government job speak to how gender conventions simultaneously shaped the private and the public spaces of daily lives. Napier's career was defined as much by her continual struggles against economic, sex, and gender discrimination, financial insecurity, childcare dilemmas, and a paternalism that spoke nicely but played mean as it was by her significant and important accomplishments.

NOTES

1. Georgiana McCall, "Early Trailblazer," *Macon Telegraph and News*, October 19, 1986; Frannie to Viola Ross Napier (vrn), February 14, 1919, folder 5D, Viola Ross Napier Papers, Middle Georgia Archives, Washington Memorial Library, Macon, Ga., hereafter cited as vrn Papers; Hermie to vrn, April 3, 1919, to vrn from her stepmother, April 13, 1919, folder 5D, vrn Papers; Hendley Varnier Napier Jr., Obituary, undated clipping [April 7, 1919?], folder 30B, vrn Papers. On the role of public school teachers in Georgia during this time, see Ann Short Chirhart, *Torches of Light: Georgia Teachers and the Coming of the Modern South* (Athens: University of Georgia Press, 2005), 73–85.

2. Lorraine Gates Schuyler, *The Weight of Their Votes: Southern Women and Political Leverage in the 1920s* (Chapel Hill: University of North Carolina Press, 2006), 6–11. On interpretations that focus on the waning of women's political power in the decade after suffrage, see Nancy F. Cott, *The Grounding of Modern Feminism* (New Haven: Yale University Press, 1987), 8; J. Stanley Lemons, *The Woman Citizen: Social Feminism in the 1920s* (Urbana: University of Illinois Press, 1973); Elna Green, *Southern Strategies: Southern Women and the Woman Suffrage Question* (Chapel Hill: University of North Carolina Press, 1997).

3. On the efforts to defeat the amendment in southern states both by antisuffragists and states' rights suffragists, see Marjorie Spruill Wheeler, *New Women of the New South: The Leaders of the Woman Suffrage Movement in the Southern States* (New York: Oxford University Press, 1993), 172–84.

4. A. Elizabeth Taylor, "The Last Phase of the Woman Suffrage Movement in Georgia," *Georgia Historical Quarterly* 43 (March 1959): 11–28; Elizabeth Gillespie McRae, "Caretakers of Southern Civilization: Georgia Women and the Anti-Suffrage Campaign, 1914–1920," *Georgia Historical Quarterly* 82 (Winter 1998): 801–28.

5. Wheeler, *New Women of the New South*, 191.

6. Nancy MacLean, *Behind the Mask of Chivalry: The Making of the Second Ku Klux Klan* (New York: Oxford University Press, 1995), 17; Cynthia Rymph, *Republican Women: Feminism and Conservatism from Suffrage through the Rise of the New Right* (Chapel Hill: University of North Carolina Press, 2006), 23. Rymph notes that in 1920, the Democratic Convention adopted twelve of fifteen proposals of the League of Women Voters for their platform.

7. "No Intention of Padding List of Woman Suffrage Supporters," *Macon Daily Telegraph*, June 19, 1919; "Leader of Antis Warning against Joining 'League of Suffragettes,'" *Macon Daily Telegraph*, August 30, 1920; "1,000 Women Hear Mrs. Harrold Discuss Issues in Present Race," undated clipping, Harrold Family Scrapbooks, Middle Georgia Archives, Washington Memorial Library, Macon, Ga.; "Forty Women Sign Registration Cards in Regular Man Fashion," *Macon Daily Telegraph*, September 3, 1920; "Election of Woman Pleases Women Here," *Macon Daily Telegraph*, September 23, 1921. On maternalist language and its presence in postsuffrage politics, see Robin Muncy, *Creating a Female Dominion in American Politics, 1890–1935* (New York: Oxford University Press, 1991),

124–25, 131; Georgina Hickey, *Hope and Danger in the New South City: Working-Class Women and Urban Development in Atlanta, 1890–1940* (Athens: University of Georgia Press, 2003), 4.

8. Chirhart, *Torches of Light*, 109, 112.

9. Viola Ross Napier, handwritten autobiographical account, folder 40, VRN Papers; Marion Napier Smith, typescript, folder 40, VRN Papers; Georgiana McCall, "Early Trailblazer"; Sam Hays, "Remembering Georgia's Woman of Firsts," *Atlanta Journal-Constitution*, January 11, 1987, 6H.

10. VRN to Edith Moriarty, May 5, 1923, folder 8A, VRN Papers; "Law Partnership Established by Macon Women," *Atlanta Constitution*, February 1921?, VRN Papers; Hays, "Remembering Georgia's Woman of Firsts."

11. "Mrs. Viola Ross Napier in Favor of Jail with a Yard," April 8, 1923; William Miller to VRN, July 21, 1923, box 2, folder 8B; Ivory Thomas to VRN, December 1, 1926, box 2, folder 8E; Robert Ryans to VRN, February 2, 1927, box 2, folder 2E, VRN Papers.

12. Hays, "Georgia's Women of Firsts"; Helen Ross Rogers to VRN, November 11, 1920, folder 5F, VRN Papers; Edgar Alfred Ross to VRN, February 14, 1921, folder 6A, VRN Papers; E. L. Stephens to VRN, February 12, 1921, folder 6A, VRN Papers.

13. Hays, "Georgia's Women of Firsts"; Helen Ross Rogers to VRN, November 11, 1920, folder 5F, VRN Papers; Edgar Alfred Ross to VRN, February 14, 1921, folder 6A, VRN Papers; E. L. Stephens to VRN, February 12, 1921, folder 6A, VRN Papers.

14. On H. Augustus Howard, see A. Elizabeth Taylor, "The Origin of the Woman Suffrage Movement in Georgia," *Georgia Historical Quarterly* 28 (June 1944): 64–79. H. Augustus Howard to VRN, May 23, 1921, May 28, 1921, June 10, June 22, 1921; VRN to Howard, June 8, 1921; VRN to Judge H. D. Humphries, October 6, 1921, Miriam Howard to VRN, October 20, 1921; Wheeler Williams to VRN, December 14, 1921; H. Augustus Howard to VRN, January 9, 1922, folder 6C, VRN Papers. By the time Napier accepted the Howard case, P. C. Herrington, a male attorney, was a partner in her firm. For correspondence, clippings, petitions, and Howard's courtroom statements, see folder 6C, VRN Papers.

15. Hays, "Remembering Georgia's Woman of Firsts"; Emory C. Pharr, "Mrs. Viola Ross Napier in Favor of Jail with a Yard," *Macon Daily Telegraph*, April 8, 1923; VRN to William D. Anderson, February 7, 1926, folder 8D, VRN Papers; Boyce M. Eden to VRN, May 16, 1923, VRN Papers; VRN to Richard Lawton, October 27, 1922, VRN Papers; Nell Battle Lewis and Kate Burr Johnson, "The North Carolina Conference for Social Service," *Journal of Social Forces* 1 (March 1923): 266–68; John Egerton, *Speak Now against the Day: The Generation before the Civil Rights Movement in the South* (Chapel Hill: University of North Carolina Press, 1994), 130.

16. Questionnaire of the League of Women Voters for Congressional and Legislative Candidates in the State of Georgia, folder 17, VRN Papers; VRN to Mrs. E. B. Chamberlain, June 26, 1922, folder 7B; O. B. Bush to VRN, May 15, 1922; O. B. Bush to VRN, May 24, 1922, folder 7A, VRN Papers.

17. VRN, "Why Women Should Vote," typescript, folder 40, VRN Papers.

18. Chirhart, *Torches of Light*, 143–48.

19. Marion Napier Smith, "Viola Ross Napier Biography," undated typescript, VRN Papers.

20. VRN, "Experiences in the Legislature," handwritten account, folder 40, VRN Papers.

21. C. E. Benns to VRN, June 1, 1922, VRN Papers; Hays, "Remembering Georgia's Woman of Firsts"; VRN to Edith Moriarty, May 5, 1923, folder 8A, VRN Papers.

22. VRN, "Interesting People I Met," undated typescript, folder 22, VRN Papers.

23. J. H. Ennis to VRN, September 15, 1922, folder 7A; Richard Lawton to VRN, September 21, 1922, folder 7A; Charles Stewart to VRN, September 25, 1922, folder 7A, VRN to J. H. Milner, October 23, 1922, folder 7A, To VRN from Mrs. Marvin Williams, October 4, 1922, folder 7A, VRN Papers.

24. "Mrs. Napier Urges Repeal of Clause Exempting Women," *Macon Telegraph*, August 8, 1923; 1925 Business and Professional Woman's Club Legislative Program, typescript, folder 17, VRN Papers.

25. William Miller to VRN, July 21, 1923, folder 8B; "General Assembly of Georgia, 1923–24," Legislative Directory, folder 27, VRN Papers; Numan V. Bartley, *The Creation of Modern Georgia* (Athens: University of Georgia Press, 1983), 172.

26. W. A. Winburn to VRN, February 16, 1923, VRN to Winburn, February 20, 1923, folder 8A, Mrs. E. B. Chamberlain to VRN, June 16, 1923, folder 8A, VRN Papers.

27. "Mrs. Napier's Bills," undated clipping [1923?], *Atlanta Georgian*, VRN Papers; M. L. Duggan to VRN, December 23, 1923, folder 9D; Rhonda Kaufman to VRN, August 21, 1923, folder 8B, VRN Papers.

28. VRN to Little Viola and Hendley Napier, June 22, 1923, and July 2, 1923, folder 8B, VRN Papers; "Woman Enters Tax Job Race," *Macon Telegraph*, September 2, 1923.

29. J. W. Holley to VRN, February 20, 1925, and February 24, 1925, folder 8d, VRN Papers.

30. "Actions of House Keeps Assembly Steadily on Job," *Atlanta Constitution*, July 17, 1925, 1; "First of Children Code Bills Lost in Lower House," *Atlanta Constitution*, July 18, 1925, 1; "Legislative Calendar for 1925," *Atlanta Constitution*, June 28, 1925; "Georgia Legislators Pledge Support to Proposed New Child Welfare Code," *Atlanta Constitution*, July 12, 1925, 8; "Mrs. Napier's Bills," *Atlanta Georgian*, undated clipping [1925?], VRN Papers.

31. Louise Leonard to VRN, July 28, 1926; VRN to William Anderson, February 7, 1926, VRN Papers; VRN to Sam Rutherford, September 13, 1924, folder 8B; Joseph W. Holley to VRN, February 20, 1925; VRN to Joseph Holley, February 24, 1925, folder 8D, VRN Papers; Account of Viola Ross Napier campaign expense account, folder 20, VRN Papers.

32. William D. Anderson to Viola Ross Napier, J. F. Malone, and Nat Winship, February 7, 1926; Bartley, *The Creation of Modern Georgia*, 160.

33. VRN to Mr. Sutlive, September 19, 1924, VRN Papers; VRN to Sam Rutherford, September 13, 1924, VRN Papers; Governor Clifford Walker to VRN, April 20, 1926, VRN Papers; W. H. Stanford to VRN, September 11, 1924, VRN Papers.

34. Mary Raoul Mills to VRN, September 1, 1927, VRN Papers.

35. *Macon Daily Telegraph*, May 22, 1935; Macon Business and Professional Women's Clubs to W. T. Anderson, October 2, 1942, VRN Papers.

36. VRN to Raymond Martin, July 18, 1927, VRN Papers.

37. Rosemary Lyons Jones, "Pen Shots of Macon Women Making Careers," *Wesleyan Alumnae*, November 18, 1934.

38. "Mrs. Viola Ross Napier," *Macon News*, June 29, 1962; Hays, "Remembering Georgia's Woman of Firsts"; VRN to Hermie, January 22, 1931, folder 9A, VRN Papers.

39. VRN to John A. Jones, November 30, 1946, folder 9D, VRN Papers; copy of her first pension check, folder 32, VRN Papers.

40. Marion Napier Smith, handwritten note, folder 40, VRN Papers.

41. News release from office of Max Cleland, February 17, 1987, folder 15, VRN Papers; "Napier Is Still Recording Firsts," *Macon Telegraph and News*, January 31, 1987; "Funeral Services Planned Saturday for Mrs. Napier," undated clipping [June 30, 1962?], VRN Papers.

42. Ellamae Ellis League to VRN, January 15, 1954; VRN to Ellamae Ellis League, January 21, 1954, VRN Papers.

Mary Hambidge
(1885–1973)

A Vision of Beauty, Symmetry, and Order

ROSEMARY M. MAGEE

An ecstatic vision of oneness with nature and the universe informed the work of Mary Crovatt Hambidge. In every part of her life, she sought to find and express the interconnectedness of beauty, symmetry, and order. A weaver of textiles, as well as a thinker and social reformer, these qualities became interwoven in the very texture of her life and work. In 1944, Hambidge established a foundation that subsequently gave birth to the Hambidge Center for the Creative Arts and Sciences. Nestled in the woods and mountains of North Georgia, the Hambidge Center offers a retreat program where people from many walks of life have found time for solitude, reflection, and creative endeavors. Thus, Hambidge's grand dream of eternity has had an enduring effect on the lives of artists, writers, scientists, and creative thinkers in Georgia and around the world.

Born in Brunswick, Georgia, on December 20, 1885, Mary Crovatt Hambidge came from a family that was part of the southern aristocracy. Her father, Alfred J. Crovatt, originally from Charleston, South Carolina, was a lawyer and judge who served as the mayor of Brunswick. He represented the "New South," working with both northern and western industrialists; he helped to found the Jekyll Island Club, "whose membership roster carried exclusively millionaire's names."[1] Although he was never an official member, he and his family maintained close friendships with some of the members who had cottages on the island. Her older brothers, Alfred Hayne Crovatt and William Cecil Crovatt, both attended Emory University and served in the military.[2]

With little interest in the social world of her parents, Mary Crovatt attended Lee School for Girls, a finishing school, in Cambridge, Massachusetts, after which she fled to New York where she worked as an artist's model while she

MARY HAMBIDGE

artist and founder of the Hambidge Art Foundation and the Weavers of Rabun.

Hambidge Center, Rabun Gap, Ga.

tried to find work singing. She enrolled in whistling lessons in order to become
a professional whistler. Eventually, she found success singing with a trained
mockingbird named Jimmy. Demonstrating a rebellious streak throughout her
life, she was subsequently described as presenting "a striking figure" with "intense blue eyes and an enigmatic smile, and to the end of her life she was always
aware of the impression she made."[3]

While in New York, around 1914, she met Jay Hambidge (1867–1924), an artist and art historian. Nearly twenty years her senior, and already married with
children, he worked as an illustrator, often sending Mary drawings enclosed in
his love letters. As Mary Hambidge would say, she "lived for years on the verge
of extinction until she met Jay Hambidge."[4] Fulfilling both her creative and romantic yearnings, Jay Hambidge's scholarly pursuits also strengthened their attraction to one another. Collaborators as well as lovers, they provided mutual
financial as well as moral support; his scholarship created a philosophical basis
for her life and work while her work elaborated and extended his theories into
a whole new realm. They were devoted to each other until his sudden death in
1924, but their relationship continued to inspire Mary Hambidge's work for the
rest of her life. Although Hambidge took his last name and referred to Jay as her
husband, no legal record of their marriage exists.[5]

As a scholar, Jay Hambidge made a name for himself by developing an important theory of art, which he called "dynamic symmetry." In a letter dated
September 2, 1918, Jay wrote to Mary Hambidge: "I have made a most astonishing discovery and I want you to know about it first. . . . I have solved the whole
problem of dynamic symmetry and in the most picturesque way."[6] Mary took
his theories very seriously, not only incorporating them into her life and work
but even into her daily routine, seeking to create a way of life that brought
dynamic symmetry out of the strict domain of art and into the realm of the
spiritual, practical, and ecological. In this way, Mary had a significant effect on
Jay's life and work by transforming dynamic symmetry into an ideology that
stretched well beyond the realm of academia.

As an illustrator, Jay Hambidge became convinced that design was not purely
instinctive, and he spent much of his life incorporating mathematical equations
into design. Out of this work, he developed the concept of dynamic symmetry,
which refers to the proportion of things that grow in nature. According to his
theories: "Dynamic symmetry in nature is the type of orderly arrangement of
members of an organism such as we find in a shell or the adjustment of leaves

on a plant. There is a great difference between this and the static type. The dynamic is a symmetry suggestive of life and movement."[7] Using the golden ratio derived from the mathematical Fibonacci sequence and other similar ratios, Jay Hambidge developed mathematical calculations that correlate to growth in nature. To test his theories, he studied ancient Greek art, becoming convinced that the secret of the beauty of Greek design rested in the intentional utilization of dynamic symmetry. By relying on ratios, he realized that it becomes possible to draw humans, plants, and flowers as they appear in nature.

In his theory, Jay Hambidge sought to avoid estimation and approximation in design, uniting art and arithmetic by demonstrating growth patterns in nature: "As moral law without intellectual direction fails, ends in intolerance, so instinctive art without mental control is bound to fail, to end in incoherence. In art the control of reason means the rule of design. Without reason art becomes chaotic. Instinct and feeling must be directed by knowledge and judgment."[8] Jay Hambidge's insistence that a rule exists to provide a foundation for design created a sensation in the world of art. His insights into design and art prompted Yale University to fund a research trip to Greece for him to further his studies in ancient Greek art and its use of dynamic symmetry. He measured artistic details on temples, vases, and statues, proving that the proportions and ratios evident in the design of the ancient Greeks were identical to the ratios that govern all growth in nature. As a result of his work, in 1920 he published *The Greek Vase*, a study of the design forms of the Greek vase in relationship to dynamic symmetry, which reviewers praised as creating a connection to the possible "scheme of the universe."[9] Jay Hambidge's discoveries stretched beyond the art world, influencing designs generated by Tiffany as well as the Chrysler Corporation. After Jay died suddenly at age fifty-seven in 1924, Mary Hambidge collected her husband's writings and shaped them into the book *Elements of Dynamic Symmetry*. For her, the principles of dynamic symmetry were essential to a full and complete understanding of the meaning of life—and her belief in the theory was to shape every dimension of her life, work, and thought.

Mary Hambidge first incorporated the principles of dynamic symmetry into her weaving. In 1919, while in Greece with Jay, she came upon a weaving school run by local women. It was an inspirational event: "The moment I saw the looms and the Greek women at them," Hambidge states, "I knew that I had found the important thing for me."[10] Apprenticing with them, she set out to learn how to spin and eventually how to weave. The connection the Greek women and their weaving had to the earth, animals, and community, as well as to art, led Hambidge to continue weaving upon her return to New York.

She initially began making simple white tubular clothing, layered and gathered with sashes, based on classical Greek drapery. Demonstrating contempt for commercial textiles, she learned to create her own fabric using ancient techniques. As her skill increased she incorporated the colors of nature, from acid green to tree-bark brown. She dyed her own thread, adding a few accentuating graphics along the border of the pieces. Her friend and future benefactor, Eleanor Steele, an heiress and highly regarded opera singer, secured for Hambidge costume-design jobs for various theater productions.[11] In 1924, after Jay's death, Mary Hambidge moved to Connecticut, "designing and weaving clothing based on the principles of dynamic symmetry, including the costumes used by Ted Shawn's dance company in the revival of the Delphic festivals, Delphi, Greece, and the costumes for the production of 'Phoebus and Pan,' Little Theatre Opera Company, New York."[12] Hambidge began incorporating figures measured with Jay's principle of dynamic symmetry into her work. Hambidge also used the dynamic symmetry formula to generate motifs for clothing.[13] One dress, with a lotus design on its front, is based on a watercolor in the Hambidge archive.[14] For Hambidge, weaving satisfied both a practical need and a spiritual void, as it allowed her to feel a connection to her environment: "When you're weaving, it's the most fascinating thing. . . . You become part of it. You're related to it. . . . All the beauty and perfection is in the raw material. You draw it out and are one with it."[15]

During a visit to a friend after Jay's death, Mary Hambidge spent time in the North Georgia mountains. While there, she was pleased to discover that a weaving culture already existed. Hambidge's dream to extend Greek weaving into a way of life further came to fruition when again Eleanor Steele acted as her benefactor by purchasing nearly eight hundred acres of mountain land on Betty's Creek in Rabun County, which laid the groundwork for what would later become the Jay Hambidge Art Foundation, founded in 1934 and incorporated in 1944 as a nonprofit organization to promote "Agriculture and Handcraft" as "the basis of a creative life."[16] Hambidge saw the potential of the land to create a sustainable community that connected craft to farming, and her first step was to create the Weavers of Rabun cooperative, which encouraged the Appalachian woman to retrieve her looms and spinning wheels from the attic, training young women in the forgotten craft of weaving. An article on the weaving cooperative published in the *Atlanta Constitution* states: "More than fifty of the mountain folk, young girls and aging women, have united in an original community enterprise." The weaving "is modern and based upon nature."[17]

Beyond the weaving cooperative, Hambidge saw a future for the citizens of Rabun Gap, despite the fact that the people there initially referred to her as "That Woman."[18] Originally inhabited by the Cherokee and then settled by Protestant families from England, Scotland, and Northern Ireland, Rabun Gap developed into a staunchly independent, agrarian community that resisted outsiders. Many reformers came through the area, but one of its most notable was a local: Andrew Jackson Ritchie. Ritchie, Rabun Gap's first college graduate, worked his way through Harvard College and then decided to leave a faculty position at Baylor University to found the Rabun Gap Industrial School. Financed by donations from the Carnegie Corporation, John D. Rockefeller Jr., and Ernest Woodruff of Coca-Cola, the Rabun Gap Industrial School aimed to remedy the "extreme conditions of isolation, illiteracy, and poverty that prevailed in the country."[19]

Like Ritchie, Hambidge sought to improve the lives of those in the area. She imagined the entire population engaging in craftwork sponsored by the foundation. While her plan was to begin with weaving, which was an art form already indigenous to the area,[20] she thought that pottery and furniture making eventually could be added. Hambidge also wanted a summer school to offer classes on these crafts and the principles of dynamic symmetry and to serve as an outreach center for other educational endeavors.[21] Yet her dreams stretched even further. Again, with the help of benefactors, Hambidge opened a shop on Madison Avenue in New York City in 1937. Displaying samples in the shop allowed customers to make customized orders for fabric (including fabric for furniture) and scarves. In a statement for Rabun Studios, Hambidge described her mission: "Our work is created by human beings, not produced by machines. . . . We believe that the future happiness of America lies in the development of its own natural resources, in training the hands of its people to use these resources and in educating the minds of its people to form them into beauty."[22] Although the shop was not profitable, it served customers as diverse and famous as Greta Garbo, Georgia O'Keefe, and Jackie Gleason. It also became a meeting space where artists and designers converged.

Hambidge's dedication to weaving brought her increased recognition. She won a gold medal at the Paris exposition of 1937. The fabrics she designed were included in the "Textiles USA" exhibit at the Museum of Modern Art in New York. Closer to home, she exhibited her work at both the University of Georgia and Georgia Institute of Technology. As her reputation spread, she was asked to weave the sails for President Harry Truman's yacht, the *Williamsburg*. Fashion designers also sought her out. American designer Laura Willis collaborated with her to develop fabric for a collection of gowns, suits, and dresses in 1962.[23] The prestige of the collection prompted Mary to organize a fashion show in

Rabun Gap to highlight the work of the weavers to the local audience, an event reported in the *Atlanta Constitution*.[24] Although she never established formal relationships with other weaving schools in the South, her influence was known throughout the handcraft community. Her work was clearly related to the Appalachian Craft Revival, which had begun at the start of the twentieth century, spawning centers that promoted women's financial independence throughout the region. As Philis Alvic, historian of the movement, notes about Mary Hambidge, "With her charming and flamboyant personality, she was able to get many people to help her in developing a weaving business launched from her mountain home."[25] She relied on both modern and traditional weaving techniques, influenced by the separate worlds of Greece, New York City, and Appalachia.

Thus, Mary Hambidge contributed to a broader culture of weaving. The weaving cooperative reflected a trend throughout the Appalachian Mountains to preserve handcrafts, while also providing women with an income. The Penland Weavers and Potters in North Carolina, Berea College in Kentucky, and the Pi Beta Phi Settlement School in Tennessee were schools begun in the 1920s and 1930s to advocate the revival of mountain handcrafts.[26] These programs "offered a creative outlet, stimulated and sharpened handwork and intellectual abilities, fostered individual talents, and developed the aesthetic senses. Crafts classes promoted social interaction, and one's identification as a craftsperson became a source of mutual respect within communities."[27] The Arts and Crafts movement, as it came to be called, also saw middle-class Americans purchasing these handcrafts out of an interest in rural ways of living and working. The production of products based on folk crafts for mass consumption came from a sentiment that industrialization was erasing significant aspects of regional identity and eliminating American traditions.[28]

Mary Hambidge's primary interest in folk culture was related to others' opposition to industrialism, but she was not as committed to preserving Appalachian ways of life. Whereas the other schools sought to revive the tradition of the mountains and provide a source of income for the women, Hambidge saw her mission as encouraging others to take up their forgotten looms. She gave demonstrations of weaving and carding in Virginia, Connecticut, and other places along the East Coast.[29] The impetus that Hambidge's weaving provided to Rabun Gap was unplanned, but once she recognized the needs of the community, she became more fully committed to improving their homes and lives. The Southern Highland Handicrafts Guild awarded Hambidge honorary membership in their organization because of her important work advocating weaving.[30]

Hambidge's endeavor differed from these cultural-improvement projects because she based her designs on dynamic symmetry, not on the Appalachian culture. She created a work environment for the women in Rabun Gap, and

she used her influence to improve their living conditions, but the emphasis of
the Jay Hambidge Art Foundation was dynamic symmetry and the values of
sustainability she learned while in Greece. When her employees began to leave
the foundation in order to work at the nearby James Lee & Son's carpet mill,
she mourned that their "common minds" cared more about making money
than art.[31] She wrote, "When I first came here, [the mountain people, essentially
self-sufficient then] were wonderful. But the minute the outside world comes in,
they're ruined. I tried my best to keep them from being ruined." Although her
attitude toward the women at Rabun Gap was patronizing, Hambidge's respect
for their skill eventually brought their talents to a wide audience.

The success of the weaving cooperative in North Georgia did not detract from
Hambidge's dedication to seek further the unity and balance she witnessed in
the Grecian weavers' lives: "Here, buried away in the mountains of the northern
part of the State, I found people very much like the people I had known and
loved in Greece, living much the same kind of life."[32] With the bounty of the
land, she developed her property so that she and the weavers could live off the
land as much as possible. She purchased cows and a bull and built a milking
shed to provide milk, cheese, and butter. Produce from tenant farmers provided
the basis of many meals, and with the establishment of a gristmill, they ground
their own cornmeal and whole-wheat flour. She also purchased sheep and silk
worms that could provide the raw materials for the women's weaving. With the
women weaving and men working on the land, she oversaw the building of a
sawmill, which cut the timber they used for additional buildings. Hambidge's
desire to establish a sense of community and to enhance the lives of those
around her was not limited to the people she worked with daily. She also began
to seek improvement to the lives of the impoverished residents of Rabun Gap.
In a letter listing the accomplishments of the Jay Hambidge Art Foundation, she
summarized that the foundation provided plumbing, electricity, glass windows,
and good roofs for the entire valley and helped to prevent land erosion. In addition to these improvements, she petitioned the county to provide a mobile
dental clinic for the people of Rabun Gap.[33] Although no official documentation of these actions exist outside of her correspondence, Hambidge's summary
demonstrates her intended concern for the conditions she found in the area.

Mary Hambidge sought to create a self-sufficient community for those individuals who, in her words, "need a place like this to grow and develop; whose
ideals are more powerful than the urge for riches; whose powers of creation need

enhancement and nourishment."[34] In addition, she believed this community could be a place where someone could build a studio or home; and if the person left or died, the studio would revert back to the foundation, thus keeping the property intact while adding new facilities as well. She envisioned that the board of directors of the foundation might also live there permanently, with the life of the compound based on work (farming, building, and raising livestock and sheep), study (classes in Greek and dynamic symmetry), and artistic creation (writing, composing, weaving, throwing pots, and woodworking). Income, she anticipated, would come from the sale of crafts and rental of studios to transient artists; food and shelter would come from the land; and cultural enrichment would come from those living there—as well as from guest lecturers, performers, and even exchange students from Greece. It would be a community immune to outside pressures—a self-contained, working unit bound by a sense of organic order: "As all of this work has been and is based on a nature principle I wanted it to start from a small seed and gradually develop from within into a healthy plant, following its own natural pattern, just as the oak grows from the acorn."[35]

Whereas she imagined expansive growth based on the foundation of Jay's principles of dynamic symmetry, the management of such a complex and idealistic enterprise was fraught with challenges. There were complicated financial matters and legal questions that Mary Hambidge did not have the expertise or patience to understand. Given her ideals, she was inclined to trust others, thereby subjecting herself to those who took advantage of her. Difficulties, such as problematic water lines and reservoirs, were part of running such a multifaceted organization. Industrialization and changes in labor laws that emerged in the aftermath of World War II required shifts in her relationship to workers and sales, both in Rabun County and New York City.[36] Eventually, minimum-wage laws closed the shop in New York, the books on dynamic symmetry went out of print, factories offered better wages to the mountain people in Rabun Gap, and the county laid a highway through the middle of the amphitheater she had established for Greek theater–style performances. In short, the external world intruded on the idyllic community she had worked so hard to establish. In response, Hambidge shifted her efforts from weaving to encouraging the creative potential of individual artists by providing them a mountain retreat, thereby opening the foundation's doors to those who needed a place to work.[37]

Mary Hambidge addressed many of life's questions, writing down her thoughts, ideas, and reflections also dedicated to her belief in dynamic symmetry. She believed that all aspects of life are interrelated.[38] Hambidge extracted from the idea of dynamic symmetry Jay's language regarding arrangement, interrelation, and perfection to develop an organizing principle for life. Mary Hambidge's philosophical ramblings, found scattered throughout her notes, journals, poetry, and quotations, were not published until 1975 (two years after her death), collected in the volume *Apprentice in Creation: The Way Is Beauty*.[39] This volume offers a compendium of poems and fragments of her thought previously stored randomly in drawers, suitcases, and boxes collected after her death by Aspasia Voulis, a friend of Mary Hambidge who also served as assistant director of the Hambidge Center. Many of these scraps of paper had been revised over time in order to achieve greater clarity of thought.

Her writings consistently convey the sense of a person dedicated to the ideals of beauty, order, and symmetry. A motif that runs throughout her writing is the importance of nature to the full experience of life. Some of the fragments address the relationship between nature, animals, and humans, while others describe recurring patterns that appear in nature. Imagery of birds, rocks, and other parts of nature make up her poetry. Living in the midst of the wildness and beauty of the mountains of North Georgia clearly influenced her awareness of the relationship between nature and creativity.

Mary Hambidge's vision had a political dimension. She protested the industrialization of the South, particularly when the higher wages of the factories enticed Hambidge's weavers to become factory workers. Instead, she increasingly promoted the values indigenous to the southern region: "The South has got to learn to stay at home and work. Georgia's gold mine is in her people. The trend must be toward the land. They can go from agriculture through the crafts to the arts. Many artists today don't have their roots in the earth—that's why their work hasn't grown. It's surface art, with no depth. The most important thing in life is to learn to use your hands, to create useful and beautiful things. Out of our craftsmen the artists and writers will develop."[40] Mary viewed the industrialization of the South as destroying the strong culture she found in Rabun Gap and elsewhere in North Georgia. Her utopian community sought to preserve a way of life that was not rooted in industrialization. She brought like-minded people together to resist a mechanistic society. The foundation and its reliance on food and wood from the land was Hambidge's way of building a utopia explicitly at odds with the principles of industrialization.

Hambidge's beliefs had company. Twelve southerners based in Nashville, Tennessee (at Vanderbilt University), who came to be known as the Agrarians, issued a manifesto arguing that southern culture contained a regional, agrarian identity that provided the antidote to the ills of modernity. In *I'll Take My Stand*

(1930), they advocated for values such as the need for spiritual fulfillment, aesthetic experience, and leisure and lamented the presence of northern industry and the intervention of the national government.[41] *I'll Take My Stand* became a popular as well as a controversial treatise on southern culture.

Mary Hambidge's resistance to industrialization and related governmental policies went beyond rhetoric. When the U.S. government tried to provide Hambidge health insurance and a stipend through social security, she protested. After falling ill in 1968, she wrote to a social security official: "You have been misinformed by someone—I did not apply for social security because I do *not* believe in it. I do *not* wish to be supported by the govt but prefer to *work* for what I believe in. So please take me off your list. All this govt. support is completely *corrupting* the *People* of America."[42] Hambidge made a point of putting her beliefs into practice. This inclination often included writing letters to government officials in support of Greek politics and against the proposed highway running through her property. By resisting government intervention, even when it came to attending to her own needs, Hambidge reiterated her philosophical investment in the rewards of self-sufficient labor.

Throughout all of these writings, Hambidge continued to imagine the potential of dynamic symmetry as a guiding philosophy in her life: "Man's development occurs in pattern. First he *grows* in pattern—then he *feels* in pattern—then he *thinks* in pattern and finally *creates* in pattern. Pattern development is simultaneous with his own development."[43] The emphasis on growth, patterns, and the details to be found in nature reflect Jay Hambidge's theories of dynamic symmetry. In addition, many fragments reveal visions she experienced that contributed to her philosophy of life: "Once I had a vision. I became one with the Universe. I saw life as one great and perfect whole with all the parts related by a law of beauty, symmetry, and order. I seemed to be suspended in eternity. I lost consciousness of the world. When I came to I was changed. I experienced both an ecstasy and a torture—ecstasy in the beauty that had been revealed, torture in the throes of its revealment and realization."[44] In Mary Hambidge's vision, she has taken Jay's mathematical language of dynamic symmetry and moved toward a mystical perception of the world.

Mary Hambidge's writings display a woman developing a strong sense of independence, an extraordinary commitment to imaginative enterprises, and a fine capacity for thinking and reflecting. They express her struggle against materialism and the mechanistic structures of the world around her; in much of her writing, social constraints seem not to exist. Her voice comes across as alone yet harmonious with nature while yearning for a life of simplicity and a philosophy of creativity. She remained throughout an "apprentice" to the way of beauty she initially saw manifested in the lives of the weavers she had studied with in Greece.

Her intellectual forebears, as indicated by the various sources she quoted, and those compiled in *Apprentice in Creation*, include the romantic poets Percy Bysshe Shelley and William Wordsworth, who sought the sublime in nature, and the philosopher Alfred North Whitehead, who pursued the relationship between mathematics and metaphysics in a kind of process philosophy with interconnected constructs of matter, meaning, and time. Similarly influenced by transcendentalism, with its emphasis on nature and spirituality, she sought to create a kind of utopian community, uniting art and science. Resisting the corrosive effects of industrialism, she believed (like Thoreau) that only individuals, not political systems, could transform the world—but only when in close harmony with nature. Through self-fulfillment, and by surrounding oneself with like-minded people, it becomes possible to transcend social constraints. In addition, Mary Hambidge quotes her relative contemporary, the writer and diplomat Dag Hammarskjold (1905–1961), who on a more global stage struggled with some of the same questions Mary Hambidge contemplated. Hammarskjold, also a seeker of depth and meaning, writes, "I am being driven forward / Into an unknown land."[45] Indeed, *Markings*, the Hammarskjold journals, edited after his death by W. H. Auden in 1964, demonstrates a similarity in structure and substance to the collected writings of Mary Hambidge.

Establishing the Hambidge Center allowed Mary Hambidge to create a non-profit organization with dynamic symmetry at its core. In 1952, the mission of the Hambidge Center moved beyond the original concept of a self-sustaining community and was enlarged to include a working-artists retreat center. One of her most ardent students and advocates was Eliot Wigginton, who founded the Foxfire movement in Rabun County. As he was to say after her death: "Foxfire was born on her kitchen table, issue after issue came out of the little studio of mine, and when *The Foxfire Book* was published, I called her in the acknowledgements 'the most remarkable woman I have ever met.' I meant it."[46] Like many of her relationships, Hambidge's friendship with Eliot Wigginton developed tensions over time, mostly around issues of practicality and principle. Wigginton noted that as Foxfire began to highlight the "mountain people—a breed she had never really loved as a whole and never really felt deserved that much credit or attention," Hambidge became uneasy.[47] However, as with Wigginton, all those who encountered her were impressed by the strength and persistence of her convictions.[48] Indeed, her very personality sought to embody the theories she promoted, as people who knew her emphasized her "dynamism."[49]

With Mary Hambidge's deteriorating health, she turned over the foundation to the Hambidge Center's board to ensure continuity in its mission. After her death in 1973 at the age of eighty-eight, the Jay Hambidge Art Foundation was renamed the Hambidge Center for the Creative Arts and Sciences to honor the visions of both Jay and Mary Hambidge and to reflect more accurately its full scope and mission. The Hambidge Center began to focus its resources on its residency program and its role as a community-arts organization. Among the oldest artist residency programs in the United States, the Hambidge Center's mission supports the arts by providing individuals the setting, the solitude, and the time necessary for creativity while preserving the surrounding pristine natural environment. Under the direction of Mary Nikas Beery, a schedule of art, crafts, and music workshops emerged as well as activities promoting the study of nature.[50] Similar programs have continued into the present with subsequent directors, so that in the decades since Mary Hambidge's death, the Hambidge Center has expanded the number of artists served, as well as its own physical resources. New cottages, beyond the original log cabin, farmhouse, and gristmill, have been added; a pottery kiln and a pottery studio have been built, while several of the original buildings have been renovated or restored. The Hambidge Center, listed on the National Register of Historic Places as a rural historic district, serves as a natural repository for native plants and provides a protected site for endangered species.

The principles of dynamic symmetry, as Mary expanded on Jay Hambidge's artistic theories, became incorporated into a place dedicated to beauty, nature, and art. Always rebellious, she was bold enough to consider herself a visionary:

> I have the gift of second sight
> I see into the past.
> I see into the future.
> I see the destruction that could
> come if we let it.
> I see the beauty that would evolve
> if we mold it.[51]

Drawing from a past informed by the ancient Greeks, she insisted on creating a future with beauty at its center. Her desire for oneness with nature and her commitment to the principles of dynamic symmetry provided an interwoven texture of meaning throughout her life. Her dedication to the relationship between creativity and nature continues in the mission of the Hambidge Center. Further-

more, she prefigured environmental values and the necessity of sustainable living, beliefs she brought forward from the past into her own lifetime and which
are becoming increasingly more important in the twenty-first century. In these
ways, Mary Hambidge was indeed a visionary whose life work embodies the
desire to discover and sustain beauty, symmetry, and order.

NOTES

1. Nathan James, "What Did Mary Say?," *Brown's Guide to Georgia* 10, no. 10 (1982): 52.

2. Letter from Alfred Crovatt, Mary and Jay Hambidge Papers, 962:5 Atlanta History Center.

3. Mary Nikas Beery, "Mary Lee Crovatt Hambidge," unpublished manuscript, 4.

4. Quoted in Eliot Wigginton, *Mary Crovatt Hambidge* (Rabun Gap, Ga.: Hambidge Center,
n.d.), rpt. of issue of *Foxfire* 7, no. 3 (1973): 2.

5. Jay Hambidge was already married when he began his relationship with Mary Crovatt. This
essay refers to Jay as Mary's husband since that is how she referred to him.

6. Reprinted in Mary Hambidge, *Apprentice in Creation: The Way Is Beauty*, ed. Aspasia Voulis
(Rabun Gap, Ga.: Hambidge Center, 1973), 325.

7. Jay Hambidge, *Elements of Dynamic Symmetry* (New York: Brentano's Publishers, 1926), xviii.

8. Ibid., xix.

9. Claire Gaudet, "An Appreciation of Dynamic Symmetry by an English Critic," *The Diagonal* 1,
no. 6 (1920): 127–28.

10. Bo Emerson, "Reaching for the Stars, I Stumbled in a Sack of Wool, and inside Found the
Golden Fleece!," *Atlanta Journal-Constitution*, November 10, 1996, M3.

11. Eleanor Steele, later Eleanor Steele Reese, believed in the ideals she learned from Mary. As an
heiress, Eleanor provided Mary Hambidge with a monthly stipend to enable her to carry out her
vision until Mary's death, as indicated in Eleanor's correspondence. Eleanor Steele to Mary Hambidge, June 20, 1938, Mary and Jay Hambidge Papers, 962:52, Atlanta History Center.

12. "Mary Crovatt Hambidge and the Center She Founded," Mary and Jay Hambidge Papers,
962:41, Atlanta History Center.

13. Raymonde Alexander, "Georgia Mountains Inspire Creations by Top Designer," *Atlanta Constitution*, January 5, 1963, 21; Mary and Jay Hambidge Papers, 962:43, Atlanta History Center.

14. Virginia Gardner Troy, "The Great Weaver of Eternity," *Surface Design* 23, no. 4 (1999): 8.

15. Wigginton, *Mary Crovatt Hambidge*, 2.

16. Philis Alvic, *Weavers of the Southern Highlands* (Lexington: University of Kentucky Press,
2003), 108.

17. Lamar Q. Ball, "Making Fabrics by Hand," *Atlanta Constitution*, March 9, 1941, 10A; Mary and
Jay Hambidge Papers, 962:0S4.91, Atlanta History Center.

18. Mary Hambidge is quoted in St. John, Wylly Folk, "Weavers of Rabun . . ." *Atlanta Journal
Magazine*, October 10, 1948; Mary and Jay Hambidge Papers, 962:0S4.91, Atlanta History Center.

19. Ibid., 465.

20. Ritchie, "The Weavers of Rabun," *Sketches of Rabun County History* (n.p.: n.p., 1948), 415.

21. Mary Hambidge to George Parmly Day, April 29, 1946, Mary and Jay Hambidge Papers, 962:7,
Atlanta History Center.

22. Rabun Studios Card, Rabun Gap, Ga.: Weavers of Rabun, n.d.

23. Alexander, "Georgia Mountains Inspire Creations by Top Designer," 21.

24. Ibid., 21.

25. Alvic, *Weavers of the Southern Highlands*, 96.

26. Ibid., 96.

27. Jane Becker, *Selling Tradition: Appalachia and the Construction of an American Folk, 1930–1940* (Chapel Hill: University of North Carolina Press, 1998), 83.

28. See David E. Whisnant, *All That Is Native & Fine: The Politics of Culture in an American Region* (Chapel Hill: University of North Carolina Press, 2009).

29. "Society Woman Urges Loom in Every American Home," *Daily News*, March 1936; Mary and Jay Hambidge Papers, 962:0S4.91, Atlanta History Center.

30. Southern Highland Handicraft Guild Award is part of Mary's archive at the Atlanta History Center. Mary and Jay Hambidge Papers, 962:54, Atlanta History Center.

31. James, "What Did Mary Say?," 52–53.

32. Mary Hambidge to Mr. Zikakis, December 20, 1949, Mary and Jay Hambidge Papers, 962:7, Atlanta History Center.

33. Mary Hambidge, undated letter, Mary and Jay Hambidge Papers, 962:7, Atlanta History Center.

34. Quoted in Wigginton, *Mary Crovatt Hambidge*, 3.

35. Mary Hambidge, letter to George Parmly Day, April 29, 1946, Mary and Jay Hambidge Papers, 962:7, Atlanta History Center.

36. Wigginton, *Mary Crovatt Hambidge*, 5.

37. "Mary Crovatt Hambidge and the Center She Founded," Mary and Jay Hambidge Papers, 962:41, Atlanta History Center.

38. Hambidge, *Apprentice in Creation*, 323.

39. Ibid.

40. Wylly Folk St. John, "Weavers of Rabun . . ." *Atlanta Journal Magazine*, October, 10, 1948, 21; Mary and Jay Hambidge Papers, 962:0S4.91, Atlanta History Center.

41. Louis D. Rubin Jr., "Torchbook Introduction," *I'll Take My Stand* (New York: Harper and Row Publishers, 1962), viii–xiii.

42. Mary Hambidge, letter to Mr. Collins dated September 27, 1968.

43. Ibid., 39.

44. Ibid., 5.

45. Quoted in *Apprentice in Creation*, n.p.

46. Wigginton, *Mary Crovatt Hambidge*, 7.

47. Ibid., 8.

48. Eliot Wigginton first visited the Hambidge Center as a child with his father. He subsequently built a cottage and resided on Hambidge property. Wigginton founded *Foxfire* as a way to teach high school students at Rabun Gap–Nacoochee School basic writing skills. The students wrote stories they learned from their family about earlier eras in southern Appalachia. The magazines were eventually published as books and found a wide audience both in and outside the South, also serving as the basis for an award-winning play.

49. Alvic, *Weavers of the Southern Highlands*, 110.

50. An article in *Brown's Guide to Georgia* describes the difficulties the Hambidge Center faced in the decade following Mary's death. See James, "What Did Mary Say?," 50–55, 82–88.

51. Hambidge, *Apprentice in Creation*, 125.

Gertrude "Ma" Rainey
(1886–1939)

"Hear Me Talkin' to You"

STEVE GOODSON

They called her the "Mother of the Blues." At her peak, in the mid-1920s, Gertrude "Ma" Rainey toured with her company in a $13,000 Mack bus, her name proudly painted on the side.[1] Her bandleader, Thomas Dorsey, later recalled with a healthy measure of awe the power of her onstage presence:

> The room is filled with a haze of smoke, she walks into the spotlight, face decorated with Stein's Reddish Make-up Powder. She's not a young symmetrical streamed-lined type; her face seems to have discarded no less than fifty some years. She stands out high in front with a glorious bust, squeezed tightly in the middle. . . . When she started singing, the gold in her teeth would sparkle. . . . She possessed her listeners; they swayed, they rocked, they moaned and groaned, as they felt the blues with her.[2]

Gertrude Pridgett was born on April 26, 1886, in Columbus, Georgia, the second of five children. Her parents, Thomas and Ella (Allen) Pridgett, had come to Columbus from Alabama. Thomas died in 1896, a dismal year in a dreary decade for African Americans in Georgia. Political upheaval, wrenching economic distress, and widespread racial violence characterized the South of the 1890s, and 1896 stands out as the year in which the U.S. Supreme Court in effect authorized racial segregation with its infamous *Plessy v. Ferguson* decision. Gertrude would grow to adulthood in an increasingly stratified and volatile region. African American women at this time found themselves at the very bottom of the American racial hierarchy. Typically, in addition to the daily indignities of the Jim Crow system, they faced onerous low-wage employment (usually in domestic service); high rates of infant mortality and widowhood; vulnerability to the sexual advances of white male employers; and the serious problems that arose from living in neighborhoods that were the last to receive city services, such as water and proper sanitation.[3] But through her music—and in particular through a new musical style to which she helped give birth—Gertrude would assert her dignity, her autonomy, and her humanity, all the while tacitly encouraging her listeners to do the same.

The girl who would become Ma Rainey performed publicly for the first time at the age of fourteen as a member of a small troupe that appeared at Columbus's Springer Opera House. At seventeen, Pritchett married an older stage performer, William "Pa" Rainey. As a song-and-dance team, the couple worked for a dozen years in the traveling black tent shows that crisscrossed the South. They performed with many of the leading black minstrel troupes of the day—of which the Rabbit Foot and Silas Green companies were the best known—and frequently wintered in New Orleans, where Ma had the opportunity to sing with such jazz luminaries as Kid Ory, King Oliver, and Louis Armstrong. From 1914 to 1916 the couple appeared with Tolliver's Circus and Musical Extravaganza, billing themselves as "Rainey and Rainey, Assassinators of the Blues." Gertrude eventually headed her own shows, as "Madame Gertrude Rainey," though her moniker was eventually shortened to "Ma," in part because of her relationship with "Pa" Rainey, but also in fond recognition of her warm maternal nature. Her troupe, the Georgia Smart Set, included a female chorus line and a five-piece band.[4]

Perhaps of necessity on the tent-show circuit, she became a versatile performer, skilled as a dancer, a comedian, and a singer in a variety of styles. Her enduring fame, however, would come from her abilities with a new musical genre that developed simultaneously with her career. Some mystery surrounds the circumstances under which Ma first became acquainted with the blues. Musicologist John Wesley Work Jr. interviewed her in the late 1930s and learned that Rainey had "heard them [the blues] in 1902 in a small town in Missouri where she was appearing in a show under a tent. She tells of a girl from the town who came to the tent one morning and began to sing about the 'man' who had left her. The song was so strange and poignant that it attracted much attention. 'Ma' Rainey became so interested that she learned the song from the visitor, and used it soon afterwards in her 'act' as an encore." The audience reacted so enthusiastically to the new song that Ma began to highlight it in her shows. According to the interview, after she had repeatedly been asked what type of song this was, "one day she replied, in a moment of inspiration, 'It's the *Blues*.'"[5]

Scholars have questioned the dating of the story—1902 might have been placing the incident a bit early—and are skeptical of Rainey's claim to have named the blues. But the gist of the story seems to be true, meaning that Rainey "served as both midwife to the new music and as an important early champion."[6] She thus

GERTRUDE "MA" RAINEY
at the peak of her career.
Ma Rainey House, Columbus, Ga.

became "the single or at least the earliest link between the male country blues artists who roamed the streets and back roads of the South and their female counterparts," opening a rich if relatively short-lived era of successful female blues singers.[7]

Descended from the communal spirituals and work shouts of slavery, blues
originated in the rural Deep South near the end of the nineteenth century. This
new musical form served the needs of men and women who experienced the
grinding economic and social realities of an impoverished region that remained
fiercely committed to the principle of white supremacy. Any number of performers, listeners, and scholars have attempted to capture in words the essence of this
powerfully expressive style. British chronicler Paul Oliver sees the blues as "a
state of mind" and the "music which expresses this condition. The blues reflect
the cry of the forgotten man and woman, the shout for freedom, the boast of the
virile man, the wrath of the frustrated, and the ironical chuckle of the fatalist; but
this is not all: they also reflect the agony of insecurity, the poverty and hunger of
the workless, the despair of the bereaved and the cryptic humour of the cynic."[8]
Like countless others, Thomas Dorsey grounded the blues in human relationships: "It would be hard to explain to anyone who has never had a love craving,
or had someone they loved dearly to forsake them for another, a wounded heart,
a troubled mind, a longing for someone you do not have with you, and many
other things I could mention."[9] Perhaps musician/producer Willie Dixon cut to
the quick of the issue: "The blues ain't nothing but the facts of life."[10]

Despite this grim foundation rooted in bleak realities, commentators have
stressed that the ultimate purpose of the blues is transcendence—of poverty,
of oppression, of personal isolation and frustration. According to famed African American poet Langston Hughes, "The blues are sad songs, but with an
undercurrent of hope and determination in them. Thus it was with Negro life
for a long time, with pools of prejudice and segregation at the doorstep, but
with hope and determination always there."[11] James Baldwin went even further,
claiming that "the acceptance of this anguish one finds in the blues, and the
expression of it, creates also, however odd this may sound, a kind of joy."[12]

Numerous writers have noted the parallels between the blues and the church,
between the blues singer and the preacher. Historian Lawrence Levine observes
that "blues performed some of the functions for the secularized masses that religion did: it spoke out of a group experience; it made many individual problems—
dislocation, loneliness, broken families, economic difficulties—seem more common and converted them into shared experiences."[13] Musician Sidney Bechet
saw strong similarities between African American spirituals and the blues: "One
was praying to God and the other was praying to what's human. It's like one was
saying, 'Oh God, let me go,' and the other was saying, 'Oh, Mister, let me be.' And

they were both the same thing in a way; they were both my people's way of pray-ing to be themselves, praying to be let alone so they could be human."[14]

Whatever the power of the new music, however, some individuals doubted its commercial appeal. While black performers of other styles were being re-corded by the early 1890s, record companies proved unwilling to sign black blues artists before 1920. Multitalented performer, songwriter, and promoter Perry Bradford worked indefatigably to change the minds of white executives, insisting that "fourteen million Negroes . . . will buy records if recorded by one of their own." After being turned down by Victor and Columbia, Bradford fi-nally broke through with the smaller Okeh Company, for which, in February 1920, Mamie Smith recorded "That Thing Called Love" and "You Can't Keep a Good Man Down." The record sold stunningly well—even without any efforts on Okeh's part to promote it—and on August 10 of the same year Smith found herself hurried back into the studio to make her historic recording of "Crazy Blues." This record also sold phenomenally—seventy-five thousand copies the first month and more than one million within a year. Suddenly, a rush was on to record black artists, and company after company entered the market to release what were tellingly listed and promoted as "Race" records.[15]

The women who would go on to be acclaimed as the greatest female blues singers of the decade—Ma Rainey and Chattanooga native Bessie Smith—would have to wait until 1923 for their opportunities to make records. By the early twenties the two women had known each other for more than a decade, having worked together in southern venues such as Atlanta's 81 Theatre. Ac-counts of Rainey's influence on Smith vary—there was even a widely circulated but apocryphal story that Rainey had kidnapped the young Smith and molded her into a star. In any case, Smith did later concede her debt to Rainey's style, remarking that the first time she heard Ma perform "she proceeded to cry all over the place."[16] Still, Smith reached the studio first, in February 1923, and, as it turned out, inadvertently did much to guarantee her legacy by committing her-self to Columbia Records. Eight decades later, her recordings maintain a warmth and clarity that Rainey's reissues would never achieve. Thirty-seven-year-old Ma Rainey, on the other hand, who cut her first eight records in Chicago in December of 1923, signed with Paramount, a company that played a leading role in the distribution of race music but which produced a technologically inferior product. Even in their most recently remastered form, Rainey's recordings often sound as if they were made at the far end of a corridor, behind a closed door.[17]

Both women sang in a style that has come to be known as the "Classic Blues." Rainey's biographer Sandra Lieb emphasizes how this genre differed from the rural "country blues" of the Deep South:

In contrast to the improvised and traditional nature of early country blues, the Classic Blues . . . were a highly sophisticated form of paid entertainment, sung by professional women performers who had years of experience in tent shows and who could act, dance, and do comedy as well as sing. Instead of being drifters or neighbors who sang for local parties on Saturday night, the blues "queens" were self-conscious stars; they wore makeup, elaborate gowns, and jewelry, and they appeared in traveling revues complete with a stage and footlights. . . . Unlike folk blues singers, Classic Blues singers did not accompany themselves, and their accompanists were usually solo pianists or jazz bands composed of music hall professionals, rather than harmonica players and guitarists.[18]

The audience for this new style of music was swelled by the Great Migration, the mass movement of hundreds of thousands of African Americans from their homes in the poor and segregated South to the industrial cities of the North. The shift from ancestral rural homeland to the factories and teeming streets of the big city could be wrenching and alienating. For all of the opportunities for economic progress that the North offered, such a dramatic relocation often brought a keen longing for what had been left behind. Ma Rainey, Bessie Smith, and their counterparts provided a cultural bridge that helped these men and women hang onto the "old ways . . . precisely at the time when they were attempting to adjust to the city where such ways were held in disdain."[19] This burgeoning audience, along with the new eagerness of the record companies to reach them, helped produce what one scholar has termed the "blues decade," a brief moment in which black—and even white—audiences responded to exciting music rooted in the African American South: "At no time before or since has there been as much attention concentrated on the idiom either in sheer recording output, live performances, or creative composition and arrangement."[20]

If the Classic Blues represented in part a creative tug of war between the country blues of the South and the more sophisticated commercialism of the urban North, Ma Rainey played a key role in keeping the music moored to its roots. She—and to a lesser extent, Bessie Smith—helped tilt the recorded music toward the "rural, downhome, 'moanin'" style of the blues, a trend that would accelerate as the twenties wore on.[21] Rainey, "steeped in the folk blues of her people," served as the "prime link between country blues and black show business" and, along with other Classic Blues singers, "transform[ed] a folk tradition to popular art."[22]

Rainey's career took off quickly after the release of her first recordings. In 1924 she recorded eighteen additional sides, which Paramount publicized heavily in the African American press. Paramount also booked Rainey on a tour of the southern and midwestern theaters linked by the Theater Owners' Book-ing Agency (TOBA). Organized in 1909, at its peak TOBA placed African American performers on a circuit that included some sixty-seven theaters that offered a wide array of variety entertainment at ticket prices of twenty-five cents to a dollar a show. In need of a band to accompany her on tour, Rainey hired Thomas Dorsey, a native of Villa Rica, Georgia, and an accomplished blues pianist, songwriter, and arranger. Dorsey put together the Wildcats Jazz Band, which included, in addition to Dorsey on piano, musicians who played the saxophone, clarinet, trombone, and drums.[23]

From his vantage point at the head of the band, Dorsey provided the most vivid and detailed descriptions of Ma Rainey on stage. The 1924 tour opened at Chicago's Grand Theater, one of the Southside's prominent venues. There was some preshow apprehension about her appearance in a large city outside of her southern stomping grounds, so Paramount cautiously downplayed her on the program as an added attraction. Dorsey recalled, "I don't think Ma had ever appeared in Chicago. The only singing she did around Chicago was for the record company. . . . We felt that if we had an opening in Chicago, it would give us a good tryout for the show before we hit the circuit. . . . She had fame, but . . . she wanted to get into a big theater where there was going to be a crowd."[24] The results, as Dorsey recalled, were spectacular:

> I shall never forget the excited feeling when the orchestra in the pit struck up her opening theme, music which I had written especially for the show. The curtain rose slowly. . . . Ma was hidden in a big box-like affair built like an old Victrola. . . . A girl would come out and put a big record on it. Then the band picked up the Moonshine Blues. Ma would sing a few bars inside the Victrola. Then she would open the door and step out into the spotlight with her glittering gown that weighed twenty pounds and wearing a necklace of five, ten and twenty dollar gold-pieces. The house went wild. It was as if the show had started all over again. Ma had the audience in the palm of her hand. Her diamonds flashed like sparks of fire falling from her fingers. The gold-piece necklace lay like a golden armor covering her chest. They called her the lady with the golden throat. . . . When Ma had sung her last number and the grand finale, we took seven [curtain] calls.[25]

The 1920s did not "roar" for all Americans, but—for a while—they certainly roared for Ma Rainey. When she appeared again at the Grand in January 1925, "audiences lined up from the box office to the streetcar tracks."[26]

The years 1924 to 1928 marked the peak of Rainey's career. She toured the TOBA circuit, appeared in independent engagements, and recorded in Chicago. By the time she made her final recording in 1928, she had cut more than ninety-two sides for Paramount. Although she demonstrated her versatility as a singer and songwriter by performing in a variety of styles, most of her songs embodied blues structures and imagery. Remarkably for any recording artist of this period, but especially for an African American female artist, Rainey wrote or co-wrote about half of the songs that she recorded. Whether composed by herself or by others, however, her recordings are characterized by certain persistent themes. By examining these themes, we can get an idea of the issues that were important not only to Rainey herself but to the audiences that attended her shows and bought her records.

References to alcohol, for example, appear frequently in her work. Rainey made all of her records during the period of national Prohibition, but the musical world she created is awash in liquor and beer. The characters who populate her songs drink for a variety of reasons. Sometimes alcohol provides the fuel for a sexually adventurous lifestyle:

> Papa likes his bourbon, mama likes her gin
> Papa likes his bourbon, mama likes her gin
> Papa likes his outside women, mama like her outside men
> ("Barrel House Blues")[27]

Alcohol also serves in Rainey's songs as a desperately needed means of easing stress and anxiety. In "Dead Drunk Blues," the song's narrator vows, "Daddy, I'm going to get drunk just one more time. . . . 'Cause when I'm drunk, nothing's gonna worry my mind."[28] In "Dream Blues," liquor provides a respite from tormented nights:

> Had a dream last night and the night before
> Had a dream last night and the night before
> Gonna get drunk now, I won't dream no more[29]

The grim pitfalls of drinking can sometimes spark a resolve to quit:

> I been drinkin' all night, babe, and the night before
> But when I get sober, I ain't gonna drink no more
> 'Cause my friend left me, standin' in my door
> ("Moonshine Blues")[30]

A frequent accompaniment of alcohol, and another pervasive presence in Rainey's fictional world, is violence. It can come as the result of male abuse, as in "Black Eye Blues":

> Nancy and her man had just had a fight
> He beat Miss Nancy 'cross the head[31]

It can be directed at a rival, as in "Black Dust Blues," in which one woman places a curse on another:

> It was way last year when my trouble began
> It was way last year when my trouble began
> I had a fuss with a woman, she said I took her man
>
> She sent me a letter, says she's gonna turn me down
> She sent me a letter, says she's gonna turn me down
> She's gonna fix me up so I won't chase her man around[32]

In a number of Rainey's songs the violence has fatal consequences:

> I walked in my room the other night
> My man walked in and begin to fight
>
> I took my gun in my right hand,
> "Hold him, folks, I don't wanta kill my man."
>
> When I did that, he hit me 'cross my head
> First shot I fired, my man fell dead
>   ("Cell Bound Blues")[33]

In one striking song, coauthored by Rainey, serious domestic violence is discounted by a grateful lover:

> I woke up this mornin', my head was sore as a boil
> I woke up this mornin', my head was sore as a boil
> My man beat me last night with five feet of copper coil
>
> He keeps my lips split, my eyes as black as jet
> He keeps my lips split, my eyes as black as jet
> But the way he love me makes me soon forget
>   ("Sweet Rough Man")[34]

A constant backdrop in this world of drinking and violence is a callously repressive justice system, designed and operated exclusively by whites. Jail or the risk of arrest is a common concern in the songs concerning alcohol:

> Went to bed last night and, folks, I was in my tea
> I went to bed last night and I was in my tea
> Woke up this morning, the police was shaking me. . . .
>
> They carried me to the courthouse, Lordy, how I was cryin'
> They carried me to the courthouse, Lordy, how I was cryin'
> They give me sixty days in the jail and money couldn't pay my fine

> Sixty days ain't long when you can spend them as you choose
> Sixty days ain't long when you can spend them as you choose
> But they seem like years in a cell where there ain't no booze
> ("Booze and Blues")[35]

Another ominous possibility was relegation to the chain gang:

> The judge found me guilty, the clerk he wrote it down
> The judge found me guilty, the clerk he wrote it down
> Just a poor gal in trouble, I know I'm county road bound
>
> Many days of sorrow, many nights of woe
> Many days of sorrow, many nights of woe
> And a ball and chain, everywhere I go
> ("Chain Gang Blues")[36]

By far the most common theme in Rainey's work, however, is the troubled nature of the interactions between women and men. More than half of her recordings deal with broken relationships. In some two dozen songs, a man has abandoned the narrator to loneliness and longing. In "Army Camp Harmony Blues," for example:

> My man is leavin', cryin' won't make him stay
> Lord, my man is leavin', cryin' won't make him stay
> If cryin'd do any good, I'd cry my poor self away[37]

Such abandonment can have harsh economic consequences, as in the musically upbeat "Lawd, Send Me a Man Blues":

> Who gonna pay my board bill now?
> Had a good man, and he turned me down
> Landlord comin', knock on my door
> I told him my good man don't stay here no more[38]

Of course, a man who does not leave can be problematic as well. He can stay out late, drink heavily, cheat, or ignore his partner. The man in "Don't Fish in My Sea," one of the few songs co-written by Rainey and Bessie Smith, is guilty of all of these failings:

> My daddy come home late this mornin', drunk as he could be
> My daddy come home late this mornin', drunk as he could be
> I know my daddy's done gone bad on me
>
> He used to stay out late, now he don't come home at all
> He used to stay out late, now he don't come home at all
> I know there's another mule been kickin' in my stall

> I ain't had no lovin' since God knows when
> I ain't had no lovin' since God knows when
> That's the reason I'm through with these no-good triflin' men[39]

As this final stanza suggests, however, a mistreated woman has choices, and Rainey lays out many of these options in her recordings.[40] The abused partner can swear off men entirely, as the narrator above does, or she can go out and find another man, like the narrator in Rainey's self-penned "Little Low Mama Blues," who wavers between complete despair and the defiant conviction that "I'm little and low, can get a man anywhere I go."[41] As a body, Rainey's recordings range between these poles of passive heartache and confident agency. Crying is one option, as in "Those All Night Long Blues":

> All night long, all night long, there's just one man on my mind
> Can't sleep a wink at night for cryin'
> All night long, Lord, my worries just renews
> And I suffer with those all night blues[42]

Sometimes the misery is such that it threatens mental stability:

> Here I'm upon my knees, play that again for me
> 'Cause I'm about to be losin' my mind
>
> Boys, I can't stand up, can't sit down
> The man I love is done left town
>
> I feel like screamin', I feel like cryin'
> Lord, I've been mistreated, folks, and don't mind dyin'
>   ("Moonshine Blues")[43]

And can even lead to thoughts of suicide:

> I felt like going on the mountain, jumping over in the sea
> I felt like going on the mountain, jumping over in the sea
> When my daddy stay out late, he don't care a thing 'bout me
>   ("Deep Moaning Blues")[44]

Movement is a very common response to unhappiness in Rainey's songs, many of which involve tramping the urban sidewalks:

> Lord, what's the matter, mama can't be treated just right
> Lord, what's the matter, mama can't be treated just right
> Got my clothes in my hand, walk the streets all night
>   ("Runaway Blues")[45]

Frequently, in this age of newly increased mobility, the narrator flees her troubles by taking to the rails:

> Lord, I wants my ticket, show me my train
> I wants my ticket, show me my train
> I'm gonna ride till I can't hear them call your name
> ("Grievin' Hearted Blues")[46]

Sometimes the trip leads back home:

> Done bought my ticket, Lord, and my trunk is packed
> Goin' back to Georgia, folks, I sure ain't comin' back
> ("South Bound Blues")[47]

On the other hand, in many of Rainey's recordings the woman takes a more assertive role. The train rides are not always flight from heartbreak. Some of her narrators leave the men who mistreat them:

> I wade in the water, walk through the ice and snow
> I wade in the water, I walk through the ice and snow
> But from now on, papa, I won't be your dog no more
> ("Bessemer Bound Blues")[48]

While others set out to track down the men who abandoned them:

> When I get through drinkin' gon' buy a Gatlin gun
> Find my man, he better hitch up and run
> 'Cause I'm leavin' this mornin', I'm leavin' this mornin'
> I'm going to Kansas City to bring Jim Jackson home
> ("Leavin' This Morning")[49]

Occasionally the narrator warns her man that he'll want her back someday, as in "Oh Papa Blues":

> You're going to miss me, you'll long to kiss me
> You'll 'gret the day that you ever quit me[50]

By no means did all of Rainey's recordings deal with conventional male-female romance. At least one song—"Prove It On Me Blues," written by Rainey—concerns a lesbian relationship:

> Went out last night, had a great big fight
> Everything seemed to go on wrong
> I looked up, to my surprise
> The gal I was with was gone

> They say I do it, ain't nobody caught me
> Sure got to prove it on me
> Went out last night with a crowd of my friends
> They must've been women, 'cause I don't like no men[51]

In another recording—"Sissy Blues," composed by Thomas Dorsey—the narrator's heterosexual relationship is broken up by another man. This song contains some of the most sexually explicit lyrics in Rainey's catalogue:

> My man's got a sissy, his name is Miss Kate
> He shook that thing like jelly on a plate
> Now all the people ask me why I'm all alone
> A sissy shook that thing and took my man from home[52]

And in one of her most moving recordings—"Hustlin' Blues" (co-written by Dorsey)—a prostitute is desperate enough to seek legal protection from her pimp:

> It's rainin' out here and tricks ain't walkin' tonight
> It's rainin' out here and tricks ain't walkin' tonight
> I'm goin' home, I know I've got to fight
> If you hit me tonight, let me tell you what I'm going to do
> If you hit me tonight, let me tell you what I'm going to do
> I'm gonna take you to court and tell the judge on you
> Oh, judge, tell him I'm through
> Oh, judge, tell him I'm through
> I'm tired of this life, that's why I brought him to you[53]

So many of Rainey's songs deal with women's responses to strained or damaged relationships that some scholars have viewed her as a socially conscious artist who took it as her mission to dispense hard-won wisdom and coping strategies to her female listeners. Biographer Sandra Lieb writes, "It is my contention that the body of Ma Rainey's recorded songs constitutes a message to women, explaining quite clearly how to deal with reverses in love and how to interpret other areas of life."[54] Similarly, Daphne Duval Harrison argues that 1920s female blues singers "were able to capture in song the sensibilities of black women—North and South—who struggled daily for physical, psychological, and spiritual balance. They did this by calling forth the demons that plagued women and exorcising them in public. Alienation, sex and sexuality, tortured love, loneliness, hard times, marginality, were addressed with an openness that had not previously existed."[55] In the process, according to Angela Y. Davis, "women's blues provided a cultural space for community-building among working-class black women," a space in which these "women were able to autonomously work out . . . a working-class model of womanhood."[56]

Such claims certainly have validity, but we should not allow our recognition of the powerful feminist themes in Rainey's music to constrain our sense of the broader scope and importance of her work. Like any great artist, she produced material rich enough to bear multiple interpretations and to speak to varied audiences and their needs. Richard K. Spottswood notes that Rainey's recordings "were deeply imbued with her own personality and outlook—that of the weary veteran who's been there and seen it all, whose vulnerability to pain and heartbreak is tempered by a residual toughness, if not cynicism, that gives her blues universality and timelessness."[57] These qualities of "universality and timelessness" are well worth emphasizing, as they indicate why Rainey's music remains powerful to listeners today, long after the original social and historical context in which it was created have passed. As much as these songs are about black migrants from the South, the travails of working-class black women, and the 1920s, they are also—in a broader sense—about what it is to be a human being of whatever gender or race in any time. So while Sterling Brown's famous poem "Ma Rainey" specifically concerns the heartfelt connection that southern African Americans felt with the singer ("She jes' catch hold of us, somekindaway"), Brown's lines suggest how Rainey's work could be meaningful to anyone living out their existence in this troubled and troubling world:

> O Ma Rainey,
> Sing yo' song;
> Now you's back
> Whah you belong,
> Git way inside us,
> Keep us strong . . .
> O Ma Rainey,
> Li'l an' low;
> Sing us 'bout de hard luck
> Roun' our do';
> Sing us 'bout de lonesome road
> We mus' go . . .[58]

Whatever the true nature of her appeal to her contemporaries, however, Rainey's commercial viability could not withstand the cultural, technological, and economic hammer blows delivered in the late 1920s and early 1930s. Records, radio, and talking motion pictures offered deadly competition to the theatrical circuits in which Rainey graced the stage. In addition, the ever-continuing centralization of the American commercial entertainment industry meant the increasing dominance of white middle-class tastes and the squeezing out of minority genres and performers. Even the record companies that continued to record blues began emphasizing male over female performers because, ironically, male artists could be had more cheaply than could popular female performers such as Rainey.[59] Most damaging of all was the onset of the Great Depression, which decimated the recording business: record sales fell from more than $100 million in 1927 to $6 million in 1933. African American artists in particular faced complete disaster—the average sale of a "race" record declined from ten thousand copies in the mid-1920s to two thousand in 1930 and then to four hundred in 1932.[60] Paramount, Rainey's label, collapsed altogether, as did the TOBA circuit, which closed its doors for good in 1930.[61]

Under such dire conditions, Rainey's career could not help but suffer. Her recording career over after 1928, Rainey continued to tour the South but in increasingly constricted circumstances. Though her talent remained, the trappings faded, as her luxurious touring bus gave way to a patched-together house trailer, and imitation pearls replaced the gold coins on her necklace. Falling income made it difficult for her to maintain her reputation as a generous employer, and low wages and primitive touring conditions drove away band members. When her sister Malissa died in 1935, Rainey gave up the road and retired to her hometown of Columbus, Georgia, to live in a house she had built for her family.[62]

Fortunately, Ma Rainey had saved during her flush times and remained a shrewd businesswoman. Though her fame and performing career had ended, she purchased and ran two theaters in Rome, Georgia. She also became an active member of the Friendship Baptist Church, of which her brother was a deacon. Four years after her return to Columbus, however, on December 22, 1939, Rainey died of heart disease. She was laid to rest in the family plot in Columbus's Porterdale Cemetery. "With her," notes William Barlow, "passed the era of the traveling black minstrel troupes, as well as one of the most compelling blues styles ever captured on record."[63]

In recent decades, Ma Rainey has rebounded from obscurity as scholars, artists, civic agencies, and new generations of fans have celebrated her legacy. In 1994 the U.S. Postal Service honored Rainey on a postage stamp, and in the first decade of the twenty-first century Columbus used city and federal funds, along with money raised during a 1997 benefit concert by blues legend B. B. King, to rescue and restore her home, which is now open to the public.[64]

A significant tribute to Rainey came in the form of a 1982 play by Pulitzer Prize–winning playwright August Wilson. *Ma Rainey's Black Bottom* is set at a

1927 recording session in Chicago. At one point in the play, Ma Rainey's character attempts to explain the blues:

> I never could stand no silence. I always got to have some music going on in my head somewhere. It keeps things balanced. Music will do that. It fills things up. The more music you got in the world, the fuller it is. . . . White folks don't understand about the blues. They hear it come out, but they don't know how it got there. They don't understand that's life's way of talking. You don't sing to feel better. You sing 'cause that's a way of understanding life. . . . The blues help you get out of bed in the morning. You get up knowing you ain't alone. There's something else in the world. Something's been added by that song. This be an empty world without the blues. I take that emptiness and try to fill it up with something.[65]

More than seven decades after she breathed her last at age fifty-three, our lives are still fuller because of Ma Rainey and her music.

NOTES

1. Sandra Lieb, *Mother of the Blues: A Study of Ma Rainey* (Amherst: University of Massachusetts Press, 1981), 39. I rely heavily upon Lieb's fine book for Rainey's biographical information.

2. Quoted in Michael W. Harris, *The Rise of Gospel Blues: The Music of Thomas Andrew Dorsey in the Urban Church* (New York: Oxford University Press, 1992), 89.

3. Jacqueline Jones, *Labor of Love, Labor of Sorrow: Black Women, Work, and the Family from Slavery to the Present* (New York: Basic Books, 1985), chap. 4.

4. Lieb, *Mother of the Blues*, 1–10; William Barlow, *"Looking Up at Down": The Emergence of Blues Culture* (Philadelphia: Temple University Press, 1989), 155–56. Lieb states that Rainey was eighteen at the time of her marriage, but the date she gives for the marriage—February 2, 1904—would have meant that the new bride was still two-and-a-half months short of her eighteenth birthday. Lieb also notes that Ma's "relationship with Pa becomes very shadowy after their early collaboration. . . . At some point they adopted a son, Danny, who worked as a dancer in the show. . . . Apparently in the late teens the Raineys separated and Pa died; Ma was later remarried to a younger man not connected with show business, who sometimes accompanied her on tour" (*Mother of the Blues*, 18).

5. Quoted in Lieb, *Mother of the Blues*, 1–3.

6. Richard K. Spottswood, "Country Girls, Classic Blues, and Vaudeville Voices: Women and the Blues," in *Nothing But the Blues: The Music and the Musicians*, ed. Lawrence Cohn (New York: Abbeville Press, 1993), 93.

7. Chris Albertson, *Bessie* (New York: Stein and Day, 1972), 26; Spottswood, "Country Girls," 105.

8. Paraphrased by Derrick Stewart-Baxter, *Ma Rainey and the Classic Blues Singers* (New York: Stein and Day, 1970), 8.

9. Harris, *Rise of the Gospel Blues*, 60.

10. Daphne Duval Harrison, *Black Pearls: Blues Queens of the 1920s* (New Brunswick: Rutgers University Press, 1988), 6.

11. Quoted in Angela Y. Davis, *Blues Legacies and Black Feminism: Gertrude "Ma" Rainey, Bessie Smith, and Billie Holiday* (New York: Pantheon, 1998), 145.

12. Quoted in Harrison, *Black Pearls*, 64–65.

13. Lawrence W. Levine, *Black Culture and Black Consciousness: Afro-American Folk Thought from Slavery to Freedom* (Oxford: Oxford University Press, 1977), 235. See also Harris, *Rise of the Gospel Blues*, 60.

14. Quoted in Levine, *Black Culture and Black Consciousness*, 236–37.

15. Barlow, *"Looking Up at Down,"* 127–28; Harrison, *Black Pearls*, 44–49. The Bradford quote is from Barlow, *"Looking Up at Down,"* 127.

16. Michelle R. Scott, *Blues Empress in Black Chattanooga: Bessie Smith and the Emerging Urban South* (Urbana: University of Illinois Press, 2008), 114, 119–20; Albertson, *Bessie*, 27; Lieb, *Mother of the Blues*, 15–16.

17. Lieb, *Mother of the Blues*, 20–23; Spottswood, "Country Girls," 93–95.

18. Lieb, *Mother of the Blues*, 60. See also Stewart-Baxter, *Ma Rainey*, 6–8; and Jeff Todd Titon, *Early Downhome Blues: A Musical and Cultural Analysis* (Chapel Hill: University of North Carolina Press, 1994), xvi–xviii.

19. Harris, *Rise of the Gospel Blues*, 60; Lieb, *Mother of the Blues*, 169.

20. Harrison, *Black Pearls*, 220; Lieb, *Mother of the Blues*, 45, 165.

21. Harris, *Rise of the Gospel Blues*, 91; Lieb, *Mother of the Blues*, 77–78, 165–66; Stewart-Baxter, *Ma Rainey*, 35, 42; Spottswood, "Country Girls," 92–93.

22. Spottswood, "Country Girls," 93; Lieb, *Mother of the Blues*, 165; Harrison, *Black Pearls*, 219.

23. Lieb, *Mother of the Blues*, 25–30; Harrison, *Black Pearls*, 17, 23–24.

24. Harris, *Rise of the Gospel Blues*, 87–88.

25. Quoted in Lieb, *Mother of the Blues*, 28–30.

26. Ibid., 36.

27. Quoted song lyrics are from Davis, *Blues Legacies and Black Feminism*. For "Barrell House Blues," see pp. 200–201.

28. Davis, *Blues Legacies and Black Feminism*, 213.

29. Ibid., 215.

30. Ibid., 234.

31. Ibid., 204.

32. Ibid., 203.

33. Ibid., 210

34. Ibid., 247.

35. Ibid., 208.

36. Ibid., 210–11.

37. Ibid., 200.

38. Ibid., 225.

39. Ibid., 214.

40. Sandra Lieb stresses this point in *Mother of the Blues*. See, for example, p. 128.

41. Davis, *Blues Legacies and Black Feminism*, 227.

42. Ibid., 248.

43. Ibid., 234.

44. Ibid., 213–14.

45. Ibid., 239.

46. Ibid., 221.

47. Ibid., 245–46.

48. Ibid., 201.

49. Ibid., 226.

50. Ibid., 237–38.

51. Ibid., 238.

52. Ibid., 242–43.

53. Ibid., 222–23.

54. Lieb, *Mother of the Blues*, xvi.

55. Harrison, *Black Pearls*, 221.

56. Davis, *Blues Legacies and Black Feminism*, 44, 46. Similarly, Hazel V. Carby argues: "The blues women did not passively reflect the vast social changes of their time; they provided new ways of thinking about these changes, alternative conceptions of the physical and social world for their audience of migrating and urban women and men, and social models for women who aspired to escape from and improve their condition of existence" (*Cultures in Babylon: Black Britain and African America* [London: Verso, 1999], 36; see also 8, 10, 14, 18).

57. Spottswood, "Country Girls," 93.

58. Quoted in Davis, *Blues Legacies and Black Feminism*, 140.

59. Lieb, *Mother of the Blues*, 37–40.

60. Barlow, *"Looking Up at Down,"* 133.

61. Lieb, *Mother of the Blues*, 44.

62. Ibid., 46–47.

63. Barlow, *"Looking Up at Down,"* 164; Lieb, *Mother of the Blues*, 46–48.

64. Sheila Dewan, "Columbus Journal: After Years of Neglect, Rebirth for a Blues Singer's House," *New York Times*, March 28, 2008, http://www.nytimes.com/2008/03/28/us/28rainey.html?emc=eta1#.

65. August Wilson, *Ma Rainey's Black Bottom: A Play in Two Acts* (New York: Plume Books, 1985): 82–83.

Lillian Smith

(1887–1966)

Humanist

JOHN C. INSCOE

What accounts for the fascination that Lillian Smith continues to evoke among southern scholars today? Hers was a unique voice in the mid-twentieth century that was ahead of its time in terms of the hard truths and harsh judgments she poured out about the inequities and injustices of southern society, first and foremost in terms of race, but she also touched on other facets of southern life, including politics, gender, religion, and economics. No other white southerner of her generation was as openly and unabashedly critical of the region and its inherent flaws. In that volatile era in which Jim Crow's strange career began to wane as an emergent civil rights movement made itself felt, Smith should have been a major player. And yet, despite the celebrity derived from her sensationalistic (some would say scandalous) first novel, *Strange Fruit*, in 1944, and her nonfiction jeremiad *Killers of the Dream* in 1949, she found herself increasingly marginalized or ignored as the great national discussions over civil rights and racial justice reached full volume.

Smith greatly resented the fact that her voice was not more fully heard or acknowledged. She once likened herself to Cassandra, the mythic Trojan princess blessed with a gift of prophecy but cursed to never be believed. Margaret Rose Gladney appropriately titled her edited collection of Smith's correspondence *How Am I to Be Heard?*, a reference to Smith's constant frustration in her latter years.[1] She seemed genuinely hurt when she wrote in the early 1960s: "When southern writers are discussed, I am never mentioned; when women writers are mentioned, I am not among them . . . Whom, among the mighty, have I so greatly offended."[2] One could argue that it was because she had offended so many of those "mighty" that she never fully enjoyed the credit or acclaim she rightly deserved. Her no-holds-barred, take-no-prisoners critiques were never aimed only at the rabid racists and political conservatives who would have been the most obvious targets of her wrath; she also took on those southern moderates who might well have been her allies and promoters had she not been so quick to condemn them for their failure to express the same level of urgency and moral outrage that she herself did.[3] Perhaps even more frustrating was the failure of African Americans to give her what she felt was her due, though she rarely—if ever—acknowledged their neglect or their criticism of her work.[4]

Yet since her death in 1966, no other Georgia woman, other than perhaps Flannery O'Connor, has inspired as much scholarly attention and analysis as has Lillian Smith; certainly no other southern liberal of her era has been scrutinized as fully by as many historians.[5] I would argue that much of this ongoing fascination with Smith lies in the power of her prose. Few others brought as much passion, as much anger, as much emotional fervor to their writing. She had a flair for metaphor, analogy, parables, anecdotes, and other forms of literary expression, and used them all as much to probe the southern psyche as to condemn the region's institutions and social practices. Much of what so distinguished Smith's writing is that she conveyed often familiar truths about the South and its sins in such intimate and yet compelling terms. To some, her rhetorical flourishes often overwhelmed her message. As one critic noted of *Killers of the Dream*, "Reading it is somewhat like eating seven courses of soufflé."[6]

But even more vital to the power of Smith's work, I would suggest, is the sheer humanity that pervades it all. Her contemporaries often stressed the stridency and uncompromising condemnation that she poured out with such vim, vigor, and vitriol. Atlanta journalist Ralph McGill called her "a modern, feminine counterpart of the ancient Hebrew prophets Amos, Hosea, Isaiah and Micah." Virginius Dabney saw her as a southern version of that most radical of northern abolitionists, William Lloyd Garrison. Far more recently, Fred Hobson noted that Smith saw the South "as virtually a nightmare society, a culture nearly as dark as that portrayed by Hawthorne as he looked back on his harsh ancestral Puritan New England."[7]

Yet what her fellow southern liberals seemed to overlook (though certainly not Hobson and other recent scholars) were the remarkably fresh, vividly rendered emotional and psychological insights that distinguish the best of her work. No one else was so adept at interweaving personal feelings and experiences with regional and even universal truths. Regardless of how shrill, caustic, or unrelenting she or her "volcanic temperament" appeared to her contemporaries, what we take from her work now are those profoundly human and humane observations that remain as poignant and meaningful as they should have been to readers at the time. Sometimes these are conveyed in intimate anec-

LILLIAN SMITH
Courtesy of the Hargrett Rare Book and Manuscript
Library, University of Georgia Libraries.

dotes of personal experiences and encounters, and sometimes in more abstract, imaginative form, which proved equally effective because she kept the human dimensions so central to her analysis. Despite her initial recognition—and notoriety—as a novelist, her nonfiction best reflects her knack for storytelling, and for wrapping her sharpest barbs in such creative and unexpected imagery and example that continue to resonate with scholars today and that make so much of her work so effective a teaching tool in southern history classrooms. Those qualities, as much as anything, account for the enduring appeal of her prose and for the continued interest in the woman who produced it.

Smith was not a native Georgian, although her father was from Ware County, in the state's southeastern piney woods, and her mother from a rice-planting family in Camden County, near St. Mary's. Soon after they married in 1884, Calvin and Anne Smith moved across the state line to the small mill town of Jasper, Florida, where he ran a lumber and turpentine business that made the Smiths the town's most prosperous residents. It was there that Lillian was born on December 12, 1897, the seventh of nine children, and there that she spent her childhood and adolescence. In 1912 her father bought a summer home in Clayton, in the north Georgia mountains; three years later, with his enterprises in Jasper faltering, and just as Lillian graduated from high school, he moved the family to Clayton where he established a hotel and later, a summer camp for girls.[8]

Lillian's collegiate education was sporadic; it included a year at nearby Piedmont College and a little more than that at the Peabody Conservatory in Baltimore, where she studied piano. In 1922 she went to China to teach music at a Methodist mission school, but returned home in 1925 to take over from her aging parents the management of the Laurel Falls Camp for girls. Though she traveled extensively, Lillian made the Smith house on Old Screamer Mountain in Clayton her home base for the rest of her life, most of which she shared with Paula Snelling, a Macon native she came to know as a counselor at Laurel Falls. Together, Smith and Snelling shared responsibility for the camp until it closed in 1948, and in the long off-seasons they produced a series of magazines and journals through which Smith honed her writing skills, made connections with intellectuals and activists in both the North and the South, and found her voice as a sharp critic of the oppression and exploitation that so marred her native region.[9]

As early as 1936 she was writing as vehemently as anyone else in the country—and certainly more so than any other southern white—about the insidious nature of segregation. Far more than mere southern tradition, or southern "custom," she argued, segregation was "an ancient psychological mechanism used by men . . . whenever they want to shut themselves away from problems which they fear and don't have the strength to resolve." It is "more a way of death" than a way of life in the South; it is both "cultural schizophrenia and "spiritual lynching" where both the "lynched and the lynchers are our own people, ourselves, our *children*." "The white man himself is one of the world's most urgent problems today," she declared, "not the Negro, nor other colored races. We whites must learn to confess this." Here already were many of the key elements of Smith's unique take on the region's racial injustices that she would repeat and expand upon over the course of her career. If these were the hard truths that would repel so many of her fellow southern intellectuals, also evident in this tirade is that deeply humanistic stance that infused nearly all of her writings. In the same piece, she insisted these were problems that would never be solved simply by "putting a loaf of bread, a book and a ballot in everyone's hand." None of these would mean much "so long as we refuse to acknowledge Negroes as human beings in need of that which makes them human."[10]

The sources of Smith's liberal views on race remain unclear. Some suspect that it was her years in China and subsequent trips to Brazil and India that heightened her awareness of and empathy for oppressed peoples worldwide, including those in the South.[11] She also immersed herself in fields as varied as Freudian theory, Paul Tillich's theology, and Gandhi's pacifism, all of which helped shaped her perspectives on her native region. Certainly parental influence had little to do with Smith's liberalism, a point she makes abundantly clear in print. "The mother who taught me what I know of tenderness and love and compassion taught me also the bleak rituals of keeping Negroes in their place," she once wrote. Of her father, to whom she felt much closer and admired much more, she stated that he, "who rebuked me for an air of superiority toward schoolmates from the mill and rounded out his rebuke by gravely reminding me that 'all men are brothers,' trained me in the steel-rigid decorums I must demand of every colored male. They who taught me split my body from my mind and both from my soul, taught me also to split my conscience from my acts and Christianity from southern tradition."[12]

In 1944 *Strange Fruit*, Smith's first published novel, appeared. Although she had completed it three years earlier, publishers had been reluctant to take on a work they found far too inflammatory given the interracial romance at its center. From a literary standpoint, it is a cumbersome and awkwardly plotted work, and yet it was that plot that attracted so much attention and generated such strong reaction almost as soon as it appeared. Set in a small south Georgia town (modeled on Jasper), Smith's protagonist is Nonnie Anderson, a young African American woman and college graduate, who returns home and resumes a clandestine love affair with Tracy, the son of a white physician, who had just returned home from service in the First World War. When Nonnie finds she is pregnant, their relationship becomes strained, and her own siblings' resentment of her affair eventually leads to Tracy's murder, which in turn sparks mob violence that culminates in a horrific lynching, all of which Smith describes in graphic detail. The miscegenation, the violence (and the role of religion in fueling it—this all takes place during the week of an August tent revival), and her pointed commentary on southern racism and class conflict all generated controversy. Along with its ban in Boston due to perceived obscenity, these factors made the book a best seller and Smith a national celebrity; at the same time, it made her a pariah among her fellow white southerners, who nevertheless contributed to the novel's healthy sales.[13]

The "triangulation of sex, sin and segregation," which Smith had long seen as central in explaining the southern psyche, was fully evident in *Strange Fruit*, but would become even more pronounced five years later with the publication of *Killers of the Dream*, her nonfictional, semiautobiographical diatribe against all of those forces—racism, violence, poverty, ignorance, and oppression—that so crippled the human spirit and killed so many dreams for white and black southerners alike. That 1949 book entails a mix of genres and reads more like a series of disparate essays than a coherent narrative. Although Smith once labeled the work a memoir, its autobiographical passages are fleeting and anecdotal. Far more of its content consists of sociological and historical analysis, editorial commentary, parables, and allegory, much of it previously published in her journals and elsewhere. Substantially expanded and revised in 1961, the book became Smith's most distinctive and full-bodied commentary on the South and her most lasting legacy as both writer and social critic.

As with most of her critiques of the region, Smith never limited her analysis to herself or her family. She made clear that the schizophrenic nature of southern racism that she attributed to her parents was far more pervasive, and she generalized in far more damning terms just how insidious it had become:

> One day, during your childhood or adolescence, a Negro was lynched in your county or the one next to yours. A human being was burned or hanged from a tree and you knew it had happened. But no one publicly condemned it and always the murderers went free. And afterward, maybe weeks or months or years afterward, you sat casually in the drugstore with one of those murderers and drank the Coke he casually paid for. A "nice white girl" could do that but she would have been run out of town or perhaps killed had she drunk a Coke with the young Negro doctor who was devoting his life to service to his people.[14]

Again, it is her sense of the hypocrisy, the blindness, and the contradictions that so typified the racism of those more genteel southerners that would have—or should have—resonated so among southern readers, who may well have recognized themselves in such scenarios.

Such descriptions reflect Smith's unique application of personal, psychological, and even spiritual analysis of the "sick society" she found the South to be. Among her more sustained concerns were the impact such problems had on children, suggesting that they somehow sensed the injustices of their world and yet were gradually indoctrinated into the belief system behind those injustices. She opens *Killers of the Dream* with the rather startling statement: "Even its children knew that the South was in trouble." Yet she fully recognizes how completely they succumbed to the racism so central to that "trouble." In one of her most quoted passages, she proclaimed:

> From the time little southern children take their first step they learn their ritual, for Southern Tradition leads them through its intricate movements. And some, if their faces are dark, learn to bend, hat in hand; and others, if their faces are white, learn to hold their heads high. Some step off the sidewalk while others pass by in arrogance. Bending, shoving, genuflecting, ignoring, stepping off, demanding, giving in, avoiding. . . . So we learned the dance that cripples the human spirit, step by step by step, we who were white and we who were colored, day by day, hour by hour, year by year until the movements were reflexes and made for the rest of our life without thinking.[15]

While she revealed remarkably little about her adult life or personal feelings in her published work, Smith had much to say about her childhood struggles with the perplexities of race. These revelations often came through oblique references or fleeting anecdotes, and yet they reflect her continuing fascination with what she called the "haunted childhoods" and "crippling spirit" that southern racial mores imposed on most of its young people, white or black. "I began to understand slowly at first more clearly as the years passed," she wrote, "that the warped, distorted frame we have put around every Negro child from birth is around every white child also."[16] Of course, the white child she most likely had in mind was herself. In a variety of writings over the years, she described her childhood traumas and confusions, always suggesting that her own experiences typified those of most of her generation (a claim that she could hardly make regarding her adult life.) As she noted in her preface to the revised *Killers of the Dream*, "I realize this is personal memoir, in one sense; in another sense, it is Every Southerner's memoir."[17]

In the most extended of such personal revelations, Smith described a strange childhood encounter that has become the most often cited and discussed passage in the book. When Lillian was ten years old, her parents took in what a local social worker assumed was a white girl who had been found in the "colored section" of Jasper, living in a broken-down shack with a black family who had just moved there. The assumption was that she had been kidnapped. Janie, as she was known, was brought to the Smith household, shared a room with Lillian, and was generally made a part of the family. She was, Smith wrote, "dazed by her new comforts and by the interesting activities of my big lively family; and I was as happily dazed, for her adoration of me was a new thing; as time passed a quick, childish and deeply felt bond grew up between us."

Then one day, a phone call from a black orphanage led to nervous meetings, whispered conferences, and finally an announcement made by Lillian's mother that Janie would be returning to the black family she had been taken from. The only explanation offered was that Janie was found to be "colored." In response to repeated queries from Lillian in all her innocence and confusion as to why Janie had to leave, how she could be colored, and why she couldn't continue to play with or ever see her roommate and friend again, he mother finally said, "You're too young to understand. And don't ask me again, ever again, about this!" "Mother's voice was sharp but her face was sad and there was no certainty left there," Lillian wrote. "I knew something was wrong. I knew my father and mother whom I passionately admired had betrayed something which they held dear. And they could not help doing it. And I was shamed by their failure and frightened, for I felt they were no longer as powerful as I had thought."

If her disappointment in her parents is the most apparent lesson conveyed in this story, even more moving is the disappointment she felt in her own ten-year-old self. Wracked by guilt and confusion on the night before Janie was to be taken away, Lillian went to the piano and began to play, as she said she always did when she was in trouble. As she stumbled through a number, Janie came over and sat on the piano bench beside her. "Feeling lost in the deep currents sweeping through our house that night, she crept closer and put her arms around me and I shrank away as if my body had been uncovered. I had not said a word, I did not say one, but she knew, and tears slowly rolled down her little white face." In describing those few moments on a piano bench, Smith captured not only the full extent of the pain felt by both little girls, but also the gross inhumanity of racism and intolerance that few other white writers have expressed in such poignant terms. She could have left it at that, but she concluded with a simple, almost childlike statement expressing the moral of the story: "Something was wrong with a world that tells you that love is good and people are important and then forces you to deny love and humiliate people."[18] Smith acknowledged that her experience with Janie was "an incident that has rarely happened to other southern children," but only at one level. "It was an acting out," she insisted, "a private production of a little script that is written on the lives of most southern children before they know words. Though they may not have seen it stated this way, each southerner has had his own private showing."[19]

While it was often a stretch for Smith to suggest that her own feelings and experiences typified those of most southern white children, she found it far easier to universalize other equally traumatic experiences she felt in other relationships they may have known—those with their nurses or caretakers. She spoke with great affection and regret about Aunt Chloe, who lived behind the Smith household and proved a particularly important part of her young life when she was consigned almost fully to her nurse's care after the birth of Smith's baby sister. This beloved cook provided young Lillian with the nurture she needed to overcome the sense of displacement or even abandonment that a newborn sibling could provoke. "I was once more the center of someone's universe," she wrote of Aunt Chloe's care. "What did it matter that this universe encompassed only one room in a little back-yard cabin? It filled my need and I loved her."[20]

As with Janie, Smith found the inevitable breaking of that bond to be devastating. Alternating between singular and plural first-person pronouns, she blurred her own feelings with those of most children of her class: "These intimacies fill our memories and do strange things now to our segregated grown-up lives." Of herself, she wrote that Aunt Chloe, "who had given me refuge when a little sister took my place as the baby of the family, who soothed, fed me, delighted me with her stories and games, let me fall asleep on her deep warm breast, was not worthy of the passionate love I felt for her but must be given instead a half-smiled-at affection similar to that which one feels for one's dog."[21]

Smith employed even more striking imagery in generalizing from this scenario and the psychological damage it imposed. Shifting from first to third person, and from feminine to masculine pronouns, she suggested that one of the most profound relationships of a white southerner's life is that which tied him to "two women whose paths will take them far from each other." It is as if "he were fastened to two umbilical cords which wrap themselves together in a terrifying tangle," creating a dual relationship that so many white southerners have had with "two mothers . . . each of a different culture that centered in different human values," all of which make "the Oedipus complex seem by comparison almost a simple adjustment." Well after the break is made, even as a southern boy moves into adolescence, he is drawn to his old mammy and "wants to stay in her lap forever; but he slips away shamefaced, remembering *this* mother is not 'fitten,' as she herself says, to sit in the living room or eat at the table with the rest of the family." He is learning, she reiterates, "a desolating lesson that shrinks the heart when we think of its human implications." Only Lillian Smith could move so easily between Freudian theory and moral remorse, and in so doing, create so indelible an impression on those who read her even now.[22]

Much of Smith's role as "teacher" came in the lessons she sought to convey to the girls she faced around campfires each summer at Laurel Falls. That constant contact with children and adolescents may well explain why childhood perspectives and vulnerabilities remained so central a theme in her writing. As Rose Gladney has noted, it provided her with "emotional access to her own childhood." Childless herself, Smith took very seriously the opportunity and responsibility she had to shape her girls' values and help them realize their full human potential. Gladney has suggested that Smith saw the camp as a laboratory through which she could both observe and shape the socialization process of her many campers. "Through the camp," Gladney writes, "she also came close to recreating the world she wanted to live in, a world where every child could experience esteem, where individual creativity could be encouraged by a supportive community, where old ideas could be questioned and new ones explored, and where differences could be appreciated."[23]

Smith urged her counselors to study psychology, child development, and mental hygiene, stating, "I have read many such books, but even if I had read everything written on the subject, it would not be enough. You and I must have a common background of knowledge—a common purpose." As to what that purpose was, she is just as clear: "Unless we produce behavior changes in our children, we have *done nothing*."[24] She confided to a correspondent in 1941, "I sometimes think perhaps our work with girls who will someday be the women leaders of the South may be of some definite value. We have this year, as usual, worked on many genuinely interesting projects with them in racial relationships, and there is always up here much discussion of the South and its problems."[25] Two years later, she informed Eleanor Roosevelt, "Because I am known for my work with children of wealthy southern families, I have had a fortunate position in the South, and made the most of it." And yet, she sometimes considered these responsibilities to be as much of a burden as an opportunity, once musing, "I am the kind of person who has to give as much creative energy to a child as to a book—and sixty little girls, each with her own emotional problems, can by the end of the summer, have a desiccating effect on the spirit."[26]

In *Killers of the Dream*, Smith devoted several chapters to the moral and historical lessons she sought to instill in her campers, which led some of them in turn, to confide in her. One seventeen-year-old told her that in the dining car on a train trip to New York with her father several months earlier, she had noticed the president of one of Atlanta's black colleges eating behind drawn curtains: "I said, 'Daddy, did you see that? He's the president of a college!' And Daddy

said, 'That's where colored folks are supposed to sit. You mustn't get silly notions, honey.' But she couldn't let the matter rest, and couldn't finish her dinner.
"I know it was morbid," Smith quoted her as saying, "but I kept looking at all
those faces wondering why they felt they had to have a curtain between them
and a college president, just to eat their dinner. And it began to seem so crazy!"

Yet the young Atlantan's response was not as morally clear-cut as one might
expect, especially coming from Smith, for whom there was often little shading
or ambivalence in her sense of right and wrong. The girl confided that she had
real doubts as to whether she could, or should challenge her father's wisdom, or
at least his authority, on this and other matters of decorum and social values. "I
want so much to go home and be decent about things. Not make folks mad—
just live what I believe is right. But how? Tell me how." This provided just the
opening Smith needed to launch into a discourse on the South's long legacy
of racial oppression and how it had evolved.[27] It was not the inequity itself but
rather the doubts raised about her father's value system that proved so troubling
to Smith's camper; and it was no doubt a dilemma Smith could identify with
at a very personal level, given the troubling inconsistencies in her own father's
sense of human decency.[28]

Smith often viewed major developments in southern race relations, both positive and negative, through the perspectives of her campers. In the summer of
1946 she wrote a letter to their parents in which she reported that the girls "were
very upset about the lynching near Monroe, Georgia and have asked questions
that are hard for a grown-up to answer." This was a particularly shocking incident, one of the worst of the post–World War II years, in which two black
couples in a car were ambushed by a group of white men, taken to a remote spot
on Moore's Ford Creek in Walton County, and shot.[29] Especially troubling were
the girls' questions regarding whether the two women who were lynched had left
children behind, and if so, who would care for them, now that their parents were
gone. They also asked her how those children felt about living in America; and
did they hate white people for what a few did to their parents. Smith admitted
that these were difficult questions to answer. Even harder was how to respond to
the girls' inquiries as to what they could do to help. "I think the most heartbreak-
ing and frustrating thing for all of us who feel decent inside ourselves is to know
what to do," she told their parents. "If we don't find some way for our children
to express their kindly feelings I fear that they may find it easier psychologically
not to have decent feelings but to grow instead a hard shell of indifference and
blindness to protect themselves from questions that are hard to answer."[30]

As free-wheeling and widely cast as the targets of her attacks could be, Smith
was selective in terms of which societal ills she targeted and with which victims

she sympathized. For all her attention to the economic inequities and lack of opportunity inherent in southern racism, the plight of poor whites rarely evoked in her the same levels of sympathy or concern. Such a blind spot in her social conscience seems especially striking, given that she spent the majority of her life among the humble white Appalachian residents of Rabun County, Georgia, who far outnumbered the marginal black populace that made their homes in that highland setting. (In fact, her correspondence includes numerous references to the local black community of Ivy Hill—in which she took a real interest and with which she seems to have maintained regular contacts. She gives far less attention to the county's preponderance of mountain whites, though her feelings toward them, as reflected in her private correspondence, seem to have been both sympathetic and respectful.)[31]

Poor whites were integral to Smith's condemnation of the South's social and economic shortcomings, but she portrayed them—in print at least—only in generic or abstract terms, often as pawns or stooges, easily manipulated to serve the corrupt agendas of their social betters. To her, they were little more than willing victims of class exploitation, to which they were especially susceptible because of their own racism, much of it bred by their own insecurities on the economic ladder. Poor whites, Smith claimed, became the "yes men, the moral henchmen quieting their leaders' uneasy consciences." (Even here, guilt was never far from the surface.) In her own version of "herrenvolk democracy," she conveyed more contempt than sympathy for those poor whites whose skin color was all that was needed to make them "forget that [they] were eaten up with malaria and hookworm; make [them] forget that [they] lived in a shanty and ate pot-likker and corn bread, and worked long hours for nothing. Nobody could take away from [them] this whiteness that made [them] and [their] way of life 'superior.'" She expressed even more disdain for their exploiters, noting that "though they did nothing about starved minds and bodies, nothing about health and jobs, demagogues did keep their starved spirits alive here on earth with the drug of white supremacy and Negro-hate."[32]

In a 1943 essay entitled "Two Men and a Bargain," Smith provided an even more extended version of that class exploitation by means of an intricate parable in which Mr. Rich White made a bargain with Mr. Poor White. The former proposed that if he would continue to employ only the latter in his factories; in return, Mr. Poor White would accept the long hours and low wages offered him as long he didn't have to compete with blacks for them. In return, he'd be given free range to do whatever it took—to make sure the black man stayed in his place. "I've learned a few things about making a living you're too no-count to learn," Mr. Rich White told his fellow bargainer, "things about jobs and credit, prices, hours, wages, votes, and so on. But one thing you can learn easy, any white man can, is how to handle the black man. . . . You boss the nigger, and I'll boss the money." Nor did it end there. Mr. Rich White made the offer even more attractive: "If you don't have much to do, and begin to get worried-up inside and mad with folks, and you think it'll make you fell a little better to lynch a nigger occasionally, that OK by me too; and I'll fix it with the sheriff and the judge and the court and our newspapers so you won't have no trouble afterwards."[33]

Smith clearly recognized and understood the rampant manipulation and race-baiting that made the Jim Crow South the "Solid South" as well, and she was astute enough to see the psychological, economic, and social dynamics that allowed it to operate as effectively and as long as it did. Her ability to describe those realities through such abstract and yet recognizably human terms rendered her message all the more potent—and teachable—than more conventional forms of analysis or editorializing would have been.

Only once in her published work did Smith ever describe any personal contact with poor whites, and it came in the midst of an otherwise rather innocuous and nostalgic piece she wrote for *Life* magazine in 1961 on her memories of childhood Christmases with her large family. Toward the end of that essay, Smith wrote of a remarkable act of generosity by her father that made one such holiday memorable. As he and his family struggled to make ends meet, in what she called "our year of austerity," the year in which they were forced to move up to Rabun County after his business in Jasper failed, Calvin Smith invited a chain gang to have Christmas dinner with the family. Disturbed after having encountered the convicts in the shabby railroad cars in which they lived while assigned to state road work in the area, he came home and declared to his wife that "there's more misery in the world than even I know; and a lot of it unnecessary." He then proposed the Christmas visit, and Mrs. Smith reluctantly agreed.[34]

At noon on Christmas Day, the Smiths watched forty-eight men in stripes, both white and black, along with their guards, heading toward their house. According to his admiring daughter, Calvin "moved among them with grace and ease," and broke the early awkward moments with a warm welcome. The "wonderful absurdity" of the situation soon had them "all laughing and muttering Merry Christmas, half deriding, half meaning it." Three of the guests—specifically a killer, a rapist, and a bank robber—pitched in to put the meal on the table, Lillian notes wryly. "My sister and I served the plates. The murderer and his two friends passed them to the men. Afterward, the rapist and two bank robbers and the arsonist said they'd be real pleased to wash up the dishes."[35]

While this story comes across as more of an amusing anecdote than is typical of Smith's writing, it is a tale with a moral. When the chain gang left after a satisfying visit for all concerned, Calvin gathered his family around him, as "the old look of having something to say to his children settled across his face." He began his lecture: "We've been through some pretty hard times, lately, and I've been proud of my family. Some folks can take prosperity and can't take poverty; some can take being poor and lose their heads when money comes. I want my children to accept it all: the good and the bad, for that is what life is." He went on to talk about their recent guests, reminding his children that they were merely men who had made mistakes, as would they all at some point in their lives. "Never look down on a man," he told them. "Never. If you can't look him straight in the eye, then what's wrong is with you."[36]

Despite this sermon with which Smith closes her story, it is obvious that she has told it more as a tribute to her father than as a transformative moment in her own consciousness. While she never made white poverty or misfortune nearly as central to her writing as she did racism, it is also curious that Smith never chronicled nearly so definitive a turning point in terms of her racial conversion as in this minor anecdote in a nostalgic holiday piece on a lesson taught about less fortunate whites.

In 1954 Smith published a follow-up of sorts to *Killers of the Dream*, entitled *The Journey*. It was only somewhat more coherent in structure than its predecessor, largely because Smith centered her narrative on an extended trip she made to coastal Georgia in 1951 in search of family roots and her own early memories. Both sets of her grandparents were from the region, and she visited her grandmothers regularly there as a child. Given that agenda and the evocative sense of her own past inspired by the places she visited, there are slightly stronger autobiographical and more introspective threads running through this narrative, and yet, she continued the free-flowing, almost stream-of-conscious approach to her musings about family, self, and much else.

Perhaps the most notable difference in *The Journey* and *Killers of the Dream* is that Smith's tone changed dramatically from her earlier diatribes against southern racism and exploitation. Race was no longer her central concern by the early 1950s, or so she tried to claim. (Even on the eve of *Killers of the Dream*'s publication, she confided to a friend: "I hope to God I am through with race when I finish this book.")[37] Amid seemingly random and fleeting portraits of her relatives and childhood reminiscences about visits to see them, Smith's primary focus in *The Journey* was on human disabilities—both physical and mental—and the means by which modern society and modern science coped with the challenges posed by those handicaps, with children, as always, at the forefront of her musings. It's a far more uplifting message than anything she wrote in *Killers*, and unusually optimistic in outlook.[38]

And yet, Smith could never fully ignore race, and it is no surprise that two of the most compelling passages in *The Journey* have to do with African Americans, even as they contrast sharply with her harsh indictments of five years earlier. Early in her trip, while traveling along coastal back roads on a Sunday afternoon, she passed a small church around which a group of rural blacks were gathering for a service. What struck her most about their socializing was how much they laughed, and what she perceived as its transformative effect into something "fresh and new, cleaned of tensions, freed of resentment." Laughter of that magnitude "struck down the Whiteness, struck down poverty, struck down sweat and shame, laid it flat on the earth, made it nothing." Smith went on to muse: "Here on the coast, tucked in by creeks and marshes, moving slow as the tide were people floating in a back eddy of time. They knew so little of what has tightened the hearts and minds of the rest of the world; and yet, I had the feeling that maybe they knew more, deep down in them, where knowledge is a real thing."

As they moved on into the church, Smith drove closer and continued to reflect on the meaning of what she observed: "They had left the laughter outside and hate and shame with their whiskey bottles and their six-day life and were singing to God of something that He and they understood." Inspired by that moment, and what she heard coming from inside that small church, Smith launched into a remarkable treatise on the power of religion in the lives of southern blacks, and she managed to do so through her own youthful memories: "All my childhood I had listened to it: this never-ending dialogue between human beings and their God. . . I heard that wordless song, sung by women over washtubs, in kitchens, out under the oak trees when a white baby was being put to sleep." She continued, "I had heard it, too, in the little churches on the edge of town; I would lie in bed at night listening to those sounds that pounded like the sea against an iron wall. . . and I knew, even then, that they were talking over the white race's head to God, and in doing it, they made of the white man no more than an overseer; their Master was on their side." Ruminating in even more historical terms, Smith reasoned that "because so long ago a few white folks decided that their slaves had no souls and hence needed no Bible or no preacher to help them die, our South and the whole world were given the most poignantly beautiful death songs a folk ever created. . . How strange and lovely, sometimes, are the wages of sin."[39]

Such passages are vintage Smith, and utterly unlike those of any other commentator on black or southern life. And yet, this was one of the few times in Smith's nonfiction in which she observed a black community and wrote firsthand about the spirit, the feelings, the response of its members to the oppressive world in which they struggled. It is a far more uplifting message than she could have conveyed even a few years earlier, and it suggests that she had in the interim come to a new appreciation for the resiliency and resourcefulness— both religious and psychological—with which African Americans endured the subjugation and limitations against which she had once railed so unrelentingly.

Equally extraordinary is an encounter shortly afterward that allowed Smith to express an even more optimistic view of southern whites and their capacity to overcome the hatred and prejudices so ingrained in their culture. Smith stopped overnight at a motor court near Waycross, Georgia, where she was befriended by the middle-aged couple who served as her hosts. In the midst of a long, late-night conversation, Timothy and Ellen told her of a recent incident they had experienced there. Late one stormy evening, a car had pulled up in front of the motor court, but merely sat there with the headlights on and no one emerging from it. Eventually, Tim went out to the car, where he found two African American women, "well dressed and terribly scared." They nervously told him that they knew of no place to go in the storm, and asked if he could direct them to a black family who might take them in for the night. "I got sick at my stomach," Smith quotes Tim as saying:

> Here was a place supposed to be open to strangers. And this was America; my country; theirs, too; and I loved it and was proud of it and had good cause to be. . . . Yet, *this* question could be asked.
>
> I said—and God help me, do you know I was more scared than when I got the shrapnel in my hip at Argonne!—I said, If you would care to stay here, there is a vacant room and I believe you would be comfortable.
>
> One stared at me as if I had accosted her. The other never looked up. I don't know what they were thinking—a white man had—I just don't know what came into their minds. But there was no trust in their faces. So I called my wife. Ellen came out in the rain and invited them in. We put them in room seven. We both went with them and got them settled. They paid the fee and filled out a card. And I heard Ellen say as quietly as her mother would have spoken, "If you ladies would like breakfast, we begin to serve at seven o'clock." I almost yelled "*Ellen, what in the name of God are you saying! This is Geor . . .*" And then, inside me suddenly, I knelt down.
>
> Yeah, I asked Him to forgive me for my sin. I saw it as plain as Saul of Tarsus saw on the road to Damascus. I had done what was right to do but with only half of me. And Ellen had done what was right with her whole heart.

The story doesn't end there. For Ellen spoke up at that point, and said simply: "Because of Henry's letter, Tim." They told Lillian that the women had politely declined their offer of breakfast, saying that they needed to be on the road by six. Later that evening though, Ellen told her husband, "Tim . . . there comes a time in a life when if you don't go the second mile, you'll never take another step. You'll sit there the rest of your days justifying why you didn't move. That time has come for me." Tim replied, "OK, Ellen. My muscles feel like a little hike might be the very thing to take the kinks out of them, too." And at five-thirty the next morning they took a breakfast tray to room 7. "There was nowhere, and we knew it, for them to get a cup of coffee."

Only at that point in the story do they explain the letter Ellen received from Henry. He was their younger son, fighting in Korea, and he had written several weeks earlier about an incident in which he was wounded in his leg and was left behind by his company as nightfall approached. Grappling in the dark, Henry stumbled onto something hard, heard an American voice speaking softly and then felt a hand pull him down to the ground. He blacked out, and only later when he came to, did he realize this man had bandaged his leg. They couldn't see each other, and given the proximity to North Korean troops, they lay side by side, eventually overcoming the stillness by whispering to each other, and finding out that they were from Georgia and Alabama. They fell asleep, and Henry awoke at dawn and noticed a black arm resting across his chest. "And I lay, Mother, and looked at it. And you know all I was thinking for you and Dad have thought it too." This black man from Alabama named Bud had risked his own life to save that of a white Georgian. "And I knew something," Henry told his parents. "I knew when I went home, I was going to have Bud come visit me. And if I haven't got the guts to do it—because I know you and Dad have—then I hope a bullet will get me. I'd deserve a communist prison but I'd settle for a little less." Smith concluded the story with a simple quote from Tim as to why they'd done what they did for their black guests. "We were sort of getting ready for Bud's visit," he chuckled.[40]

Smith was at her best in recounting such episodes, and in seeing in them omens or portents of the goodness that she—at least at times—felt were inherent in most southern whites. By presenting both cause and effect—an act of kindness by a black man toward a white in Korea that led his parents in Georgia to defy southern tradition and respond in kind, Smith doubled the moral imperatives at play. And yet the very nature of Tim and Ellen's kindness was so far afield from the mores of that time and place that they surprised even themselves. The guilt, shame, and second thoughts with which this couple—or Tim at least—wrestled were equally integral to Smith's message here and to the emotional resonance of his "conversion."

Such is the power of Smith's vision and her articulation of it. The momentary sense of optimism brought on both by such personal, privately shared incidents were reinforced by the far more momentous action of the Supreme Court in 1954 in the *Brown* decision that occurred just as she completed her book—a development in which she reveled, calling it "every child's Magna Carta."[41] She greatly admired Martin Luther King Jr. and was quick to applaud his leadership of the Montgomery bus boycott. In an approving letter, she informed Dr. King in March 1956 that "I, myself, being a Deep South white, reared in a religious home and the Methodist church, realize the deep ties of common songs, common prayer, common symbols that bind our two races together on a religio-mystical level, even as another brutally mythic idea, the concept of White Supremacy, tears our two peoples apart." She assured King that his way was "the right way." "Only through persuasion, love, goodwill, and firm nonviolent resistance," she insisted, "can change take place in our South."[42]

Even the brutal murder of Emmett Till in the summer of 1955 did not deter Smith from her resilient optimism during those years. In response to concerns by Vermont writer Dorothy Canfield Fisher over the increased racial tensions evident in the South, Smith attempted to put Till's death in a broader perspective that would have very much surprised those who saw her purely as a critic of her native land. "We all, all of us who are decent people, were deeply shocked," she informed Fisher in March 1956. But "only the angry Mississippians were given a voice" in the newspaper accounts of the crime and subsequent trial. "One child who came South to visit his grandparents was killed. But every summer, thousands of little colored children come South to visit their grandparents and go back home unharmed."

Then, as she so often did, Smith illustrated that claim by relating to Fisher an experience she had had on a train the previous August, the same month in which Till was murdered. Traveling from Georgia to New York, she boarded the train in Toccoa along with two "small colored girls" who were returning home after a summer with their grandparents, who put them on the train. During the trip, she befriended the girls, who told her how much they enjoyed helping their grandpa and grandma on their farm. Enchanted, Smith asked the children to join her in the dining car, and despite a few raised eyebrows, no one made a fuss. She concluded her story by stating that, after the girls had returned to their compartment and had gotten ready for bed, Smith—bunking just across the narrow aisle from them—heard "a chanting of little voices." She opened the door of her compartment and saw the girls "kneeling in the aisle in their pink and blue pajamas with their heads on the bed, saying their prayers. 'Now I lay me down to sleep . . . if I should die before I wake, I pray . . .'" Smith went on to lecture Fisher:

But you see, they did not die. They got home safely and they had a pleasant, comfortable trip back North. They had also had a fine vacation, a completely secure one, down South. There were thousands of these children who came South last summer and returned safe and sound. That does not justify the death of the Till boy, nor does it make it less cruel or barbarous; but it does help us see the total picture in an honest perspective to be reminded that after all, murder came to only one of these children.[43]

As the civil rights movement kicked into full gear, Smith took a great interest in how it unfolded and in the people on the front lines. In the fall of 1960 she was invited to speak at a meeting of Student Non-Violent Coordinating Committee (SNCC) workers in Atlanta, just as they were staging a series of sit-ins protesting segregated lunch counters at Rich's and other department stores in downtown Atlanta. While she considered being part of those demonstrations, she limited her involvement to what she did best—a war of words. In letters to store owner Richard Rich, Atlanta mayor William Hartsfield, and other influential Atlantans, she urged them to give in to SNCC demands, insisting that "its symbolic significance" was what mattered most: "It hurts to feel shunned; hurts to feel second-class; hurts to be pushed around."[44]

Smith was gratified to see young people leading the charge in this campaign, and praised Jane Stembridge, a young white woman who managed SNCC's Atlanta office and became a regular correspondent of Smith's, for her leadership of the sit-ins. "Everything seems to me, at this distance, to have been managed beautifully," she wrote in October 1960. "And this is *you*, Jane . . . One acts in the mind, in the imagination, in the heart as well as out in the world with one's body. You are making an impact with your ideas, your guidance, your suggestions, your restraints, your values." She encouraged Stembridge to remain visible in her protest, stating that "it is still a good symbol to those who understand that segregation hurts the whites as much as Negroes," reiterating a theme she long pushed hard in her writings.[45]

Yet that optimism, once spurred by the promise of the *Brown* decision, King's leadership, and SNCC's activism, was already beginning to diminish for Smith, perhaps clouded by the cancer that would sap much of her energy and spirit until her death in 1966. In 1960 she described her native region to Paul Tillich, a close confidante: "Full of cruelty and blindness; stiff and rigid in some of its ways, so resilient and warm in others; dragging itself and the full country toward chaos. Sometimes I am not confident that we shall make it." Despite being embraced by Atlanta's SNCC workers at least, she also felt frustration at what she saw as her own lack of influence. "Sometimes as I write, talk, work trying like a Cassandra to warn my people," she confided to Tillich, "I feel the words are breaking to pieces against my own face."[46] On the other hand, she still on occasion entertained delusions of grandeur. Just months after her discouraging words to Tillich, she told another friend: "Some day I rather think *Strange Fruit* and *Killers of the Dream* will give me the Nobel Prize. I am patient; I know my worth; I know my historical value to this country."[47]

In part, that sense of worth lay in her recognition of *how* she had made her case. She once said of her writings: "I say nothing that people in their hearts do not already know, but I try to say it in such a way that their imaginations will be stirred and some of their energies released that are now tied up in conflict." She chided historians, most of whose work she felt was "very, very white," and singled out Charles Beard as a particular culprit, stating that "he was so intent on selling his idea of the economic interpretation of history that he brushed off much that is psychological and human and 'racial.'" She concluded, "Real history, in my opinion, has never been written and won't be until historians are willing to deal seriously with men's feelings as well as with events."[48] In response to critics who suggested that she was too passionate in her analysis of southern society, she wrote to her publisher regarding the revised edition of *Killers of the Dream* in 1961: "Too much feeling? Perhaps. I could snip off a little of the pain, rub out a few words. But no; let's leave it, for it may be the most real part of the book."[49]

At about the same time, she acknowledged how central children had always been in her concerns for and focus on the South. In 1960 she told a friend that she was working on a children's book, and confided that "this returning to children in my imagination gave me immense relief and rest; I still miss their love and belief in me; no other group, in my South, or even in this country has ever given it to me. But these children did, for twenty-five years." When "weary and worn," she mused, "it is good to call them together in my imagination and renew our old bonds."[50]

Historian Bruce Clayton once noted of Smith that "her genius and greatness of soul was her abiding sensitivity, her empathy, her heartfelt willingness to try to put herself in others' shoes."[51] Those qualities were certainly at the heart of her humanist perspective, as was her constant focus on young people, for whom she felt such responsibility and with whom she identified so closely. While she may have been selective as to the recipients of that empathy and abiding sensitivity, it is those traits—often unappreciated by contemporaries, diverted perhaps by the sheer vehemence of her assaults—that have since emerged as fully integral components of her writing and her character. And it is those qualities, no doubt, that account for the remarkable staying power and

continuing fascination by historians and literary scholars in both the woman
and her work in the near half century since her death.

NOTES

1. Margaret Rose Gladney, ed., *How Am I to Be Heard: Letters of Lillian Smith* (Chapel Hill: University of North Carolina Press, 1993).

2. Lillian Smith (hereinafter LS) to Frank Spencer, March 8, 1956, quoted in Gladney, *How Am I to Be Heard?*, 165; and in Fred Hobson, *Tell about the South: The Southern Rage to Explain* (Baton Rouge: Louisiana State University Press, 1983), 307. Smith actually enjoyed some newfound respect and new readers when a new edition of *Killers of the Dream* appeared in 1961, but biographer Anne Loveland notes that she was never able to overcome her perpetual "sense of persecution" and sensitivity to slights, real and imagined, which Loveland suggests may have been exacerbated by medications prescribed as part of her cancer treatments. See Anne Loveland, *Lillian Smith: A Southerner Confronting the South* (Baton Rouge: LSU Press, 1986), 241–44; and Will Brantley, *Feminine Sense in Southern Memoir: Smith, Glasgow, Welty, Hellman, Porter, and Hurston* (Jackson: University Press of Mississippi, 1993), 39–40.

3. Smith claimed that her strongest objection to these moderates was not so much their caution as the fact that "they refuse to let others move faster, or to speak more clearly or perhaps even more persuasively than they." Smith actually named the "chief villains," journalists all, in a 1957 letter to Harry Golden: Hodding Carter, Jonathan Daniels, Virginius Dabney, and especially Ralph McGill, whom she claimed "does not like to believe in the existence of anyone in the South who dares to speak out more plainly than he; he is God . . . and when God says, 'this is not the time to speak out plainly,' He punishes those who seem deaf to his Words" (LS to Harry Golden, December 15, 1957, quoted in Loveland, *Lillian Smith*, 145–46). See also James C. Cobb, *Away Down South: A History of Southern Identity* (New York: Oxford University Press, 2005), 196, in which he quotes Smith as calling them "victims of temporary moral and psychic paralysis" and declaring that "moderation never made a man or a nation great."

4. The fullest treatment of this topic is a senior history thesis produced at the University of Georgia by Jenaé Moxie, "Southern Rage to Explain or Misplaced Self-Importance? Black Georgians' Responses to Lillian Smith's *Strange Fruit* (senior thesis, May 2012).

5. For quick overviews on Smith and her work, see articles "Lillian Smith," "*Killers of the Dream*," and "*Strange Fruit*" in *The New Georgia Encyclopedia*, http://www.georgiaencyclopedia.org, and reprinted in *An NGE Companion to Georgia Literature*, ed. Hugh Ruppersburg and John C. Inscoe (Athens: University of Georgia Press, 2007), 261–63, 389–92, 393–94. The current body of work on Smith includes a full biography, Loveland, *Lillian Smith*; a briefer biography and literary assessment of her writings, Louise Blackwell and Frances Clay, *Lillian Smith* (New York: Twayne Publishers, 1971); and her published correspondence, Gladney, *How Am I to Be Heard?* She holds a prominent place in broader studies, including Hobson, *Tell about the South*, 307–23; Hobson, *But Now I See: The White Southern Racial Conversion Narrative* (Baton Rouge: Louisiana State University Press, 1999), chap. 1; Morton Sosna, *In Search of the Silent South: Southern Liberals and the Race Issue* (New York: Columbia University Press, 1977), chap. 9; John Egerton, *Speak Now against the Day: The Generation before the Civil Rights Movement in the South* (New York: Knopf, 1994); Grace Elizabeth Hale, *Making Whiteness: The Culture of Segregation in the South, 1890–1940* (New York: Pantheon, 1998), chap. 6; Brantley, *Feminine Sense in Southern Memoir*, chap. 2; McKay Jenkins, *The South in*

Black and White: Race, Sex, and Literature in the 1940s (Chapel Hill: University of North Carolina Press, 1999), chap. 4. Darlene O'Dell, *Sites of Southern Memory: The Autobiographies Katherine Du-Pre Lumpkin, Lillian Smith, and Pauli Murray* (Charlottesville: University Press of Virginia, 2001), chap. 3; Cobb, *Away Down South*, 193–97; Jennifer L. Ritterhouse, *Growing Up Jim Crow: How Black and White Southern Children Learned Race* (Chapel Hill: University of North Carolina Press, 2006); Jennifer Jensen Wallach, *"Closer to the Truth than Any Fact": Memoir, Memory, and Jim Crow* (Athens: University of Georgia Press, 2008), 113; and most recently, Robert H. Brinkmeyer Jr., *The Fourth Ghost: White Southern Writers and European Fascism, 1930–1950* (Baton Rouge: LSU Press, 2009); and numerous articles and essays, a sampling of which includes Randall Patton, "Lillian Smith and the Transformation of American Liberalism, 1945–1950," *Georgia Historical Quarterly* 76 (Summer 1992): 372–92; Roseanne V. Camacho, "Race, Region, and Gender in a Reassessment of Lillian Smith," in *Southern Women: History and Identities*, ed. Virginia Bernhard, Betty Brandon, Elizabeth Fox-Genovese, and Theda Perdue, 157–76 (Columbia: University of Missouri Press, 1992); Bruce Clayton, "Lillian Smith: Cassandra in Dixie," *Georgia Historical Quarterly* 78 (Spring 1994): 92–114; and Jay Watson, "Uncovering the Body, Discovering Ideology: Segregation and Sexual Anxiety in Lillian Smith's *Killers of the Dream*," *American Quarterly* 32 (1998): 387–99. See also two unpublished dissertations: Patricia Bryan Brewer, "Lillian Smith: Thorn in the Flesh of Crackerdom" (PhD diss., University of Georgia, 1982); and Kathleen Atkinson Miller, "Out of the Chrysalis: Lillian Smith and the Transformation of the South" (PhD. diss., Emory University, 1984).

6. Blackwell and Clay, *Lillian Smith*, 99.

7. Hobson, *But Now I See*, 19.

8. Loveland, *Lillian Smith*, chap. 1; and "Autobiographical Notes" in box 1, of Lillian Smith Papers, Hargrett Rare Book and Manuscript Library, University of Georgia Libraries. Smith reveals more about her parents, grandparents, and siblings in an essay, titled "Memory of a Large Christmas," that was commissioned by *Life* magazine and appeared in its issue of December 15, 1961, pp. 90–94. The essay was expanded and later published as a book, *Memory of a Large Christmas* (Athens: University of Georgia Press, 1998). The latter version is cited in subsequent notes.

9. For a collection of her strongest writings during those years, see Helen White and Redding S. Sugg Jr., eds., *From the Mountain: Selections from Pseudopodia, the North Georgia Review, and South Today* (Memphis: Memphis State University Press, 1972).

10. Lillian Smith, "Addressed to White Liberals," *New Republic*, September 14, 1936, 331–34.

11. Egerton, *Speak Now against the Day*, 262; and Hobson, *But Now I See*, 19–20.

12. Lillian Smith, *Killers of the Dream* (1949; rev. ed., New York: W. W. Norton, 1961), 27. For the fullest and most perceptive analyses of *Killers of the Dream*, see Brantley, *Feminine Sense in Southern Memoir*, 47–85; and Wallach, *"Closer to the Truth,"* 113–23.

13. The fullest treatments of *Strange Fruit* and the controversy it generated include Sosna, *In Search of the Silent South*, 188–92; Loveland, *Lillian Smith*, chap. 4; Blackwell and Clay, *Lillian Smith*, chap. 3; and Jenkins, *South in Black and White*, chap. 4. The most revealing perspectives on the novel come from Smith herself, much of it captured in her correspondence before and after its publication. See Gladney, *How Am I to Be Heard?*, 70–84 passim. See Moxie, "Southern Rage to Explain or Misplaced Self-Importance?" for black southerners' reservations about *Strange Fruit*.

14. Smith, *Killers of the Dream*, 97–98.

15. Ibid., 25, 96. *Killers of the Dream* is divided into four sections, and biographers Louise Blackwell and Frances Clay note that the first sentence of each section contains the word "child" or "childhood" (Blackwell and Clay, *Lillian Smith*, 98).

16. Smith, *Killers of the Dream*, 39.

17. Ibid., 21.

18. Ibid., 34–39.

19. Ibid., 30.

20. Ibid., 130–31, 133.

21. Ibid., 28–29.

22. Ibid., 133. Several critics have noted that Smith rarely depicted individual blacks as full-bodied, multidimensional characters. See, for example, Wallach, *"Closer to the Truth,"* 118–19.

23. Gladney, *How Am I to Be Heard?"* 8, xvi. Gladney makes an additional point here by following this statement with this one: "Not surprisingly, it was a world composed almost entirely of women, and Lillian Smith was in charge." For other analyses of Smith's relationship to children and childhood, see Hale, *Making Whiteness*, 246–50; and O'Dell, *Sites of Southern Memory*, 84, 90–93. For a broader study of the socialization of southern children on matters of race, that builds on many of Smith's concerns, see Ritterhouse, *Growing Up Jim Crow*.

24. LS to Counselors, May 20, 1932, in Gladney, *How Am I to Be Heard?*, 23.

25. LS to William C. Haygood, August 15, 1941, in ibid., 50–51.

26. LS to Eleanor Roosevelt, December 14, 1943, and LS to Laurel Falls parents, June 1945, both in ibid., 63, 93.

27. Smith, *Killers of the Dream*, 55–56. This passage forms the end of chapter 2. Chapter 3, "Unto the Third and Fourth Generation," consists of Smith's response to this perplexed teenager. For accounts of Laurel Falls Camp and Smith's relationship with her campers, see Loveland, *Lillian Smith*, 12–20, 191; and Margaret Rose Gladney, "A Chain Reaction of Dreams: Lillian Smith and the Laurel Falls Camp," *Journal of American Culture* 5 (Fall 1982): 50–56. See also a 2004 documentary film, *Miss Lil's Camp*, made by Suzanne Niedland and Anberin Pasha.

28. This is one of a number of occasions where Smith expressed contempt specifically for the ill treatment of distinguished black men and women. In a typical passage, she pleaded with southern readers to exercise civility and respect toward "Negro college presidents, teachers, ministers, lawyers, community leaders, and artists," who deserved to be addressed as Mr. or Mrs. or Miss. Smith; see "Addressed to Intelligent White Southerners," in White and Sugg, *From the Mountain*, 118–19. More cryptically, she later confided to a friend, "I am not popular with the Negroes because I have never been 'for' Negroes; I am for quality people, regardless of color" (LS to Joan Titus, Thanksgiving weekend, 1959, in Gladney, *How Am I to Be Heard?*, 236).

29. For full accounts of the Moore's Ford lynching, see Laura Wexler, *Fire in the Canebrake: The Last Mass Lynching in America* (New York: Scribners, 2003); and Wallace H. Warren, "'The Best People in Town Won't Talk': The Moore's Ford Lynching of 1946 and Its Cover-Up," in *Georgia in Black and White: Explorations in the Race Relations in a Southern State, 1865–1950*, ed. John C. Inscoe, 266–88 (Athens: University of Georgia Press, 1994).

30. LS to Laurel Falls Parents, midsummer 1946, in Gladney, *How Am I to Be Heard?*, 106.

31. The Ivy Hill community was adjacent to her camp's property on Old Screamer Mountain. One of her first short stories, though never completed or published, was set there. In instructions drawn up a month before her death, Smith indicated that all members of that community were to be invited to the memorial service she wanted held after she died (Gladney, *How Am I to Be Heard?*, 9, 353–54). For the fullest treatment of her attitude toward the Appalachian world in which she lived and those poor mountain whites she came to know there, see Robert C. Poister, "At Home on the Mountain: Appalachia in Lillian Smith's Life and Work," *Appalachian Journal* 37 (Spring/Summer 2010): 268–85.

32. Smith, *Killers of the Dream*, 164, 165.

33. This essay—first published in *South Today* 7 (Spring 1943): 6–10—was expanded and became a full chapter in *Killers of the Dream* (quotes from pp. 176, 177).

34. Smith, *Memory of a Large Christmas*, 60–62.

35. Ibid., 62.

36. Ibid., 63.

37. LS to George Brockway, June 1949, in Gladney, *How Am I to Be Heard?*, 125.

38. Very few Smith scholars give any attention to *The Journey*. The best analysis of it comes in Loveland, *Lillian Smith*, 106–13.

39. Lillian Smith, *The Journey* (Cleveland: World Publishing Co., 1954), 30–33.

40. Ibid., 146–49.

41. LS, letter to the editor, *Atlanta Constitution*, May 31, 1954, in Gladney, *How Am I to Be Heard?*, 146.

42. LS to Martin Luther King Jr., March 10, 1956, in ibid., 193.

43. LS to Dorothy Canfield Fisher, March 10, 1956, in ibid., 197–98. Equally revealing in this account is Smith's suggestion that the Jim Crow restrictions on railroad cars—and even in the waiting room in Toccoa—had eased considerably by 1955.

44. Loveland, *Lillian Smith*, 215–17, quote on p. 216.

45. LS to Jane Stembridge, October 22, 1960, in Gladney, *How Am I to Be Heard?*, 257–58.

46. LS to Paul Tillich, December 1960, in ibid., 263.

47. LS to Jerry Bick, October 27, 1961, in ibid., 288.

48. LS to George Brockway, June 1949, in ibid., 126.

49. Smith, "Letter to My Publisher," in *Killers of the Dream*, 21–22.

50. LS to Ruth Nanden Ashen, September 9, 1960, in Gladney, *How Am I to Be Heard?*, 249. Smith never completed the children's book she referred to in this letter.

51. Clayton, "Lillian Smith," 103–4.

Margaret Mitchell
(1900–1949)

"What Living in the South Means"

KATHLEEN ANN CLARK

❀ ❀ ❀

Writing to her friends Clifford and Helen Dowdey in August 1938, two years after the publication of *Gone With the Wind* had brought her fame and fortune, Margaret Mitchell reflected on the price to be paid for "peace and happiness" in the South: "I couldn't live any other place in the world except the South. . . . I believe, however, that I see more clearly than most people . . . just what living in the South means. There are more rules to be followed here than any place in the world if one is to live in any peace and happiness." And yet, the author insisted, the benefits of southern life were well worth the cost: "Having always been a person who was perfectly willing to pay for everything I got, I am more than willing to pay for the happiness I get from my residence in Georgia." As an individualistic and at times rebellious woman from a prominent Atlanta family, Mitchell was keenly aware of both the costs and the benefits of her particular southern existence. Perhaps, by the age of thirty-seven, when she penned the letter to the Dowdeys, Mitchell really had come to terms with the many "rules to be followed" in order to reap the benefits afforded an elite white woman in pre–World War II southern society. However, there is ample evidence from her life and writings—particularly during the years of adolescence and young adulthood—to suggest that such an unequivocal accommodation, if in fact it was achieved, did not come easily. In striking contrast to her later claims of satisfaction with southern life, Mitchell struggled throughout her adolescence and young adulthood to define an independent white female identity, a struggle that was nourished and ultimately stymied within the social order of Jim Crow.[1]

Born on November 8, 1900, Margaret Munnerlyn Mitchell grew up in a household that embodied contradictory impulses shaping white female roles and identity in the turn-of-the-century South. Mitchell's mother, May Belle Mitchell, was a suffragist active in the Georgia movement throughout Margaret's childhood and adolescence. Advocating for political rights on the grounds that women's exclusion from the right to vote unfairly discriminated against women property holders, May Belle gave voice to oft-repeated economic arguments of women suffragists in Georgia, who—like many elite women throughout the history of the women's rights movement—crafted a feminist ideology that was fundamentally rooted in distinctions of class and race. In the speeches she delivered throughout the state, May Belle castigated a system that enfranchised men whom she believed to be the distinct inferiors of "quality" women such as herself: "If you stretch your neck a little bit, you can look down Decatur Street [in Atlanta] and see the drunken bums being thrown out of the saloons on the sidewalk. And because they are men, though they haven't been paid a dime and the city and the county have supported them all their lives, they are entitled to vote and we are not. Is that fair?"[2]

May Belle's unshakable commitment to expanding the rights of women—or at least a select group of women—impressed her young daughter. Indeed, one of Margaret's earliest and most vivid memories was of a suffrage rally in Atlanta conducted by Carrie Chapman Catt. As there was no one at home to take care of Margaret, who was a toddler at the time, her mother took her along to the rally: "Mother tied a Votes-for-Women banner around my fat stomach, put me under her arm, took me to the meeting hissing blood curdling threats if I did not behave, set me on the platform between the silver pitcher and the water glasses while she made an impassioned speech. I was so at my eminence that I behaved perfectly, even blowing kisses to gentlemen in the front row."[3] In addition to her championing of women's suffrage and other civic reforms, May Belle was also a firm believer in the importance of higher education and professional opportunities for women; she made it clear that she expected Margaret to take her studies seriously, and to develop into a strong and capable woman.

In her desire for increased educational, professional, and even political opportunities for women, May Belle Mitchell exemplified a number of uneven changes that were occurring in white women's lives in the late nineteenth and early twentieth-century South. As Anne Firor Scott first argued more than thirty years ago, and as more recent southern women's historians have largely confirmed, white southern womanhood underwent significant alterations in the decades following the Civil War, a time when increasing numbers of women enhanced their capacity for independence and self-possession through more practical education, the postponement or even avoidance of marriage, public activism, and paid employment. At the same time, cultural definitions of ideal

MARGARET MITCHELL

Kenan Research Center at the Atlanta History Center.

southern womanhood began to place a greater emphasis on the qualities of a woman's intellect and capacity for self-reliance than in the past.[4]

And yet if May Belle Mitchell embraced ongoing developments toward a more independent white womanhood, she also exhibited the profound ambivalence that persisted in the South regarding such changes. Thus, even as May Belle adopted some feminist principles and urged Margaret to develop a foundation for self-reliance, she also insisted that her children master the exacting etiquette that reflected and reinforced their social position, and she pressed upon Margaret in particular the importance of maintaining a "respectable" reputation as a developing young woman. These contradictory expectations must have been especially confusing for Margaret, who was supposed to develop independence and capability while simultaneously remaining faithful to conservative southern traditions that celebrated (and demanded) female domesticity and submissiveness. As Mitchell's biographer, Darden Asbury Pyron, points out: "May Belle Mitchell . . . pressed two worlds [upon Margaret]. On the one hand . . . she must know the rules and perform her part as belle and proto-lady. On the other hand, she demanded that her daughter 'do what the boys do.'"[5] Neither May Belle nor Margaret's father, Eugene Mitchell, questioned the social conventions that sustained their way of life as an elite white family in early twentieth-century Atlanta. On the contrary, both parents took great pains to school Margaret and her brother, Stephens, in the history and culture that worked to secure their privilege, and Eugene in particular cultivated a reputation for conservative principles. "Among those who knew him as a man, Eugene Mitchell left an invariable impression," argues Pyron. He was "inflexibly conservative, severely decorous, socially reactionary, and relentlessly proper."[6]

The Mitchells' simultaneous embrace of certain feminist ideals and the stringent rules of Jim Crow society necessarily bequeathed an ambiguous legacy to their only daughter, which was only reinforced by the conflict and uncertainty in the broader culture as Atlanta underwent significant transformations during the early 1900s. To many city residents, young women's growing presence in places of employment, commercial entertainments, and other public venues was an especially worrisome sign that rapid industrialization and urbanization were threatening to undermine morality and unravel the social order. Indeed, the rapid expansion of Atlanta's economy, coupled with other changes wrought by brisk industrial development and urban growth, did provide unprecedented opportunities for female mobility and independence during the early 1900s in Atlanta, as in many cities throughout the country. As Georgina Hickey has demonstrated, civic leaders who were anxious to reassert control over their city focused on reinforcing a conservative gender ethos and reiterating the necessity of female "protection" and domesticity to moral discipline and social order.[7] These efforts came to a head when Mitchell herself was a young teenager. The brutal murder of Mary Phagan, who was a young factory worker (and nearly the same age as Mitchell) in 1913, and the lynching of her accused killer, the Jewish industrialist Leo Frank, two years later, reflected a wide range of social anxieties about the challenges posed by industrialization to existing social controls in Atlanta, especially in regard to young women and female sexuality.[8]

After graduating high school in 1918, Mitchell left Atlanta for college in the North, a move that enabled many young southern women to experience new freedoms, expand their sense of self, and develop lives that challenged southern gender conventions, at least to a degree.[9] But Mitchell's time at Smith College in Massachusetts was cut short by tragedy. In January of 1919, partway through her first year, May Belle was stricken with the flu during an epidemic that raged across the country that year. Although Margaret sped home, she was not in time—her mother succumbed to the illness on January 25, one day before Margaret was able to reach Atlanta. During her illness, as she prepared for the possibility of death, May Belle composed a long letter to her only daughter in which she reflected on her own life and attempted to leave some final instructions: "I must warn you of one mistake that a woman of your temperament might fall into," she wrote. "Give of yourself with both hands and overflowing heart, but give only the excess after you have lived your own life." Just as quickly as she gave her blessing to individual pursuits, however, May Belle hurried to make a retraction. She continued, "This is badly put. What I mean is that your life and energies belong first to yourself, your husband and your children. Anything left over after you have served these, give and give generously, but be sure there is no stinting of love and attention at home." She concluded the letter by writing, "Care for your father when he is old, as I cared for my mother . . . [yet] never let his or anyone else's life interfere with your real life." Adding to this mix of decidedly contradictory advice, May Belle emphasized throughout the letter that her own happiness and satisfaction had come from her family, and particularly a happy marriage and loving children.[10]

Thus, Margaret Mitchell—bright, sensitive, and highly impressionable—came of age in the midst of contradictory impulses regarding white female agency and independence in the early twentieth-century South, impulses that were brought to bear on her formative relationships and experiences as she emerged into young adulthood. If her mother's dedication to woman suffrage was among Margaret's earliest recollections, so too did she have a prime opportunity as a young child to absorb her society's vivid warnings as to the dangers facing white girls and women. Margaret was just five years old on September 22, 1906, when several thousand whites undertook a rampage through black neighborhoods in central and suburban Atlanta, attacking individual African Americans and black-owned businesses. By the time the carnage ended three days after it started, there were dozens of (mostly black) fatalities, many more who were badly injured, and considerable property damage inflicted, especially in predominantly black areas of the city. As was the case in other communities that experienced outbreaks of white-on-black violence during the period, local newspapers and politicians had kept up a steady drumbeat of "news" regarding alleged assaults by black men on white girls and women in the days and weeks leading up to the riot in Atlanta. Echoing the charges that swirled around the city and state during the summer of 1906, the *Atlanta Journal* portrayed the African American man as so outside his appropriate "place" in southern society that he was now out to "destroy" the one thing "he cannot attain," that is, "the fair young girlhood of the South."[11]

May Belle Mitchell was away from the city visiting friends in New York at the time of the riot, but the rest of the family was at home. Writing to his wife in the aftermath of the violence, Eugene described the excitement of the crowd, which had been whipped into a frenzy by rumors "that negro mobs had been formed to burn the town." Rumors reached Eugene that Jackson Hill, where the Mitchells lived, was destined to be a particular target; men "went down the street warning every man to get his gun and be ready at a moment's warning." Without a gun in the house, Eugene searched for alternative weapons, but it was five-year-old Margaret who came up with the idea of a sword that was kept in the home as a family heirloom. "I adopted the suggestion," Eugene reported. As he sat up all night guarding the house, he could hear pistols and guns being fired off in different parts of the city.[12]

Not only was Margaret present for the riot, but she was clearly attuned to the sense of danger that gripped her father and other white Atlantans as rumors spread of rampaging black mobs and repeated assaults on white women. With the imagination and creativity that would mark her future writings, she inserted herself into the unfolding drama and did her best to help protect her home and family. Not yet six years old when the riot occurred, Margaret was nonetheless witness to a set of events that would stand as a defining moment in race relations in the city in the coming decades.

❀ ❀ ❀

Out of these desultory conditions, Margaret Mitchell endeavored to shape her own modern, southern female identity; considerations of race and class were absolutely inextricable from both the opportunities and the dilemmas she faced as a young woman in her quest to achieve a measure of female freedom and individuality in her life and writing. And yet, the connections between race, class, and gender have gone largely unexamined in scholars' treatments of Mitchell. While many historians have astutely analyzed Mitchell's efforts to explore and resolve various conflicts over gender and sexuality in her life and writings, particularly *Gone With the Wind*, and others have examined her treatment of race, these analyses have tended to remain separate, leaving Mitchell's endeavors to redefine southern womanhood as somehow distinct from her whiteness and the broader racial and class context of Jim Crow.[13] But Mitchell's efforts to forge an independent and sexually mature female identity, in both her writing and her life, were both facilitated and, ultimately, curtailed by the social mores of her community and her own faithfulness to southern hierarchies of race and class.

Early on, Mitchell tried repeatedly to chart a nontraditional course for herself in both her life and writings, consistently taking on personas that defied conventional expectations—as a child she was known as "Jimmy" the tomboy; as a rebellious flapper and ambitious newspaper reporter she adopted the moniker "Peggy"; and then, as a married woman who nonetheless sought to retain a measure of autonomy and would go on to publish the best-selling novel of all time, she settled on "Margaret Mitchell." In the years following the publication of *Gone With the Wind*, however, the now-famous author assumed the role of a prim and proper southern matron, telling reporters that she preferred to be known simply as "Mrs. John Marsh," and claiming to identify much more with the demure and retiring Melanie than the defiant and unruly Scarlett in her novel. Even in her earlier phases of more openly rebellious behavior, however, Mitchell was always torn between her desire to reject the limitations placed on her as a woman on the one hand, and her steadfast loyalty to the southern values of her family and community on the other.

Mitchell's struggles—between her own desires for independence and her commitment, as she put it, to a "conservative" life—are especially apparent in her choices and writings as a maturing adolescent and young adult in the 1910s and early 1920s. As a child, Margaret had been a self-described "tomboy" and showed many signs of rebellion against the strictures of traditional southern femininity. She often dressed as a boy, was an enthusiastic baseball player and equestrian, and frequently cast herself as either the male lead or an exceptionally adventurous female character in the many stories and plays she wrote and directed for her neighborhood "gang." The nickname "Jimmy" suited her well as a young child, as it went along with her boyish appearance and activities.[14] As a teenager, she continued to enjoy male/masculine role-playing, and surviving photographs from the period frequently show Margaret in pants and taking an assertive stance. Even when dressed in more feminine attire, she tended to look directly and boldly into the camera—a gaze that embodied the "manly" self-possession of the lead female character in *Lost Laysen*, a novella that Mitchell composed (from a male narrator's point of view) when she was fifteen: "She looked at you as straight and steady as a man without any coquetry or anything like that."[15]

While her early writing and role-playing afforded Mitchell opportunities to take on masculine attributes, and even experiment with male identities, she found it difficult to integrate her conflicting desires for independence and love, Jazz Age freedoms and a "conservative" reputation, as she matured from an adolescent into a young woman. Her late teens and early twenties marked an extremely tumultuous and unstable period. Even as she maintained an active—even frenetic—social life, Margaret (or "Peggy") confessed to one of her closest confidants that she was "as acutely unhappy as it is humanly possible to be and remain sane."[16] "I've got things that many a girl has sold her soul to get—social position, money enough to buy what I want, looks and brains sufficient to get by, a family who loves me, friends who care for me, and a few men who would marry me if I loved them. A girl is a fool, a damn fool, not to be happy with all that, wouldn't you think? Well, I'm not and I don't know why."[17]

Margaret's transition to adulthood transpired at a time of family upheaval that no doubt exacerbated her sense of uncertainty and indirection. In 1917, a terrible fire raged through a wide swath of Atlanta, destroying not only Margaret's childhood home on Jackson Street (the family had since moved to a new house on Peachtree Street) but also nearly a dozen other properties owned by extended family members. The following year, Margaret suffered the death of her fiancé, Clifford Henry, a young soldier whom Mitchell had met and fallen in love with sometime during the spring of 1918, when Atlanta was overrun with troops from nearby Fort McPherson and Camp Gordon. Fast on the heels of Henry's demise came May Belle's death in early 1919. Although she finished out her freshman year at Smith, Margaret returned to Georgia for good in June, taking up housekeeping for her bereft father, her brother Stephens, and her grandmother, Annie Fitzgerald Stephens, with whom she had a particularly contentious relationship. This was the life she would continue, even through her first, and by all accounts disastrous, marriage. In 1922 Margaret wed Berrien "Red" Upshaw, a former University of Georgia football player and ne'er do well, and divorced him in 1923 after a miserable year that included at least one incident of violence by Red against Margaret.[18]

During the period between her withdrawal from Smith and her marriage to Upshaw, Margaret juggled the responsibilities of household management with the whirlwind social life of an Atlanta debutante and (as she later described herself during this period) "flapper." Pretty, clever, and vivacious—not to mention an inveterate flirt—Margaret never lacked for male admirers, even as some of her behavior offended more-traditional constituents of Atlanta society. At a charity ball held at the Georgian Terrace during the spring of 1920, Margaret and a male partner stunned the crowd with their enthusiastic performance of the Apache Dance. A physically vigorous and highly sensual routine that had been popularized in recent movies starring Rudolph Valentino, the Apache Dance enacted an Indian brave's rough and demeaning treatment of his squaw—and her enjoyment of it all. As Mitchell's biographer, Darden Pyron, describes it, the dance elevated "misogyny to terpsichorean art. . . . With cigarette dangling from vicious lips, [the brave] slings his maiden this way and that; she slides away only to crawl back in supplication. The dance involved considerable slapping and other mayhem alternating with histrionic poses [not to mention a passionate kiss]. All in all, Mitchell loved it." Others were less enthusiastic. A few months later, Margaret was singled out for exclusion from the local chapter of the Junior League, a vital—and conservative—social institution for elite women in Atlanta. This rebuke stung—Mitchell reportedly never forgot it—but it did not slow her down or dent her popularity with men, and she continued to enjoy a hectic schedule of dating, parties, and excursions of various sorts.[19]

In spite of her popularity and outward exuberance, Margaret expressed deep ambivalence about her life, and especially her future, in letters she wrote to two male contemporaries—Henry Love Angel, a devoted, but ultimately unsuccessful, suitor of Mitchell's during the late 1910s and early 1920s, and Allen Edee, a close friend and confidante from her days at Smith, with whom she kept a particularly voluminous and intimate correspondence between the summer of 1919 and the fall of 1921. Mitchell was unenthusiastic about the prospect of marriage, even as she actively courted male attention, comradeship, and love—and wrote, almost obsessively, about the various men she dated in her letters to Edee. In one especially vivid correspondence, Mitchell described her several "close calls" with engagement, "I've skidded along the edge of matrimony a few times since I've been home but never seriously, because as you say, Al, it's a serious proposition to belong to one man for the rest of your natural life or till you relieve the boredom by putting arsenic in his soup."[20] Or, as she put it in another letter, "I'm not going to marry. I'm *not* engaged and don't intend to be either, for I'm having too good a time to tie up."[21] More reflectively, she wrote in the late summer of 1921, in one of her final letters to Edee before she embarked on her ill-fated (and to her friends inexplicable) marriage to Upshaw, "Somehow, Al, I don't seem able to love beyond a certain stage. . . . [Several suitors] are just my pals. . . . I realize that happiness lies in a husband and children. I don't believe much in happiness. I know I can never be really happy, but my best chance lies in love. And I can't love. Peculiar state of affairs, n'est-ce pas?"[22]

One person who must have found Mitchell's aversion to marriage especially painful was Henry Love Angel. Angel and Mitchell had been friends and neighbors from their early teenage years. After Mitchell returned to Atlanta following her mother's death, Angel emerged as a particularly ardent admirer, and the two spent a great deal of time together over a period of three years, between Angel's honorable discharge from the army in summer of 1919, and the fall of 1922, when Mitchell married Upshaw. Mitchell's letters to Angel during this period indicate that the two were on quite intimate terms, but—for whatever reason— she turned down his repeated requests for marriage. Apparently, the ritual of proposal and refusal became a well-known routine and source of humor among their friends. Surviving photos include a picture of Angel, down on his knees, sliding a ring on Margaret's finger as she feigns approval, in a tongue-in-cheek performance for the camera.[23]

Even as she skirted marriage to Henry Love Angel or anyone else, Mitchell did not seem able to work out a viable alternative. Surely, she could not count on support from either her father or her brother—Stephens criticized higher education as the "ruination" of women, and her father, at the very least, was opposed to Mitchell pursuing a career. Perhaps a young woman less committed to her family or more definite about her own educational or professional goals would have been able to persevere in the face of such opposition. But Mitchell—barely twenty years old—felt no such certainty. Although she ostensibly left Smith to care for her family, it was never clear that she was truly committed to a college education, much less a medical career—these were much more her mother's vision for Margaret's life, rather than her own dreams or goals. The times she did express wistfulness at the lost opportunity to pursue a career in her letters to Allan Edee were in reference to journalism, not medicine.[24] But even those allusions, brief and isolated amidst dozens of intimate letters, did not really convey a great sense of loss at having to leave Smith. Instead, Mitchell's letters, diary, and later recollections suggest that even as she missed some aspects of school and longed for a way out of conventional domesticity, she was ultimately more comfortable back home in the South, in spite of her protests that she had given up "all the worthwhile things that counted" when she returned to Atlanta to "keep house and keep my family and home intact and take Mother's place in society."[25]

Sprinkled throughout Mitchell's letters to Edee are hints that Mitchell's time away from the South was intensely challenging, and that her northern experiences undermined her view of the world in ways that made it even more difficult for her to adjust to life back at home. She complained to Edee, "I learned very much in the year that I was away from home—from girls and men and books and life and sorrow—till when I came home I had an acute case of mental indigestion."[26]

Margaret's departure from home opened up feelings of freedom and opportunity that she found exhilarating. But she was also confounded by alien practices at the northern college. "I never found my level," she later reflected, "I was a misfit." One incident that particularly struck her then-roommate was the explosion that occurred when Margaret was placed in a history class with one of the handful of African American students then attending the college. As Florence Grandin later recalled, Margaret was incensed. She "vowed and declared that she would go and see the dean or the president if she had to, but she was not going back to that class! I never really knew just whom she did see, but by some artful strategy she won her point, and . . . she was changed to another history class."[27]

It is impossible to know whether Mitchell would have moved past her initial ambivalence and settled on a clearer academic and professional path, as did many other southern women at northern colleges, had May Belle not died. Instead, she returned home after just one year away, unsettled and unsure of what she wanted to do. Back in Atlanta, she talked frequently of going back up North to see Edee and other friends from her days at Smith, but each time she found a reason not to go, falling back on her duties to her father and brother, "But who'd keep house and look after my menfolks? I couldn't leave them alone and unprotected—to say nothing of undarned and unfed!"[28] And, in spite of her whirlwind social life and multiple male "pals," she repeatedly insisted to Edee that she had returned to Atlanta to lead a "conservative" life and to be "the kind of girl 'they'd' want to marry."[29] She continued to express vague yearnings to "escape" her current life circumstances, but Mitchell's brief sojourn to the North seemed ultimately to reaffirm her loyalty and devotion to the South, even as she struggled to find her own path forward there.[30] At Smith, she was well known for her fiery denunciation of "damn Yankees" and stalwart defense of the Confederacy, and throughout the rest of her life she would nurse a deep and abiding sense that the South was a region apart from the rest of the country, one that outsiders were bound to misrepresent—just as the teacher in the history class at Smith, whom Mitchell thought to be a descendant of a well-known New England abolitionist, had (she believed) misunderstood and mistreated Margaret in the wake of her outburst. Utilizing a line of argument that had long been typical of white southerners' defense against northern charges of racial injustice, she wondered whether the professor, Dorothy Ware, had "ever undressed and nursed a Negro woman or sat on a drunk Negro man's head to keep him from being shot by the police."[31] Significantly, Mitchell would later take care to model her own version of ideal race relations in *Gone With the Wind*, especially in the character of Scarlett's mother, Ellen O'Hara, who represented the kind of concern and forbearance Mitchell believed characterized twentieth-century white elites' paternalistic duties (and burdens) vis-à-vis African Americans. Moreover, the author repeatedly expressed her wish that the success of *Gone With the Wind* would help to overturn more oppressive (and to Mitchell's mind, false) images of southern slavery and race relations that had characterized in an earlier best-selling novel: abolitionist Harriet Beecher Stowe's *Uncle Tom's Cabin*. Whatever misgivings Mitchell had about the limits placed on her in the South, she was fiercely loyal to the region; and her time at Smith College—while it may have made it difficult for her to adjust to life in Atlanta—ultimately reinforced her determination to defend her home and community.

Mitchell's ambivalence about her options as an independent-minded and yet "conservative" young southern woman is also at the heart of *Lost Laysen*, the novella that she wrote as a teenager, and which was kept hidden in Henry Love Angel's private collection for several decades. It is not known precisely why Mitchell made the gift of *Lost Laysen* to Angel, but it is clear that both the course of their relationship and the novella, which tells a story of a young white woman's misadventures on a South Pacific island, were characterized by similar themes—in particular, the struggles of a young woman to achieve and maintain her independence in a society that expected and in many ways compelled white female dependence, and the especial difficulties Mitchell had in fashioning a mature and assertive sexual identity (either for herself or her white female characters). The novella also compellingly demonstrates what many scholars have had difficulty seeing in Mitchell's life and work: attachments to race and class privilege were inextricable from the dilemmas she faced and choices she ultimately made as a young and, later, middle-aged woman.

In *Lost Laysen*, the heroine Courtenay Ross (named after Mitchell's close childhood friend and confidante) is a privileged and beautiful young woman who has made the unexpected decision to become a missionary, much to the dismay of her most determined suitor, Douglass Steele, an extremely wealthy and handsome young man, "one of the big athletes of America . . . about 23, broad of shoulder and lean of hips."[32] In spite of Steele's impeccable credentials and utter devotion to Courtenay, she repeatedly rebuffs his proposals of marriage. Instead, she has determined to journey to Laysen, described by the author as "a volcanic island of the Tongas group . . . peopled mostly by Japanese, Chinese, and a few whites," vaguely located (for the story's purposes) somewhere in the South Pacific.[33] As the novella opens, "Miss Ross" has set sail on a ship bound for Laysen, leaving a despondent Douglass Steele waving helplessly from the shoreline—a vision of humbled, indeed humiliated, masculinity that clearly delights Courtenay, and sharply contrasts with her own steely gaze and dignified pose. At the sight of Steele helplessly "running up and down making wild signals," Courtenay begins "to explode with laughter and double up as with a cramp."[34] And yet, when he succeeds in scrounging up a boat—and two "natives"—to bring him out to her ship, Courtenay is happy—if a bit bemused—to accept his company, and he travels with her to Laysen (unsuccessfully importuning her the entire time to leave and return with him to the United States to be married).

Mitchell's identification of missionary life as an avenue for Courtenay Ross's independence, and most specifically avoidance of marriage, links her to legions of young white female contemporaries who envisioned imperial ventures—and missionary work in particular—as a means to their own advancement in the late 1800s and early 1900s. As historian Patricia Hill explains, "Foreign missions were the focus of ambition and the stuff of dreams of young women" at a time when the United States was an emerging imperial power.[35] A number of popular novels written for girls, such as Kate Douglas Wiggin's *Rebecca of Sunnybrook Farm* (1904), featured female missionaries as protagonists.[36] And, in the early decades of the twentieth century, thousands of women seized on the country's expanding imperialist ventures to forge new and unique roles for themselves, working in a variety of capacities—as reformers, educators, writers, and photographers, in addition to working as missionaries. These women's real-life adventures and achievements were in turn regularly featured in popular magazines and newspapers. As Hill notes, foreign work had become a new career option for women, "akin to teaching, nursing, social work," but offering something more as well. Facilitating foreign missions and other work abroad promised women "a life of travel and adventure beyond the wildest dreams of a district schoolteacher."[37]

It is not surprising, then, that the teenage Mitchell envisioned missionary work as an alternative to marriage and path to adventure for the young female protagonist in *Lost Laysen*. A key facet of white women's self-promotion as uniquely *capable* imperialists (missionary or otherwise) was their claim to special abilities—as women—to domesticate, and thereby civilize, indigenous non-white and "barbaric" peoples.[38] So, too, did Mitchell's "Miss Ross" declare that she could not marry Douglass Steele because she had "work to do"—the work of transforming "Chinks" and "Japs," portrayed in the novella as alternately slothful and violent, into a more refined people. "I *am* a missionary," she insisted, "I'm going to wash dirty little Japs and teach 'em not to stick knives in people."[39]

As Mitchell makes clear, just the sight of Courtenay Ross, as a beautiful and—presumably—chaste white woman, powerfully affects the vulgar and uncouth men about her on the ship, a process Mitchell portrays, both literally and figuratively, as whitening the men on board. The narrator of the novella, a rough and hardscrabble Irish seaman who has lived and worked in the South Pacific for many years, recalls his transformation at the onset of the story, "I guess I was forgetting that I was a white man and turning yellow when—*she* came."[40] Upon the moment he first lays eyes on "Miss Ross," the first "good" woman he has come across in five years, the seaman feels compelled to change his ill-mannered ways, reaching up—for the first time in his memory—to remove his hat in her presence, and rushing off at the earliest opportunity to shave a long-neglected beard.

In spite of Ross's stated commitment to missionary work and obvious ability to tame at least some of the wildness around her, no one in *Lost Laysen*—not even, it would seem, Courtenay Ross herself—ever fully believes that she is truly cut out for missionary work. As the ship's captain laughingly declares to a shipmate, "She's about as psalm singing as you are!"[41] Indeed, there is little, if anything, in Mitchell's depiction of Courtenay Ross to suggest that she is destined to find fulfillment via pious and self-abnegating devotion to others, no matter how exotic or savage, any more than Margaret was fated to follow May Belle's example by blending capable household management with civic reform. Ross's attempt to acquire independence via missionary work is clearly doomed from the start, and the general sentiment on board the ship bound for Laysen is that, in the end, she will marry Douglass Steele. As Bill Duncan, the Irish seaman and narrator who also loves her states matter-of-factly to Steele, "You are the little lady's kind and someday—you'll—marry her."[42]

Even as Mitchell portrays one set of choices—both "domestic," albeit in different ways—for a young white woman like Courtenay Ross, she also hints at other more alluring, but also dangerous, possibilities. A particularly intriguing aspect of the novella, given contemporary obsessions with interracial sex, is Ross's obvious fascination with both the working-class Irishman Bill Duncan (who refers to himself as "turning yellow" at the onset of the story) and a resident "half-breed—Jap and Spanish," named Juan Mardo. Whereas Mitchell portrays Ross as merely tolerating, in a comradely sort of way, the attentions of Douglass Steele, she depicts the would-be missionary as physically excited—if somewhat frightened—by the bodies of Duncan and Mardo. In the second of two quite intimate scenes during which Ross nurses a shirtless Duncan after a fight, the narrator relates, "I sat at her feet . . . and for the second time in two days before her without my shirt. I felt her cool hands slide over my shoulder with its hard packs of muscle and down my arm. I looked up into her eyes then and I caught a fleeting glance of pure terror . . . 'God made you well, Mr. Duncan,' she said softly."[43] Equally striking is Mitchell's portrayal of Mardo as alluring *and* dangerous, "possessing the devils [sic] own dark beauty. He had soft black eyes that slanted slightly and a soft, red woman's mouth that always sneered. His hair was soft and black and silky and his yellow brown skin was soft. Oh! he *looked* soft and gentle all right but if ever there was a fiend out of Hell, it was Juan Mardo!" Ross's response when she learns that Mardo, as Duncan warns her, intends "to have you—any way he [can] get you!" is not fearfulness but exhilaration. "Ye Gods!" she says with a gasp and a grin, "This *is* thrilling!"[44]

Ross—who, although named for Mitchell's childhood friend is portrayed as physically and temperamentally resembling the author herself—is sexually enlivened by the "yellow" (and working-class) Duncan and "half-breed" Mardo, in striking contrast to her rather tepid, if not downright cold, responses to the ultrawhite, elite Steele. Thus, Mitchell strongly implies that Ross can only be sexually excited or satisfied by a nonwhite, working-class man. In this mixed-race/class context, it is also possible for Mitchell to imagine more flexible gender roles—she repeatedly emphasizes masculine qualities in Courtenay, such as her direct gaze and lack of fear, and pointedly suggests that there is something inherently exciting about Mardo's "softness" as well. Mitchell's portrayal of Ross's sexuality as enlivened by Duncan and Mardo also mirrors the sexually charged kiss in the Apache Dance that was apparently so objectionable to Atlanta matrons. In addition, it would seem to reflect Mitchell's exposure to the titillating stories of miscegenation that circulated widely in American newspapers between 1900 and 1920, and that frequently featured scandalous (and increasingly illegal) unions between white women and Asian American—or "Mongolian"—men, very often specified as Japanese or Filipino. Splashed across the pages of newspapers throughout the country, sensationalist stories and images of white women being seduced by "Mongolian" men "captivated readers partly for the enticing lure of the forbidden, the new and exotic possibilities they pitted against traditional morality," argues historian Peggy Pascoe.[45]

Having hinted at a potential escape from the frigidity of respectable white womanhood for Courtenay Ross, however, Mitchell immediately retreats into a well-worn script, a la Thomas Dixon's *The Clansman* and D. W. Griffith's recently released *Birth of a Nation*. These were narratives that Mitchell knew well, and in fact they played a key role in her imagination as a budding author and playwright. She particularly admired Dixon, whose novels she consumed voraciously. In fact, one of her most elaborate theatrical productions as a teenager was of the Dixon novel *The Traitor*, which pitted heroic Klansmen against an array of malevolent black and white forces.[46] Indeed, so faithfully did Mitchell portray Dixon's work that her parents gave her a stern lecture on the dangers of copyright infringement.

In *Lost Laysen's* climax, Steele fights mightily to fend off Mardo and his henchmen from an attack on Ross until, vastly outnumbered, he succumbs to multiple stab wounds. Left to fend for herself against the relentless assault, Ross takes her own life, rather than submit herself to "Mardo and his Japs." And so, in the end, Mitchell concludes Ross's quest for adventure and self-fulfillment with catastrophe; indeed, the very island of Laysen itself is convulsed in a volcano and sinks into the sea during a terrible storm that sets the scene for the fatal battle. And yet, the deaths of Steele and Ross also achieve redemption of sorts. In death—and only in death—are Steele and Ross returned to their appropriate and complementary roles as brave defender and virtuous maid, a balance that was impossible to achieve while Ross was alive and persisted in her quest for independence and excitement via relationships (both tutorial and sexual) with nonwhite men. When Bill Duncan and the ship's captain come upon the now-quiet battle scene, a short time after combat has ended, they are devastated by the demise of Steele and Ross, but also heartened by what they can tell of each one's actions during the assault. Surveying the evidence that Steele fought fiercely to protect Courtenay, suffering dramatic knife wounds as he struggled against multiple opponents—"long slashes, reaching from shoulder to waist, small deep stabs and short jagged hacks," the captain exclaims, "He . . . was a *man*—that boy! . . . God in heaven, Bill, but there must have been a fight. . . . No doubt the boy threw several overboard."[47] In spite of her earlier flirtations, Ross, too, rises to the occasion and is finally able to perform her assigned role to perfection. "The little lady heard Juan Mardo coming . . . she used [a knife given to her by Duncan]. God bless her brave little heart—she wasn't afraid to die!" Ross committed suicide, just as she should, a woman "who placed her honor far—far higher than her life."[48]

Written when Mitchell was a maturing adolescent, and presented as a gift to a devoted suitor whom she was unable to bring herself to marry, *Lost Laysen* strikingly expresses the young author's struggles to navigate a forward course for her own life amidst competing social forces and internal needs. The novella is also suggestive of the ways in which racial and class considerations informed Mitchell's own ambivalences regarding female independence. On the one hand, the interracial and interclass context of *Lost Laysen* make possible Mitchell's exploration of white female independence and sexual adventure. On the other hand, it is precisely this interracial (and interclass) context that makes it necessary to punish—indeed, annihilate—any such impulses toward white female freedom, sexual or otherwise. Only in death can Mitchell's characters successfully stave off nonwhite (or gender-bending) forces, both internal and external, and perfectly fulfill their society's expectations for white female self-abnegation and male mastery.

In her own life, Mitchell's inability to enact a mature, autonomous female identity was given particularly acute expression in her sexual self-fashioning, which in turn directly mirrored contemporary portrayals of respectable white women as naturally sexually passionless—the victims of male (and most typically nonwhite male) sexual aggression, rather than self-possessed sexual agents. Mitchell took precisely such pains to deny any sexual desire or agency of her own, and instead dwelled repeatedly—even obsessively—on fantasies of rape, or attempted rape. Indeed, part of Courtenay Ross's attraction to Bill Duncan and Juan Mardo is the seeming potential for assault. Mitchell repeatedly dwells on the contrast between Ross's diminutive stature and Duncan's heft—"at least 6 ft 3, of hard bunchy muscle," and she portrays the burly seaman as struggling to keep his "hunger" for Ross in check, even as he swears he would die "a hundred deaths" rather than harm her. And from the story's very beginning, it is clear that Mardo is both sexually dangerous and appealing to Ross, as Duncan resignedly confesses, "He *was* good to look at."[49]

Although Mitchell herself obviously enjoyed—even thrived on—male company as a young woman, she took umbrage at any suggestion that she was willingly physically intimate with any man. In her letters to Edee, she took pains to convince him that her dates never moved beyond a chaste kiss or two. Or, if a relationship did become more physical, she emphasized that it was only because a man forced himself on her. Mitchell loved to relate tales of adventure and mishap to Edee, and some of her most vivid and energetic stories involved narrow escapes from overly lustful companions, such as one date, whom Mitchell described only as "the cave man." She expressed relief when he returned to college after the summer, for she had found him to be particularly "unmanageable," a fact that she attributed to his time abroad during the war. "He had lived in France for 18 months and his methods of attack were disconcertingly direct."[50] Mitchell used this and other stories to illustrate a point—which she insisted on repeatedly—that she had "drawn a line that men can't pass except by force."[51] In striking contrast to her vivid stories featuring male aggression, she literally could not bring herself to portray a kiss from the "female point of view"—she confessed to Edee that she was stuck in writing a particular story because it called for such a kiss, and, try as she might, she could not figure out how to depict it.[52]

In the summer of 1920, Mitchell complained to Allen Edee that she felt like a "dynamo going to waste." She was contemplating a return to school, though not to Smith. "I've made up my mind that sometime, somehow, I'm going away, *somewhere!*"[53] But Mitchell did not return to school, nor did she leave Atlanta. In August of 1921, she wrote the letter to Edee in which she confessed that she didn't seem "able to love beyond a certain stage," and in September, she wrote to Henry Angel that she loved him, but could not marry him. One year later, she married Red Upshaw—much to the surprise and consternation of her family and friends, who could see little to recommend a man whom they perceived as unlikable, unstable, and incapable of taking responsibility for his life. Paradoxically, it was Upshaw's immaturity that contributed to Mitchell finally embarking on her longed-for career as a writer. Feeling she needed to take some responsibility for the couple's disastrous financial state, Mitchell went to work for the *Atlanta Journal*, a job she loved and thrived in until she quit, upon marrying her second husband, John Marsh, in 1925.[54]

Shortly before she agreed to marry Marsh, however, Mitchell once again felt "an urge most violent to escape from something," and departed from Atlanta. This time she traveled to Cuba, with a plan to travel on to Panama, Honolulu, and Tahiti, and with the intention of supporting herself as a journalist as she went. She never made it past Cuba. As she later summarized her experiences there in an article for the *Journal*, she quickly realized that the "tropics" were an uncomfortable place for a white woman traveling alone, absent the protection that white men—and the carefully guarded rules of Jim Crow—provided at home. The men of Cuba, she reported disdainfully, "have as much chivalry in their souls as hungry sharks." And the local police "are no comfort to an enraged young American woman who has run the gauntlet of smirking dandies—twisting their tiny black moustaches and insolently murmuring remarks as the lady passes by."[55]

Not long after her precipitous return to Atlanta, Mitchell and Marsh became engaged; they were married on July 4, 1925—a date that amused Margaret, as she later claimed, for it was a "queer way to celebrate Independence Day."[56] Soon after, Margaret, who was restricted to her home as a consequence of a foot injury, began to write the epic story of the South that would eventually become *Gone With the Wind*.

In 1936, the publication of her novel transformed Margaret Mitchell into one of the most famous women in the country. While Mitchell had indeed settled down to a fairly domestic existence over the previous decade, having quit journalism soon after marrying Marsh, she had not simply retreated into a conventional home life. Neighbors had been surprised, and perhaps a bit shocked, when Mitchell—in a small but notable rebellion against the tradition of wives' merging their identity with that of their husband—placed a nameplate on the door of the newlyweds' first apartment that boldly stated the names of the occupants as "John Marsh and Margaret Mitchell." The apartments where she and Marsh resided were known for their boisterous gatherings of friends, rather than the pitter-patter of little feet—the marriage did not result in any children, and for years Mitchell threw herself into writing the manuscript that would eventually become *Gone With the Wind*.

With fame came unyielding attention, however, and Mitchell and Marsh struggled to maintain a semblance of privacy, even as Mitchell committed herself to responding personally to the hundreds, and then thousands, of letters that poured in to her from admiring readers from around the world. Now well into her thirties, the "Mrs. John Marsh" who presented herself—warily—to the public was careful to prune away any hint of the "wild woman" who had hoarded male beaus, scandalized Atlanta matrons, and attempted an escape to Cuba many years before. Invariably described as modest and demure in the press, she now appeared to epitomize the qualities of restrained southern womanhood that had so eluded her throughout much of her life. To anyone acquainted with the earlier versions of Mitchell, this latest performance must have been somewhat remarkable—not unlike the sudden transformation of her character, Courtenay Ross, from a strong and fearless adventurer into the personification of defenseless white womanhood at the conclusion of *Lost Laysen*. And yet, there was continuity as well in Margaret Mitchell's desire to chart an individualistic course while retaining her social standing and defending the region's racial order—a feat she finally accomplished by becoming a successful author whose renown came from writing a phenomenal vindication of the Confederate South that simultaneously offered up a paternalistic rendering of race relations and a highly ambivalent portrait of white southern womanhood. In the decade that followed the publication of her novel and the subsequent release of the Hollywood film, Margaret and John lived a relatively quiet existence, devoting much of their energy to nursing their health and defending Mitchell's copyright, until she died tragically after being hit by a speeding driver on Peachtree Street on August 16, 1949. Throughout that decade, there was little—at least to the public eye—to suggest the headstrong young woman who had rebelled, however ambivalently, against southern convention. As Mitchell herself explained, there were "rules to be followed" in the South, and she, at least, had determined that the benefits outweighed the sacrifices that were necessary to keep them.

NOTES

1. Letter from Margaret Mitchell to Mr. and Mrs. Clifford Dowdey, August 22, 1938, reprinted in *Margaret Mitchell's "Gone With the Wind" Letters, 1936–1949*, ed. Richard Harwell (New York: Macmillan, 1976), 222–23.

2. May Belle's argument for woman suffrage, as recalled by her son, Stephens Mitchell, quoted in Darden Asbury Pyron, *Southern Daughter: The Life of Margaret Mitchell and the Making of* Gone With the Wind (1991; Athens: Hill Street Press, 2004), 40. For additional biographical material on Mitchell, consult Anne Edwards, *Road to Tara: The Life of Margaret Mitchell* (New Haven: Ticknor & Fields, 1983); and Elizabeth I. Hanson, *Margaret Mitchell* (Boston: Twayne Publishers, 1991).

3. Margaret Mitchell, quoted in Pyron, *Southern Daughter*, 43.

4. Anne Scott's groundbreaking study of southern white women was published in 1970. See Scott, *The Southern Lady: From Pedestal to Politics, 1830–1930* (Chicago: University of Chicago Press, 1970). Since that time, historians have debated the precise nature and degree of change in various aspects of white women's position, but there is certainly a general consensus that the events of the Civil War and Reconstruction, as well as economic and political developments associated with the "New South," propelled significant alterations in southern white women's lives. Important works include Drew Faust, *Mothers of Invention: Women of the Slaveholding South in the American Civil War* (Chapel Hill: University of North Carolina Press, 1996); LeeAnn Whites, "'Stand by Your Man': The Ladies Memorial Association and the Reconstruction of Southern White Manhood," in *Women of the American South: A Multicultural Reader*, ed. Christine Anne Farnham, 133–49 (New York: NYU Press, 1997); Caroline E. Janney, *Burying the Dead but Not the Past* (Chapel Hill: University of North Carolina Press, 2008); Karen Cox, *Dixie's Daughters: The United Daughters of the Confederacy and the Preservation of Confederate Culture* (Gainesville: University Press of Florida, 2003); Jane Turner Censer, *The Reconstruction of White Southern Womanhood, 1865–1895* (Baton Rouge: Louisiana State University Press, 2003); and Georgina Hickey, *Hope and Danger in the New South City: Working-Class Women and Urban Development in Atlanta, 1890–1940* (Athens: University of Georgia Press, 2003).

5. Pyron, *Southern Daughter*, 47.

6. Ibid., 16.

7. Hickey, *Hope and Danger*.

8. Nancy MacLean, "The Leo Frank Case Reconsidered: Gender and Sexual Politics in the Making of Reactionary Populism," *Journal of American History* 78 (December 1991): 917–48.

9. On southern women's experiences at northern colleges, see Joan Marie Johnson, *Southern Women at the Seven Sister Colleges: Feminist Values and Social Activism, 1875–1915* (Athens: University of Georgia Press, 2008).

10. Letter from May Belle Mitchell to Margaret Mitchell, as quoted in Pyron, *Southern Daughter*, 90–91.

11. Quotation appearing in Gregory Mixon, *The Atlanta Riot: Race, Class, and Violence in a New South City* (Gainesville: University Press of Florida, 2005), 1. See also David Fort Godshalk, *Veiled Visions: The 1906 Race Riot and the Reshaping of American Race Relations* (Chapel Hill: University of North Carolina Press, 2009).

12. Eugene Mitchell's account of the riot appears in Pyron, *Southern Daughter*, 31.

13. In the historical literature on Mitchell, Drew Faust has written a notable essay that considers the role of race in limiting Mitchell's (and Scarlett's) pursuit of independence in "Clutching the Chains That Bind: Margaret Mitchell and *Gone With the Wind*," *Southern Cultures* 5, no. 1 (1999): 5–20. On the other hand, Grace Elizabeth Hale argues that "Mitchell constructs no racial drama" in *Gone With the Wind*. See Grace Elizabeth Hale, *Making Whiteness: The Culture of Segregation in the South, 1890–1940* (New York: Vintage Books, 1998), 263. Mitchell's biographer, Darden Pyron, has also taken issue with the notion that race was vital to Mitchell's identity and conflicts as a woman and author. See Pyron, *Southern Daughter*, 216. An important early attempt to grapple with the significance of race for Mitchell and *Gone With the Wind* is the provocative article by Joel Williamson, "How Black Was Rhett Butler?," in *The Evolution of Southern Culture*, ed. Numan V. Bartley, 87–107 (Athens: University of Georgia Press, 1988). More recently and much more thoroughly, the literary scholar Elizabeth Young has challenged scholars to analyze much more the relationships among race, gender, and sexuality in Mitchell's *Gone With the Wind*. See *Disarming the Nation: Women's Writing and the American Civil War* (Chicago: University of Chicago Press, 1999), chap. 6. See also Tara McPherson, *Reconstructing Dixie: Race, Gender, and Nostalgia in the Imagined South* (Durham: Duke University Press, 2003).

14. Pyron, *Southern Daughter*, 28–30, 49–52; Jane Eskridge, ed., *Before Scarlett: Girlhood Writings of Margaret Mitchell* (Athens: Hill Street Press, 2000).

15. Margaret Mitchell, *Lost Laysen*, ed. Debra Freer (New York: Scribner, 1996), 68.

16. Letter of Margaret Mitchell to Allen Edee, November 18, 1919, reprinted in *Margaret Mitchell, a Dynamo Going to Waste: Letters to Allen Edee, 1919–1921*, ed. Jane Bonner Peacock (Atlanta: Peachtree Publishers, 1985), 49.

17. Ibid., 50.

18. Pyron, *Southern Daughter*, 74–94.

19. Ibid., 107 (quote), 108–9.

20. Letter of Margaret Mitchell to Allen Edee, March 4, 1920, in Peacock, *Margaret Mitchell*, 65.

21. Letter of Margaret Mitchell to Allen Edee, October 12, 1919, in ibid., 37.

22. Letter of Margaret Mitchell to Allen Edee, August 1–2, 1921, in ibid., 119.

23. Introduction to Mitchell, *Lost Laysen*.

24. Letters of Margaret Mitchell to Allen Edee, September 13, 1919, July 31, 1920, in Peacock, *Margaret Mitchell*.

25. Letter of Margaret Mitchell to Allen Edee, October 21, 1919, in ibid., 42.

26. Ibid., 46.

27. Florence Grandin quoted in Pyron, *Southern Daughter*, 84–85.

28. Letter of Margaret Mitchell to Allen Edee, March 13, 1920, in Peacock, *Margaret Mitchell*, 72.

29. Letter of Margaret Mitchell to Allen Edee, October 12, 1919, in ibid., 37–38.

30. Joan Marie Johnson argues that women who returned to the South after going north to college "had to negotiate a new path for themselves to take the place of the freedom they had experienced at school." See Johnson, *Southern Women*, 76.

31. Mitchell quoted in Pyron, *Southern Daughter*, 85.

32. Mitchell, *Lost Laysen*, 74–76.

33. Ibid., 67.

34. Ibid., 73.

35. Patricia Hill, *The World Their Household: The American Women's Foreign Mission Movement and Cultural Transformation, 1870–1920* (Ann Arbor: University of Michigan Press, 1985), 9.

36. Popular novels featuring female missionary antagonists included not only *Rebecca of Sunnybrook Farm* and *New Chronicles of Rebecca* by Kate Douglas Wiggin but also Emma Dorothy Eliza Nevitte Southworth's *Fair Play* and Ellen Glasgow's *Barren Ground*. See Hill, *The World Their Household*, 8–18.

37. Hill, *The World Their Household*, 124.

38. Laura Wexler, *Tender Violence: Domestic Visions in an Age of U.S. Imperialism* (Chapel Hill: University of North Carolina Press, 2001); Louise Michele Newman, *White Women's Rights: The Racial Origins of Feminism in the United States* (New York: Oxford University Press, 1998).

39. Mitchell, *Lost Laysen*, 87.

40. Ibid., 67.

41. Ibid., 71.

42. Ibid., 109.

43. Ibid., 83.

44. Ibid., 99.

45. Peggy Pascoe, *What Comes Naturally: Miscegenation Law and the Making of Race in America* (Oxford: Oxford University Press, 2010), 85–104.

46. Introduction to Mitchell, *Lost Laysen*, 14; Thomas Dixon Jr., *The Traitor: A Story of the Fall of the Invisible Empire* (New York: Doubleday, 1907).

47. Mitchell, *Lost Laysen*, 120–21.

48. Ibid., 122–23.

49. Ibid., 70, 79–80.

50. Margaret Mitchell to Allen Edee, September 13, 1919, in Peacock, *Margaret Mitchell*, 32.

51. Margaret Mitchell to Allen Edee, March 26, 1920, in ibid., 77.

52. Ibid., 81–83.

53. Margaret Mitchell to Allen Edee, [August 1, 1921] in ibid., 104.

54. Pyron, *Southern Daughter*, chaps. 7–9.

55. Mitchell quoted in Pyron, *Southern Daughter*, 196.

56. Mitchell quoted in ibid., 200.

Frances Freeborn Pauley

(1905–2003)

Working for Justice in Twentieth-Century Georgia

KATHRYN L. NASSTROM

The life story of Frances Freeborn Pauley is that of a political activist whose career spanned the twentieth century. At the center of the story is a middle-class white woman, with northern roots and a southern upbringing, who carved out an ever-expanding role for herself in the social and political movements of the twentieth century. Frances came of age politically between the suffrage generation and the generation that grew up with contemporary feminism, and like many of her cohort, she rarely presented the explicit critique of gender roles that was characteristic of both early and late twentieth-century feminism. Instead, her outlook on politics was shaped by the economic concerns of the Depression era, followed by the changing race relations of the postwar period. Nonetheless, throughout her activist career Frances worked with women who fully believed that they, along with men, should define and shape the social and political world. Beginning in the 1930s and extending into the 1990s, a core set of commitments—public education, health and welfare, the civil rights of the oppressed, and the needs of the poor—animated a lifetime of advocating, educating, organizing, and lobbying. In the struggle for social, racial, and economic justice, Frances exhibited a dogged determination and a willingness to learn by doing. "It's just a matter of starting, just putting your foot in the road and saying you're going to do something about it," she maintained.[1] Hers is a political career, not in the traditional sense of office holding and the formal exercise of power, but in a broader definition of politics in which the political efficacy of all citizens matters and the distribution of power and resources in a society is at stake. One can't leave Frances's story without feeling her deep commitment to meaningful democracy.

Frances Freeborn, born on September 11, 1905, in Wadsworth, Ohio, became a southerner at the age of three when her family relocated to Georgia. "One of my earliest memories is my mother telling me that when people call you a 'damn Yankee,' just smile. That was a good lesson for me, because I always talked too much. And I remember being proud that I was a 'damn Yankee.'" A consummate storyteller as well as activist, Frances often used such simple vignettes to encompass a range of experience and meaning. Condensed in these few words are her ambiguous identity as both a northerner and a southerner, the importance of her mother's influence, and a hint that Frances, just like a damn Yankee, would try to leave her mark on the South. In the Methodist church, the faith of her family, Frances observed that women practiced the Social Gospel. Her mother, Josephine Andrews Freeborn, visited the day nursery at Atlanta's Fulton Bag and Cotton Mills and delivered medicine to the sick, thus imparting this tradition to her daughter. Frances accompanied her mother on one occasion to visit the nursery school, and the memory remained vivid. "I was so horrified. I still can smell how the room smelled, and I can see how dirty those children were. Cotton mills were awful, just awful. You know, poverty and degradation are something you have to see and touch and smell." Josephine suffered from an extended illness that curtailed her activities, but Dorothy Tilly, secretary of children's work for the Woman's Missionary Society of the Methodist Episcopal Church, South, nurtured Frances's early development in the church's youth group.[2] Methodist women were in the vanguard of white women's efforts to ameliorate the many problems associated with urbanization and industrialization: overcrowded cities, unsafe working conditions, high rates of disease, and poor health generally. Atlanta was the site of the earliest mission work of Methodist women in Georgia with the establishment of the Trinity Home Mission Society, a ministry to poor women and children, black and white, in downtown Atlanta in 1882. By the time the Freeborns settled in nearby Decatur, Methodist women sponsored settlement houses, homes for unwed mothers, kindergartens, and Sunday schools. In the broad-gauged reform movement of the early twentieth century known as progressivism, churchwomen initiated much of the social welfare thrust and worked with municipal officials to deliver the meager beginnings of a public health and welfare system in the metropolitan Atlanta area of Fulton and DeKalb Counties.[3]

Like many children raised in the South, Frances first learned about race relations in the domestic setting, but family custom again set the Freeborns apart. The family hired an African American domestic helper not, as was common in

FRANCES FREEBORN PAULEY

whose career of social activism spanned the twentieth century.
Francis Freeborn Pauley papers, box 4, folder 2, Manuscript,
Archives, and Rare Book Library, Emory University.

their neighborhood, as a nursemaid for Frances and her brother, but as a cook who also provided more general domestic help. Josephine Freeborn paid her domestic workers a higher wage, limited the hours she required of them, and (in a nearly unthinkable act for a southerner) invited them to enter through the front door. Frances's formative experience of domestic service in the South was with a day worker, not a "mammy," with all the complex connotations of racial intimacy and power that relationship called up. While the Freeborns enjoyed the same advantage as all southern white, middle-class households—white domesticity and comfort were almost uniformly predicated on the low-cost labor of working-class blacks, especially black women—the distinctions the Freeborns drew mattered. Josephine Freeborn did not require, and Frances did not experience, such a thoroughly personalized and exploitative form of service. It would be some time before Frances developed a critique of southern employment patterns, but her childhood provided some of the ground on which she would later link poverty, labor, and racial practices.[4]

Frances came of age in the 1920s, a time of increasing secularism and expanding models for female behavior. She recalled being the first girl at Decatur High School to bob her hair, a momentous act at the time. "Boy, did I make a splash. That was my new freedom, to cut my hair." When she enrolled at nearby Agnes Scott College in the fall of 1923, theater captured her imagination. Other reform-minded women of her generation merged the new opportunities afforded by a college education with their Christian upbringing; many spent their college years working in the YWCA, with its roots in Protestant evangelical reform.[5] While Frances's choice was at once more secular and artistic, she too sensed that a college education prepared an individual for civic engagement. "Agnes Scott certainly taught me to be a serious student, a very serious citizen, that life is real, life is earnest. This was the attitude of the faculty as a whole."

After graduation, Frances faced a choice, as all college graduates do, about what to do with the next phase of her life. Initially, she devoted herself to theater. She gave private drama lessons, directed plays for the Decatur school system, continued to study playwriting with faculty from Agnes Scott, and joined a civic theater group known as the Drama Workshop. Playwriting allowed Frances to give artistic expression to a growing social consciousness. The Drama Workshop was part of an effort to develop a "sectional drama" that reflected ordinary people and places in the South.[6] In the workshop's 1930 season, Frances presented "The Poor Farm," drawing on her church youth group's mission work at the DeKalb County Poor Farm. These visits helped Frances understand poverty on a personal level and avoid a reductionist view of the poor as a social type. Frances's later activism exhibited a flair for the dramatic, which she often attributed to her training in the theater, but as a formative experience the theater was about representing the diversity of the South in the spirit of social realism and, perhaps most fundamentally, about forms of artistic expression that encouraged empathy.

The onset of the Great Depression ended Frances's budding career in civic theater. In 1930 the workshop lost its ticket receipts in a bank failure, and the group hobbled through one last season. As the Depression worsened, simply making do was challenge enough.[7] Recently married (to William C. Pauley on May 25, 1930) and raising two small daughters (Joan born in 1930 and Marylin in 1935), the Depression was for Frances, as for many, a lesson in neighborliness. "All the neighbors got together and tried to figure out the cheapest way to buy the best food and feed our families. There was quite a lot of bartering that went on." The Pauleys, however, survived not only by borrowing and bartering but also through government assistance. Bill Pauley's landscape architecture business was in danger of going under until he began to take on projects funded by the New Deal's Public Works Administration and Works Progress Administration, and with those programs Frances experienced firsthand the benefits of an activist government. With three working men in the family—husband Bill Pauley, father William Freeborn, and brother Elbridge Freeborn—the Pauleys made out better than most, but the Depression left a tremendous impression on Frances and would be a turning point in her life of activism.

In identifying the start of what would become a lifetime of effecting change, Frances said simply, "The first thing I ever remember organizing was during the Depression." She reached adulthood at the onset of the Great Depression and the implications of that demographic fact can almost not be overstated. Her family and church predisposed her to helping others, her college education taught her that citizens have a duty to their society, but the Depression created a particularly pressing context for action. Frances began in the Junior Service League of Decatur, a well-heeled beginning to a life of activism that eventually strayed quite far from the Junior League model. Nonetheless, it was observing the wan and hollow faces of hungry children who didn't have a nickel to come to the Junior League's puppet show that made Frances decide that "something had to be done." That "something" became two related but distinct projects: the formation of the DeKalb Clinic, a county public health clinic, and the introduction of a school lunch program in the county.

Public health was one of the most pressing problems in Depression-era Georgia. Despite the inroads made by progressivism in the early part of the century, Georgia's public health profile was dismal: the state ranked consistently in the top three for malaria deaths, only one town had a milk supply that met the standards of the U.S. Public Health Service, and much of the housing—in Atlanta the majority—was substandard. Georgia's director of public health concluded that the state's primary need was for additional funds for public health and medical care. Only the infusion of federal aid in the context of the New Deal purchased for the state a minimal level of public health protection.[8] Faced with this need, Frances's solution was to organize "a couple of us ladies" who "got together with the county's public health director and decided that we would try to set up a clinic." These "ladies" were the same church women who had taken the lead in establishing a variety of clinics in DeKalb County, first made available to African Americans and later to needy white citizens as well.[9] Presbyterian women established a medical clinic for blacks in 1919 that survived the onset of the Great Depression and became a model for later clinics. Methodist women, for their part, opened a dental clinic for blacks in 1933 and over the course of the Depression laid plans for adding services to whites. The final consolidation of these independent clinics into the DeKalb Clinic occurred in 1939 and represented a partnership of private and public services. Folded into the DeKalb Clinic, from the public sector, were the small beginnings of municipally financed health care delivery, generally focused on disease prevention and maternal and child health.[10] That this also represented Frances's "first" organizing meant that she came of age as an activist in a time of growing public responsibility for social welfare. She never forgot that lesson.

The story of the development of the DeKalb Clinic had a personal dimension as well, and one of the keys to Frances's success as an organizer was her willingness to learn. Although Frances often emphasized that her childhood differed from that of other southerners, she nonetheless came to recognize that she grew up in a world of thoroughgoing racial prejudice. The clinic offered an opportunity for an alternate education. As she assisted on "well-baby day," Frances observed that the county's African American population took greater advantage of the clinic's services than did whites. In the South, where whites more typically viewed blacks as carriers of disease, Frances noted instead that black families sought out preventive care.[11] The lesson was profound: the prevalence of disease among African Americans was not the result of racial inferiority; rather, access to medical resources determined health. Frances's work in the clinic likewise encouraged an understanding of health problems among poor whites, especially mill villagers who suffered from malnutrition and the harmful effects of harsh working conditions. For all that Jim Crow had done to depress the standard of living for blacks in the South, when it came to health care, poor whites, particularly mill workers, faced an equally daunting, if different, array of health problems.[12] Frances took as her charge doing all she could to make that health care more widely available. As vice president of the clinic, she raised funds from the rich and powerful, and she traveled deep into neighborhoods to publicize the clinic's services.

The school lunch program, a direct outgrowth of Frances's work in the DeKalb Clinic, extended Frances's activist education as she came to know middle-class black social reformers of her day for the first time. When malnourished children made their way to the clinic, the need to provide proper meals became obvious at the same time that the federal government provided the means to meet that need.[13] Frances met Maude Hamilton, the principal of a black school in nearby Scottdale, who had already brought the New Deal school lunch program to her own school. Frances, working with school authorities, arranged for Hamilton to speak to the white principals about the program, contacted the federal agency in charge of the program, equipped schools with the necessary kitchen facilities, and raised funds to cover those costs. And, once again, she learned critical lessons. Both the public health clinic and the school lunch program alleviated some of the hardship of the Great Depression and provided services to the needy of both races. But with the school lunch program, the racial roles were reversed. Whereas the clinic was begun by white women as an act of charity toward African Americans, Hamilton, a black woman, led the way with the school lunch program. Even under the confines of segregation, Frances and the white principals were supplicants seeking guidance from Hamilton.[14]

Nonetheless, such racial reversals had their limits; segregation was sidestepped, not confronted. When Hamilton came to speak to the assembled school principals of DeKalb County, she waited in another room. Similarly, when a grand jury inspected the clinic and found that black and white patients shared a waiting room, it instructed the clinic to segregate the races. The staff complied. Frances recalled that the clinic readily accepted the "natural line" that separated blacks from whites in the clinic. "We weren't thinking about real desegregation and what that would require." For most southern white liberals of the period, desegregation was not yet thinkable; rather, they worked to improve the conditions of African Americans within the confines of segregation. Frances was no exception.[15]

While neither Frances nor any of her white colleagues in the clinic and school lunch program challenged segregation, change was underway, which can best be appreciated in generational terms. Frances went into the Great Depression under the tutelage of women like Dorothy Tilly, imbued with the spirit of benevolence and charity, which, in the segregated South, amounted to no small measure of dissent within a discriminatory racial order. Nonetheless, most women of Tilly's generation mixed heartfelt charity with some degree of condescension, and they did not envision African Americans as capable of changing their own status. For the next generation, the Great Depression opened up new vistas. The particular circumstances of a government program available to blacks as well as whites, an adept Hamilton who first seized the opportunity, a young Frances Pauley open to new approaches—all of these conspired to position Frances as someone who could and would chart a different course. In Frances's interactions with Hamilton, it is possible to see how a later generation had formative experiences that, were they ready to accept them, moved them beyond earlier models of interracial reform.[16] In this the role of the federal government was critical, as the New Deal introduced a third party into southern race relations. Despite the fact that the New Deal institutionalized racial discrimination in many of its projects and did not directly confront southern racial patterns, the New Deal on the local and personal level had many consequences, some unintended. In Frances's experience, it was not a government program that African Americans got belatedly, in half measures, if at all. Quite the opposite.[17] Frances Pauley's New Deal, it is no exaggeration to say, changed her life.

As the Depression waned in Georgia, Frances continued to work as a volunteer, but her volunteerism took her squarely into Georgia politics in the 1940s. Like many women of her race and generation, she channeled a growing political interest into the League of Women Voters, that relatively little studied outgrowth of the much-studied women's suffrage campaign of the early twentieth century.[18] From the mid-1940s through the early 1960s, the league was Frances's avenue into the critical questions of democracy and desegregation as they moved to center stage in the political life of the South and the nation after World War II.

The war that pulled the country out of the Depression changed the South, as it did the nation, profoundly. One of the most evident changes was a quickened struggle for civil rights among African Americans. During the war, the U.S. Supreme Court outlawed two linchpins of white supremacy: the poll tax in 1942 and the white primary in 1944. After the war, returning veterans translated the fight against Nazism and fascism abroad into struggles over democracy at home. They found those who had remained on the home front also ready to challenge the racial status quo. Locally, in metropolitan Atlanta, a massive black voter registration drive in early 1946 increased the number of black registered voters from seven thousand to twenty-four thousand. In that same year, the Georgia League of Women Voters went on record in support of black voting rights.[19] As a member, then officer, and finally president of the Georgia League from 1952 to 1955, Frances helped open up Georgia politics.

When Frances joined the league, a citizen had to put up a good fight simply to learn what was happening in the legislature. "We had to do a lot of the stuff that now you can just walk in a clerk's office and get. To get a roll call vote you would have to get permission to read the journal, and to get permission to read the journal was kind of like getting in Heaven." The league's most basic tasks, then, were simply observation and reporting on how the government was being run. In the league, Frances further developed a nascent sense, shared by many American progressives of that time, that information and education were critical starting points in addressing social and political problems. They believed that the facts, once widely known, would move people to do the right thing. The centerpiece of the league's program, locally and nationally, was voter education and citizenship training.[20] This seemingly unobjectionable program was neither routine nor accepted by many Georgia politicians in the 1940s. When two political commentators surveyed the political landscape of Georgia in 1947, they concluded that only two organizations were making a serious effort at voter education: the League of Women Voters and the Citizens Fact-Finding Movement, an information-gathering agency formed in 1938 that had its roots in the league.[21]

The league was, even more importantly, about effecting political change, and in the 1940s this meant confronting Georgia's county unit system, which V. O. Key, in his classic study of southern politics in the late 1940s, described as "unquestionably . . . the most important institution affecting Georgia politics."[22] In what was essentially an indirect system of election, each county in the state carried two, four, or six unit votes, depending on its population. Victory went to the candidate who amassed the most unit votes, rather than the largest popular vote. The practical impact of the system was to weigh heavily the vote in Georgia's numerous rural counties and to diminish significantly the political clout of the much smaller number of urban counties. For the league, with its commitment to representative democracy, this was a critical matter, and the imbalance of political representation only intensified during Frances's time with the league as Georgia continued a trend toward urbanization that the Depression and World War II had fueled. Who got to vote and how those votes counted was also a racial issue, as most of the state's politically active African Americans resided in urban areas.

The League of Women Voters had been working against the county unit system for some time, but the issue came to a head in 1952 when Governor Herman Talmadge, himself a beneficiary of rural rule in Georgia, sought to extend the county unit's reach by writing it into the state constitution. To oppose Talmadge, the league joined a coalition representing liberal forces in Georgia to form an umbrella organization, Citizens against the County Unit Amendment. Their goal was to influence the public to reject the amendment when it came up for a popular vote on the November ballot. Frances remembered it as an exhausting but exhilarating fight: "It was the first time I had just worked day and night without making the bed, without doing anything, just putting your whole self into it. We just simply had to win, and we did, but by a hair." Of the league's and Frances's leadership, Pulitzer Prize–winning journalist Julian LaRose Harris enthused, "It was inspiring to meet women who were providing leadership for both men and women in what proved to be an astonishingly successful effort to save Georgia from political bankruptcy. . . . As for yourself, I have seldom seen an iron hand so effectively masked by a glove so seemingly soft and pliant."[23] Frances, with a tendency to state matters more prosaically, found the origins of her leadership in the realities of intergroup conflicts within the coalition: "Finally they decided that the only trustworthy group was the League. That's one thing, the League has always kept its skirts clean."

The image of a squeaky-clean League of Women Voters, echoing as it does the claims of early twentieth-century suffragists, the foremothers of the league, that women would clean up politics with their votes, suggests an intriguing connection between gender and politics in postwar Georgia. Political corruption in the state—buying votes, bribing officials, tampering with electoral returns— extended into the 1940s and 1950s.[24] More generally at stake in postwar Georgia was the basic issue of democratic citizenship in a complex society: which individuals and groups have access to the political process and to political power? Citizens against the County Unit Amendment brought together a number of predominantly urban interests (including city mayors, urban legislative delegations, organized labor, and newly reenfranchised black voters) who would benefit from adherence to the "one person, one vote" principle. These were often perceived to be special interest groups that marshaled their vote as a bloc. The league, by contrast, presented itself as above the political fray, as an advocacy organization for good government. "In the public interest" was a favorite league phrase to describe the character of its work. It did not seek to be, nor did it present itself as, a special interest group for women. Instead, informed and responsible action by all citizens was its stated mission.

Despite its carefully honed rhetoric of neutrality, the league was quite plainly throwing its weight behind certain political tendencies in Georgia. The opposition, well aware of this, often responded to the league's rhetoric by identifying women in the organization as the so-called good government crowd and levying guilt by association. If the league supported organized labor, then it was communist inspired; if it advocated for black voting rights, then it was led by "nigger lovers." In this climate, the league directed its efforts at the public at large, toward the court of public opinion. League women were rarely the first or the most outspoken advocates to call for political reforms, such as the abolition

of the county unit system. But, when the members of the league—generally
educated, well heeled, and hardly radical—spoke in a measured and reasoned
tone, the tide of racial hyperbole ebbed just a bit. In the early 1950s, on the eve
of the civil rights movement, while black activists were registering black voters
and demanding access to the ballot, and while the courts were chipping away at
racially discriminatory voting regulations, the League of Women Voters helped
cast these changes as reasonable, even desirable. The uncoupling of skin color
from the capacity for citizenship required activists on the one hand and, on the
other, advocates who simply made the proposition look reasonable. The irony,
however, was that the league, by not calling attention to itself as a women's
organization representing women's interests, seems, as a result, to have disappeared somewhat into the historical woodwork.

At the same time that the league joined the battle over the county unit system,
it had its own internal conflicts over race and democracy. Frances worked to
make the Georgia league itself more democratic, an effort that mirrored what
was happening in the national organization.[25] With a group of fellow renegades,
Frances helped elect a state league president who resided outside the metropolitan Atlanta area, a new departure for the league, which was dominated by urban
interests. Frances, first as vice president and later as president of the league,
"pushed organization," and as a result the Georgia league became a presence
in a number of smaller cities and towns where there had not previously been
a League of Women Voters. An additional achievement of this organizational
push was opening the membership of the league to nonwhite women. At a time
when many state and local members resisted admitting black women, believing
it was "right" but not "expedient," Frances pushed ahead.[26] At her first convention as president of the DeKalb league in 1947, the membership accepted new
bylaws eliminating the clause that limited membership in the organization to
white women. Over the next decade, as Frances moved into more active service
in the state league, the desegregation agenda went forward, despite—but also
in part because of—growing racial tensions in the South: "We lost some people.
One or two Leagues that were weak folded. But new members came in, a growth
of new people. A lot of people like to join something if it's doing something. So
we got good people in the League."

Frances remained for the rest of her life committed to making meaningful
participation in democracy possible for an ever-expanding range of citizens.
Over time, she moved beyond the league's limited and well-heeled constituency
and toward an increasingly grassroots and participatory model of citizenship.
That said, the work of the league years should not be discounted. Frances's aim
was to make one of the few women's organizations that was seriously interested

in women's political participation stretch its own thinking about representative democracy. To do this, Frances implemented the League of Women Voters' program of voter education and citizenship training on a scale that most women in the Georgia league were unprepared, at least initially, to countenance. Furthermore, Frances, in leading the league into the county unit fight and the desegregation of its own ranks, also took the membership of the league into the very real political fights of the 1940s and 1950s, where they stood the chance, for those women who could be pushed to change, of making a difference. In the 1940s and 1950s, and throughout most of her life, Frances chose not to work with the most radical spirits, but, instead, to move along the South's ordinary citizens. This was even more true of the school desegregation fight that was looming on the political horizon.

Frances's three-year term as Georgia league president coincided with the U.S. Supreme Court's *Brown* decision, delivered on May 17, 1954, outlawing segregation in public education. With it, desegregation moved squarely to the center of Frances's political focus. In many ways, Frances was simply responding to an issue and a series of events set in place by the NAACP's two-decades-old legal assault on segregation, but her personal commitment to public education had deep roots in family history. It was a point of pride for her that her ancestors were early supporters of public education in Ohio and Georgia. Come the 1950s the NAACP presented Frances with a struggle she could believe in. As the civil rights organization pushed an agenda of desegregation, and as the courts increasingly approved, Frances and her associates in the league worked to undermine southern resistance to desegregation by recasting desegregation not as a threat to southern society but, first, as a matter of law and order and, second, as a matter of children's education. Those two potent themes in American political discourse became the ground on which Georgia made a peaceful, if token, transition to desegregation.

From her position in the League of Women Voters, Frances first tackled desegregation as a legislative matter. In late 1953 Governor Herman Talmadge, anticipating a decision from the Supreme Court, proposed an amendment to the state constitution, which the legislature adopted, allowing the state to divert public funds to private schools in the event of a court order to integrate schools. That proposition went to the Georgia electorate in November 1954. Just two years after the county unit fight, Frances found herself in another constitutional battle. Even more so than it had with the county unit amendment, the league led the fight against the private school amendment. While Frances had hoped to reconvene the county unit coalition, school desegregation, she found, was a different matter. Whereas the county unit fight could be approached as "governmental philosophy," the private school amendment was "nothing but a race issue." Those who persevered were largely women, the leadership of several statewide women's organizations, including the League of Women Voters and United Church Women, an interfaith group that had been dedicated to progressive social change for several decades. "At that time, even more than now," Frances explained, "women arranged for the children." To Frances's great disappointment, the private school amendment passed. By a slim margin, Georgia voters approved of its leadership's plans to circumvent the Supreme Court's mandate. Georgia went into the post-*Brown* era with a legislature and a citizenry that appeared ready to resist federal law.

By late 1958 a school desegregation suit for the Atlanta schools was working its way through the courts on a collision course with state laws that made it a felony to spend tax money for integrated public schools and vested the governor with the power to close any public school upon its integration and set in motion the funding of private schools. These laws, passed in 1955 and 1956, further signaled the depth of political resistance to *Brown*. Faced with a recalcitrant governor and legislature, Frances turned her attention, as she had with the county unit fight and the public school amendment, toward a politics of public opinion formation. For this next round, Frances joined with a group of middle-class white Georgians, the majority of them women and many with league training, to launch Help Our Public Education (HOPE) to preserve public education in Georgia through information dissemination, organizing, and lobbying. It was HOPE that first articulated the proposition that children's education and the preservation of public schools was more important than allegiance to segregation. (And school closures were no idle threat, as the experience of Prince Edward County, Virginia, and Little Rock, Arkansas, had revealed.) HOPE's activities ranged from holding public meetings and large-scale petition drives to providing members with stickers to place on their checks that declared: "If schools shut down this account may also close." Frances's tasks in HOPE reflected the skills she had honed in the League of Women Voters; she organized and directed much of the lobbying effort, and she traveled the state establishing HOPE chapters. All told, HOPE was an educational campaign of impressive scope, mobilizing thirty thousand white Georgians in support of preserving public schools. Its achievement was to chart a course away from Massive Resistance and toward the beginnings of compliance with the *Brown* decision. Nowhere was the success of HOPE's strategy more evident than in the terms by which Governor Ernest Vandiver, who had declared previously that "not one" black child would sit next to a white child in a Georgia school, announced his retreat. "We cannot abandon public education," he declared in 1961, and he called one piece of his enabling legislation a "child protection amendment."[27] On August 30, 1961, the Atlanta public schools desegregated peacefully. After the violence and turmoil surrounding school desegregation in Little Rock and New Orleans in previous years, peaceful desegregation was no small achievement, and one that city officials quickly translated into a public relations coup.

HOPE women shared in the celebration. Some, however, were sobered by what little had in fact been accomplished. School desegregation in Atlanta constituted the enrollment of nine African American high school juniors and seniors in four previously all-white schools. The token extent of desegregation meant that much work was still ahead, and the majority of the white support for desegregation ran only so deep as preserving public schools for their own children. Frances was among that much-smaller number of white Georgians who dedicated themselves to the then-emerging civil rights movement.

The same years in which Frances joined the debate over school desegregation involved a great deal of personal growth related to changing race relations: "I had made a resolve within myself in 1954 that I was not going to belong to, give my efforts to, give my money to, or support in any way anything that was segregated. That's what I believed and I decided that I'd better live up to it." To meet this personal commitment, Frances first faced her own ignorance. While she had worked on matters related to the well-being of Georgia's African Americans since the Great Depression, she realized, "I hadn't really known black people." As a result, Frances set about a program of interracial self-education. She made her way to events at Atlanta University so as to meet politically active African Americans; she joined the integrated Women's International League for Peace and Freedom, whose Atlanta chapter was predominately black; she began attending the weekly luncheon discussion series, known as the Hungry Club, at Atlanta's black YMCA; and she organized interracial discussion groups, along the lines of the Great Books series, through the American Fund for Political Education. She also put herself under the tutelage of Sadie Mays, an African American social reformer and the wife of Benjamin Mays, president of Morehouse College. "That was wonderful to have a friend like that because it meant well for my education. She never minced words," Frances recalled. Nonetheless, Frances struggled to find her role, as a white woman, in a black-initiated and black-led movement. "Can't you help *with*—and *not* for?" she wondered. Over the course of the 1960s, Frances answered her own question and took her political cues increasingly from African Americans. The road to that answer, however, was hardly an easy one, and she went through stages of guilt and shame over white privilege. Ultimately, she turned her insecurity toward a deepened sense of responsibility to act as a southern white woman, whatever advantages and disadvantages that social role afforded her. This new identity, rooted in a growing interracialism and a willingness to take unpopular stands, would sustain Frances in the years ahead.

Frances extended her commitment to interracial activism during the years between 1961 and 1967 when she served as executive director of the Georgia Council on Human Relations, the Georgia state arm of the Southern Regional Council, which was an interracial organization formed during World War II. It was her first professional and her first paid position. The job entailed traveling the state in order to organize local interracial councils and to plan a program of desegregation activity. Frances had two constituencies for this work, one quite familiar, one new. Her years with the League of Women Voters and HOPE provided contacts with liberal and moderate whites around the state, although more women than men initially. Over time, Frances turned the council into a biracial and mixed-sex organization, often relying on Vernon Jordan, who was doing statewide organizing for the NAACP at the time, to introduce her to black leadership around the state. It is difficult for those who were not raised under Jim Crow to appreciate the enormousness of these tasks:

> Time after time, town after town, that I went into, it would be the first interracial meeting that they had ever had. In some cases, this was before the Civil Rights Act, and this made it much more difficult. Anytime you had anything that was interracial, you really were breaking the law. Unless you decide you are going to break the law and have civil disobedience, which I highly approve of, you had to plan it and do it. It's not just a matter of casually asking a few people in for tea.

Beneath the legal obstacles lay the human dimension: "We were all trying to make sense out of this thing called racism and prejudice."

Frances most often described her role as executive director of the Georgia Council as being a "bridge." She was the bridge bringing blacks and whites together in local councils, but she was also a bridge between black activists and white officialdom in many small towns and counties and occasionally a bridge between various black-led organizations in the shifting combination of cooperation and competition that characterized the movement at the organizational level. At its worst the work was tiring and discouraging. "Albany is a sick, sick, sad, sad town," Frances sighed in 1963. Nonetheless, Frances's gift was to enjoy the process and relish the victories. Three years later she rejoiced: "Had a *good* meeting in Albany at *Court House.* A real wonderful occasion—over 100 present. Visited the integrated nursery—17 Negroes, 14 whites—*Unbelievable* in Albany." Frances's strength as an organizer lay in working closely with people, searching out the possible, and helping them find their own way over time.

Such was the general nature of organizing for the movement, but Frances's involvement with the Albany Movement, one of the more storied episodes of the civil rights movement, allows us to compare her perspective on Albany against the volumes that have been written about it and examine what is unique about her perspective for understanding the civil rights movement. Albany, Georgia, a small city in the southwest corner of the state, became a center of movement activity in the fall of 1961. A coalition of local organizations, aided by activists from the Student Nonviolent Coordinating Committee (SNCC), launched a citywide campaign for integrated public facilities and voting rights. In just a few short months, the Albany Movement saw over one thousand activists head to southwest Georgia's jails. In December of 1961 the arrival of Rev. Martin Luther King Jr., followed by his well-publicized arrest, transformed Albany into a national symbol of the movement in the Deep South—and eventually a symbol of its failure. By most accounts, the Albany Movement collapsed in 1962 when sustained mass protests did little to undermine Jim Crow. Laurie Pritchett, Albany's police chief and himself a symbol of white intransigence, reportedly crowed that the city remained as segregated as ever.[28]

For Frances's perspective we have two distinct but reinforcing views, one from letters and a diary she kept during this period, the other from her retrospective oral history interviews. The diary is a chronicle, Frances's ordering and interpretation of events as they unfolded. It reflects the often chaotic nature of the civil rights movement and the day-to-day shifting of forces and fortunes. Perhaps because Frances herself was a female observer and participant, many more women appear in her chronicle than is typical of accounts of Albany. In relation to the existing literature on the Albany Movement, with its emphasis on the role of Rev. Martin Luther King Jr., the most interesting aspect of Frances's diary is that it only records King's presence once, almost in passing: "July 9, 10, 1962: Court—verdict of King and Abernathy." The weight of Frances's chronicle is with local people and the movement on the community level.

Frances's retrospective assessments were shaped, quite naturally, by the passage of time and, more especially, by the debate that has swirled around the events of Albany ever since, debates among and between participants, journalists, and scholars. Frances, cognizant of the controversy over King's role, devoted far more time to him in her oral histories than in her diary. She stated emphatically, on numerous occasions, that King was called to Albany by the Albany Movement: "You know, there's a lot of controversy about whether King just went or whether SNCC asked him to come to Albany. Well, I'll have you know SNCC asked him. I heard it. They got on the phone and called him." Frances characterized the events of 1961–62, in which King figures prominently, as a "fizzle," and King's departure left the movement adrift: "When King left, there was deep depression, and various factions blaming each other that they hadn't succeeded." Still, she maintained, "The thing that people don't realize is that King played such a small part. He came in and he didn't really stay so very long. It wasn't such a big part that he played. The whole Albany Movement was the people there, and the same thing was true of the whole movement. It was a grassroots movement." Famous individuals passed through Frances's stage, but they mattered because of what they brought to a local struggle.

When Frances described her work in Albany, the events to which King was central serve as prelude to the heart of her own story. She took pride in having "stuck it out" in Albany and having later expanded her Georgia Council program throughout southwest Georgia. Working in and around Albany through 1967, Frances offered a perspective of social change in the area that reaches well beyond the King years. Indeed, her work in Albany began in earnest in 1962, as she entered a more proactive than reactive stage and slowly built a viable local council. This was no easy task. Frances's diary is a record of the fits and starts of organizing, and her oral histories describe painful failures. When she sent a letter to white households in Albany, urging white citizens to use the pressure of public opinion to bring about social change, the response was overwhelmingly negative: "I got 278 answers that told me to go to hell, in no uncertain terms. I think I got one positive response from somebody that didn't live there. I was surprised. I thought there'd be some decent people." Initially, Frances had trouble rustling up even a handful of sympathetic whites.

Slowly, however, the rewards of having "stuck it out" emerged. By 1965 Frances had contacts not only throughout southwest Georgia but in each of Georgia's 159 counties.[29] The Southwest Georgia Council, availing itself of new antipoverty funds available from the federal government's War on Poverty, established a number of government programs that operated on an integrated basis. Among these was an integrated day care center that Carol King, wife of Albany's most famous black attorney, established in the late 1960s, which became one of the first Head Start programs in the country. Moreover, the Georgia Council expanded into new concerns, organizing welfare rights groups. From Frances's perspective, Albany was indeed changing in the late 1960s, in marked contrast to most of the literature on Albany that suggests a dispirited movement, fundamentally unable to alter the deeply racist patterns of Albany.[30]

The next phase of Frances's career took her, for the first time, away from the volunteer sector. In 1968, at the age of sixty-two, she took a position as civil rights specialist in the Atlanta regional office of the Office of Civil Rights, a division of the Department of Health, Education, and Welfare (HEW). Frances joined HEW at an exciting time. The Civil Rights Act of 1964 had banned discrimination in schools and other institutions receiving federal funds, and the expanding Office of Civil Rights aimed to implement the law with rigor. At the same time, the U.S. Supreme Court undermined the systematic evasion of the *Brown* decision that prevailed across the South. In the *Alexander v. Holmes County* decision of 1969, the court mandated that desegregation take place "at once." In this context, Frances approached her work with a relish: "We had the law, and if you discriminated, you did not get federal funds. That was what the law said and what the government meant. So it was a lot of fun, because you had some power behind you, which I had not ever had before."

Frances spent the bulk of her HEW years as the coordinator of operations for the state of Mississippi, although she worked in a number of southern states. Frances's goal was to urge voluntary compliance with the school desegregation provisions of the Civil Rights Act, and she presented school authorities with workable plans and then nursed them through the process. Frances is an example of a civil rights activist who took the organizing impetus of the movement into the federal bureaucracy. What were the possibilities for working in the spirit of an organizer within the government? Could the movement be sustained by "going inside?" For some movement activists, such behavior was, by definition, selling out. For Frances, the question did not resolve itself so easily.[31] As a bureaucrat, she was forced to leave behind most of the grassroots organizing that consumed her energies during the Georgia Council years. With the council, she had enjoyed the luxury of setting her own schedule and returning time and time again to groups and communities that sought her help. HEW was a different matter, and Frances regretted not having the time to engage in community organizing. Yet even as the character of her work changed, Frances believed her goals for HEW were consistent with her years in the movement. Much as she had with the council, Frances was seeking to be a bridge, but with HEW the span was even wider, reaching from black communities, through local school boards, to the federal government, in order to harness the energy of the movement to the world of public policy.

Frances believed she was part of the "most successful team in the country," an assessment that flies in the face of the now prevalent view of school desegregation as failed policy. Despite the very real problems of continuing segregation and discrimination against black students within supposedly integrated schools, over the course of the early 1970s school desegregation took hold, demonstrating the beginnings of a successful policy that are now often forgotten. By 1973 the eleven southern states had achieved the most significant degree of desegregation of any sector in the nation, with nearly half of black children attending desegregated schools.[32] There were, however, limits to what was possible, particularly after President Richard M. Nixon came into office and scaled back the scope of the HEW desegregation push. Following a run-in with the Mississippi Republican party, precipitated by her refusal to accept desegregation plans that she deemed ineffective, Frances found HEW to be an increasingly inhospitable place to work. She left the agency in February 1973. Frances remained, however, a thoroughgoing supporter of desegregation—as it might have been.

Whereas Frances would have felt justified in retiring, at the age of sixty-seven she turned her formidable organizing skills to poverty, or, more accurately, back to poverty. With the Georgia Poverty Rights Organization (GPRO), which came into being over the course of 1974 and 1975, Frances made the poor, a constituent part of her activism since the Great Depression, the focus of her attention: "They were the ones that hadn't had a chance to have their voices heard. So it just seemed logical to try to get poor people together and have them realize that they did have strength and power."

Frances and the cadre of friends and associates who launched the GPRO did so under inauspicious circumstances. In the mid-1970s, the U.S. economy experienced a period of economic malaise that combined recession with high rates of inflation—"stagflation," as economists inelegantly labeled the problem. While some parts of the Southeast enjoyed a much-ballyhooed "Sunbelt boom" in the 1970s and 1980s, the poor of the region saw inflation cut into meager wages and welfare subsidies. The benefits of Sunbelt growth extended primarily to corporations in the form of low taxes and a pro-business environment and secondarily to workers in the professional sector. Moreover, the surge of employment and wealth was concentrated in metropolitan Atlanta, while the rest of Georgia was poorer than Mississippi, long the bellwether for poverty and discrimination in the region.[33] As the federal government retreated from its War on Poverty, government services to the broad range of the populace, and particularly to the poor, lagged even further behind.[34] Frances and her colleagues in the GPRO believed that the poor deserved better from the state of Georgia.

Frances's work with the GPRO followed her HEW stint but came most directly out of the Georgia Council years. Toward the end of her tenure with the council, Frances expanded her mandate to include establishing welfare rights groups around Georgia, sometimes in conjunction with, sometimes independent of, a local council. Then, during her HEW years, Frances helped establish a Poverty Rights Office at Emmaus House, a social service program run by the Episcopal Church in south Atlanta. Emmaus House became Frances's base for her anti-poverty organizing. After her retirement from HEW, Frances grafted an advocacy organization onto the program of Emmaus House. Whereas the Poverty

Rights Office helped the poor obtain services to which they were entitled, the GPRO aimed as much at prevention as amelioration. It intended to educate the poor about the workings of government and help them influence the legislature to attend to their needs. Toward that goal, the GPRO organized poverty rights chapters in numerous cities and towns, provided education on the ins and outs of Georgia politics, facilitated lobbying activities for the poor (including an annual Poor People's Day at the Capitol), and deployed Frances as its volunteer lobbyist.

As the culmination of a lifetime of activism, the GPRO brought together the numerous threads of Frances's earlier work. Her well-honed organizing skills helped her establish the GPRO on a statewide basis, and Frances's associates in the GPRO ranged across her affiliations and over the several decades of her activism. A core commitment to expanding democratic citizenship linked the work that Frances did with women in the League of Women Voters and African Americans in the civil rights movement to a new commitment to political participation among the poor, while political skills from the League of Women Voters years helped Frances decide how best to influence recalcitrant legislators and policy makers. Moreover, in the GPRO, Frances brought together the many levels of education that interested her: educating the poor to best represent themselves, educating the public and the legislature on the needs of the poor, and educating herself. Her ongoing fascination with the workings of government meant that she simply enjoyed using her association with the Poverty Rights Office to learn about the range of social services available to the poor: "It certainly did train me in putting together all of the various agencies and how they fit in with poor people." Finally, Frances returned to the volunteer world, where she had always been happiest and most productive.

It is hard to pick a retirement date for Frances Pauley, but certainly the pace of her activism slowed in the latter half of the 1980s, and as the 1990s progressed, her visits to the legislature became less frequent. Even so, Frances added new concerns, such as homelessness and gay rights and AIDS activism to her repertoire, and new organizations, such as AID Atlanta and the Open Door Community for the homeless, benefited from her advice and counsel. While Frances threw herself into the work, with still considerable energy as she aged, her activism mattered as much as an example and inspiration for others as for those things that she herself did. Buren Batson, a close friend and colleague since the poverty rights years, described Frances as bringing legitimacy to issues that the gay community was raising, whether related to AIDS, police brutality, or gay rights.[35] Frances no longer had to "do," she could simply "be." Frances Pauley died of natural causes on February 16, 2003, at the age of ninety-seven.

NOTES

1. All quotations to Pauley's words, unless otherwise indicated, are taken from Kathryn L. Nasstrom, *Everybody's Grandmother and Nobody's Fool: Frances Freeborn Pauley and the Struggle for Social Justice* (Ithaca: Cornell University Press, 2000). Much of this chapter is reprinted from the chapter "'Talking for a Purpose': Storytelling and Activism in the Life of Frances Freeborn Pauley" in the same book. Copyright © 2000 by Cornell University. Used by permission of the publisher Cornell University Press.

2. Arnold Shankman, "Dorothy Eugenia Rogers Tilly," in *Notable American Women: The Modern Period: A Biographical Dictionary*, ed. Barbara Sicherman and Carol Hurd Green, with Ilene Kantrov and Harriette Walker (Cambridge, Mass.: Belknap Press of Harvard University, 1980), 691–93.

3. Thomas Mashburn Deaton, "Atlanta during the Progressive Era," (PhD diss., University of Georgia, 1969), chap. 7; Workers of the Writers' Program of the Works Projects Administration in the State of Georgia, comp., *Atlanta: A City of the Modern South* (New York: Smith & Durrell Publishers, 1942), 72–80; Mary E. Frederickson, "'Each One Is Dependent on the Other': Southern Churchwomen, Racial Reform, and the Process of Transformation, 1880–1940," in *Visible Women: New Essays on American Activism*, ed. Nancy A. Hewitt and Suzanne Lebsock (Urbana: University of Illinois Press, 1993), 296–324; Anne Firor Scott, *The Southern Lady: From Pedestal to Politics, 1830–1930* (Chicago: University Press of Chicago, 1970), chap. 6; Elna C. Green, ed., *Before the New Deal: Social Welfare in the South, 1830–1930* (Athens: University of Georgia Press, 1999). African American women were also undertaking a great deal of social welfare work at this same time. For one treatment of such work, also in the metropolitan Atlanta area, see Jacqueline Anne Rouse, *Lugenia Burns Hope: Black Southern Reformer* (Athens: University of Georgia Press, 1989). Frances, however, was socialized into a white women's network of reform and only later began to learn of interracial work.

4. For a description of the typical patterns of black–white relations in domestic service, from which the Freeborns varied, see David M. Katzman, *Seven Days a Week: Women and Domestic Service in Industrializing America* (New York: Oxford University Press, 1978), 194–95, 202, 274. On the political economy of domestic service in the South, see Tera W. Hunter, *To 'Joy My Freedom: Southern Black Women's Lives and Labors after the Civil War* (Cambridge, Mass.: Harvard University Press, 1997), esp. 111.

5. Jacquelyn Dowd Hall, *Revolt against Chivalry: Jessie Daniel Ames and the Women's Campaign against Lynching* (New York: Columbia University Press, 1974), 82–83.

6. Playbill, Drama Workshop, n.d., in Frances Pauley Papers, Special Collections Department, Robert W. Woodruff Library, Emory University, Atlanta, Ga.

7. On the Great Depression and New Deal in Georgia, see Numan V. Bartley, *Creation of Modern Georgia* (Athens: University of Georgia Press, 1983), 172–77; Kenneth Coleman, gen. ed., *A History of Georgia* (Athens: University of Georgia Press, 1977), 263–66, 310–18; Clifford M. Kuhn, Harlon E. Joye, and E. Bernard West, *Living Atlanta: An Oral History of the City, 1914–1948* (Atlanta: Atlanta Historical Society; Athens: University of Georgia Press, 1990), chap. 7; Douglas Lee Fleming, "Atlanta, the Depression, and the New Deal" (PhD diss., Emory University, 1984).

8. T. F. Abercrombie, "History of Public Health in Georgia, 1733–1950" (Atlanta: Georgia State Board of Health, n.d.), 139; Kuhn, Joye, and West, *Living Atlanta*, 32.

9. By 1918 white southern Methodist women had made work with African Americans the focus of their domestic program. Frederickson, "Each One Is Dependent," 310.

10. Annual Report, 1938–39, Junior Service League of Decatur, in Frances Pauley Papers, Special Collections Department, Robert W. Woodruff Library, Emory University, Atlanta, Ga.; Mary

Walker Fox, *The Sesquicentennial Celebration, 1823–1973: The First Methodist Church, Decatur, Georgia* (Decatur, Ga.: First United Methodist Church, 1973); J. R. Evans, "Annual Report of the DeKalb Clinic, Inc.," [1940?], in Pauley Papers; Social Planning Council, *A Report on Health and Welfare in DeKalb and Fulton Counties* (Atlanta: Social Planning Council, 1943).

11. This was the prevalent view in the South, including among white reformers. See Glenda Elizabeth Gilmore, *Gender and Jim Crow: Women and the Politics of White Supremacy in North Carolina, 1896–1920* (Chapel Hill: University of North Carolina Press, 1996), 170.

12. Edward H. Beardsley, *A History of Neglect: Health Care for Blacks and Mill Workers in the Twentieth-Century South* (Knoxville: University of Tennessee Press, 1987), vii.

13. School lunch programs of the New Deal were a vital link in women's New Deal activism. See Martha H. Swain, "A New Deal for Southern Women: Gender and Race in Women's Work Relief," in *Women in the American South: A Multicultural Reader*, ed. Christie Anne Farnham (New York: New York University Press, 1997), 252; and *Ellen S. Woodward: New Deal Advocate for Women* (Jackson: University Press of Mississippi, 1995), 336–37.

14. On the theme of white women learning from black women, see Frederickson, "Each One Dependent on the Other," 308, 311–12; and Gilmore, *Gender and Jim Crow*, chap. 7.

15. For the argument that white liberals of the 1930s emphasized economic and class issues over race but still made significant steps to include blacks in government programs, see Peter J. Kellogg, "Civil Rights Consciousness in the 1940s," *The Historian* 42 (November 1979): 21–22; Morton Sosna, *In Search of the Silent South: Southern Liberals and the Race Issue* (New York: Columbia University Press, 1977), 60–64; Tracy Elaine K'Meyer, *Interracialism and Christian Community in the Postwar South: The Story of Koinonia Farm* (Charlottesville: University Press of Virginia, 1997), 18–19.

16. For treatments of white women's interracial reform activity that aim to expand the discussion beyond the question on how racist white women were or weren't, see Frederickson, "Each One Dependent"; and Gilmore, *Gender and Jim Crow*. My analysis from a generational perspective was aided by Jacquelyn Dowd Hall and Anne Firor Scott's review essay, "Women in the South," in *Interpreting Southern History: Historiographical Essays in Honor of Sanford W. Higginbotham*, ed. John B. Boles and Evelyn Thomas Nolan, 495–505 (Baton Rouge: Louisiana State University Press, 1987).

17. On racial discrimination within the New Deal in Georgia, see Kuhn, Joye, and West, *Living Atlanta*, 214; Ann Wells Ellis, "'Uncle Sam Is My Shepherd': The Commission on Interracial Cooperation and the New Deal in Georgia," *Atlanta Historical Society Journal* 30 (Spring 1986): 47–63. Even though much of the New Deal was discriminatory in both intent and practice, in other ways it encouraged a growing challenge to the southern racial order, among both politically active African Americans and some white liberals. See Douglas L. Smith, *The New Deal in the Urban South* (Baton Rouge: Louisiana State University Press, 1988).

18. On the League of Women Voter's general significance to twentieth-century politics, apart from its role as the successor to the women's suffrage campaign, see Susan Ware, "American Women in the 1950s: Nonpartisan Politics and Women's Politicization," in *Women, Politics, and Change*, ed. Louise A. Tilly and Patrician Gurin (New York: Russell Sage Foundation, 1990). The league's own historians have placed more emphasis on the years before World War II, but good overviews of the organization's history can be found in Louise M. Young, *In the Public Interest: The League of Women Voters, 1920–1970* (Westport, Conn.: Greenwood Press, 1989); and League of Women Voters of the United States, *40 Years of a Great Idea* (Washington, D.C.: n.p., 1960). On the league's significance in relation to the county unit fight and school desegregation in Georgia, see Paul E. Mertz, "'Mind Changing Time All Over Georgia': HOPE, Inc., and School Desegregation, 1958–1961," *Georgia Historical Quarterly* 77 (Spring 1993): 41–61. Sometimes references to the league's importance are well

buried in footnotes or mentioned only in passing. Numan V. Bartley notes that the league led the civic groups that opposed the private school amendment in Georgia; see *The Rise of Massive Resistance: Race and Politics in the South during the 1950s* (Baton Rouge: Louisiana State University Press, 1969), 55n21. Harold Paulk Henderson describes the importance of the league to the poll tax issue in *The Politics of Change in Georgia: A Political Biography of Ellis Arnall* (Athens: University of Georgia Press, 1991), 85–86. Martin Gruberg notes that the Georgia League of Women Voters was credited with eliminating the poll tax in *Women in American Politics: An Assessment and Sourcebook* (Oshkosh, Wis.: Academia Press, 1968), 90.

19. Resolution, Georgia League of Women Voters, May 10, 1946, League of Women Voters of Georgia Records, Georgia Department of Archives and History, Atlanta, Ga. For a description of Atlanta's 1946 voter registration drive, see Kathryn L. Nasstrom, "Down to Now: Memory, Narrative, and Women's Leadership in the Civil Rights Movement in Atlanta, Georgia," *Gender & History* 11 (April 1999): 113–44.

20. Ware, "American Women in the 1950s," 282–83.

21. Calvin Kytle and James A. Mackay, *Who Runs Georgia?* (1947; Athens: University of Georgia Press, 1998).

22. V. O. Key Jr., *Southern Politics in State and Nation* (New York: Vintage Books, 1949), 119.

23. Letter from Julian LaRose Harris, to Frances Pauley, January 8, 1953, in Frances Pauley Papers, Special Collections Department, Robert W. Woodruff Library, Emory University, Atlanta, Ga. Frances's papers contain numerous letters praising her for her work on the county unit fight.

24. Kytle and Mackay, *Who Runs Georgia?*, 79–85.

25. In 1944 the League of Women Voters underwent a significant restructuring intended to place more decision making in the hands of local leagues. The league, which had been a federation of state leagues, became an association of individual members. At the same time, the league changed its name from the National League of Women Voters to the League of Women Voters of the United States. See League of Women Voters of the United States, *40 Years of a Great Idea*, 36–37.

26. "Brief Stating Georgia's Position Re 'White' in By-Laws," October 23, 1946, Papers of the League of Women Voters of the United States, Manuscript Division, Library of Congress, Washington, D.C.

27. Vandiver quoted in Kathryn L. Nasstrom, "Women, the Civil Rights Movement, and the Politics of Historical Memory in Atlanta, 1946–1973" (PhD diss., University of North Carolina at Chapel Hill, 1993), 197.

28. Participants, journalists, and scholars have all written extensively on the Albany Movement. For two reviews of the literature on Albany, from very different perspectives, see Michael Chalfen, "'The Way Out May Lead In': The Albany Movement beyond Martin Luther King, Jr.," *Georgia Historical Quarterly* 79 (Fall 1995): 560–67; Joan C. Browning, "Invisible Revolutionaries: White Women in Civil Rights Historiography," *Journal of Women's History* 8 (Fall 1996): 186–204. To cover the major groups, on King, see Taylor Branch, *Parting the Waters: America in the King Years, 1954–63* (New York: Simon and Schuster, 1988); on SNCC, see Clayborne Carson, *In Struggle: SNCC and the Black Awakening of the 1960s* (Cambridge, Mass.: Harvard University Press, 1981), chap. 5; and for a perspective on white southerners, see David L. Chappell, *Inside Agitators: White Southerners in the Civil Rights Movement* (Baltimore: Johns Hopkins University Press, 1994), chap. 6.

29. Letter from Frances Pauley, to Maxwell Hahn, July 8, 1965, Southern Regional Council Papers, microfilm edition, series 4, State Councils, reel 142 (Ann Arbor, Mich.: University Microfilms International, 1984).

30. As David Chappell notes, the central question asked of the Albany Movement was whether it was a failure (Chappell, *Inside Agitators*, 220–21). Michael Chalfen, in "The Way Out May Lead In," suggests significant successes for the Albany Movement, in contrast to most of the literature on Albany. Significantly, Chalfen also follows developments in Albany beyond 1962.

31. Charles M. Payne has a subtle discussion of both ongoing resistance and co-optation among activists who sought to work within the power structure beginning in the 1960s in *I've Got the Light of Freedom: The Organizing Tradition and the Mississippi Freedom Struggle* (Berkeley: University of California Press, 1995), chap. 12.

32. Much of the attention to "resegregation" emphasizes the very real obstacles on the way to effective desegregation; nonetheless, it also tends to obscure the extent to which desegregation had taken hold in the late 1960s and early 1970s as a result of court orders and administrative action. For reminders of that progress, see Gary Orfield, Susan E. Eaton, and the Harvard Project on School Desegregation, *Dismantling Desegregation: The Quiet Reversal of* Brown v. Board of Education (New York: The New Press, 1996), 8.

33. Bartley, *Creation of Modern Georgia*, 233

34. For an overview of southern economic development and its relation to poverty in this period, see David R. Goldfield, *Black, White, and Southern: Race Relations and Southern Culture, 1940 to the Present* (Baton Rouge: Louisiana State University Press, 1990), 244–55.

35. Interview with Frances Pauley and Buren Batson, Atlanta, Ga., June 11, 1997.

Kathryn Dunaway

(1906–1980)

Grassroots Conservatism and the STOP ERA Campaign

ROBIN MORRIS

❀ ❀ ❀

"Mercy!" cried Lee Wysong as she fell into a hug with Kathryn Dunaway in the halls of the Georgia Capitol. The longtime friends had just heard the announcement from the state senate: the Equal Rights Amendment had failed once again. The floor vote on January 21, 1980, was the third defeat of the Equal Rights Amendment in Georgia.[1]

Kathryn Dunaway and her network of conservative women repeatedly stopped the Equal Rights Amendment from passing in Georgia. Through this work, Dunaway recruited and trained many Georgia women for political activism. Together, these women shifted the language of southern conservatism to emphasize family values rather than white supremacy. This new pro-family focus in turn paved a way for southern states to join and, indeed, lead the national conservative movement.

Dunaway's political development reflects well-documented trends in women's participation in maternalist politics in the twentieth century. Like thousands of other women, Dunaway found her way into politics through motherhood. Historians have recognized this link between women's unpaid work in the home and activism in the public sphere as maternalist politics. Suffragists pushed for the vote on the grounds that women's responsibility to raise moral citizens meant that women had the obligation to participate in government to prevent corruption and to ensure healthy living conditions in cities where children lived. Maternalism depended on separate spheres: women performed the critical work of raising the nation's future citizens while, ideally, men earned wages outside the home.[2]

Connections between maternalism and Progressive era reforms are well documented. Women advocated for suffrage, social welfare programs, and family wages for labor all under the banner of motherhood.[3] The activism of Kathryn Dunaway and her peers makes a case for extending the consideration of maternalism to the rise of the New Right in 1970s America. For Dunaway the battle against the Equal Rights Amendment and abortion rights was grounded in ideas of separate spheres and women's role of caring for the children. Motherhood was more than her private life; it was also her political character. An examination of gender in the development of the New Right illuminates the evolution of the cultural and social issues embraced by the Pro-Family movement.

Recent histories of the New Right that have focused on class and race as primary thrusts of realignment have obscured the gendered convergence of southern local and national politics. Focusing on conservative gender politics, such as the anti-ERA and anti-abortion issues espoused by Kathryn Dunaway, offers a critical lens through which we may view southern political realignment as well as the rise of the New Right nationally. Certainly, studies of Massive Resistance (i.e., to the Civil Rights movement) have contributed to our understanding of southern conservatism in the twentieth century. However, unlike busing and voting rights, the ERA allowed southern legislators to resist a progressive issue without mentioning race. Instead, STOP ERA developed language focused on protection of all mothers and children, and, by extension, provided the basis for the Pro-Family movement.[4]

Other recent histories have considered gender as a building block in the creation of the New Right. Historians have shown how women worked both inside and outside of conservative political movements. One of the best-known conservative women organizers of the century is Phyllis Schlafly; long ignored by history, she is now receiving recognition for her contributions to national right-wing politics. Scholars have also recognized the work of women at the local levels, supporting campaigns or hosting educational meetings in homes. As a state leader, Kathryn Dunaway offers a middle ground between the national and the local. An examination of figures like Dunaway operating at the state level—organizing local women all across the state, but networking with women leaders in other states—places narratives of grassroots activism and national context into conversation.[5]

Kathryn Caldwell Fink was born in Charlotte, North Carolina, on September 2, 1906. Following her father's work, the family moved to Harrison, Tennessee, and New Orleans, Louisiana, before settling in Atlanta. She attended the Girls' High School of Atlanta, where she was assistant editor of the school yearbook and editor in chief of the monthly news and literary magazine. Her

KATHRYN DUNAWAY

with Speaker of the Georgia House of Representatives Tom Murphy.
Kathryn Fink Dunaway Collection, Manuscript, Archives, and Rare Book
Library, Woodruff Library, Emory University, Atlanta, Georgia.

senior yearbook pinpointed her chief characteristic as "Pep" and her main pastime as "writing editorials."[6] Both those traits would help her years later in her political work.

After graduating high school in 1925, she went to work for Sears Roebuck in Atlanta. She met John Dunaway through church activities at Peachtree Road United Methodist Church, and the two married on a Thursday afternoon in April 1928. John Dunaway studied law at Emory and opened a corporate law firm that grew with Atlanta's businesses. Kathryn's limited political involvement included working on her husband's successful campaign for the Georgia House of Representatives in 1940. After a single term, John Dunaway chose not to run again, preferring to focus on his legal career.[7]

Aside from regular voting—she would later boast that she had voted in "each and every election since 1928"—and her husband's campaign, Dunaway was otherwise uninvolved in most political activities before 1960.[8] A stay-at-home mother, she aligned her activities with her children's and believed she was raising not just her own two sons and a daughter, but three American citizens. Of this time in her life, she later remembered, "My activities were primarily centered in our home and in [the children's] guidance and development into wholesome, responsible, Christian adults and citizens."[9] The Dunaways had two sons, John Allen Jr. and Marshall, and a daughter, Louise, which kept Kathryn active in the Parent Teacher Association from 1936 through 1956, when the youngest, Marshall, graduated from high school. She was also a Cub Scout den mother and a leader for Campfire Girls. With her youngest son out of college in 1960—the same year she changed her party affiliation to Republican—Dunaway began to fill her time with political activities.[10] She also became active in the Daughters of the American Revolution (DAR) and the Sandy Springs Women's Club. On her women's club application, she identified her talents as voice, cooking, flower arranging, and added "government" as a write-in category.[11]

In 1963 Dunaway helped establish the North Fulton chapter of the Georgia Federation of Republican Women (GFRW). Later, she wrote that she had supported "all Republican candidates during . . . city, county, state, and national elections since 1963."[12] By 1965 she was the North Fulton chapter president and third vice president of the state organization. Her daughter, Louise Dunaway Grovensteen, was secretary of the local chapter. In March 1965 the fledgling group reported dues-paying membership of sixty-six women, with more unpaid members on the rolls.[13] Between 1963 and 1966 Dunaway helped plant six more GFRW chapters in the Atlanta area. Through all these activities, Dunaway was an important contributor to the rapid growth of the Republican Party in 1960s Georgia. In 1966 the National Federation of Republican Women (NFRW) honored the Georgia Federation with the Silver Tea Service Award for the greatest growth. The state federation boasted sixty-two new local clubs established from 1965–66. Georgia won the Silver Revere Bowl for the addition of 1,642 new members across the state.[14]

In February 1965 Dunaway testified against disarmament before the Senate Foreign Relations Committee and greeted Senator Fulbright with "salutations from the deep South and from that state, which after 100 years, voted Republican again for Barry Goldwater." The next day, the NFRW's first vice president, Phyllis Schlafly, testified before the same committee.[15] Schlafly and Dunaway had both been active in the national DAR and Republican Federation of Women circles for a few years. The details of their initial meeting are not known, but through these organizational affiliations, Phyllis Schlafly and Kathryn Dunaway formed a friendship of nearly two decades. In addition to a personal friendship, Dunaway and Schlafly maintained a political network that made Georgia a critical state in Schlafly's growing national network of conservative women.

At home in Atlanta, Kathryn Dunaway supported GFRW canvassing projects for Barry Goldwater's campaign and organized volunteers in the Fifth Congressional District. In 1966 she coordinated Fifth District telephone polling for Republican gubernatorial candidate Howard "Bo" Callaway.[16] GFRW volunteers organized extensive monthly phone surveys that covered the state of Georgia. The 1966 gubernatorial election was the first time in decades that state voters actually had a choice between two parties.[17] Still, the election pitted two pro-segregation Georgia businessmen against each other. Democrats nominated famed segregationist restaurateur Lester Maddox, while the Republicans nominated one-term congressman Callaway. Either way voters chose, they elected a governor opposed to civil rights. Thus, the GFRW phone surveys emphasized the difference in style. A question in the October surveys asked, "If you were asked to describe the quality you dislike most about Lester Maddox, would you say it is his appearance, his inexperience, his extremist views, or his irresponsibility?"[18] Dunaway organized the surveys in her district, including recruiting the volunteers and collecting the results for analysis each month. Dunaway and her volunteers were just a part of the statewide efforts of over 1,100 women conducting the fourteen surveys that reached over 25,000 Georgians. GFRW president Lee Ague estimated the statewide totals at "over 15,000 woman hours . . . providing a contribution to the campaign which in monetary value would exceed $60,000."[19]

In working for Republican candidates even before the GOP had a strong presence in Georgia, Dunaway was at the fore of the shift away from the Solid South of the Democratic Party. Many southerners cast their first GOP vote for Barry Goldwater in 1964. South Carolina senator Strom Thurmond publicly switched party affiliation that year, one of the highest-ranking southern Democrats to do so. Dunaway did not give reason for her change in party affiliation in 1963, outside of her firm beliefs in anticommunism and national defense. However, that she and a few other Republican women were already organized allowed the spark of Goldwater's nomination to spread quickly across Georgia in 1964. The women were not simply committed to Goldwater but also to the Republican Party and a strong two-party electoral system in the strongly Democratic South. Through her volunteer leadership, Dunaway developed networks of women committed to and active in Republican politics in Georgia. With each year, her network of conservative women grew stronger both within Georgia and throughout the nation.

Along with her GFRW volunteerism, Dunaway continued to support conservative causes. As DAR Constitution Week Chair, Dunaway successfully lobbied Governor Carl Sanders to proclaim Saturday, April 11, 1964, as "Return the Bible to Our Schools Day" in Georgia. In 1962 the Supreme Court had ruled school prayer unconstitutional in *Engle v. Vitale*. Dunaway also organized celebrations of the U.S. Constitution at area high schools during the 1960s.[20] Thus, Dunaway's early political activism called on her experience as a mother raising Christian citizens.

Interestingly, Kathryn Dunaway was not active in Massive Resistance efforts to prevent integration of schools or other public facilities. Historians have shown how women often entered political activism through desegregation politics.[21] Certainly, Dunaway opposed civil rights legislation. In a letter to Senator Hubert Humphrey, she opposed the 1964 Civil Rights Act as "90% federal control," but argued that it would "hamper free enterprise," rather than citing fears of race mixing. Her letter to Senate Majority Leader Mike Mansfield, aside from opposing the Civil Rights Act, protested the shipment of wheat to the Soviet Union.[22] The same year, she sent a donation to Americans for National Security, an organization focused on maintaining strong national defense at the height of the Cold War.[23] She worked against the fluoridation of Atlanta's water supply in the early 1960s, a popular right-wing cause.[24] Her opposition to civil rights was just one component of her conservative worldview. Perhaps the fact that her children had all graduated from high school by the time of the most heated desegregation battles explains why she did not get involved. However, a primary political concern over civil rights may have led John and Kathryn Dunaway to support strongly segregationist Democrats for elected office, particularly in local Georgia politics. Race was just one component of her Cold War worldview. She and her husband were early converts to the national Republican Party, not only because of civil rights but because of broader Cold War politics.

In 1967 Kathryn Dunaway was first vice president–elect of the GFRW and in line to be the organization's president in 1969. That year, the election for NFRW president in 1967 pitted conservative Phyllis Schlafly against the more moderate Gladys O'Donnell. Dunaway threw her support behind her friend Schlafly. During the NFRW campaign, she hosted Schlafly for the Georgia leg of a national speaking tour, and the two women traveled throughout the state together. Schlafly later thanked Dunaway for "dedication above and beyond the call of even your famous southern hospitality."[25] At the national meeting, Schlafly lost in a very hotly contested election, with each side accusing the other of unfair practices. Conservatives viewed Schlafly's defeat as part of party-wide punishment for all members of the right wing who had pushed so strongly for Barry Goldwater's nomination in 1964. After Goldwater's humiliating defeat, the Republican Party leadership had tried to position itself for a stronger showing in future elections.[26]

After losing the NFRW election, Schlafly resigned from the NFRW to create the Eagle Forum to reach conservative women. Kathryn Dunaway immediately became a charter member. In protest over what she considered irregular voting at the NFRW convention, Dunaway resigned from the GFRW.[27] She also wrote to newly elected president Richard M. Nixon to encourage him to appoint Schlafly to an "appropriate position" in his administration.[28] Nixon did not appoint Schlafly to a position, and instead she set about organizing conservatives outside the structure of party politics. Schlafly encouraged her supporters remaining in the NFRW to send the minimum amount of one dollar to the organization. The rest of the dues normally earmarked for NFRW should go to Schlafly's new Eagle Trust Fund, "a new conservative war chest." Those who sent money to the fund automatically received the brand new, four-page *Phyllis Schlafly Report* every month.[29] The first issue of the *Phyllis Schlafly Report* went out to three thousand women, including Kathryn Dunaway, in August 1967.[30] The newsletter covered topics of interest to conservatives, including national defense, prayer in schools, and federal economic policy. Schlafly challenged her readers "in every community [to] develop and train a corps of qualified, attractive speakers on the major issues of the day so [they] can engage the liberals on the battleground of the media."[31]

In February 1972 the *Phyllis Schlafly Report* took on the issue of the proposed Equal Rights Amendment (ERA) before the U.S. Congress. Schlafly's headline asked readers, "What's Wrong with Equal Rights for Women?" The article addressed the amendment, which read, in part, "Equality of rights under the law shall not be denied or abridged by the United States or by any State on account of sex."[32] Schlafly argued that current laws respected differences between men and women, the most basic of which was "that women have babies and men don't." She told any reader who did not "like this fundamental difference . . . to take up [their] complaint with God because He created us this way."[33]

The ERA, authored by the National Women's Party founder Alice Paul, had been introduced in every U.S. Congress since 1923. Usually, the amendment died in committee. However, with the political weight of second-wave feminism and recognition of women as powerful constituents, the ERA passed both houses of the U.S. Congress with minimal resistance in the spring of 1972 before moving to state legislatures for final approval.

Congress allowed a period of seven years for three-fourths of the states to ratify the ERA, but hardly anyone expected it would take that long. Before the end of the first day, Hawaii ratified the ERA. By the end of the first year, twenty-two states ratified the amendment. Eight states passed it in 1973. The ERA had great momentum and looked certain to receive the approval of the thirty-eight states needed for ratification. Mamie K. Taylor, chair of the Georgia Commission on Women ERA Steering Committee, emphasized that Georgia needed to lead on the ERA. With so much momentum behind the amendment, she wanted Georgia to move quickly to be one of the crucial states to ratify the amendment rather than just hopping on after the fact as it had with suffrage.[34]

With the amendment only five states away from ratification in 1973, Phyllis Schlafly mobilized her national network of conservative women to form state chapters of Stop Taking Our Privileges Equal Rights Amendment (STOP ERA). Schlafly would later remember Kathryn Dunaway as "my first and best state chairman" of the STOP ERA campaign.[35] When Phyllis Schlafly formed STOP ERA, she selected each state chair personally from her trusted conservative contacts. With its early legislative session, Georgia became a key state in the ratification for both sides. Victory or a defeat in an early state could set a tone for later battles in Florida, Illinois, and unratified others. As the decade progressed, Georgia also became significant as home to the pro-ERA president and first lady, Jimmy and Rosalynn Carter.

STOP ERA attacked the amendment from several angles. First, they argued that the "so-called Equal Rights Amendment," as they regularly called it, was unnecessary. As Dunaway wrote, "To say that men are in the Constitution and women are not is to display an ignorance of the U.S. Constitution."[36] ERA opponents argued that any unfair laws and practices should be handled with targeted legislation, preferably at the state level. The all-inclusive amendment, they maintained, was too broad and left interpretation up to the Supreme Court. Without mentioning specific cases, Dunaway warned, "We have seen some stunning examples of the total disregard for the will of the people by the Supreme Court."[37] Georgia voters probably thought immediately of school desegregation or busing cases.

With Vietnam present in Americans' minds, STOP ERA warned that the amendment would require women to register for military draft. Dunaway challenged American masculinity on the question of the draft: "Have the men of this nation sunk so low that they are willing to have their daughters, sisters, and wives shipped to a foreign country to fight a war while the men keep the home fires burning?"[38] In such statements, she linked traditional gender roles with national security to argue that any change threatened both foreign and domestic affairs. Opponents also warned Americans that the amendment would require women to contribute to the family income and hence endanger housewives.

ERA opponents further warned that housewives would lose alimony in cases of divorce and Social Security benefits in cases of widowhood. When the U.S. Supreme Court affirmed a woman's right to an abortion in the 1973 *Roe v. Wade* decision, STOP ERA linked with abortion opponents to warn that the amendment would protect abortion rights. Throughout Georgia, Kathryn Dunaway distributed copies of an Eagle Forum pamphlet titled *The Abortion Connection*, with an illustration of two strings wrapping around each other to form a shape. One string was "Equal Rights Amendment" while the other was "abortion." The pamphlet warned, "The abortionists want to lock abortion forever into the U.S. Constitution through ERA" and told readers, "the same people support abortion and ERA . . . almost always." Thus, to fight the ERA, one also had to fight abortion, and vice versa.[39] Less common, though not unheard of, messages in opposition to the ERA included warning parents about unisex dormitories, sports teams, and bathrooms. By the end of the 1970s STOP ERA had also linked the amendment with homosexual rights, particularly homosexual marriage rights, to which they were opposed.

Because she had the connections in place from her GFRW and DAR experience, Dunaway immediately launched an effective Georgia STOP ERA campaign once Schlafly tapped her for the post in 1973. Dunaway set about selecting regional chairs to head up the efforts in each congressional district in the state, copying the organizational strategy she had learned in GFRW canvassing. District coordinators organized women at the precinct levels, the most local units. By dividing the state up in such a way, Dunaway sat atop the communications network and needed to make only a few phone calls in order to mobilize the grassroots.

Furthermore, having local women leading different regions reinforced the message that the amendment was a local battle. The system also empowered women across the state to meet with legislators in order to influence legislation in the upcoming session. Additionally, women working in their own towns already had relationships with clergy, councilmembers, and other local leaders who could help in the anti-ERA campaign. Importantly, women working at the local level also had networks with their PTAs, church groups, women's clubs, and other volunteer organizations that might provide means for educating voters about the dangers of the ERA. Dunaway wanted to enable women to be their own legislative advocates.

Before Georgia's STOP ERA was firmly established, the Georgia House Special Judiciary Committee held public hearings on the ERA in February 1973. Each side had one hour and forty-five minutes to present arguments. The *Atlanta Journal* reported that the amendment supporters "appeared generally younger than the opponents." Pro-ERA speakers used their advantage of opening the debate to refute some of the more extreme arguments of anti-ERA activists. The Georgia state coordinator for the National Organization for Women (NOW) apologized to representatives "that our time should be taken on such a non-issue as public restrooms." Other pro-amendment speakers included representatives from the League of Women Voters and Church Women United, who testified that rape laws would remain unchanged and the family unit would not be harmed by the ERA.[40]

Then the anti-ERA side took the stand. With only a few weeks of organization, Kathryn Dunaway did not yet have the control over the opposition message she would develop in later years. She had invited some, but not all, of the anti-ERA speakers. Phyllis Schlafly flew in to testify about the amendment's danger to women as well as to lend a national name to the STOP ERA movement in the state. Of the Georgia women represented, Mrs. Russell Kelly of Moultrie told representatives that American women did not need the protections of a constitutional amendment "because we are protected by our men." Other opponents before the Special Judiciary Committee included "quite a few older women from church groups and conservative organizations."[41]

Age, however, was not the only problem for the opposition in the initial legislative committee hearings on the ERA. National States' Rights Committee chairman J. B. Stoner also gave his testimony. He proudly admitted to being a white supremacist and warned that the ERA would force women into military service and lead to "race mixing in the barracks," and would "legalize prostitution."[42] Reacting to Stoner's racist testimony, one woman worried, "I wish he would leave. He hurts us, bad."[43]

Dunaway learned the lesson. Within a few years, she distributed a "Check List for Witnesses to Speak against ERA." She explained, "It is important to schedule a variety of witnesses with a good distribution of age, religion, color, economic group, organizational affiliations, political party, and geographic section of the state." She suggested diverse women, including female lawyers, "representatives of various religious faiths," teachers, "a draft-age girl," a "senior woman who was a suffragette," female veterans, union workers, and a "black woman or minister or representative of the NAACP or Urban League."[44]

After that initial legislative hearing in 1973, the Georgia STOP ERA organization strengthened and streamlined the opposition message. While linked issues of race and sex were certainly behind some legislators' and constituents' opposition to the amendment, STOP ERA refrained from overt racial messages for the remainder of the decade. The women in STOP ERA embraced a new gendered language of conservatism, focusing on home, family, and motherhood. By shunning racist language, the women also hoped to appeal to socially conservative African American legislators and voters who exercised recently won voting power all over the state.

The Special Judiciary Committee decided to postpone the ERA until the next session for a full floor debate. Eight other states passed the ERA in 1973, though, making the stakes for STOP ERA in unratified states like Georgia even higher for 1974. The amendment was only eight states shy of passage.

Kathryn Dunaway, Lee Wysong, and other STOP ERA volunteers spent the remainder of 1973 strategizing for the next session. They held training sessions to educate women in each district about the opposition message. Each district coordinator contacted her legislator and reported back to Dunaway. Mrs. Allen Jones of Sandersville reported, "We have heard from twenty of the men. . . . Eight are against, five definitely for and seven undecided. . . . Hope you all get a better response than we did." Margaret Scharmitzky of Thomasville happily reported her legislator opposed the ERA. Erin Sherman boasted that the Valdosta STOP ERA was educating voters and legislators about the dangers of the amendment.[45] The volunteer efforts statewide to educate volunteers and to log legislators' opinions prepared STOP ERA for the next session.

In late January 1974 the Special Judiciary Committee passed the ERA with no recommendation, allowing the full Georgia House to vote on the amendment for the first time in Georgia. Dunaway was ready. STOP ERA ladies gave every legislator a loaf of freshly baked bread bearing the note: "From the breadmaker to the breadwinner." The gift, along with a few words against the amendment, spoke volumes to the largely male legislature. The "breadwinner," assumed to be male, made both money and laws to support the housewife and children. The "breadmaker," assumed to be female, stayed home to raise the children and maintain the household. The gift of fresh bread reinforced the idea that homemakers nourished the family. Legislators did not know, however, that lobbying efforts took up Dunaway's baking time, and that another of her political connections donated the bread. Privately, Dunaway thanked Mr. Chester Gray Mom's Bakery in Atlanta "for the donation of the many small loaves of [their] delicious bread." Her note did not acknowledge the irony of passing off the store-bought bread as homemade.[46] Legislators did not have to know that fighting the ERA had already taken valuable baking time from STOP ERA volunteers. They only needed to get the message that Georgia's women wanted them to vote no.

Georgia's first lady, Rosalynn Carter, also a housewife, recalled visiting the Capitol the day before the 1974 ERA vote. She wore an "I'M FOR ERA" button as she journeyed through the halls to meet her husband. Carter remembered the corridors packed with anti-ERA demonstrators. The demonstrators wore red STOP ERA buttons and carried stop signs emblazoned with the stop sign logo. "They were camped all over the capitol, lobbying legislators very effectively," she wrote. "I was booed all the way in, and . . . we were booed all the way out." Significantly, Carter did not recall any noteworthy presence of pro-ERA demonstrations.[47] Rosalynn and Jimmy Carter remained advocates of the ERA and would battle Dunaway and the Georgia STOP ERA volunteers from the White House in years to come.

Georgia legislators debated the amendment for four hours on January 30, 1974, before ultimately voting it down in a 104–70 vote. In his speech opposing passage, Rep. W. W. Larsen of Dublin asked, "Where would we have been when we were attacked at Pearl Harbor if we had to line up men and women equally?" Rep. Dorsey Matthews of Moultrie warned that the amendment "stinks of communism." Echoing the message of STOP ERA, the legislators opposed the amendment based on the perceived threat to national security. The only two women in the legislative body voted for the amendment.[48] Jeanne Cahill, chair of the pro-ERA and governor-appointed Georgia Commission on the Status of Women (CSW), called the vote "a slap in the face of equality and justice," but reminded ERA supporters that "in a state that took 138 years to ratify the first ten amendments [i.e., the Bill of Rights] . . . 70 votes for equality is rather impressive."[49] She vowed to work through the next year to make sure Georgia passed the ERA in 1975.

Meanwhile, Kathryn Dunaway celebrated momentarily before regrouping for the 1975 session. In June 1974 Phyllis Schlafly rewarded Dunaway's success in stopping the ERA by appearing at an Atlanta Victory Luncheon to raise funds for further Georgia STOP ERA work.[50] Even with a comfortable margin of victory, Dunaway continued to recruit more women, train those already on board, and press legislators to oppose the ERA. Because every House seat was up for election that fall, Dunaway directed the women at local levels to meet personally with every candidate, regardless of party affiliation or previous voting record. Before Election Day women were to meet with every candidate to ascertain his or her position on the ERA so that STOP ERA would know whom to endorse. After the election, she told them to develop a relationship with the winner, regardless of party affiliation, and to "convince the undecided—and especially the newly elected members—of the evils of this amendment."[51] Within a few years, Dunaway began compiling this information into a Georgia STOP ERA voting guide. Between Election Day and the vote on the ERA, Dunaway asked women to recruit friends to write legislators. Senator Ebb Duncan of Carollton divided his numerous letters into three piles—letters from outside his district, pro-ERA letters from his district, and anti-ERA letters from his constituents. Revealing the effectiveness of Dunaway's local emphasis, Duncan's letters from inside his district ran 8 to 1 against the ERA. Senator Lee Robinson of Macon said his letters were 9 to 1 against the amendment.[52]

The 1975 General Assembly session brought another defeat for the amendment, this time by a 33–22 vote in the Senate. The debate lasted only one hour. Senator Hugh Gillis of Soperton celebrated: "We have the most beautiful and gracious ladies in the South. . . . Let's show the nation that we respect our ladies." The Senate's sole woman, Virginia Shapard of Griffin, replied in debate, "Passage of the ERA will not make a woman a lady, nor will it prevent her from being one."[53] While only four states were needed to pass the ERA by the time of the Georgia vote in February, passage looked doubtful for 1975. Fred Schlafly, Phyllis's husband, wrote Kathryn Dunaway to thank her for her phone call telling them of the critical senate vote and to congratulate her for "slowing down" the national momentum with her work in Georgia.[54] Kathryn Dunaway and other ERA opponents were so effective in "slowing down" the amendment in Georgia that it did not reach the floor of either house again for five years.

While the ERA languished in committee, Kathryn Dunaway expanded her battle against other incarnations of the feminist movement. The National Organization for Women and other pro-ERA groups organized a boycott of all unratified states. Participating organizations refused to hold conventions and encouraged members not to vacation in any state that had not passed the ERA. Dunaway responded to the boycott of her state by asking national STOP ERA allies to visit Georgia. Speaking to a group of Atlanta broadcasters in the spring of 1978, Dunaway challenged, "Will Atlanta, Georgia, and other states sacrifice their womanhood for a few more greedy dollars? Or are we willing to advertise our city as the most beautiful, the most hospitable city in America, filled with exciting historical and fun areas?"[55] Her calls for conservatives to visit were not enough, however, and estimated losses of convention revenue to Atlanta by November 1978 were $21.3 million.[56]

One convention that had to be in Atlanta was the 1977 Georgia meeting for the observance of International Women's Year. The United Nations declared 1975 the International Women's Year and held a conference in Mexico City on the topic of women's issues around the world. In celebration, President Gerald Ford selected 1977 as International Women's Year (IWY) in the United States and budgeted $5 million to pay for fifty state meetings and one national meeting to discuss the status of American women. Ford's appointments to the National Commission did not please ERA opponents. Ford appointed Senate ERA sponsor Birch Bayh and House ERA sponsor Martha Griffiths. Feminist congresswoman Bella Abzug sat on the committee, as did media personality Barbara Walters.[57] Schlafly was not invited, nor were any other ERA opponents. As if the millions in federal money was not insult enough, the pro-ERA composition of the committee guaranteed the vehement opposition of conservative women to IWY. As a final affront, the National Commission proclaimed ratification of the ERA its "highest priority." The National Commission acted on that priority with the January 1976 establishment of ERAmerica, co-chaired by television star Alan Alda and feminist Margaret Heckler.[58] Spinning the losses to their advantage, though, STOP ERA forces adopted the position of the underdog, relying on the funding and goodwill of private citizens to battle big government.

Women of the Eagle Forum, STOP ERA, DAR, and other conservative groups first fought the apportionment of taxpayer funds. Immediately, Dunaway set about opposing all IWY meetings and any federal funding for them. She sent a letter of protest to Georgia's U.S. senator Sam Nunn, who replied that he had favored only $3 million. In a statement that did little to dissuade Dunaway, Nunn mentioned that the $5 million was a compromise from the $10 million that the National Commission requested.[59] Working through other conservative networks, Dunaway introduced a resolution at the Georgia Republican Party Convention to request that the president and Congress "immediately cease funding and abolish the International Women's Year Commission."[60] The $5 million funding stayed in the budget and became a rallying cry for conservatives. Georgia's share of the national IWY funds totaled $66,252. Schlafly encouraged STOP ERA state organizations to hold garage sales, bake sales, and craft bazaars to raise 5 percent of their state's federal allocation to fund the local fight against IWY.[61]

Kathryn Dunaway was the sole conservative appointed to the Georgia Co-ordinating Committee on the Observance of International Women's Year, the committee charged with planning the state women's meeting. On the letter-head, she was the only one of thirty-seven members to identify by her husband's name, "Mrs. John Dunaway," making a statement against feminism every time a letter went out.[62] At the same time, she led Georgia STOP ERA women in creating the IWY Citizen's Review Committee (IWY CRC), which trained women to spot violations of the nonlobbying clause of the IWY funding and to report high-pressure tactics by pro-ERA and pro-abortion attendees. Since Georgia was only the third state meeting held, the IWY CRC observers felt a strong responsibility to record violations in order to prepare other states' conservatives for their own meetings.

Before Georgia's IWY meeting in May 1977, Dunaway prepared the Citizens' Review Committee for their tasks. She invited Phyllis Schlafly to visit Atlanta, and the two hosted a training workshop at the First Baptist Church of Atlanta.[63] Dunaway had received reports from Vermont's conservatives, fresh from their own state meeting. Georgia women studied Vermont's plan and developed a strategy. Dunaway personally chose at least one person to attend each workshop of the state IWY meeting. That leader was responsible for raising the conserva-tive view during the discussion period. Knowing her supporters would be out-numbered, Dunaway told them to use the "Buddy System for support," so that no woman would be the only conservative in the room. She also encouraged the leaders to document the sessions with tape recorders.[64]

Finally, May 6–7, 1977, came and women arrived from all over Georgia to discuss the status of women, including education, abortion, health care, divorce, rape, and the ERA, among many other issues. Each of the IWY CRC delegates came prepared with three workshop observation forms in order to record events, discrepancies, and unfair practices in sessions. In particular, the women were to watch for "anything calling for more government control," "violations of Roberts Rules of Order," "anything which will take rights away from people under the guise of 'doing good,'" and "half-truths or twisted truths."[65] Dunaway reminded her workers, "Do not be intimidated. . . . Maintain your dignity at all times—even if you are treated rudely. A soft voice and a smile work miracles."[66] Her strategy was to fight feminism with femininity.

Each workshop ended with a vote on recommendations on the workshop topic. The Georgia IWY CRC warned, "Affirmative votes on these questions will add support to the IWY program." Therefore, to avoid "an increase in government spending and government interference," the IWY CRC told its delegates to vote "(A) Strongly Disagree, (B) Disagree, or (C) Neutral" on all issues.[67] Dunaway had planned every detail from the note-taking strategies to the voting slate. She considered numerous cases in which a housewife attending her first political meeting might be intimidated and prepared women for every scenario. Dunaway sought to empower any conservative woman willing to join her in fighting feminism.

Dunaway organized the IWY CRC hospitality suite at the conference hotel, where the conservative ladies could rest with a cup of coffee in the company of like-minded women. Because they feared conference organizers would disrupt their work, the CRC workers had to keep their mission secret. Anyone who came into the CRC hospitality suite had to be escorted by "someone we know" or should be able to show proof of CRC membership upon demand. National CRC chair Rosemary Thompson reminded women "to avoid talk about our activities on elevators or at lunch."[68] Women turned in their workshop reports in the hospitality suite where more women and some husbands compiled the findings into a report. Dunaway, Thompson, and national STOP ERA co-chair Elaine Donnelly presented the findings at a press conference at the close of the IWY meeting.[69]

After the state IWY meeting, Dunaway wrote her own report about the meeting. She sent her findings to state and federal legislators as well as to STOP ERA leaders in other states. Filling four legal pages, Dunaway's report outlined irregularities ranging from materials missing from some participants' registration packets to suspected voting fraud. She protested that keynote speaker Bella Abzug openly endorsed the ERA and even read a telegram of support from President and First Lady Carter. Dunaway offered reports on individual workshops upon request, but asserted, "There was active suppression of views different from IWY." Her primary advice for other state leaders included, "WATCH FOR INFILTRATION" and "REMAIN LADIES AT ALL TIMES."[70] Once again, Dunaway's network extended both throughout Georgia and beyond state lines to aid conservative women in other states.

The women of STOP ERA did not succeed in preventing the Houston IWY meeting, nor did they stop many feminist proposals from becoming formal recommendations in the IWY final report to President Carter. Using recommendations from other states, CRC delegates at Mississippi, Oklahoma, and Utah state meetings managed to elect some conservative women delegates—or, in Mississippi's case, five conservative men—to the large Houston meeting. Feminists still greatly outnumbered conservatives, though.

In protest, Phyllis Schlafly organized an event she called the Pro-Family Rally at another Houston venue. Georgia STOP ERA organized a bus trip to Houston for any women who wanted to attend the Pro-Family Rally. Dunaway sent the trip details to ministers throughout the state, asking them to inform congregants about the national rally. She also requested that the ministers honor Family Week in Georgia by preaching on a topic related to the Christian family on Sunday, November 20—the final day of the Houston IWY conference.[71]

Thousands of men and women attended the Pro-Family Rally, including many from Georgia. Opening the Pro-Family Rally, Schlafly thanked her husband for allowing her to attend the meeting. In contrast to the IWY meeting, the Pro-Family Rally featured many men as speakers. They included several religious figures, emphasizing their idea of America as a Christian nation and the family, not the individual, as the basic unit of society. Phyllis Schlafly and a number of prominent conservative speakers called for defeat of the ERA, an end to legal abortion and protection for families from homosexual activists. National CRC chairman Rosemary Thompson described the outlook of the group, "We're a pro-family, pro-American, anti-lib anti-NOW organization." Schlafly contrasted her meeting with the official IWY meeting that she predicted "will show them off for the radical, anti-family, pro-lesbian people they are."[72] Media outlets covered both meetings, often questioning the ability of feminism to survive the pro-family threat. While conservatives did not stop the IWY recommendations from passing, they did garner attention for the rising tide of the New Right of women and families in America.

Even with the success of the Houston IWY meeting and the boycott of unratified states, no additional states passed the ERA. As the seven-year deadline approached, pro-amendment groups lobbied Congress for additional time to pass the ERA. Frustrated but not discouraged, Dunaway mounted a refocused campaign in 1978. She told the STOP ERA women all over Georgia to meet with legislators to convince them to oppose extension, saying that "we don't care whether he is pro or con on ERA. We only care that he vote against the . . . Time Extension Bill." She mourned, "The plain fact is that, whatever you already did on this subject was NOT enough! . . . Whatever you did before must be multiplied by 100 times within the week after you receive this letter if this crooked ERA Time Extension Bill is to be defeated!"[73] While many in Georgia's delegation opposed extension, the bill had enough support from other states' legislators to succeed. The original 1979 deadline was null. Pro-ERA groups had until March 22, 1982, to get the final three states.

Undeterred, Phyllis Schlafly still declared victory over the first round of the ERA battle. She celebrated with an "End of an E.R.A." gala. Recognizing Dunaway's value to the campaign, Schlafly invited her friend to walk in with her and sit at the head table.[74] With the momentum they had built over the first seven years, STOP ERA forces knew they just had to keep up hope and hard work for what they hoped would be the final three years.

※ ※ ※

The year 1980 was much different for the ERA in Georgia. It was the first time the amendment had come up since Jimmy Carter had assumed the presidency. But, the Republican Party was gaining ground in Georgia. West Georgia College professor Newt Gingrich had finally succeeded in his third campaign for a seat in the U.S. House of Representatives, defeating the pro-ERA state senator Virginia Shapard. In late 1979 Schlafly had again visited the Atlanta area on a speaking tour, in recognition of the value of defeating the amendment in Carter's home state.[75] Kathryn Dunaway was battling stomach cancer privately, which only seemed to push her harder to defeat the amendment in her lifetime.

President Jimmy Carter wielded his influence in hopes of securing a much-needed domestic policy victory before a heated campaign season. The Iran hostage crisis was dragging on, and Carter faced a challenge from Senator Ted Kennedy within his own party. Carter received a telegram from a pro-ERA voter in Pennsylvania charging, "Ted Kennedy is from a ratified state. You aren't. Don't you think that it's about time for Georgia to ratify the ERA?"[76] In an effort to win a major victory and secure women's support, Carter instructed his administration to be aggressive in Georgia. Administration staff went to Georgia to lobby in person, while First Lady Rosalynn Carter made several personal phone calls to state legislators. The president phoned Governor George Busbee to ask him to pressure legislators.[77]

Carter's Special Assistant for Women's Affairs Sarah Weddington organized for a showdown in the Georgia House. Her background research on the state's ERA story revealed that "there was strong lobbying by Stop-ERA groups. . . . Brought in hundreds of people and passed out sandwiches and cake and stayed there until they beat it down. *Good* lobbyists." Dunaway was not mentioned by name, but her strategy was all over the report. An anonymous legislator predicted that "ERA has about as much chance of passing as I do of walking on Lake Lanier." The memo on Georgia predicted "a bleak outlook. Sorry." [78] The research turned out to be accurate in its predictions. Despite the intense pressure from the administration in Washington, the Georgia Senate defeated the ERA for a third time on January 21, 1980.

Aware of all the Washington pressure, Kathryn Dunaway admitted, "We thought they [the senators] wouldn't resist the pressure. We were looking for the worst, but praise the Lord, we got the best." The most the senators could do was delay the vote for a few minutes. Initially, Carter's supporters in the state senate tried to delay voting by a day so that a defeat would not influence the Iowa caucuses the next day. However, anti-ERA legislators thrice voted down any delays. The vote continued with a vote of 32–23 against the amendment. "It was just wonderful, wonderful, wonderful," gushed Dunaway.[79] Her grassroots efforts had established conservative voting power in local districts and provided a bulwark against pressure from as high up as the White House.

ERA advocates in Atlanta and in the Carter Administration immediately began to spin the story. They explained that the vote was close, and the pro-ERA groups had finally begun a powerful grassroots organization to encourage ratification. What they did not say, however, was that Dunaway had been nurturing her grassroots coalition for much longer. For more than twenty years, Dunaway had been building a network of conservative women. By the time the ERA left the U.S. Congress for state ratification in 1972, Dunaway already had a strong volunteer base. By 1980 the group had developed strong relationships with legislators, pastors, and women all across Georgia. Whatever the pro-ERA forces could accomplish at the grassroots in a couple of years could not compete with what Dunaway had accomplished over twenty years.

Of course, Dunaway did have the advantage of working in what even Weddington recognized as "the extremely religious, conservative nature of Georgia."[80] Even with the general conservatism of the state on her side, however, Dunaway managed a skillful campaign against an amendment that had once seemed destined for passage even in her state. Several legislators recognized Dunaway's natural ability for political work. Democratic leader and longtime Speaker of the Georgia House Tom Murphy wrote, "Mrs. Dunaway not only has opinions. She acts."[81]

That was her final battle in the Georgia House. Kathryn Dunaway died from stomach cancer on September 16, 1980. On her watch, the grassroots conservative forces had grown and organized. Near the end of the ERA battle, Fred Schlafly, Phyllis's husband, praised Dunaway: "I love to tell Phyllis and the other wonderful girls in all the states which have defeated ERA that your work is even superior to what everyone else did because you have stopped ERA in Carter's own state for eight hard fought years. What you have accomplished should be described as the greatest political victory of the second half of the twentieth century."[82] While Fred Schlafly's flattery was certainly over the top, he did sum up the significance of the political work of the Georgia housewife turned political strategist. She had organized women throughout the state effectively enough to resist pressure from numerous better-funded groups, national organizations, celebrities, and experienced politicians. Dunaway did not live to vote for Ronald Reagan in 1980, but she did write him to scold his decision in "appointing so many women's libbers to [his] women's advisory committee" during his campaign.[83] Even with conservatives, Dunaway did not let up.

In the 1981 session of the Georgia General Assembly, legislators recognized the absence of the woman they had come to expect would greet them with baked goods and conservative pamphlets. Senate Resolution 177 expressed "deepest sympathy" for Dunaway's death. The resolution praised her decades of political activism "supporting those causes which she strongly believed in" and called her a "shining example of the positive influence which all citizens can have on the democratic process."[84]

Dunaway's successors honored her legacy by keeping the amendment down in Georgia until the extended time period for ratification ended in 1982. Dunaway's friend and longtime co-chair Lee Wysong assumed leadership of Georgia STOP ERA, assuring conservatives and liberals alike, "There won't be any lag in the Stop ERA effort because I think that continuing to oppose ERA and achieve ultimate success would be the greatest tribute we can pay."[85] The final defeat for ERA came on January 21, 1982, when the Georgia House of Representatives once again defeated it by a wide margin.[86] Dunaway's legacy extended further than the defeat of ERA, however. Stone Mountain STOP ERA organizer Sue Ella Deadwyler wrote to John Dunaway, "I thank the Lord that Kathryn taught me how to work the Capitol!"[87] Women like Deadwyler lived all over Georgia and now had the skills and confidence to meet with legislators and host political meetings on their own. With the ERA finally laid to rest, the numerous women that Dunaway had trained were now free to pick up other work of the conservative movement in Georgia.

NOTES

1. Jerry Schwartz, "Georgia Senators Say No to ERA," *Atlanta Constitution*, January 22, 1980, 7A.

2. Molly Ladd-Taylor, *Mother-Work: Women, Child Welfare, and the State, 1890–1930* (Urbana: University of Illinois Press, 1995), 3.

3. For further reading on this, see Ladd-Taylor, *Mother-Work*; Seth Koven and Sonya Michel, eds., *Mothers of a New World: Maternalist Politics and the Origins of Welfare States* (New York: Routledge, 1993); Linda Gordon, *Pitied but Not Entitled: Single Mothers and the History of Welfare, 1890–1935* (Cambridge, Mass.: Harvard University Press, 1994); Susan Ware, *Beyond Suffrage: Women and the New Deal* (Cambridge, Mass.: Harvard University Press 1987).

4. For further reading on the history of race and the rise of the New Right in the South, see Matthew D. Lassiter, *The Silent Majority: Suburban Politics in the Sunbelt South* (Princeton: Princeton University Press, 2006); Kevin M. Kruse, *White Flight: Atlanta and the Making of Modern Conserva-*

tism (Princeton: Princeton University Press, 2007); Joseph Crespino, *In Search of Another Country: Mississippi and the Conservative Counterrevolution* (Princeton: Princeton University Press, 2009) Pete Daniel, *Lost Revolutions: The South in the 1950s* (Chapel Hill: University of North Carolina Press, 2000); Earl Black and Merle Black, *The Rise of the Southern Republicans* (Cambridge, Mass.: Belknap Press of Harvard University, 2003).

5. Donald T. Critchlow, *Phyllis Schlafly and Grassroots Conservatism: A Woman's Crusade* (Princeton: Princeton University Press, 2005); Catherine E. Rymph, *Republican Women: Feminism and Conservatism from Suffrage through the Rise of the New Right* (Chapel Hill: University of North Carolina Press, 2006); Lisa McGirr, *Suburban Warriors: The Origins of the New American Right* (Princeton: Princeton University Press, 2001). Donald T. Mathews and Jane Sherron de Hart's *Sex, Gender, and the Politics of ERA: A State and the Nation* (Oxford: Oxford University Press, 1990) is an important work in our understanding of the Equal Rights Amendment and the contentious politics surrounding it, particularly those debates in a southern state. They emphasize women's organizing both pro- and anti-ERA and offer analysis of the arguments on either side.

6. Letter from Kathryn Dunaway to Director of Census, June 15, 1971, and *Halcyon*, Yearbook of the Atlanta Girls' High School, 1925, Louise Dunaway Grovensteen papers, personal collection of Laura Dunaway Green, Lilburn, Ga.

7. Marshall Dunaway, interview with the author, Thomasville, Ga., August 19, 2006.

8. "Biographical Statement," folder 13, box 2, Kathryn Fink Dunaway Papers, Manuscript and Rare Book Library, Woodruff Library, Emory University, Atlanta. This collection is unprocessed, but I have tried to identify folders clearly here. These will change once the collection is processed. Hereafter cited as Dunaway Papers.

9. Biographical sketch, folder 29, box 1, Dunaway Papers.

10. "Biographical Statement," folder 13, box 2, Dunaway Papers.

11. Application for Sandy Springs Woman's Club, undated, folder 8, box 2, Dunaway Papers.

12. "Governmental Activities of Kathryn Fink Dunaway," undated, folder 29, box 1; NFRW news release, September 18, 1966, folder 10, box 7, Dunaway Papers.

13. Members of GFRW chapters 1965, folder "Cauble," box 3, Estelle Lee Ague Papers, Georgia Archives, Morrow, Ga. This collection is unprocessed and few items are in folders or envelopes. As of August 2011, this collection was moved to the Donna Novak Coles Women's Movement Collection, Georgia State University, Atlanta, Ga. Hereafter, cited as Ague Papers.

14. "News Release," NFRW, September 18, 1966, folder 10, box 7, Dunaway Papers.

15. Dunaway testimony before Senate Foreign Relations Committee, February 22, 1965, folder 2, box 3; "Biographical Sketch," undated, folder 13, box 2. While there is no date on this sketch, the latest dates listed indicate that it was probably written in 1965 or 1966. "Governmental Activities of Kathryn Fink Dunaway," undated, folder 29, box 1; NFRW news release, September 18, 1966, folder 10, box 7, Dunaway Papers.

16. Letter from Lee Ague to Lila Byrd, September 6, 1966, folder "Fulton County," box 3, Ague Papers.

17. In 1962 federal courts ruled against Georgia's county unit system in statewide politics. This ruling allowed for the rise of a two-party South even as more people moved into suburban areas. For more on the end of the county unit system and its effect on the 1966 elections, see Harold Paulk Henderson, "The 1966 Gubernatorial Election in Georgia" (PhD diss., University of Southern Mississippi, 1982).

18. John H. Friend Company, Political Opinion Surveys, October 10, 1966, and November 1966, no folder, box 9, Ague Papers.

19. Lee Ague, "President's Report to NFRW Board of Directors Meeting," January 24–25, 1967, no folder, box 4, Ague Papers.

20. Governor Carl E. Sanders, "Proclamation," April 11, 1964, folder 20, box 7, Dunaway Papers.

21. Daniel, *Lost Revolutions*. Daniel examines the roles of women on both sides of desegregation in Little Rock, Ark. Matthew Lassiter, *Silent Majority*, focuses on Charlotte, N.C., and Atlanta. Kevin M. Kruse, *White Flight*, focuses on Atlanta.

22. Letter from Kathryn Dunaway to Hubert Humphrey, March 2, 1964; letter from Kathryn Dunaway to Senator Mike Mansfield, March 2, 1964, folder 6, box 1, Dunaway Papers. In these letters, she cites the American Conservative Association's rating for each of the senators—Humphrey at 1 percent and Mansfield at 8 percent.

23. Letter to Patriot from Americans for National Security, April 30, 1964, folder 14, box 1, Dunaway Papers.

24. National Committee against Fluoridation, Inc. to Supporter, April 20, 1963; letter from Bernard L. Lefoley to Edward A. McLaughlin, August 11, 1961; letter from Bernard D. Hirsch to M. A. Mott, September 7, 1961, folder 5, box 1, Dunaway Papers.

25. Phyllis Schlafly to Kathryn Dunaway, October 30, 1967, folder 8, box 1, Dunaway Papers.

26. For more information on the NFRW election, see Catherine E. Rymph, *Republican Women: Feminism and Conservatism through the Rise of the New Right* (Chapel Hill: University of North Carolina Press), 2006, 177–87; Carol Felsenthal, *Phyllis Schlafly: The Sweetheart of the Silent Majority*, (Chicago: Regnery Gateway), 1981, 179–94; and Critchlow, *Phyllis Schlafly and Grassroots Conservatism*, 147–57.

27. Minutes of the GFRW Board of Directors Meeting, September 21, 1968, folder "GFRW Board meeting—2/15/69," box 3, Ague Papers.

28. Harry S. Flemming to Kathryn Dunaway, January 24, 1970, folder 3, box 1, Dunaway Papers.

29. Warren Weaver Jr., "Defeated Leader Sets Up a Rival Group for Republican Women," *New York Times*, August 9, 1967, 21.

30. Weaver, "Defeated Leader."

31. "Why Don't Conservatives Do Their Homework?," *Phyllis Schlafly Report*, February 1970, box 11, Dunaway Papers. Hereafter, *PSR*. For this paper, I have not checked the veracity of Schlafly's presented facts. The importance here is not the assertions but her language in presenting them.

32. Jane Mansbridge, *Why We Lost the ERA*, (Chicago: University of Chicago Press, 1986), 9–11; Donald T. Critchlow, *Phyllis Schlafly and Grassroots Conservatism*, 213–17; Donald G. Mathews and Jane Sherron De Hart, *Sex, Gender, and the Politics of ERA: A State and the Nation* (Oxford: Oxford University Press, 1990), 45–52.

33. *PSR*, February 1972. While I work from the original 1972 report, the content of this article is reprinted along with other significant *Phyllis Schlafly Report* articles in Phyllis Schlafly, *Feminist Fantasies* (Dallas: Spence Publishing Company, 2003).

34. Letter from Jeanne Cahill to Commission on the Status of Women, February 6, 1974, folder 3; Minutes of the Commission on the Status of Women Meeting, November 28, 1972, folder 2, Georgia Commission on the Status of Women Papers, Department of Human Resources, Georgia Archives, Morrow, Ga. Henceforth, CSW papers.

35. Phyllis Schlafly, interview with the author, June 8, 2009.

36. Kathryn Dunaway, Georgia STOP ERA Press Release, January 16, 1980, folder 17, box 4, Dunaway Papers.

37. Ibid.

38. Ibid.

39. "The Abortion Connection," published by the Eagle Forum, undated, folder 1, box 3, Dunaway Papers.

40. Bill Montgomery, "Women's Rights Backers Say Men's Room Is Safe," *Atlanta Journal*, February 7, 1973, 2A.

41. "Protest Equal Rights Bill," *Memphis (Tenn.) Tri-State Defender*, February 17, 1973, in Georgia Files, Eagle Forum Archives, Eagle Forum Library and Archives, St. Louis, Mo. Henceforth, Eagle Forum Archives. While I was initially not allowed into the archives, Deb Pentecost, Eagle Forum Archivist, generously photocopied all the Georgia files. These did not indicate folder numbers.

42. "Protest Equal Rights Bill."

43. Montgomery, "Women's Rights Backers."

44. STOP ERA of Georgia, "Check List for Witnesses to Speak against ERA," folder 8, box 4, Dunaway Papers. This list does not have a date.

45. Mrs. Allen Jones to Kathryn Dunaway, December 27, 1973, folder 26, box 1; Margaret Scharmitzky to Kathryn Dunaway, January 12, 1974, folder 27, box 1, Erin Sherman to Kathryn Dunaway, folder 29, box 1, Dunaway Papers.

46. Kathryn Dunaway to Chester Gray, February 6, 1974, folder 20, box 1, Dunaway papers.

47. Rosalynn Carter, *First Lady from Plains* (Boston: Houghton Mifflin Company, 1984), 102–3.

48. Sam Miller, "Equal Rights Amendment Defeated by Ga House," *Atlanta Daily World*, January 31, 1974, 2.

49. Letter from Jeanne Cahill to Commission members, February 6, 1974, CSW Papers.

50. Kathryn Dunaway and Lee Wysong to Friend, June 1, 1974, folder 23, box 1, Dunaway Papers.

51. Kathryn Dunaway and Lee Wysong to STOP ERA members, November 1974, folder 2, box 7, Dunaway Papers.

52. Sarah Cash, "How the ERA Battle was Lost," *Atlanta Journal-Constitution*, March 2, 1975, 4G.

53. William Cotterell, "ERA Rejected by Georgia Senate," *Washington Post*, February 18, 1975, A2.

54. Letter from Fred Schlafly to Catherine [*sic*] Dunaway, February 18, 1975, folder 4, box 2, Dunaway papers.

55. Kathryn Dunaway speech to Georgia Association of Broadcasters, Inc., April 20, 1978, folder 3, box 1, Dunaway Papers.

56. Corporate Responsibility Planning Service Report #580–49, June 11, 1979, folder 18, box 16, Papers of the Office of the First Lady, Carter Library.

57. Phyllis Schlafly, "Federal Financing of a Foolish Feminist Festival," *Daughters of the American Revolution Magazine* 112 (March 1978): 192.

58. "International Women's Year Commission—Report on ERAmerica Formation" January 15, 1976, Subject File 1976–1982, box 132, Records of ERAmerica, Manuscript Division, Library of Congress, Washington, D.C.

59. Sam Nunn to Kathryn Dunaway, May 20, 1976, folder 1, box 1, Dunaway Papers.

60. Resolution introduced at Republican Party of Georgia, undated, folder 18, box 4, Dunaway Papers.

61. STOP ERA Fundraising Project, undated, folder 2, box 3, Dunaway Papers.

62. Georgia Coordinating Committee on the Observance of International Women's Year, folder 22, box 4, Dunaway Papers. In 1978 committee member Eliza Paschall voiced her opposition to the ERA. Dunaway's papers do not give any insight into how or why she was selected for the Georgia Coordinating Committee on IWY.

63. Kathryn Dunaway to Friend, April 7, 1977, folder 10, box 1, Dunaway Papers.

64. "Instructions for Workshop Leaders," folder 1, box 4, Dunaway Papers.

65. Ibid.

66. "IWY Workshop Report Form," folder 1, box 4, Dunaway Papers.

67. Citizens' Review Committee for IWY Handout to Georgia Delegates, folder 1, box 4, Dunaway Papers.

68. Rosemary Thompson to Citizens' Review Chairman, June 5, 1977, folder 2, box 1, Dunaway Papers.

69. "Instructions for IWY Conference," undated, folder 1, box 4, Dunaway Papers.

70. Georgia Eagles to Eagles in Other States, "Be Prepared for the IWY Meetings," undated, folder 9, box 4, Dunaway Papers.

71. Letter from Kathryn Dunaway to Pastors, November 9, 1977, folder 4, box 2, Dunaway papers.

72. Susan Fraker, "Women vs. Women," *Newsweek*, July 25, 1977, 34.

73. Kathryn Dunaway to STOP ERA friend, May 23, 1978, folder 3, box 1, Dunaway Papers.

74. Phyllis Schlafly to Kathryn Dunaway, March 17, 1979, folder 3, box 1, Dunaway Papers.

75. Memo from Linda Tarr-Whelan to Judy Carter, November 28, 1979, folder 1 ERA-Georgia [2], box 31, Sarah Weddington Papers, Special Assistant for Women's Affairs, Jimmy Carter Presidential Library and Museum, National Archives and Records Administration, Atlanta, Ga. Hereafter, Sarah Weddington Papers.

76. Letter from Patricia Mollo to Jimmy Carter, Catasqua, Pa., June 15, 1979, folder 10, box 33, Sarah Weddington Papers.

77. "First Lady's Telephone Calls," January 19, 1980; "President's Calls," January 19, 1980, folder 1, box 31, Sarah Weddington Papers.

78. "Background on Georgia," unsigned, January 1, 1980, folder 1, box 31, Sarah Weddington Papers.

79. Jerry Schwartz, "Georgia Senators Say No to ERA," *Atlanta Constitution*, January 22, 1980, 7–A.

80. Ibid.

81. Tom Murphy to Georgia Mother's Committee, November 7, 1975, folder 10, box 2, Dunaway Papers.

82. Fred Schlafly to Kathryn Dunaway, January 3, 1980, folder 11, box 1, Dunaway Papers.

83. "Georgia STOP ERA Chairman Dies," newspaper clipping, undated, ERA Georgia files, Eagle Forum Archives.

84. Senate Resolution 117, "A Resolution Expressing Regrets at the Untimely Passing of Mrs. Kathryn Dunaway," ERA Georgia files, Eagle Forum Archives.

85. Tony Cooper, "Leading ERA Opponent Kathryn Dunaway Dies," *Atlanta Constitution*, September 17, 1980, 1–2C.

86. "ERA Defeated in Georgia House; Third Major Setback in 2 Weeks," *Miami Herald*, January 22, 1982, 8A, photocopy in ERA-Georgia Collection, Eagle Forum Archives.

87. Ibid.

Hazel Jane Raines
(1916–1956)

Georgia's First Woman Pilot and Her
"Band of Sisters" during World War II

PAUL STEPHEN HUDSON

Enshrined in 1989 with a group of six other pilots inducted into the Georgia Aviation Hall of Fame at Robins Air Force Base in Warner Robins, Georgia, Hazel Jane Raines is hailed as "Georgia's First Lady of Flight."[1] Indeed, Hazel Raines was the first woman in Georgia to earn a pilot's license, doing so in Macon in 1938. That year she was the first woman in the state to pilot solo, and in 1939 she was the first Georgia woman to earn a private pilot's license. In 1940 Raines was the first woman aviator to make a solo flight of significant distance in Georgia, from Macon to Athens.[2] Raines's greatest achievements, however, were during World War II. She flew military aircraft overseas in the first cohort of twenty-five women pilots in the British ATA (Air Transport Auxiliary). Later, she was a leader among the 1,074 aviators in the United States WASP (Women's Airforce Service Pilots) on the home front in America.

Thus, the air service career of Hazel Raines can be interpreted in the broad historical context of American women breaking new ground during the World War II era. More than "Georgia's First Lady of Flight," Raines should be viewed as one of the best American women pilots of the 1940s wartime era. She was among the first American women aviators who worked in transport and training situations as close to combat as legal regulations allowed. As such, she was part of a unique and ambitious group of women obliged to deal with multiple cultural and official forces—including the U.S. Army Air Force, military pilots, the media, and Congress—that were skeptical of using women in wartime aviation.

There was little indication in Hazel Raines's early life that she would become an outstanding pilot. Born on April 21, 1916, in Waynesboro, Georgia, Hazel was sickly as a child, the result of a heart condition she had all her life.[3] Nevertheless, she had a strong will and determination, and she pursued a high level of education, graduating in the class of 1936 from the distinguished Wesleyan College, a women's institution in Macon, Georgia.[4] Raines studied music in the school's conservatory.[5] Hazel's schooling may have further imbued her with a sense of equality and self-confidence. To advocates of higher education for women, nothing was worse than an education that confined students to subjects or vocations based on gender stereotypes, and many young women found college to be a liberating experience that opened up new possibilities for independence.[6]

The youngest of three girls, Hazel was to be different from her older sisters Frankie and Martha, who did not attend Wesleyan and grew up to marry and have children. It was soon after graduation from college that Raines dramatically broke from the expectations of traditional southern womanhood and entered what had been a man's world of aviation in Georgia. According to family stories, it was on a dare that she decided to take flying lessons at tiny Herbert Smart Field in Macon. On hot summer days at the airfield, Raines blended in well, typically wearing a short-sleeved shirt, slacks, and brown leather flying boots.[7] It appears that Raines gained respect from pilots who liked her passion for flying and, seeing her talent for aviation, encouraged her in a mentoring spirit.

The preeminent role model for American women pilots of Raines's 1930s generation was the famous aviatrix (then a contemporary term for a female aviator) Amelia Earhart. In 1929 Earhart had helped organize the first support group for American women in aviation, of which she became president. She named the informal group the Ninety-Nines because of its number of charter members determined "to discuss the prospects for women's pilots."[8] She made a solo flight over the Pacific from Honolulu to Oakland, California, in 1935. That same year in Georgia there was a highly publicized celebration, which suggested that at least some in the state had become more progressive in recognizing women's achievement. In Atlanta, Oglethorpe University president Thornwell Jacobs proclaimed 1935—the year before Hazel Raines graduated from Wesleyan—as the "Year of the Woman." He invited ten distinguished women to receive honorary doctorates at May commencement to recognize their careers in "public advancement." All had college connections and created lives outside of mar-

HAZEL JANE RAINES

Courtesy Georgia Women of Achievment; image detail by Hilary Coles.

riage. For example, Annie Jump Cannon, a distinguished astronomer, had graduated from Radcliffe and Wellesley. Martha Berry had founded Berry College in Rome, Georgia, in 1902. Amelia Earhart, who had attended Columbia University, represented aviation. In her featured speech, she contended that in flying, women deserved the opportunities that men had. "Machines have come to the rescue of women," Earhart declared. She acknowledged that men typically had more strength than women, but noted that "[flying] machines . . . equalize matters."[9] The popular Earhart symbolized a growing acceptance of women as pilots; her 1932 solo nonstop transatlantic flight had led to a Distinguished Flying Cross from the United States and also the Legion of Honor of France.[10]

Thus, a measure of openness toward women pilots was beginning to emerge just as Hazel Raines and a relatively small cohort of American women sought to advance their own careers and make inroads into a male-dominated profession in the mid-1930s. By 1940 Raines, seeking solo flying hours to qualify for a commercial license, had begun flying Taylor-craft airplanes—a brand of old-time, high-winged fabric aircraft similar to the Piper Cub and manufactured in Alliance, Ohio—to deliver them to southern cities. In a performance review of Raines, L. J. Mercure of the Civil Aeronautics Authority noted that her "flying is superior to that of the average licensed male pilot," and in 1941 Hazel Raines received a flight instructor's rating and was ready to embark on a career in aviation.[11] However comfortable the country had become with a handful of outstanding female pilots or "women of the year," most Americans continued to associate women first and foremost with family and domesticity, and their ongoing ambivalence regarding expanding work roles for women in general—and female aviators specifically—would be clearly reflected in the years to come, as Raines and other women pilots endeavored to claim a place for themselves in wartime aviation.

The economic mobilization of World War II significantly transformed women's relationship to the labor movement—at least temporarily. Wartime circumstances legitimized women's working in unprecedented areas to meet national necessities, and the defense industry presented striking opportunities. In aviation, women became involved in war-related industries, such as producing parts and parachutes. Piloting planes, however, meant high-profile careers that created general uncertainties about what was considered men's and women's work for the first generation of American women aviators.[12] Seeking to grab hold of the opportunities for advancement that the war seemed to promise even as they still encountered considerable skepticism regarding women's role in military aviation, women pilots sorely needed a new leader—Amelia Earhart had mysteriously disappeared in her flight to circumnavigate the equator in 1937.

The legendary Jacqueline Cochran (1906–80), one of the most gifted rac-
ing pilots of her era, ultimately became mentor to Hazel Raines and other top
women flyers. By 1938 Cochran was widely known as the best woman pilot in
the United States—she had set transcontinental speed and altitude records for
all pilots, regardless of gender. Cochran, who assumed the presidency of the
Ninety-Nines, also had keen political and administrative skills.[13]

Undaunted by ongoing efforts to restrict women's role in aviation, Cochran
aggressively sought opportunities for women pilots in England during wartime
mobilization. Fluid conditions meant that flying as "women's work" might be
redefined if set in a new location.[14] In 1940 the ambitious Raines was twenty-four
and ready to seize the moment. Her father, Frank, had recently died of a stroke
at age sixty-one, and though Hazel was eager for new flying assignments, this
inevitably meant leaving her mother, Bessie, in Macon. In the years that followed, Hazel corresponded regularly with her mother, and her letters reflect a
complex relationship between mother and daughter as Hazel embarked on a
groundbreaking and at times hazardous career. Hazel was unquestionably devoted to her mother and wanted approval; but at the same time she had chosen
a demanding and unconventional life and had no intention of "settling down."
Because there was an element of risk in flying, Hazel often wrote letters of reas-
surance.[15] Seeking to allay her mother's fears, Hazel downplayed the dangers she
faced as well as the challenges presented to women as they attempted to gain acceptance and respect among fellow pilots and male military leaders more generally. Only occasionally did she let slip an ironic comment or note of frustration
that hinted at obstacles she and other women pilots faced.

By 1942 Jacqueline Cochran was able to secure U.S. approval for American
women pilots to assist British flyers in England's ATA (Air Transport Auxiliary),
where gender barriers had been broken after the outbreak of World War II.
Originally intended as a civilian organization to transport mail and medical
supplies in Britain during World War II, ATA began to serve as ferry pilots. Their
roles included more strategic details, including delivery and transport of new,
repaired, and damaged military aircraft from factories to air stations overseen
by the Royal Air Force (RAF). ATA flyers thus freed British combat aviators for
their particular wartime duties.[16]

It was in this context that Hazel Raines became involved in government aviation in the U.S. Civilian Pilot Training Program (CPTP) in 1941. It had begun
in 1939 to link flight training with colleges and universities so the United States
could keep pace with the burgeoning military flight training air academies for
young pilots in Nazi Germany and Fascist Italy. After the outbreak of World
War II, the CPTP became much more important strategically.[17] Raines taught

flying as one of its six women instructors—and the only Georgian—in hopes of commencing an air service career if America entered the war. Training pilots first in Cochran, Georgia, and then in Fort Lauderdale, Florida, the experienced Raines had logged more than 1,300 hours of government documented flight time. She held memberships in the Macon Aero Club and the National Aeronautical Association. She naturally was a member of the Ninety-Nines, the support group for women pilots.[18] Her record of flight hours arrested the attention of Jacqueline Cochran just as she was compiling lists of the best, most experienced women aviators in the United States.[19]

"I was teaching flying when the telegram from Miss Jacqueline Cochran arrived asking me if I would be interested in flying planes in England," a thrilled Raines later related, adding: "Me, a two bit Flight instructor and a gal trying to make her way in Aviation and Bang**—Outa [*sic*] the blue comes a telegram, of all things, from the top aviatrix asking me, quote—'Can you fly to New York Thursday March 5th [1942] for interview.'"[20] A few months after the Japanese attack on Pearl Harbor, Raines underwent a successful interview in New York City with Cochran, who accepted Georgia's premiere woman pilot as a contract flier for the English Ferry Pool Service. (A helpful Macon doctor wrote a letter that satisfactorily explained the asthma and heart problems that surfaced on Raines's physical exam.) Cleared for processing in Montreal, Canada, Raines, amid much excitement, passed all other tests, thus becoming one of an accomplished cohort of twenty-five American women flyers—and the only Georgian—approved to receive contracts to fly for the British ATA.[21] Ironically, these civilian pilots were to become the first United States women to fly military aircraft.

Planning required that Raines and her fellow pilots leave from Canada, because the United States would not issue passports for women to travel to a war theater. "We were going to England to do our bit—our part, all because America, the land of the free and the home of the brave, would not give us a chance," Hazel later wrote in a highly personal memoir that had, for her, uncharacteristically biting irony. Setting sail from Halifax, Nova Scotia, Raines and three women aviators traveled Top Secret status on a British Merchant Navy fruit ship laden with aluminum as part of a convoy, with corvette and destroyer escort, bound for England on a journey that took twenty-seven days.[22] Arriving early, Raines and eleven cohorts became the first of the twenty-five American women aviators to join the British ATA.

At Air Transport Auxiliary Headquarters at White Waltham, Maidenhead, England, Hazel and her cohorts began intensive training that was to make them extraordinarily experienced aviators by any standard. Versatility in flying was the keynote of all pilots for the ATA, whose official motto in Latin, *Aetheris Avidi*, was freely understood to be "Any aircraft, anywhere." Superiors expected ATA aviators, after completion of their training, to fly any plane assigned to them, even if they had to consult the Ferry Pilots' Notes to learn basic information on an aircraft before taking off.[23]

The important ferry pilot support role for the RAF meant that ATA pilots wore heavy blue wool uniforms indicating military service. Still, they were civilian contract employees and lived in homes of private British citizens. They flew at random in a series of fourteen flyer pools from Southampton in the south of England to Lossiemouth in Scotland, spelled with stretches of intensive flight training.[24] "We are being taught the technical and theoretical side of flying as well as the practical," Hazel related in a letter to her mother in May 1942. By the next month Raines was deeply tanned from the sun and wind as she flew open cockpit airplanes on longer trips. After passing one flight test on what she vaguely called "heavy equipment" (her letters were always subject to wartime censorship), Hazel gratefully sighed to her mother: "Never did I dream I'd be flying the stuff I am now." Tellingly, her assessment was more sober to a male pilot friend flying in England: "never would I have the chance to fly such equipment in the United States."[25] Raines never forgot her first flight on a single-seat fighter plane, which, for security reasons, she did not identify in a letter to her mother. It was the "largest aeroplane [an arcane term from the 1930s] I had ever seen," Raines remembered. She admitted taking charge of her "knocking knees," but then assumed control of the plane. This achievement led to a "promotion to Second Officer and two Yank stripes on my shoulder," Raines related.[26]

It was not long before Raines regularly flew Hurricanes and Spitfires for the ATA. A surviving scrapbook photo shows Raines in uniform as she is dwarfed by a great Spitfire, the elite elliptical-winged warplane manufactured by Supermarine and powered by Rolls Royce engines, the pride of British Fighter Command. Raines admitted once she was happiest when she had a "nice new machine and . . . a long hop to make" as she flew over England viewing "a beautiful patchwork quilt effect when flying about 3,000 feet."[27] Though she never noted it explicitly, it appears abundantly clear that Raines was thrilled she was not in Macon anymore. Never did she express a desire to return.

Raines and her cohort of American women ATA pilots flew their ferry missions in the aftermath of the Battle of Britain, in which RAF losses in the summer of 1940 had been heavy, including 915 fighter aircraft.[28] When Raines and her fellow flyers arrived in London in the spring of 1942, the city had undergone the worst assaults of "the Blitz," but bombing still continued. "As for air raids," she observed, "the people take about as much notice to a siren as a telephone ringing and go on their way."[29] Indeed, the German Luftwaffe still patrolled the

English skies as a combat zone. Moreover, British Bomber Command in late May 1942 executed a strategic plan, committing most of the RAF planes to a "Thousand Bomber" raid on Cologne, Germany, followed by similar assaults on Essen and Bremen. The dramatic air strikes absorbed losses but garnered such favorable publicity that nobody dared suggest an end to the campaign. "Behind the recent 1,000 plane Royal Air Force raids on Germany," a correspondent wrote, "are the pilots of the British Ferry Service. They are the ones who make possible the RAF performances that have astonished the democratic world."[30] British bombers needed a steady stream of escort fighter planes such as those Raines and her fellow pilots ferried. In 1942 British and American factories produced peak numbers of new aircraft that needed transporting, making the ATA role even more important.[31]

Ferry aviators such as Hazel Raines piloted both new replacement and older disabled aircraft, transporting planes from factories to bases and fighter squadrons, often flying the length of Britain, never using instruments for navigation nor radio beam contact in order to prevent detection, while having no ammunition for guns. Flying damaged planes was particularly perilous. A persistent hazard was flying in restrictive air corridors hemmed in by hazardous hydrogen gas–filled barrage balloons, suspended on heavy cables and situated in the base of clouds up to five thousand feet, expressly designed to take down aircraft. It also was not uncommon for ferry pilots to encounter German v-1 rocket bombs fired over the English Channel from occupied France.[32]

In addition to Hurricanes and Spitfires, the proficient Raines flew nearly every other kind of British fighter-type aircraft. Indeed, Raines flew some airships, such as one particular RAF Tiger Moth, in which she lay down fully extended in order to reach the rudder bars. (She successfully flew the plane in a prone position in which she could not see where she was going, pulling up periodically to make adjustments when she could view her checkpoint positions.) "I will have flown practically every type [twin engine] Aeoroplane built by the United States and Great Britain," Raines noted proudly.[33] Raines relished her job, to fly a variety of planes that were markedly varied in airworthiness as well as in speed, handling, and navigation capabilities. Medical officers at White Waltham, monitoring Raines's health issues and aware of her determination to do her duties, instituted special monthly physical examinations for her, which she appreciated and always passed successfully.[34]

Raines's flight logbooks indicate that she crashed once, on March 2, 1943, when she suddenly experienced engine trouble while flying a flak-damaged Spitfire. She did not parachute, but rather attempted a wild crash landing while trying to save the plane, which lost both wings as it removed the second story of a thatched cottage in a remote English village. There were no casualties on the ground. Raines later admitted she did not remember anything "after seeing the houses come up in my face." News accounts reported the surprise of "two broad-shouldered Britons" when they attempted to "dig out the dead man" from the mangled Spitfire, only to find Raines, "who spoke in the accents of her native Georgia." Crawling out of the wreckage, Raines took off her parachute unaided; and then, instinctively reflecting her standard ATA pilot's crash procedure training, in a clear voice she gave the required order: "London—guard that plane!" Only then did Raines allow herself to be taken to a hospital. Afterward, Raines remembered none of the details of the crash; but she had executed the proper military regulation and chuckled, "That shows training accounts for something in a crisis!"[35]

Although she downplayed it in letters to her family, Raines's crash in the damaged Spitfire was obviously a narrow brush with death. She suffered head injuries and eye trouble, and was grounded from flying by doctors for three months while she received intense medical supervision, but eventually her doctors approved her return to service. Undaunted, Raines wanted to continue her contributions to the war effort, which she believed were more useful in Britain as an ATA flyer than anything she might do in the United States. "You feel you are part of it all," Raines wrote. She loved the "wonderful feeling it is to deliver a Fighter Aircraft to a Fighter Squadron of Boys that are really just standing there waiting for you to bring them something to fight with."[36] Meanwhile, back in the United States, Jacqueline Cochran wrote a group letter to Raines and two of her fellow pilots, saying "I heard about Hazel's accident, and I do hope you are quite recovered." But Cochran was particularly concerned about Hazel's ATA colleague Evelyn Hudson, who had not fared as well—when she was ferrying a Wellington British bomber, she had crashed and broken her back.[37]

Because of their notable achievements and dramatic breaking of gender barriers by ATA women pilots in service to Britain's RAF, Raines was among a select group who occasionally had random opportunities to meet some of the most significant women of their times. For example, at the ATA command base at White Waltham on October 26, 1942, Raines was present during a formal inspection performed by Eleanor Roosevelt, America's most influential advocate for women in aviation. Indeed, she had called the small number of ATA women pilots "a weapon waiting to be used."[38] Raines and Roosevelt struck up a conversation about places they had in common, especially Macon and Warm Springs, Georgia. Still, Hazel was not the type to be overawed. "Even tho we did hafta put on skirts for the occasion, stand in the rain for half an hour and almost freeze to death," she wryly related, "I guess it was worth it."[39]

Later in 1942, and shortly before Christmas, while spending time in a Canadian hospital near Maidenhead receiving treatment for chronic ailments, Raines met an eccentric middle-aged Red Cross helper who, unknown to her, was the legendary Lady Nancy Astor. She only identified herself as a Virginian and brashly wanted to meet the patient from Georgia. She offended Raines by questioning how "a Southern girl would come off her dignity and do such an unladylike thing as fly." Raines, expressing what she significantly called her psychological "inner self," told off the visitor in no uncertain terms. "I started in on her and told her just what I thought of flying, as well as people who do," she recalled, adding, "I was of the opinion that the women of today were doing a man's job in a woman's world with unfaultering ability and finesse, and to me if a woman of her integrity could not see it in that light, she must be a very narrow-minded person." Lady Astor admired the candor of the plucky young American and finally introduced herself. Thinking it was a joke, an exasperated Raines exclaimed, "So what!" After the visitor left, the patients in the ward, convulsed with laughter, informed the nonplussed Hazel she had just dressed down the famous Lady Nancy Astor.[40]

The next day Lady Astor visited Raines again and invited her for Christmastime at the Astor estate Cliveden, a fabulous family mansion in Buckinghamshire overlooking the River Thames.[41] When Lady Astor teasingly mentioned that she wanted to introduce her four eligible sons to her guest in the hopes that one might fall for a daughter of the South, Raines declined. "I told her that was not what I was looking for in life," she firmly said.[42] Although she dated occasionally, Hazel never expressed any interest in marriage, and aviation always remained the real passion in her life. "The rest of the girls have been going the way 90% of females go—After [*sic*] the tall, dark, handsome pilots," Raines once wrote, adding "They can have them—just give me a big shiny aeroplane!"[43] She never did marry, but devoted her entire life to a personally rewarding aviation career.

After her crash and three months of recovery, Raines did not fly again until June 1943. Her flight logbooks indicate that Raines, who now had a scar on her right temple, no longer flew Hurricanes and Spitfires but rather piloted less heavy British equipment, mainly twin-engine Oxfords and Fairchilds. She was obliged to fly without a helmet due to the pressure on her head.[44] Medical reports indicate that she had a fairly marked postconcussion syndrome, and doctors recommended ophthalmic surgery. Indeed, Raines complained of occasional mistiness of vision and difficulty in judging distances, so perhaps her medical condition was a factor in her decision to leave the British ATA.[45]

Raines returned to Macon in August 1943 and enjoyed a brief mother–daughter reunion. Raines, who had been promoted to captain in the ATA, never

would return to the war theater in England and at that time became interested
in the work of her mentor, Jacqueline Cochran, now director of the new U.S.
Women's Airforce Service Pilots (WASP), a branch of the Army Air Force (AAF).
Cochran believed that Raines's impressive service in England with her cohort
of American women pilots had been invaluable. It critically demonstrated the
need to organize in America a flying group similar to the women's service rendered to the British ATA. "I am convinced," Cochran wrote to Hazel and some
of her women colleagues, "that if you girls hadn't gone to England, and were not
doing the grand job that you are, that this [WASP] program would never have
gotten started, so, in my opinion, I can't overestimate how much I feel you have
contributed to women in aviation."[46] The AAF, founded in 1941, was probably the
most innovative service branch, in part because it was not locked in to convention and army custom. The AAF not only employed women as pilots but also in
a variety of other occupations, including as air traffic controllers, tower radio
operators, and radio mechanics.[47]

In November 1943 Hazel Raines donned the Santiago blue uniform of the
U.S. WASP, based at its new headquarters at Avenger Field in Sweetwater, Texas.
It was the only flight school in the history of aviation devoted exclusively to the
training of women cadets.[48] Raines became a member of the 44-W-4 class (the
fourth women's trainee class of 1944). Her wartime experience with Spitfires
and Hurricanes as an English ferry pilot perhaps accounted for the quiet "big-
sisterly confidence" noted by trainees, most of whom had not made solo flights.
They learned that Raines, who personally knew the great Jackie Cochran, was
somewhat of a legend in women's aviation.[49] Raines characteristically did not
balk as she studied to fly the relatively elementary PT "trainer" planes while
helping her classmates, who were in reality a kind of next generation to follow
the pioneering Georgian in the new field of women's aviation. The Wesleyan
Conservatory–educated Raines took the duty of post bugler, which reminded
her of her days in Georgia, and she cheerfully noted, "Seems like old times toot-
ing a horn again, but I like it." Because of her experience and mentoring contributions, superiors awarded Hazel Raines the highest office a student could hold
in a trainee class: squadron commander.[50]

In her WASP training, Raines continued to grow in aviation proficiency. She
began instrument training—a technique of flight with inestimable value in all
kinds of weather, which had been denied to ATA flyers—and made the highest
grade issued on instrument rides up to that time for any of the WASPs. Still,
Jackie Cochran advised Raines to accelerate all training to prepare to fly B-26
twin engine heavy bombers. Having been exempted from cross-county flying
because of her extensive flight hours in Britain, Hazel finished the entire course

of study two months before her squadron members and was allowed to graduate from WASP training early. Afterward, she performed test flying of light twin-engine aircraft after their engines had been repaired. "I have decided I like English fog better than Texas dust," pilot Raines laconically commented.[51]

Again following Cochran's advice, her protégé successfully sought an assignment to tow-target flying "since they only fly the best equipment in those squadrons." Raines began transition training in Texas and Arizona to pilot B-26 bombers on "target missions" at altitudes up to twenty thousand feet. She served as squadron commander for tow-target pilots at Pecos Army Air Field in Pecos, Texas. Although no longer flying in a war zone, Raines still faced danger in drills where she served as a tow-target flyer, in which male air gunner trainees practiced shooting from B-17s with live ammunition. "Of course the target is trailing behind us at some 500 feet, so we don't have a thing to worry about," Raines glibly assured her mother in late 1944 while recounting various experiences at Kingman Army Airfield in Arizona.[52]

Meanwhile Jacqueline Cochran had lobbied unsuccessfully to clarify a technical point that had become increasingly controversial—full military status of the WASPs, which the U.S. Army Air Force had not recognized. Cochran encountered increasing resistance from many quarters, most notably military pilots who, with World War II demobilization looming, wanted jobs held by WASP aviators. Cochran's efforts were to no avail and the U.S. government disbanded the WASP on December 20, 1944. After demilitarization and deactivation, Hazel Raines was among a group of 1,074 women who had collectively flown about sixty million miles for the U.S. Army Air Forces without formal recognition. Among them there had been thirty-eight deaths of women in service (with a ratio of one to about sixteen thousand hours of flying, which was comparable to male aviators performing similar work).[53] WASPs were not only disappointed at their denial of military status but also dismayed at an abrupt lack of post-war flying opportunities in aviation. They began to experience what historian William Chafe has called the "strange paradox of change"—women's sphere of work had been expanded, yet traditional attitudes toward their "place" had remained largely unchanged.[54] "The girls who went to the airlines, trying to fly, were not allowed in. It was for men only," remembered Leonoa Golbinek. It would be many years before WASPs would be able to feel some pride and solidarity as forerunners for women in the U.S. Air Force.[55]

Raines kept in her scrapbooks a copy of the last Women's Airforce Service Pilots graduation address, delivered on December 7, 1944, in Sweetwater, Texas, by General Henry "Hap" Arnold, pioneer aviator and legendary commander of the U.S. Army Air Forces. He eloquently praised the groundbreaking work of the WASP flyers—a fact that must have been bittersweet to his audience in light of the organization's impending deactivation. Arnold, who initially had been skeptical of women aviators in the military, had been won over by their sterling performance. He saluted the "young women who have been making Aviation history . . . [as] pioneers in a new field of wartime service," unequivocally declaring that "more than two years since WASP started flying with the Air Forces, we can come to only one conclusion—the entire operation has been a success. It is on the record that women can fly as well as men."[56] Indeed, the caliber of piloting that Hazel Raines and her cohort of women pilots displayed during World War II helped establish the fundamental ideal of gender equality in American aviation today. They were integral to what historian David M. Kennedy has described as the "social . . . upheavals of wartime [that] laid the groundwork . . . for an eventual revolution in women's status."[57] Indeed in its own time the WASP—the first American wartime service unit comprised entirely of women who performed functions traditionally associated with men—was exceedingly controversial. By taking on roles and missions previously associated with the masculine, Hazel Raines and her cohort of women pilots implicitly challenged assumptions of male supremacy in wartime culture.[58]

Jacqueline Cochran was deeply frustrated at the final deactivation of the WASPs, not only because they had broken gender barriers, but also because they were successful beyond question, as even General Arnold had come to acknowledge. Although Hazel Raines did not for security reasons mention in her letters everything she did as a WASP, it is clear that she contributed significantly to help prove the skill of women flying in many critical areas that Cochran later enumerated. "We were proving a point about women flyers," she declared, "providing competent pilots to the ferry operation, towing targets was a nasty job—working on tracking and searchlight operations, simulated strafing, smoke laying, and performing other chemical missions, radio control flying, taking care of basic and instrument instructing, engineering test flying, as well as handling the administrative and utility flying."[59]

As World War II drew to a conclusion, a disappointed Raines found that, due to the summary demilitarization of the WASP, all she was acknowledged to have contributed was three years of "volunteer nonmilitary service" to her country. She also found herself without a job or benefits. Worse in a sense for her, Raines's increasing heart problems reached such a critical point that she could no longer fly. Although she always loved her family and Georgia, she firmly ruled out returning home, making it clear to her mother, "I think you understand me when I say I don't want to go back to Macon."[60] It was too provincial for her, for Raines's wartime experiences had made her an independent woman. All of her versatile aviation work—accumulating about 6,400 flying hours in all kinds of weather, piloting more than forty types of aircraft, some of them damaged, from light trainers to fighter planes and twin-engine ships—had given Raines the self-confidence to make her own way.[61] "What about Women after the War?" the *New York Times* asked as early as 1943. While answers varied, the conventional one was the "emergency" was over and that women should return home.[62]

Raines declined to return home; instead, she left the country. She learned Portuguese and subsequently taught a course called Theory of Flight on a one-year contract for the Air Ministry of Brazil in Sao Paulo. She did good work, and her superiors requested that Hazel teach LINK instrument flying as well.[63] Ironically Raines, who was a civilian contract employee, found that she was required to wear the khaki uniform of the Brazilian Air Force. However, Raines's only connections with aviation in this role were academic and she had been a woman of action. "I'm not doing what I like to do most and you know that is flying," she wrote to her mother. Returning to the United States, Raines found herself a kind of icon and role model to women pilots. At a conference sponsored by the Texas Ninety-Nines in 1947, for example, Hazel Raines was a featured speaker with Nancy Love, the first woman to fly the B-17 Flying Fortress. In 1948 Raines served as WASP honor representative in a memorial service for her departed cohorts—the thirty-eight women pilots who had lost their lives during World War II.[64]

In 1949 Raines began a successful effort to serve in the United States armed services, where postwar opportunities for women had become limited. She applied for and received a reserve commission as second lieutenant in the new U.S. Women's Air Force (WAF) and began in an organized reserve program at Lackland Air Force Base in San Antonio, Texas. When the Korean Conflict began in 1950, Raines immediately volunteered to serve active duty in the WAF. Raines and her fellow aviators of the old WASP group all faced one common problem: because the program had not been fully militarized, there literally were no official records, much less honorable discharges, to document how well they had served their country. Raines, however, appealed directly to the WAF. She acknowledged the unfortunate technicality that she "had never before been service connected," but at the same time tactfully suggested that "I am qualified somewhere along the line . . . that would afford justification for my recall." By the end of the year, Atlanta papers proudly reported, "Hazel Raines, of Macon, Georgia . . . is the first WAF reservist to be returned to active duty on a mobilization assignment."[65]

When Hazel Raines received her commission in November 1950 at Maxwell Air Force Base in Alabama to serve as an officer in the U.S. Air Force, she was the only woman to stand with a group of nineteen men. She had broken yet another gender barrier. As she at long last pledged allegiance to the United States in an officer induction ceremony, the patriotic Raines was thrilled. "It really gave me goose bumps . . . as I stood there with my right hand upraised, repeated the oath of office, and for the first time realized and felt I had been accepted for duty with our United States Air Forces," she later wrote.[66]

Past her time to fly, Raines served in various personnel and administrative staff positions, recruiting and mentoring women pilots for the U.S. WAF. Having grown up in Jim Crow Georgia, Raines was obliged to make adjustments as the U.S. military desegregated, but it was no problem. When she first met a black female officer, a "colored captain," who was helping to break the color line in the military, Raines was matter of fact. "Yes, I know this is the first time I have had to live with a colored person but believe me after talking with her for ten minutes, I forgot all about the fact that she is black and I am white," she related to her mother.[67] The Air Force later transferred Raines to London, where she was assigned as an adjutant to a large communications squadron that was 90 percent men. "My first crack at serving as an officer in a male Squadron," she noted.[68] Whatever Raines's assignments in Europe were, she did not relate them in her letters, and they remain a bit of a mystery. She was dispatched to various NATO countries, including Portugal, Italy, Greece, and Germany. "Wish I could tell you more about my job but I can't," she told her mother apologetically.[69] In Wiesbaden, Germany, in the summer of 1956 she was hospitalized for back and leg pain.

Because of chronic heart problems, Hazel was accustomed to frequent, relatively short, stays in hospitals. After her release in Wiesbaden, Raines returned to England, where she was again hospitalized, this time for neurological examinations and treatment. In her final letter to her "Dearest Mother," on August 27, 1956, Hazel wearily reported that her legs felt like rubber. "Well, it has been a long haul, tiresome at times," she noted, clearly fatigued, and then with buoyed spirits added she would be "glad when I am strong enough and can go back to active duty." And her last lines sent to Georgia were affectionate as always: "Take care and give my love to all the family."[70]

First Lieutenant Hazel Jane Raines died on September 4, 1956, in London after she had been released from the hospital.[71] A Western Union telegram relayed the sad news to her mother, Bessie P. Raines, in Macon. There was no question that Hazel would be interred in her native state. The Central of Georgia Railroad transported her remains by way of Dover Air Force Base, Delaware, and consigned them to the Hart Mortuary on Cherry Street in Macon.[72] Hazel Jane Raines is buried in the family plot at Riverside Cemetery with her parents. Regina Trice Hawkins says she never heard her grieving grandmother Bessie talk about Hazel afterward. The dutiful proud mother, who died in 1971 at age eighty-six, had carefully saved all of her youngest daughter's letters, from which historians now know a remarkable story. Indeed, Hazel Raines's life and times is one of those countless resilient threads in the epic tapestry of what writer Tom Brokaw has called the Greatest Generation: "They came of age during the Great Depression and the Second World War and went on to build modern America—men and women whose everyday lives of duty, honor, achievement, and courage gave us the world we have today."[73] However, it is also part of a larger story of women's only partially successful struggle to be accepted, acknowledged, and rewarded as equals to men at that time.

A final assessment of Hazel Jane Raines as a woman of achievement in Georgia starts with her setting precedents and breaking gender barriers as the state's first licensed woman pilot in the late 1930s. However, her career entered a much wider area of military service in the critical years from 1942 to 1945 during World War II, when she was a vital part of a cohort of courageous women flyers led by Jacqueline Cochran. As the first American women to fly military aircraft, at least for a short time, they helped establish the foundation for a new age in aviation in the United States.

For women aviators of Raines's generation, flying was an exceedingly difficult field because all programs were experimental. They thus needed to achieve exceptional job performance by exceeding or equaling the work of men. The clear success of Hazel Raines with her cohort of women pilots significantly furthered continued social change in American attitudes toward military aviation directed by men who, up until the 1940s, had barred participation of women altogether. In the war theater in England and on the Home Front in America, Raines operated with her highest level of competitive achievement as a pilot; however, due to the nature of her work, her greatest success was not that of an isolated individual. Rather, Hazel Raines excelled against the odds in every sense as not only a role model but also a key supporting leader in the chain of command of a small but proficient women's flying community, performing its own unique contributions within limited opportunities in the important wartime world of military aviation.

NOTES

1. Along with Hazel Jane Raines, the 1989 inaugural class of inductees to the Georgia Aviation Hall of Fame included the following distinguished pilots born in the state: Ben Epps Sr. (1888–1937)

of Athens, the first Georgian to fly an airplane; Eugene Jacques Bullard (1894–1961) of Columbus, World War I pilot and the first black combat aviator; Frank O'Driscoll Hunter (1894–1962) of Savannah, World War I ace; Guy Orlando Stone (1894–1980) of Glenwood, pioneer World War I pilot and aviation historian; Hamilton McWhorter III (1894–1982) of Athens, World War II ace; and Robert Lee Stone (1908–2006) of Waynesboro, World War II ace and author of the classic wartime memoir *God Is My Co-Pilot* (1943). See Natalie D. Saba, "Hazel Raines (1915–1956)," *New Georgia Encyclopedia* (http://www.georgiaencyclopedia.org/articles/business-economy/hazel-raines-1916-1956 [accessed November 25, 2013]), for her 1989 induction into the Georgia Aviation Hall of Fame.

2. For a useful summary of Raines's career, see Saba, "Hazel Raines (1916–1956)." For Raines's first solo flight in Georgia, see "Macon Aviatrix Reaches Goal by Circular Route," *Athens Banner Herald*, October 22, 1940. It is not clear why women did not fly in Georgia until so late. Perhaps it was because of the patriarchal nature of a southern state that had such little regard for women's rights that it adamantly refused ratification of the Nineteenth Amendment in 1920. Harriet Quimby was the first licensed woman aviator in the United States, in New York in 1911, and Amelia Earhart received her pilot's license in California in 1921. See Thomas A. Scott, ed., *Cornerstones of Georgia History: Documents That Formed the State* (Athens: University of Georgia Press, 1995), 177; Claudia Oakes, *U.S. Women in Aviation through World War I* (Washington, D.C.: Smithsonian Institution, 1979); and Doris L. Rich, *Amelia Earhart: A Biography* (Washington, D.C.: Smithsonian Institution, 1989).

3. "Raines, Hazel J.," *Riverside Cemetery Online*, Riverside Cemetery, Macon, Ga., http://www.riversidecemetery.com (accessed July 8, 2010).

4. "History of the College," Wesleyan College website, http://www.wesleyancollege.edu/about/history.cfm (accessed December 1, 2012).

5. Registrar's Office Records, Wesleyan College, Macon, Ga.

6. Amy Thompson McCandless, *The Past in the Present: Women's Higher Education in the Twentieth-Century American South* (Tuscaloosa: University of Alabama Press, 1999), 53.

7. Regina T. Hawkins, *Hazel Jane Raines: Pioneer Lady of Flight: A Biography in Letters* (Macon, Ga.: Mercer University Press, 1996), 2.

8. Pamela Feltus, "The Ninety-Nines," U.S. Centennial of Flight Commission, http://www.centennialofflight.gov/essay/Explorers_Record_Setters_and_Daredevils/99s/ (accessed December 15, 2009).

9. See Paul Stephen Hudson, "'In Service to Humanity for the Good of the World': Thornwell Jacobs and the Awarding of Oglethorpe University Honorary Doctorates," *Atlanta History: A Journal of Georgia and the South* 44 (Spring 2000). Jacobs awarded Earhart a unique doctor of public service honorary degree.

10. Rich, *Amelia Earhart*.

11. Hawkins, *Hazel Jane Raines*, 3.

12. See William H. Chafe, *The Paradox of Change: American Women in the 20th Century* (New York: Oxford University Press, 1991), 121–72; and Ruth Milkman, *Gender at Work: The Dynamics of Job Segregation during World War II* (Urbana: University of Illinois Press, 1987), 49–64.

13. Deborah G. Douglas, *United States Women in Aviation, 1940–1945* (Washington, D.C.: Smithsonian Institution Press, 1990); Nina McGuire and Sandra Wallus Sammons, *Jacqueline Cochran: America's Fearless Aviator* (Lake Buena Vista, Fla.: Tailored Tours Publishing, 1997). Jacqueline Cochran, who was born as Bessie Lee Pittman near Mobile, Ala., married aircraft mechanic Robert Cochran in Blakely, Ga., in 1920. Mrs. Bessie Cochran, after a divorce, changed her name to Miss Jackie Cochran. This woman of extraordinary achievement was enshrined in the Georgia Aviation Hall of Fame in 1992.

14. Milkman, *Gender at Work*, 49.

15. Hawkins, *Hazel Jane Raines*, vii. This indispensable book on Hazel Raines includes transcripts of narratives, letters, medical reports, articles from her scrapbooks, flight logbooks, and photographs. These materials compiled by Hawkins on her aunt make for a unique collection of original sources on Raines's air-service career.

16. E. C. Cheeseman, *Brief Glory: The Story of ATA* (Leicester, England: Harborough Publishing Company, 1946), 58.

17. Roger Guillemette, "Civilian Pilot Training Program (CPTP)," U.S. Centennial of Flight Commission, http://www.centennialofflight.gov/essay/GENERAL_AVIATION/civilian_pilot_training/ (accessed July 17, 2008).

18. Hawkins, *Hazel Jane Raines*, 3. Raines was also a member of the unofficial pilots group Short Snorters, whose membership card was a dollar bill with one's name on it (Mary M. Holtzclaw, "Girl Trains Men to Fly—Hazel Raines of Macon, Ga., Gets Her Men into U.S. Air Corps," *Atlanta Journal*, July 20, 1941).

19. "Local Girl Air Instructor Desires to be U.S. Bomber Pilot despite Male Snickers," *Fort Lauderdale (Fla.) Times*, August 11, 1941; U.S. Trade, Inc., "British Air Transport Auxiliary: Hazel Jane Raines," ATA Members, 2001, http://www.airtransportaux.org/members/raines.org (accessed July 16, 2008).

20. Hawkins, *Hazel Jane Raines*, 7.

21. Douglas, *U.S. Women in Aviation*, 115. In an effort first organized by Briton Pauline Gower, the ATA began employing eight English women pilots to ferry single-engine Tiger-Moth trainer planes around England in 1940. See Pamela Feltus, "Women in the Military in World War II," U.S. Centennial of Flight Commission, http://www.centennialofflight.gov/essay/Air_Power/Women/ AP321.htm (accessed July 16, 2008). Jacqueline Cochran remembered: "The 'going off to war' giddiness probably originated in Montreal, where the American women were checked out in powerful, complicated aircraft. There was a feeling of exhilaration among the forty girls. Fifteen failed to pass. That's how we ended up with twenty-five" (Jacqueline Cochran and Maryann Bucknum Brinkley, *Jackie Cochran: An Autobiography* [New York: Bantam Books, 1987], 189).

22. Hazel Raines, "Top Secret," "Sea Legs," "Columbus Versus Hazel," "My Trip O-Var" [*sic?*], transcription of handwritten narratives in Hawkins, *Hazel Jane Raines*, 12–17.

23. Feltus, "Women in the Military."

24. Cheeseman, *Brief Glory*, 77; Diana Barnato Walker, *Spreading My Wings: One of Britain's Top Women Pilots Tells Her Remarkable Story* (Sparkford, England: Patrick Stephens, 1994), 66. In the brief history of the ATA, from 1940 to 1945, there were in its two training units 166 women pilots compared to 1,152 male flyers.

25. Hazel to "Dearest Mother" [Mrs. Frank G. Raines], May 28, 1942; June 5, 1942; June 14, 1942; and Hazel to Lt. William L. Wood Jr., August 20, 1942, in Hawkins, *Hazel Jane Raines*, 20, 21, 24, 33.

26. Hazel to "Dearest Mother," November 5, 1942, in ibid., 47.

27. Hazel to "Dearest Mother," June 19, 1942, in ibid., 25; Hazel to "Dearest Mother," September 20, 1942, and September 26, 1942, in ibid., 37. The legendary Spitfire had wingspans of thirty-six feet and stood eleven feet, five inches tall, with a take-off weight of 6,770 pounds. See Alfred Price, *Spitfire: A Documentary History* (London: MacDonald and Janes, 1977). Raines described what is most likely a Spitfire as "a wonderful ship—a single seater fighter and one you perhaps read about every day in the papers as having taken part in a raid over Germany—an English fighter." Raines flew the liquid-cooled v-12 powered Spitfires at speeds of about 230 miles per hour. Hazel to "Dearest Mother," November 20, 1942, in Hawkins, *Hazel Jane Raines*, 48–49.

28. C. L. Sulzberger, *World War II* (New York: McGraw-Hill Book Company, 1970), 52. Still, the RAF claimed to have shot down 2,698 Luftwaffe planes in the epic Battle of Britain.

29. Hazel to "Dearest Mother," November 5, 1942, in Hawkins, *Hazel Jane Raines*, 48.

30. Kathleen Harriman, "Macon Girl Flouts Death to Ferry RAF Planes: Miss Hazel Raines One of Pilots Who Makes Giant Air Raids Possible," *Atlanta Journal*, June 18, 1942. Originally printed in London, this article, when reprinted, gave local emphasis by highlighting Hazel Raines in the Atlanta paper.

31. John Pimlott, *The Atlas of World War II* (London: Courage Books, 2006), 104; R. A. C. Parker, *The Second World War: A Short History*, rev. ed. (New York: Oxford University Press, 2001), 133, 153.

32. Diana Barnato Walker, *Spreading My Wings* (Sparkford, England: Patrick Stephens, 1994), 51, 157.

33. Hazel to "Dearest Mother," November 3 and November 5, 1942, in Hawkins, *Hazel Jane Raines*, 42–48.

34. Hazel to "Dearest Mother," February 2, 1943, in ibid., 65.

35. Reproduction of page in Hazel Raines's flight log book, ibid., 68. Raines noted that she crashed in Kingston, a town near London. For an account of the crash, see Zera Pendleton Nottingham, "Macon Girl Is in Crack-up While Flying in England," *Macon Telegraph*, June 20, 1943.

36. Hazel to "Dearest Mother," April 23, 1943, in Hawkins, *Hazel Jane Raines*, 78–79.

37. Jackie [Cochran] to "Grace, Hazel and Kay [two unidentified women ATA flyers with Hazel Raines]," May 20, 1943, in ibid., 81–82.

38. Feltus, "Women in the Military in World War II."

39. Hazel to Martha [her sister], October 27, 1942, in Hawkins, *Hazel Jane Raines*, 41.

40. Hazel to "Dearest Mother," December 23, 1942, in ibid., 57. Viscountess Nancy Witcher Astor (1879–1964) was born Nancy Langhorn in Danville, Va. She moved to England and married Viscount Waldorf Astor, becoming a prominent member and hostess of the social elite with a reputation as a witty and interesting expatriate American. She was the first woman to serve as a British member of Parliament. See Anthony Masters, *Nancy Astor: A Biography* (New York: McGraw-Hill Book Company, 1981).

41. Hazel to "Dearest Mother," December 23, 1942, in Hawkins, *Hazel Jane Raines*, 58. Built in 1851, the massive three-story Cliveden estate, rendered in the Italian style, became the home of the Astor family in 1893. In the 1930s the house became a fashionable gathering place for prominent political and artistic personalities known as the Cliveden Set. In 1942, when Raines visited Cliveden, Viscount Waldorf Astor turned the estate over to the British National Trust under the provision that his family could continue to live there. See C. Quigley, *The Anglo-American Establishment: From Rhodes to Cliveden* (London: CS&G Associates, 1981).

42. Hazel to "Dearest Mother," December 23, 1942, in Hawkins, *Hazel Jane Raines*, 59.

43. Hazel to "Dearest Mother & All," March 25, 1942, in ibid., 8.

44. Hazel to Martha [her sister], May 27, 1943, in ibid., 85–86.

45. Memorandum, Air Transport Auxiliary Headquarters nr. Maidenhead, Berks., Ophthalmic Specialist, American Dispensary London re S/O Miss H. Raines, July 10, 1943, in ibid., 89–90.

46. Jackie [Cochran] to "Grace, Hazel and Kay [two unidentified ATA women flyers with Hazel Raines]," May 20, 1943, in ibid., 82.

47. Leisa D. Meyer, *Creating GI Jane: Sexuality and Power in the Women's Army Corps During World War II* (New York: Columbia University Press, 1996), 94.

48. Jean Hascall Cole, *Women Pilots of World War II* (Salt Lake City: University of Utah Press, 1992), 23.

49. "Hazel Raines, English Ferry Pilot among Trainees of 44-w-4," *The Avenger* [base publication of Women's Airforce Service Pilots, Avenger Field, Sweetwater Texas], November 5, 1943, in Hawkins, *Hazel Jane Raines*, 102.

50. "Experiences of Woman Ferry Pilot Told Rotary," *Abilene (Tex.) Rotater*, February 18, 1944; Hazel to "Dearest Mother," November 4, 1943, and November 9, 1943; (Personal memories of Hazel Raines, Macon, Georgia); Hazel to "Dearest Mother, "December, 27, 1943, (all correspondence is datelined Avenger Field, Sweetwater, Tex.), in Hawkins, *Hazel Jane Raines*, 113, 103, 104, 109.

51. Hazel Raines to "Dearest Mother," February 29, 1944, and March 10, 1944, Hawkins, *Hazel Jane Raines*, 114, 115; Hazel Raines to "Dearest Mother," May 30, 1944, in ibid., 121.

52. Hazel to "Dearest Mother," September 28, 1944, Hawkins, *Hazel Jane Raines*, 124.

53. See Molly Merryman, *Clipped Wings: The Rise and Fall of the Women's Airforce Service Pilots (WASPs) of World War II* (New York: New York University Press, 1998). Not until 1977 did the U.S. government, under President Jimmy Carter, approve former WASP aviators for full military recognition and benefits. Senator Barry Goldwater (R-Ariz.), a former ferry pilot, sponsored the legislation.

54. Chafe, *Paradox of Change*, 166.

55. Cole, *Women Pilots*, 135. Chapter 10, "Deactivation and Beyond," relates many memoirs of the WASPs.

56. War Department, Bureau of Public Relations, Press Branch, address by General H. H. Arnold, Commanding General, Army Air Forces, Before WASP [Women's Airforce Service Pilots] Ceremony, Sweetwater, Tex., Thursday December 7, 1944, in Hawkins, *Hazel Jane Raines*, 133–35. General Henry Harley "Hap" Arnold (1886–1950) was a five-star general in the U.S. Army and later the U.S. Air Force, the only individual to hold both such distinctions at the same time. Arnold, an aviation pioneer who learned flying from the Wright Brothers, was commanding general of the U.S. Army Air Forces from 1941 to 1945. See Thomas M. Coffey, *Hap: The Story of the U.S. Air Force and the Man Who Built It* (New York: Viking Press, 1982).

57. David M. Kennedy, *Freedom from Fear: The American People in Depression and War, 1929–1945* (New York: Oxford University Press, 1999), 857.

58. Merryman, *Clipped Wings*, 2–3.

59. Cochran and Brinkley, *Jackie Cochran*, 207.

60. Hazel to "Dearest Mother," October 28, 1944, in Hawkins, *Hazel Jane Raines*, 127.

61. "Hazel Raines, 1916–1956," Georgia Museum of Aviation Flight and Technology Center, Warner Robins, Ga., www.museumofaviation.org.

62. Nancy Woloch, *Women and the American Experience*, 4th ed. (Boston: McGraw-Hill, 2006), 466–67.

63. Hazel to "Dearest Mother," July 1, August 15, and August 25, 1945, in Hawkins, *Hazel Jane Raines*, 142, 145–46, 148–49.

64. Hawkins, *Hazel Jane Raines*, 172.

65. Hazel J. Raines, 2nd LT USAFR, Yukon, Okla., to Colonel Geraldine P. May, Director, Women in the Air Force, Pentagon Building, Washington, D.C., May 17, 1950, in ibid., 177–78; Mary M. Holtzclaw, "Georgia's Flying Lady: Is First WASP Recalled by Air Force," *Atlanta Journal and Constitution Magazine*, December 17, 1950.

66. Hazel to "Dearest Mother," November 28, 1950, in Hawkins, *Hazel Jane Raines*, 179.

67. Hazel to "Dearest Mother," January 8, 1953, in ibid., 187.

68. Hazel to "Dearest Mother," September 16, 1954, in ibid., 197.

69. Hazel to "Dearest Mother," October 12, 1954, in ibid. See also chap. 5, "WAF Advisor," in ibid., 199, 198–209.

70. Hazel to "Dearest Mother," August, 27, 1956, Hawkins, *Hazel Jane Raines*, 213.

71. "Raines, Hazel J.," *Riverside Cemetery Online.*

72. Transcription of telegraph, Western Union: Commander Dover AFB Delaware, to Mrs. Bessie P. Raines, College Street, Macon, Ga., September 20, 1956, in Hawkins, *Hazel Jane Raines*, 214.

73. The author uses this poignant quotation on the back cover of his book on the subject (Tom Brokaw, *The Greatest Generation* [New York: Random House, 1998]).

Carson McCullers

(1917–1967)

"The Brutal Humiliation of
Human Dignity" in the South

CARLOS DEWS

❀ ❀ ❀

Carson McCullers once said of her native South, "I must go home periodically to renew my sense of horror."[1] Although celebrated as one of the most important southern writers of the twentieth century—all her major works were set in the South and suffused with the language and atmosphere of the region—McCullers felt great ambivalence toward the South, escaped from it to what she considered a more tolerant New York City, and, with the exception of brief trips, after the age of twenty-two spent little time below the Mason-Dixon Line.[2] One could read the Georgia writer's work as an extended homage to her native region; however, with the knowledge of her mixed feelings toward the South, it is possible to see her work in a different light. An examination of Carson McCullers's relationship with the South, specifically the Georgia of her childhood and adolescence, provides a new lens through which to view her work that takes the reader beyond the previous emphasis on loneliness, spiritual isolation, and the psychological experience of the adolescent girl and instead into the realm of politics and McCullers's engagement with the social, cultural, and political issues relevant to the American South in the first half of the twentieth century. Her five novels, *The Heart Is a Lonely Hunter*, *Reflections in a Golden Eye*, *The Ballad of the Safe Café*, *The Member of the Wedding*, and *Clock without Hands*, can be read as extended argument with the South over the issues that were of greatest concern to McCullers and any other southerner with any progressive leanings at the time: namely, racial and gender inequality, classism and economic injustice, the hypocrisy of religious fundamentalism, anti-intellectualism, xenophobia, and homophobia.

CARSON MCCULLERS

Carson McCullers Center for Writers and Musicians.

Lula Carson Smith McCullers was born in Columbus, Georgia, into a solidly middle-class family on February 19, 1917, the daughter of Lamar Smith and Marguerite Waters Smith. Racially segregated, politically and culturally conservative, with an economy based on exploitative mill labor, Columbus in 1917 exhibited all the hypocrisy, injustice, and economic and social fault lines that would propel McCullers away from her hometown and influence all her major work.[3]

The economic life of Columbus at the time of McCullers's birth in 1917 was controlled by a small group of families who had accumulated their wealth through the mills that operated on the waterpower of the Chattahoochee River that ran through the city. These families, operating as an economic oligarchy, resisted unionization of their mills and exploited their employees, who had few other work opportunities. With the exception of a small mercantile class, to which McCullers's family belonged, the vast majority of the citizens of Columbus, both black and white, were dependent on the low wages and non-union working conditions of the city's mills. Poor whites worked long hours for little pay, and black citizens, living under the Jim Crow–era segregationist policies, had fewer work opportunities, earned lower wages, and lived with few legal recourses for any injustices they encountered. Housing, education, medical care, and businesses were racially segregated, and black citizens were prevented from voting by the Jim Crow policies established after the post–Civil War Reconstruction era.

Virginia Spencer Carr, the author of the most comprehensive biography of the writer, wrote of McCullers's sensitivity toward the racism of her hometown: "Even as a child she knew intuitively that the blacks were treated as second-class citizens, and sometimes she probed her father with such questions as why 'colored people' had their own drinking fountains and why most fountains said 'White Only.' . . . She also wondered why colored people lived in little brown houses and tar paper shacks and seemed so poor, and why white people never worked for colored people. She could never get the answers she wanted."[4]

Without the social programs instituted during the Great Depression, mill workers during McCullers's childhood were at the mercy of the changeable markets for their products and were left destitute during slow periods. Mill workers in Columbus participated in a national strike in February 1919 calling for an eight-hour workday, but an attempt at organizing the workers in the city's industries in May 1919 was violently put down by anti-unionists, ending the drive for unionization.[5]

Although she focused on them less than she did the twin issues of racial and economic injustice, McCullers was also troubled by the restrictions placed on women and girls and the hatred of gay, lesbian, bisexual, and transgendered people. Opportunities for women were severely limited by traditional notions of proper behavior and the limits on ambition exercised by the fundamental-ist Christian denominations that were predominant in the South. In 1917, the year of McCullers's birth, the first woman, Stella Akin,[6] was admitted to the Georgia bar and in 1919, two years after her birth, the state of Georgia rejected the Nineteenth Amendment to the United States Constitution, which would guarantee women the right to vote. Georgia would finally ratify the Nineteenth Amendment in February 1970.[7] The hatred faced by gay men, lesbians, and bi-sexual and transgender individuals in the homophobic atmosphere at the time was also of great concern to McCullers. But during the years she lived in the South, 1917–39, the very idea of advocating for the rights of gay, lesbian, bi-sexual, or transgender individuals was untenable. Despite this, in drafting *The Heart Is a Lonely Hunter*, her first novel, at age nineteen, McCullers included a transgender character she intended to treat sympathetically. In addition, the internalized homophobia of one of her main characters was a major theme of her second novel.

McCullers's ambivalence toward the South can be traced to the influence of a small number of family members and friends and the firsthand experiences she had growing up in Georgia during the 1920s and 1930s. The source of McCull-ers's sensitivity to the suffering of others because of their differences, economic circumstances, and/or race is due primarily to the influence of her mother and grandmother, her childhood piano teacher, the man she called her "first adult friend," and the man who would become her husband.

McCullers's maternal grandmother, Lula Caroline Waters, was a strong in-dependent matriarch who raised her children by herself after her husband died from alcoholism, and she exerted considerable influence on the household in which McCullers was raised.[8] Although a member of the First Baptist Church of Columbus, McCullers's grandmother demonstrated her independence by drinking alcohol. McCullers included in her autobiography an anecdote about her grandmother, obviously told to her by her mother, that illustrates just how unconventional her grandmother could be:

> Once towards the last of her illnesses, some ladies from the Woman's Christian Temperance Union came to call. . . . Mommy said mischievously, "Is it time for my toddy yet Lamar? I think it would be delicious now." "Would any of you ladies like to join us?" Daddy asked. But already the WCTU were fleeing in horror. "To tell you the truth Lamar, those WCTU ladies are awfully narrowminded, although I guess it's wicked of me to say so." "Very wicked," my Daddy said, as he poured her toddy.[9]

Her grandmother's home, in which McCullers's family lived until her grand-mother died, was located in the center of downtown Columbus. This location gave McCullers the unique opportunity to experience the life of her hometown and see the diverse experiences of its citizens, from the wealthy families who lived in mansions nearby to the working poor who walked by her home on their way to work in the mills along the river. McCullers's family moved to a nearby suburban development in 1926, but it is the atmosphere of her grandmother's house, within sight of all that went on in her hometown, that readers find recreated in the settings of McCullers's novels and short stories.

McCullers's desire to escape the South and her sense that she was different from the other children with whom she was growing up was nurtured by her mother from a very early age. Marguerite Waters Smith encouraged her daughter to pursue any creative pursuits that attracted her attention, anticipating the revelation of her true talent and the ability for which she would eventually gain renown. Her mother treated the young Lula Carson like a sibling or companion rather than as a daughter, did not force her to attend school every day, and allowed her to smoke and drink at an early age. She supported Carson's wearing clothes that incurred the teasing and ridicule of their more staid neighbors and her daughter's classmates. Carr details McCullers's eccentric behavior and dress:

> Most of Carson's high school classmates thought her eccentric. She usually stood
> out in a crowd because she dared to be different. Her skirts and dresses were always
> a little longer than those worn by the popular girls whose clubs and cliques gave
> them prestige among their peers. She also wore dirty tennis shoes or brown Girl
> Scout oxfords when the other girls were wearing hose and shoes with dainty heels.
> When Carson was younger, some of the girls gathered in little clumps of femininity
> and threw rocks at her when she walked nearby, snickering loud asides and tossing
> within hearing distance such descriptive labels as "weird," "freakish-looking," and
> "queer."[10]

Thanks to her mother's influence, McCullers did little to accommodate the cultural expectations placed upon her as a white middle-class young woman. Her mother's influence was clearly effective in fostering both the desire to be different and the courage not to care what others thought of her unconventional behavior. As McCullers's friend Janet Flanner said, "Carson was enough to drive any small town right off its rocker and stood out among New Yorkers, even, as an eccentric of the first water."[11]

The year 1930, when she was thirteen years old, marked a turning point in Carson McCullers's life. Not only did she leave the South for the first time that summer—she visited an aunt and uncle who lived in Ohio—and change her name from the very southern-sounding double name of Lula Carson to the simple and somewhat gender-ambiguous Carson, but back home she also met Mary Tucker, the piano teacher and wife of an army officer based at nearby Fort Benning who would change her life.

McCullers first met Mary Tucker after hearing her perform at a recital in Columbus. McCullers had fantasized about being a concert pianist, with her mother's encouragement, and meeting and then studying with Mary Tucker taught McCullers that the study of piano could be the means by which she could escape the South. McCullers described Tucker in her autobiography: "Mrs. Tucker was to me the embodiment of Bach, Mozart, and all beautiful music, which at age thirteen had enveloped all my soul. . . . I yearned for one thing; to get away from Columbus and to make my mark in the world. At first I wanted to be a concert pianist, and Mrs. Tucker encouraged me in this."[12] Tucker also introduced McCullers to the person she would describe as her "first adult friend," Edwin Peacock, a fellow Georgian who encouraged Carson's reading of philosophy and political theory and with whom Carson shared a love for fine music. McCullers wrote that Peacock introduced her to Marx and Engels in addition to music, and she learned to understand the roots of African American poverty and severe hardship. She had long realized "that there was something fearful and wrong with the world," she later recalled, but before meeting Peacock, she had never "in any way thought of it intellectually."[13]

Edwin Peacock, cultured, well educated, homosexual, and politically progressive, not only influenced McCullers by encouraging her to read and to develop her musical skills but also supported her decision to leave behind her ambition for a career in music after a series of illnesses left her without the stamina for the long hours of practice needed for such a career. He instead encouraged her to pursue her secondary dream, writing fiction. Peacock's influence on McCullers is obvious in her first novel, *The Heart Is a Lonely Hunter*. The political consciousness exhibited in the work is clearly indebted to him, and McCullers honored Peacock's importance in her political, emotional, and cultural development by basing the central character of the novel, John Singer, in part, on Peacock.

McCullers graduated from Columbus High School in 1933, and in 1934, at age seventeen, sailed from Savannah to New York City, ostensibly to study piano at the Juilliard School of Music but actually to pursue her newfound ambition to write. Working various jobs to support herself, she studied creative writing at Columbia University and at Washington Square College of New York University. The realization of her dream to escape the South was tempered during her studies in New York by loneliness, depression, and frequent respiratory illnesses that forced her to return to Columbus for nursing by her mother. Nevertheless, through her classes with Whit Burnett and Dorothy Chatfield Bates, McCullers was encouraged by her New York experience and knew that her future was in the city.

Home from New York in the summer of 1935, Edwin Peacock introduced McCullers to her future husband and the person most responsible for enabling her departure from the South and her eventual success as a writer. McCullers wrote in her autobiography of meeting Reeves McCullers, the importance Edwin Peacock played in their meeting, and how she and her future husband bonded over their mutual disdain for the South. In June 1935 McCullers met Reeves at Peacock's apartment. At that first meeting, McCullers realized immediately that he was not only charming but also "a liberal," which was particularly striking to her, living in a "backward Southern community," as she described Columbus.[14]

In addition to their shared political philosophy, Carson and Reeves both wanted to write fiction and to find a place outside the South that would support them creatively and politically. The couple married on September 30, 1937, and divorced in 1941, but their shared disdain for the South never abated. During World War II, as Carson and Reeves considered remarrying, the prospect of having to return to the South to live frightened them. Looking ahead to his discharge from the army, Reeves was afraid that he might have to ask Carson to return to the South if he were to be assigned to a southern base: "I would like for us to be together but it is only reluctantly that I drag you down South again. Perhaps it won't be for long."[15]

Unfortunately, at the time of their marriage in 1937, the economic conditions of the Great Depression limited the young couple's choices. Reeves could only find work as a debt collector in Charlotte and Fayetteville, North Carolina, where the couple moved after their marriage. The atmosphere of the boarding house in which they lived provided McCullers with motivation to write her way out of their situation and place: "Our aim in life during those days was to go to New York, and often we would just look at the parked cars with New York license plates and dream about the time when we, too, could go to the magic city."[16] Around the time of their move to North Carolina in April 1938, McCullers submitted an outline and six chapters of her first novel, *The Heart Is a Lonely Hunter*, to Houghton Mifflin and was offered a contract for the book. She finished the manuscript for the novel in less than a year. The couple moved to New York in the summer of 1940 when the book was published. With the publication of *The Heart Is a Lonely Hunter*, McCullers's dreams of fame as a writer and escape from the South were finally realized and, with the exception of brief visits, she would never live there again.

In *The Heart Is a Lonely Hunter* McCullers confronted the South on all the issues that motivated her escape. Dr. Mady Copeland, a black physician, represents the struggle against racism. McCullers described Dr. Copeland as representing "the bitter spectacle of the educated Negro in the South."[17] Jake Blount is the frustrated labor organizer who is driven to near madness by the futility of organizing mill workers. In an early outline of *The Heart Is a Lonely Hunter*, the nineteen-year-old writer included a character who would not appear in the novel when published in 1940. McCullers described Lily Mae Jenkins as "an abandoned, waifish Negro homosexual" and included a brief bit of dialogue with which another character describes him: "Lily Mae is right pitiful now. I don't know if you ever noticed any boys like this but he cares for mens instead of girls. When he were younger he used to be real cute. He were all the times dressing up in girls' clothes and laughing. Everybody thought he were real cute then. But now he getting old and he seem different. He all the time hungry and he real pitiful."[18] With Lily Mae Jenkins, McCullers intended to address the plight of homosexuals and transgender individuals in the South at the time. It is impossible to know why she removed the character from the final manuscript of the novel, but had he remained in the novel Lily Mae Jenkins would have been one of the first sympathetically represented openly homosexual characters in all of southern literature.

Although she ultimately did not include Lily Mae Jenkins as a character in *The Heart Is a Lonely Hunter*, McCullers did include two characters through whom she engaged what were for her the intertwined issues of sexual/gender freedom, creativity, and a desire for escape from the South. With Biff Brannon, the owner of the significantly named New York Café, McCullers subtly addressed gender ambiguity and confused sexuality. McCullers described Brannon: "Biff comes to his own curious conclusion that marital relations are not the primary functions of the sexual impulse. He believes that human beings are fundamentally ambi-sexual."[19] McCullers described Mick Kelly, the most autobiographical of the characters in the novel, as having "great creative energy and courage. She's defeated by society on all the main issues before she can even begin, but still there is something in her and in those like her that cannot and will not be destroyed."[20] At the end of the novel it is unclear if Mick Kelly will be able to escape her circumstances in her native Georgia and be able to find an outlet for her great creative energy, or if Biff Brannon will find a community supportive of his ambisexual nature. This is not surprising, since at the time she was writing the novel about Mick and Biff, McCullers herself was still unsure if her own desire to escape the South would be met.

Shortly after McCullers moved to New York City in 1940, Klaus Mann, the son of the German novelist Thomas Mann, asked her to write an article about the connections between writers of the American South and the Russian realists. While considering the origins of the characteristics of the southern writing of her contemporaries, then being described as "Southern gothic,"[21] McCullers provided an explanation for how she could remain simultaneously indebted to the South for her artistic inspiration and have considerable antipathy toward the region. In her essay "The Russian Realists and Southern Literature," McCullers described what she saw as the fundamental connection between the world depicted by Gogol, Dostoevsky, and Chekhov, among others, and the way of life that she was familiar with from having grown up in Columbus, Georgia, in the first half of the twentieth century: "The circumstances under which Southern literature has been produced are strikingly like those under which the Russians functioned. In both Old Russia and the South up to the present time a dominant characteristic was the cheapness of human life."[22] In rejecting the label of "gothic" for the realistic literature being produced by southerners in the first half of the twentieth century, McCullers found common ground with the juxtaposition of the tragic and comic in the work of the Russian realists and her contemporary fellow southern writers, championing their reporting of the moral confusion of their native milieu and absolving them of any "spiritual responsibility," as she describes it, for what they have reported. Carson came to understand the South as a colony that was used in and by the rest of the nation, as she was struck by similarities she perceived the South and old Russia, each with a "distinct peasant class."[23] She continued:

> In both the South and old Russia the cheapness of life is realized at every turn. The thing itself, the material detail, has an exaggerated value. Life is plentiful; children are born and they die, or if they do not die they live and struggle. And in the fight to maintain existence the whole life and suffering of a human being can be bound up in ten acres of washed out land, in a mule, in a bale of cotton. . . . Life, death, the experiences of the spirit, these come and go and we do not know for what reason, but the *thing* is there, it remains to plague or comfort, and its value is immutable.[24]

With this essay McCullers provided her readers with both a justification for her ambivalence toward her native state and region, the American South, but also a potential explanation for why the South, despite her personal and political antipathy toward it, remained influential in informing both the settings and thematic content for her creative work. In the same way that McCullers credits the cheapness of life in her native South as the explanation for the characteristics of southern literature that was being called "Southern gothic" at the time, particularly the simultaneous use of the tragic and comic, the sacred and profane, and the high minded and low, she provided her readers with a further understanding of how she can both set all of her major work in the very location of her experience of the cheapness of human life and simultaneously provide a critique of that very place. She honors the South by turning to it for her creative inspiration but at the same time uses her depiction of it, realistically, as a harsh critique. Should her critique be taken to heart, the very South on which she depends for her inspiration would cease to exist, just as the Russian revolution brought to an end the world depicted by the Russian realists.

McCullers wrote this essay at a time when she thought that, at last, she had escaped the South once and for all. With the success of *The Heart Is a Lonely Hunter* and her subsequent introduction into the literary world of New York, she had every reason to believe that, should she choose to do so, she could turn her back on the South and the aspects of the region that she hated so. Her essay was perhaps a parting shot from an escaped daughter. McCullers had found success in the work she set in the South and clearly felt that the ideas, themes, settings, and characters that she wanted to engage in her work were best explored in the place with which she was most familiar and to which the themes she wanted to involve were especially indebted; however, she continued to find the South an intolerable and intolerant place to live.

After completing the manuscript for *The Heart Is a Lonely Hunter* but still living in Fayetteville, North Carolina, McCullers completed a second novel, based on the story she had heard of the killing of a peeping tom at Fort Bragg in nearby Beufort, North Carolina. *Reflections in a Golden Eye* was first serialized in the October and November 1940 issues of *Harper's Bazaar*. McCullers described the setting and characters in the first paragraph of the novel: "There is a fort in the South where a few years ago a murder was committed. The participants of this tragedy were: two officers, a soldier, two women, a Filipino, and a horse."[25] While the novel is ostensibly about obsessive love, infidelity, and the corrosive effects of denying one's own nature, the novel can also be read more broadly as a critique of the South's hypocrisy regarding sexuality and a statement on the results of the stifling of individuality and anti-intellectualism in the South.

The military base where the novel is set is a microcosm of the region. The regimentation of the military stands in for the religious fundamentalism and moral rigidity of southern culture and the enforced conformity of southern traditional notions of masculinity and sexuality. McCullers addresses the twin issues of the South's response to what it sees as sexual deviance and the catastrophic results of the South's hypocrisy.

McCullers addressed another negative aspect of the South in this novel. She presented the stunted nature of women in the South, with the dual curse of lowered expectations and rigidity of roles—where the options of wife and mother or provider of flattery or sexual gratification for men were the two broadest categories for women. With Captain Penderton, McCullers represented the oppressive nature of a society that did not allow the truthful expression of sexual desires.

In a climactic scene in the novel, Captain Penderton, the self-loathing homosexual army officer, plays cards with his wife, Leonora, and his wife's lover, Major Langdon. While discussing how serving in the military would "make a man" of Langdon's effete, and assumed homosexual, Filipino houseboy, Anacleto, Captain Penderton has an epiphany and, for the first time, states his understanding of the hypocrisy around him: "'You mean,' Captain Penderton said, 'that any fulfillment obtained at the expense of normalcy is wrong, and should not be allowed to bring happiness. In short, it is better, because it is morally honorable, for the square peg to keep scraping about the round hole rather than to discover and use the unorthodox square that would fit it?' 'Why, you put it exactly right,' the Major said. 'Don't you agree with me?' 'No,' said the Captain, after a short pause."[26] This realization on the part of Captain Penderton marks a turning point for the character. He can no longer live his life as he had before, denying his own desire and continuing to participate in the hypocritical system. Penderton's thoughts here reflect those of McCullers. She could have remained in the South and continued to feel like the square peg attempting to fit into a round hole, or she could find a place that provided the freedom for her to live her life as she wanted.

The unorthodox elements of *Reflections in a Golden Eye* did not go unnoticed in McCullers's hometown. Recovering from an illness in the early months of 1941, McCullers returned to Columbus from New York to find herself in the center of a firestorm over her latest work. With Reeves serving in the army, McCullers returned home to Georgia at the time of the publication of *Reflections in a Golden Eye* to face the response of her hometown and of Ft. Benning, the nearby army base. She wrote in her autobiography: "The Ku Klux Klan even called me and said, 'We are the Klan and we don't like nigger lovers or fairies. Tonight will be your night.' I naturally called my Daddy and he quit work and came with a policeman to stand vigil over me."[27]

This hateful response to her work would only prove to McCullers that her negative thoughts about the South were well founded and that her work, by refusing to ignore the South's backwardness, would only push her further away but also confirm that her work was relevant. Like Captain Penderton, McCullers had realized that she could no longer cooperate with a system that was as morally corrupt as the South and that she could not sacrifice satisfaction for the sake of normalcy in such a corrupt system. McCullers, and her character Captain Penderton, had realized what McCullers's friend and fellow southerner Ralph McGill would describe: "There is a special guilt in [southerners], a seeking for something had—and lost. It is a consciousness of guilt not fully knowable, or communicable. Southerners are the more lonely and spiritually estranged, I think, because we have lived so long in an artificial social system that we insisted was natural and right and just—when all along we knew it wasn't."[28]

When McCullers's father died in 1944, McCullers's mother sold the family home and business in Columbus and moved north to live with her daughter in New York. She bought a large home in Nyack, New York, the place McCullers would call home for the rest of her life. With her mother now with her to provide her with the care her frequent illnesses required, McCullers had almost no ties to the South. Nonetheless, her imagination remained anchored in her native state.

After the publication of her first two novels, McCullers began work on a novel that, despite being her most metaphorical and least traditionally realistic, would nonetheless continue to engage with issues relevant to her relationship with the South. *The Ballad of the Sad Café*, set in a small southern mill town, is ostensibly the lyrical story of jealousy and obsession in a triangular love relationship involving an Amazon-like Miss Amelia; a hunchbacked midget, Cousin Lymon; and an ex-convict, Marvin Macy. Of McCullers's five novels, *The Ballad of the Sad Café* is the only work that does not address racism; in this novel she limited the scope of her concern to the lives of the poor workers and the fate of those who are different and fail to find an escape from the limited opportunities of small-town life in the South. The brief novel appeared in the August 1943 issue of *Harper's Bazaar*. The work was later published by Houghton Mifflin in a 1951 omnibus edition of the author's work, *The Ballad of the Sad Café: The Novels and Stories of Carson McCullers*.

With the opening lines of *The Ballad of the Sad Café* McCullers paints the scene of the South as she experienced it as a child—a place with little beyond dead-end work, miserable living conditions, and the church:

> The town itself is dreary; not much is there except the cotton mill, the two-room houses where the workers live, a few peach trees, a church with two colored windows, and a miserable main street only a hundred yards long. On Saturdays the tenants from the near-by farms come in for a day of talk and trade. Otherwise the town is lonesome, sad, and like a place that is far off and estranged from all other places in the world. The nearby train stop is Society City, and the Greyhound and White Bus Lines use the Forks Falls Road which is three miles away. The winters here are short and raw, the summer white with glare and fiery hot. . . . These August afternoons—when your shift is finished there is absolutely nothing to do; you might as well walk down to the Forks Falls Road and listen to the chain gang.[29]

In a novel that is most often described as her most gothic, McCullers used some of the same language she had used three years earlier in her article on the Russian realists' influence on southern writers and the misuse of the term "gothic" to describe her fellow southern writers' simultaneous use of the comic and tragic to address what she called "the cheapness of human life." In her most direct statement regarding the lives of the exploited mill workers in the town in which she set *The Ballad of the Sad Café*, McCullers echoed her earlier article in explaining the impact the establishment of the café in the town had on its patrons and by doing so what it was that she saw missing from southern society. McCullers explained that it was not only the "warmth, the decorations, and the brightness" that made the café so vital to the people in the mill town. There was a deeper reason that had to do with a rare sense of pride and human dignity enjoyed by the café's patrons:

> Often after you have sweated and tried and things are not better for you, there comes a feeling deep down in the soul that you are not worth much. . . . The people in the town were likewise proud when sitting at the tables in the café. They washed before coming to Miss Amelia's, and scraped their feet very politely on the threshold as they entered the café. There, for a few hours at least, the deep bitter knowing that you are not worth much in this world could be laid low.[30]

The café in the unnamed town of *The Ballad of the Sad Cafe* provided what the institutions of the South claimed but failed to provide—a sense of belonging, and unconditional acceptance.

The early 1950s marked the beginning of a significant deterioration of Mc-Cullers's health. At age thirty-three her most productive years were behind her, and with the exception of the novel that she began during the 1950s, she would produce little work during the following decade.

In a 1958 article in *Esquire*, McCullers wrote her most direct statement of her relationship with the South and her indebtedness to the region:

> People ask me why I don't go back to the South more often. But the South is a very emotional experience for me, fraught with all the memories of childhood. When I go back South I always get into arguments, so that a visit to Columbus in Georgia is a stirring up of love and antagonism. The locale of my books might always be Southern, and the South always my homeland. I love the voices of Negroes—like brown rivers. . . . This is particularly true of Southern writers because it is not only their speech and the foliage, but their entire culture—which makes it a homeland within a homeland. No matter what the politics, the degree or non-degree of liberalism in a Southern writer, he is still bound to this peculiar regionalism of language and voices and foliage and memory.[31]

After decamping to New York, McCullers discovered that her body had escaped, yet her imagination and memory remained rooted in the South. Setting her work in the South goes far beyond simply a matter of writing what McCullers knew. The South was more than a setting for all her work; it was the site for the drama and trauma that had shaped her own life and thus was the necessary place for her to return in creating a fictional world in which to reenact those dramas. McCullers's thematic concerns were inextricably linked with the South, Georgia, and Columbus, and it was necessary for her to engage the themes that recur in her work in the place from which they sprang. The South was where McCullers's imagination was born, nurtured, and continued to thrive.

Despite her failing health, the end of her marriage to Reeves, his suicide in 1952, and the emotional devastation of her mother's death in 1955, McCullers continued to work during the 1950s on what would be her final novel. She spent more than ten years working on *Clock without Hands*, beginning in 1950 at the time of the success of the stage adaptation of her novel *The Member of the Wedding*. In *Clock without Hands*, published in September 1961, McCullers focused primarily on issues of racial and economic injustice, with a secondary concern for sexuality and gender. During the ten-year period during which she wrote *Clock without Hands*, most of the significant milestones of the modern civil rights movement happened, including the *Brown v. Board of Education* decision of the Supreme Court (May 1954), the murder of Emmett Till (August 1955), Rosa Parks's defiance of bus segregation (December 1955), the founding of the Southern Christian Leadership Conference (1957), and the desegregation of the Little Rock Public Schools (September 1957).

Perhaps McCullers's most underappreciated work, *Clock without Hands* is set during 1954 at the time of the *Brown v. Board* decision and concerns the intersecting lives of three main characters in the fictional town of Milan, Georgia. The title of the novel suggests the timeless nature of southern tradition and the resistance of the South to the influence of progressive development. Although framed around the story of a pharmacist, J. T. Malone, who is dying of cancer, the novel primarily concerns the lives of Judge Fox Clane, a senile racist judge fighting against the winds of progress that threaten the traditional South that he champions; Jester Clane, the grandson Fox has raised since the death of the boy's parents, who struggles with his confusion over his sexuality and his birthright as a privileged citizen in the racist and backward community; and Sherman Pew, an orphaned gay mulatto who, as is revealed late in the novel, is the illegitimate son of the judge's dead son and thus Jester's half-brother.

Most of McCullers's early works anticipated political and social concerns, but *Clock without Hands*, her most overtly political work, engaged contemporary issues head on. Early in the novel Judge Clane characterizes the time of change in which he finds himself: "Have you ever stopped to consider that the South is in the vortex of a revolution almost as disastrous as the War Between the States?"[32] In declaring his independence from his birthright to the traditional racist privilege into which he was born and raised, Jester Clane declares to his grandfather, "For one thing, I question the justice of white supremacy."[33] Like McCullers, who refused to accept things in the South as they were, the narrator of the novel declares of Jester Clane: "Some people were content to live their mortal lives and die and be buried in Milan. Jester Clane was not one of them."[34] Sherman Pew, named for the Union general William T. Sherman and the church pew on which he was discovered, represents in the novel the black southerners of the civil rights movement era—politically aware and engaged and demanding his rights as a citizen: "I vibrate with every injustice that is done to my race."[35] Sherman Pew, lacking the means to leave the South, no less wishes to escape the oppression the region represented: "Still a nigger would rather be a lamppost in Harlem than the Governor of Georgia."[36]

In a passage reminiscent of W. J. Cash's 1929 book *The Mind of the South*, McCullers also provides in *Clock without Hands*, in the voice of Judge Clane, an economic explanation for the hatred of the poor white southerner for the descendants of former slaves:

the Judge went on, "you and I have our property and our positions and our self-respect. But what does Sammy Lank have except those slews of children of his? Sammy Lank and poor whites like that have nothing but the color of their skin. Having no property, no means, nobody to look down on—that is the clue to the whole thing. It is a sad commentary on human nature but every man has to have somebody to look down on. So the Sammy Lanks of this world only have the Nigra to look down on. You see . . . it is a matter of pride. You and I have our pride, the pride of our blood, the pride of our descendants. But what does Sammy Lank have except those slews of white-headed triplets and twins and a wife worn out with child-bearing sitting on the porch dipping snuff?"[37]

Near the end of the novel, McCullers provides the most perceptive and subtle meditation on race and the South in her body of work and demonstrates once again her passionate engagement with the contemporary issues most relevant to the South:

Drawn to broodings on atrocities, he felt that every evil was reserved for him personally. So he lived in a stasis of dread and suspense. This attitude was supported by facts. No Negro in Peach County had ever voted. A schoolteacher had registered and been turned down at the polls. Two college graduates had been turned down likewise. The Fifteenth Amendment of the American Constitution had guaranteed the right to vote to the Negro race, yet no Negro Sherman had known or heard tell of had ever voted. Yes, the American Constitution itself was a fraud. . . . Since his imagination enveloped all disaster, he felt that any evil he read or heard about could just as well have happened to himself. This state of anxiety made Sherman take the old Judge more seriously than he would have under calmer conditions. Slavery! Was the old Judge planning to make slaves of his race? It did not make sense. But what the fuckin hell made sense in the relation between the races? The Fifteenth Amendment had been put at nought, the American constitution was a fraud as far as Sherman was concerned. And justice! Sherman knew of every lynching, every violence that had happened in his time and before his time, and he felt every abuse in his own body, and therefore lived in his stasis of tension and fear.[38]

The sensitivity toward Sherman displayed in this passage is similar to the representations of black characters that led Richard Wright to write, in reviewing *The Heart Is a Lonely Hunter*: "To me the most impressive aspect of *The Heart Is a Lonely Hunter* is the astonishing humanity that enables a white writer, for the first time in Southern fiction, to handle Negro characters with as much ease and justice as those of her own race."[39]

At the time of her death from a cerebral stroke, on September 19, 1967, there was reason for Carson McCullers to be hopeful about the South, at least as far as race relations were concerned. In 1964 and 1965 President Lyndon Baines Johnson had signed the historic Civil and Voting Rights Acts that would were intended to undo the entrenched Jim Crow policies. McCullers would not live to see if these legal changes brought about actual changes in the lives of people in the South and transformed the South into a place McCullers might have been drawn back toward. But there were very negative developments that soon followed that would have tempered any enthusiasm McCullers might have had about the civil rights legislation. Less than a year after her death, Martin Luther King and Robert Kennedy were assassinated, and Richard Nixon won the presidency in 1968 with his southern strategy.

In her biography of McCullers, Virginia Spencer Carr described McCullers's concerns over the 1967 riots in Detroit and Newark: "She told [John] Huston that Congress had recently defeated a rat control measure, and that the one solution—to rebuild the slums, which should have been done at least two decades earlier—still had not been put into effect. She found it intolerable that white men continued to have employment privileges over blacks even though their skills were inferior or equal."[40]

One can speculate that the South, her home state of Georgia, and her hometown of Columbus would still feel as equally oppressive and frightening to Mc-

Cullers today as it did to her when she lived there. Although there have been superficial changes in the culture and politics of the South, very little has changed in McCullers's hometown. She might feel the same today as she did when she left Columbus for New York for the first time in 1936. Like many other states in the South, Georgia remains significantly racially segregated and homophobic—the citizens of Georgia approved a constitutional amendment in 2008 prohibiting gay marriage—strongly influenced by fundamentalist Christianity. Columbus's economy is still largely in the hands of the same families that have controlled it since the nineteenth century, and, according to the 2000 census data, had a child poverty rate of close to 22 percent.[41] It is likely that McCullers would see too many similarities between the Georgia she escaped in 1937 and the Georgia of today and still prefer her adopted New York to her native state.

NOTES

1. Carson McCullers, quoted in a letter from her friend Eleanor Clark to Virginia Spencer Carr (Virginia Spencer Carr, *The Lonely Hunter* [Athens: University of Georgia Press, 2003], 9).

2. Although Lula Carson Smith only took the name of McCullers when she married Reeves McCullers in 1937, because she is known as a writer as Carson McCullers, I use the name McCullers for her throughout this chapter.

3. Important to note here is that the culture of Columbus, and the aspects of the town that caused McCullers to be so critical of it, was not unique. In fact, many small southern cities, like Columbus, exhibited the same levels of intolerance and economic degradation. Although no book yet published examines these issues in detail on Columbus, Ga., there are two important books that examine race, employment, and culture in two Georgia cities very similar to McCullers's Columbus: Michelle Brattain's *The Politics of Whiteness: Race, Workers, and the Culture in the Modern South* (Athens: University of Georgia Press, 2004) examines Rome, Ga.; and Douglas Flamming's *Creating the Modern South: Millhands and Managers in Dalton, Georgia, 1884–1984* (Chapel Hill: University of North Carolina Press, 1992). These two volumes provide detailed analyses of the political, social, and cultural atmosphere from which McCullers wished to escape.

4. Carr, *Lonely Hunter*, 21.

5. John Lupold, "Columbus," *New Georgia Encyclopedia*, April 30, 2008, http://www.georgia encyclopedia.org/nge/Article.jsp?id=h-2208 (accessed October 12, 2013).

6. "Stella Akin," *GeorgioInfo*, http://georgiainfo.galileo.usg.edu/stellaakin.htm (accessed October 12, 2013).

7. "1919," *GeorgiaInfo*, http://georgiainfo.galileo.usg.edu/1919.htm (accessed October 12, 2013).

8. Carr, *Lonely Hunter*, 10, 12, 17–18, 20, 40.

9. Carson McCullers, *Illumination and Night Glare: The Unfinished Autobiography of Carson McCullers* (Madison: University of Wisconsin Press, 1999), 7.

10. Carr, *Lonely Hunter*, 299–300.

11. Ibid., 9.

12. McCullers, *Illumination and Night Glare*, 13–14.

13. Ibid., 13.

14. Ibid., 16.

15. Ibid., 149.

16. Ibid., 19.

17. Carson McCullers, "Author's Outline of 'The Mute,'" in Carson McCullers, *The Mortgaged Heart* (London: Penguin, 1975), 133.

18. Ibid., 140–41.

19. Ibid., 135.

20. Ibid., 131.

21. Southern gothic is a "style of writing practiced by many writers of the American South whose stories set in that region are characterized by grotesque, macabre, or fantastic incidents" ("Southern Gothic," *Encyclopedia Britannica Online*, December 5, 2009, http://www.britannica.com/EBchecked/topic/556752/Southern-Gothic [accessed October 12, 2013]).

22. Carson McCullers, "The Russian Realists and Southern Literature," in McCullers, *Mortgaged Heart*, 258.

23. Ibid., 260.

24. Ibid.

25. Carson McCullers, *Complete Novels* (New York: Library of America, 2001), 309.

26. Ibid., 384.

27. McCullers, *Illumination and Night Glare*, 30–31.

28. Ralph McGill, *The South and the Southerner* (Boston: Little, 1963), 217.

29. McCullers, *Complete Novels*, 397.

30. Ibid., 442–43.

31. Carson McCullers, "The Flowering Dream: Notes on Writing," in McCullers, *Mortgaged Heart*, 284–85.

32. McCullers, *Complete Novels*, 619.

33. Ibid., 633.

34. Ibid., 692.

35. Ibid., 677.

36. Ibid., 740.

37. Ibid., 786.

38. Ibid., 741–42.

39. Richard Wright, "Inner Landscape," *New Republic* 103 (August 1940): 195.

40. Carr, *Lonely Hunter*, 534.

41. See, Columbus, GA-AL, diversitydata.org, http://diversitydata.sph.harvard.edu/Data/Profiles/Show.aspx?loc=352 (accessed December 4, 2013).

Mabel Murphy Smythe

(1918–2006)

Black Women and Internationalism

MARY ROLINSON

❀ ❀ ❀

In June 1981, during her final week as deputy assistant secretary of state for Africa, Mabel Murphy Smythe sat down with Ruth Stutts Njiiri of the Phelps-Stokes Fund for an interview. Expressing her hopes for the future of U.S. diplomacy under the recently inaugurated administration of Ronald Reagan, she declared,

> We have a sterling asset in the interest that black Americans have shown in African affairs, as well as other affairs—and I wouldn't for a moment restrict black American input to areas that are related to Africa or even other parts of the [D]iaspora. It seems to me that we have such a special relationship available to us there that Africans respond to, and as a result it is important for them to see a George Dalley or an Ann Holloway or a Mabel Smythe explaining American foreign policy.[1]

In qualifying this statement Mabel Smythe revealed a tension she carried within herself throughout her life: pride and identity in both her African heritage and her American citizenship. In her forty-five-year career in such diverse roles as professor, editor, cultural liaison, and U.S. ambassador, she seized opportunities to open doors to women and African Americans while simultaneously furthering peaceful relations, intercultural understanding, and U.S. influence throughout the world.

How she became an advocate for people of African ancestry is not as mysterious as her conviction that the U.S. government was essentially a force for good internationally. Her youth was spent in Jim Crow Atlanta, Georgia, during the 1920s and the Depression era 1930s, but her major overseas diplomatic career began in 1965 as wife of the U.S. Ambassador to Syria, where she regularly faced jeers of "imperialist!"[2] She knew from earlier international experiences that the

MABEL MURPHY SMYTHE

Favorite publicity photo of the diplomat and scholar,

c. 1965. Photo in author's personal collection.

United States wielded great power, but not always in ways other nations appreciated or accepted. She wanted to change that because she felt the United States had high ideals and values, but rarely lived up to them in an international context.

Despite Mabel and Hugh Smythes' efforts to represent the best of U.S. intentions toward the Syrian people, they found themselves fleeing hostilities in Damascus in early June 1967. In late May the ever-unflappable Mabel had sent a letter of warning to her parents, Josephine and Harry Murphy, in Atlanta, telling them not to worry and that "we may shortly be evacuated until we see what the Middle East will do."[3] By June 5 all Americans and embassy staff had evacuated to Rome, and Hugh Smythe took down the U.S. embassy's flag and left Syria just hours before the Six-Day War began.[4] The hostilities between Israel and the surrounding Arab states led Syria to sever diplomatic ties with the United States, ushering in a tumultuous new phase in Middle East relations. In the context of the last forty-five years of the United States' Mideast diplomacy, there are few more critical turning points than this one. Mabel and Hugh Smythe represented the United States in Syria precisely when President Lyndon Johnson inserted the United States decisively into the conflict by sponsoring the land-for-security United Nations resolution number 242 that challenged the Arab states to recognize Israel's right to exist.[5]

The Smythes each held doctoral degrees, had prior experience working with the State Department and at the United Nations, and were well aware of the profound implications of their duties as U.S. representatives in this delicate situation. The Johnson administration had selected the Smythes for this sensitive, hardship post based on their proven credentials rather than on their wealth or political influence. In fact, while Americans read news reports of the evacuation and learned of Ambassador and Mrs. Smythe, few realized until they saw photographs that the United States' diplomats in this crisis were African Americans.[6]

Mabel Murphy Smythe's presence at the center of geopolitics in the 1960s and beyond opens another window on African American women's diverse forms of activism. What much of the recent historical literature emphasizes is that the 1960s saw many politically engaged African Americans, especially local grassroots women, pouring their energies into achieving legal recognition of their civil rights. In the years after passage of the Civil Rights Act (1964) and the Voting Rights Act (1965), some African Americans reacted with disappointment and disgust at the slow pace of social and economic change. But there is also a growing literature on the activism and protest tradition of American blacks in the international realm of anticolonialism and human rights.[7] By taking a different approach from many of these internationalist African Americans who criticized, protested, and petitioned against U.S. international policies and practices, Mabel Smythe became an agent of the United States in its efforts to influence the rest of the world during the Cold War by working within the system and pressuring U.S. policymakers to live up to the American ideals of equality in the global context.

While most American blacks saw their destinies unfolding in the local or national arenas of courtrooms, schools, and even sometimes the streets, Mabel Murphy Smythe found her way to the international stage and the most serious diplomatic challenges facing postwar America. The personal odyssey of her life took her to Japan during the U.S. occupation after World War II; to the offices of the United Nations and U.S. State Department; to international work projects in dozens of newly independent African countries as a facilitator for U.S. college students; and eventually to an appointment as U.S. Ambassador to Cameroon and Equatorial Guinea under President Jimmy Carter.[8] The influence of her activist mother and the determination of her father to give Mabel the best education available led her on an extraordinary path out of segregated Atlanta. Mabel's realization that she had to leave the South and even the United States itself to function as a full American citizen guided her choices through the modern civil rights movement, second-wave feminism, and the politics of the Cold War and international diplomacy. Her professional trajectory put her in the forefront of global humanitarian activism. She became a pioneer among African American women in promoting human rights and addressing economic disparity through internationalism in education, politics, economic development, and cultural exchange.

As Mabel Murphy Smythe's internationalist perspective on humanitarian problems emerge from her interviews, one can barely fathom the sweeping social changes that occurred during her lifetime. In February 2006, when she died at age eighty-eight at her sister's home in Tuscaloosa, Alabama, from complications of Alzheimer's disease, an African American woman, Condoleezza Rice, was serving as the nation's first female African American Secretary of State. Both of these women had received PhD degrees, and both had strikingly similar formative experiences separated by nearly two generations. Rice had grown up in a middle-class African American family in strictly segregated and notoriously violent Birmingham in the 1960s; Mabel Murphy had grown up four decades earlier in a rigidly segregated Atlanta during the 1920s, when the Ku Klux Klan's headquarters were located on Peachtree Street and Mayor Walter Sims was a known Klan sympathizer. Atlanta had a history of racial violence it badly wanted to overcome, but the city's African American community remained scarred from the infamous 1906 Atlanta Race Riot that had lasted three days and left dozens of black citizens murdered.[9]

A decade before the riot, local, national, and even international black organizing persisted in Atlanta, springing mainly from the city's African American
centers of higher education. Atlanta University had inaugurated a series of conferences to address the high mortality rate of urbanized African Americans,
and Lugenia Burns Hope, the wife of Morehouse College president John Hope,
had followed up by organizing the Neighborhood Union to improve education,
housing, and healthcare for the city's black population. In a more international
realm, Gammon Theological Seminary had hosted a well-attended pan-African
conference as early as 1896. Even earlier, in 1895, the year of the Cotton States
and International Exposition, black women had convened the Atlanta Congress
of Colored Women, establishing a critical mass of national and international
networks for later black women's organizations like the National Association of
Colored Women (NACW) that formed in the following year.[10] Yet even though
some of Atlanta's black leaders were challenging social and racial issues beyond
regional parameters, the 1906 riot revealed that locally, the city remained mired
in racial strife and hopes of rapid structural change were misplaced, It would
require a long struggle to remedy the abysmal conditions of poverty, inadequate
housing, disfranchisement, and undereducation of the average black Atlantan.[11]
The trauma of the riot did not paralyze an already active black community in
the city; it seemed to have kindled more strenuous efforts of black and white
leaders to improve the Gate City's image and living conditions.

By the 1920s black Atlanta had made some significant progress. There were
a few residential and academic enclaves where the most fortunate African
Americans could live in relative safety and prosperity. Surrounding the campus of Atlanta University, families like the Murphys could interact with enlightened white people, attend excellent schools, and imagine futures in which
full American citizenship might be enjoyed. Mabel's early development in this
unusual milieu enabled her to pursue lofty goals. By reaching many of them,
Mabel opened the doors for black women like Condoleezza Rice to have influence in academia and world diplomacy.

Two or more generations of family prosperity and educational excellence
were perhaps prerequisites for Mabel navigating these untraced paths. Both of
Mabel's parents had grown up in Camden, South Carolina. Her father, Harry S.
Murphy, attended Hampton Institute in Virginia and later completed his college
degree at the University of Wisconsin in 1916. He used his education to teach
literature to black college students, first at Langston College in Oklahoma and
then at Alabama State Normal School in Montgomery. Three years after his
third daughter, Mabel, was born on April 3, 1918, Harry Murphy moved his family from Montgomery to Atlanta, worked briefly for Standard Life Insurance,

and soon opened a printing business, the House of Murphy, on Auburn Avenue, the premiere black commercial strip in downtown Atlanta.[12]

The Murphys had a comfortable existence and more advantages than most black people during Mabel's years at home during the 1920s and 1930s, and she was well aware that she was privileged and very much a member of the black elite.[13] They chose to buy a home in the up-and-coming, prosperous section of the West Side right across from the Morehouse College campus.[14] Atlanta's most affluent black citizens had begun to migrate to the West Side from the older and prestigious Victorian-era neighborhood situated around Auburn Avenue, just east of the downtown center at Five Points. The West Side's attraction was two-fold. Homes were developed and built new by black real estate pioneers like Hemon Perry, and they surrounded the key African American higher learning institutions in the city: Atlanta University, Spelman Seminary, and Morehouse College (formerly Atlanta Baptist College).[15]

As idyllic as things might have seemed for the Murphy family, this enclave of black affluence and higher education did not provide an impenetrable barrier to the problems of the larger community, and a serious racial incident exploded right in seven-year-old Mabel's neighborhood in 1925. Seventy years later she vividly remembered witnessing a frightening episode in front of her home at 357 West Fair Street.[16] The regular streetcar driver was not on duty, and a white substitute driver had slapped an older black woman during a disagreement. By the time the streetcar made its next cycle past the Murphys' house, a crowd of men from Morehouse had heard about the incident and had become enraged. They surrounded the streetcar, unhooked the power cable, and smashed windows until the terrified driver was rescued. The disturbing memory became Mabel's first awareness of racial conflict, but also her first sense of black community solidarity.[17] Throughout the rest of her life, Mabel could discuss in a matter-of-fact manner the violence and unfairness associated with racism, but she never spoke with bitterness or resentment. At all times she seems to describe segregation, discrimination, and prejudice from the perspective of an observer and not a victim.

A sense of security and collective responsibility held black communities together in the highly segregated decades of the 1920 and 1930s, and the fragile cocoon of safety in which Mabel Murphy grew up allowed her a childhood free from daily humiliations and racism. Mabel's mother appreciated the black fraternal ideal that endorsed voluntary racial separation in an age of forced racial segregation. When asked about a 1922 zoning ordinance that attempted to keep black Atlantans from moving north of Ashby Street on Atlanta's West Side, Josephine Murphy related her preference for the retention of tight-knit, separate black communities as opposed to integrated ones.[18] For the most part the West Side community in which the Murphy family lived felt secure and comfortable. Outside of its protective boundaries, however, the larger society was beset with racial prejudice and misunderstanding.

Mabel's mother cherished the black community that generally protected her children from feelings of hatred and inferiority, but she also consistently applied her own personal and social approach to bringing about fairness and understanding between the races.[19] In the Murphy household, Josephine Murphy modeled reconciliation in two important ways: by getting to know another's point of view; and by helping others to be successful in their education and work. Mabel later employed this model broadly in her career as an educator and diplomat, embracing multiculturalism in education and collaborative problem solving in international aid programs. She consistently promoted the idea that all people and nations had important lessons to learn from one another, even though one might be in a more advantaged position in terms of economic development or education.

Mabel's parents, who were immersed in politics and issues of citizenship in Atlanta from the 1920s through the 1970s, also raised their daughters with high expectations for political engagement and participation. In Atlanta city elections as well as those of other municipalities around the South, voting in nonpartisan special elections and on bonds was still possible despite the disfranchisement of blacks through the poll tax and the Democratic white primary. As a child, Mabel canvassed black neighborhoods with her mother for black voter registration.[20] While leader of the women's auxiliary of the Atlanta NAACP in the 1930s, Josephine Murphy worked diligently to educate the black Atlanta electorate by promoting attendance at the city branch's Citizenship Schools and by speaking to churches and civic organizations to encourage the masses to get organized and vote.[21] Mabel was nurtured in a community of race women like Lugenia Burns Hope, her mother's good friend, and had frequent contact with the most dedicated and service-oriented black women of Atlanta. These women profoundly influenced Mabel as she grew up and came of age, and we can see the lasting legacy of their work in her strategy of working within existing structures and institutions to pressure government authorities to create change.

In some ways, Mabel's childhood resembled that of a privileged white girl more than that of a typical black girl. But Mabel grew up around black activists who kept the goal of racial progress and the plight of the less fortunate in the fore. In addition, her extraordinary family history gave her a traceable African identity. On two direct ancestral lines, Josephine Murphy could connect her children to African relatives, one set from Nigeria and one set from

Sierra Leone. The Nigerian cousins descended directly from Scipio Vaughan, an enslaved Yoruba man of the Egba people of Nigeria, who was legendary in Camden, South Carolina, for having purchased his children's freedom in the 1850s and admonishing them to return to Africa to find their people. Two of the Vaughan sons eventually did so, and one of them later returned to Camden for a visit in 1889. Ties between the Nigerian and American sides of the family were reestablished then and continue to this day.[22] Eight-year-old Mabel first met her Nigerian cousins when Aida Arabella Vaughan Moore, the first African woman to graduate from Oxford University (and Scipio Vaughan's granddaughter), came to the United States in 1926 to enroll her daughter Kofo at Vassar College. The pride the Mabel's mother took in her family took in their African origins profoundly reinforced Mabel's embrace of African cultural ties and differences.

Josephine Murphy's elite class identity also influenced Mabel's sense of self. Mabel grew up knowing that generations of the Dibble family had lived in prosperity and with high social and political status. Mabel often spent summers with Eugene Sr. and Sallie Lee Dibble, her maternal grandparents, in Camden. Mabel relished these times partly because her grandfather was a very wealthy landowner and grocer, and his grandchildren could enjoy prestige in this small southern town, even among white citizens, many of whom were Eugene Dibble's customers. Eugene Dibble had political clout extending back to 1878, at which time he had served a two-year term in the South Carolina legislature representing Kershaw County. The Dibbles could indulge their grandchildren in a large home, filled with modern conveniences and local black domestic servants who cooked and cleaned. Although the Dibbles lived in the center of town, Eugene Dibble took Mabel out to the tenant farms on his land holdings so she could experience country life and understand the realities of farming families. Mabel's Camden memories supplemented her understanding of class differentiation among African Americans and revealed to her the pervasive poverty in rural black populations.

Despite these opportunities for exposure, being a legacy of the patriarchal Eugene Dibble Sr. was a double-edged sword. In the first generation, each of Eugene Dibble's three male children became college-trained professionals, while his two daughters received only normal school certificates. Even though Josephine Dibble Murphy loved her father and her alma mater, Atlanta University, she harbored some resentment over her father's limitations and gender discrimination.[23] Eugene Dibble's patriarchal regulations became an oft-repeated grievance heard among the Murphy granddaughters, Doris, Sarah, and Mabel. Their mother, Josephine, told them that her father had placed priority on sending his sons to professional school because he believed education beyond a teaching degree was a waste of money on his daughters, "who would just be getting married anyway."[24] In her eighties, this inequity lingered in Mabel's mind, even as she reflected on earning her doctoral degree in economics and law at the University of Wisconsin in 1942. She no doubt understood that her mother's determination not to perpetuate this gender discrimination had been a catalyst for Mabel's ambitions and the high-powered professional career that followed. Mabel clearly recognized and regretted that her mother's considerable achievements in social and political work never rewarded her with the status she deserved among men.

Harry and Josephine Murphy valued education as a vehicle for success of the individual and the larger society. They spent large portions of their family budget to give their children the best possible educational and cultural opportunities. The Murphy daughters attended the private Oglethorpe Elementary School on the Atlanta University campus instead of one of Atlanta's segregated public schools. This grammar school mainly served the children of faculty members at Spelman, Morehouse, and Atlanta University. A large number of these faculty members were white and had come to Atlanta from areas outside the South. A number of the black alumni who were still in Atlanta were able to enroll their children at Oglethorpe, and Josephine Murphy seized this opportunity for Mabel. This little-known setting of integrated education in 1920s Atlanta enabled Mabel and her sisters to form friendships with white children and to compete with them for academic excellence.[25]

Upon reaching the eighth grade, even though her mother had been instrumental in organizations that pressured the city into building a public high school for Atlanta's black students in 1924 (Booker T. Washington High School), Mabel moved into the Atlanta University Laboratory High School, which continued the academic mission of Oglethorpe with a demanding but progressive curriculum in coeducational but all-black classrooms. Her experiences as a child in both an integrated school and coeducational setting gave her self-assurance. She never thought to question the convention that she might be intellectually inferior to males or whites because she had proven she was not, every day at school. She graduated from the AU Lab School in 1933 as valedictorian and posted the highest SAT score of any student who had ever attended the school.[26] From 1933 through 1936 Mabel attended the all-black and female Spelman and remained close to her family in Atlanta. One of her educational mentors was Jesse B. Blayton, a former student of her father and Atlanta's first black Certified Public Accountant. His interest in her scholastic aptitude and his subsequent encouragement of her ambition steered Mabel toward the field of economics.

Before her senior year in college, because of her extraordinary academic record and with the recommendation of the white president of Spelman, Florence Read, a 1909 graduate, Mabel earned a partial scholarship to Mount Holyoke College in South Hadley, Massachusetts. Her parents, who viewed this as a potentially life-changing opportunity to broaden Mabel's horizons beyond the segregated South, had used every connection they had to get her in, and when she was accepted they took out an endowment loan that took many years to pay off.[27] She had been only sixteen when she matriculated at Spelman, and so at only nineteen she entered Mount Holyoke, one of the most elite women's colleges in America. Harry Murphy believed that by interacting with the northeastern American elite, Mabel could get the exposure and make the connections that could open the way into the upper ranks of American education, business, and politics.

Mabel earned her first Bs at Mount Holyoke, but also found real contentment and purpose there. Her first living experience outside the South finally fulfilled and challenged her academically and placed her in an environment where her intellectual ability could flower and her color would not automatically limit her opportunities. Harry Murphy knew these things from his own experiences at University of Wisconsin. Over forty years later, Mabel described wistfully that at Mount Holyoke, for the first time in her life, she did not have to play down her intelligence and inquisitiveness among her peers for fear that they might feel overawed by her intellectual ability. Surprisingly, instead of feeling like an outsider as the only southern black woman there, she felt a sense of belonging "because most of the students seemed to have the same kind of goals and concerns that I did and the same kind of family background and so on."[28] The Mount Holyoke women noticed her uniqueness, however, and she was called on to speak to the students about "growing up black in the South." Mabel gave a memorable impromptu talk to her classmates including examples of how black people's talents were stultified because of segregation, discrimination, and poverty. She found herself articulating that even someone as fortunate as she would have to find a more accepting and democratic situation than Atlanta in which to develop completely as a person. Evidently the exposure and comfort she found at the prestigious Seven Sister college in Massachusetts provided an important bridge to a life well outside of the confines of the segregated South; with the exception of two short stints at southern colleges as a teacher and visits to her family and friends in Atlanta, she never did return South.[29] Circumstances on the rural Massachusetts campus globally pointed Mabel toward an international perspective. In the summer of 1936, as she prepared to move to New England, the Axis alliance had been established, the Spanish Civil War and the Second Sino-Japanese War had begun, the Italian overthrow of Abyssinia (an event much protested in the black press and which garnered the African nation African American volunteers from Harlem) was consolidated, and Berlin held the Summer Olympic games in which African American sprinter Jessie Owens competed and won, flouting the claims of Aryan racial superiority espoused by the host nation's leader. Mabel Murphy could have remained an insular nineteen-year-old in the pastoral setting of South Hadley, but this would have been unlikely. Her year at Mount Holyoke in 1936–37 was also the last academic year for Mary Emma Woolley, who retired as the college's president after thirty-seven years' service. President Woolley contributed singularly to the internationalist perspective of the college and its women. Woolley's focus on Asia, in particular, had much to do with the seventy-six alumnae living and working in Japan and China as early as 1921. Woolley, although deeply devoted to her "girls," only once missed the Mount Holyoke 1932 commencement ceremony because she was the only U.S. woman delegate to the Conference for the Reduction and Limitation of Armaments in Geneva.[30] The militaristic aggression around the world in the later 1930s no doubt disappointed Woolley and became a further impetus for challenging the Mount Holyoke women to action. In fact, the promotion of international peace became a theme during Mabel's career, showing clearly when she went to Japan during the United States' postnuclear occupation and as she discussed the feasibility of war-free zones with Syrian officials and later among African leaders.

As a 1937 graduate from Mount Holyoke at age nineteen, Mabel's options for a career were not only limited by being young and black, but also because it was another Depression year and she was a woman. As in the case of her ambitious and educated mother, one of her only employment opportunities was teaching. So with prospects to be an educator, she left Massachusetts and moved to Peach County, Georgia, where she taught a diverse range of subjects at an esteemed black land grant college in central Georgia, Fort Valley Normal and Industrial School. Although she was barely twenty at the time, the Fort Valley faculty welcomed a known quantity like Mabel Murphy, whose talents and family many in Georgia already knew.

Mabel was not destined to remain long at Fort Valley, however. After her first year teaching, she spent time in Atlanta, where she met and married Hugh H. Smythe of Pittsburgh, a master's student of sociology at Atlanta University.[31] Soon after they married, the couple traveled to Northwestern University in Evanston, Illinois, on matching Rosenwald Fellowships. Mabel shortly completed a thesis, "Some Methods of Capital for a Consumers' Cooperative," and earned an MA degree in economics, while Hugh pursued a degree in anthropology.[32] Mabel moved on quickly to earn her PhD in economics and law at her father's alma mater, the University of Wisconsin, in 1942. However, Hugh's time as a student was cut short when the army drafted him. Foiled in his efforts to enroll in officer training, he served four months at the rank of private before the army leadership at Fort Sill, Oklahoma, honorably discharged him.[33] Disappointed and bitter at the racial segregation and discrimination in the army, he returned to Northwestern and completed his PhD three years after Mabel.[34] Hugh Smythe thus became the first black anthropology PhD to earn a degree under the preeminent scholar of African Studies in the United States, Melville Herskovits. Throughout his career, however, Hugh held academic positions in sociology because the black colleges and universities where he could find a position early on did not have anthropology departments.[35]

Hugh and Mabel struggled in an early example of what is now a fairly common phenomenon: the academic couple. She made a number of concessions to his career out of simple pragmatism. As an African American, his opportunities were limited, but as a man, they usually turned out to be more plentiful than hers. Mabel seemed to understand this reality, and this practical outlook required her to be flexible and to accommodate his opportunities for foundation grants, teaching jobs, and consultancies. This flexibility within the Smythes' marriage became evident almost immediately after they wed in 1939.[36]

Over the next four decades, Hugh Smythe built an academic career as a sociologist, becoming a long-standing member of the faculty of Brooklyn College in New York, a consultant and representative to various United Nations and international commissions, and eventually the United States Ambassador to Syria. Hugh Smythe would have been considered a feminist by contemporary standards, and with this enlightened mindset he provided encouragement to Mabel that catalyzed her career. Although he was the more ambitious of the two, he recognized her extraordinary intellectual and literary gifts and consistently pushed her forward in her academic and professional endeavors.[37] Their parallel educational achievements, however, did not often translate into equal opportunities.

In 1946 the Smythes' only child, Karen Pamela, was born. With their two doctorates and a baby, this African American couple faced an almost insurmountable challenge. Where would they be able to get positions in the mainstream of U.S. academe at the same institution, or at least in the same city? How could black scholars like the Smythes imagine teaching at white universities when so many black academics before them had been denied? How would a black woman get a job in competition with other black men? Who would hire a woman who had a baby?

Ironically, even though the army had seriously discriminated against men like Hugh, World War II had provided an opening for Mabel and other black women before Karen Pamela was born. Mabel had gained teaching experience during her three wartime years as assistant professor of economics at the all-black Lincoln University in Missouri while many American men were serving in the military. Talented women filled openings in many previously exclusively male jobs during the massive societal mobilization for war, and Mabel's life-long fan and sister Sarah also found an unusual opportunity as a major in the Women's Army Auxiliary Corps (waacs), the first women in American history to enlist as soldiers.[38]

But in 1946 the problem of finding jobs together reemerged. Mabel and Hugh both took academic positions at Tennessee Agricultural and Industrial Institute (later known as Tennessee State), the black teacher's college in Nashville, but this was not the caliber of institution that the couple felt was commensurate to their educational attainments. Nevertheless, they encountered another irony by being discriminated against by predominately white universities outside the legally segregated South, while finding themselves much more employable in the South because of its segregated institutions. Ultimately, however, Hugh and Mabel found living in the South intolerable in part because they both had serious concerns about the Janus-faced black administrators who confronted the dilemma of seeking funding from a white supremacist state government. The Smythes understood that to speak frankly and openly about their grievances, even tactfully and sympathetically, was not pragmatic.[39] They clearly understood that if they could not go along with Jim Crow higher education and the way it was consistently and unapologetically underfunded, they would have to go elsewhere.

These trying circumstances led the Smythes to consider novel and adventurous options. The following year they were appointed as two of thirty-four American professors willing to teach for at least a year in a Japanese university through a program set up by the U.S. Institute for Educational Exchange (usiee). In their quest to be fully accepted as American academics, they had to leave the United States altogether and take on one of the most challenging assignments in the postnuclear age. This first experience outside of the United States for Hugh and Mabel Smythe became the cornerstone of their internationalist futures.[40]

The usiee placed Hugh at Yamaguchi University and Mabel at Shiga University in Hikone. These universities were both on the main island of Honshu but were separated by an eleven-hour train ride. They visited each other every few months for a weekend, and Hugh did most of the traveling because Mabel kept Karen Pamela, at that time a toddler, with her. They wrote each other almost daily for the two years they spent in Japan, and their correspondence contains much about their students and colleagues and surprisingly little discussion of the devastation of Hiroshima and Nagasaki or political commentary about the transformation of Japanese society under the U.S. occupation. Also absent is any inkling that their skin color placed them at a social disadvantage among the Japanese, who had encountered over three thousand black soldiers of the Twenty-Fourth Infantry Regiment stationed at Camp Gifu some thirty miles from Hikone, where Mabel lived. Even though some American black internationalists had tried to forge ties with the Japanese in the earliest years of the twentieth century, after World War II, divisions signified by Japanese racial classifications such as *kokujin-hei* (black soldier) or *kurombo* (a pejorative for a person of African descent) were more prominent.[41] Nevertheless, much can be gleaned from lengthy correspondence regarding the couple's tireless assistance to Japanese individuals in their quest to receive educational opportunities in the United States.[42]

While in Japan, both Mabel and Hugh became deeply committed to solving social and political problems from a global perspective in which all cultural frames of reference are appreciated and respected. Mabel described her awakening this way:

> I started out, like many Americans, seeing the world as a pyramid, with us at the apex and everybody else at the bottom struggling to get up, but I began to understand that there are people who had pride in their way of doing things and didn't really want to become Americans. . . . I still have a feeling of comradeship with Japan over some of the things that the Japanese like and do and think. I think their ability to concentrate on what they want to accomplish and just brush hardships aside and go ahead is a marvelous thing.[43]

She appreciated their difference in social and cultural conduct but found commonality with what she perceived as Japanese perseverance against the odds. She and Hugh believed some of their Japanese students might beat the odds by finding places at U.S. universities. Both of the Smythes spent countless hours helping individual Japanese students find placement and contacts in the American academy, something many had concluded was their best option for acceptance into the world community.[44]

In the universities at Hikone and Yamaguchi, the Smythes met hundreds of students and dozens of faculty members who had ambitions to go to the United States, and for the best candidates they would do all they could—lobby, negotiate, translate, and proofread applications—to help them. They identified the best and most suitable candidates for American education and made Herculean efforts to fulfill these students' ambitions to immerse themselves in the United States' culture of higher education and democracy.[45]

In the beginning, the Smythes faced scores of rejections and other complications in trying to convince white universities to sponsor Japanese students to attend, so they began to see the possibilities for intercultural understanding while selling the idea to the black college presidents. Very early on they met Ryokichi Hirono, an extremely gifted student who wanted to go to college in the United States. Mabel called upon her mother to sponsor this particular student to attend Morehouse, and Josephine Murphy made arrangements for his tuition and lodgings with Dr. Benjamin Mays, the Atlanta college's president. In addition to Morehouse taking on Ryokichi Hirono, Bennett College for women in Greensboro, North Carolina, accepted and funded Shoko Yoshikane, who became extremely popular and maintained close ties with the Smythes and the Murphys for decades. She was featured in the popular black magazine *Jet* after her first semester at Bennett and was described as "the most popular girl on campus."[46] In the 1990s Ryokichi Hirono came to the United States as an influential trade negotiator for Japan with American corporate and political figures. Kichi, as Mabel affectionately called him, was a special source of pride to the Murphy family, because Mabel was his first economics professor and Josephine was his surrogate mother and sponsor while he attended Morehouse.[47] Dozens of Japanese students took and passed the Fulbright exams under the direction of Hugh and Mabel Smythe, and a good many of those matriculated at historically black colleges and universities (HBCUs) thereafter. Even though some white Americans in Japan discouraged Japanese students from going to black institutions, most of them took the advice of Mabel and Hugh and had rewarding experiences.[48]

These types of international scholarships were not unknown or unprecedented. A number of African students had matriculated at HBCUs already. Mabel believed that the enrollment of Japanese students would build logically upon this earlier pan-African focus at black colleges and would provide more global interaction with Asian culture. The Smythes began to think also that students from Japan who attended HBCUs could return home from the experience and help to discredit pervasive racist stereotypes of black people. In addition, Japanese students could see firsthand the unequal opportunities based on race in the United States and could expose the hypocrisy of America's Cold War rhetoric.[49]

In early autumn 1951 Mabel and Hugh had taken their first international voyage and crossed the Pacific on an ocean liner from California to get to Japan; but they left Japan twenty-seven months later to return home via Hong Kong, India, the Suez Canal, and Europe, furthering their international exposure. Back in the United States in the summer of 1953, Mabel immediately joined the NAACP's legal team, serving for a year as deputy director of nonlegal research for the school desegregation cases that resulted in the Supreme Court's *Brown v. the Board of Education* decision. She then accepted a teaching position at the New Lincoln School, a progressive and self-consciously multicultural institution that originated as the Columbia University laboratory school. Mabel quickly received a promotion to head of the high school at New Lincoln, a post she held intermittently until 1969. Her position at the head of this cosmopolitan secondary school with its experimental and culturally progressive pedagogy and curriculum allowed her to reside in New York where Hugh had become a faculty member at Brooklyn College. Residency in New York also allowed her to accept appointment to a number of United Nations educational and cultural commissions and to have easy access to international flights to Africa and other global destinations.

Mabel's interest in international work and cross-cultural education overlapped with that of a black Tennessee native, Reverend James H. Robinson, whom she had met while briefly teaching at Tennessee State after the war. In 1938 Robinson had founded a Presbyterian congregation at the Church of the Master in Harlem, and in 1954 he became the founder of Operation Crossroads Africa, a program that recruited black and white U.S. college students to perform good works and good-will missions in African countries every summer. Robinson became an influential professional connection for the Smythes as he visited them and spoke at their universities in Japan about blacks in America and about the essential importance of cross-cultural understanding in American actions and behaviors in Asia and Africa as these areas emerged from the shadow of colonialism. Although Rev. Robinson couched his views of American democratic ideals in the language of Christian benevolence (something the Smythes did not do), his Crossroads organization became another outlet for Mabel's international agenda of cross-cultural education. Mabel became the group leader for three of these summer groups, including the first group that went to Nigeria in 1958. The Crossroads Africa program was so innovative and successful in promoting cross-cultural interactions that the Peace Corps program set up under the Kennedy administration used it as a model.[50]

Back in Atlanta at the same time, 1959, Mabel's mother became president of the multiracial Atlanta chapter of the Women's International League for Peace and Freedom (WILPF). As an American delegate she attended the group's international conference in Stockholm, and in 1964 its international conference in Moscow. At this second meeting the WILPF sought a ban on nuclear testing, the abolition of the House UnAmerican Activities Committee (HUAC), and the elimination of war.[51] Founded in 1915 by Jane Addams, the WILPF had spent nearly fifty years trying to change the social and economic conditions that led

to war, and to nobody's surprise the WILPF eventually became vocal in opposing the war in Vietnam in 1963.[52] Then in her seventies, Josephine continued
to take her humanitarian interests beyond her race, gender, and community
to the international stage; the rich correspondence between the Murphys and
the Smythes reveal an overlapping interest in global humanity that, because of
her age and educational credentials, Mabel was much better positioned to employ within the apparatus of U.S. government institutions than her pioneering
mother would have been.[53]

Beginning in the late 1950s the United States moved cautiously but expec-
tantly toward new and fruitful relationships with African countries. These areas
held bountiful untapped resources but were also burdened with pressing health,
education, and development needs. The African continent, by 1980 would possess forty-eight independent governments, many of them new and fragile de-
mocracies, finally free of colonial domination. Mabel's formal experiences in
African nations coincided with the independence movements of Ghana, Nigeria, and many others in the late 1950s and early 1960s, and thus the Smythes
were well positioned to become leaders in the work of forging relationships
between African nations and the United States.

In 1960 Hugh and Mabel Smythe coauthored *The New Nigerian Elite* and
became recognized experts in the field. Their collaboration on this publication
involved Hugh conducting 156 interviews in the emerging independent nation
of Nigeria in order to describe the characteristics of the people who would
assume political power under independence; Mabel, the writer, drew on her
Nigerian experiences with Crossroads, her connections with Nigerian cousins,
and her analytical and literary gifts.[54] The Kennedy administration needed the
Smythes' type of expertise for its many humanitarian, economic, and strategic
ambitions in postcolonial Africa. *The New Nigerian Elite* served as a primer for
understanding the new leadership class emerging in newly independent Nigeria
and placed the names Mabel and Hugh Smythe on a short list known colloqui-
ally in Washington and New York as "the Africa crowd."

Beginning in 1961, every year until Hugh's appointment to Syria, Mabel was
appointed to a new U.S. advisory committee on educational or cultural exchange, the State Department Advisory Council on African Affairs, or a U.S.
UNESCO Commission. She also continued to participate in selection, orientation, and leadership of American college students through Crossroads Africa,
the Women's Africa Committee, and the U.S. Advance Committee on Educational Exchange.[55]

In 1965 President Lyndon Johnson appointed Hugh Smythe to serve as U.S.
Ambassador to Syria. For two years, until the Six-Day War, Mabel served as

hostess at the ambassador's residence in Damascus, learned Arabic, and traveled widely in the Middle East.[56] The strict Muslim subordination of women
was an adjustment for her, although she took cultural differences and the inevitable anti-American protests in stride.[57] She continued her own academic and
educational work and kept up a correspondence with her mother in Atlanta
and her daughter, Pamela, who undertook a diverse college career at Brandeis
University, NYU, and finally the University of Madrid.

After the evacuation from Syria, Hugh was reassigned as Ambassador to
Malta, and Mabel returned to New York from a leave of absence as principal
of the New Lincoln School. She then spent the summer of 1968 in Malta, again
as the ambassador's wife, reprising the subordinate woman's role in this predominately Catholic, British-influenced Mediterranean island between Libya
and Sicily. She mingled frequently with the American community living there
and had a number of significant interactions with the admiral of the U.S. Navy
Sixth Fleet. Ever concerned about the U.S. image abroad, she recommended to
him that the U.S. sailors could help build and paint Maltese schools while on
shore in addition to picking up the thousands of beer cans they had strewn on
the beaches.[58] In 1969 she resigned from the New Lincoln School to move into
more-concentrated international educational recruitment and publication as
the Vice President for Research and Publications of the Phelps Stokes Fund, an
organization that was founded in 1911 with the mission of educating the "under-
privileged" of Africa as well as African Americans and American Indians. Over
subsequent years, Mabel continued in a variety of leading roles in facilitating
African faculty and student exchanges with U.S. universities.

Mabel Smythe's diverse professional experiences coalesced in the 1960s as
African Americans asserted their legal rights and claimed a share of political
power, and the United States responded to an increasingly vocal constituency
concerned about African affairs. This predominantly black interest group began
to gain influence, first under the Kennedy and Johnson administrations and
later under the Carter administration—when human rights became a major
concern in many African nations and also a prominent foreign policy issue.
President Jimmy Carter appointed the first female black ambassador to Africa
when he chose Mabel Murphy Smythe to serve in Cameroon and later Equatorial Guinea in west central Africa. Only Patricia Roberts Harris, former dean
of Howard University Law School and Carter's HEW Secretary, preceded Mabel
as the first black woman appointed to an ambassadorship (to Luxembourg in
1965). Unlike many diplomatic appointments, Mabel's did not follow a political
reward tradition. President Carter chose her because she was highly qualified
and prepared in the field of African sociology and economics as well as by her

extensive travel and connections in sub-Saharan Africa. Mabel's expertise in Africa, particularly in Nigeria, Cameroon's neighbor to the northwest, and her record of service in diplomacy in Syria and Malta were put to use in the highest ranks of government as a chief of mission for the U.S. State Department.

The high and low points of her life, however, coincided in May and June of 1977. Sadly, two weeks before she left for her Cameroon post, Hugh Smythe died of cancer. He had lived to see her nomination and had implored her to go forward after he had been informed of his terminal condition. She expeditiously organized his affairs and with a heavy heart took on this extraordinary responsibility and opportunity without her husband, best friend, and intellectual partner of thirty-seven years.[59]

In Yaounde, the capital of Cameroon, she became well acquainted with El Hadj Ahmadou Ahidjo. The French-speaking, Muslim president had held power in the country since its independence in 1958, and he had cultivated good relations with the United States. Cameroon had had a fairly peaceful and stable existence since independence under Ahidjo's highly centralized one-party government. Mabel used creative strategies to enhance positive relations, to foster educational exchange, and to position Cameroon to be a strong ally in Carter's ambitious plans to further international human rights through engagement and economic development. She instituted a vibrant program of cultural events at the U.S. Cultural Center in Yaounde, and facilitated the exchange of faculty between the university in Yaounde and institutions in the United States. Among many other cultural and educational activities she sponsored, she also facilitated economic and developmental encroachments into Cameroon. She oversaw the opening of a Chase Bank in Douala, garnered matching funds for modern fisheries and farming projects for local communities, hosted hundreds of Peace Corps volunteers, and coordinated the evacuation of Chad during its political turmoil.[60]

After a tour of Africa, Carter's vice president, Walter Mondale, commented on the potential for Cameroon to serve as a model of American-African cooperation and also on Mabel's exemplary work and diplomatic skills.[61] Patricia Derien, Assistant Secretary of State for Human Rights, also visited Cameroon, and Ambassador Smythe made a special point to have her visit the Anglophone section of the country that comprised the beleaguered minority population. The gesture reinforced Mabel's dedication to inclusiveness and gave her a way to demonstrate to the Francophone president how even the most symbolic acts can help in building bridges.[62]

Although Cameroon experienced an economic boom in the late 1970s, it had its share of economic structural problems and difficulties between formerly

French and English dominated areas. The encouragement of Islam by President Ahidjo contributed to tensions within the country also, but compared to its neighbor to the southeast, the Republic of Equatorial Guinea, Cameroon was a model of moderation and capitalist development.[63] On November 20, 1979, Mabel became dual ambassador to Cameroon and Equatorial Guinea, a former Spanish colony that had just endured a three-year anti-Spanish reign of terror under the dictator Francisco Macias Nguema. U.S. government leaders felt that President Carter needed to show support for a coup that had eliminated Macias in order to support the United States' strong NATO ally, Spain, and to stabilize the country, which had become a resource area for Soviet and Chinese fishing and a staging area for Cuban fighters in the Angolan War. Mabel's mission in Equatorial Guinea, thus, was strategic, humanitarian, and urgent—a far cry from the developmental, educational, and cultural focus of her work in Cameroon.[64]

Seven months later, however, she received a job promotion in the State Department. In June 1980 she resigned her ambassadorships and moved to Washington, D.C., as Deputy Assistant Secretary of State for African Affairs.[65] Her superior at the State Department in African Affairs was Dick Moose, who had visited her at her post in Yaounde the previous year and given her the highest rating on her evaluation. He noted the large number of personnel, Agency for International Development missions, Peace Corps volunteers, and the $10 million budget she had so ably overseen. Her French was excellent, she was popular with the Cameroonians, and she had traveled extensively throughout the country despite the difficulty of reaching some regions.[66]

In her new role at the State Department, Mabel used her experience in the U.S. Foreign Service to offer didactic advice on how to communicate and negotiate effectively with African leaders. She also lambasted the state department for its ill-advised appointment of single men for post positions abroad. She detailed how posting married couples and even entire American families was essential for morale purposes and for reflecting the true nature of American society and values abroad.[67] She lobbied and counseled the Office of Foreign Service recruitment and the Congress for more black representation in the foreign service and state department.

The election of Ronald Reagan in November 1980 brought a new political party to the executive branch and eventually new foreign service personnel. Mabel left the State Department in June of 1981 and moved to Northwestern University, the institution that had awarded her Master's degree forty-one years earlier. She was named the Melville Herskovits Distinguished Professor of African Studies and coordinator of the new African Studies program. She shared her unparalleled personal and professional knowledge of Africa with Northwestern's students for five years.

In 1985, at the age of sixty-seven, Mabel married Robert Haith and moved back east to Washington, D.C. Although she was extremely active as a board member for numerous colleges and foundations, she never sought a full-time position after her Northwestern years in the 1980s. She remained active as a promoter of intercultural education and understanding with a specific focus on sub-Saharan Africa. She received a number of honorary degrees and accumulated many awards from both black and white organizations.[68] She joined the Spelman College Board of Trustees and donated the exquisite collection of West African art she had collected to her alma mater. After Mabel Murphy Smythe-Haith's death in early 2006, family members fulfilled her request by spreading her ashes on the Spelman campus in the Atlanta neighborhood that watched her grow up.

Raised in Jim Crow Atlanta where few black girls could be shielded from racism and also nurtured intellectually by an elite black community, Mabel Murphy Smythe took every advantage and opportunity presented to her and directed her life's work toward multicultural education and helping the United States develop a more enlightened and tolerant foreign policy. Her personal experience, beginning at home with her parents, Josephine and Harry Murphy, allowed her to view the United States as a deeply flawed but worthy nation, and she chose to work within systems of education, philanthropy, and government to seek peace and human progress for African Americans and non-Americans alike. As she matured as an adult, she sought to make her contribution outside of Atlanta, of Georgia, and of the South. Along the way, she remained aware of stark economic inequalities and their consequences for the American poor, women, and underdeveloped countries, but she maintained an economist's and social scientist's belief in policy-based solutions. At the height of her diplomatic career, Mabel solidified the link between the U.S. government and Africa in places like Cameroon while the festering issue of apartheid in South Africa came to the fore. How to approach postindependence African leaders in ways that recognized their dignity and national pride became better understood through her efforts at the State Department and through exchange programs that brought African students like Barack Obama Sr. from Kenya to the United States to study. Her focus on economic development and promotion of peace and education for Africans gave the United States credibility even as the nation aggressively and sometimes counterproductively sought to undermine the opposing influences of the USSR, China, and Cuba in underdeveloped and politically fragile African countries. By the 1960s, when she became engaged directly with Africa, no longer was Africa just a place of great interest and concern to African Americans but a place of profound possibilities for U.S. investment and importance to global security. Taking advantage of the opportunities that parents like Harry and Josephine Murphy had fought to create for their children, Mabel Smythe balanced her role as an agent of the U.S. international agenda and her personal mission to promote intercultural understanding and peace. After facing the many obstacles blocking African Americans and women before the dramatic societal reforms during the years of her early career, she recognized clearly that she was poised by her experiences and education to take advantage of new pressures on politicians and institutions to hire blacks and women in the 1960s and 1970s. Mabel Murphy Smythe faced the challenges that her race and gender posed, but she believed that class barriers and restricted economic opportunities were the real obstacles for individual Americans and also for the nations of the world.

NOTES

1. See Mabel Murphy Smythe interview with Ruth Stutts Njiiri, June 2–3, 1981, 120, Oral History Project on Former Black Chiefs of Mission, Phelps-Stokes Fund, Schomburg Center for Research in Black Culture, New York, N.Y. (hereafter cited as MMS interview with RSN).

2. "A Free Man's Kin Is Wife of Envoy to Syria," *Atlanta Constitution*, n.d., in "Dibble Family" clipping file, Robert W. Woodruff Library, Atlanta University, Atlanta, Ga.

3. Mabel M. Smythe to Josephine Dibble Murphy and Harry Murphy Sr., May 29, 1967, box 3, Josephine Dibble Murphy Papers, Special Collections and Archives, Robert W. Woodruff Library, Atlanta University Center, Atlanta, Ga. I would like to thank my graduate research assistant, Cathy L. Freeman, for her help with this project.

4. Mabel Murphy Smythe (Haith) interview with Ann Miller Morin, May 2 through October 23, 1986, 44–53, Foreign Affairs Oral History Project, Women Ambassadors Series, Association for Diplomatic Studies and Training, Foreign Service Institute (hereafter cited as MMS-H interview with AMM). See also MMS interview with RSN, 31.

5. Allen P. Dobson and Steve Marsh, *United States Foreign Policy since 1945*, 2nd ed. (New York: Routledge, 2006), 118–25; Kenneth W. Stein and Samuel W. Lewis, *Making Peace among Arabs and Israelis: Lessons from Fifty Years of Negotiating Experience* (Washington, D.C.: U.S. Institute of Peace, 1991), xv–xvi, 4–7; Thomas F. Brady, "Syrian Chief Says U.S. Has 'Lust to Dominate': Attassi Assails Britain, Iraq and Lebanon in Speech He Charges Baath Opponents 'Please Imperialists,'" *New York Times*, March 9, 1966, accessed August 17, 2010, from ProQuest Historical Newspapers (document ID: 79969212).

6. An exception would have been readers of Tor Eigland, "Our Man in Damascus: U.S. Ambassador Hugh Smythe Serves on Syrian Hot Spot," *Ebony*, December 1966, 29–36. See also Robert B. Semple Jr., "Johnson Picks 6 New Envoys, 4 of Them Career Diplomats," *New York Times*, July 9, 1965, 8, accessed August 17, 2010, from ProQuest Historical Newspapers (document ID: 96705380).

7. See Brenda Gayle Plummer, *Rising Wind: Black Americans and U.S. Foreign Affairs, 1935–1960* (Chapel Hill: University of North Carolina Press, 1996); Penny M. Von Eschen, *Race against Em-*

pire: Black Americans and Anti-Colonialism, 1937–1957 (Ithaca: Cornell University Press, 1997); Mary Dudziak, *Cold War, Civil Rights: Race and the Image of American Democracy* (Princeton: Princeton University Press, 2000); and Carol Anderson, *Eyes off the Prize: The United Nations and the African American Struggle for Human Rights, 1944–1955* (New York: Cambridge University Press, 2003).

8. Hugh H. and Mabel M. Smythe Papers, Library of Congress, Washington, D.C. (hereafter cited as Smythe Papers, LOC).

9. John M. Matthews, "Studies in Race Relations in Georgia, 1890–1930" (PhD diss., Duke University, 1970), 167–71. See also David Godshalk, *Veiled Visions: The 1906 Atlanta Race Riot and the Reshaping of American Race Relations* (Chapel Hill: University of North Carolina Press, 2005).

10. "Negro Problems to Be Discussed," *New York Times*, May 4, 1896.

11. Wilson Jeremiah Moses, *The Golden Age of Black Nationalism* (New York: Oxford University Press, 1988), 119–21.

12. *Atlanta City Directory*, 1923–26.

13. Mabel Murphy Smythe-Haith, interview with author, April 17, 1999 (hereafter cited as MMS-H interview with author, with date).

14. MMS-H interview with AMM; David Lewis and August Meier, "History of the Negro Upper Class in Atlanta, Georgia, 1890–1958," *Journal of Negro Education* 28 (Spring 1969): 130–39.

15. Lewis and Meier, "History of the Negro Upper Class," 130–39. Morris Brown College and Clark College would eventually be located in the same district. This consortium of schools is now referred to as the Atlanta University Center.

16. MMS-H interview with author, March 26, 1999. The Murphys lived in this house until it was razed to add new buildings to the AU Center. See also *Atlanta City Directory*, 1923–27.

17. MMS-H interview with author, April 16, 1999.

18. Mrs. H. S. Murphy, private interview held in her home with Michael L. Porter, Atlanta, Ga., April 19, 1973, quoted in Michael Leroy Porter, "Black Atlanta: An Interdisciplinary Study of Blacks on the East Side of Atlanta, 1890–1930" (PhD diss., Emory University, 1972), 25–26.

19. MMS-H interview with author, March 26, 1999.

20. Darlene Clark Hine, ed., *Black Women in America: Law and Government* (New York: Facts on File, 1997), 157.

21. Mary Gambrell Rolinson, "Community and Leadership in the First Twenty Years of the Atlanta NAACP, 1917–1937," *Atlanta History* 42, no. 3 (1998): 15–21.

22. Era Bell Thompson, "The Vaughan Family: A Tale of Two Continents," *Ebony*, February 1975, 53–64.

23. One of the most notable of Mabel's Dibble uncles was Eugene Dibble Jr., who in 1923 became the first black man to head the medical department of a Veteran's Administration hospital. He was a highly respected leader who held this position at the Tuskegee VA hospital for over forty years. During his tenure, however, the notorious Tuskegee syphilis experiment took place. See Susan Reverby, *Examining Tuskegee: The Infamous Tuskegee Syphilis Experiment and Its Legacy* (Chapel Hill: University of North Carolina Press, 2009).

24. MMS-H interview with author, April 16, 1999.

25. Clarence A. Bacote, *The Story of Atlanta University: A Century of Service* (Atlanta: Atlanta University, 1969), 35, 143–44, 276; Myron W. Adams, *A History of Atlanta University* (Atlanta: Atlanta University Press, 1930), 98–99. The first black woman member of the Georgia General Assembly, Grace Towns Hamilton, also attended Oglethorpe Elementary University campus and described it

this way: "There was some question raised about the children of faculty attending the [Oglethorpe] School, which was the elementary. . . . And the children of faculty went there. And when there was some state visitor, this was discovered, and that became the basis for the state demanding that the charter of the University be changed, or they would sacrifice their money. Unless the charter clearly said for the education of black youth. And the Trustees of Atlanta University did not want to do that, and did not do it" (Grace Towns Hamilton interview with Jacquelyn Hall, July 19, 1974, 9, Southern Oral History Program Collection, G-0026, University of North Carolina, http://docsouth.unc.edu/sohp/html_use/G-0026.html [accessed November 7, 2008]).

26. Sarah M. Palmore (Mabel's sister), interview with the author, June 24, 2010; MMS-H interview with AMM, 15–16.

27. Hine, *Black Women in America*, 157.

28. MMS-H interview with AMM, 23–25.

29. Mount Holyoke admitted very few black women before the 1960s, whereas Wellesley and Vassar had a record of admitting the largest numbers in earlier years. See Joan Marie Johnson, *Southern Women at the Seven Sister Colleges: Feminist Values and Social Activism, 1875–1915* (Athens: University of Georgia Press, 2008), 99, 123.

30. Anne Carey Edmonds, *A Memory Book: Mount Holyoke College, 1837–1987* (South Hadley, Mass.: Mount Holyoke College, 1988), 85–86.

31. MMS interview with RSN, 55–56.

32. Mabel Murphy Smythe, "Some Methods of Capital for a Consumers' Cooperative" (master's thesis, Northwestern University, 1940).

33. Honorable Discharge and Enlistment Record of Hugh H. Smythe, Mabel M. Smythe-Haith Collection, W. S. Hoole Special Collections Library, University of Alabama, Tuscaloosa, Ala.

34. MMS-H interview with AMM, 20–24; Mabel Murphy Smythe, "Tipping Occupations as a Problem in the Administration of Protective Labor Legislation," (PhD diss., University of Wisconsin–Madison, 1942).

35. Mark Anderson, "The Complicated Career of Hugh Smythe . . . Anthropologist and Ambassador: The Early Years, 1940–1950," *Transforming Anthropology* 16, no. 2 (2008): 128–46.

36. Marianne A. Ferber and Jane W. Loeb, eds., *Academic Couples: Problems and Promises* (Urbana: University of Illinois Press, 1997), 90, 100.

37. Mabel M. Smythe and Hugh H. Smythe, Japan correspondence, 1951–1953. This correspondence is in the author's personal collection.

38. "WAACS: First Women Soldiers Join Army," *Time*, September 7, 1942, 75–81.

39. MMS-H interview with AMM, 25–26.

40. MMS-H interview with author, April 16, 1999.

41. Yasuhiro Okada, "Race, Masculinity, and Military Occupation: African American Soldiers' Encounters with the Japanese at Camp Gifu, 1947–1951," *Journal of African American History* 96, no. 2 (2011): 179–86.

42. Smythe Papers, LOC, Washington, D.C., box 44, Mabel M. and Hugh Smythe, Japan correspondence, 1951–53.

43. MMS-H interview with AMM, 33.

44. Hine, ed., *Black Women in America*, 158; George Goodman Jr., "Dr. Hugh Smythe, Worked for Dubois," *New York Times*, June 26, 1977, 26.

45. This magazine reference to *Jet*, November 15, 1952, taken from Hugh H. Smythe to Mabel M. Smythe, January 12, 1953, Japan Correspondence; Mabel M. Smythe to Sarah M. Palmore, April 9,

1990 (letter in author's possession); Mabel M. Smythe to Hugh H. Smythe, Japan correspondence, especially November 1952–February 1953.

46. *Jet*, November 15, 1952, found in Hugh H. Smythe to Mabel M. Smythe, January 12, 1953, Japan Correspondence.

47. Mabel M. Smythe to Sarah M. Palmore, April 9, 1990 (letter in author's possession).

48. Mabel M. Smythe to Hugh H. Smythe, Japan correspondence, November 1952–January 1953.

49. Mabel M. Smythe and Hugh H. Smythe, "Race, Culture, and Politics in Japan," *Phylon* 13, no. 3 (1952), 192–98; Mabel M. and Hugh H. Smythe, "Report from Japan: Comments on the Race Question," *The Crisis*, March 1952, 159–64.

50. Adelaide Cromwell and Martin Kilson, eds., *Apropos of Africa: Sentiments of Negro American Leaders on Africa from the 1800s to the 1950s* (London: Frank Cass and Company, 1969), 136–37; MMS-H interview with AMM, 39–40.

51. Josephine Dibble Murphy, "Women for Peace and Freedom," *The Crisis*, December 1965, 636–38.

52. Catherine Foster, *Women for All Seasons: The Story of the Women's International League for Peace and Freedom* (Athens: University of Georgia Press, 1989), 8; *Who's Who of American Women: A Biographical Dictionary of Notable Living American Women*, 3rd ed., 1964–65 (Chicago: The A. N. Marquis Company, 1965, 737.

53. JDMP correspondence files.

54. Hugh H. Smythe and Mabel M. Smythe, *The New Nigerian Elite* (Stanford: Stanford University Press, 1960). For reviews, see Immanuel Wallerstein in *American Anthropologist* 63 (June 1961): 614–15; and *Book Review Digest* (1962): 1125–26.

55. Shirelle Phelps, ed., *Who's Who among African Americans* (Detroit: Gail, 1998), 946.

56. Goodman, "Dr. Hugh Smythe," *New York Times*, June 26, 1977, 26.

57. "A Free Man's Kin Is Wife of Envoy to Syria," *Atlanta Constitution*, n.d., in "Dibble Family" clipping file, Robert W. Woodruff Library, Atlanta University, Atlanta, Ga.

58. MMS-H interview with AMM, 51–52.

59. MMS-H interview with author, March 10, 1999.

60. Smythe Papers, LOC.

61. White House Central Files, CO 27, January 20, 1977–January 20, 1981, Jimmy Carter Library, Atlanta, Ga.

62. MMS interview with RSN, 86–87.

63. David Birmingham and Phyllis Martin, eds., *History of Central Africa: The Contemporary Years since 1960* (New York: Longman, 1998), 43–55.

64. MMS interview with RSN, 110–16.

65. Name File, "Mabel Murphy Smythe," White House Central Files, Jimmy Carter Library, Atlanta, Ga.

66. Smythe Papers, box 20, folder 1, LOC, Washington, D. C.

67. Smythe Papers, box 19, folder 3, LOC, Washington, D.C.

68. *Who's Who*, 1213–14.

Mary Flannery O'Connor

(1925–1964)

A Prophet for Her Times

SARAH GORDON

❀ ❀ ❀

At the time of her untimely death at age thirty-nine, Flannery O'Connor had published thirty-one short stories and two novels and had established herself as a fiction writer of some interest, although her work was often mistakenly and simplistically labeled "southern gothic" and, at least initially, seemed to resist interpretation. Famously stating that she could wait a hundred years to be understood, O'Connor has not had to wait that long. Indeed, since 1964 O'Connor's oeuvre has drawn readers from around the world and provoked vast critical commentary. She is now considered one of the finest fiction writers in America, and her reputation has moved well beyond her region and her time. Nevertheless, O'Connor is something of an anomaly in modern and contemporary literature—a profoundly Christian writer whose satiric vision is both arresting and disturbing to readers, as she intended it to be.

Like T. S. Eliot, one of the early influences on her work, O'Connor understood that she was not writing for an audience that accepted her traditional Christian point of view; she wrote that, in order to awaken the slumbering children of God, the writer had to use drastic means: "To the hard of hearing, you shout, for the almost blind, you draw large and startling figures."[1] Unquestionably O'Connor saw herself as akin to that street-corner prophet, the embarrassing figure we'd rather walk right by, the one whose message we don't want to hear. In her writing and in her personal life, O'Connor was singularly focused, as though she were aware of the brevity of her time on earth.

Mary Flannery O'Connor, born into two of Georgia's oldest Catholic families, was both a woman of her time and place and an outsider by inclination and by choice. At the time of her birth in Savannah as the only child of Edward

Francis and Regina Cline O'Connor, Mary Flannery, as she was called then, became a part of the lively and self-sufficient Irish American community. The location of the O'Connor townhouse on Charlton Street in Lafayette Square just across from the Cathedral of St. John the Baptist and within walking distance of O'Connor's first parochial school afforded the young O'Connor the schooling in her faith that would set the course of her life's work and, simultaneously, mark her as detached observer, in this world but not of it.

A shy, precocious, and extremely protected child, Mary Flannery nonetheless could on occasion exhibit rebellion. Her mother Regina, whose family's roots were in middle Georgia (Locust Grove and, later, Milledgeville), was extremely careful with her young daughter. Relatives recall that Regina kept a list of suitable playmates for her daughter and sent home any child who was not on the list. Imaginative and often strong willed, Mary Flannery demonstrated early on a talent for storytelling and art. Regina often hosted a gathering of children for the Let's Pretend story hour on the radio on Saturday mornings, serving refreshments to her daughter and friends. Mary Flannery especially loved climbing to the third-floor bathroom with a few of those friends, to sit in the claw-foot tub and read stories aloud. One friend recalled that Mary Flannery constantly interrupted her reading of a story to insist on hearing a passage again. An early instance of O'Connor's perhaps innate sense of the absurd involved her teaching a chicken to walk backward, an event that was captured in a brief, now famous Pathe newsreel.

Clearly doted on by her parents, Mary Flannery understood that Regina made and enforced the rules and that Ed, the warm and indulgent father, was her kindred spirit. Biographer Brad Gooch reports that when O'Connor was nine, she drew a cartoon showing a child walking with her parents. The balloon of dialogue from the mother's mouth says, "Hold your head up, Mary Flannery, and you are just as bad, Ed." The child replies, "I was readin' where someone died holding up their head."[2] Mary Flannery folded poems and notes for her father into his napkin at dinnertime, and in the course of his business day, Ed proudly showed them to his friends. Regina, however, dominated the household, with a clear eye to family propriety and social status.

In her years at two parochial schools in Savannah, Mary Flannery did not especially distinguish herself—prone to provoking the nuns and sometimes performing poorly. Indeed, at the beginning of the sixth grade, Mrs. O'Connor removed her daughter from St. Vincent's and enrolled her in Sacred Heart, perhaps because of Mary Flannery's conflicts with the nuns at St. Vincent's or because Sacred Heart was located in a more prosperous neighborhood. Such a move was undoubtedly shocking to the O'Connors' insular, close-knit Irish

MARY FLANNERY O'CONNOR

Courtesy of the Flannery O'Connor Collection, Georgia College & State University.

Catholic neighborhood in Savannah, but it demonstrates Regina O'Connor's determination and her singular focus on her daughter and her welfare. In only a few more years, the family would leave Savannah because of Ed's faltering business career; the three lived for nearly two years in Atlanta, where Mary Flannery attended the public North Fulton High School.

For Regina and her daughter, however, city life was not tenable. Ed, therefore, moved the two to Regina's family home in Milledgeville, where Mary Flannery was enrolled in the Peabody Laboratory School, affiliated with the Education Department at Georgia State College for Women, an institution at that time largely devoted to teacher education. For a time, Ed O'Connor came to Milledgeville only on weekends. After he became ill with lupus, he was forced to give up his job and to live permanently at the Cline house.

The teenage O'Connor seems to have settled in nicely and was considered a bright and talented young woman by her high school teachers. Her imagination given free rein, O'Connor began cartooning in earnest and even sent some of her work to the *New Yorker* magazine, reporting in the high school newspaper that she was spending her time collecting rejection slips. The move to Milledgeville, away from the rather closed Catholic community of Savannah, proved momentous for the young writer, for although she continued to be under her mother's protective oversight, O'Connor's world widened a bit to include non-Catholic friends in a richly historic college town, albeit a place small and rather provincial. Milledgeville and its sometimes eccentric inhabitants would be grist for the writer's mill her entire life. As her friend Sally Fitzgerald liked to observe, O'Connor in Milledgeville "was like a silver miner at the Comstock Lode," finding plenty of material to satisfy her keen appetite for the banal and the strange.

The illness and death of Edward O'Connor from lupus erethematosis in 1941 was a tremendous blow to his fifteen-year-old daughter. In a portent of things to come, Mary Flannery decided to remain in Milledgeville with Regina and to attend college at Georgia State College for Women (GSCW), where she completed an accelerated three-year program, majoring in social science. As a day student, O'Connor walked the two blocks to campus, thus remaining under her mother's watchful eye. Although she was involved in campus life as a writer and cartoonist and often invited friends to lunch at the Cline house on Greene Street, Mary Flannery was still at home, now in a household full of female relatives and the occasional boarder. The writer and her mother regularly attended mass at Sacred Heart Catholic Church, continuing the long history of the Cline family in Catholic leadership in Milledgeville. Paradoxically, O'Connor's life appeared to be opening up at the same time that much remained the same; the constancy of Roman Catholicism and of her mother's presence were undoubtedly consol-

ing in her grief. The church, for that matter, would continue to be O'Connor's
strength and consolation to the end of her days. On the decidedly more human and personal side, Flannery O'Connor's relationship to her mother was,
without question, the most important and most complicated of her life. Regina
O'Connor was her protector, her provider, and the source of her daughter's
greatest amusement and exasperation. Regina O'Connor was at Flannery's side
when she died on August 3, 1964, from the same disease, lupus, that had killed
Flannery's father; Regina died in 1995 at age ninety-nine, outliving her daughter
by more than thirty years.

Mary Flannery's time at GSCW, from 1942 to 1945, coincided with the quarter-
ing of the WAVES on campus for the war effort. O'Connor and her classmates
were obviously fascinated by the uniformed presence of these military women;
for her part, O'Connor used them as fodder for her cartoons, published in the
college literary magazine, newspaper, and yearbook. Following the drawing
style of James Thurber, O'Connor echoed his acerbic content as well, demonstrating the satirist's eye and a real sense of life at a woman's college. In honor
of the presence of the WAVES, Bob Hope broadcast his NBC radio show from the
campus in May of 1943. In a further demonstration of their wartime solidarity,
many of the GSCW students volunteered to roll bandages and engage in other
patriotic endeavors, but there is no evidence that O'Connor involved herself
in this effort. Her apparent detachment was characteristic; O'Connor would
always keep a safe distance from historical and political reality.

The fact that O'Connor's family possessed a certain elevated status in
Milledgeville—her grandfather Peter Cline was the town's first mayor—virtually ensured that Mary Flannery was a part of the elite, if not elitist, social
milieu of the historic town. Milledgeville was spared during Sherman's march
to the sea, and from Reconstruction on, the town preserved the racist hierarchy of most southern towns at this time. In O'Connor's time, African Americans lived in substandard housing and depended on white property-owners
for employment. In fact, it is safe to say that the young O'Connor shared the
prevailing racism of the time, whether that racism was implicitly or overtly
manifested. Mary Flannery O'Connor knew no African Americans except
those hired by her family as servants, even though one or two black families
in town had distinguished themselves as professionals. At the end of her life,
O'Connor witnessed the beginning of the civil rights movement and the heroic
efforts of the charismatic Martin Luther King Jr., a fellow Georgian for whom
O'Connor expressed admiration. However, O'Connor was not above telling a
racist joke, as readers of her private correspondence have learned.[3] At the very
least, O'Connor's ambivalence about race testifies to a troubled conscience, one

that genuinely sought in her published fiction to slough off the old ways in favor of acknowledgment of the full humanity of African Americans, in spite of her limited background and experience.

When Mary Flannery O'Connor left Milledgeville in 1945 for the graduate program in journalism at the University of Iowa, she entered for the first time a world without Regina's oversight and protection. In Iowa City she boarded off campus with nonsouthern women who were not especially devout. Soon after classes began O'Connor, who by now was calling herself simply "Flannery," realized that journalism was not a good fit for her and approached Paul Engle, of the newly established Writers' Workshop, for admission to that program. Engle claims to have recognized O'Connor's genius early on, even though her nasal southern accent and her shyness were initial stumbling blocks to her participation in a program that called for reading one's own work aloud and participating in class discussion. In 1947 O'Connor completed the requirements for the MFA with her collection *Geranium and Other Stories*. This thesis reveals a young writer struggling to find her voice, and, in at least one story, "The Turkey," beginning to acquire that humorous ironic edge that would characterize the later work. "Geranium" anticipates a recurrent theme in all of O'Connor's work—displacement—and reflects her own sense of uprootedness and homesickness in Iowa. That story would be reworked and published twice again; the version entitled "Judgement Day" was one of the last writing projects near the end of her life.

Another story from the thesis collection, "Wildcat," a weak attempt at capturing a black man's fear of death, is the only time O'Connor would use an African American protagonist. Indeed, O'Connor's black characters often serve as chorus figures or catalysts to the plight of the central white characters. Fifteen years after O'Connor's death, her friend Sally Fitzgerald, in her introduction to O'Connor's collected letters, *The Habit of Being*, defended O'Connor's treatment of blacks by insisting that O'Connor felt that she could not "'get inside'" the heads of African Americans (O'Connor's own wording, repeated by Fitzgerald) and attributes that failure to O'Connor's "humility." Fitzgerald suggests that perhaps O'Connor wanted "to give dignity and meaning to the lives of individuals" with "far fewer champions," that is, the poor whites, not recognizing that African Americans have had far fewer defenders than poor whites.[4] However, despite the absence of black protagonists in her mature fiction, O'Connor constantly excoriates the bigotry and racism of her white characters.

In *Wise Blood*, O'Connor's first novel (1952), Hazel Motes, the Christ-haunted protagonist, is imbued with the bigotry of most white southerners in the mid-twentieth-century South. Attempting to prove that there is no sin, no Fall, and thus no need for redemption, Motes asserts that "Jesus is a trick on niggers,"[5] a satiric echo of Marx's familiar idea that religion is the "opiate" of the people. For poor whites in the rural South, Motes's use of the black man as scapegoat would have been commonplace. O'Connor clearly wants the reader to recognize Motes's provincialism and racism. In a similar fashion, O'Connor's "The Artificial Nigger," published in her first collection, *A Good Man Is Hard to Find* (1955), presents the ignorant and countrified Mr. Head escorting his grandson Nelson to the city for the first time to show him the metropolis and, in covering his own pitiful inadequacy, to teach the boy racial superiority. Indeed, before the two leave home, Mr. Head warns Nelson that he may not like the city, for "it'll be full of niggers."[6] The boy has never seen an African American, and when, on the train into the city, Mr. Head questions the boy about the black man who has just walked down the aisle ("What was that?"), the boy answers in a series of observations that are, in Mr. Head's mind, incorrect. First, the boy responds with the obvious, "A man." When Mr. Head asks, "What kind of man?" the boy answers "A fat man" and then "An old man," not seeing skin color as a descriptor. His grandfather answers smugly, "That was a nigger."[7]

When the two bumpkins manage to get lost in the city, Mr. Head is not a heroic guide to his grandson. In fact, he ends up denying Nelson, his own flesh and blood, and nearly losing the boy's trust, in one of the most moving scenes of alienation in modern American literature. Later, the two are reconciled before the plaster statue of a black boy, when Mr. Head, feeling it incumbent upon him to proffer his wisdom, concludes, "They ain't got enough real ones here. They got to have an artificial one."[8] Although "The Artificial Nigger" was the author's favorite story, its ending has generated much commentary, especially concerning Mr. Head's revelation. So relieved is he to be reconciled to his grandson via the clever, albeit racist remark, and to be home again once more, that he avers that "he was forgiven for sins from the beginning of time, when he had conceived in his own heart the sin of Adam, until the present, when he had denied poor Nelson" and that "since God loved in proportion as He forgave, he felt ready at that instant to enter Paradise."[9]

Just how seriously do we take the prideful Mr. Head's revelation? Throughout the story, as Louis D. Rubin and others have observed, old Mr. Head is presented in mock-heroic fashion. Is it not possible that we are to see his final epiphany as a self-aggrandizing delusion? And what about the story's use of race? Is the issue of Mr. Head's bigotry, which, after all, unites grandfather and grandson in the climactic moment, set aside as incidental to the old man's certainty that he is forgiven—not forgiven for racism, it should be said, but forgiven for his arrogance and for his betrayal of his own flesh and blood? On the other hand,

Mr. Head has also recognized that "his true depravity had been hidden from him, lest it cause him despair";[10] perhaps Mr. Head has not yet recognized the depravity of his racism. In fact, this provincial, ignorant man would not likely recognize himself as racist; like many others, he needs to believe himself superior to the African American to confirm his own worth. At the least, we might argue, he has experienced searing insight into the sin of which he is capable— his prideful attempt to control the visit to the city, his denial of relationship with his grandson, his self-serving betrayal of Nelson, and, perhaps, most of all, his fear of the unknown, signaling his lack of trust in God. O'Connor suggests that perhaps this insight and consequent guilt will open the old man up to a deeper humanity. We can only hope.

The problematic ending of this story, with its ambiguous treatment of racial prejudice, reveals an unevenness of tone rather unusual in O'Connor's work. For the most part, her white racist protagonists condemn themselves by their own use of dehumanizing, bigoted language, emanating from them as freely and easily as it does today in provincial areas of this nation. The dialogue of Mrs. McIntyre in "The Displaced Person," Mrs. Cope in "A Circle in the Fire," and Ruby Turpin in "Revelation" are fine examples of these characters' sense of superiority to others, especially African Americans. Sophisticated readers will recognize O'Connor's sharp irony in these characters.

Flannery O'Connor, educated at Iowa in the New Critics and their emphasis on the work of art itself, not on its historical context and its author's life, never centered a narrative on historic and social reality. O'Connor believed that even getting near a soapbox was death to the quality of her work. However, she sometimes made reference to history and social issues in developing characters and pursuing her deeply theological point of view. In *A Good Man Is Hard to Find*, two stories illustrate this point. "A Late Encounter with the Enemy" presents the ancient Confederate soldier "General" Tennessee Flintrock Sash, who is content to let his community believe he was a general when he actually served as a foot soldier. General Sash makes his last public appearance onstage at the graduation of his granddaughter Sally Poker Sash from a teacher certification program at a state teachers' college, familiar territory to O'Connor. Painted boldly with O'Connor's satiric brush, the general is a man for whom history—specifically, the events of the war in which he is supposed to have been a hero—has no meaning whatsoever. The problem is not that his memory has failed as a result of the aging process, but, more subtly, that his life has never had meaning.

O'Connor implicitly asks, What gives life meaning and purpose? Surely not the prideful and silly self-regard of an old soldier who allows his backward-looking southern community to lionize him and the cause for which he presumably fought! Taking aim at the sentimental nostalgia of her native region for the antebellum South and the Confederate cause, O'Connor achieves a direct hit. General Sash is hauled out, a living relic, for all of the local tours of homes and Civil War anniversaries; his granddaughter, moreover, is the epitome of the community's foolishness when she thinks of General Sash standing behind her on the stage at her graduation: "See him! See him! My kin, all you upstarts! Glorious upright old man standing for the old traditions! Dignity! Honor! Courage!"[11] Southern pride and family pride are both assaulted here, for perhaps in no region of the country is family history, especially white family history, more venerated. O'Connor will have none of it. Later, in a scene of deserved comeuppance, poor Sally Poker has a nightmare in which she is calling out, "See him! See him!" and when she turns around, the general is sitting behind her naked in his wheelchair, with a "terrible expression on his face."[12]

Like many of us, O'Connor suggests, General Sash has forgotten the simple fact of his own mortality and has lived a frivolous and pointless life, allowing himself to be used to summon up a lost cause that has become even more "lost" by the community's foolish veneration of it. O'Connor's Irish ancestry and Catholicism would seem to ally her with fellow Georgian Margaret Mitchell, whose *Gone With the Wind* had become by the early 1950s the South's (and the world's) most revered narrative of the Civil War. O'Connor was acutely aware of this fact, especially as she was urged by her mother to write another *Gone With the Wind*. "A Late Encounter" may be read as O'Connor's retort to Mitchell's popularity, which O'Connor disdained. In response to the obsession of her region with Mitchell's novel, O'Connor eschewed material about "the war." For O'Connor, only the Incarnation, the divine entry into human history, gives meaning to history. General Sash hears the graduation speaker offer up a garbled version of George Santayana's popular admonition "Those who do not learn from the past are doomed to repeat it": "If we forget our past . . . we won't remember our future and it will be as well for we won't have one"[13]—gobbledygook that illustrates the chaos of General Sash's life. For O'Connor, the acknowledgment of guilt, both individual and communal, and the recognition of the need for forgiveness are essential to a fully realized humanity. This wildly comic story marks the only time O'Connor will significantly use the Civil War in her work.

A second story from the 1955 collection, "The Displaced Person," contains O'Connor's most extensive use of World War II and the Holocaust. The title character, Mr. Guizac, is a Pole who has been displaced by the German invasion and, to Mrs. McIntyre's initial delight, relocated with his family to her southern farm. Inordinately pleased by Mr. Guizac's industry and hard work that make him far superior to her white tenants and the African Americans, Mrs. McIntyre believes Mr. Guizac to be her "salvation."[14] With that terribly ironic appellation, O'Connor goes on to imply that Mrs. McIntyre is Hitlerian in outlook; she has no understanding of or compassion for the Guizac family, merely observing that "one fellow's misery is another fellow's gain."[15] She sees Mr. Guizac solely in terms of his value as a productive worker on the farm, just as she does all of her workers. Mrs. McIntyre is therefore horrified when Mr. Guizac seriously disrupts her understanding of the way things work on "her" place by attempting to arrange a marriage between his cousin in a concentration camp to Sulk, one of "her" black workers, to free the girl from the camp and certain death. Feeling completely victimized, Mrs. McIntyre realizes that she will have to fire the best worker she has ever had. To her credit, however, she has great difficulty in firing Mr. Guizac. Weeks pass as she struggles with her conscience: "This is my place," she tries to reassure herself. "I say who will come here and who won't," she continues. "I am not responsible for the world's misery."[16]

Mrs. McIntyre's foil in her willful ignorance of "the world's misery" is the ignorant and sly Mrs. Shortley, who, in the first third of the narrative, fears the success of the Guizacs, who threaten her own family's place on the farm. Supplying comic relief and exemplifying O'Connor's ear for the rhythms of southern speech, Mrs. Shortley has only the vaguest understanding of geography, history, and current world affairs, her slim knowledge deriving from newsreels. Her grasp of cultural and linguistic difference is so weak that, upon the arrival of the Guizacs, she observes to Mrs. McIntyre, "They can't talk," adding, "You reckon they'll know what colors even is?"[17] She remembers the newsreel she has seen "of a small room piled high with bodies of dead naked people all in a heap, their arms and legs tangled together, a head thrust in here, a head there, a foot, a knee, a part that should have been covered up sticking out, a hand raised clutching nothing."[18] She realizes that this "kind of thing . . . was happening every day in Europe where they had not advanced as in this country" and imagines that the Guizacs, "like rats with typhoid fleas, could have carried all those murderous ways over the water with them directly to this place."[19] The hilarious Mrs. Shortley in her ignorance and fear indeed reflects the ignorance and fear of Mrs. McIntyre herself, who, in her position of power, also does not perceive the humanity and suffering of the Guizacs. Proud and superior, Mrs. McIntyre is forced to move from a selfish, self-serving, and fragmented view of humanity to one of wholeness and community.

O'Connor's personal library contains several books by the Swiss Jewish convert to Catholicism Max Picard. Picard's *Hitler in Our Selves* (1947) is especially apposite to O'Connor's understanding of history. Picard explains that Hitler's rise to power was the result of a fragmented, distracted modern consciousness, tragically dissociated by its increasing reliance on technology and by the ensuing chaos of modern urban life. Both technology and urbanization disguise the heart's emptiness. Picard writes that the radio "perceives, registers, and judges" for the individual, that it "suspend[s]" the "distinction between the momentary and the permanent," and that the factory-made tool, the machine, "threatens to destroy."[20] The tractor in "The Displaced Person" figures in both the success of Mrs. McIntyre's farm under Mr. Guizac's tenure and in his death (his murder, as it were). In fact, to Mrs. McIntyre, Mr. Guizac himself might as well be another well-run machine.

Images of the fragmented and of discontinuity are present throughout "The Displaced Person," in repeated references to the piles of bodies of Holocaust victims in Mrs. Shortley's memories of the newsreels and in her important "vision": "The children of wicked nations will be butchered. . . . Legs where arms should be, foot to face, ear in the palm of hand."[21] These newsreel images capture the most horrifying catastrophe of her time, but the ignorant Mrs. Shortley does not understand it. Similarly, her employer, Mrs. McIntyre, values people solely in terms of their usefulness to her. She has Hitler within herself; she will not recognize the humanity of the people with whom she lives and on whom she depends for her farm's success. They are only hands and feet, obedient to her will. As Picard notes, "With the Nazis, man counted solely according to his efficiency, solely as fuel for the efficiency-machine per se. That machine had to function; it was immaterial what it burned up and whether it was beast or man or God."[22] The world of the momentary and the efficient has no eyes to see, according to Picard; "the man of the instant lacks the steady look; he merely blinks."[23] Moreover, "he lives in a state of nothingness; he is an empty zero, he rants, he commands, he relies on slogans."[24]

Although these descriptions of the Hitlerian "zero" may seem unrelated to Mrs. McIntyre, struggling to manage her farm help, she reflects Picard's description of the "dictatorship of the command" that was Hitler.[25] In a Hitlerian economy, language itself is degraded, and actions therefore have no meaning:

> It is because they are uncontrolled by the word that these actions are horrible. They are without sense because they are beyond the Logos, and so they try to find some sense in themselves, in action, that is. Action must follow upon action, each to give sense to its predecessor, each to explain the other; that is why action is incessantly heaped upon action.
>
> . . . [The command] appears as the magical word by which anything can be performed, and Hitler appeared as the great magician who, by one word, conjured action upon action or rather forced them out of their secret abodes, which were known only to Hitler. This appeared as something superhuman.[26]

To her spiritual credit, Mrs. McIntyre is for a time reluctant to fire Mr. Guizac. Weeks after Mr. Shortley has returned to the farm, Mr. Guizac is still there. When Mrs. McIntyre finally believes she has the will to fire the displaced person, she allows the machine to remove her "problem." Appropriately and tragically, Mrs. McIntyre's last image of Mr. Guizac alive is of "his legs lying flat on the ground" beneath the tractor, the smaller one of the two on the farm. Mr. Shortley, meanwhile, has backed out the larger tractor from the shed, and when Mrs. McIntyre, Mr. Shortley, and Sulk hear the brake slip, the tractor is described (in what could be Max Picard's own phrasing) as "calculating its own path,"[27] as though it had life and will. Only the three onlookers have life and will and the capacity to save Mr. Guizac's life, but they refuse to speak, their silent complicity taking care of the "problem." The implicit allusion to Hitler's extermination of the Jews could not be more obvious.

Picard writes that, despite the modern emphasis on the momentary, there is another kind of "moment which is altogether different." Indeed, "this great moment . . . lifted out of the course of the commonplace, this moment of truth during which we are confronted with eternity" is what O'Connor would surely have called "the moment of grace."[28] Mrs. McIntyre experiences just such a moment when she recognizes what Picard might call "the Hitler" in herself, when she sees that she has failed to acknowledge Mr. Guizac's sacred humanity. Thus she is most profoundly displaced by the fact of her own participation in the Fall. The place that she has claimed as her own, the farm, is not hers, nor are the human lives in her employ. In a parody of the disunity and fragmentation with which she has viewed her employees, Mrs. McIntyre is beset by "a nervous affliction," one leg becomes "numb," and "her hands and head [begin] to jiggle." Later, her vision "grows steadily worse," and she "[loses] her voice altogether."[29] Deliberately emphasizing the collapse of Mrs. McIntyre's "parts," O'Connor dramatizes both the physical and spiritual breakdown of the protagonist, a curious mirroring of the disconnected arms and legs of the Holocaust victims in the newsreels. At the story's conclusion we are told that Mrs. McIntyre's sole visitor is the old priest, who feeds the peacock and instructs the mute (and perhaps uncomprehending) Mrs. McIntyre in "the doctrines of the Church."[30]

At the time of the publication of her first book, *Wise Blood*, O'Connor was back in Milledgeville, having been forced to return home in 1950 because of the onset of lupus. She would spend the rest of her short life at Andalusia farm with her mother, completing her best work there. The return was clearly a profound adjustment for O'Connor, although none of her letters are self-pitying. Readers of these letters are usually stunned to find so little mention of her debilitating illness and to discover that, in instances in which she does allude to it, she often finds humor in her condition, which was a roller-coaster ride for the last fourteen years of her life. The steroids that she took caused her bones to deteriorate, necessitating the use of crutches. Photographs of the author in the last decade of her life often show her thinning hair and moon-shaped face, also the result of her medications. Nevertheless, her adjustment to life on the farm with Regina was swift. Many commentators believe that the return to her own "postage stamp" of central Georgia was completely salutary for her fiction, as Faulkner's return to Oxford had been for his mature work. In Milledgeville and Baldwin County, O'Connor found her material and her true voice. Although she lived in a time of much political and social change in the South and in the United States—years marked by the Cold War, the 1954 *Brown v. Board of Education* decision mandating school desegregation, the beginnings of the civil rights movement, the rise of Martin Luther King Jr. and his philosophy of nonviolent civil disobedience, the increasing presence in the South of the Ku Klux Klan, the election of the nation's first Catholic president, John F. Kennedy in 1960, and Kennedy's assassination in 1963—O'Connor rarely alluded to these events in her fiction. Front and center in her work are always the local, the bizarre, and the obsessed to demonstrate the spiritual numbness—the profound nihilism—of her day.

Unlike her Georgia contemporary Lillian Smith, who boldly took on the racist and segregationist society of the South, O'Connor never took a public stand on political and social issues. O'Connor had learned the New Critics' lesson well: fiction with the purpose of social change was usually inferior art. Her high standards, set by her literary mentors John Crowe Ransom, T. S. Eliot, Austen Warren, Allen Tate, Caroline Gordon, and Robert Penn Warren, were based on the premise that art must never serve temporal causes. In this view, she also followed another of her masters, James Joyce, even relying on his concept of a narrative's epiphanic moment to create her idea of the moment of grace.

Joyce's *Dubliners* and *A Portrait of the Artist as a Young Man* were profoundly influential on O'Connor's fiction. In *A Portrait* Stephen Daedalus proposes a notion of art as static, not kinetic; art moves beyond easy appeal to the emotions toward a transcendent radiance (consonantia). Clearly indebted to Thomas Aquinas for this aesthetic, Joyce had nonetheless wrenched himself free of the Roman Catholic Church and, unlike O'Connor, believed that artistic freedom could exist only apart from the Church. Joyce was, however, haunted by the Church for the most of his life. O'Connor, on the other hand, used the epiphanic moment as the character's opportunity for divine grace, as is evident in the grandmother's revelation at the conclusion of "A Good Man Is Hard to Find" and Ruby Turpin's life-changing vision in "Revelation."

Yet O'Connor does indeed have a cause, albeit one expressed for the most part with great artistry and subtlety: our human need for God. She would not have viewed religious conviction as in any way similar to a political or social agenda, so deeply immersed was she throughout her life in the tenets of her Catholic faith. Political and social allegiance are temporary and transient; religious belief is concerned with the nontemporal, the eternal. O'Connor would never have espoused the social gospel movement that came to prominence in Christianity shortly after her death.

O'Connor's privately held conservatism was of a piece with that of Russell Kirk, a convert to Catholicism whose popular book *The Conservative Mind* (1953) O'Connor owned and admired. Kirk and O'Connor met in 1955 at the home of Brainerd and Fanny Cheney in Smyrna, Tennessee, and although they never became close friends, each greatly respected the other. Kirk was an admirer of Edmund Burke and observes that Burke never used the word "conservative," preferring instead to speak of "preservation," a term that signaled to Burke and later to Kirk the necessity of guarding "the heritage of civilization."[31] Conservatives adhere to the principle that "a transcendent moral order exists" to which society should try to "conform" itself; that "the principles of social continuity" should be upheld, with "necessary change" being "gradual and discriminatory"; that the "principle of prescription," that is "of things established by immemorial usage," should be upheld; that the "principle of prudence" should be adopted in all public measures; that the "principle of variety," by which the diversity of civilization be maintained by the survival of "orders and classes, differences in material condition, and many sorts of inequality," with the observation that "the only true forms of equality" exist "before a just court of law" and at "the Last Judgment"; and, finally, that "the principle of imperfectibility" chastens us to recognize man's inability to create a "perfect social order."[32] That this last principle echoes the Christian doctrine of original sin is no accident. Kirk, a zealous Catholic convert, criticizes the "liberals and idealists" who believe they can achieve a perfect social order.

O'Connor's fictional presentation of politically and socially conservative ideas is, however, more complicated than Kirk's influence might suggest. To be sure, O'Connor's intent in reminding us of our mortal weakness is essentially theological. For example, while it is perfectly possible to read "Everything That Rises Must Converge," "The Lame Shall Enter First," and "The Enduring Chill" as critical of secular efforts to "engineer" social change, when we look closely at these works, we recognize that O'Connor's satirical object is not the efforts themselves but the egotistical and self-serving characters whose motives for social change are often juvenile, irresponsible, and even dangerous.

In "Everything That Rises Must Converge," O'Connor confronts the changing South and especially the civil rights movement, although her intent is not
political. Julian, the protagonist, is reluctantly escorting his doting mother on
the bus to her weight-loss class at the YWCA. Feeling superior to and deeply re-
sentful of his mother, he considers her clinging to her southern past and to her
family, appropriately named the Godhighs, to be provincial and embarrassing.
At the outset of the trip, he decides that he will teach her a lesson, entertaining
the fantasy that he will introduce a black woman to her as the woman he loves.
O'Connor here alludes to a common fear among white southerners after the
1954 Supreme Court decision that miscegenation would be the inevitable result
of school desegregation. However, the childishness of Julian's desire to shock
his mother is evident early in the story; his liberalism, in fact, derives from his
own unhappiness at having no family fortune and no future and simultaneously
from his wish to feel morally superior to his mother. Charity begins at home; we
understand that Julian does not have a charitable and loving heart, but rather,
a crippled and mean-spirited one. His mother may appear to us as foolish and
benighted, but she at least has loved and believed in her ne'er-do-well son despite his arrogance and pretension. The conclusion of Julian's journey is a tragic
one; he, not his mother, learns the profoundest lesson of all. As he watches
her collapse on the sidewalk, presumably from a stroke, he knows that he is
"postpon[ing] from moment to moment his entry into the world of guilt and
sorrow."[33] But he will enter that realm and soon. O'Connor suggests that Julian
is a phony liberal, not necessarily that liberalism in itself is wrong.

A similar situation occurs at the center of "The Enduring Chill," in which Asbury bears striking resemblance to Julian: dependent on his mother, to whom
he feels intellectually and cultural superior, Asbury is a foolish ne'er-do-well
who presumes an artistic sensibility but who hasn't yet come to terms with who
he really is. Asbury wants to dramatize the tragedy of his imminent death by
summoning a sophisticated Jesuit priest with whom he can truly communicate
and by engaging in "communion" with the two African Americans who work
for his mother on the farm. Again we detect in the background of this narrative
the social change effected by the civil rights movement; O'Connor mercilessly
attacks Asbury's presumed sophistication and liberalism and reveals him to be
a hollow, cowardly man. As I and others have observed,[34] O'Connor's model
for both Julian and Asbury is, in part, her closest liberal friend, Maryat Lee, a
southern transplant to New York City who was active in attempts to achieve
equal rights for African Americans. O'Connor also indulges in a bit of self-
indictment in these stories, especially as she was forced, because of her illness,
to return home to Milledgeville to live with her mother. One frequently finds

such self-chastisement in O'Connor, from the characterization in "Good Country People" of Joy-Hulga Hopewell, who possesses both a PhD in philosophy and a wooden leg (the two oddly linked in her moment of grace) to Asbury in "The Enduring Chill."

In "The Lame Shall Enter First," the appropriately named Sheppard, a social worker, is a version of the fervent social scientist Rayber who appeared in *The Violent Bear It Away* (1960). Sheppard is the genuine article, a social "engineer" unable to face the grief and neediness of his son, Norton, who has just lost his mother. Instead, Sheppard seeks to provide a dangerously bright, clubfooted delinquent, Rufus Johnson, with secular enlightenment and opportunity. Sheppard is determined to find a proper-fitting shoe for the clubfoot, introduce both boys to the wonders of science through the purchase of a microscope and a telescope, and attempt to debunk Rufus Johnson's fundamentalist religious upbringing and save both boys from what he considers childish superstition. However, as is the case with Julian and Asbury and Rayber in *The Violent Bear It Away*, the worldly, presumably sophisticated atheist receives the lesson in humility and human limitation. While this lesson may seem to be a warning against the arrogance of human attempts at social change, it is more particularly a caution against human pride itself, the human presumption that, by our own unaided efforts, we can effect significant and lasting change. In this respect, O'Connor has affinities with both Nathaniel Hawthorne and Joseph Conrad, two writers influential to her work. In Hawthorne's "The Birthmark," for instance, we find a similar emphasis on the foolishness of human attempts at perfection. In Conrad's *Heart of Darkness*, a novel with a decidedly more political cast than "The Birthmark," Conrad offers a compelling admonition about the limits of human "civilization," casting doubt on inflated ideas of human potential and disregarding the darkness of much human motivation and behavior.

In 1960 O'Connor was approached by the nuns at Our Lady of Perpetual Help Cancer Home in Atlanta to write the story of Mary Ann, a twelve-year-old child with a disfiguring malignancy on her face. Wary of such a task, O'Connor suggested that the sisters write the story themselves; she would provide editorial assistance and an introduction. One of the most revelatory of O'Connor's works, the introduction to *A Memoir of Mary Ann* unequivocally states the author's disdain for the doctrine of human perfectibility. In a full examination of the mystery of human suffering, especially the suffering of children, O'Connor clearly separates herself from all purely humanist attempts to "solve" the problem and offers insight into her creation of those "social engineers" Sheppard and Rayber. Such people are "detached from the source of tenderness,"[35] that is to say, Christ, and without that connection to the One who is the standard for all love and giving, their charitable works can become poison. Noting that one of the arguments of our time against the goodness of God uses the suffering of children to discredit belief (Camus's Dr. Rieux, Dostoevsky's Ivan Karamazov), O'Connor writes that "in this popular pity, we mark our gain in sensibility and our loss in vision": "If other ages felt less, they saw more, even though they saw with the blind, prophetical, unsentimental eye of acceptance, which is to say, of faith. In the absence of this faith now, we govern by tenderness. It is a tenderness which, long since cut off from the person of Christ, is wrapped in theory. When tenderness is detached from the source of tenderness, its logical outcome is terror. It ends in forced labor camps and in the fumes of the gas chamber."[36] This bold and haunting statement is key to understanding O'Connor's spirituality and, by extension, her political conservatism.

From our twenty-first-century vantage point, we might expect Flannery O'Connor, a white woman writer from a relatively privileged background, to have acquiesced to the social roles assigned to a woman of her class and situation, and in her public behavior, O'Connor was generally perceived to toe the line of gentility and manners. However, in her private correspondence and in her published writing, O'Connor often resisted prescribed female roles; her letters often offer scathing attacks on the encoded behavior for white southern womanhood. When she was forced to attend tea parties and receptions, she was reportedly quiet, at times even churlish. Yet her attitude is complicated; for example, O'Connor's private penchant for the casual and comfortable as opposed to the socially acceptable but often superficial (if not hypocritical) is in some measure contradicted by the emphasis in her prose on the necessity for stability and order in traditional society. Following the lead of Russell Kirk, she wrote in her essays of the importance of a mannered society (see especially "The Fiction Writer and His Country" and "The Catholic Novelist in the Protestant South"), believing that the established customs of such a hierarchy maintained a necessary, if not necessarily admirable, balance and stability. Perhaps we might conclude that O'Connor preferred the idea of tea parties and formal receptions to the reality of such events.

In this same way, O'Connor adhered to the unwritten codes of behavior of both her patriarchal society and her patriarchal Church. She saw no problem with the treatment of women in the Roman Catholic Church, never questioning the sexism of that institution. As I have argued more extensively elsewhere, O'Connor never seemed to grasp that the patriarchal church throughout history viewed women as inferior, unclean, and even dangerous.[37] Had O'Connor, for example, read her Georgia contemporary Lillian Smith's *Killers of the Dream* (1947)—and there is no evidence whatsoever that she did—she might have been led to consider the tangled knot of racism, religion, and sexuality in the South. When asked by Betty Hester and Maryat Lee to consider feminism, O'Connor shrugged off the subject. In response to Betty Hester's suggestion that the Catholic Church stifled women, O'Connor writes, "Don't say the Church drags around this dead weight [sexism], just say the Rev. So&So drags it around, or many Rev. So&Sos. The Church would as soon canonize a woman as a man and I suppose has done more than any other force in history to free women."[38] To be sure, O'Connor is writing these words in the mid-1950s, a time when few women were speaking out about women's issues and well before the second wave of feminism in the twentieth century. However, that this thoughtful woman argues that the Church has been liberating to women, that, in fact, no other institution has "freed" them more completely, certainly seems misguided to some readers.

The spiritual journey as it is depicted in western culture is usually a male one, and it is perhaps not surprising that O'Connor's protagonists in her two novels of spiritual quest are male. Her chief literary influences were male writers— Hawthorne, Conrad, Flaubert, James, Eliot, Joyce, Faulkner—whose views of women were often reduced to the stereotypical polarities of the virgin and the whore. Though O'Connor claims to have read the modernist women writers— Dorothy Richardson, Virginia Woolf, and Djuna Barnes, for example—she dismisses them as "the nuts."[39] Furthermore, in her published work O'Connor appears to have often adopted male writers' view of woman as temptress or woman as flesh. However, in the unpublished drafts of *Wise Blood*, Sabbath, the wife of Hazel in this version, is the visionary whose "spells" of revelation cause Hazel to lock her in their apartment. Sabbath's role changes completely in the published novel, in which she is reduced to ancillary status and, as temptress, is merely one of the obstacles in Hazel's journey to salvation, the familiar male narrative frame in western literature. O'Connor (like many of us who grew up female in the mid-twentieth century) unconsciously accepted the archetype of the journey to enlightenment as that of the hero. This is what O'Connor's culture and her religion taught.

In her short fiction, on the other hand, O'Connor's satire is directed at both male and female, and often females are granted the opportunity for grace. Perhaps, however, the short stories do not present the archetypal spiritual journey but are, rather, comically satiric attacks on smugness and pride. As many critics have observed, southern attitudes emphasizing the need for a southern white woman to "do pretty" are harshly satirized; Joy/Hulga Hopewell ("Good Country People"), Sally Virginia Cope ("A Circle in the Fire"), and the child protagonist of "A Temple of the Holy Ghost," all spirited and rebellious females, defy the status quo. As much as O'Connor ridiculed the popularity and sentimentality of *Gone With the Wind*, some of her own female characters are as "contrary" and strong-willed as Scarlett O'Hara.[40]

The social ideas of Flannery O'Connor were in large measure a product of her place and time in history. She breathed in the air of a racist society, she was not above the use of the "n" word in her private correspondence, and she certainly followed the teachings of the patriarchal Roman Catholic Church. To make these observations, however, is in no way to diminish O'Connor's brilliance as a writer; indeed, it would appear the height of anachronistic condescension to charge O'Connor with a lack of feminist insight. O'Connor saw by the light of her Catholic faith, which underlies all of her published writing. As she wrote to John Lynch in 1955, "I feel that if I were not a Catholic, I would have no reason to write, no reason to see, no reason ever to feel horrified or even to enjoy anything. . . . I have never had the sense that being a Catholic is a limit to the freedom of the writer, but just the reverse."[41] If the stringency of O'Connor's belief strikes us as anomalous or as even medieval, we can be only more dazzled by the power of her imagination within those confining limits.

NOTES

1. Flannery O'Connor, *Collected Works*, ed. Sally Fitzgerald (New York: Library of America, 1988), 806.

2. Brad Gooch, *Flannery: A Life of Flannery O'Connor* (New York: Little Brown, 2009), 27.

3. See O'Connor's unpublished letters to Maryat Lee in the Flannery O'Connor Collection, Russell Library, Georgia College and State University, Milledgeville, and her unpublished letters to Betty Hester in Archives and Special Collections in Woodruff Library, Emory University, Atlanta.

4. Flannery O'Connor, *The Habit of Being: Letters of Flannery O'Connor*, ed. Sally Fitzgerald (New York: Farrar, Straus and Giroux, 1989), xix. See also Ralph Wood, "Where Is the Voice Coming From? Flannery O'Connor on Race," *Flannery O'Connor Bulletin* 22 (1994): 90–118; and Sally Fitzgerald, "Letter to the Editor," *Flannery O'Connor Bulletin* 23 (1995): 175–82.

5. O'Connor, *Collected Works*, 43.

6. Ibid., 212.

7. Ibid., 216.

8. Ibid., 230.

9. Ibid., 231.

10. Ibid.

11. Ibid., 253.

12. Ibid.

13. Ibid., 260.

14. Ibid., 294.

15. Ibid.

16. Ibid., 315.

17. Ibid., 287.

18. Ibid.

19. Ibid.

20. Max Picard, *Hitler in Our Selves*, trans. Heinrich Hauser (Hinsdale, Ill.: Regnery, 1947), 58, 59, 63.

21. O'Connor, *Collected Works*, 301.

22. Picard, *Hitler in Our Selves*, 73.

23. Ibid., 81.

24. Ibid.

25. Ibid., 95.

26. Ibid., 94–95.

27. O'Connor, *Collected Works*, 325.

28. Picard, *Hitler in Our Selves*, 66; O'Connor, *Habit of Being*, 367.

29. O'Connor, *Collected Works*, 326.

30. Ibid., 327.

31. Russell Kirk, *The Essential Russell Kirk: Selected Essays*, ed. George A. Panichas (Wilmington, Del.: Intercollegiate Studies Institute, 2007).

32. Ibid., 7, 8, 9.

33. O'Connor, *Collected Works*, 500.

34. See Sarah Gordon, *Flannery O'Connor: The Obedient Imagination* (University of Georgia Press, 2000).

35. Ibid., 830.

36. Ibid., 830–31.

37. Gordon, *Flannery O'Connor*, chaps. 4–5.

38. O'Connor, *Habit of Being*, 168.

39. Ibid., 98–99.

40. See a fuller discussion of this in Gordon, *Flannery O'Connor*, 204–10.

41. O'Connor, *Habit of Being*, 114.

Coretta Scott King

(1927–2006)

Legacy to Civil Rights

GLENN T. ESKEW

❀ ❀ ❀

World renowned for her human rights activities during and after the modern civil rights struggle, Coretta Scott King created a lasting legacy by establishing the process through which the nonviolent movement is memorialized in annual ceremonies, monuments, and institutes. Her vision resulted in the Martin Luther King Jr. Center for Nonviolent Social Change in Atlanta and the King national holiday observed every January in the United States. More than anyone else, Coretta Scott King deserves credit for the memorialization of the movement that propagates a new ideology of tolerance in America. Her tireless devotion to the cause of social justice as symbolized in the life of her martyred husband resulted in the first official civil rights commemoration and codified the ritual whereby nonviolence would be recalled through ceremonies celebrating diversity in America. Coretta Scott King's upbringing, the training she received as a student, her role as wife and mother, and her activities on behalf of social justice before the death of her husband prepared her for the leadership role she played after 1968 promoting nonviolent social change at home and abroad.[1]

A native of Heiburger, Alabama, Coretta grew up in the Black Belt, where plantation owners and small farmers raised cotton. In the two-room house of Obadiah Scott, his wife, Bernice McMurry, gave birth to Coretta on April 27, 1927. The newborn joined an older sister, Edythe, and then a younger brother, Obie, as the couple's only children. On the farm, the family raised foodstuffs, from vegetables to livestock, and the cash crop cotton, which Coretta learned to chop and pick, helping neighbors during the fall harvest for extra money to pay for school. She was surrounded by extended family who farmed and timbered, African Americans who were independent landowners.[2]

As members of Mount Tabor African Methodist Episcopal Zion Church, the paternal Scott and maternal McMurry families exposed Coretta to a traditional culture of Protestant religion she embraced. In her youth she looked forward to attending church services on Sundays as a weekly social occasion, and the experience instilled in her a genuine religious conviction.[3] At great sacrifice the Scott family paid the tuition for the children to attend good schools, for Coretta's mother advised: "You get an education and try to be somebody. Then you won't have to be kicked around by anybody and you won't have to depend on anyone for your livelihood—not even on a man." When Coretta was old enough she joined her sister at Lincoln High School in Marion. Founded by freed slaves in 1867 and supported by the northern American Missionary Association, Lincoln boasted of an integrated faculty—half black and half white—that taught a rigorous curriculum of college prep courses. Of the white teachers, all but one came from the North. They lived in integrated housing, which local white people in the Black Belt town found scandalous, despising them as "radicals and 'nigger lovers'" according to Coretta, who saw them as "brave and dedicated." The music teacher recognized the quality of Coretta's singing and gave her voice lessons. The musical programs at Lincoln provided a model Coretta Scott King used in her Freedom Concerts of prose and song performed years later to raise money for the movement. At Lincoln she experienced the "beloved community" later described by her future husband, Dr. Martin Luther King Jr.[4]

Lincoln High School arranged for its chorus to tour colleges in the Midwest, thereby introducing the Scott girls to educational opportunities outside the South. Sister Edythe integrated Antioch College in Yellow Springs, Ohio, and Coretta followed in 1945. Founded by the great educator Horace Mann, the liberal arts institution encouraged students to "be ashamed to die until you have won some victory for humanity." Coretta Scott took the words to heart. As one of the only African Americans at Antioch, she dealt with the difficulties of desegregating society while developing an "understanding of [her] own personal worth" achieved through the college's program based "on the total development of the individual." As she recalled, "Antioch's pioneering, experimental approach to educational problems reaffirmed my belief that individuals as well as society could move toward the democratic ideal of brotherhood."[5]

Attending Antioch during World War II, Coretta Scott met people who, through their own witness for social justice, awoke in her a human consciousness that steadily expanded to the universal. She supported conscientious objectors who bravely opposed military service, and she joined the college chapter of the National Association for the Advancement of Colored People (NAACP).

CORETTA SCOTT KING
at the Democratic National Convention, New York City, 1976.
Library of Congress.

During former U.S. vice president Henry Wallace's 1948 presidential campaign, Scott attended the Progressive Party's national convention as a student delegate and Young Progressive, revealing her commitment to radical causes that never wavered throughout her life. She worked in a college-sponsored settlement house in the slums of Cleveland, roomed with white girls, and dated a Jewish man. She confronted racial discrimination in the North when student teaching at an elementary school. And at Antioch under the training of its black director of music she began to seriously study singing.[6]

After graduating in 1951, Coretta Scott received admission to the New England Conservatory of Music in Boston. She wanted a stage career like that of Paul Robeson, whom she had heard at Antioch. A scholarship covered tuition, but not room and board, so Coretta worked part time for her landlady, being taught by Irish maids how to scrub the floors by hand. At the school she gave vocal recitals with the orchestra.[7]

A classmate shared Scott's phone number with a theology student named Martin Luther King Jr., who telephoned one evening. She took King's call and remembered his comments at first sounding like those of "a typical man" but with a "smoothness" and "intellectual jive" that she "enjoyed," at least enough to join him for lunch. On a wet January day in 1952 they met on a blind date, each putting on their best appearances, with Martin arriving in his new green Chevy and Coretta dressed stylishly in a light blue suit, black coat, and scarf. Her superficial dismissal that he was too short changed when he spoke and "radiated so much charm" that his looks improved. As the date ended and he drove her back to the conservatory, King confessed to a startled Coretta: "The four things that I look for in a wife are character, intelligence, personality, and beauty. And you have them all. I want to see you again." A relationship blossomed.[8]

A group of black graduate students studying in Boston that included Martin and Coretta began to socialize and discuss the intellectual ideas they confronted in class. Here they debated G. W. F. Hegel's dialectic, Karl Marx's critique of capitalism, and theological evaluations of industrialization, such as Walter Rauschenbusch's progressive social gospel and the corrective offered by Reinhold Niebuhr with his focus on humanity's selfishness and the unequal distribution of power in a capitalist society. King led these heady discussions, but Scott joined in the debate as the two mutually respected each other's opinions. She recalled, "I was impressed by the breadth of his mind," while Martin made it clear he did not "want a wife I can't communicate with." He described Coretta as "an attractive young singer whose gentle manner and air of repose did not disguise her lively spirit." A shared intellect and mutual understanding sustained them throughout their sixteen years of life together.[9]

While seemingly different, the young lovers came from similar backgrounds. King hailed from a prominent black middle-class family in Atlanta. Although his father, Mike King, descended from poor sharecroppers in Middle Georgia, his mother, Alberta Williams, came from the family of Reverend Adam Daniel Williams, the Baptist minister who had developed Ebenezer Baptist Church into one of the city's largest black congregations. His parents had married in 1926 and moved into the Williams household at 501 Auburn Avenue around the time that Mike King became the associate pastor of Ebenezer Baptist. Here the Kings gave birth to and raised their three children on black Atlanta's renowned "Sweet Auburn." After attending Atlanta's inferior segregated public schools, M. L. followed his older brother A. D. to Morehouse College, where their father and grandfather had studied. Martin then left Atlanta for Crozer Theological Seminary in Chester, Pennsylvania, and later attended Boston University's School of Theology for his doctorate.[10]

The young couple experienced resistance from King's family. During the summer of 1952, Martin returned to Atlanta to assist "Daddy King" in the pulpit, while Scott remained in Boston to study. She traveled to Atlanta in August to stay with her friend Mary Powell and attended Sunday services at Ebenezer, where she watched with pride as Martin ministered to the congregation that had ordained him a few years before. Meeting his family, Scott received a lukewarm reception, as "Daddy King" made clear he wanted his son to marry into one of Atlanta's better black families because they "have much to share and much to offer." With fight in her eyes, a determined Scott retorted, "I have something to offer too." The students returned to school. By November Martin informed his mother that "Coretta is going to be my wife." Traveling up to Boston, the parents confronted the lovers to break up the relationship, but Martin explained to his father: "She's the most important person to come into my life, Dad. I know you don't really approve, but this is what I have to do." On June 18, 1953, Daddy King officiated at the wedding of Martin and Coretta at the Scott's house in Marion.[11]

The newlyweds embarked on an unconventional marriage. Coretta had made it clear to Martin that while she would be the devoted wife, she wanted no part of a traditional patriarchal structure that relegated her to a subservient role in the relationship. She convinced Daddy King to drop from the wedding vows the commandment insisting wives be submissive to their husbands. Her prior misgivings regarding marriage to a minister had given way to an acceptance of the duties of pastor's wife. Back in Boston to complete their degrees, Coretta faced a difficult academic year because she had changed majors out of performance, requiring additional courses and teaching practice in the public schools, while Martin had to finish his doctoral dissertation and search for a pulpit. Within the household, King discussed job options with his new wife, and although he heard her desire to live in a North free from legal segregation, that did not prevent him from accepting an offer down South. In June 1954 Coretta graduated from the New England Conservatory of Music with a degree in music education. The next month the couple left Massachusetts for Alabama.[12]

Despite her misgivings, Coretta Scott King found life in Montgomery rewarding. As the minister's wife, she joined the music committee and co-chaired the cultural committee. King gave birth to their first child, Yolanda Denise, on November 17, 1955. Three weeks later a bus driver ordered Rosa Parks to relinquish her seat to a white passenger and then had her arrested for violating Montgomery's ordinance on segregated seating in public transportation. The act of civil disobedience prompted a protest that launched the modern civil rights movement.[13] During the tense and exciting year of the bus boycott that followed, Coretta offered Martin strong support and a welcome escape from the pressures of leading the Montgomery Improvement Association (MIA) as its president, thereby playing a crucial role in the success of the movement. It was she who called to him on that first day of the boycott, December 5, 1955, when black Montgomery pledged not to ride, "Martin, Martin, come quickly!" and then exclaimed about the bus that passed by the living room window, "Darling, it's empty!" Coretta was in that same room a month later visiting with a parishioner, Mary Lucy Williams, when vigilantes lobbed dynamite at the house in an attempt to blow it up and kill the family. The women heard the thud of the bomb on the porch and fled to the nursery in back when the explosion occurred. Coming from a mass meeting, King found the roof caved in and the windows shattered, but his wife and daughter, Yoki, and their friend safe. The assassination attempt unified the MIA behind a court case that once filed and carried through the appeals process resulted in the desegregation of Montgomery's buses on December 20, 1956.[14]

The success of the Montgomery bus boycott not only won Martin Luther King Jr. national praise as a new civil rights leader but also led to numerous speaking engagements for Coretta Scott King. Across the country she addressed church groups and performed at fundraisers. On December 6, 1956, she headlined an event for the New York–based group In Friendship on behalf of the MIA. Like the song and word performances she had staged at Lincoln High School years before, Coretta Scott King combined spirituals with a recitation on the bus boycott that ended with her declaration: "We are determined that there shall be a new Montgomery, a new Southland, yes, a new America, where freedom, justice, and equality shall become a reality for every man, woman, and child." Indeed, the couples' experiences had moved them from simply supporting the protest to becoming committed to human rights.[15]

The Kings joined with other civil rights leaders in plans to extend the non-violent struggle beyond Montgomery. On January 10 and 11, 1957, a hundred black pastors gathered at Atlanta's Ebenezer Baptist Church to organize a new regional protest group, and although more bombings in Montgomery forced Martin to miss the opening session, Coretta Scott King chaired the meeting, spoke to the delegates, and distributed the action items, with the outcome being the formation of the Southern Christian Leadership Conference (SCLC).[16]

Invitations to travel to Africa and India enabled the Kings to study firsthand nonviolence and the worldwide freedom fight against colonial rule. Newly elected President Kwame Nkrumah welcomed the Kings to Accra where they witnessed the transition of power from the British colony of the Gold Coast to the independent state of Ghana in 1957. The abject poverty they saw in Nigeria compromised any promise after imperialism. When the Friends Service Committee financed their travel to India in March 1959, the Kings arrived as pilgrims, meeting with Prime Minister Jawaharlal Nehru and discussing Gandhi's rejection of materialism, calls for tolerance, and teachings of satyagraha, or soul force. The Kings joined others in founding the Committee for a Sane Nuclear Policy (today known as Peace Action) in 1957.[17]

Returning to Montgomery, Martin tried to balance the demands placed on him by the newly organized SCLC with his responsibilities at Dexter Avenue Baptist Church while Coretta oversaw a growing family. The couple celebrated the birth of their first son, Martin Luther King III, on October 23, 1957. In 1960 the Kings moved back to Atlanta, where Daddy King arranged for Martin to copastor at Ebenezer while also leading the SCLC that had headquartered on Auburn Avenue.[18]

Still searching for its proper role, the SCLC scrambled to respond to the spontaneous demands for equal access symbolized by such protests as the sit-ins that broke out in 1960 and the Freedom Rides that followed in 1961. The media expected King, as a recognized civil rights leader, to participate in such demonstrations. Both Martin and Coretta did, often with ambiguous results, but they nonetheless revealed their commitment to the movement. When students planned a sit-in at Atlanta's premier lunch counter of Rich's Department Store in October 1960, they convinced Martin to join, and his arrest provoked a national response. After Georgia officials jailed King in the Reidsville state penitentiary, presidential candidate John F. Kennedy called Coretta to express his concern, while his brother and campaign manager Robert F. Kennedy negotiated with Georgia governor Ernest Vandiver to influence King's release. News of the telephone call to Coretta encouraged black voters to support Kennedy, who won the November election over Nixon by a slim margin. Thus inextricably linked together, the Kennedys and Kings began a decade that forever changed America.[19]

With Martin busy leading the civil rights campaigns in Albany and Birmingham, Coretta remained in Atlanta with their young children and their newborns. During the protests in Albany, she gave birth prematurely to Dexter Scott King on January 30, 1961. On March 28, 1963, the week before the Birmingham campaign began, she gave birth to Bernice Albertine King. With Yoki at seven and a half and Marty at five and a half, the thirty-five-year-old mother had her hands full. The frequent absence of their father strengthened her authority, and the children remained committed to their mother.[20]

Yet, Coretta Scott King added to her family obligations a full calendar of civil rights activities, including speaking engagements and concerts. In March 1962 she traveled to Geneva, Switzerland, for the Women's Strike for Peace where representatives from seventeen countries called for disarmament, and there she found the Soviet delegates more encouraging than the American diplomatic corps. Coretta believed that women had the power to unite the world for change, so subsequently she served on the Women's International League for Peace and Freedom. She accompanied her husband to Oslo, Norway, when he received the Nobel Peace Prize in 1964. Invitations in America sent her to cities outside the South, such as Cleveland and Cincinnati, Ohio. On November 14, 1964, she began a series of Freedom Concerts. The first occurred in New York, where she interpreted "The Story of the Struggle from 1955–1965" and sang spirituals such as "Walk Together, Children," along with songs such as "Witness," set by Hall Johnson; "No Crystal Stair," arranged by Francis Thomas; and Hamilton Forrest's "He's Got the Whole World in His Hands." These performances raised more than $50,000 for civil rights groups.[21]

Once her babies became toddlers, Coretta Scott King felt she could rejoin her husband on the frontlines of the civil rights struggle. She traveled to Selma in February 1965 as racial tensions escalated. When Malcolm X arrived unannounced to speak with Martin, who had just been arrested, Coretta met with him instead, and then took to her husband in jail the black Muslim's message of encouragement. The next month Coretta and Martin headed the Selma to Montgomery march as it wove through the downtown of Alabama's capital, and she recalled that upon seeing Dexter Avenue Baptist Church she felt her heart swell with pride over the distance traveled in the ten years since the bus boycott. The Kings participated in the Meredith March through Mississippi in 1966 as the southern movement splintered into factions. By then the SCLC had expanded its reach into the North.[22]

Emphasizing that white supremacy knew no region and that poverty accompanied racism, the Kings moved into a tenement building in the Chicago ghetto to underscore the need for fair housing and antipoverty programs. With children in tow the winter of 1966, the family settled into the slums as the SCLC organized a protest of poor housing conditions. On July 10, 1966, some fifty thousand people rallied at Soldier's Field, listened to speeches and the great Mahalia Jackson's singing, and marched with the Kings to Chicago's city hall to deliver their demands to Mayor Richard J. Daley. Federal reform followed with the Fair Housing Act of 1968, but the experience left the Kings feeling the extent of racism in America with its integral links to poverty and violence.[23]

The King family struggled with the materialism of life in a consumer society. Since their days debating Marxism in Boston, the couple had rejected the driving consumption of capitalism. In a 1965 interview in *Playboy* magazine, Martin renounced materialism, explaining that the struggle for freedom "is not one that should reward any participant with individual wealth and gain." Similarly, Coretta Scott King noted the young couple had failed to accumulate material goods such as wedding china when they first married. With children, however, her attitude changed, as she worried about their well-being. To provide a safe environment and a college preparatory education while also emphasizing integration, the parents placed their children in one of Atlanta's premier private schools. Yet the King family lived modestly, at first in a yellow house on Johnson Avenue that was to be demolished by the state to build Freedom Parkway, then in a brick ranch house that the couple bought in 1965 at 234 Sunset Avenue in the Vine City neighborhood adjacent to Atlanta University. Outwardly, the family appeared average, while inwardly they required personal assistance from domestic help typical of busy professionals. Increasingly, the Kings enjoyed the finer things in life such as nice clothes befitting the prosperous middle class.[24]

Since her days at Antioch, Coretta Scott King had questioned war, and with the growing conflict in Vietnam she spoke out in favor of peace. She joined Dr. Benjamin Spock and others as keynote speakers at the November 27, 1965, peace rally in Washington, D.C., that attracted 35,000 antiwar protesters. That year, Martin first voiced his opposition to the conflict in Southeast Asia, calling for negotiations, but criticism silenced him until his famous speech at Riverside Church against the Johnson Administration's prosecution of the war in 1967, an action that reaffirmed Coretta's position.[25]

Demonstrating how far the Kings had traveled in their intellectual journey for human rights, they proposed with the SCLC in 1968 a Poor People's Campaign to bring together impoverished blacks from the rural South and urban North, West Coast Latinos, Appalachian whites, and Native Americans. In a bid to transcend racism, these destitute people would descend on Washington, D.C., to pressure Congress to adopt federal policies that end poverty. A protest in Memphis by striking garbage men seeking a living wage crystallized the broader campaign and received the support of the SCLC. The day after Martin spoke at a mass meeting in Memphis, an assassin shot him dead as he stood on the balcony of the Lorraine Motel. In Atlanta with the children that April 4, 1968, Coretta Scott King received the news stoically, having steeled herself in anticipation of such an outcome. The foreboding did not lessen the pain felt by the family over the tragic loss. To many people, the sniper's bullet ended the era of reform.[26]

Within weeks of King's murder in Memphis, Coretta Scott King announced her intention to create a "living, productive" memorial out of the historic district where he had lived and worked that could honor the man while carrying on his message in a dual mission that since then other civil rights commemorations have followed. Three months after King's burial in Atlanta's South View Cemetery, a blue ribbon committee chaired by vice mayor Sam Massell convened to determine "how Atlanta can fittingly memorialize" its most famous son. Listening to the wishes of the widow, who wanted to focus on King's life and not his death, the committee recommended a memorial near King's birth home and Ebenezer Baptist Church. The area had suffered during the postwar decline of the urban center as affluent African Americans moved to Atlanta's west side suburbs. Massell's committee built on the nascent historic preservation movement then trying to save the nearby Victorian community of Inman Park by designating the adjacent neighborhood along Auburn Avenue as a "King Shrine Area." The committee's goal was to "preserve the character" of the black business district, which it recognized as "possessing historical significance." In addition, Massell asked Vice President Hubert Humphrey to select Atlanta as the site for any federal commemoration of King. Anticipating just such a possibility, Coretta Scott King expressed the desire that her husband's remains be reentombed in any memorial "the city or the nation may erect in Atlanta." Her efforts faced competition from other monuments, such as the King Memorial Chapel planned by Morehouse College that received $250,000 from the Rockefeller Fund in July 1968.[27]

Still in mourning, Coretta rejoined the movement. Within weeks of King's death she participated in the April 27, 1968, student-led antiwar march down Fifth Avenue in New York City, the Poor People's Campaign in Memphis, and the Charleston Hospital Strike, but the days of demonstrations seemed over. She kept her late husband's speaking engagements, telling thousands assembled before the Lincoln Memorial that women should rise up to save the soul of the nation. Harvard University invited her to speak, and she became the first woman to deliver its Class Day address. She traveled to Europe, preaching in St.

Paul's Cathedral in London, meeting the pope in Rome, and receiving awards in Italy and then India.[28]

Upon returning home, Coretta Scott King determined that building an institute in Atlanta designed to promote nonviolent social change would create the "living, productive" memorial she envisioned. Here she could rely on family members, especially her sister, Edythe Scott Bagley, and her sister-in-law, Christine King Farris, for support. Her attorney, Archer Smith, helped the King heirs settle their father's estate. Given that the family members had inherited King's property—both real and intellectual—they recognized the need to form a trust known as the King Estate that could own the property for them, handle issues of copyright, and determine licensing fees. Family members also saw the wisdom in organizing a nonprofit entity separate from the estate through which they could memorialize the man. Initially, Coretta Scott King named the nonprofit the Martin Luther King, Jr., Memorial Center and managed its activities from her basement at 234 Sunset Avenue. She served as president and chief executive officer while King's sister, Christine King Farris, a professor at Spelman College, served as treasurer. The nonprofit later became the Martin Luther King, Jr., Center for Non-violent Social Change, Incorporated, through which these two women dominated the memorialization effort in Atlanta.[29]

On the first anniversary of King's birthday after his death, Coretta Scott King inaugurated the King Day Celebration. Joined by her family, numerous civil rights leaders, and politicians, she called on Congress to declare the Monday closest to King's January 15 birthday a national holiday and thus recognize the slain civil rights leader in a fashion similar to that reserved for Presidents George Washington and Abraham Lincoln. Rather than another day off from work and an excuse for department store sales, Coretta Scott King envisioned the holiday as a national celebration of nonviolence. Four days after King's assassination, Michigan Congressman John Conyers had introduced legislation in the U.S. House of Representatives, and later that year in the U.S. Senate, Edward Brooke of Massachusetts had revived the issue by calling for a national commemoration. In support, the SCLC led a petition drive that collected three million signatures. Although the effort stalled at the federal level, individual states ratified legislation that officially observed the King holiday—Illinois in 1973, Connecticut and Massachusetts in 1974, and New Jersey in 1975. In time, the observance in Atlanta came to include a parade and a ritualistic service at Ebenezer Baptist Church where Coretta Scott King presided over dignitaries who spoke and where she delivered a "State of the Dream" address that evaluated race relations over the past year while charting a course for the future. As she explained, "I believe that the best way to commemorate Martin Luther King,

Jr.'s birthday is to recommit ourselves to his unfinished work for social and economic justice." Symbolically, the events recognized King's life, but the rhetoric focused on present-day concerns and agendas for the future.[30]

From the outset, Coretta Scott King understood the nation needed her martyred husband because his image suggested the movement's success in bringing about racial equality, and so she courted congressional support for a national holiday and federal funding for an Atlanta commemoration. Looking to Congress for help seemed odd given the family's belief that a larger conspiracy stretching back to Washington surrounded King's death. Nevertheless, the federal government played a key role in Coretta Scott King's plans to memorialize the man and his message. Wearing the mantle of the martyr's widow, Coretta Scott King approached potential donors such as the Nixon Administration, which declined to offer money, and the Ford Foundation, which gave the first gift in December 1969, money used to process and make available to scholars some of King's papers.[31]

To make a "living, productive" memorial, rather than a monument, Coretta Scott King favored a library and archive—similar to the conceptualized John F. Kennedy Presidential Library—that could promote the study of nonviolent approaches to reform. Hence she proposed a "depository" for King's papers, those she personally retained, those of his associates in the movement, and those held elsewhere. Coretta Scott King anticipated a building of striking design with an archive for scholarly study of Kingian nonviolence, space for exhibits, offices for herself and the King Center staff, an auditorium for lectures, and a suitable memorial space in which to entomb King's remains so that pilgrims might pay homage. Recognizing the need to concentrate the memorial around the historic sites on Auburn Avenue, she began buying property between Ebenezer Baptist Church and the birth home using money donated by well-wishers. She hired the minority architectural firm Bond-Ryder to design the King Center, and principal architect J. Max Bond proposed a complex of buildings on a memorial campus revolved around a new gravesite. On a somber King Day Celebration in January 1970, the family relocated the martyr's remains to a marble sarcophagus positioned adjacent to Ebenezer Baptist Church in the block-long section of the projected King Center. The crypt added a traditional monument to Atlanta's King Shrine Area.[32]

Three events in 1975 substantially advanced Coretta Scott King's vision. As part of its January 15 King Day Celebration, the family broke ground for the proposed administrative building and archive to be housed in its King Center complex. Several dignitaries participated, such as Atlanta's first black mayor, Maynard Jackson, who had been elected in the fall of 1973 in a showing of black political empowerment. Others present included former mayor Ivan Allen Jr.;

Jesse Hill of the Atlanta Life Insurance Company, who had headed the building committee that launched the $10 million capital campaign to pay for the
proposed building; and family friends Harry Belafonte, singer Marvin Gaye,
and celebrity boxer Muhammad Ali, who all participated in a fundraiser that
night. Also in January 1975 Coretta joined Mayor Jackson in unveiling plans
for a $2.8 million King Community Center funded with federal grants and a
$1 million donation from Coca-Cola's Robert W. Woodruff to be located across
Auburn Avenue from the King Center. Once completed, the city-owned facility
housed offices for Atlanta Legal Aid, a branch of the Atlanta Public Library, a
gymnasium and recreation room staffed by the city's parks department, and
a childcare program. Finally, the U.S. Department of the Interior announced
the listing of the King Birth Home on the National Register of Historic Places,
signifying federal recognition of the area. Increasingly, Coretta Scott King's abstract memorialization of nonviolence appeared real.[33]

As calls for a national holiday in honor of King grew, the King Center dedicated the Interfaith Peace Chapel that flanked the "permanent entombment of
Dr. King" in 1977. Four months later the King Estate completed its restoration
of the birth home, giving the house the appearance it had when King had lived
there from 1929 to 1941. The process of historic preservation pleased family
members, who arranged for the King Center staff to conduct interpretive tours
of the site. With the birth home, King's crypt, the reflecting pool, and the perpetual flame, the King Shrine Area became one of Atlanta's top tourist attractions.[34]

Yet Coretta Scott King's efforts drew opposition from movement veterans
who advocated social reforms and pushed the King Center to develop an activist agenda. Initially, she had been named the first woman to serve on the SCLC
board of directors, as she stepped in to fulfill her dead husband's schedule. But
given that, in the words of Andrew Young, "[the other board members] didn't
want her to play any kind of policy role in the organization," and they were
"incapable of dealing with a strong woman like Coretta, who was insisting on
being treated as an equal," she withdrew from the organization, as did several
of King's top aides, including Young. Those who remained, such as the Rev-
erends Joseph Lowery and Hosea Williams, "criticized Mrs. King for devoting
her time to creating a memorial center to her husband," rather than fighting to
end hunger and unemployment. Thus, by 1975, the SCLC staged protests that
disrupted wreath-laying ceremonies at King's grave and the groundbreaking of
the community center.[35]

Coretta Scott King responded directly to the antimemorial demonstrations.
In 1974 she helped assemble more than a hundred labor and business, civil
and women's rights, and religious groups behind economic opportunity into

a national coalition called the Full Employment Action Council, of which she served as co-chair. She stated, "I believe in jobs for people," then pushed the center to also schedule training seminars on civil disobedience. Voter Education Project Director John Lewis, the former chairman of the Student Nonviolent Coordinating Committee, headed the King Center's inaugural weeklong Summer Institute on Nonviolence and Social Change in July 1976. Held at the Gammon Theological Seminary, the institute attracted fifty participants and positive coverage in the media. Coretta Scott King modified the King Day Celebration to include a conference on a major social issue, selecting unemployment in 1976 and 1977 in order to "develop 'an agenda' for the nation." This resulted in her co-chairing a national committee that convinced Congress to adopt the Humphry-Hawkins Full Employment and Balanced Growth Act. With a social strategy for the King Day Celebration and a new summer institute on nonviolence, she had answered her critics and redoubled her efforts to both memorialize the movement and advocate for social and economic justice.[36]

Once Democrats regained control of the White House in 1976, Coretta Scott King found a receptive audience in Washington willing to support her objectives. President and Mrs. James E. Carter joined industrialist Henry Ford II at the October 1979 groundbreaking for the $8 million Freedom Hall centerpiece of the King Center with its auditorium, gift shop, and classrooms anchoring the corner of Boulevard and Auburn Avenues. An analysis by the *Atlanta Constitution* revealed Coretta Scott King's success while also pointing to serious problems in the management of the facility and the fulfillment of its mission. First and foremost, she had created "a thirteen million dollar complex of monuments and buildings in the heart of what the government officially calls a 'stricken area' surrounded by poor people.'" Before Ford's fundraising campaign for the $8 million, she had raised $6 million in public and private funds. The public saw the tangible results of donations in the form of brick and mortar contributions, yet the day-to-day expenses of running a civil rights memorial to nonviolent social change had proven far more costly and remained virtually invisible to the public. Officially, from 1968 to 1978 the King Center had paid Coretta Scott King a yearly salary of $1, a gesture similar to that of Martin Luther King's refusal to accept payment from the SCLC, but of course both organizations picked up any expenses incurred in the line of work. In reality, the King Center posted an annual budget of $750,000 in 1979. Income from rents and other investments, royalties, and speeches offset Coretta's cost-of-living expenses. As Dexter Scott King later recalled, "We watched it all come up out of nothing—the reflecting pool and arched, covered walkway known as 'Freedom Walkway.' Next the administration building went up, then adjacent to it, Freedom Hall.... The construction of the center was rewarding to Mother, because it was her insurance that her husband's message and spirit would endure."[37]

As if to recapture the movement, Coretta Scott King published a memoir in 1969, *My Life with Martin Luther King, Jr.*, and to promote nonviolent social change released another book in 1983, *The Words of Martin Luther King, Jr.* In response to an extensive interview that resulted in what Coretta recalled as "several paragraphs about what I was wearing and two muddled sentences that somehow managed to convey the opposite of what I actually said," adding, and "it wasn't the first time," she began publishing a syndicated column in 1985 carried by such newspapers as the *Boston Globe*, *Detroit Free Press*, *Dallas Morning News*, and *Los Angeles Times*.[38]

Demonstrating through actions her commitment to nonviolent social change, Coretta Scott King embraced a broad global agenda for human rights. During the Carter Administration she served as a public delegate to the United Nations. In 1983 she headed the Coalition of Conscience, which represented more than eight hundred civil and human rights organizations as they marked the twentieth anniversary of the March on Washington with the largest demonstration in the Capitol up to that time. Joined by three of her children on August 13, 1985, she picketed before the South African embassy in Washington, D.C., and suffered arrest, helping galvanize support for the divestment campaign against apartheid. The next year she traveled to South Africa and met Winnie Mandela, then wife of jailed activist Nelson Mandela. The dualism of the King Center's mission as memorial and center for social change enabled her to maintain such a politically engaged approach. Ostensibly "a memorial, research, and educational institution," it also served in her words as "a people's lobby for sanctions against South Africa, gun control, and amnesty for political prisoners." It worked "for nuclear disarmament, and for legislation to protect voting rights, to eliminate job discrimination, and to put people back to work."[39]

Searching for permanent funding, Coretta Scott King announced the goal of a $13.5 million endowment for the King Center, but although IBM and Coca-Cola loaned staff support, other corporations were less enthusiastic about contributing. An executive explained that Atlanta's Citizens & Southern Bank failed to donate because "they really don't have a tangible program coming out of there." Perhaps a more honest assessment would reveal disagreement over the activist agenda. Not only had the private sector expressed concerns about the King Center, but the public sector raised questions as well, as criticism of the family's handling of the historic site steadily increased.[40]

While the King Center's annual budget doubled between the 1970s and 1980s, internal reports decried "a serious cash flow problem" and "severe financial crisis." On the eve of President Carter's failed reelection bid, Congress authorized in October 1980 the Martin Luther King Jr. National Historic Site and Preservation District, initiating direct federal intervention over parts of the "King Shrine Area" that in time evolved into nearly complete control of the King memorial. On King Day in 1982, Coretta Scott King dedicated Freedom Hall and then retired the remaining $10 million debt on the buildings by 1984. With a reputation as Georgia's number 1 tourist attraction, drawing a half-million visitors in 1985, it would seem a success, but expenses outpaced revenues as the King Center turned over to the National Park Service tours of the Birth Home in 1984. With the announcement that Atlanta would host the Olympics, park officials recognized an opportunity to expand its role in the district beyond that of restoring historic shotgun houses, a fire station, running a visitor kiosk, and leasing out house tours. With support from Georgia's congressional delegation and Atlanta's political leadership, the National Park Service proposed in a 1986 report the building of a visitor's center on Auburn Avenue across from the King Center that could at last provide interpretation of the site, adequate bathrooms, and parking for tourists.[41]

Having successfully completed the construction of the King Center, Coretta Scott King turned her attention to gaining the national holiday in honor of Coretta and Martin's interpretation of nonviolence. A decade had passed since Conyers proposed his initial legislation, but with an endorsement by President Jimmy Carter, the bill finally reached a congressional committee for review in 1979. Voted out to the floor, it failed by five votes to garner the necessary two-thirds required to pass the House. Coretta Scott King redoubled her efforts, assisted by Stevie Wonder's 1980 hit "Happy Birthday." She presented to Congress a petition supporting the holiday signed by six million people. In the fall of 1983, U.S. Speaker Tip O'Neill pushed Conyers's legislation through the House of Representatives and—despite a filibuster by North Carolina's Jesse Helms—it passed the Senate. Although President Ronald Reagan had initially opposed the King Holiday, he signed Public Law 98-144 on November 2, 1983, in a Rose Garden ceremony attended by the King family. To promote the celebration, Congress authorized the Martin Luther King Jr. Federal Holiday Commission in 1984. Coretta arranged for Lloyd Davis, who through the U.S. Department of Housing and Urban Development had been assigned by the Carter Administration to work with the King Center, to oversee the holiday efforts. The first federal observance of King Day occurred on January 20, 1986, with President Reagan speaking in Washington and the Reverend Jesse Jackson in Atlanta. Congress renewed the commission's charter in 1989, but with its shoestring budget, Davis found completing objectives difficult. Despite some holdouts—

most notably Arizona and South Carolina, which waited until 1992 and 2000, respectively—most states and communities joined in the celebration of non-violent social change.[42]

Having accomplished the goals she set in 1968—securing the national holiday and creating a historic site that both memorializes the movement and promotes social and economic justice—Coretta Scott King decided in 1988 that it was time for a change in leadership at the King Center. The problems that remained—finding revenues to fund an endowment to keep the King Center open as a memorial site and to finance its programs—could be left to her successor. Since the beginning, the King family and its closest advisors had tightly controlled the board of directors. Unwilling to see the memorial fall into hands outside the family, Coretta called her children together in the fall of 1988 to discuss its future. With Yolanda involved in acting, Martin engaged in local politics, and Bernice in the ministry, only Dexter remained available, and he accepted the responsibility while expressing ideas of his own that he tried to implement following his installation in April 1989. Four months later, he resigned in frustration, leaving his mother to resume her role as president of the King Center.[43]

As an international human rights leader, Coretta Scott King often hosted foreign dignitaries when they visited Atlanta. In June 1990 she welcomed South Africa's Nelson Mandela to the city, awarding him the first Martin Luther King Jr. International Freedom Award; she returned Mandela's favor of a visit in 1994, when she attended his inauguration in Pretoria as president of South Africa. The King Day Celebration in January 1992 attracted the largest crowd yet, with three hundred thousand people marching in its annual parade down Auburn Avenue. The following year, on April 30, 1993, an all-star salute featuring Stevie Wonder, Robert Guillaume, Cicely Tyson, and cohosted by Phil Donahue and Dionne Warwick paid tribute to Coretta Scott King on the twenty-fifth anniversary of her founding of the King Center, at a $150 a ticket event that attracted 1,500 people. The next week, on May 6, she lost the lawsuit the King Center had filed against Boston University in a bid to retrieve the papers King had donated to the school in 1964. It was a bitter blow, for she had seen the return of these manuscripts as crowning her achievement of creating the country's leading archive on the civil rights movement. The failure of the court case crushed her spirit, and within months it convinced her to hand the King Center back to her son. At Coretta Scott King's insistence, the board of directors reelected Dexter King as president and chief executive officer.[44]

With his mother's full support, Dexter aggressively changed the way the King Center and the King Estate did business. Heretofore, many of Martin Luther King's speeches, statements, tracks, and even books remained in a readily accessible and hazy public domain where his Kingian nonviolence reached a wide audience. To defend its title to King's intellectual property as presented in the media, the King Estate filed suit against CBS over the rebroadcast of the "I Have a Dream" and other speeches. The legal expenses topped $1 million, but the King Estate won its claim to control the public broadcast of King's intellectual property in a decision reached in 2000. Although Coretta Scott King had convinced Congress to create the King Federal Holiday Commission as a governmental agency to assist community service projects as part of the national holiday observance to encourage nonviolent social change, Dexter Scott King and the King Estate—which trademarked King's image—ordered the commission in 1995 to cease and desist from using for free King's likeness to promote the holiday, an act that led to the disbanding of the commission in September 1996. Instead, the King Estate endorsed a line of products using King's image on checks, limited edition ceramic statuettes by Lladro, and most notoriously ads in newspapers selling cellular phones. When the King Estate's appeals failed to overturn the ruling that defended Boston University's claim to King's papers, the heirs decided to sell what remained of his manuscripts. Critics accused the King Estate of shamelessly marketing and profiting from Dr. King's legacy.[45]

Dexter Scott King banned rangers from conducting tours of the King Birth Home. He explained that "the history of the civil rights movement and the legacy of Dr. King shall not reside with the National Park Service, but shall forever remain in the care and custody of the King family." His real complaint, however, focused on the visitor center, for the initial agreement had left the Park Service in a "support role," but once it planned to put "up something directly in competition" with the King Center, it had broken that agreement. The removal of rangers from the King Center properties forfeited a $534,000 lease agreement with the federal government, a serious financial blow especially given that the center had run substantial deficits in eight of the previous ten years. Reports suggested the compensation paid Coretta Scott King had declined with the deficit from $176,000 in 1992 to $114,922 in 1993. The conflict convinced corporations to back off pledges. As Dexter King evaluated the King Center's negative financial situation, the Park Service proceeded with construction plans to meet its deadline for the Summer 1996 Centennial Olympics, convincing him to renegotiate with federal officials the management of the site and even to offer to sell the family residence at 234 Sunset with all of King's personal belongings still intact, including the Impala in the garage, so that the Vine City house might be preserved as another civil rights shrine.[46]

Having retired from active work at the King Center, Coretta Scott King nevertheless continued to advocate for human rights. She had long supported women's issues, serving on the National Organization for Women's National Advisory Board. At a public address in the Mayor's Conference Room in Washington in 1983, she endorsed the efforts of the D.C. Chapter of the National Gay and Lesbian Task Force and the D.C. Coalition of Black Gay Men and Women to link the rights of homosexuals with the Civil Rights Act of 1964. Speaking at the Palmer House Hotel in Chicago in 1998, she remembered the sacrifices of gays and lesbians active in the movement and called on the civil rights community to condemn homophobia as bigotry. Despite criticism from conservative black pastors and opposition from family members, Coretta Scott King stepped up her efforts on behalf of gay rights. She addressed the 1999 AIDS Memorial Quilt Initiative in Atlanta. She invited the National Gay and Lesbian Task Force to participate in the planning of the fortieth anniversary of the March on Washington in 2003. She opposed a congressional effort in 2004 to ban gay marriage. Indeed, her efforts made her one of the best-known advocates for the rights of lesbian, gay, bisexual, and transgendered people within the African American community.[47]

The nation's leading civil rights celebrity insisted on remaining in her house at 234 Sunset Avenue on the west side of Atlanta until a home invasion in 1996 convinced the family she had to move. In return for her participation in a beauty makeover on a broadcast of Oprah Winfrey's television show on May 5, 2003, the Hollywood mogul purchased for Coretta Scott King a condominium on the 39th floor of Park Place, a gated community on Peachtree Road in upscale Buckhead, where Elton John and Janet Jackson had flats. Since 1991 she had owned Unit #402 in the Cedar Chase Condominiums in Atlanta. She maintained an active social life, attending formal affairs and state events with visiting dignitaries, occasionally taking with her a male companion but in later years more often her friend, the poet Maya Angelou.[48]

Meanwhile, the King Estate continued to settle affairs in a fashion often at odds with her original vision for the King Center. Having turned matters over to her son Dexter, and with Christine King Farris likewise surrendering authority to her son, Isaac King Farris, and the two first cousins hiring their friend Phillip Jones of Intellectual Properties Management, the King Estate reevaluated licensing agreements, such as signing in 1997 a multimillion-dollar contract with Time Warner Trade Publishing to reprint King's books. The King Estate offered to sell King's papers to Emory University, Stanford University, and the Library of Congress, before putting them on the auction block at Sotheby's where, at the midnight hour, the City of Atlanta bought them for $32 million in June 2006. Under Coretta's leadership, the King Center had seen as competition civil rights institutes in Birmingham and Selma, but Dexter saw opportunity, smoothing the way for his mother to attend events at the National Civil Rights Museum in Memphis. Both he and the Memphis staff embraced conspiracy theories surrounding the assassination of his father. Calling for a federal investigation of the crime, Dexter met with the man convicted of King's assassination, James Earl Ray, and convinced his mother to endorse calls for a new trial. Coretta Scott King had long opposed the death penalty, arguing that "morality is never upheld by legalized murder." Criticism of Dexter's managing the King Center from his Malibu home convinced him to turn day-to-day affairs over to his brother Martin in January 2004 while retaining leadership control. As the siblings disagreed publicly over what to do with the facility, their mother struggled to raise an endowment to sustain her dream. Having suffered a stroke and confined to a wheelchair, Coretta Scott King nevertheless dazzled attendees at the King Center's Salute to Greatness fundraiser on January 14, 2006, in what became her last public appearance.[49]

The nation marked the death of Coretta Scott King by affording her a state funeral. While seeking help at the holistic Santa Monica Health Institute in Rosarito Beach, Mexico, the civil rights activist, now seventy-eight years old and vegan, died of complications from ovarian cancer on January 30, 2006. Coretta Scott King became the first woman to lie in state in the rotunda of the Georgia Capitol. Tens of thousands of mourners passed by her coffin there and at Ebenezer Baptist Church. The networks broadcast the three-hour funeral held at New Birth Missionary Baptist Church in Lithonia, where her daughter, the Reverend Bernice King, preached the eulogy before four United States presidents, the governor of Georgia, and millions of viewers across the world. The family arranged a fairytale farewell as a Cinderella-like hearse took her body to the Auburn Avenue site for internment, ultimately in the crypt with her husband, as dozens of white doves ascended into the air. Surrounded by the troubled King Center she had worked so hard to construct and only weeks after the annual observance of the King National Holiday she had helped convince Congress to pass, Coretta Scott King left her legacy memorializing the movement for nonviolent social change in the hands of her children, the nation, and the world.[50]

NOTES

1. The best analytical and thorough treatment of Coretta Scott King (csk) to date is Laura T. McCarty, *Coretta Scott King: A Biography* (Westport, Conn.: Greenwood Press, 2009), but the series limits its scope and size to 150 pages. McCarty also wrote the entry for the online *New Georgia Encyclopedia* (http://www.georgiaencyclopedia.org/articles/history-archaeology/coretta-scott

-king-1927-2006 [accessed December 6, 2013]). An excellent analysis that places Coretta Scott King within the context of black leadership is provided by Vicki Crawford, "Coretta Scott King and the Struggle for Civil and Human Rights: An Enduring Legacy," *Journal of African American History* 92, no. 1 (2007): 106–17. See also the entry by Minoa D. Uffelman, "Coretta Scott King," in the online *Encyclopedia of Alabama* (http://www.encyclopediaofalabama.org/face/Article.jsp?id=h-1489 [accessed December 6, 2013]). There are a half-dozen accounts for young adults and children, such as Lisa Renee Rhodes, *Coretta Scott King* (Philadelphia: Chelsea House Publishers, 1998), and the one written by fellow civil rights activist Octavia Vivian, *Coretta: The Story of Coretta Scott King*, commemorative ed. (Minneapolis: Augsburg Press, 2006). She is virtually absent from the volume of essays *Women in the Civil Rights Movement: Trailblazers and Torchbearers, 1941–1965*, ed. Vicki L. Crawford, Jacqueline Anne Rouse, and Barbara Woods (Brooklyn, N.Y.: Carlson Publishing, 1990). A definitive biography of Coretta Scott King by a scholar is terribly needed. The papers of Coretta Scott King are held by the family and closed to researchers.

2. Coretta Scott King, *My Life with Martin Luther King, Jr.* (New York: Holt, Rinehart and Winston, 1969), 20–25; *Atlanta Journal-Constitution*, February 7, 2006, D4, D6.

3. Edythe Scott Bagley with Joe Hilley, *Desert Rose: The Life and Legacy of Coretta Scott King* (Tuscaloosa: University of Alabama Press, 2012), 3–31, goes into great detail about the McMurry and Scott families; CSK, *My Life*, 29–31; *Atlanta Journal-Constitution*, February 7, 2006, D14, D16.

4. CSK, *My Life*, 32–39, quote on 36; Bagley, *Desert Rose*, 58–66.

5. CSK, *My Life*, 39–45; Bagley, *Desert Rose*, 67–87. For a description of the progressive college on the eve of Coretta Scott's admission, see Algo D. Henderson and Dorothy Hall, *Antioch College: Its Design for Liberal Education* (New York: Harper & Brothers Publishers, 1946). While his daughters attended Antioch, Obie Scott opened a store adjacent to his house located near Mount Tabor AME Church.

6. Her son recalls his mother's friendship with conscientious objectors while at Antioch, see Dexter Scott King, with Ralph Wiley, *Growing Up King: An Intimate Memoir* (New York: Warner Books, 2003), 163; Clayborne Carson, Ralph E. Luker, Penny A. Russell, and Pete Holloran, eds., *The Papers of Martin Luther King, Jr.*, vol. 2: *Rediscovering Precious Values* (Berkeley: University of California Press, 1994), 13.

7. In *Desert Rose*, 92–95, Bagley describes her sister's nearly destitute early weeks in Boston. She also notes that Coretta received funds that Alabama paid black students to maintain segregation by sending them outside the state for their graduate training. See also CSK, *My Life*, 46–51.

8. Coretta Scott King quotations regarding her first conversation with King cited in David J. Garrow, *Bearing the Cross: Martin Luther King, Jr., and the Southern Christian Leadership Conference* (New York: William Morrow, 1986), 45; King quoted in CSK, *My Life*, 55; Bagley, *Desert Rose*, 96–101.

9. Garrow, *Bearing the Cross*, 45–47; Coretta's evaluation of Martin quoted in CSK, *My Life*, 59; Martin's view of Coretta quoted in Martin Luther King Jr., *Stride toward Freedom: The Montgomery Story* (New York: Harper & Row, 1958), 23.

10. Martin Luther King Sr. with Clayton Riley, *Daddy King: An Autobiography* (New York: William Morrow, 1980), 148–51; Christine King Farris, *Through It All: Reflections on My Life, My Family, and My Faith* (New York: Atria, 2009), 3–42.

11. The anecdote is confirmed in Farris, *Through It All*, 74. Coretta Scott King, *My Life*, 65–69. Daddy King later said, "I don't believe there was any girl who could have fitted into Martin's life as Coretta did." Martin's quote to his father cited in MLK Sr., *Daddy King*, 151.

12. CSK, *My Life*, 46–93.

13. Carson et al., *Papers of MLK* 2:289–90; CSK, *My Life*, 101–7. For an account of the bus boycott, see Garrow, *Bearing the Cross*, 11–82.

14. MLK Jr., *Stride toward Freedom*, pp. 53, 135–37; CSK, *My Life*, 126–30; J. Mills Thornton III, *Dividing Lines: Municipal Politics and the Struggle for Civil Rights in Montgomery, Birmingham, and Selma* (Tuscaloosa: University of Alabama Press, 2002), 76–77; Clayborne Carson, Stewart Burns, Susan Carson, and Pete Holloran, eds., *The Papers of Martin Luther King, Jr.*, vol. 3: *Birth of a New Age, December 1955–December 1956* (Berkeley: University of California Press, 1997), 114–15. The bombing took place on January 30, 1956, and tour director Shirley Cherry or other guides at the Dexter Parsonage Museum, 309 South Jackson Street, in Montgomery, will show visitors the crack in the cement porch where the dynamite landed.

15. MLK Jr., *Stride toward Freedom*, 134–35; CSK, *My Life*, 138–145. She titled the spoken performance "Portrait of the Montgomery Bus Boycott."

16. CSK, *My Life*, 149–53; MLK Jr., *Stride toward Freedom*, 175–77. A thorough analysis of the formation of the SCLC may be found in Adam Fairclough, *To Redeem the Soul of America: The Southern Christian Leadership Conference and Martin Luther King, Jr.* (Athens: University of Georgia Press, 1987); a copy of the valentine Martin King sent Coretta in February 1957 is reproduced in Clayborne Carson, Susan Carson, Adrienne Clay, and Virginia Shadron, eds. *The Papers of Martin Luther King, Jr.*, vol. 4: *Symbol of the Movement, January 1957–December 1958* (Berkeley: University of California Press, 2000), 136.

17. CSK, *My Life*, 154–58, 172–80. On the Kings witnessing the independence of Ghana, see Carson et al., *Papers of MLK*, 4:145–49, 155–67, 304; on India see Clayborne Carson, Tenisha Armstrong, Adrienne Clay, and Susan Carson, eds., *The Papers of Martin Luther King, Jr.*, vol. 5: *Threshold of a New Decade, January 1959–December 1960* (Berkeley: University of California Press, 2005), 4–12, 135–36.

18. Carson et al., *Papers of MLK*, 5:328–32.

19. Clifford M. Kuhn, "'There's a Footnote to History!': Memory and the History of Martin Luther King's October 1960 Arrest and Its Aftermath," *Journal of American History* 84, no. 2 (1997): 583–95. The Republicans in the White House were also anxious about King according to MLK Sr., *Daddy King*, 174–77.

20. On the birth of Dexter and Bunny and her views on raising children, see CSK, *My Life*, 212–16.

21. CSK, *My Life*, 247–49; Xernona Clayton with Hal Gulliver, *I've Been Marching All the Time* (Atlanta: Longstreet Press, 1991).

22. CSK, *My Life*, 256–58; Manning Marable, *Malcolm X: A Life of Reinvention* (New York: Viking, 2011), 411–12.

23. CSK, *My Life*, 276–90.

24. Andrew Young, *An Easy Burden: The Civil Rights Movement and the Transformation of America* (New York: HarperCollins, 1996), 163, 328; Dexter Scott King, *Growing Up King*, 101–7. Dexter describes the King children attending the Galloway School, although in ninth grade he transferred out to Frederick Douglass High School. The King family employed people to cook, clean, and do yard work. Spelman College student Gwendolyn Hall Middlebrooks helped with the children.

25. Through the Committee for a Sane Nuclear Policy, the Kings associated with Dr. Spock, who encouraged the civil rights leaders to oppose the war in Vietnam. See telegrams from Benjamin Spock to Martin Luther King Jr., April 30 and September 8, 1965, and letter from Spock to King, May 4, 1965, Martin Luther King Jr. Papers, Digital Archive, Martin Luther King Jr. Center for Nonviolent Social Change, Atlanta; CSK, *My Life*, 291–95; Dexter Scott King, *Growing Up King*, 163.

Dexter King notes his mother's opposition to the war in Vietnam, a policy his father first expressed publicly in February 1965.

26. CSK. *My Life*, 308–27; Bagley, *Desert Rose*, 233–45.

27. *Atlanta Journal*, June 4, 1968, 1-A. The *Atlanta Constitution*, July 15, 1968, 13A, notes that More-house College had received $700,000 of a $3 million goal earmarked as memorials to King by June 10. The paper reported that most Atlantans favored a library as a memorial to King.

28. *Atlanta Constitution*, January 14, 1979, 2-B; CSK, *My Life*, 337–38, 344–47; Rhodes, *Coretta Scott King*, 118–21. Edythe remained Coretta's closest companion for the rest of her life, with the two sisters communicating almost daily. See *Atlanta Journal-Constitution*, February 2, 2006, D-16; Bagley, *Desert Rose*, 246–53.

29. Dexter Scott King, *Growing Up King*, 70, 76, 164, 198–203. At first Coretta managed the King Center at 234 Sunset, then from space at the Interdenominational Theological Seminary; then from 503 Auburn Avenue, the house adjacent to the 501 Auburn Avenue King birth home; and finally from the administrative offices constructed in the King Center Complex. See Farris, *Through It All*, 141.

30. *Atlanta Constitution*, January 15, 1969, 5-A; Frances Romero, "Martin Luther King, Jr., Day," *Time*, January 18, 2010; McCarty, *Coretta Scott King*, 65–67; Coretta Scott King, "The Movement for Economic and Social Justice 1994 and Beyond," in *Reflections of the Dream: 1975–1994*, ed. Clarence G. Williams (Cambridge, Mass.: MIT Press, 1996), 279.

31. On her conversations with Nixon see *Atlanta Journal-Constitution*, September 28, 1969, 2-A; *Atlanta Constitution*, December 29, 1969, 5-A; Ford Foundation, *Report 1969*, Ford Foundation Grant #07000089, "Support of Afro-American Studies Program," Office of the Vice President, Finance and Administration, $100,000, 12/04/1969–12/03/1970; *Atlanta Constitution*, June 10, 1968, 13-A.

32. In many ways, CSK's behavior mirrored that of Jacquelyn Kennedy, as both women responded to the assassinations with quiet dignity and steady determination to take the memories of their husbands and turn them into living memorials. The Kennedys envisioned three components: a museum on the presidency, an archive, and an educational institute on public affairs. Initially they planned, with Professor Arthur M. Schlesinger Jr., a memorial at Harvard University in what became the John F. Kennedy Institute of Politics, but by 1975 they abandoned placing the presidential library in Cambridge, locating it on Boston Harbor instead, in a building designed by I. M. Pei, that opened in 1979. The *Atlanta Voice*, January 19, 1969, 1, suggests that like the strategy followed by the Kennedys, CSK initially planned for the memorial shrine to incorporate Ebenezer and the birth home, while the activist Institute for Non-violent Social Change would be housed at Atlanta University. Noted historian and civil rights activist Dr. Vincent Harding inaugurated the work from Spelman College. See *Atlanta Journal*, June 4, 1968, 1-A; April 27, 1993, A-1, A-3, D-1; April 29, 1993, A-12, E-2. Despite criticism of the practice, CSK kept MLK's papers in the basement at 234 Sunset. Fulton County, Georgia Superior Court, book 5825, p. 408, warranty deed dated May 18, 1973; book 6022, 312, 319, warranty deeds dated November 28, 1973. Coretta Scott King also purchased rental property as investments for herself. See book 6032, p. 433, among other deeds.

33. Frederick Allen, *Atlanta Rising: The Invention of an International City, 1946–1996* (Marietta: Longstreet Press, 1996), 180–82; *Atlanta Constitution*, September 17, 1975, 6-A. Black contractor Herman Russell built the community center, which was designed by architect Joe Robinson. The city constructed the adjacent MLK Natatorium on top of an old warehouse in 1978 (*Atlanta Constitution*, January 16, 1975, 1-AF).

34. *Atlanta Constitution,* April 4, 1977, 3-A.

35. *Atlanta Constitution,* January 16, 1975, 1-AF; Young, *An Easy Burden,* 478–79. Ella Baker had served as SCLC's first director but not on its board.

36. *Atlanta Constitution,* July 27, 1976, 4-A; July 28, 1976, 28-C; July 29, 1976, 5-C; April 4, 1977, 3-A; John Lewis with Michael D'Orso, *Walking with the Wind: A Memoir of the Movement* (New York: Simon and Schuster, 1998), 413–19.

37. *Atlanta Constitution,* October 4, 1978, 2-B; January 14, 1979, 2-B; October 18, 1979, A-1, A-21, A-22; Dexter Scott King, *Growing Up King,* 70–71, 91–93, 113.

38. Dave Astor, "Coretta Scott King's Accomplishments Include a Syndicated Column," *Editor and Publisher,* January 31, 2006.

39. Police arrested Yolanda, Bernice, and Martin III along with Coretta. See McCarty, *Coretta Scott King,* 92–97; and Farris, *Through It All,* 176–88.

40. *Atlanta Constitution,* January 7, 1985, C-2; November 17, 1985, D-11; January 17, 1986, A-1, A-12. The endowment drive attracted $500,000 from an Atlanta foundation and corporate support from the Stroh Brewery Company.

41. Glenn T. Eskew, "Exploring Civil Rights Heritage Tourism and Historic Preservation as Revitalization Tools," in *Past Trends and Future Prospects of the American City: The Dynamics of Atlanta,* ed. David L. Sjoquist, 309–27 (Lanham, Md.: Rowman and Littlefield, 2009).

42. McCarty, *Coretta Scott King,* 80–86. See also RG220, Martin Luther King Jr. Federal Holiday Commission, Accession #97-0001 to #97-0026, containing the correspondence of Lloyd Davis and Coretta Scott King regarding the holiday efforts located in the National Archives, Southeastern Region, Morrow, Ga.

43. Dexter Scott King, *Growing Up King,* 157–70. On the children see *Atlanta Journal-Constitution,* April 28, 2002, C-3; January 19, 2004, D-1, D-4. Hosea Williams continued to criticize the King Center and its national holiday observance; see *Atlanta Constitution,* January 16, 1990, D-1.

44. *Atlanta Journal-Constitution,* June 30, 1990, A-19; January 12, 1992, D-4; May 1, 1993, B-2; May 7, 1993, A-1, C-1; June 20, 1993, G-1. The election of Dexter Scott King is reported in the *Atlanta Journal-Constitution,* October 22, 1994, B-1; his December 1994 installation is reported in the *New York Times,* January 17, 1995, A-11.

45. *New York Times,* April 14, 1995, A-1; Cynthia Tucker, "Assault on a Legacy," *Birmingham News,* May 28, 1995; Cynthia Tucker, "Martin Luther King's Own Family Did More to Demean His Legacy than Bigots like Helms," *Birmingham News,* January 15, 1996; *Atlanta Journal-Constitution,* October 22, 1994, B-1; January 1, 1995, A-1; January 17, 1995, C-1; June 16, 1996, G-1; January 19, 1997, R-5; October 26, 2001, D-7. On the King papers see *Atlanta Journal-Constitution,* October 27, 1999, A-3; November 14, 1999, E-1. On the marketing of King see *Atlanta Journal-Constitution,* January 12, 1999, B-1. Dexter Scott King explained the need to market licensed goods to compete with bootlegged products being produced in China and sold illegally. He explained the King Estate was protecting its control of the King image using the same rationale as the Elvis Presley right of publicity law in Tennessee.

46. *Atlanta Journal-Constitution,* January 1, 1995, A-1; May 21, 1996, B-1; June 16, 1996, G-1; November 20, 1996, B-2. On the Park Service facility fulfilling the needs of visitors see *Atlanta Journal-Constitution,* January 16, 1999, C-1; Dexter Scott King, *Growing Up King,* 207–9, 261–65.

47. Gil Gerald, "The Trouble I've Seen," in *Freedom in this Village,* ed. E. Lynn Harris, 67–82 (New York: Carrol and Graff Publishers, 2005); McCarty, *Coretta Scott King,* 128. Beverly Guy Sheftall

and Jonetta Cole hope to edit speeches by Coretta Scott King into a volume that would secure her reputation as a leading radical.

48. *Atlanta Journal-Constitution*, May 3, 2003, C-1; Fulton County, Georgia Superior Court, book 14402, p. 11.

49. Dexter Scott King, *Growing Up King*, 253–56; *Atlanta Journal-Constitution*, May 3, 2003, C-1; December 24, 2005, A-1; February 7, 2006, D-16.

50. The CSK Estate manages property while the CSK Foundation perpetuates memory. See *Atlanta Journal-Constitution*, February 3, 2006, A-1; February 8, 2006, A-1.

Rosalynn Carter
(1927–)

The President's Partner

SCOTT KAUFMAN

During the past century, the first lady of the United States has adopted an increasingly activist role. Eleanor Roosevelt traveled overseas on goodwill missions and fought for greater rights for African Americans. Jacqueline Kennedy promoted the arts, while Lady Bird Johnson encouraged environmentalism. Pat Nixon endorsed volunteerism; Betty Ford fought for passage of the Equal Rights Amendment (ERA) and greater awareness of the danger posed by breast cancer; Nancy Reagan had influence over her husband's schedule; Laura Bush denounced the nation of Myanmar for human rights violations. Yet of the nation's first ladies since World War II—indeed, one could argue that of *all* first ladies— none was more involved in her husband's administration than Rosalynn Carter. While in some respects she followed precedents set by her predecessors, such as endorsing policies of a maternalist nature, she broke new boundaries, involving herself in political and personnel decisions as no president's wife had before her. In the process, she generated a debate over the proper role of the first lady.

Eleanor Rosalynn Smith was born in August 1927 in Botsford, Georgia. Her father, William Edgar, worked as a bus driver and auto mechanic in the nearby town of Plains, while her mother, Frances Allethea (or simply "Allie" to those who knew her), was a seamstress. Living conditions for the Smiths—who by 1936 had added two more sons and a daughter to their family—were not easy. Edgar had lost his life savings in 1926 when the bank in Plains had failed. The family home lacked an indoor bathroom or central heating. Summertime heat and humidity required keeping the windows open; while this would not necessarily be a problem, it was for the Smiths, for cars or wind kicked up dust from a nearby road, which then blew into the house. Cleaning, thus, became all the

ROSALYNN CARTER

First Lady of the United States, First Lady of Georgia, author, reformer.

Jimmy Carter Presidential Library.

more of a chore. Despite such difficulties, Rosalynn remembered a happy childhood. Though strict parents, Edgar and Allie doted on their children. Rosalynn herself spent her free time with her siblings and with other children in the neighborhood or, when alone, read, sewed, and played with her dolls.[1]

Religion and education became central to Rosalynn's life. Allie, whose mother and father were devout churchgoers, insisted that her children attend church weekly. Edgar regretted his failure to get an education and did not want his kids to make the same mistake. To please her father, Rosalynn pushed herself hard in school. While there, she met two teachers who had a particularly strong influence upon her: Thelma MacArthur and Julia Coleman, Rosalynn's seventh- and eight-grade instructors, respectively. MacArthur encouraged her students to read newspapers and listen to the radio. Coleman believed that a well-rounded pupil was one who knew not just the three Rs, but who also had an appreciation for music and art. From these teachers the future first lady began "to discover a world of interesting people and faraway places,"[2] and developed an appreciation for cultural diversity.

Rosalynn's happy childhood came crashing down during her eighth-grade year when she learned her father had terminal cancer. "I was devastated. . . . My childhood really ended at that moment," she recounted. Edgar passed away shortly thereafter, meaning that Allie and the Smith children had to assume new responsibilities, such as overseeing the family finances. Those duties grew the following year when Allie's mother died and her father moved into the house. Though the Smiths had some money coming in from Edgar's insurance and from renting out the farm, it was not enough to cover the bills. Allie thus got employment as a school lunchroom worker and then as a postmistress, leaving it up to Rosalynn to watch over her brothers and sister. Additionally, Allie used her oldest daughter as a sounding board, discussing with her matters ranging from money to jobs.[3]

Rosalynn had, in short, at the age of thirteen become the cohead of the household, acting as adviser to her mother and role model to her siblings. One can assume that role was not easy. On the one hand, she came from family in which, she later wrote, "the women always have worked, and worked hard." Moreover, she looked up to her mother, who became the epitome of an accomplished, strong, independent woman. On the other, she had an inner insecurity, driven by an uncertainty as to whether she could all at once meet her mother's expectations, do her part to help the family survive, and get the education her father wanted her to obtain. She started to question her faith in God. Her mother, however, assured her that God would look over the family. Encouraged, Rosalynn regained her faith and kept up with her school studies. Her good grades made her more confident in her abilities. By the time she entered high school, her siblings were all old enough to fend for themselves, so Rosalynn got work as a hairdresser. Having a job, followed by her graduation as her high school class's valedictorian, only added to her inner strength.[4]

The future first lady had plans to leave Plains and travel after graduation. But World War II, as well as her mother's concerns about paying for the education of Rosalynn's siblings, moved Rosalynn to attend nearby Georgia Southwestern Community College. It was during her sophomore year that she fell for Jimmy Carter. The two had known one another for quite some time. Aside from the fact that only six hundred people lived in Plains, there were connections between the Carters and Smiths. Lillian Carter, Jimmy's mother, was a local nurse who had cared for Edgar during his final days. Jimmy's father, James Earl Sr., had been one of Edgar's customers. Finally, one of Jimmy's sisters, Ruth, was Rosalynn's best friend. Yet Jimmy had shown little interest in the eldest Smith daughter; though only three years separated them, he had considered her too young for him.[5]

It was here that Ruth (and fate) stepped in. In the summer of 1945 Jimmy, who at the time was attending the U.S. Naval Academy, came home on leave. Ruth invited Rosalynn to join her on a Carter family get-together. Rosalynn and Jimmy talked, and afterward, he invited her to join him on a double date. The two were immediately taken with each other and began a whirlwind romance that culminated in their marriage in July 1946. Afterward came seven years of nearly constant moving and the birth of three children: John ("Jack"), James Earl III ("Chip"), and Donnel Jeffrey. With her husband oftentimes at sea, Mrs. Carter had to assume ever more responsibility for the family's welfare. She took up knitting and sewing, cooked, paid the bills, and fixed anything that broke. While she missed Jimmy when he was away, her life gave her an opportunity to see new places. It also taught her to become strong and independent, which she came to love. "[I] was more content than I had been in years," she wrote.[6]

Rosalynn's happiness took a blow in 1953 when Jimmy learned his father was dying of cancer. He decided to quit the navy, return to Plains, and assume control of the family's peanut warehouse. Though he had a brother, Billy, he concluded that Billy—who was still in high school—was not old enough to take on that burden. The result was one of the biggest fights Jimmy and Rosalynn would ever have. Despite its hardships, she enjoyed being a navy wife. Returning to Plains would mean living near both his family and hers, and she feared that Allie and Lillian would try to run her life. But Jimmy refused to budge. After a long car trip during which the couple barely spoke to each other, they arrived back in Georgia.[7]

The first two years for the Carters were difficult. They lacked an income, had to live in government housing, amassed a $90,000 debt in 1954 because of a poor crop caused by drought, and could not get loans from the local banks. But better weather in 1955 and assistance from the company that supplied fertilizer to the Carters generated a large harvest and a good profit. Recognizing he could not oversee the company alone, Jimmy asked Rosalynn for assistance, so she took over management of the firm's ledgers. The Carters' young sons helped as well, destroying weeds and labeling bags of peanuts. Rosalynn soon realized that her husband had come to see her as a partner in the company: "[He] would come to me and say, 'Does this work; should we continue to do this in the business. . . . Are we making money on that?' And I could advise him." His confidence in her made her feel both indispensable and increasingly self-assured.[8]

By 1956 the Carters had made enough money to move into their own home. Jimmy also began to take on other pursuits, such as serving on the county school board. It was his first real taste of politics, and it made him interested in seeking further public office. In 1962 he told Rosalynn of his decision to run as a Democrat and seek a seat in the state senate. Though taken aback, she supported him, believing he could do good for Georgia. With Jimmy away on the campaign trail, she took on additional duties to make sure the family business stayed afloat. When she had free time, she supported him by calling voters and mailing letters. The combined effort culminated in a victory for the future president. Because his new job required Jimmy to spend several months a year in Atlanta, Rosalynn had to assume even more burdens. But she was more than happy to accept them: "I felt very, very important, because he couldn't have done it at all if I hadn't managed the business."[9]

In 1966 Jimmy again surprised his wife by announcing his intention to run for the governorship. Leaving the family business in the hands of Billy and his wife, Sybil, Rosalynn, Jack, and Chip went on the campaign trail with Jimmy. (Jeff, who was only fourteen, tagged along with his mother or stayed with Lillian.) Despite a vigorous effort Jimmy failed to win. Undaunted, he began preparations for another gubernatorial bid in 1970. As the Carters laid the foundation for the upcoming campaign, Rosalynn learned she was pregnant. She had always wanted a daughter and, to her delight, got her wish with the birth of Amy in 1967.[10]

The 1970 campaign was much more intimidating for Mrs. Carter than that of 1966. Naturally shy before crowds, she, as well as her sons, had limited their role four years earlier to giving brochures to voters. Furthermore, Jimmy had announced his 1966 bid only three months before the election, thereby leaving little opportunity for her to give speeches. This time, the campaign would be longer and would require her to explain to crowds why they should cast their lot for her husband. Additionally, she had a young daughter to worry about. But she was determined to see Jimmy to victory. With Allie or Lillian available to watch over Amy, Rosalynn took on a grueling schedule, giving numerous speeches. On the inside, she hated it. "She was *really* terrified of public speaking," recalled Mary Hoyt, who became Mrs. Carter's press secretary in 1976.[11] Outside, though, she appeared calm and collected. After a relentless campaign, Jimmy emerged victorious.

Being Georgia's first lady meant a new slate of responsibilities for Rosalynn. She had to entertain guests, which required hiring a kitchen staff and a housekeeper to oversee those personnel. She got a nanny for Amy and a personal assistant who maintained schedules for both her and Amy. With the help of this staff, Mrs. Carter hosted numerous events at the governor's mansion. In the process she tried to avoid extravagance. In part this was because of a limited entertainment budget. But it was also because she and her husband were fiscal conservatives. Jimmy's father had been an anti–New Dealer who regarded Franklin Roosevelt's domestic policy as a waste of money; though not as cost-conscious as Earl Sr., the Georgia governor saw merit in limiting expenditures. Rosalynn had learned to make do in a family with limited financial means, especially after her father's death. As part of this effort to rein in spending, Mrs. Carter sought to avoid buying new outfits. It just so happened that she wore the same dress size as several women in her circle, including Edna Langford, a longtime friend; Judy, Langford's daughter who married the Carters' son Jack in 1971; Caron Griffin, who would wed son Chip in 1973; and Annette Davis, Jeff's girlfriend. Borrowing their dresses gave Mrs. Carter a wide choice of outfits without having to purchase new garments. She also made an effort to hold "large functions on successive days. The same flowers could be used, the menu could be coordinated, and it saved taking down tables and putting them up again."[12]

Mrs. Carter, however, wanted to do more than simply be a hostess. She had an interest in two issues, mental health and the ERA. Her concern for mental health originated from two sources. One was that two cousins of Jimmy's themselves coped with mental disability. The other came from questions she had received during the 1970 campaign from people who wanted to know what her husband would do, if elected, to help the mentally handicapped. Her support for the ERA stemmed from her own struggle to achieve greater equality in her marriage and her desire that other women be able to do the same, and from a broader determination to protect women's rights.[13] Helping the mentally ill or convincing Georgians to ratify the ERA would mean more than just personal accomplishment for Rosalynn. She knew that her successes would reflect well on her husband, which could assist him should he seek reelection. With her personal staff now in place, her sons in college or at work, and her nanny watching Amy, Mrs. Carter could devote time to this agenda.

Jimmy had promised during the campaign to do more to help the mentally ill, and following his inauguration he established the Governor's Commission to Improve Services to the Mentally and Emotionally Handicapped. Its members included the first lady, laypersons, and experts in the field. Mrs. Carter, determined to learn more about mental illness, attended every meeting of the commission, spent one day a week volunteering at a nearby hospital, and visited medical facilities throughout the state. Several months after its establishment, the commission issued its report. It called for giving more responsibility for treating mental illness to community health centers rather than to larger institutions; this would permit patients to get care at home or at least closer to their loved ones. The governor adopted the recommendation. By 1974 the number of community health centers in Georgia had grown to 134, nearly six times as many as when Carter was elected.[14]

Rosalynn had less success with the ERA. The women's rights movement of the early 1900s—oftentimes referred to as the "first wave" of feminism—from which women had gained the right to vote, had combined a maternalist desire to reform America in ways to help the poor and needy with an effort to promote peace. Yet despite the achievement of suffrage, women still were expected to be housewives and mothers, with opportunities for employment and pay disproportionate to those of men. A growth in the number of women attending college as the 1960s progressed, the finding of a 1963 presidential commission which attested to limited educational and job prospects for women, and the publication that same year of Betty Friedan's book *The Feminine Mystique*—in which Friedan found that many women did not enjoy being relegated to the home—engendered a "second wave." This postwar feminist movement concentrated on a woman's social, political, and economic equality and called for such things as an end to disparities in employment, educational opportunities, and income; giving women access to both contraception and abortions; and passage of the Equal Rights Amendment.[15]

Assisted by the election between 1966 and 1970 of lawmakers supportive of the ERA, proponents of the amendment saw it passed by Congress and sent to the states for ratification. Here, though, the ERA ran headlong into powerful conservative grassroots opposition led by Phyllis Schlafly. She and her allies argued that the amendment would make women eligible for the draft, lead to unisex restrooms, promote homosexuality, oblige the government to fund abortions, and most important, break down the traditional family structure by which men worked and women acted as homemakers and family caregivers. Establishing a nationwide organization called STOP (Stop Taking Our Privileges) ERA, and with the help of like-minded lawmakers such as Senator Sam Ervin of North Carolina, Schlafly convinced enough states not to ratify the amendment that by 1974 it was still eight short of the thirty-eight required for it to become law.[16]

One of those states that planned to consider the ERA in 1974 was Georgia. Mrs. Carter understood that most voters in the state opposed the amendment, which explained her admission that she "made a few phone calls, but had done very little else for the futile cause." That said, she hoped to see Georgia's lawmakers endorse it. As she remarked, "My first priority is being a homemaker and taking care of my husband and family," but she also "wanted her rights." Governor Carter apparently misunderstood his wife's position, for a few days before the state's vote he told anti-ERA protestors that while he wanted to see the amendment passed, his wife did not. Her husband's statement came as "a bombshell" to Rosalynn. "How could you?" she protested. When she realized that he had mistaken her true stance, she attempted to clarify it by wearing an "I'M FOR ERA" button past anti-ERA demonstrators and telling reporters her true feelings on the issue.[17] It was not enough: both houses of the state legislature rejected the amendment.

Trying to further her agenda forced Mrs. Carter again to face up to her aversion to public addresses. It was not until six months into her tenure as Georgia's first lady that she accepted an invitation to speak. The request had come from the Georgia Association for Retarded Children, and both of the Carters saw it as a chance to highlight their commitment to aid those with mental disabilities. The speech went well, yet it had proven a difficult experience for Rosalynn; for months, she rejected other requests to give a public address. Finally, the governor stepped in. "Write down a few words that will remind you of the things you want to say," he suggested, "and then just get up and talk about them." She took his advice after accepting an invitation to talk to the Atlanta Women's Chamber of Commerce. The event went without a hitch. "I did it! I did it!" she excitedly told her husband. While the nerves remained, her self-confidence had taken another step forward.[18]

And it was just in time, for in 1974 Jimmy announced his decision to run for the U.S. presidency. The signs looked encouraging. The Democratic Party had made changes so that the average voter rather than party leaders had the greatest say in choosing the party's presidential candidate, and an increasing number of states had turned to primaries to select the nominee. In the meantime, the country under the current president, Gerald Ford, had seen a rise in both unemployment and inflation, while the Watergate scandal, which had occurred during the administration of Ford's predecessor and fellow Republican, Richard Nixon, still resonated in the minds of many Americans. Lastly, the activism of the 1960s, especially that represented by the gay and women's rights movements, had upset religious conservatives. If Carter played his cards right, he could use his credentials as a Washington outsider, a religious devotee, and a fiscal conservative to win the election. On the one hand, Rosalynn was nervous about the idea of being the wife of a presidential candidate, for it would mean even more speaking appearances. On the other, his victory would, she believed, create a government more open, honest, and competent. Moreover, she would have the opportunity to bring her agenda to the entire country.

Jimmy's decision to run for the presidency was also important for his relationship with his wife. For a couple who had wed at a time when men were supposed to be the breadwinners and women housewives and mothers—a perception reinforced in the immediate postwar era by government propaganda, social "experts," advertisements, and popular culture—it appeared the Carters were in a way unique, for they almost immediately after their wedding day had begun developing a relationship that was increasingly one of equals. In fact, many married couples sought to adopt "socially prescribed roles" while simultaneously pushing for egalitarianism.[19] Thus, the Carters were like many others who had been wed after World War II. For the Carters, the point at which their partnership reached full maturity came with Jimmy's decision to seek the country's highest office. While on the telephone one day, he asked his wife to pack his suitcase. "Do it yourself," Rosalynn told him. "I have to get my own things ready." Her response made him realize that he had to give more consideration to her responsibilities and feelings. From then on, he wrote, "we carved out an unprecedented concept of equality and mutual respect." She seconded him. "That was kind of the turning point. He's been packing his suitcase ever since."[20]

The entire Carter family—minus Amy, who either traveled with her mother or stayed behind in Plains with Allie or Lillian—began an intense campaign. They had assistance from friends such as Langford as well as volunteers nationwide who became known as the "Peanut Brigade." Mrs. Carter was involved in all aspects of the campaign. As in Georgia in 1970, she maintained a grueling schedule, spending as many as eighteen hours a day speaking, attending receptions and town meetings, and visiting various businesses. She helped her husband plan the campaign's strategy, convincing him to run in every primary. Finally, she coached him on his speeches. Jimmy's naval training as a nuclear engineer had taught him to see the complexity that oftentimes existed in specific issues; his problem was explaining that complexity in simple terms. Rosalynn tried to help him on that score. For instance, Greg Schneiders, who worked for the Carter campaign and later served as the president's deputy assistant for communications, recalled that the Carter team decided to interview voters and find out what they would ask Jimmy if given the chance. "One of them was what he'd do about crime, and [Jimmy] went on in great detail about the root causes of crime and social issues." When Rosalynn suggested saying simply that "'we'd put more criminals in jail,'" her husband replied, "'Well, the fact of the matter is we don't even have jails to put them in, even if we could get all these people and could convict them all. We don't have any place to put them.' And she said, 'Well, I know that, and you know that, but I think you ought to just say it anyway.'"[21]

Onlookers saw in Mrs. Carter someone determined to win. "Sometimes it's hard to tell which of the Carters—Jimmy, or his wife Rosalynn—is running harder for President," commented *People* magazine in March 1976. Some started to call her the "steel magnolia," suggesting that while her small frame and soft southern accent made her appear feminine and charming, she was in fact cold, tough, and prepared to do whatever it took to achieve victory on Election Day. The incumbent first lady, Betty Ford, shared that perception. Rosalynn Carter, she stated, was "saccharin sweet but always ready to stick a knife in your back."[22]

The Carter campaign paid off. In July the Georgia governor formally received the Democratic Party nomination, and four months later, he defeated Ford for the presidency. While some at the time questioned how much Mrs. Carter had done to help her husband's victory, others were certain. "Through the years," commented New Hampshire's *Union Leader*, "successful primary candidates often have been aided a great deal by their wives. . . . But none had the impact of Rosalynn Carter."[23]

Now that she was first lady of the United States, one of the expectations was that Mrs. Carter would host numerous events at the White House. To assist her in this effort, Rosalynn relied on her staff, especially her social secretary, Gretchen Poston; Jane Fenderson, the first lady's appointments secretary; Press Secretary Mary Hoyt; and Evan—and later, his wife, Edith—Dobelle, chief of protocol. The gatherings she held reflected her long-standing interest in cultural diversity and included dinners for visiting officials, the White House Jazz Festival, stock-car night, the annual Easter egg roll, and a series of Sunday night music performances, the last of which aired on national television. The selection of events impressed observers. "It adds up to a mix of entertainment that, while still all American in most cases, offers more variety than the White House has seen for years," noted *U.S. News and World Report*.[24]

While it was the traditional role of the first lady to act as hostess, Mrs. Carter, as in the case of her tenure in Georgia, wanted to be anything but. It is ironic that her first name was Eleanor, like that of one of the nation's most activist first ladies, Eleanor Roosevelt. Influenced by the early feminist movement, Mrs. Roosevelt had endorsed a greater role for women in politics, an increase in government aid for the disadvantaged, passage of civil rights legislation, and promotion of world peace.[25] The media assumed Rosalynn would follow in her famous predecessor's shoes. Though Mrs. Carter downplayed the comparisons with Mrs. Roosevelt, she made clear, even before Jimmy's inauguration, that she had no intention of being a traditional first lady. She planned not just to continue the agenda she had developed in Georgia but to expand it. In addition to mental health and the ERA, the first lady promoted aid for the elderly, the immunization of children, and volunteerism.

Mrs. Carter had several reasons for adopting such a substantive agenda. For one, it would allow her to maintain the independence she had come to enjoy. Furthermore, these programs, if implemented, would create what she called "a caring society," whereby communities, states, and the federal government would help those in need.[26] On this score, she reflected the "Social Gospel," a theological doctrine dating back to the late 1800s that called for doing Christ's work via aid to the disadvantaged. Finally, these programs would not only complement those of her husband's, but, if successful, would reflect well on him and his administration.

Of these initiatives, the centerpiece was mental health. To the first lady and officials within the executive branch, the nation's mental health care system required substantial reform. About 10 percent of Americans required mental health care, concluded the White House, but health insurance covered only about a tenth of a person's bills for mental health treatment. While there were numerous institutions in the country that provided mental health care, such as nursing homes, mental hospitals, and community health centers, they lacked integration.[27] This increased a person's difficulty in receiving adequate mental health assistance.

A month after his inauguration, President Carter announced the establishment of the twenty-member President's Commission on Mental Health. Mrs. Carter had hoped to act as the body's chair, but federal law prohibited nepotism in the executive branch with regard to hiring or promoting individuals. The headship thus went to Tom Bryant, who had overseen the Office of Economic Opportunity's Emergency Food and Medical Services Program under President Lyndon Johnson. Though unhappy that she could not officially lead the committee, Rosalynn received the position of honorary chair. Ultimately, though, she served as the committee's de facto head.[28]

In its report issued in the spring of 1978, the commission made 117 recommendations on such topics as community support and insurance coverage for, as
well as the rights of, those with mental disabilities. The commission made clear
that instituting these suggestions required action not just at the federal level but
also at the state and local. For instance, most individuals with mental illness were
likely to seek help locally from friends, family, doctors, or religious leaders. It was
important, argued the commissioners, to strengthen these support networks and
to improve coordination between them and local mental health centers. Furthermore, the commission called for money to establish local community health
centers where they did not exist and to improve the services of those that did.[29]

It was one thing to make recommendations but another to turn them into a
bill for submission to Congress. Here Mrs. Carter faced an obstacle in the form
of the Department of Health, Education, and Welfare (HEW), and its secretary,
Joseph Califano. In a sense, Califano and his staff were in a catch-22. They had
received orders from the president to reform the welfare system and establish a
national health insurance program, two major initiatives themselves. As those
proposals came from the Oval Office, HEW believed it had to give them priority.
Meanwhile, Jimmy's fiscal conservatism had moved him to demand that any
new initiatives require a minimal amount of additional spending. Thus, HEW
allocated only $83 million in the 1980 budget to implement the mental health
commission's recommendations, or one-fifth of what HEW itself had estimated
would be needed to fully fund the commission's proposals. When Califano refused to provide additional funding, Mrs. Carter went to both James McIntyre,
the head of the Office of Management and Budget, and her husband, and got a
promise of $150 million.[30]

To convince Congress to support this appropriation, Mrs. Carter in February 1979 testified on Capitol Hill, becoming only the second first lady—the first
being Eleanor Roosevelt—to do so. She admitted that her husband wanted to
curtail spending, but "no other problem facing society touches so many families
or leaves them so vulnerable." President Carter submitted the legislation, called
the Mental Health Systems Act, to Congress three months later, yet lawmakers
were slow to act on it. When she learned in August that the bill was stuck in the
House Commerce Committee, the first lady called that body's chairman, Harley
Staggers (D-W.Va.), and convinced him to push it through. Two months later,
Capitol Hill passed the bill. Unfortunately, the act's life was not long. After his
inauguration in January 1981, President Ronald Reagan cut much of the funding
for the mental health program. It was, wrote the first lady, "a bitter loss."[31]

Mrs. Carter's interest in mental health intersected with another part of her
agenda, aid for the elderly. Her work on the commission made her realize that

many mental health workers and doctors lacked the training needed to meet the needs of the aged. She also had personal connections to the issue. Her mother had worked to age seventy, her mother-in-law had joined the Peace Corps at age sixty-three, and her husband had an uncle in his eighties who worked as a salesman. Older Americans, realized the first lady, could play an active and useful role in society. And with both life expectancy and the number of elderly individuals on the rise, it was important to make sure that persons in their later years received greater attention.[32]

Mrs. Carter successfully lobbied for various bills to help the elderly, finding assistance from Nelson Cruikshank, the president's counselor on aging, and Claude Pepper, the seventy-six-year-old Democratic representative from Florida. Under the 1977 Rural Health Clinics Act, recipients of Medicare and Medicaid received greater access to health care. In 1978 Capitol Hill amended both the 1967 Age Discrimination in Employment and the 1965 Older Americans Act. Under the former, lawmakers banned mandatory retirement in the federal government and raised mandatory retirement in the private sector from sixty-five to seventy years of age. In the latter, Congress consolidated several federal programs, appropriated more money for health and nutrition programs for the aged, and established an ombudsman to look into nursing home complaints.[33]

Mrs. Carter perceived a connection between mental health and aid for the elderly, and the third part of her domestic agenda, volunteerism. She had learned while first lady of Georgia that programs designed to help those in need were most effective when "people in the community are interested in them, want them to work and assume some kind of responsibility for them." Volunteerism offered other advantages. It cost almost nothing and thus met the president's desire to control spending. It would promote an ethic of altruism within the country. And a successful volunteer program (or programs) would reflect well on her husband's administration. Accordingly, the first lady encouraged Americans to provide time and money for neighborhood beautification and to assist the needy. Furthermore, she urged federal support (moral and sometimes financial) for various programs designed to help the disadvantaged. She secured about $3 million in government funds for Project Propinquity (now Communities in Schools), which aimed at keeping youth in impoverished neighborhoods in school. She also endorsed Green Door, a program to help mentally ill patients in Washington, D.C., leave the hospital and live normal lives.[34]

Aside from volunteering their time to aid the needy, Americans could take time to have their children immunized. This program developed from the first lady's friendship with Betty Bumpers, the wife of Arkansas Democratic senator Dale Bumpers. Together, the first lady and Mrs. Bumpers started a campaign to convince Americans to immunize their children. By October 1979, this campaign had reached its goal of having 90 percent of American children immunized against measles, while other diseases had seen dramatic reductions.[35]

Aid for the mentally handicapped and elderly, volunteerism, and immunization of children—all were maternalist in nature, and in that respect made Rosalynn Carter similar to Eleanor Roosevelt. But here the comparisons end, for in other ways, Rosalynn went further than her famous predecessor. Eleanor Roosevelt had strongly opposed the Equal Rights Amendment. She believed that the ERA would undermine laws designed to protect poor working women and children; proponents of the amendment concluded that without it, women would continue to face injustice. It was not until the mid-1940s that Mrs. Roosevelt changed her mind: the United Nations Charter, which the former first lady believed was vital to defend world peace, called for "equal rights of men and women," and it would have been inconsistent for her to endorse the Charter and not the ERA.[36]

For her part, Mrs. Carter from the beginning had endorsed the ERA. However, ratification still was four states short when she entered the White House. Through lobbying, Rosalynn succeeded in convincing a state lawmaker in Indiana to cast a decisive vote in favor. With the support of her husband, Vice President Walter Mondale, and members of Congress, she had the deadline for ratification extended from October 1979 to 1982. That was as far as she got. STOP ERA and its allies prevented any other state from ratifying the amendment by the 1982 deadline. It was, Mrs. Carter later wrote, the "greatest disappointment" of her agenda of initiatives.[37]

Though busy pursuing this domestic agenda, Mrs. Carter did not limit her role to just that. She took part as well in the development of the administration's foreign policy. Eleanor Roosevelt had encouraged peace efforts in the early 1930s, denounced the anti-Semitism apparent in Germany as the decade progressed, and visited U.S. troops overseas engaged in fighting against America's enemies during World War II. Lady Bird Johnson had gone to Greece to attend the funeral of that nation's king, while Pat Nixon had observed efforts to help earthquake victims. Mrs. Carter again went further. A few months after his inauguration, Jimmy asked his wife to travel to Latin America. What made this trip important was not that Mrs. Carter would be going abroad; rather, she would travel not as a goodwill ambassador but as the president's official representative, with the purpose of holding substantive discussions with foreign leaders. This was something no other first lady had done. Leaving on May 30 with a delegation that included Hoyt, Assistant Secretary for Interamerican Affairs Terence Todman, and Robert Pastor, the Latin American expert on the National Security Council (NSC), Mrs. Carter over the next two weeks met with officials in Jamaica, Costa Rica, Ecuador, Peru, Brazil, Colombia, and Venezuela. Though initially she encountered a standoffish response, it quickly became clear to those she met that she had the power to speak for the U.S. president. Consequently, they became more willing to discuss serious matters, including U.S. economic assistance, President Carter's arms control and human rights initiatives, and drug control.[38]

Mrs. Carter's trip had both symbolic and real impacts. Before her departure, she and the administration had come under criticism for sending a woman, and one who had neither been elected nor appointed to her post, to a part of the world that did not hold women in high regard. Dante Fascell, a Democratic representative from Florida, had commented, "The Latinos are macho and they hate gringos and women. What else do you want to know?" Yet the *New York Times* found by the end of her junket that the impression she had left with officials in Latin America was "a favorable one." Back in the United States, a Roper poll determined that 55 percent of Americans believed it "appropriate for a First Lady to represent the country on a diplomatic mission," while 68 percent felt she had done "a good or excellent job." More substantively, the White House in July announced $4 million in aid to Colombia, including three helicopters to fight drug production; during her visit to Colombia, the president of that nation, Alfonso López Michelson, had asked for helicopters to combat the drug trade. Jamaican prime minister Norman Manley had requested economic assistance, and after Mrs. Carter's return to the United States, Washington announced $63 million in economic aid for that country.[39]

In 1979 Mrs. Carter traveled to Thailand to visit Cambodian refugee camps. Shocked by the conditions in which the refugees lived, she determined to do all she could to help. Upon her return to the United States, she contacted United Nations Secretary General Kurt Waldheim and convinced him to coordinate an international relief effort. She made public appeals for help, while President Carter, assured he would have bipartisan support, requested congressional assistance. Ultimately, nearly $500 million in aid was raised for the Cambodian refugees, with almost one-quarter of it coming from the U.S. government.[40]

In addition to trips abroad, the first lady involved herself in foreign affairs in other ways. She sat in on the daily foreign policy briefings NSC adviser Zbigniew Brzezinski gave the president. During the Senate debate over whether to ratify the Panama Canal treaties, which would turn control of the canal from the United States to Panama, Mrs. Carter contacted the wives of Senators Edward Zorinsky (D-Neb.) and Paul Hatfield (D-Mont.), and asked them to convince their husbands to vote in favor. She helped persuade her husband to directly involve himself in peace talks between Egypt and Israel, which eventually led to the Camp David Accords. When Egyptian president Anwar Sadat and Israeli prime minister Menachem Begin appeared to come to agreement, she urged Jimmy to sign the accords then and there, lest Sadat and Begin change their minds. During the Iran hostage crisis of 1979–81, in which militants held more than three dozen Americans hostage in the Iranian capital of Tehran, she suggested that the United States embargo Iranian oil imports and even raised the possibility of bombing Tehran; the president accepted the former suggestion but rejected the latter, fearing that it could lead to the hostages' deaths. She endorsed her husband's decision to call upon the military to try to rescue the hostages—an effort that ended in failure—and was the driving force behind using connections Jimmy's brother Billy had with Libya in the hopes that the Libyans could convince Iran to release the Americans. News of the approach to Libya created a firestorm, especially after the U.S. public learned of the first lady's role. The president rejected the criticism, commenting that the decision to ask for Libyan assistance ultimately was his.[41]

Personnel was another area in which Mrs. Carter made her influence felt. According to Jimmy's cousin Hugh, it was Mrs. Carter who "tipped the scales" in favor of the Democratic nominee's decision to name Minnesota senator Mondale as his running mate (though in truth, Jimmy himself preferred Mondale over the other possible choices). The first lady convinced the president in 1978 to hire Jerry Rafshoon as communications assistant. With Jimmy's poll numbers falling as his first year in office came to a close, it was important for him to shore up his support. Rafshoon, Mrs. Carter believed, could help the president better get his message across to the American people. Rosalynn had promised during the presidential campaign to use her influence in the Oval Office to get women appointed to high posts, and she did just that, urging her husband to hire Sarah Weddington, who became a special assistant to the president, and Anne Wexler, who served as deputy undersecretary of commerce.[42]

Rosalynn had less luck when it came to Jimmy's decision to appoint Bella Abzug as co-chair of the National Advisory Committee on Women. Abzug was a prominent feminist, an outspoken proponent of the ERA, and a critic of those who resisted the amendment's passage. Mrs. Carter feared that Abzug could turn away voters in those states that had yet to decide on ratification. Midge Costanza, who headed the White House Office of Public Liaison, had successfully fought the first lady on the appointment, contending that the administration needed "the strongest woman we can find." The president ended up firing Abzug in 1979 after she charged him with curtailing funding for programs for women.[43]

Of the president's appointees, though, it was Secretary Califano who received most of the first lady's vituperation. Regarded as a liberal within the Democratic Party, Califano's views did not mesh with the administration's more conservative orientation. For Mrs. Carter, however, the HEW secretary's key error was his "tepid support for mental-health funding." Following talks with his advisers, including his wife, the president in July 1979 decided to shake up his cabinet. Among those sacked was Califano. Though the HEW head realized that there existed a "cultural chasm between President Carter and me," the cabinet shakeup left him dumbfounded. He did not realize until after he left the White House that it had been the first lady who had pushed hardest for his removal from office.[44]

Mrs. Carter had not supported the idea of full cabinet shakeup, believing it would hurt her husband's presidency. Indeed, it did, as Americans began to wonder if Carter's administration "was falling apart." That the first lady sensed the danger of her husband's decision with regard to the cabinet pointed to a keener understanding than he of politics. Indeed, Jimmy himself years later admitted to this: "Rosalynn's much more of a politician than I was or am. I never had much use for politics myself. I was successful in politics, but Rosalynn is much more politically sensitive than [I]."[45]

Another good example of Mrs. Carter's political astuteness was her understanding that complex ideas required simple explanations. This appeared not just in the 1976 campaign. She assisted Carter as well in his speeches as president, reading over drafts, listening to tape recordings of them, and suggesting changes. A notable example concerned an address on energy the president planned to give in July 1979. Rosalynn did not like it. The American people, she told her husband, "don't want to hear about a new program that will allocate energy to the elderly at a lower cost. They just want to be told that everything is going to be all right and that somebody understands the situation and has it under control."[46]

Mrs. Carter also had a better understanding of the possible. That the first lady brought with her an agenda of five items was a lot. But President Carter proposed a virtual laundry list of domestic and foreign policy initiatives: hospital cost containment, tax reform, welfare reform, social security reform, reorganization of the government, a comprehensive energy program, turning the Panama Canal over to Panama, resolving the Greco-Turkish dispute over Cyprus, withdrawing U.S. military forces from South Korea, signing and ratifying a Strategic Arms Limitation Treaty (SALT) with the Soviet Union, stopping the proliferation of nuclear technology, promoting human rights, controlling conventional arms sales, getting a law of the sea treaty passed, and normalizing relations with Cuba, China, and Vietnam. Mrs. Carter attempted to convince her husband that he was trying to do too much at once, but he demurred. "It was better to get 95 percent of something," the first lady remembered her husband telling her, "than it was to get just an awful 5 percent of what you really wanted."[47]

Trying to accomplish so much in so little time was bound to cause problems. It left little opportunity to vet policies before trying to put them into effect. Consequently, attention was not given to prepare the groundwork so those initiatives had a fighting chance of success or to make sure that one initiative did not interfere with another. President Carter did register some achievements, such as ratification of the Panama Canal Treaties, the Camp David Accords, normalization of relations with China, creation of the Departments of Education and Energy, and passage of environmental legislation, and his human rights policy may have freed some political prisoners. Yet his failures far surpassed his successes. He submitted to Congress a comprehensive energy program without first getting input from lawmakers or even from members of the administration who would be responsible for its implementation. Consequently, the energy bill stalled on Capitol Hill for months and, when finally passed, was far less comprehensive than Carter had wanted. The president's public attacks on the Soviet Union's treatment of its citizens made that country unwilling to proceed with signing SALT. Carter thus had to downplay human rights to get what he regarded as a far more important arms control agreement. On welfare and social security reform, hospital cost containment, normalization of relations with Cuba and Vietnam, resolution of the dispute over Cyprus, SALT's ratification, stopping the proliferation of nuclear weapons, curtailing the sale of conventional arms, signing a law of the sea treaty, and withdrawal of troops from South Korea, the president also did not register successes. While admittedly some of these failures were the result of issues beyond his control—he could not force Greece and Turkey to come to terms over Cyprus, as one example—he too often created his own problems or made them worse. For a president who wanted to achieve 95 percent of what he wanted, Carter got far less.

Maybe most important, the first lady realized the importance of having a vision. Americans want to know not just what policies the president hopes to put into practice but where he sees those initiatives taking the nation. Rosalynn understood this. Hence her talk of creating "a caring society." Jimmy, however, focused solely on individual problems to be solved. The American people were thus left with inconsistent and even contradictory policies. How could, for instance, a president who preached human rights downplay that issue to achieve a SALT agreement with a repressive Soviet government? Brzezinski later admitted that the White House failed to explain clearly to Americans "what we were do-ing and where we were heading."[48]

It is not clear if Mrs. Carter ever raised with her husband his need for a vision. It is clear, however, that her involvement in administration policy, both domestic and foreign, was a demonstration of the partnership she and her hus-band had developed. When the first lady questioned whether media reports on White House policy were accurate, the president suggested she start coming to cabinet meetings, which she did, beginning in early 1978. Appreciating how many decisions they made together, and not wanting to bring to his wife a stack of paperwork in the evening, Jimmy and Rosalynn had lunch each Thursday, during which they discussed matters ranging from policy to personnel. In fact, the president himself admitted that "aside from a few highly secret and sensitive security matters, she knew all that was going on."[49]

The media periodically mentioned unnamed staffers who disliked the influence—real or perceived—Mrs. Carter had but who feared speaking up because they knew that doing so risked repercussions from the president. "There are very few people in this Administration that I fear," one such aide commented. "And Rosalynn Carter is at the top of the list." Yet a more likely explanation for the lack of criticism was the realization that the first lady was both an asset and someone who, if they could get her ear, might help White House officials achieve their goals. Press Secretary Jody Powell regretted not using the first lady as much as he could have in getting things done in the ad-ministration's early months. Likewise, Hamilton Jordan, a close friend who later became White House chief of staff, commented, "Whenever I think the Presi-dent is pursuing an unwise course of action and I strike out with him, I try to get her on my side."[50]

Such influence aroused a nationwide debate. It was one thing for the presi-dent's wife to be a hostess, contended her detractors. Even promoting aid for the elderly or the mentally ill was okay, as those policies had a "maternal" qual-ity to them. It was quite another for the first lady, who was neither elected nor appointed, to sit in on cabinet meetings, discuss substantive issues with for-eign officials, and make policy or personnel decisions. The *Manchester Union Leader* suggested that Rosalynn "stay a little further away from the actual seat of government for this country than she has in the past," while Myra McPher-son of *McCall's* asked, "Is Rosalynn Carter Really Running the Country?" Mrs. Carter's defenders, meanwhile, saw little wrong in what she was doing. "We jump to all kinds of assumptions with president's wives," wrote Richard Cohen in the *Washington Post*, "including, in Rosalynn Carter's case, that her advice is hard-headed and practical when it is probably parochial and protective, no loftier than her husband's self-interest." Columnist Carl Rowan was even more straightforward: "I'll be damned if I ever want my country run by a president who is too dumb to consult his wife."[51]

One would have expected feminists to join individuals such as Cohen and Rowan in defending Mrs. Carter. Here was a strong, independent-minded woman who clearly had an impact not just on her husband but on the policies of the nation. She was also someone who was an outspoken advocate of the ERA, the passage of which was one of the central goals of the feminist movement. Yet interestingly, the relationship between the first lady and women's rights activists was strained. Part of the problem was the president, who abhorred abortion on moral and religious grounds—though he said he would not overturn the 1973 Roe v. Wade Supreme Court decision, which gave women the right to terminate a pregnancy—limited the use of Medicare to fund abortions, and fired Abzug. But feminists also saw shortcomings in his wife. Mrs. Carter shared her husband's position on abortion. Furthermore, she refused to make public any disagreements she did have with him. To Rosalynn, doing so would not only endanger her influence within the Oval Office but would be "a tacky thing to do." Feminists rejected such arguments. How could a woman be equal to a man if she saw herself as nothing more than an extension of her husband? "More than any other president's wife I have seen there is no independent thought or phrasing separate from his," charged women's rights activist Gloria Steinem. "I am disappointed in her altogether."[52]

Public opinion polls reflected this ambivalence within the media and the feminist movement. One, taken by the New York Times and CBS in the fall of 1980 gave Mrs. Carter a 46 percent favorable rating versus 9 percent unfavorable; this compared to a 44 percent unfavorable rating for her husband. Yet Betty Ford, who as first lady had also supported the ERA but had assumed a less activist role than Mrs. Carter, had an approval rating 25 points higher at the same point before the 1976 election.[53]

Whether the first lady could use what support she did have to assist her husband in the 1980 campaign became a key question. President Carter had announced his candidacy in December 1979 but had decided because of the Iran hostage crisis to remain in the White House. This meant that much more of the burden of helping him achieve reelection fell on his wife's shoulders than had been the case in 1976. Making matters even more difficult was the president's approval rating. While he had seen a sudden increase in support immediately after the Iran hostage crisis began in November 1979, his numbers had dipped significantly by the spring of 1980 because of a worsening economy—including double-digit inflation and a rising unemployment rate—and his seeming inability to free the hostages. On top of all of this, the president faced a challenge for the nomination from Senator Edward Kennedy of Massachusetts. The president had angered Kennedy because of his fiscal conservatism and his refusal to support the senator's call for a comprehensive national health insurance program. Realizing his precarious situation, Carter decided in April to end his Rose Garden strategy and actively campaign. By June he had obtained enough delegates to cinch up the nomination.

With the Democratic nomination in hand, the Carters and their campaign team shifted attention to the Republican candidate, Ronald Reagan. They charged that Reagan would destroy Medicare and Social Security, while his military policy could drag the United States into a war. Meanwhile, they touted Carter's accomplishments both domestically and internationally. The president, who had lagged far behind Reagan in public opinion polls, began to show signs of life. How much Rosalynn played a role in Jimmy's resurgence remains a matter of debate, but some observers believed it was significant. "Mrs. Carter [is] disarmingly effective," commented the *New York Times*'s B. Drummond Ayers. The Allentown, Pennsylvania, *Morning Call* went even further. "If President Carter is elected to a second term, it may well be largely because of the efforts of the First Lady."[54]

Ultimately, it was not enough. The economy and the hostage crisis hurt, and the single presidential debate, held a week before the election, made matters worse. Reagan appeared relaxed, humorous, and knowledgeable. Maybe most important, he asked voters if they felt better in 1980 than they did in 1976; if not, he urged them to vote for him. That question resonated with the majority of Americans, who chose Reagan the next month.

Following Reagan's inauguration, Jimmy went to Germany to meet the Americans who had recently been released by the Iranians. He then joined Rosalynn and traveled with her back to Plains. They fixed up their home, sold the warehouse business, and signed lucrative contracts for their memoirs. They also started raising money for the Jimmy Carter Library, Museum, and Presidential Center. Neither of the Carters wanted a library that focused solely on his presidency. Rather, they wanted it to be an institution that would serve vital functions, including promoting peace and fighting illness. Since opening in 1986, the Carter Presidential Center has done just that, providing a locus for academic research and for individuals seeking to combat poverty, war, and disease. The Carters themselves have traveled to nations throughout the world to monitor elections and combat malnutrition and sickness.[55]

All along, Rosalynn Carter has pursued her agenda. After leaving the White House, she and her husband became members of Habitat for Humanity, through which volunteers build homes for disadvantaged families. She celebrated President Barack Obama's signing in April 2009 of the Serve America Act. Sponsored by Senator Kennedy, the bill promotes volunteerism and expands AmeriCorps. She continues to endorse immunization of children, drawing attention to the subject in 2011 during a measles outbreak in the United States. But most of her energy has been devoted to providing aid for the elderly and the mentally handicapped. She has written books on both subjects, hosted (and continues to host) summits aimed at improving care for the aged and mentally disabled, and fought to provide those with mental disabilities the same health coverage those with physical disabilities receive. She saw the achievement of the latter in October 2008, when President George W. Bush signed a bill requiring insurance companies to provide parity in coverage.[56]

The Carters do not devote all of their attention to work. They spend time with their family, which has grown to nearly a dozen grandchildren and two great-grandchildren. Mrs. Carter was also one of several first ladies who attended the funeral of Betty Ford, who passed away in July 2011. Rivals in 1976, they had become good friends years later. Rosalynn regarded Mrs. Ford as an inspiration, commenting that her predecessor "showed me that there is life after the White House."[57]

Rosalynn Carter became first lady at a time of transition. The women's rights movement and its call for equality raised the question of whether the president's wife should act simply as hostess and promoter of "maternal" causes or be permitted a greater say in the affairs of her husband's administration. While Rosalynn's role in the White House was to the Carters a continuation of the partnership she and Jimmy had developed over the years, observers split over whether her influence, real or perceived, was appropriate for her office. On the one hand were those who saw nothing wrong with the first lady acting as an advisor to the president, if not his personal representative. On the other were those who believed that a person who had been neither elected nor appointed to office should remain outside the realm of policy.

Such ambivalence regarding the first lady continues to the present. Nancy Reagan caused a furor when Americans learned that she had seen to it to sack her husband's chief of staff, Donald Regan. Hillary Clinton came under assault when President Bill Clinton named her to head a committee to reform the nation's health care system; to many Americans, Hillary Clinton had improperly moved into the world of policymaking. Laura Bush was also an activist first lady, but the initiatives on which she focused, such as education, health, and human rights, were seen as more "maternal" in nature and thus more acceptable. Michelle Obama likewise has taken care not to stray too far from the "acceptable" role of the first lady. She has planted gardens, read to children, and made it clear that her first job will be "mom in chief."[58] There is no doubt that despite advances for women and a growing activism within the office of the first lady, presidents' wives will continue to find that their position and power within the White House are subjects of intense public scrutiny.

NOTES

1. Kathy B. Smith, "(Eleanor) Rosalynn (Smith) Carter," in *American First Ladies: Their Lives and Their Legacy*, ed. Lewis Gould (New York: Garland, 1996), 557; Elizabeth Simpson Smith, *Five First Ladies: A Look into the Lives of Nancy Reagan, Rosalynn Carter, Betty Ford, Pat Nixon, and Lady Bird Johnson* (New York: Walker and Company, 1986), 33; Rosalynn Carter, *First Lady from Plains* (Boston: Houghton Mifflin, 1984), 9–12.

2. Rosalynn Carter, *First Lady from Plains*, 13–14, 19.

3. Ibid., 15, 16–17.

4. Ibid., 17–18, 20; Ralph G. Martin, "Rosalynn," *Ladies Home Journal*, March 1979, 101.

5. Rosalynn Carter, *First Lady from Plains*, 10, 15–16, 20; Jerrold Smith, interview with David Alsobrook, June 23, 1979, transcript, Carter/Smith Family Oral History Project, Jimmy Carter Library (hereafter JCL), Atlanta, Ga.

6. Rosalynn Carter, *First Lady from Plains*, 26–27.

7. Jim Auchmutey, "Over 60 Years of Highs and Lows, Carters Find Happiness as Equals," *Atlanta Journal-Constitution*, July 6, 2006, 1A.

8. Winzola McLendon, "Meet Rosalynn Carter," *Family Circle*, October 1976, 184; Jimmy Carter, *Sharing Good Times* (New York: Simon & Schuster, 2004), 28; Kandy Stroud, "Rosalynn's Agenda in the White House," *New York Times Magazine*, March 20, 1977, 58.

9. Jimmy Carter, *Sharing Good Times*, 42; Stroud, "Rosalynn's Agenda," 58.

10. Interview with Rosalynn Carter, December 21, 1974, transcript, miscellaneous interviews, JCL; Rosalynn Carter, *First Lady from Plains*, 56, 60.

11. Mary Hoyt, interview with the author, Washington, D.C., August 19, 2005.

12. Rosalynn Carter, *First Lady from Plains*, 85–86.

13. Ibid., 69, 272; Paul Healy, "Not Really Mrs. President—But . . . ," *New York Daily News*, September 7, 1977, 45; Stanly Godbold, *Jimmy and Rosalynn Carter: The Georgia Years, 1924–1974* (New York: Oxford University Press, 2010), 216.

14. Rosalynn Carter, *First Lady from Plains*, 90–92.

15. Ruth Rosen, *The World Split Apart: How the Modern Women's Movement Changed America* (New York: Penguin, 2001), 27; Nancy Woloch, *Women and the American Experience*, 4th ed. (New York: McGraw Hill, 2005), 517–26.

16. Susan M. Hartmann, *From Margin to Mainstream: American Women and Politics since 1960* (Philadelphia: Temple University Press, 1989), 103–6, 131–37; Donald G. Mathews and Jane Sherron De Hart, *Sex, Gender, and the Politics of ERA: A State and the Nation* (New York: Oxford University Press, 1990), 28–72. See also the essay in this volume by Robin Morris on Katherine Fink Dunaway.

17. Rosalynn Carter, *First Lady from Plains*, 95–96; Goldbold, *Jimmy and Rosalynn Carter*, 217; Celestine Sibley, "Oh-Oh! Rosalynn for ERA—and He Knows It," *Atlanta Constitution*, January 18, 1974, 1A.

18. Rosalynn Carter, *First Lady from Plains*, 99–100.

19. For more on this subject, see Jessica Weiss, *To Have and to Hold: Marriage, the Baby Boom, and Social Change* (Chicago: University of Chicago Press, 2000).

20. Jimmy Carter, *Sharing Good Times*, 49–50; Auchmutey, "Over 60 Years."

21. B. Drummond Ayres Jr., "The Importance of Being Rosalynn," *New York Times Magazine*, June 3, 1979, 46; Greg Schneiders, telephone interview with the author, January 26, 2006.

22. Joyce Leviton, "Jimmy Carter Already Has a 'Running' Mate—His Tireless Wife, Rosalynn," *People*, March 13, 1976, 10; Myra McPherson, "White House Confidential," *Washington Post*, December 14, 1978, C1.

23. "1976: A National Stage for Carter," *Manchester (N.H.) Union Leader* http://www.theunion leader.com/article.aspx?articleId'38f7db01-c61f-4361-bdd8-cdd5f68f24d8 (accessed May 5, 2009).

24. "Crisis or Calm, White House Parties Roll On," *U.S. News and World Report*, March 12, 1979, 41.

25. Nancy Woloch, *Women and the American Experience*, 4th ed. (New York: McGraw Hill, 2005), chap. 17; Blance Wiesen Cook, *Eleanor Roosevelt*, vol. 1: *1884–1933* (New York: Penguin, 1992), esp. chaps. 12 and 14, and vol. 2: *1933–1938* (New York: Viking, 1999), 4–5, 67–69, 74–76, 129, 152–89, 243–47, 348–49.

26. Rosalynn Carter, "Toward a More Caring Society," *Mental Hygeine* 61, no. 2 (1977), 3.

27. Marlene Cimons, "Mrs. Carter Begins Study of Mentally Ill," *Los Angeles Times*, April 21, 1977, pt. 4, p. 1; Gerald Grob, "Public Policy and Mental Illness: Jimmy Carter's Presidential Commission on Mental Health," *Milbank Quarterly* 83, no. 3 (2005): 426, 428.

28. MaryAnne Borrelli, "The First Lady as Formal Adviser to the President: When East (Wing) Meets West (Wing)," *Women & Politics* 24, no. 1 (2002): 28–29, 37.

29. PAIA Bulletin #92, "Highlights from the Report of the President's Commission on Mental Health," April 27, 1978, President's Commission on Mental Health—Implementation, April 1978–November 1978, First Lady's Office, Project's Officer, Mental Health Project, box 7, JCL.

30. Kathy to RSC, November 14, 1978, Mental Health Memorandums, February 14, 1977–September 30, 1980, in ibid., box 2; Carter, *First Lady from Plains*, 263; "Compassion Drove Rosalynn to Testify," *Atlanta Constitution*, February 7, 1979, 20C.

31. "Statement by Rosalynn Carter, Honorary Chairperson, the President's Commission on Mental Health, before the Senate Subcommittee on Health and Scientific Research, February 7, 1979," Hearings on Mental Health, February 7, 1979, First Lady's Staff File (hereafter FLSF), First Lady's Press Office (hereafter FLPO), box 8, JCL; "Panelists' Responses," in *The Presidency and Domestic Policies of Jimmy Carter*, ed. Herbert D. Rosenbaum and Alexej Ugrinsky (Westport, Conn.: Greenwood, 1994), 544–45; Rosalynn Carter, *First Lady from Plains*, 265.

32. Rosalynn Carter, *First Lady from Plains*, 266–67; Jimmy and Rosalynn Carter, *Everything to Gain: Making the Most of the Rest of Your Life* (Fayetteville: University of Arkansas Press, 1995), 126–27; Celestine Sibley, "Portrait of Rosalynn," *Atlanta Journal*, May 14, 1977, 1A.

33. Rosalynn Carter, *First Lady from Plains*, 268.

34. John Osborne, "Rosalynn at Work," *New Republic*, August 26 and September 2, 1978, 12; David S. Broder, "Rosalynn Carter's Favorite Program," *Washington Post*, July 10, 1977, B1; Dorothy Marks, "Washington, My New Hometown," *Dossier*, January 1979, 42–43, Magazine Articles on Rosalynn Carter, FLSF, FLPO, box 50, JCL.

35. Rosalynn Carter, *First Lady from Plains*, 162.

36. Cook, *Eleanor Roosevelt*, 1:356–59; Jane Mansbridge, *Why We Lost the ERA* (Chicago: University of Chicago Press, 1986), 9.

37. Myra MacPherson, "Indiana Ratifies the ERA—with Rosalynn Carter's Aid," *Washington Post*, January 18, 1977, A1; Rosalynn Carter, *First Lady from Plains*, 271.

38. Rosalynn Carter, *First Lady from Plains*, 181–201.

39. Ibid., 177; David Vidal, "Ambassador Rosalynn Carter," *New York Times*, June 14, 1977, 18; Hoyt to RSC, September 15, 1977, Hoyt Chron: July–September 1977, box 28, FLSF, FLPO, JCL; "U.S. to Aid Colombia Stop Flow of Drugs," *Washington Post*, July 9, 1977, A3; "U.S. Announces Aid for Jamaica," *New York Times*, November 9, 1977, A26.

40. Rosalynn Carter, *First Lady from Plains*, 279, 282; "Discussant: Kathryn E. Cade," in Rosenbaum and Ugrinsky, *Presidency and Domestic Policies*, 533.

41. Howard Norton, *Rosalynn: A Portrait* (Plainfield, N.J.: Logos International, 1977), 89, 98; Jimmy Carter, *Keeping Faith: Memoirs of a President* (Fayetteville: University of Arkansas Press, 1995), 176; Rosalynn Carter, *First Lady from Plains*, 252, 294; Donnie Radcliffe, "The View from the Rose Garden," *Washington Post*, March 28, 1980, F1; Kenneth W. Thompson, ed., *The Carter Presidency: Fourteen Intimate Perspectives of Jimmy Carter* (Lanham, Md.: University Press of America, 1990), 232; K. B. Smith, "(Eleanor) Rosalynn (Smith) Carter," in Gould, *American First Ladies*, 569; Burton I. Kaufman and Scott Kaufman, *The Presidency of James Earl Carter, Jr.*, 2nd ed. (Lawrence: University Press of Kansas, 2006), 230; *Public Papers of the Presidents of the United States, Jimmy Carter, 1980–81*, 2:1487–88.

42. Hugh Carter and Frances Spatz Leighton, *Cousin Beedie and Cousin Hot: My Life with the Carter Family of Plains, Georgia* (Englewood Cliffs, N.J.: Prentice-Hall, 1978), 158; John Osborne, "Rosalynn," *New Republic*, August 19, 1978, 10; Marks, "Washington, My New Hometown" 44.

43. Scott Kaufman, *Rosalynn Carter: Equal Partner in the White House* (Lawrence: University Press of Kansas, 2007), 56; Suzanne Braun Levine and Mary Thom, *Bella Abzug: How One Tough Broad from the Bronx Fought Jim Crow and Joe McCarthy, Pissed Off Jimmy Carter, Battled for the Rights of Women and Workers, Rallied against War and for the Planet, and Shook Up Politics along the Way* (New York: Farrar, Straus and Giroux), 201.

44. Tom Morgenthau et al., "The President's Partner," *Newsweek*, November 5, 1979, 39; Joseph A. Califano Jr., *Inside: A Public and Private Life* (New York: Public Affairs, 2004), 369; Joseph A. Califano Jr., telephone interview with the author, December 6, 2006.

45. Morgenthau et al., "President's Partner," 39; Kaufman and Kaufman, *Presidency of James Earl Carter, Jr*, 179; President and Mrs. Carter, interview with the author, Carter Center, Atlanta, Ga., June 15, 2006.

46. Rosalynn Carter, *First Lady from Plains*, 286.

47. Thompson, *Carter Presidency*, 229.

48. Zbigniew Brzezinski, *Power and Principle: Memoirs of the National Security Adviser, 1977–1981* (New York: Farrar, Straus, Giroux, 1983), 57.

49. Rosalynn Carter, *First Lady from Plains*, 165–66; Jimmy Carter, *Keeping Faith*, 34, 59

50. "Mrs. President," *Newsweek*, August 6, 1979, 23; Martin Tolchin, "Rosalynn Carter: An Adviser in Her Own Right," *New York Times*, May 30, 1978, B1.

51. "Who Elected Rosalynn?," *Manchester (N.H.) Union Leader*, December 19, 1979; and Carl Rowan, "President Should Consult Rosalynn," *Washington Star*, August 3, 1979, Carter, Rosalynn [6], FLSF, FLPO, box 41; and Myra MacPherson, "Is Rosalynn Carter Really Running the Country?" *McCall's*, March 1980, FLSF, FLPO, box 50, JCL; Richard Cohen, "Rosalynn Carter's Role: Resolving the Mystery," *Washington Post*, July 31, 1979, C1.

52. Kaufman, *Rosalynn Carter*, 56–57; Rhonda Amon, "Rosalynn Carter: Jimmy's Doing Great Things," *Newsday*, December 3, 1978, Carter, Rosalynn [3], FLSF, FLPO, box 40, JCL; Sally Quinn, "Have You Heard What They're Not Saying about Rosalynn," *Washington Post*, June 25, 1978, K1; Mathews and De Hart, *Sex, Gender, and the Politics of ERA*, 94.

53. Leslie Bennetts, "The Wives' Campaign: Enormous Effort, Uncertain Impact," *New York Times*, October 28, 1980, A30; Gil Troy, *Mr. and Mrs. President: From the Trumans to the Clintons* (Lawrence: University Press of Kansas, 2000), 231.

54. B. Drummond Ayres Jr., "Barbs and Gossamer Line First Lady's Political Trail," *New York Times*, October 12, 1980, 34; "If Carter Gets Re-elected, Give Credit to First Lady," *Allentown (Pa.) Morning Call*, October 10, 1980, FLSF, FLPO, Box 46, JCL.

55. Kaufman, *Rosalynn Carter*, 144–63.

56. Susan Milligan, "President Signs $5.7 Billion Measure to Boost Volunteerism," *Boston Globe*, April 22, 2009, http://www.boston.com/news/nation/articles/2009/04/22/president_signs _57_billion_measure_to_boost_volunteerism/ (accessed October 16, 2013); Liz Szabo, "Rosalynn Carter, Vaccine Advocate," *USA Today*, November 15, 2011, 5D; Gianna Caserta, "Former First Lady Hosts Annual Caregiver Summit at GSW," WALB-TV, October 25, 2012, http://www.walb.com/ story/19919104/former-first-lady-hosts-annual-caregiver-summit-at-gsw (accessed October 16, 2013); "Rosalynn Carter Co-hosts Town Hall Meeting at South Georgia Technical College," *Americus Times-Recorder*, October 24, 2012, http://americustimesrecorder.com/local/x688452474/ Rosalynn-Carter-co-hosts-Town-Hall-meeting-at-South-Georgia-Technical-College (accessed October 16, 2013); "Mental Health Legislation We Need," *Washington Post*, September 19, 2008, A18.

57. William M. Welch, "Betty Ford Eulogized as One Who Helped Many," *USA Today*, July 13, 2011, 4A.

58. "Michelle Obama's No. 1 Role Remains 'Mom in Chief,'" *USA Today*, January 18, 2009, http:// www.azcentral.com/news/election/election08/articles/2009/01/18/20090118inaug-michelle0118 .html (accessed May 6, 2009).

Alice Tallulah-Kate Walker

(1944–)

On All Fronts

DEBORAH G. PLANT

❀ ❀ ❀

In *Hard Times Require Furious Dancing*, author-activist Alice Walker extols the virtues of dance, its ability to release stress and teach balance—physical and metaphysical—and its transformative magic within and throughout African culture. Having perceived the healing effects of dance, Walker declared that she had learned to dance anew. At a family celebration designed to dance away the sorrows of those gathered, Walker observed the next generation of her family engaged in "a spirited line dance." She confidently contemplated, "Though we have all encountered our share of grief and troubles, we can still hold the line of beauty, form, and beat—no small accomplishment in a world as challenging as this one.[1]

Throughout her career as a writer and revolutionary, Alice Walker has strived to use her art to portray the "grief and troubles," as well as the beauty and spirit, of African Americans in all their complexity. In "Duties of the Black Revolutionary," Walker writes, "A man's life can rarely be summed up in one word; even if that word is black or white. And it is the duty of the artist to present the man *as he is*."[2] For Walker, being a black revolutionary has meant being one with the people, and, at times, being the voice of the people as well as a voice for the people. Indeed, for Walker, art and politics are inextricable—her writing has always been a form of political as well as literary expression. In addition to being a writer, being a black revolutionary has also entailed assuming the role of teacher or educator. Walker has held several writer-in-residence and lecturer positions within the academy, teaching general courses on African American literature and courses specifically on black women writers. She is also credited with developing and teaching the first course on black women writers while at Smith College in 1973. Walker has wanted not only to cultivate her own liter-

ALICE TALLULAH-KATE WALKER

Emory University Photo Video.

ary and political voice but also to give voice to writers who have been excluded from the American literary canon and silenced or ignored within the African American literary canon. She realized that her own education "had left crucial areas empty, and had, in fact, contributed to a blind spot in my education that needed desperately to be cleared if I expected to be a whole woman, a full human being, a black woman full of self-awareness and pride."[3] Born in 1944 in Wards Chapel near Eatonton, in Putnam County, Georgia, the youngest of eight children in a family whose livelihood depended on sharecropping, Alice Malsenior Walker would come to know how challenging the world could be.[4] Walker traces her paternal ancestral line through the early 1800s to May Poole, her great-great-great-great-grandmother. Sold on the auction block in Virginia, May Poole then "walked to Eatonton with a baby straddled on each hip."[5] Albert Walker, May Poole's great-great-great-grandson and Walker's great-grandfather, inherited land from his Scottish slaveholding father. However, with his cotton crop destroyed by boll weevils for several successive years, Albert Walker lost his land and social standing and became a tenant farmer to a local white family. His son, Henry Clay Walker (Alice Walker's grandfather) assuaged his despair over the turn of fortune with drink and sport.

Alice Walker's mother, Minnie Tallulah (Lou) Grant (1912–93), was also from a family established in Putnam County, Georgia. Though Minnie Lou saw Henry Clay Walker's son, Willie Lee, as a sober and hardworking young man, Willie Lee lived in the shadow cast by his father and was thus deemed unacceptable in the eyes of William Grant—Minnie Lou's father—as a potential spouse for his daughter. Despite William Grant's disapproval, Minnie Lou loved and conceived a child with Willie Lee. The couple married six months later, on June 1, 1930.[6] The love, courage, and determination the couple shared would prove to be their mainstay in a Jim Crow South where white supremacy was the presumed order of the day. Longstanding racial division and enmity was exacerbated by the challenges ushered in during the Great Depression. Willie Lee and Minnie Lou Walker eked out a living as sharecroppers for the same white family that had hired Henry Clay Walker as a tenant farmer. The unsavory prospects of both tenant farming and sharecropping compelled Willie Lee Walker to seek more profitable employment as a laborer, though he would again and again have to return to tenant farming or sharecropping to feed his family.[7]

Even as President Herbert Hoover created relief programs to mitigate the suffering of the masses during the Great Depression and Franklin Roosevelt promised Americans a New Deal, the welfare of blacks was secondary to that of whites, and southern whites frequently gave themselves the authority to deny blacks those resources that were available. Minnie Lou Walker would tell Alice the story of receiving a government voucher to obtain flour from the local relief agency. Having put on a hand-me-down dress she had received from a sister living in the North, Mrs. Walker proceeded to run errands and redeem her voucher. Mrs. Walker's "nice" dress was seen by the white woman issuing the food supplies with an invidious eye: "Anybody dressed up as good as you don't need to come here begging for food."[8] Though Mrs. Walker proclaimed her right to resources as a taxpaying citizen and not a beggar, she was denied the flour. This story would later become the basis of Walker's short story "The Revenge of Hannah Kemuff."

By the time Alice was born in 1944, the Walker family's annual income ranged between $200 and $300.[9] In a depressed economy, however, even that income felt like prosperity, as Mrs. Walker could boast of paying the midwife Miss Fannie three dollars for her services: "'We wasn't so country then,' says Mom, / 'You being the last one— / And we couldn't, like / We done / When she brought your Brother, / Send her out to the / Pen / And let her pick / Out / A pig."[10] Baby Alice's entry into the world, nonetheless, had preceded the arrival of the midwife. Her unassisted birth would be interpreted, by some among the community, as a good omen. Mrs. Birda Reynolds, the local school teacher present at Alice Walker's birth, would express the general observation and consensus of kith and kin: "Alice was a very alert baby, and we could all tell, by the way her eyes took in everything, that she was going to be special."[11]

In defiance of landlords who espoused the opinion that black children had "no need for education," Mrs. Walker sent Alice, at age four, to join Mrs. Reynolds's first-grade class at East Putnam Consolidated, a school Walker's father helped to build. Superior at spelling and recitation, and thoughtful as well as attentive in class, young Alice was considered a prodigy.[12] The brilliance everyone witnessed appeared to fade some years later, simultaneously, with the sight in her right eye. In 1952, at the age of eight, one of her brothers shot a BB gun pellet into her eye during a game of cowboys and Indians. As Walker shares in her essay "Beauty: When the Other Dancer Is the Self," she was bereft of not only her sight in the damaged eye, but also her self-esteem: "For six years I do not stare at anyone, because I do not raise my head." Doted upon as cute and smart, the child who took in everything no longer gazed outward at the world around her. Embarrassed by the cataract that formed over her wounded eye, she cast her sight downward and inward. In hopes of shielding their child from the cruel taunts of children in her new school in Milledgeville, the Walkers took Alice back home to live with her grandparents. Feeling isolated and abandoned, Alice became pensive, introspective, and an observer of those around her. She took refuge in books and writing poetry.[13]

During the summer of 1958 Walker's eldest brother Bill (Willie Lee) and his wife, Gaynell, invited Alice to Boston, where the couple had relocated. Bill had arranged for Walker to be seen by ophthalmologist Dr. Morriss Henry at Massachusetts General Hospital, where the cataract was removed. Though the sight in her eye was permanently lost, the removal of the scar tissue allowed Walker to raise her head again and look out on her world with a confident smile. Her self-esteem returned and her social life and academic performance improved. She was voted queen of Butler-Baker High School and graduated valedictorian of the class of 1961. Walker's next step compelled her to look beyond Eatonton and the limited and servile occupations that would be open to a young black girl in a Jim Crow town.

The injustices Walker saw and experienced in Eatonton were part of the wider national story of a racially stratified America. As Walker came of age, African American resistance to systematic racial oppression in the South was also on the rise. African Americans across the South organized demonstrations and campaigns to end segregation and gain their civil rights. Walker had watched televised accounts of Charlayne Hunter (Gault) and Hamilton Holmes in 1960, as they braved the integration of the University of Georgia. She observed the unfolding of events surrounding the desegregation of the University of Mississippi. And she watched, in the same year, as Martin Luther King Jr. was handcuffed and pushed into a police van for leading a protest march against an Atlanta department store. This event Walker describes as "a turning point": "At the moment I saw his resistance I knew I would never be able to live in this country without resisting everything that sought to disinherit me, and I would never be forced away from the land of my birth without a fight."[14]

In August 1961 Mr. Willie Lee Walker drove his youngest daughter to the Greyhound bus station. Recipient of a paid scholarship, she was headed to Spelman College in Atlanta, Georgia. She was seventeen years old. Mrs. Minnie Lou Walker gifted her daughter with a typewriter, a sewing machine, and a suitcase, items purchased dearly on her maid's salary. Community elders raised seventy-five dollars in support of Alice Walker's future.[15] Walker boarded the Greyhound bus to Atlanta with the determination to "excel in the Arts," and with the courage to resist the forces of ignorance and bigotry that promised a continued "history of dispossession." Alice deliberately took a seat at the front of the Greyhound bus in the Eatonton bus station. A white woman passenger complained, and the driver demanded that Walker move to the rear of the bus: "I moved. But in those seconds of moving, everything changed. I was eager to bring an end to the South that permitted my humiliation."[16] Like her parents— who demanded living wages, built schools, and defied landlords—Alice Walker, too, was committed to taking a stand for human freedom and dignity. In Atlanta she would enter a new chapter in her life as a Spelman College student, and she would join the front lines of the Black Freedom Movement.

At Spelman, Walker was academically successful. She met and liked Staughton Lynd and Howard Zinn, both history professors and political activists who influenced her progressive ideas and encouraged her activism. She studied Russian history with Zinn, and she read and was impressed by Russian authors like Turgenev, Gorky, Gogol, Tolstoy, and Khmatova: "I read all the Russian writers I could find," especially Tolstoy, whose work "taught me the importance of diving through politics and social forecasts to dig into the essential spirit of individual persons," and "Dostoyevsky, who found his truths where everyone else seemed afraid to look."[17] These writers would have a lasting impression on Walker as she, a professed writer, would be moved to examine her own relationship to the land of her birth. "The Russian writers I admired had one thing in common: a sense of the Russian soul that was directly rooted in the soil that nourished it." Walker pondered the reality that William Faulkner, Eudora Welty, and Flannery O'Connor could remain in the land of their birth, but black writers, like Richard Wright, constantly exposed to "petty insults and legally encouraged humiliations," were compelled to forsake their heritage.[18]

Walker's studies, her political activism, and her travels to Helsinki, as a delegate to the 1962 World Youth Peace Festival, and then to Russia, broadened her national and international perspectives. Her experiences encouraged an openness that allowed for a romantic interest in David DeMoss, a white exchange student she met at Spelman. She would also meet Robert Allen, an African American student at Morehouse College. Over time, these two individuals would factor significantly in Walker's life.[19] Though successful academically and socially, Walker was discontented with the environment at Spelman, which she considered to be provincial and repressive, particularly after Howard Zinn was fired in the summer of 1963. She felt creatively stifled and politically repressed. "There is nothing here for me," she concluded. "It seems almost a matter of getting away or losing myself—my self—in this strange unreal place."[20]

Disheartened by the dismissal of Zinn, but emboldened by President John F. Kennedy's stance against segregation and his call for civil rights legislation, Alice Walker and David DeMoss joined the August 28, 1963, March on Washington. Perched on the limb of a tree some distance from the Lincoln Memorial where Martin Luther King Jr. spoke, Walker was moved by the cadence of King's "I Have a Dream" speech and its message. She felt her soul rise. She heard the speeches of John Lewis, James Farmer (whose speech was read), Walter Reuther, Josephine Baker, Rosa Parks, and a host of other civil rights activists.

In King's speech, Walker heard the sound of her own hushed voice. "And when he spoke of 'letting freedom ring' across 'the green hills of Alabama and the red hills of Georgia,'" King enabled her to see clearly that she was a native daughter of the South—with a claim to the land: "Those red hills of Georgia were mine, and nobody was going to force me away from them until I myself was good and ready to go." King urged those from the South to return: "Go back to Mississippi; go back to Alabama, go back . . . to Georgia . . . knowing that somehow this situation can and will be changed. . . . With this faith we will be able to hew out of the mountain of despair a stone of hope."[21]

Walker returned to Georgia but briefly; she completed the fall semester at Spelman and then traveled to New York to begin the spring semester of 1964 at Sarah Lawrence College, her transfer facilitated by Staughton Lynd. In her new academic home, she felt nurtured as a writer. Not only was her political activism encouraged, it was expected, as graduates of the college were expected to "change the world."[22]

At the end of a successful and optimistic spring term, Walker headed to Liberty County, Georgia, to join a group of civil rights workers on a voter registration drive. After the group was attacked and no community support was forthcoming, Walker opted to leave Georgia and engage in community development projects in Kenya, and then she later traveled to Uganda. There, in a village near Kampala, Walker was surprised by a visit from David DeMoss, who was in Tanzania as a Peace Corps worker. In the ecstasy of the moment, Walker and DeMoss had sexual relations. In the fall of 1965, Walker "returned to school healthy and brown, and loaded down with sculptures, and orange fabric—and pregnant."[23] She was devastated. She contemplated suicide. Adoption was not an option. Neither was raising the child. She informed DeMoss of her decision: "The letter was very matter-of-fact . . . just like Alice. She wanted to get an abortion. I was against it. But of course, it was her choice."[24]

But abortion was illegal. *Roe v. Wade* would not be decided until 1973. Yet Walker was desperate. A doctor was found, and friends and well-wishers, including DeMoss, contributed to the cost of the abortion. As she recovered, Walker "wrote without stopping." Each morning she would shove a cache of poems under the door of Muriel Rukeyeser, who sent the poems to her literary agent, Hiram Hayden, at Harcourt, Brace. The collection, titled *Once* was published in 1968. The volume included sketches of Africa, suicide poems Walker described as "the period of waiting," poems of struggle, and love poems.[25]

Walker was pleased that her collection of poems was published, but she found more significance in the actual writing of the poems, "which clarified for me how very much I love being alive."[26] This joie de vivre inspired the writing of the short story "To Hell with Dying" and saw Walker through the completion of her undergraduate work at Sarah Lawrence College, which culminated with an honors thesis on Albert Camus. Walker earned her Bachelor of Arts degree in 1966. Thereafter, she moved to New York City, where she was employed as a caseworker for the Department of Welfare for a short period of time. Though she had been offered a $2,000 Merrill Writing Fellowship to study and conduct research in Senegal, Walker was more compelled by the protests that swept across America and the continuing foment of unrest in the South.[27] Mississippi was a focal point for civil rights activists, a place where campaigns of intimidation were the rule of the day—a place that had become infamously renowned for the murders of Emmet Till, a black teenager who reportedly whistled at a white woman; Medgar Evers, an NAACP field director; and the Freedom Riders James Chaney, Andrew Goodman, and Michael Schwerner. In the face of such terrorism, Walker would stand: "Instead [of going to Africa] I caught a plane to Mississippi, where I knew no one personally and only one woman by reputation. That summer marked the beginning of a realization that I could never live happily in Africa—or anywhere else—until I could live freely in Mississippi.[28]

Walker elected to stake her claim in Mississippi, where she joined forces with the NAACP Legal Defense Fund (LDF), Inc., headed by Miriam Wright (Edelman). In defiance of the 1964 Civil Rights Act and the 1965 Voting Rights Act, the white power structure in Mississippi denied black citizenship and nullified black voting rights through myriad stratagems, including evicting blacks from their homes. Walker's task was to take depositions from blacks, mostly poor sharecroppers, in Greenwood, Mississippi. She was paired with Melvyn Levanthal, a Jewish American New York University Law School student and civil rights worker. An intern with the NAACP LDF, his task was to draft lawsuits informed by depositions collected by Walker and others.[29] Two tenacious and stalwart spirits, Walker and Levanthal were drawn to each other. "I loved Mel because he was passionate about justice," writes Walker, "and he was genuinely passionate about me." They married the following year on March 17, 1967, in New York City. The couple chose to continue their activism in Mississippi, a state where their interracial marriage was constitutionally illegal. Yet, Walker declared, "We intended to stand our ground. . . . We came to Mississippi to kill the fear it engendered as a place where black life was terrifyingly hard, pitifully cheap."[30]

Nina Simone sang these lyrics in her popular protest song "Mississippi Goddam": "Alabama's gotten me so upset / Tennessee made me lose my rest / And everybody knows about Mississippi Goddam."[31] Anne Moody's 1968 memoir *Coming of Age in Mississippi* condemns the halting and haunting poverty ex-

perienced by black people in rural Mississippi.[32] Her memoir also champions
the courage of activists like herself, who would face down the fear that was
engendered in Mississippi. More than any other place in the South, Mississippi
was perceived as ground zero of the Civil Rights movement. Although antiseg-
regation and voting rights legislation had been passed, another wave of activism
was necessary to have the laws enacted. It was not enough for Alice Walker that
the laws had been officially changed. It was utterly important to her that they be
practically applied to everyday life. Walker was determined to live freely in the
world, anywhere—including Mississippi. Her "illegal" marriage would deny the
codes of Mississippi law as Mississippi denied federal law. Her activism would
bring into reality the promise of civil rights legislation, and the activism of Mel
Levanthal would challenge those who dared not to comply.

Known as "Mr. Civil rights," Levanthal continued as staff attorney for the
NAACP LDF, fighting school segregation. He was firm in his conviction and determined in his action: "We *will* have quality education for every child." Walker
worked as a black history consultant to the Friends of the Children of Mississippi Head Start program. She also became writer-in-residence at Jackson State
University in 1968. She was recommended for the position by author Margaret
Walker, a professor at the university who was best known for her epic poem
"For My People" and her historical novel *Jubilee* (1966). Alice lived her politics
and walked her path as a writer, and, against the odds, her career began to flour-
ish. She was determined that her work would document the racial conditions
in the South, telling the story of the denial of black humanity. It would testify
to the will of black humanity to soar, and it would bear witness to the faith and
grace of a people continuously under pressure.[33]

Walker's literary career might be conceived as having three phases. From the
publication of *Once* in 1968 to the publication of *The Color Purple* in 1982, Walker's poetry, fiction, and nonfiction works focused mainly on African Americans
in the rural South. As she decried their oppressive existence, she depicted the
ways in which they struggled to survive and maintain their human dignity.
Works of this period chronicle the defeats and the triumphs of the civil rights
movement and the women's liberation movement. For as Walker brought her
lens to focus on the social stratification of and enmity between the races, she
also looked closely at the plight of black women who were subject to both racial domination within the larger American society and sexual domination and
domestic violence within the African American community.

Temple of My Familiar (1989) initiates the second phase of Walker's oeuvre,
which includes the controversial *Warrior Marks* (1993) and culminates with the
publication of *By the Light of My Father's Eyes*, published in 1998. Heretofore

the story of African American folk in the agrarian South was predominant. This focus does not fade into the background so much as it becomes the guiding inspiration of Walker's ever-expanding reach, vision, creativity, and humanity. *Temple* takes the reader from rural Georgia to South America, Africa, Europe, and points in between. *Possessing the Secret of Joy* (1992) and *Warrior Marks* both evince Walker's geographical and cultural expansiveness, as they reflect her growing attention to international human rights issues.

The Way Forward Is with a Broken Heart (2000) heralds the third phase of Walker's writing. This work—like *The Absolute Goodness of the Earth* (2003) and *Now Is the Time to Open Your Heart* (2004)—is symbolic of the optimism that infuses Walker's later writing. As her reach embraces humanity across the globe, it extends to include the natural environment and Earth itself. Even as the depth and breadth of Walker's work expand, there is one ever-constant theme and focus: the feminine principle. In the first phase of her writing, this focus entailed the documentation of the black female experience in America and the representation of black womanhood in literature, film, and the political arena. In the second phase, the author documents and explores the female experience in other cultures, particularly in Africa, Native America, and Europe. As this focus continues into the third phase, it transcends the natural realm into the spiritual and the historical realm into the mythic.

These periodic demarcations of Walker's literary career are neither rigidly distinct nor absolute, as her entire oeuvre is reflected, for example, in the poems collected in *Once*. From civil rights to international human rights, from social justice to environmental justice, and from planetary existence to transcendent spirit, what is intrinsic to Walker's literary work and political activism is an investigation into truth, freedom, and love.

Walker explored these themes in her first work of long fiction, which she wrote during the height of the struggle for racial justice in Mississippi. As writing was essential to Walker's creative expression and was also a vital aspect of her political activism, she would continue her literary efforts under the most trying of circumstances. In the midst of social and political turmoil, Alice Walker made steady progress on her first novel manuscript, "The Third Life of Grange Copeland." She was also pregnant. Three days after completing the book, Rebecca Grant Levanthal was born.[34] As Walker embraced the miracle that was Rebecca, she was anxious about the hostile environment into which Rebecca was born, and, as a writer, she was also concerned about how being a mother would change her life. "It helped tremendously that by the time Rebecca was born I had no doubts about being a writer," states Walker. As writing was an essential aspect of Walker's being, she would also come to embrace the essentiality of "The Child": "To some of us—artists, writers, poets, jugglers—The Child is perceived as threat, as danger, as enemy. In truth, society is badly arranged for children to be taken into happy account. How many of us can say we have never forgotten 'The Child'? I cannot say this. But I can say I am learning not to forget."[35]

The Third Life of Grange Copeland, published in 1970, was a depiction of how badly arranged society could be. Walker follows the life of Grange Copeland through three generations. Grange is a tenant farmer in Green County, Georgia, during the 1920s. The optimism that attended life with his wife, Margaret, and son, Brownfield, is gradually overshadowed by anger, debt, despair, and violence. Though whites live on the periphery of the lives of the main characters, the deleterious effects of their supremacist ideology is everywhere present in the lives of the Copeland family, from the economic exploitation of their labor, to the dilapidated shacks in which they live, and, mainly, in the psychological enthrallment they suffer. Grange's self-hate and sense of inadequacy compels him to abandon his family and seek a better living "up North." His experiences in New York lead him to periods of self-reflection that restore his sense of self and a will to redeem his life. He awakens to a realization that "nobody's as powerful as we make them out to be. We got our own souls don't we?"[36] Through his love and care for his granddaughter, Ruth, Grange experiences a sense of redemption and offers a more promising path for the next generation.

Where some critics applauded Walker's ability to portray the rural South and capture the humanity of her characters, others decried the work as shallow, unrealistic, and sentimental. In letters to the editor and in her critical essays, Walker took issue with critical reviews and interpretations of her work and the work of other black writers. In a letter to her friends, colleagues, and supporters, Walker made her case: "It is important that black artists protest racist interpretations of their work, cavalier and insensitive handling of it, and white people's unfailing ability to be dishonest, when it comes to evaluating the work of black artists. . . . I refuse to accept other people's warped vision of what I am or what my experiences have been, but will challenge them wherever they are found, not only in relation to my own work but also in relation to that of other black writers and poets." She signed the letter, "On all fronts, Alice Walker."[37] As she would protest interpretations of white critics, she would also defy the dictates of Black Power politics and black cultural nationalists who charged artists with the task of depicting the black revolutionary in confrontation with a white racist society.

In her writing, Walker sought to express not just her own generation's character and experiences, but those of their forebears as well, and she especially paid homage to the creative powers and labors of prior generations of African

American women. Through essays such as the highly regarded "In Search of Our Mother's Gardens," she sought to reclaim and reinterpret the voices of her literary foremothers. In recognizing the unique expressions of their voices in quilt patterns and flower gardens as well as in poems, paintings, novels, and songs, Walker reclaimed ancestral legacies and acknowledged the individual and collective responsibility of African American people: "*We are a people. A people do not throw their geniuses away.* And if they are thrown away, it is our duty *as artists and as witnesses for the future* to collect them again for the sake of our children, and, if necessary, bone by bone."[38] So it was in 1973 that Alice Walker went "looking for Zora." Her search took her to Eatonville, Florida, where Zora Neale Hurston grew up, then to Fort Pierce, Florida, where Hurston lived in her later years and where she died. Walker's expedition culminated with her placing a marker at Hurston's gravesite, with the inscription "Genius of the South." Walker recounted the journey in her essay "Looking for Zora," originally published in 1975 in *Ms.* Magazine as "In Search of Zora Neale Hurston." Along with the work of scholar Robert Hemenway, Alice Walker's iconic search for Zora Neale Hurston resulted in a veritable literary renaissance of the author and social scientist. Walker subsequently coedited with scholar and friend Mary Helen Washington the Zora Neale Hurston reader *I Love Myself When I Am Laughing, and Then Again When I'm Looking Mean and Serious* (1979). Inspired and encouraged by both Hemenway and Walker, Georgia native Valerie Boyd, journalist, scholar, and biographer went on to write the critically acclaimed biography *Wrapped in Rainbows*, and Oprah Winfrey would produce a television film adaptation of *Their Eyes Were Watching God.*[39]

In the fashion of her literary foremother, Walker embraced "the folk," their customs, and expressions, infusing her poetry and fiction with unapologetic portraits and landscapes of the rural South of her birth. Awarded a Radcliffe Institute Fellowship from Harvard University in 1971 and 1972, Walker settled into the Cambridge, Massachusetts, area where, drawing on her experiences in the South as well as in New England, she penned a collection of short stories, *In Love and in Trouble: Stories of Black Women* (1973), and a second volume of poems, *Revolutionary Petunias and Other Poems* (1973). *In Love and in Trouble* captures the lives, loves, losses, resignations, and resiliencies of thirteen black women. The stories explore some of the predominant themes in Walker's writings: oppression and triumph over oppression, relationships—romantic, familial, interracial—self-knowledge, self-love, creativity, freedom, and the human spirit. Several stories are informed by Walker family lore and black folk tradition. "The Revenge of Hannah Kemhuff," recalls the story told by Walker's mother and is dedicated to Zora Neale Hurston. In the fictional account, Mrs.

Kemhuff is insulted and plots revenge. She avails herself of the services of Tante Rosie, a root worker. Assisted by Tante Rosie's apprentice, Mrs. Kemhuff prays a "curse-prayer," which they recite "straight from Zora Neale Hurston's book *Mules and Men*."[40]

The widely anthologized "Everyday Use" ponders the questions of value and identity and captures aspects of the Black Power movement. In this story Walker observes a growing materialism, consumerism, and a modernity that threatens family relations and distances the older from the younger generation. "The Welcome Table" looks at religious bigotry and hypocrisy in the racially segregated South, but moreover, it attempts to understand the mystery behind hate and racial prejudice. In stories like "Really, *Doesn't* Crime Pay?" and "Her Sweet Jerome," Walker questions the conventional view of marriage as a safe haven for women. Throughout the collection, the protagonists struggle against societal norms, and in using their singular means to find wholeness, they are defiant even in their defeat.

The spare but cogent verse in *Revolutionary Petunias and Other Poems* garnered Walker the Lillian Smith Award. Poems in the first half of the collection are like scrapbook photographs. In "Three Dollars Cash," there is the birth of little Alice. In "Uncles" one sees the return of northern relatives to the family homestead and is privy to the stinging insults they make and the nickel or dime they would give their nieces. Poems like "You Had to Go to Funerals" and "Burial" speak of home goings and the passage of time as the narrator cries, "Not for the dead, but the gray in my / first grade teacher's hair." And "For My Sister Molly Who in the 50s" is a portrait of the author's eldest sister and speaks of the leave taking of family and friends who could not endure the daily humiliations of the Jim Crow South. "Women" profiles Walker's mother and the women of her mother's generation. "Headragged Generals," she describes them, "With fists as well as / Hands," who anticipated the needs of the next generation.[41] The title poem is a ballad that compares Sammy Lou, a "backwoods woman," to a petunia, "incorrect" and rebellious against a final humiliation and assault on her spirit—which she could not absorb.[42] "Be Nobody's Darling," and "While Love Is Unfashionable," which is dedicated to Mel Levanthal, affirm the need to live one's own truth in the world. Both poems speak of being incorrect, unfashionable, and outcast as attributes of the revolutionary spirit requisite in the defiance of oppressive convention of whatever ilk.

In 1974 *In Love and in Trouble* won the National Institute of Arts and Letters award, and *Revolutionary Petunias* was nominated for a National Book Award. Other nominees included Adrienne Rich and Audre Lorde. As they did not cherish the competiveness and the gender and racial bias inherent in the award process, the three writers agreed that the "winner" would accept the prize on behalf of all women. Adrienne Rich, who shared the win with poet Allen Ginsberg, accepted the award on behalf of Walker and Lourde.[43] In 1974 Walker also published a biographical work, *Langston Hughes: An American Poet*, written in memory of her mentor and friend who died in 1967.

After the completion of her time in Cambridge, Walker returned to Jackson, Mississippi. Though the state manifested changes instigated and instituted by civil rights activism and court legislation, Walker found no southern comfort in the heart of Mississippi: "I became an adult there, to have been in the crux was very important. Mel and I made a difference. But we paid a price."[44] Walker and Levanthal moved to New York, where Levanthal continued his work as a civil rights lawyer, and Walker accepted a position at *Ms.* magazine as contributing editor. Her responsibilities included reading poetry and fiction submissions and writing book reviews. In her editorial position, she would introduce to *Ms.* and its readership African voices like Buchi Emecheta, African American voices like Ann Allen Shockley, and African American–Japanese voices like Ai (Florence Anthony). Walker's choices and recommendations drew controversy even within the *Ms.* house, but Gloria Steinem, cofounder of the magazine and eventual lifelong friend of the author was extraordinary in her feminist stance and in her support of Walker: "There was blatant rebelliousness, in Alice's own work and in that of other writers she brought to the magazine. She saw rebellion as key to the freedom and empowerment of women. She was far more radical than most of us in that regard."[45]

In the more diverse and progressive environment of New York, Walker completed her second novel, *Meridian*, which was published in 1976. *Meridian* explores the meaning of identity, justice, social responsibility, and freedom. The novel's protagonist, Meridian, evokes the saga of the civil rights era, a time of personal, social, and political upheaval—all spaces in which Meridian confronts the questions of her own life, that of black folks collectively, and of life itself. Having flouted the traditions of marriage and motherhood, Meridian divorced her husband and gave up her child for adoption. She became involved in the civil rights movement and continued her involvement when she moved to Atlanta to study at Saxon College, an institution that recalls Spelman College and the experiences Walker had there as a student-activist.

Through Meridian and prominent characters Truman Held, a black nationalist and Meridian's former lover, and Lynne Rabinowitz, a white civil rights activist Truman marries, Walker explores the racial, gender, and sexual politics of Black Power Movement organizations. She examines the passion, intention, confusion, and hypocrisy that characterized and complicated the lives of black and white revolutionaries and their leadership. Meridian finds herself cast out of the black nationalist circle, as she could not commit to kill "for the revolution." Rather, Meridian is compelled to investigate and ponder such questions and their consequences. Carrying the guilt of giving up her first child and aborting the second, Meridian's life is an act of atonement, a personal and political journey in quest of her own truth.

Two civil rights activists whose union was forged in the heat of the "Southern Revolution," Walker and Levanthal came to the painful conclusion that their marriage could no longer be sustained. The move to New York put some distance between the couple and the provinciality of Mississippi, but it did nothing to close the distance that had grown between them. They divorced in 1976. Levanthal went on to marry Judith Goldsmith in 1978, and Walker became reacquainted with Robert Allen. Rebecca Levanthal (later Walker) was seven years of age at the time. She would reflect on those years in her memoir *Black, White, and Jewish* (2001).

For a while after the divorce Walker would find comfort in The Sisterhood, a group of black women writers organized by Walker and June Jordan. Toni Morrison, Ntozake Shange, and Verta Mae Grosvenor were among the participants. "It was like a council," Walker remembers. "Being together was the medicine." Walker had by then a conception of her next novel, but its characters were reluctant to take form in an urban milieu. Thus, with a 1977 Guggenheim Fellowship in hand and a retainer with *Ms.*, Walker moved to Boonville, California. She would begin work on her book manuscript "The Color Purple" and solidify her relationship with Robert Allen. The following year, Walker published *Good Night Willie Lee, I'll See You in the Morning*, in memory of her father who died in 1973. The volume of poems speaks of romantic love, with its paradoxical agonies ("I loved the suffering") and offers the caveat that "needful love has to be chopped out or forced to wilt back."[46] The title poem, also the closing poem, captures a moment of grace as Minnie Lou Walker looks upon the body of her husband one last time, and whispers, "Good Night, Willie Lee, I'll See You in the Morning." The narrator observes the moment and concludes that "the healing of all our wounds is forgiveness."[47] The poem suggests that forgiveness is the balm for all wounds—those suffered between lovers, siblings, friends, spouses, races, and nations.

Walker's second collection of short stories, *You Can't Keep a Good Woman Down*, was published in 1981. As the black women in the first short story collection struggled against the conventions of a male-dominated and racially prejudiced society and within repressive personal and familial relationships, those in the second volume defy and challenge social restrictions and outmoded political policies. They are self-assertive and emboldened to move in the world on their own terms. Unlike the women in *In Love and in Trouble*, these women would not "burn themselves up." In contrast to characters in the first collection, Walker writes: "I am ready to look at women who have made the room larger for others to move in. . . . The Movement of the Sixties, Black Power, the Muslims, the Panthers . . . have changed the options of Black people generally and of Black Women in particular. So that my women characters won't all end the way they have been. . . . We have made a place to move on."[48]

Walker's characters in *You Can't Keep a Good Woman Down* are not unlike the women in blues songs sung by Big Mama Thornton, the prototype of Gracie Mae Still in "Nineteen Fifty-five," the opening story. The women in these stories pose questions about the value and quality of a black woman's life. They address the matter of selfhood and challenge the topical social issues of abortion, pornography, and sexual violence against women. "Advancing Luna," for instance, focuses on interracial rape. The protagonist engages the issue from a black female perspective, revealing a black woman's pain in a society wherein she experiences a double invisibility. The narrator-protagonist asks: "Who knows what the black woman thinks of rape? Who has asked her? Who *cares*?"[49] The reviews of the second collection describe Walker's stories as weak in characterization and plot structure, and question Walker's narrative technique. Scholar Barbara Christian reasons that Walker breaks the literary conventions by writing about "womanist" issues and, moreover, in using a "womanist process" to do so, as her stories reflect the present tense "unraveling of thought and feeling."[50]

Alice Walker coined the term "womanist," which she defines in the opening pages of *In Search of Our Mothers' Gardens: Womanist Prose*: "A black feminist or feminist of color. . . . A woman who loves other women, sexually and/ or nonsexually . . . sometimes loves individual men, sexually and/or nonsexually. Committed to survival and wholeness of entire people, male *and* female."[51] Walker conceived of "womanism" in contradistinction to "feminism," which she perceived to be exclusive, separatist, and narrowly conceived. Thus, the closing definition: "Womanist is to feminist as purple is to lavender."[52] Walker pointed out in "One Child of One's Own" that the feminist imagination tended to be white and middle class and was challenged to conceive of black women as women.[53] Walker wondered at the absence of black women from scholarly works produced by white feminists, and she questioned the approach of white women when interpreting and evaluating texts written by African American women and other women of color. In her essay "Gifts of Power," she argued for a womanist approach to black women's writing, one that honored and respected black women's history, cultural values, and traditions.

Alice Walker's appreciation for the black female condition and the promise of her legacy began with the stories of women in her own family and community in Eatonton. These stories were the creative matrix for Walker's Pulitzer Prize–winning novel *The Color Purple*. An epistolary novel, *The Color Purple* recounts the life of Celie, the novel's protagonist, through a series of letters. The first series of letters are from Celie to God. Celie is a fourteen-year-old black girl growing up in rural Georgia. She is physically, psychologically, and spiritually abused and repeatedly raped by her stepfather, Fonso. He warns Celie, "You better not tell nobody but God. It'd kill your mammy."[54] Celie's letters tell of her two children, whom she believes to be dead; a sister, Nettie, she also believes to be dead; marriage to an overbearing man who beats her; and Shug Avery, whom she nurses back to health and with whom she falls in love.

Letters from Nettie to Celie initiate the second series of letters, when Shug aids Celie in discovering the letters hidden in Albert's trunk. Through the letters, Celie learns that her sister lives, as do her children. She discovers the truth of her biological and familial world, and she is introduced to her ancestral world— Africa. In content and style, *The Color Purple* was groundbreaking. Central to the story is the loving relationship between Celie and Shug, whose relationship includes sexual love that is healing and transformative and that eventually has a positive effect on their whole community. Walker's presentation of relationships between women as sisters, mothers and daughters, friends, and lovers is visionary, as it expresses the possibilities of black womanhood as celebratory, inspiring, empowering, and as protective against the insults and assaults of white and patriarchal exploitation and domination. It is through this Sisterhood that most females in the novel overcome the trauma of sexism, domestic violence, incest, racist violence, verbal and mental abuse, and unadulterated meanness.

Gwendolyn Brooks was the first black woman to win the Pulitzer Prize in poetry. She captured the award in 1950 for her collection *Annie Allen*. In 1983, Alice Walker became the first black woman to win a Pulitzer Prize in the fiction category. She would also claim that year the American Book Award in Fiction. Some critics were wary of the accolades Walker's work received, as they looked askance at her representation of African American life. Some took issue with her use of black folk speech, her depiction of relations between black men and women, her characterization of lesbian relationships as a viable alternative to heterosexual relationships, and her portrayal of black men. These critics believed Walker's work reinforced stereotypes of black people as backward, black women as promiscuous, and black men as violent. The debate around these issues heightened as Steven Spielberg's 1984 film adaptation of the novel took the story to a mass audience.[55] The movie, featuring Whoopi Goldberg, Margaret

Avery, Danny Glover, and Oprah Winfrey, was nominated for eleven Academy Awards. Walker's novel also inspired the 2004 musical *The Color Purple*, produced by Scott Sanders, which garnered the Tony Award in 2006. The controversy around Walker's novel and the film adaptation of the novel would continue for some time. Walker's response to the controversy and her truths about *The Color Purple*, in its myriad forms, is chronicled in her 1996 publication, *The Same River Twice: Honoring the Difficult*.

As Walker endeavored to uncover and recover black women's legacies, she was also mindful of her own. She therefore compiled journal entries, unpublished essays and previously published essays, interviews, and letters into a volume titled *In Search of Our Mother's Gardens: Womanist Prose* (1983). Like the novel *The Color Purple*, the collection of prose sounded the depths of black women's lives and celebrated their ability to bloom wherever they might be planted. As *The Color Purple* broadened the American and African American literary canon, *In Search* furthered the cause of gender equality in America, offering the historical and theoretical contexts in which to understand and appreciate black women's lives and literature.

Alice Walker would augment her contribution to literature and cultural activism through the creation of a publishing enterprise. In 1984 Walker, in partnership with Robert Allen and Belvie Brooks, established Wild Trees Press. "We publish only what we love," was the guiding spirit of their endeavors.[56] Walker would be midwife to new and otherwise marginalized voices. Among the six authors published by 1988 when the press closed, was J. California Cooper's collection of short stories *A Piece of Mine* (1984), and Madi Ker Tonegoro's *The Spirit Journey: Stories and Paintings of Bali* (1988).

An internationally acclaimed writer who would continue to defy convention and the status quo, Walker and her work, life, and life choices would continue to be scrutinized. Controversy notwithstanding, Walker would always find consolation in her integrity as an artist. In "Each One, Pull One," from *Horses Make the Landscape Look More Beautiful*, Walker wrote these words, with Lorraine Hansberry in mind: "But, most of all, did we write exactly what we saw, / as clearly as we could? / Were we unsophisticated / enough to cry *and* scream?"[57] Not interested in being or not being "anybody's darling," Walker was clear that she was accountable only to the ancestors. In relation to editors and publishers of her earlier work, she had commented: "Generations of people have suffered and died so that I could be this free. And with that always in my heart, I write whatever I feel needs to be written. I work for the ancestors. Period."[58] Her fourth novel, *Temple of My Familiar*, is "literarily trying to reconnect us to our ancestors," writes Walker.[59] Through the marital, familial, and communal relationships of her major characters Carlotta, Zedé, Arveyda, Suwelo, Miss Lissie, and Hal, Walker explores the intersecting histories and cultures of peoples of the Americas, Africa, and England, over generations and through dimensions of time. Mainly through a narrative technique that honors the oral tradition, the characters tell one another their stories. Within the exchange between the storyteller and the listener unfolds the meaning of life, relationship, kinship, spirit, and freedom. In *Temple*, Walker's reach is global, its depth is mythic, and its breadth is universal, holistic, and all inclusive. As the beauty and mystery of life is lauded, humankind is reminded of its responsibility to remember and be mindful of the tenuous, interconnecting web of life.

As with Walker's writing and publication, her activism has never abated. She would continue to address social and political injustices and would do so, more increasingly, on an international scale, and her activism would extend to all life forms and the planet itself. Works like *Living by the Word* (1988) and *Anything We Love Can Be Saved: A Writer's Activism* (1997) reflect Walker's continued focus on women's liberation, protection of the earth, and an evolving holistic spirituality. As Walker's earlier works addressed the condition and the possibility of black women in American society, later works like *Possessing the Secret of Joy* (1992) and *Warrior Marks* (1993) examine the condition of women in Africa, particularly in relation to the custom of female circumcision. In *Possessing*, Tashi-Evelyn is perplexed that the suffering of women is overlooked or ignored. A character first introduced in *The Color Purple* as Tashi, then later in *Temple*, Tashi-Evelyn is the childhood friend of Adam and Olivia (Celie's children) and later marries Adam. Tashi feels compelled by cultural politics to undergo the ritual of female circumcision. This rite leads to her physical and psychological suffering. As *The Color Purple* examined the nature of domestic violence within the black family, *Possessing* brings light to another kind of "secret": "An unpopular story. Even a taboo one. An ancient story. A modern story . . . a practice that undermines the collective health and wholeness of great numbers of people in Africa, the Middle East, and the Far East and is rapidly finding a toehold in the Western World."[60]

Walker further expounded on this taboo subject in her film documentary *Warrior Marks*, directed by Pratibha Parmar, and the film's companion volume, *Female Genital Mutilation and the Sexual Blinding of Women*. Walker anchors the film and the book in an empathetic understanding of childhood wounding. She shares in *Warrior Marks* that her own injury, not unlike the circumcision of little African girls, "was a patriarchal wound." Walker's writing and activism on this issue was met with hostility and repudiation, both within the United States and abroad, and among blacks and whites. Some activists labeled Walker a cultural imperialist and stated that she might do better to pursue other causes.[61]

Walker's attention to issues concerning children and women inform her ever-expanding ecofeminism, as her works become more focused on the earth as home place, women as symbolic of the earth and embodiments of the divine feminine, and children as spiritual gifts that encourage humanity toward love, peace, and grace. Walker's 2003 poetry volume *Absolute Trust in the Goodness of the Earth* is dedicated to "the Blessed Feminine in All of us." Walker reasons in this volume that to the extent that women are comfortable and children's cries are heard, war would become obsolete. *Absolute Trust* also contains poems of mourning and hope for those lives lost during the September 11, 2001, tragedy. As in the pamphlet *Sent by Earth: A Message from the Grandmother Spirit, After the Attacks on the World Trade Center and Pentagon* (2001), *Absolute Trust* ponders "the dogs of war" and the consequences of war.

Even as Walker continues to bear witness to the horror of war, violence, and the destruction of the earth in the essays in *Overcoming Speechlessness* (2010), she also states in her poem: "The World Has Changed: / Wake up & smell / The possibility."[62] In 2007 Walker would endorse the presidential nomination of Barack Obama. In a 2009 interview she allowed that "with the election of a black man to the presidency of the United States, the world *has* changed. . . . That we continued to believe in and then to work for change, in the person of Obama, was remarkable."[63] Walker's work attests to changes in many areas of national and global society. Perspectives have been changed in relation to women and the earth, she writes, thanks in large part to feminism, feminist and womanist scholarship, and the resounding voices of indigenous peoples around the globe.[64]

The world *has* changed, and Alice Walker is a major contributor to a changed world. One of the most prolific writers of our time, Walker has been active as an instrument of change in every major social and environmental movement since her days of voter registration drives in the streets of Georgia and Mississippi. Her writings provide an incisive and adept portrayal of America as it has been, as it is, and as it can be, in the context of an international community. Through institutions like the Alice Walker Literary Society, chartered in 1997, America has begun to pay homage to a national and international treasure. Officials of DeKalb County, Georgia, declared April 24, 2009, "Alice Walker Day."[65] Alice Tallulah-Kate Walker's legacy continues. The optimism inherent in her writing and activism and in her ongoing quest to awaken the world to a transformative spirituality is recognized as one of the hallmarks of her evolving legacy. Whatever else has gone before, Walker writes that she "will / go / on / believing / that / love / is / the / future / that / I deserve / Peace / the future / whose / time / has / come.[66]

NOTES

1. Alice Walker, *Hard Times Require Furious Dancing* (New York: New Library, 2010), xvi.

2. Alice Walker, *In Search of Our Mothers' Gardens: Womanist Prose* (New York: Harcourt, Brace, Jovanovich, 1983), 137.

3. Ibid., 131.

4. Walker was named Alice Malsenior at birth. She officially changed her middle name, in 1994, on her fiftieth birthday, in honor of her mother and paternal grandmother. "Whatever the word Tallulah means in itself, to me it means 'restored' in me. . . . The word Kate means 'remembered' in me" (Evelyn C. White, *Alice Walker: A Life* [New York: Norton, 2004], 462–63). The biographical portrait of Alice Walker rendered here is largely informed by Evelyn C. White's biography on Walker, the only biography sanctioned by the author.

5. Alice Walker, *The World Has Changed: Conversations with Alice Walker*, ed. Rudolph P. Byrd (New York: The New Press, 2010), 81.

6. White, *Alice Walker*, 20–22.

7. Ibid., 24.

8. Ibid., 27.

9. Ibid., 26.

10. Alice Walker, *Revolutionary Petunias and Other Poems* (New York: Harcourt, Brace, Jovanovich, 1971), 6.

11. White, *Alice Walker*, 10–13.

12. Ibid., 14–15.

13. Alice Walker, "Beauty: When the Other Dancer Is the Self," in *In Search*, 387–89; White, *Alice Walker*, 39–40.

14. Alice Walker, "Choice: A Tribute to Martin Luther King, Jr.," in *In Search*, 143–44; White, *Alice Walker*, 60.

15. White, *Alice Walker*, 64–65.

16. Walker, *World Has Changed*, 42.

17. Ibid., 45.

18. Walker, *In Search*, 164.

19. White, *Alice Walker*, 75.

20. Ibid., 86–92.

21. Walker, *In Search*, 160.

22. Ibid., 38, 37.

23. Walker, *World Has Changed*, 35–36.

24. White, *Alice Walker*, 112.

25. Ibid., 38, 37–38.

26. Ibid., 39.

27. Ibid., 123, 133.

28. Walker, *In Search*, 163.

29. White, *Alice Walker*, 132–35.

30. Ibid., 157.

31. Nina Simone, "Mississippi Goddam," *Nina Simone in Concert* (New York: Philips Records, 1964).

32. Anne Moody, *Coming of Age in Mississippi* (New York: Doubleday, 1968).

33. Ibid., 147; Walker, *In Search*, 32.

34. Walker, *In Search*, 367.

35. Ibid., 369, 362.

36. Walker, *Third Life of Grange Copeland* (New York: Harcourt, Brace, Jovanovich, 1970), 207.

37. White, *Alice Walker*, 190–91.

38. Ibid., 92.

39. Robert Hemenway published the first extended biographical work on Zora Neale Hurston: *Zora Neale Hurston: A Literary Biography* (Urbana: University of Illinois Press, 1977). Hemenway's work would stand as the definitive portrait of Hurston until the 2003 publication of Valerie Boyd's *Wrapped in Rainbows: The Life of Zora Neale Hurston* (New York: Scribner).

40. Alice Walker, *In Love and in Trouble: Stories of Black Women* (New York: Harcourt, Brace, Jovanovich, 1973), 72.

41. Walker, *Revolutionary Petunias and Other Poems*, 5.

42. Walker, *Revolutionary Petunias and Other Poems*, 29.

43. White, *Alice Walker*, 271.

44. Ibid., 263.

45. Ibid., 306.

46. Alice Walker, *Good Night Willie Lee, I'll See You in the Morning* (New York: Harcourt, Brace, Jovanovich, 1979), 3.

47. Ibid., 53.

48. Mary Helen Washington, "An Essay on Alice Walker," in *Alice Walker: Critical Perspectives Past and Present*, ed. Henry Louis Gates and K. A. Appiah (New York: Amistad, 1993), 64.

49. Alice Walker, *You Can't Keep a Good Woman Down* (New York: Harcourt Brace, Jovanovich, 1981), 71.

50. Barbara Christian, *Black Feminist Criticism: Perspectives on Black Women Writers* (New York: Pergamon, 1985), 92.

51. Walker, *In Search*, xi.

52. Ibid., xii.

53. Ibid., 372.

54. Alice Walker, *The Color Purple* (Orlando, Fla.: Harcourt Books, 1982), 1.

55. For an overview of the critical backlash against *The Color Purple*, see Calvin Hernton's "Who's Afraid of Alice Walker: The Color Purple as Slave Narrative," in his *The Sexual Mountain and Black Women Writers: Adventures in Sex, Literature, and Real Life* (Garden City, N.Y.: Anchor, 1987), 1–36.

56. White, *Alice Walker*, 388.

57. Alice Walker, *Horses Make the Landscape Look More Beautiful* (New York: Harcourt, Brace, Jovanovich, 1984), 50.

58. White, *Alice Walker*, 293.

59. Walker, *World Has Changed*, 85.

60. Alice Walker, *Anything We Love Can Be Saved: A Writer's Activism* (New York: Random House, 1997), 126.

61. White, *Alice Walker*, 459.

62. Walker, *World Has Changed*, xix.

63. Walker, *World Has Changed*, 311.

64. Walker, *Anything We Love*, 20–21.

65. Walker, *World Has Changed*, xvii.

66. Alice Walker, *A Poem Traveled down My Arm* (New York: Random, 2003), 150–51.

Selected Bibliography

PRIMARY SOURCES

Carter, Rosalynn. *First Lady from Plains*. Boston: Houghton Mifflin, 1984.

Gladney, Margaret Rose, ed. *How Am I to Be Heard: Letters of Lillian Smith*. Chapel Hill: University of North Carolina Press, 1993.

Hunter-Gault, Charlayne. *In My Place*. New York: Vintage Books, 1993.

Lumpkin, Katharine Du Pre. *The Making of a Southerner*. 1946. Rev. ed. Athens: University of Georgia Press, 1991.

Majette, Vara A. *White Blood*. Boston: Stratford Publishing Co., 1924.

McCullers, Carson. *Complete Novels*. New York: Library of America, 2001.

———. *Illumination and Glare: The Unfinished Autobiography of Carson McCullers*. Madison: University of Wisconsin Press, 1999.

Mitchell, Margaret. *Gone With the Wind*. New York: Macmillan and Co., 1936.

O'Connor, Flannery. *Collected Works*, edited by Sally Fitzgerald. New York: Library of America, 1988.

———. *The Habit of Being: Letters of Flannery O'Connor*, edited by Sally Fitzgerald. New York: Farrar, Straus, and Giroux, 1989.

Smith, Lillian. *Killers of the Dream*. 1949. Rev. ed. New York: W. W. Norton, 1961.

———. *Strange Fruit*. 1944. Rev. ed. New York: Harvest Books, 1992.

Walker, Alice. *The Color Purple*. 1982. Rev. ed. New York: Mariner Books, 2003.

———. *Meridian*. New York: Simon and Schuster, 1976.

———. *In Search of Our Mother's Gardens*. 1983 New York: Mariner Books, 2003.

SECONDARY SOURCES

Ayers, Edward L. *The Promise of the New South: Life after Reconstruction*. New York: Oxford University Press, 1992.

Bartley, Numan V. *The Creation of Modern Georgia*. Athens: University of Georgia Press, 1990.

———. *The Rise of Massive Resistance: Race and Politics in the South during the 1950s*. Baton Rouge: Louisiana State University Press, 1969.

Beardsley, Edward H. *A History of Neglect: Health Care for Blacks and Mill Workers in the Twentieth-Century South.* Knoxville: University of Tennessee Press, 1987.

Becker, Jane. *Selling Tradition: Appalachia and the Construction of an American Folk.* Chapel Hill: University of North Carolina Press, 1998.

Bederman, Gail. "'Civilization,' the Decline of Middle-Class Manliness, and Ida B. Wells's Antilynching Campaign (1892–1894)." *Radical History Review* 52 (Winter 1992): 432–65.

Bernhard, Virginia, Betty Brandon, Elizabeth Fox-Genovese, and Theda Perdue, eds. *Southern Women: History and Identities.* Columbia: University of Missouri Press, 1992.

Black, Earl, and Merle Black. *The Rise of Southern Republicans.* Cambridge, Mass.: Belknap Press of Harvard University, 2003.

Blair, Karen J. *The Clubwoman as Feminist: True Womanhood Redefined, 1868–1914.* New York: Holmes and Meier, 1980.

Blight, David. *Race and Reunion: The Civil War in American Memory.* Cambridge, Mass.: Harvard University Press, 2001.

Brattain, Michelle. *The Politics of Whiteness: Race, Workers, and Culture in the Modern South.* Athens: University of Georgia Press, 2004.

Browning, Joan C. "Invisible Revolutionaries: White Women in Civil Rights Historiography." *Journal of Women's History* 8 (Fall 1996): 186–204.

Brown-Nagin, Tomiko. *Courage to Dissent: Atlanta and the Long History of the Civil Rights Movement.* New York: Oxford University Press, 2011.

Brundage, W. Fitzhugh, ed. *Where These Memories Grow: History, Memory, and Southern Identity.* Chapel Hill: University of North Carolina Press, 2000.

Censer, Jane Turner. *The Reconstruction of White Southern Womanhood, 1865–1895.* Baton Rouge: Louisiana State University Press, 2003.

Chapell, David L. *Inside Agitators: White Southerners in the Civil Rights Movement.* Baltimore: Johns Hopkins University Press, 1994.

Chirhart, Ann Short. *Torches of Light: Georgia Teachers and the Coming of the Modern South.* Athens: University of Georgia Press, 2005.

Cobb, James. *Away down South: A History of Southern Identity.* New York: Oxford University Press, 2005.

Cox, Karen. *Dixie's Daughters: The United Daughters of the Confederacy and the Preservation of Confederate Culture.* Gainesville: University of Florida Press, 2003.

Dailey, Jane, Glenda Elizabeth Gilmore, and Bryant Simon, eds. *Jumpin' Jim Crow: Southern Politics from Civil War to Civil Rights.* Princeton: Princeton University Press, 2000.

Daniel, Pete. *Lost Revolutions: The South in the 1950s.* Chapel Hill: University of North Carolina Press, 2000.

——. *Standing at the Crossroads: Southern Life in the Twentieth Century.* New York: Hill and Wang, 1986.

Dittmer, John. *Black Georgia in the Progressive Era, 1900–1920.* Urbana: University of Illinois Press, 1977.

Dorsey, Allison. *To Build Our Lives Together: Community Formation in Black Atlanta, 1875–1906.* Athens: University of Georgia Press, 2004.

Egerton, John. *Speak Now against the Day: The Generation before the Civil Rights Movement in the South.* New York: Knopf, 1994.

Fairclough, Adam. *A Class of Their Own: Black Teachers in the Segregated South.* Cambridge, Mass.: Harvard University Press, 2007.

Farnham, Christie Anne. *Women of the American South: A Multicultural Reader.* New York: New York University Press, 1997.

Faust, Drew Gilpin. "Clutching the Chains That Bind: Margaret Mitchell and *Gone With the Wind.*" *Southern Cultures* 5, no. 1 (1999): 6–20.

Feimster, Crystal. *Southern Horrors.* Cambridge, Mass.: Harvard University Press, 2009.

Fields, Barbara Jeanne. "Ideology and Race in American History." In *Region, Race, and Reconstruction: Essays in Honor of C. Vann Woodward,* edited by J. Morgan Kousser and James McPherson, 143–77. New York: Oxford University Press, 1982.

Flamming, Douglas. *Creating the Modern South: Millhands and Managers in Dalton, Georgia, 1884–1984.* Chapel Hill: University of North Carolina Press, 1992.

Flynn, Charles L. *White Land, Black Labor: Caste and Class in Late Nineteenth Century Georgia.* Baton Rouge: Louisiana State University Press, 1983.

Fredrickson, George M. *The Black Image in the White Mind: The Debate on Afro-American Character and Destiny, 1817–1914.* New York: Harper and Row, 1971.

Gardner, Sarah. *Blood and Irony: Southern White Women's Narratives of the Civil War, 1861–1937.* Chapel Hill: University of North Carolina Press, 2003.

Gaston, Paul M. *The New South Creed: A Study in Modern Mythmaking.* Baton Rouge: Louisiana State University Press, 1970.

Gilmore, Glenda E. *Gender and Jim Crow: Women and the Politics of White Supremacy in North Carolina, 1896–1920.* Chapel Hill: University of North Carolina Press, 1996.

Godshalk, David Fort. *Veiled Visions: The 1906 Atlanta Race Riot and the Reshaping of American Race Relations.* Chapel Hill: University of North Carolina Press, 1905.

Goldfield, David R. *Black, White, and Southern: Race Relations and Southern Culture, 1940 to the Present.* Baton Rouge: Louisiana State University Press, 1990.

Goodson, Steven. *Highbrows, Hillbillies, and Hellfire: Public Entertainment in Atlanta, 1880–1930.* Athens: University of Georgia Press, 2002.

Grant, Donald L. *The Way It Was in the South: The Black Experience in Georgia.* Athens: University of Georgia Press, 2001.

Grantham, Dewey. *Hoke Smith and the Politics of the New South.* Baton Rouge: Louisiana State University Press, 1958.

——. *Southern Progressivism: The Reconciliation of Progress and Tradition.* Knoxville, Tenn.: University of Tennessee Press, 1983.

Green, Elna C. *Before the New Deal: Social Welfare in the South, 1830–1930.* Athens: University of Georgia Press, 1999.

——. *The New Deal and Beyond: Social Welfare in the South since 1930.* Athens: University of Georgia Press, 2003.

——. *Southern Strategies: Southern Women and the Woman Suffrage Question.* Chapel Hill: University of North Carolina Press, 1998.

Hagood, Margaret Jarman. *Mothers of the South: Portraiture of the White Tenant Farm Woman*. Charlottesville: University of Virginia Press, 1996.

Hale, Grace Elizabeth. *Making Whiteness: The Culture of Segregation in the South, 1890–1940*. New York: Vintage, 1998.

———. "'Some Women Have Never Been Reconstructed': Mildred Lewis Rutherford, Lucy M. Stanton, and the Racial Politics of White Southern Womanhood, 1900–1930." In *Georgia in Black and White: Explorations in the Race Relations of a Southern State, 1865–1950*, edited by John Inscoe. Athens: University of Georgia Press, 1994.

Hall, Jacquelyn Dowd. *Revolt against Chivalry: Jesse Daniel Ames and the Women's Campaign against Lynching*. New York: Columbia University Press, 1979.

Hall, Jacquelyn Dowd, and Ann Firor Scott. "Women in the South." In *Interpreting Southern History: Historiographical Essays in Honor of Sanford W. Higginbotham*, edited by John B. Boles and Evelyn Thomas Nolan. Baton Rouge: Louisiana State University Press, 1987.

Harlan, Louis R. *Separate and Unequal: Southern School Campaigns and Racism in the Southern Seaboard States, 1901–1915*. New York: Atheneum, 1968.

Hartog, Henrik. *Man and Wife in America: A History*. Cambridge, Mass.: Harvard University Press, 2000.

Harvey, Paul. *Redeeming the South: Religious Cultures and Racial Identities among Southern Baptists, 1865–1924*. Chapel Hill: University of North Carolina Press, 1997.

Hawks, Joanne V., and Sheila L. Skemp, eds. *Sex, Race, and the Role of Women in the South*. Jackson: University Press of Mississippi, 1983.

Hewitt, Nancy A., and Suzanne Lebsock, eds. *Visible Women: New Essays on American Activism*. Urbana: University of Illinois Press, 1993.

Hickey, Georgina. *Hope and Danger in the New South City: Working-Class Women and Urban Development in Atlanta, 1890–1940*. Athens: University of Georgia Press, 2003.

Higginbotham, Evelyn Brooks. *Righteous Discontent: The Women's Movement in the Black Baptist Church, 1880–1920*. Cambridge, Mass.: Harvard University Press, 1993.

Hine, Darlene Clark. *Hine Sight: Black Women and the Re-Construction of American History*. New York: Carlson, 1994.

Hobson, Fred. *But Now I See: The White Southern Racial Conversion Narrative*. Baton Rouge: Louisiana State University Press, 1999.

———. *Tell about the South: The Southern Rage to Explain*. Baton Rouge: Louisiana State University Press, 1983.

Hunter, Tera W. *To 'Joy My Freedom: Southern Black Women's Lives and Labors after the Civil War*. Cambridge, Mass.: Harvard University Press, 1997.

Inscoe, John C. *Georgia in Black and White: Exploration in the Race Relations of a Southern State, 1865–1950*. Athens: University of Georgia Press, 1994.

Janney, Caroline E. *Burying the Dead but Not the Past: Ladies' Memorial Associations and the Lost Cause*. Chapel Hill: University of North Carolina Press, 2008.

Johnson, Joan Marie. *Southern Women at the Seven Sister Colleges: Feminist Values and Social Activism, 1875–1915*. Athens: University of Georgia Press, 2008.

Jones, Anne Goodwyn. *Tomorrow Is Another Day: The Woman Writer in the South, 1859–1936*. Baton Rouge: Louisiana State University Press, 1981.

Jones, Jacqueline. *Labor of Love, Labor of Sorrow: Black Women, Work, and the Family from Slavery to the Present*. New York: Basic Books, 1985.

Jones, LuAnn. *"Mama Learned Us to Work": Farm Women in the New South*. Chapel Hill: University of North Carolina Press, 2002.

Kammen, Michael. *Mystic Chords of Memory: The Transformation of Tradition in American Culture*. New York: Random House, 1991.

Kirby, Jack Temple. *Darkness at Dawning: Race and Reform in the Progressive South*. Philadelphia: Lippincott, 1972.

Kruse, Kevin M. *White Flight: Atlanta and the Making of Modern Conservatism*. Princeton: Princeton University Press, 2005.

Kuhn, Clifford M., Harlon E. Joye, and E. Bernard West, eds. *Living Atlanta: An Oral History of the City, 1914–1948*. Atlanta: Atlanta Historical Society; Athens: University of Georgia Press, 1990.

Kytle, Calvin, and James A. Mackay. *Who Runs Georgia?* Athens: University of Georgia Press, 1998.

Lassiter, Matthew D. *The Silent Majority: Suburban Politics in the Sunbelt South*. Princeton: Princeton University Press, 2006.

Link, William A. *The Paradox of Southern Progressivism, 1880–1930*. Chapel Hill: University of North Carolina Press, 1992.

Litwack, Leon F. *Trouble in Mind: Black Southerners in the Age of Jim Crow*. New York: Knopf, 1998.

Luker, Ralph E. *The Social Gospel and Modern American Culture*. Chapel Hill: University of North Carolina Press, 1991.

MacLean, Nancy. *Behind the Mask of Chivalry: The Making of the Second Ku Klux Klan*. New York: Oxford University Press, 1994.

Matthews, Donald T., and Jane Sherron de Hart. *Sex, Gender, and the Politics of the ERA: A State and the Nation*. Oxford: Oxford University Press, 1990.

McCandless, Amy Thompson. *The Past in the Present: Women's Higher Education in the Twentieth-Century American South*. Tuscaloosa: University of Alabama Press, 1999.

McGirr, Lisa. *Suburban Warriors: The Origins of the New American Right*. Princeton: Princeton University Press, 2001.

McPherson, Tara. *Reconstructing Dixie: Race, Gender, and Nostalgia in the Imagined South*. Durham: Duke University Press, 2003.

McRae, Elizabeth Gillespie. "Caretakers of Southern Civilization: Georgia Women and the Anti-Suffrage Campaign, 1914–1920." *Georgia Historical Quarterly* 82 (Winter 1998): 801–28.

Mixon, Gregory Lamont. *The Atlanta Riot: Race, Class, and Violence in a New South City*. Gainesville: University of Florida Press, 2005.

Muncy, Robin. *Creating a Female Dominion in American Politics, 1890–1935*. New York: Oxford University Press, 1991.

Nasstrom, Kathryn L. *Everybody's Grandmother and Nobody's Fool: Frances Freeborn Pauley and the Struggle for Social Justice*. Ithaca: Cornell University Press, 2000.

Ownby, Ted. *Subduing Satan: Religion, Recreation, and Manhood in the Rural South, 1865–1920*. Chapel Hill: University of North Carolina Press, 1990.

Pascoe, Peggy. *What Comes Naturally: Miscegenation Law and the Making of Race in America*. Oxford: Oxford University Press, 2010.

Patton, Randall L., and David B. Parker. *Carpet Capital: The Rise of a New South Industry*. Athens: University of Georgia Press, 2003.

Range, Willard. *A Century of Georgia Agriculture, 1850–1950*. Athens: University of Georgia Press, 1954.

Ritterhouse, Jennifer. *Growing Up Jim Crow: How Black and White Southern Children Learned Race*. Chapel Hill: University of North Carolina Press, 2006.

Rothman, Ellen K. *Hands and Hearts: A History of Courtship in America*. New York: Basic Books, 1984.

Rouse, Jacqueline Ann. *Lugenia Burns Hope: Black Southern Reformer*. Athens: University of Georgia Press, 1989.

Rymph, Cynthia. *Republican Women: Feminism and Conservatism from Suffrage through the Rise of the New Right*. Chapel Hill: University of North Carolina Press, 2006.

Schechter, Patricia. *Ida B. Wells and American Reform, 1865–1930*. Chapel Hill: University of North Carolina Press, 2000.

Schuyler, Lorraine Gates. *The Weight of their Votes: Southern Women and Political Leverage in the 1920s*. Chapel Hill: University of North Carolina Press, 2006.

Schweiger, Beth Barton, and Donald G. Mathews, eds. *Religion in the American South: Protestants and Others in History and Culture*. Chapel Hill: University of North Carolina Press, 2004.

Sims, Anastatia. *The Power of Femininity in the New South: Women's Organization and Politics in North Carolina, 1880–1930*. Columbia: University of South Carolina Press, 1997.

Smith, Douglas L. *The New Deal in the Urban South*. Baton Rouge: Louisiana State University Press, 1988.

Sosna, Martin. *In Search of the Silent South: Southern Liberals and the Race Issue*. New York: Columbia University Press, 1977.

Taylor, A. Elizabeth. "The Last Phase of the Woman Suffrage Movement in Georgia." *Georgia Historical Quarterly* 43 (March 1959): 11–28.

———. "The Origin of the Woman Suffrage Movement in Georgia." *Georgia Historical Quarterly* 28 (June 1944): 64–59.

Tuck, Stephen G. N. *Beyond Atlanta: The Struggle for Racial Equality in Georgia, 1940–1980*. Athens: University of Georgia Press, 2003.

Turner, Elizabeth Hayes. *Women, Culture, and Community: Religion and Reform in Galveston, 1880–1920*. New York: Oxford University Press, 1997.

Wallace-Sanders, Kimberly. *Mammy: A Century of Race, Gender, and Southern Memory*. Ann Arbor: University of Michigan, 2009.

Ware, Susan. *Beyond Suffrage: Women and the New Deal.* Cambridge, Mass.: Harvard University Press, 1987.

Wexler, Laura. *Fire in the Canebreak: The Last Mass Lynching in America.* New York: Scribners, 2003.

Wheeler, Marjorie Spruill. *New Women of the New South: The Leaders of the Woman Suffrage Movement in the Southern States.* New York: Oxford University Press, 1993.

White, Deborah Grey, *Too Heavy a Load: Black Women in Defense of Themselves.* New York: W. W. Norton, 1999.

Whites, LeeAnn. "Love, Hate, Rape, Lynching: Rebecca Latimer Felton and the Gender Politics of Racial Violence." In *Democracy Betrayed: The Wilmington Race Riot of 1898 and its Legacy,* edited by David Cecelski and Timothy B. Tyson. Chapel Hill: University of North Carolina Press, 1998.

———. "Rebecca Latimer Felton and the 'Problem' of Protection in the New South." In *Visible Women: New Essays in American Activism,* edited by Nancy Hewitt and Suzanne Lebsock. Urbana: University of Illinois Press, 1993.

Williamson, Joel. *The Crucible of Race: Black and White Relations in the American South since Emancipation.* New York: Oxford University Press, 1984.

———. *Rage for Order: Black-White Relations in the American South since Emancipation.* New York: Oxford University Press, 1986.

Woodward, C. Vann. *The Burdens of Southern History.* 3rd ed. Baton Rouge: Louisiana State University Press, 1993.

———. *The Origins of the New South, 1877–1913.* Rev. ed. with a critical essay by Charles B. Dew. Baton Rouge: Louisiana State University Press, 1971.

———. *The Strange Career of Jim Crow.* 3rd rev. ed. New York: Oxford University Press, 1974.

Contributors

ANN SHORT CHIRHART is an associate professor of history at Indiana State University in Terre Haute. She is the author of *Torches of Light: Georgia Teachers and the Coming of the Modern South* (University of Georgia Press, 2005) and coeditor of *Georgia Women: Their Lives and Times*, vol. 1 (University of Georgia Press, 2009). Her articles, published in numerous journals and collections, discuss teachers, women reformers, and African American women activists. Currently, she is working on a biography of Mary McLeod Bethune.

KATHLEEN ANN CLARK is an associate professor of history at the University of Georgia in Athens. She is the author of *Defining Moments: African American Commemoration and Political Culture in the South, 1863–1913* (University of North Carolina Press, 2005), as well as articles on a variety of subjects, including African American Emancipation Day celebrations, the author Margaret Mitchell, and historic tourism in Atlanta. She is currently writing a history of *Gone With the Wind*.

CARLOS DEWS is chair of the Department of English Language and Literature at John Cabot University in Rome. He is also the director of the John Cabot University Institute for Creative Writing and Literary Translation. He was the founding director of the Carson McCullers Center for Writers and Musicians in McCullers's hometown of Columbus, Georgia. He edited McCullers's unfinished autobiography, *Illumination and Night Glare* (University of Wisconsin Press, 1999), and *McCullers: The Complete Novels* (Library of America, 2001).

LESLIE DUNLAP is an assistant professor of history at Willamette University in Salem, Oregon. She is currently working on a manuscript entitled "No Easy Union: Temperance Women's Interracial Activism, 1873–1933," a history of Native American, African American, and white women's activism in the Woman's Christian Temperance Union.

GLENN T. ESKEW is an associate professor of history at Georgia State University in Atlanta. His most recent publication is *Johnny Mercer: Southern Songwriter for the World*, published by the Wormsloe Foundation in 2013. He is also the author of *But for Birmingham: The Local and National Movements in the Civil Rights Struggle* (University of North Carolina Press, 1997), which received the Francis Butler Simkins Prize of the

Southern Historical Association. He has published two edited volumes of essays, *Paternalism in a Southern City* (University of Georgia Press, 2001) and *Labor in the Modern South* (University of Georgia Press, 2001). He is currently working on a book manuscript that explores civil rights memorialization.

BETTY ALICE FOWLER is the grant writer and assistant to the director of the Georgia Museum of Art at the University of Georgia in Athens. She is the author of *The Art of Lucy May Stanton* (Georgia Museum of Art, 2002) and guest curator of the exhibition of the same name.

STEVE GOODSON is currently a full professor and department chair at the University of West Georgia in Carrollton. His book *Highbrows, Hillbillies, and Hellfire: Public Entertainment in Atlanta, 1880–1930* (University of Georgia Press, 2002) won the Georgia Historical Society's Bell Award as the best book on Georgia History published in 2002. With David Anderson and Patrick Huber, he is coediting *The Hank Williams Reader*, which is under contract with Oxford University Press.

SARAH GORDON, professor emerita at Georgia College & State University in Milledgeville, is the author of *Flannery O'Connor: The Obedient Imagination* (University of Georgia Press, 2000) and *A Literary Guide to Flannery O'Connor's Georgia* (University of Georgia Press, 2008), and is the editor of *Flannery O'Connor: In Celebration of Genius* (University of South Carolina Press, 2008). She edited *The Flannery O'Connor Bulletin* from 1985 to 2001 and is founding editor of *The Flannery O'Connor Review*. In addition to her work for the Board of Directors of the Flannery O'Connor–Andalusia Foundation, she is also a widely published poet whose poetry has appeared in numerous journals.

PAUL STEPHEN HUDSON is an associate professor of history at Georgia Perimeter College in Atlanta. He has published extensively in the *Georgia Historical Quarterly* and *New Georgia Encyclopedia*. His first book is coauthored with Lora Pond Mirza, *Atlanta's Stone Mountain: A Multicultural History* (The History Press, 2011). Their next project is on Butterfly McQueen. Hudson is on the board of editors of the *Georgia Historical Quarterly*.

JOHN C. INSCOE is University Professor and the Albert B. Saye Professor of History at the University of Georgia in Athens. He is the author or editor of twelve books, the latest of which is *Writing the South through the Self: Explorations in Southern Autobiography* (University of Georgia Press, 2011), which won the 2012 Lillian Smith Book Award. Since 2000 he has served as editor of *The New Georgia Encyclopedia* and secretary-treasurer of the Southern Historical Association.

SCOTT KAUFMAN is a professor of history and codirector of the Robert E. McNair Center for Government and History at Francis Marion University in Florence, South Carolina.

He is the author or coauthor of five books, including *Plans Unraveled: The Foreign Policy of the Carter Administration* (Northern Illinois University Press, 2008). His most recent project, entitled *Project Plowshare: The Peaceful Use of Nuclear Explosives in Cold War America*, is forthcoming from Cornell University Press.

ROSEMARY M. MAGEE serves as vice president and secretary of Emory University in Atlanta. In addition to her work in support of university governance, she chairs the university's strategic initiative in Creativity and the Arts. She is the editor of two volumes, *Conversations with Flannery O'Connor* (University Press of Mississippi, 1987) and *Friendship and Sympathy: Communities of Southern Women Writers* (University Press of Mississippi, 1992). She has also written essays, articles, reviews, and short stories appearing in a wide range of literary magazines and journals. A regular artist-in-residence at the Hambidge Center for Creative Arts and Sciences, she is currently completing a collection of short stories, "Fantasy Impromptu."

ELIZABETH GILLESPIE MCRAE is an associate professor of history at Western Carolina University in Cullowhee, North Carolina. Her research examines the roles white southern women played in shaping racial segregation, white supremacist politics, and the rise of the new right. She has published several articles on conservative southern women and is currently completing a book manuscript, "Raising Jim Crow: White Southern Women and the Politics of White Supremacy."

ROBIN MORRIS is Dabney Adams Hart Lecturer at Agnes Scott College in Decatur, Georgia. She received her PhD from Yale University. She is the author of "Organizing Breadmakers: Kathryn Dunaway and the Georgia STOP ERA Campaign," in *Entering the Fray: Gender, Politics, and Culture in the New South*, edited by Jonathan Daniel Wells and Sheila R. Phipps (University of Missouri Press, 2009). Currently, she is revising her dissertation for publication.

KATHRYN L. NASSTROM is an associate professor of history at the University of San Francisco. She is the author of *Everybody's Grandmother and Nobody's Fool: Frances Freeborn Pauley and the Struggle for Social Justice* (Cornell University Press, 2000), and she has published on women's history, civil rights history, and oral history in the *Journal of American History* and the *Oral History Review*, among other journals. She is also the editor of the *Oral History Review* and a series editor for Oxford University Press's oral history book series. Her current research is on autobiographies of the civil rights movement, and she is completing a book manuscript on the autobiographical literature on the Little Rock school desegregation crisis.

RANDALL L. PATTON holds the Shaw Industries Distinguished Chair in History at Kennesaw State University in Kennesaw, Georgia. He is the author of *Carpet Capital: The Rise of a New South Industry* (University of Georgia Press, 2003) and *Shaw Industries:*

A History (University of Georgia Press, 2003). Other publications include contributions to John C. Inscoe, ed., *Georgia in Black and White: Explorations in the Race Relations of a Southern State* (University of Georgia Press, 1994), and Philip Scranton, ed., *The Second Wave: Southern Industrialization from the 1940s to the 1970s* (University of Georgia Press, 2001), and articles in *Labor History* and the *Georgia Historical Quarterly*. He is currently working on a book-length study of the racial integration of the workplace in the Atlanta area, 1945–1990.

DEBORAH G. PLANT is an associate professor of Africana studies at the University of South Florida in Tampa. Her research and publications have focused on African, African American, and Afro-Caribbean writers. She is the author of several articles on African diaspora writers; two books on Zora Neale Hurston: *Every Tub Must Sit On its Own Bottom, The Philosophy and Politics of Zora Neale Hurston* (University of Illinois Press, 1995) and *Zora Neale Hurston: A Biography of the Spirit* (Rowan and Littlefield, 2011); and an edited volume on Hurston: *"The Inside Light": New Critical Essays on Zora Neale Hurston* (Praeger, 2011). Her present research and writing continue a focus on the work of Zora Neale Hurston and a forthcoming biographical work on Alice Walker.

MARY ROLINSON is a full-time lecturer in history at Georgia State University in Atlanta and a scholar of the African American experience in the twentieth century. She is the author of *Grassroots Garveyism: The Universal Negro Improvement Association in the Rural South, 1920–1927* (University of North Carolina Press, 2007), and her current research project is a biography of Ambassador Mabel Murphy Smythe that also explores the involvement of African American women in furthering international human rights.

Index